STUDENT'S SOLUTIONS MANUAL

NANCY S. BOUDREAU

STATISTICS
for Business and Economics

EIGHTH EDITION

McCLAVE ■ BENSON ■ SINCICH

Prentice Hall

Upper Saddle River, NJ 07458

Acquisitions Editor: Kathy Boothby Sestak
Supplement Editor: Joanne Wendelken
Special Projects Manager: Barbara A. Murray
Production Editor: Maat Van Uitert
Supplement Cover Manager: Paul Gourhan
Supplement Cover Designer: PM Workshop Inc.
Manufacturing Manager: Trudy Pisciotti
Michael Aveto/SIS, Inc.

ISBN 0-13-027422-4

Prentice-Hall International (UK) Limited, London
Prentice-Hall of Australia Pty. Limited, Sydney
Prentice-Hall Canada, Inc., Toronto
Prentice-Hall Hispanoamericana, S.A., Mexico
Prentice-Hall of India Private Limited, New Delhi
Pearson Education Asia Pte. Ltd., Singapore
Prentice-Hall of Japan, Inc., Tokyo
Editora Prentice-Hall do Brazil, Ltda., Rio de Janeiro

Contents

Preface

This solutions manual is designed to accompany the text, *Statistics for Business and Economics*, Eighth Edition, by James T. McClave, P. George Benson, and Terry Sincich. It provides answers to most odd-numbered exercises for each chapter in the text. Other methods of solution may also be appropriate; however, the author has presented one that she believes to be most instructive to the beginning Statistics student. The student should first attempt to solve the assigned exercises without help from this manual. Then, if unsuccessful, the solution in the manual will clarify points necessary to the solution. The student who successfully solves an exercise should still refer to the manual's solution. Many points are clarified and expanded upon to provide maximum insight into and benefit from each exercise.

Instructors will also benefit from the use of this manual. It will save time in preparing presentations of the solutions and possibly provide another point of view regarding their meaning.

Some of the exercises are subjective in nature and thus omitted from the Answer Key at the end of *Statistics for Business and Economics*, Eighth Edition. The subjective decisions regarding these exercises have been made and are explained by the author. Solutions based on these decisions are presented; the solution to this type of exercise is often most instructive. When an alternative interpretation of an exercise may occur, the author has often addressed it and given justification for the approach taken.

I would like to thank Kelly Barber for creating the art work and Brenda Dobson for her assistance and for typing this work.

Nancy S. Boudreau
Bowling Green State University
Bowling Green, Ohio

Statistics, Data, and Statistical Thinking

Chapter 1

1.1 Statistics is a science that deals with the collection, classification, analysis, and interpretation of information or data. It is a meaningful, useful science with a broad, almost limitless scope of applications to business, government, and the physical and social sciences.

1.3 The four elements of a descriptive statistics problem are:

1. The population or sample of interest. This is the collection of all the units upon which the variable is measured.
2. One or more variables that are to be investigated. These are the types of data that are to be collected.
3. Tables, graphs, or numerical summary tools. These are tools used to display the characteristic of the sample or population.
4. Conclusions about the data based on the patterns revealed. These are summaries of what the summary tools revealed about the population or sample.

1.5 The first major method of collecting data is from a published source. These data have already been collected by someone else and is available in a published source. The second method of collecting data is from a designed experiment. These data are collected by a researcher who exerts strict control over the experimental units in a study. These data are measured directly from the experimental units. The third method of collecting data is from a survey. These data are collected by a researcher asking a group of people one or more questions. Again, these data are collected directly from the experimental units or people. The final method of collecting data is observationally. These data are collected directly from experimental units by simply observing the experimental units in their natural environment and recording the values of the desired characteristics.

1.7 A population is a set of existing units such as people, objects, transactions, or events. A variable is a characteristic or property of an individual population unit such as height of a person, time of a reflex, amount of a transaction, etc.

1.9 A representative sample is a sample that exhibits characteristics similar to those possessed by the target population. A representative sample is essential if inferential statistics is to be applied. If a sample does not possess the same characteristics as the target population, then any inferences made using the sample will be unreliable.

1.11 A population is a set of existing units such as people, objects, transactions, or events. A process is a series of actions or operations that transform inputs to outputs. A process produces or generates output over time. Examples of processes are assembly lines, oil refineries, and stock prices.

1.13 The data consisting of the classifications A, B, C, and D are qualitative. These data are nominal and thus are qualitative. After the data are input as 1, 2, 3, and 4, they are still nominal and thus qualitative. The only differences between the two data sets are the names of the categories. The numbers associated with the four groups are meaningless.

1.15   a.   The population of interest is all citizens of the United States.

     b.   The variable of interest is the view of each citizen as to whether the president is doing a good or bad job. It is qualitative.

     c.   The sample is the 2000 individuals selected for the poll.

     d.   The inference of interest is to estimate the proportion of all citizens who believe the president is doing a good job.

     e.   The method of data collection is a survey.

     f.   It is not very likely that the sample will be representative of the population of all citizens of the United States. By selecting phone numbers at random, the sample will be limited to only those people who have telephones. Also, many people share the same phone number, so each person would not have an equal chance of being contacted. Another possible problem is the time of day the calls are made. If the calls are made in the evening, those people who work in the evening would not be represented.

1.17   a.   The population of interest is all employees in the U.S.

     b.   The variable of interest is whether an employee is likely to remain in his/her job in the next five years if he/she is provided with mentoring.

     c.   Since the answer to the question would be either 'yes' or 'no', the variable is qualitative.

     d.   The sample is the 1000 employees in the U.S. who were actually surveyed.

     e.   Since 62% of those surveyed indicated that they would remain in their jobs for the next five years if they received mentoring, we could infer that the majority of all workers would remain in their jobs for the next five years if they receive mentoring.

1.19   a.   Length of maximum span can take on values such as 15 feet, 50 feet, 75 feet, etc. Therefore, it is quantitative.

     b.   The number of vehicle lanes can take on values such as 2, 4, etc. Therefore, it is quantitative.

     c.   The answer to this item is "yes" or "no," which are not numeric. Therefore, it is qualitative.

     d.   Average daily traffic could take on values such as 150 vehicles, 3,579 vehicles, 53,295 vehicles, etc. Therefore, it is quantitative.

     e.   Condition can take on values "good," "fair," or "poor," which are not numeric. Therefore, it is qualitative.

     f.   The length of the bypass or detour could take on values such as 1 mile, 4 miles, etc. Therefore, it is quantitative.

     g.   Route type can take on values "interstate," U.S.," "state," "county," or "city," which are not numeric. Therefore, it is qualitative.

1.21   a.   The population from which the sample was selected is the set of all department store executives.

       b.   There are two variables measured by the authors. They are job-satisfaction and Machiavellian rating for each of the executives.

       c.   The sample is the set of 218 department store executives who completed the questionnaire.

       d.   The method of data collection is a survey.

       e.   The inference made by the authors is that those executives with higher job-satisfaction scores are likely to have a lower 'mach' rating.

1.23   a.   Some possible questions are:

           1.   In your opinion, why has the banking industry consolidated in the past few years? Check all that apply.

               a.   Too many small banks with not enough capital.
               b.   A result of the Savings and Loan scandals.
               c.   To eliminate duplicated resources in the upper management positions.
               d.   To provide more efficient service to the customers.
               e.   To provide a more complete list of financial opportunities for the customers.
               f.   Other. Please list.

           2.   Using a scale from 1 to 5, where 1 means strongly disagree and 5 means strongly agree, indicate your agreement to the following statement: "The trend of consolidation in the banking industry will continue in the next five years."

              1 strongly disagree   2 disagree   3 no opinion   4 agree   5 strongly agree

       b.   The population of interest is the set of all bank presidents in the United States.

       c.   It would be extremely difficult and costly to obtain information from all 10,000 bank presidents. Thus, it would be more efficient to sample just 200 bank presidents. However, by sending the questionnaires to only 200 bank presidents, one risks getting the results from a sample which is not representative of the population. The sample must be chosen in such a way that the results will be representative of the entire population of bank presidents in order to be of any use.

1.25   a.   The population of interest is the collection of all major U.S. firms.

       b.   The variable of interest is whether the firm offers job-sharing to its employees or not.

       c.   The sample is the set of 1,035 firms selected.

       d.   The government might want to estimate the proportion of all firms that offer job-sharing to their employees.

1.27   I.   Qualitative; the possible responses are "yes" or "no," which are nonnumerical.

       II.   Quantitative; age is measured on a numerical scale, such as 15, 32, etc.

       III.   Quantitative; the rating is measured on a numerical scale from 1 to 10, where the higher the rating the more helpful the *Tutorial* instructions.

IV. Qualitative; the possible responses are "laser printer" or "another type of printer," which are nonnumerical.

V. Qualitative; the speeds can be classified as "slower," "unchanged," or "faster," which are nonnumerical.

VI. Quantitative; the number of people in a household who have used Windows 95 at least once is measured on a numerical scale, such as 0, 1, 2, etc.

1.29 a. The process being studied is the distribution of pipes, valves, and fittings to the refining, chemical, and petrochemical industries by Wallace Company of Houston.

b. The variables of interest are the speed of the deliveries, the accuracy of the invoices, and the quality of the packaging of the products.

c. The sampling plan was to monitor a subset of current customers by sending out a questionnaire twice a year and asking the customers to rate the speed of the deliveries, the accuracy of the invoices, and the quality of the packaging minutes. The sample is the total numbers of questionnaires received.

d. The Wallace Company's immediate interest is learning about the delivery process of its distribution of pipes, valves, and fittings. To do this, it is measuring the speed of deliveries, the accuracy of the invoices, and the quality of its packaging from the sample of its customers to make an inference about the delivery process to all customers. In particular, it might use the mean speed of its deliveries to the sampled customers to estimate the mean speed of its deliveries to all its customers. It might use the mean accuracy of its invoices to the sampled customers to estimate the mean accuracy of its deliveries to all its customers. It might use the mean rating of the quality of its packaging to the sampled customers to estimate the mean rating of the quality of its packaging to all its customers.

e. Several factors might affect the reliability of the inferences. One factor is the set of customers selected to receive the survey. If this set is not representative of all the customers, the wrong inferences could be made. Also, the set of customers returning the surveys may not be representative of all its customers. Again, this could influence the reliability of the inferences made.

2.1   First, we find the frequency of the grade A. The sum of the frequencies for all five grades must be 200. Therefore, subtract the sum of the frequencies of the other four grades from 200. The frequency for grade A is:

$$200 - (36 + 90 + 30 + 28) = 200 - 184 = 16$$

To find the relative frequency for each grade, divide the frequency by the total sample size, 200. The relative frequency for the grade B is 36/200 = .18. The rest of the relative frequencies are found in a similar manner and appear in the table:

Grade on Statistics Exam	Frequency	Relative Frequency
A: 90–100	16	.08
B: 80– 89	36	.18
C: 65– 79	90	.45
D: 50– 64	30	.15
F: Below 50	28	.14
Total	200	1.00

2.3   a.   To form a relative frequency bar chart, we must first convert the percents to relative frequencies by dividing the percents by 100%. The relative frequency bar chart for Banks is:

1: Totally Satisfied and Very Loyal
2: Totally Satisfied and Not Very Loyal
3: Not Totally Satisfied and Very Loyal
4: Not Totally Satisfied and Not Very Loyal

The relative frequency bar chart for Department Stores is:

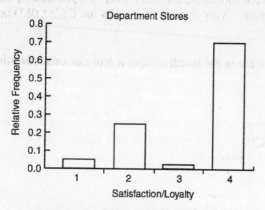

1: Totally Satisfied and Very Loyal
2: Totally Satisfied and Not Very Loyal
3: Not Totally Satisfied and Very Loyal
4: Not Totally Satisfied and Not Very Loyal

b. Since the data are qualitative, we could have described them using pie charts.

c. For the banking industry, a little over a quarter of those who are totally satisfied are very loyal. This is a relatively small percentage. However, in the department stores, only 4% of those who are totally satisfied are very loyal. This indicates that very few department store customers are very loyal.

2.5 a. We must first compute the relative frequency for each response. To find the relative frequency, we divide the frequency by the total sample size, 240. For the first category, the relative frequency is $154/240 = .642$. The rest of the relative frequencies are found in a similar manner and are shown in the table.

Response	Number of Investors	Relative Frequency
Seek formal explanation	154	.642
Seek CEO performance review	49	.204
Dismiss CEO	20	.083
Seek no action	17	.071
TOTAL	240	1.000

b. The relative frequency graph is:

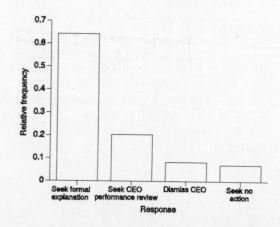

c. If the chief executive officer and the board of directors differed on company strategy, almost 2/3 of the large investors would seek formal explanation (.642). Approximately 20% (.204) would seek CEO performance review. Very few would dismiss the CEO (.083) or would seek no action (.071).

2.7 a. The variable measured by Performark is the length of time it took for each advertiser to respond back.

b. The pie chart is:

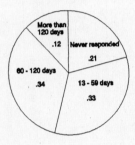

c. Twenty-one percent of .21 × 17,000 = 3,570 of the advertisers never respond to the sales lead.

d. The information from the pie chart does not indicate how effective the "bingo cards" are. It just indicates how long it takes advertisers to respond, if at all.

2.9 a. The variable measured in the survey was the length of time small businesses used the Internet per week.

b. A bar graph of the data is:

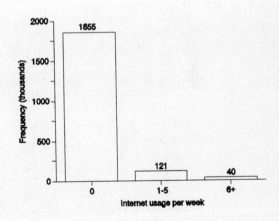

c. The proportion of the 2,016 small businesses that use the Internet on a weekly basis is (121 + 40)/2,016 = 161/2,016 = .08.

2.11 a. The Pareto diagram is:

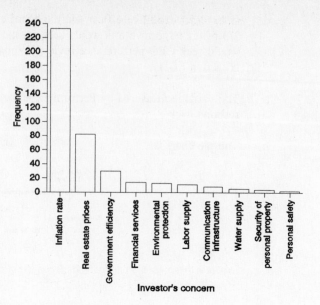

b. The environmental factor of most concern is "Inflation rate" with 233/402 = .58 or 58% of the investors indicating this as their most serious concern. The second most serious concern was "Real Estate prices." Over 20% ((82/402) × 100% = 20.4%) of the investors chose this concern. Each of the other categories were chosen by less than 10% of the investors.

c. Two factors out of 10 represent 20% of the factors. The two factors are "Inflation rate" and "Real estate prices." These two factors represent ((233 + 82)/402 = .78) 78% of the investors. This is very close to 80%.

2.13 To find the number of measurements for each measurement class, multiply the relative frequency by the total number of observations, $n = 500$. The frequency table is:

Measurement Class	Relative Frequency	Frequency
.5 − 2.5	.10	500(.10) = 50
2.5 − 4.5	.15	500(.15) = 75
4.5 − 6.5	.25	500(.25) = 125
6.5 − 8.5	.20	500(.20) = 100
8.5 − 10.5	.05	500(.05) = 25
10.5 − 12.5	.10	500(.10) = 50
12.5 − 14.5	.10	500(.10) = 50
14.5 − 16.5	.05	500(.05) = 25
		500

The frequency histogram is:

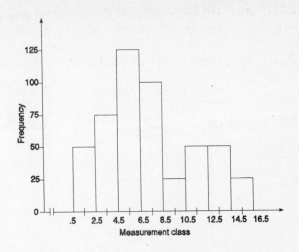

2.15   a.   This is a frequency histogram because the number of observations is graphed for each interval rather than the relative frequency.

       b.   There are 14 measurement classes.

       c.   There are 49 measurements in the data set.

2.17   a.   Using MINITAB, the stem-and-leaf displays for the two types of companies are:

            Character Stem-and-Leaf Display

            ```
            Stem-and-Leaf of Technology Companies     N = 28
            Leaf Unit = 10

                9     -0   444311000
               14      0   01334555689
                8      1   12345
                3      2
                3      3   119
            ```

            Character Stem-and-Leaf Display

            ```
            Stem-and-Leaf of Industrial Companies     N = 13
            Leaf Unit = 10

              (7)     -0   5333200
                6      0   004
                3      1   156
            ```

       b.   The stock price changes in the technology companies are much more variable than that of the industrial companies. The technology company stock price changes range from -44% to 392% while the industrial company stock price changes range from -59% to 161%. In addition, over half (7 out of 13) of the industrial companies had a negative stock price change while only 9 out of 28 of the technology companies had negative stock price changes.

       c.   In order for the stock prices to more than double, the percent change must be 100% or more. Of the 28 technology companies, 8 had stock price changes of 100% or higher. Thus, the percentage is $(8/28)*100\% = 28.6\%$.

2.19   a.   Almost half (14) of the bid prices were between $99.50 and $102.50. Seventy percent (21) of the bid prices were between $96.50 and $105.50. Only one bid price was greater than $105.50.

b. The total number of bonds with bid prices greater than $96.50 is $3 + 14 + 4 + 1 = 22$. The proportion of the total is $22/33 = .733$.

2.21 a. Using MINITAB, the stem-and-leaf display is:

```
Stem-and-Leaf of PENALTY        N = 38
Leaf Unit = 10000

(28)    0  ⓪0①①111②②222222③③33334444899
 10     1  ⓪0239
  5     2
  5     3 0
  4     4 0
  3     5
  3     6
  3     7
  3     8 5
  2     9 3
  1    10 0
```

b. See the circled leaves in part **a**.

c. Most of the penalties imposed for Clean Air Act violations are relatively small compared to the penalties imposed for other violations. All but one of the penalties for Clean Air Act violations are below the median penalty imposed.

2.23 a. Using MINITAB, the three frequency histograms are as follows (the same starting point and class interval were used for each):

```
Histogram of C1        N = 25

Tenth Performance

Midpoint   Count
   4.00      0
   8.00      0
  12.00      1   *
  16.00      5   *****
  20.00     10   **********
  24.00      6   ******
  28.00      0
  32.00      2   **
  36.00      0
  40.00      1   *
```

```
Histogram of C2        N = 25

Thirtieth Performance

Midpoint   Count
   4.00      1   *
   8.00      9   *********
  12.00     12   ************
  16.00      2   **
  20.00      1   *
```

```
Histogram of C3        N = 25

Fiftieth Performance

Midpoint   Count
   4.00      3   ***
   8.00     15   ***************
  12.00      4   ****
  16.00      2   **
  20.00      1   *
```

b. The histogram for the tenth performance shows a much greater spread of the observations than the other two histograms. The thirtieth performance histogram shows a shift to the left—implying shorter completion times than for the tenth performance. In addition, the fiftieth performance histogram shows an additional shift to the left compared to that for the thirtieth performance. However, the last shift is not as great as the first shift. This agrees with statements made in the problem.

2.25 a. The percentage of realizations of V with values ranging from .425 to .675 is approximately $13.5 + 11.5 + 8 + 6 + 5.75 = 44.75\%$.

b. The norm constraint level V that has approximately 10% of the realizations less than it is approximately .325.

2.27 a. $\sum x = 3 + 8 + 4 + 5 + 3 + 4 + 6 = 33$

b. $\sum x^2 = 3^2 + 8^2 + 4^2 + 5^2 + 3^2 + 4^2 + 6^2 = 175$

c. $\sum (x - 5)^2 = (3 - 5)^2 + (8 - 5)^2 + (4 - 5)^2 + (5 - 5)^2 + (3 - 5)^2 + (4 - 5)^2$
$+ (6 - 5)^2 = 20$

d. $\sum (x - 2)^2 = (3 - 2)^2 + (8 - 2)^2 + (4 - 2)^2 + (5 - 2)^2 + (3 - 2)^2 + (4 - 2)^2$
$+ (6 - 2)^2 = 71$

e. $\left(\sum x\right)^2 = (3 + 8 + 4 + 5 + 3 + 4 + 6)^2 = 33^2 = 1089$

2.29 a. $\sum x = 6 + 0 + (-2) + (-1) + 3 = 6$

b. $\sum x^2 = 6^2 + 0^2 + (-2)^2 + (-1)^2 + 3^2 = 50$

c. $\sum x^2 - \dfrac{\left(\sum x\right)^2}{5} = 50 - \dfrac{6^2}{5} = 50 - 7.2 = 42.8$

2.31 Assume the data are a sample. The sample mean is:

$$\bar{x} = \frac{\sum x}{n} = \frac{3.2 + 2.5 + 2.1 + 3.7 + 2.8 + 2.0}{6} = \frac{16.3}{6} = 2.717$$

The median is the average of the middle two numbers when the data are arranged in order (since $n = 6$ is even). The data arranged in order are: 2.0, 2.1, 2.5, 2.8, 3.2, 3.7. The middle two numbers are 2.5 and 2.8. The median is:

$$\frac{2.5 + 2.8}{2} = \frac{5.3}{2} = 2.65$$

2.33 The mean and median of a symmetric data set are equal to each other. The mean is larger than the median when the data set is skewed to the right. The mean is less than the median when the data set is skewed to the left. Thus, by comparing the mean and median, one can determine whether the data set is symmetric, skewed right, or skewed left.

2.35   a. $\bar{x} = \dfrac{\sum x}{n} = \dfrac{7 + \cdots + 4}{6} + \dfrac{15}{6} = 2.5$

Median $= \dfrac{3 + 3}{2} = 3$ (mean of 3rd and 4th numbers, after ordering)

Mode $= 3$

b. $\bar{x} = \dfrac{\sum x}{n} = \dfrac{2 + \cdots + 4}{13} = \dfrac{40}{13} = 3.08$

Median $= 3$ (7th number, after ordering)

Mode $= 3$

c. $\bar{x} = \dfrac{\sum x}{n} = \dfrac{51 + \cdots + 37}{10} = \dfrac{496}{10} = 49.6$

Median $= \dfrac{48 + 50}{2} = 49$ (mean of 5th and 6th numbers, after ordering)

Mode $= 50$

2.37   The median is the average of the middle two numbers (since n is even) once the measurements have been arranged in order. The median is:

Median $= \dfrac{106,161 + 152,240}{2} = 129,200.5$

The median number of passengers per cruise line is 129,200.5. Half of the cruise lines had total number of passengers greater than 129,200.5 and half had less.

The mean is: $\bar{x} = \dfrac{\sum x}{n} = \dfrac{1,581,058}{8} = 197,632.25$

The average number of passengers per cruise line is 197,632.25. Since the mean is quite a bit larger than the median, the data are skewed to the right.

2.39   a.   From the printout, the mean number of Superfund sites per county is 5.24, the median is 3 and the mode is 2. Since the mean is larger than the median and the median is larger than the mode, the data are skewed to the right. The average number of sites per county is 5.24. Half of the counties have three or fewer Superfund sites. More counties have two sites than any other number.

b.   The county with the most sites has 48 sites. This number is much larger than any other in the data set.

c.   We know that $\bar{x} = \dfrac{\sum x}{n}$. Thus, $\sum x = n\bar{x} = 75(5.24) = 393$. If we eliminate the value of 48 from the data set, then $\bar{x} = \dfrac{\sum x}{n} = \dfrac{(393 - 48)}{75 - 1} = \dfrac{345}{74} = 4.66$

If we eliminate 48 from the data set, the median is the average of the middle two numbers and is Median $= \dfrac{3 + 3}{2} = 3$

The mode is the number occurring most frequently and is still 2.

Thus, the median and the mode did not change, while the mean dropped from 5.24 to 4.66.

2.41   a.   In 1980, the median age of the U.S. population was 30. This means that half of the people in the U.S. in 1980 were less than or equal to 30 years old and half were 30 or older. In 2000, the median age is expected to be 36. This means that in 2000, half of the people in the U.S. will be less than or equal to 36 years old and half will be 36 or older. This means the population as a whole is tending to get older.

        b.   The shift in the median age to 36 in 2000 will mean that there will be proportionally fewer people in the 18 to 30 year age group in 2000 than there was in 1980.

2.45   a.   For the "Joint exchange offer with prepack" firms, the mean time is 2.6545 months, and the median is 1.5 months. Thus, the average time spent in bankruptcy for "Joint" firms is 2.6545 months, while half of the firms spend 1.5 months or less in bankruptcy.

            For the "No prefiling vote held" firms, the mean time is 4.2364 months, and the median is 3.2 months. Thus, the average time spent in bankruptcy for "No prefiling vote held" firms is 4.2364 months, while half of the firms spend 3.2 months or less in bankruptcy.

            For the "Prepack solicitation only" firms, the mean time is 1.8185 months, and the median is 1.4 months. Thus, the average time spent in bankruptcy for "Prepack solicitation only" firms is 1.8185 months, while half of the firms spend 1.4 months or less in bankruptcy.

        b.   Since the means and medians for the three groups of firms differ quite a bit, it would be unreasonable to use a single number to locate the center of the time in bankruptcy. Three different "centers" should be used.

2.47   a.   The primary disadvantage of using the range to compare variability of data sets is that the two data sets can have the same range and be vastly different with respect to data variation. Also, the range is greatly affected by extreme measures.

        b.   The sample variance is the sum of the squared deviations from the sample mean divided by the sample size minus 1. The population variance is the sum of the squared deviations from the population mean divided by the population size.

        c.   The variance of a data set can never be negative. The variance of a sample is the sum of the *squared* deviations from the mean divided by $n - 1$. The square of any number, positive or negative, is always positive. Thus, the variance will be positive.

            The variance is usually greater than the standard deviation. However, it is possible for the variance to be smaller than the standard deviation. If the data are between 0 and 1, the variance will be smaller than the standard deviation. For example, suppose the data set is .8, .7, .9, .5, and .3. The sample mean is:

$$\bar{x} = \frac{\sum x}{n} = \frac{.8 + .7 + .9 + .5 + .3}{.5} = \frac{3.2}{5} = .64$$

            The sample variance is:

$$s^2 = \frac{\sum x^2 - \frac{(\sum x)^2}{n}}{n - 1} = \frac{2.28 - \frac{3.2^2}{5}}{5 - 1} = \frac{2.28 - 2.048}{4} = \frac{.325}{4} = .058$$

            The standard deviation is $s = \sqrt{.058} = .241$

Methods for Describing Sets of Data

2.49 a. Range $= 4 - 0 = 4$

$$s^2 = \frac{\sum x^2 - \frac{(\sum x)^2}{n}}{n-1} = \frac{22 - \frac{8^2}{5}}{4-1} = 2.3 \qquad s = \sqrt{2.3} = 1.52$$

b. Range $= 6 - 0 = 6$

$$s^2 = \frac{\sum x^2 - \frac{(\sum x)^2}{n}}{n-1} = \frac{63 - \frac{17^2}{7}}{7-1} = 3.619 \qquad s = \sqrt{3.619} = 1.90$$

c. Range $= 8 - (-2) = 10$

$$s^2 = \frac{\sum x^2 - \frac{(\sum x)^2}{n}}{n-1} = \frac{154 - \frac{30^2}{10}}{10-1} = 7.111 \qquad s = \sqrt{7.111} = 2.67$$

d. Range $= 2 - (-3) = 5$

$$s^2 = \frac{\sum x^2 - \frac{(\sum x)^2}{n}}{n-1} = \frac{29 - \frac{(-5)^2}{18}}{18-1} = 1.624 \qquad s = \sqrt{1.624} = 1.274$$

2.51 a. $\sum x = 3 + 1 + 10 + 10 + 4 = 28$

$\sum x^2 = 3^2 + 1^2 + 10^2 + 10^2 + 4^2 = 226$

$\bar{x} = \frac{\sum x}{n} = \frac{28}{5} = 5.6$

$$s^2 = \frac{\sum x^2 - \frac{(\sum x)^2}{n}}{n-1} = \frac{226 - \frac{28^2}{5}}{5-1} = \frac{69.2}{4} = 17.3 \qquad s = \sqrt{17.3} = 4.1593$$

b. $\sum x = 8 + 10 + 32 + 5 = 55$

$\sum x^2 = 8^2 + 10^2 + 32^2 + 5^2 = 1213$

$\bar{x} = \frac{\sum x}{n} = \frac{55}{4} = 13.75$ feet

$$s^2 = \frac{\sum x^2 - \frac{(\sum x)^2}{n}}{n-1} = \frac{1213 - \frac{55^2}{4}}{4-1} = \frac{456.75}{3} = 152.25 \text{ square feet}$$

$s = \sqrt{152.25} = 12.339$ feet

c. $\sum x = -1 + (-4) + (-3) + 1 + (-4) + (-4) = -15$

$\sum x^2 = (-1)^2 + (-4)^2 + (-3)^2 + 1^2 + (-4)^2 + (-4)^2 = 59$

$\bar{x} = \frac{\sum x}{n} = \frac{-15}{6} = -2.5$

$$s^2 = \frac{\sum x^2 - \frac{(\sum x)^2}{n}}{n-1} = \frac{59 - \frac{(-15)^2}{6}}{6-1} = \frac{21.5}{5} = 4.3 \qquad s = \sqrt{4.3} = 2.0736$$

d. $\sum x = \frac{1}{5} + \frac{1}{5} + \frac{1}{5} + \frac{2}{5} + \frac{1}{5} + \frac{4}{5} = \frac{10}{5} = 2$

$\sum x^2 = \left[\frac{1}{5}\right]^2 + \left[\frac{1}{5}\right]^2 + \left[\frac{1}{5}\right]^2 + \left[\frac{2}{5}\right]^2 + \left[\frac{1}{5}\right]^2 + \left[\frac{4}{5}\right]^2 = \frac{24}{25} = .96$

$\bar{x} = \frac{\sum x}{n} = \frac{2}{6} = \frac{1}{3} = .33$ ounce

$s^2 = \dfrac{\sum x^2 - \dfrac{(\sum x)^2}{n}}{n - 1} = \dfrac{\dfrac{24}{25} - \dfrac{2^2}{6}}{6 - 1} = \dfrac{.2933}{5} = .0587$ square ounce

$s = \sqrt{.0587} = .2422$ ounce

2.53   This is one possibility for the two data sets.

Data Set 1: 0, 1, 2, 3, 4, 5, 6, 7, 8, 9
Data Set 2: 0, 0, 1, 1, 2, 2, 3, 3, 9, 9

The two sets of data above have the same range = largest measurement − smallest measurement = 9 − 0 = 9.

The means for the two data sets are:

$\bar{x}_1 = \frac{\sum x}{n} = \frac{0 + 1 + 2 + 3 + 4 + 5 + 6 + 7 + 8 + 9}{10} = \frac{45}{10} = 4.5$

$\bar{x}_2 = \frac{\sum x}{n} = \frac{0 + 0 + 1 + 1 + 2 + 2 + 3 + 3 + 9 + 9}{10} = \frac{30}{10} = 3$

The dot diagrams for the two data sets are shown below.

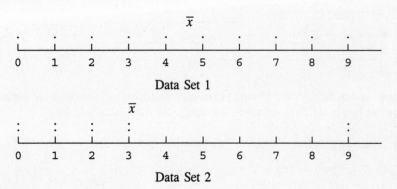

2.55   a.   For Buick, the range is:

Range = Largest − Smallest = \$36,695 − \$19,335 = \$17,360

For Cadillac, the range is:

Range = Largest − Smallest = \$48,520 − \$34,820 = \$13,700

b.   For Chevrolet, the range is:

Range = Largest − Smallest = \$45,575 − \$9,373 = \$36,202

Methods for Describing Sets of Data   15

c. No. With only the values of the ranges, we have no idea which manufacturer produces only luxury cars. The prices of luxury cars can vary over a large range of values, so the range for the prices could be very large, or if the manufacturer makes only a few luxury models which are comparably priced, the range could be small.

2.57 a. The mean value for the U.S. City Average Index for the data in the table is:

$$\bar{x} = \frac{\sum x}{n} = \frac{3607.3}{24} = 150.3042$$

The mean value for the Chicago Index for the data in the table is:

$$\bar{x} = \frac{\sum x}{n} = \frac{3622.9}{24} = 150.9542$$

b. For the U.S. City Average Index, the range = largest measurement − smallest measurement
= 153.7 − 146.2 = 7.5

For the Chicago Index, the range = largest measurement − smallest measurement
= 154.3 − 146.5 = 7.8

c. The standard deviation for the U.S. City Average Index is:

$$s = \sqrt{\frac{\sum x^2 - \frac{(\sum x)^2}{n}}{n-1}} = \sqrt{\frac{542,325.89 - \frac{3607.3^2}{24}}{24-1}} = \sqrt{5.8117} = 2.4108$$

The standard deviation for the Chicago Index for the data in the table is:

$$s = \sqrt{\frac{\sum x^2 - \frac{(\sum x)^2}{n}}{n-1}} = \sqrt{\frac{547,054.25 - \frac{3622.9^2}{24}}{24-1}} = \sqrt{7.0609} = 2.6572$$

d. The Chicago Index displays the greater variation about its mean for this time period. This is evident by the larger standard deviation and range for the Chicago Index.

2.59 a. The range is the largest measurement − the smallest measurement = 510.0 − 54.8 = 455.2

$$\sum x = 182.6 + 226.0 + 342.1 + 510.0 + 119.3 + 378.0 + 54.8 = 1812.8$$
$$\sum x^2 = 182.6^2 + 226.0^2 + 342.1^2 + 510.0^2 + 119.3^2 + 378.0^2 + 54.8^2 = 621,670.7$$
$$s^2 = \frac{\sum x^2 - \frac{(\sum x)^2}{n}}{n-1} = \frac{621,670.7 - \frac{1812.8^2}{7}}{7-1} = \frac{152,207.2943}{6} = 25,367.88238$$
$$s = \sqrt{25,367.88235} = 159.2730$$

b. The range is $455.2 million.

The variance is 25,367.88238 million dollars squared.

The standard deviation is $159.2730 million.

c. If America West had a loss of $50 million, the range would increase since the smallest measurement decreased. The data are more spread out now.

If America West had a loss of $50 million, the standard deviation would increase since the data set is more spread out. $(s = \sqrt{34,069.27667} = 184.5786 > 159.2730)$

2.61 Since no information is given about the data set, we can only use Chebyshev's Rule.

a. Nothing can be said about the percentage of measurements which will fall between $\bar{x} - s$ and $\bar{x} + s$.

b. At least 3/4 or 75% of the measurements will fall between $\bar{x} - 2s$ and $\bar{x} + 2s$.

c. At least 8/9 or 89% of the measurements will fall between $\bar{x} - 3s$ and $\bar{x} + 3s$.

2.63 a. $\bar{x} = \dfrac{\sum x}{n} = \dfrac{206}{25} = 8.24$

$s^2 = \dfrac{\sum x^2 - \dfrac{(\sum x)^2}{n}}{n - 1} = \dfrac{1778 - \dfrac{206^2}{25}}{25 - 1} = 3.357 \qquad s = \sqrt{s^2} = 1.83$

b.

Interval	Number of Measurements in Interval	Percentage
$\bar{x} \pm s$, or (6.41, 10.07)	18	18/25 = .72 or 72%
$\bar{x} \pm 2s$, or (4.58, 11.90)	24	24/25 = .96 or 96%
$\bar{x} \pm 3s$, or (2.75, 13.73)	25	25/25 = 1 or 100%

c. The percentages in part **b** are in agreement with Chebyshev's Rule and agree fairly well with the percentages given by the Empirical Rule.

d. Range = 12 − 5 = 7

$s \approx$ range/4 = 7/4 = 1.75

The range approximation provides a satisfactory estimate of $s = 1.83$ from part **a**.

2.65 a. Since the sample mean (18.2) is larger than the sample median (15), it indicates that the distribution of years is skewed to the right. In addition, the maximum number of years is 50 and the minimum is 2. If the distribution were symmetric, the mean and median should be about halfway between these two numbers. Halfway between the maximum and minimum values is 26, which is much larger than either the mean or the median.

b. The standard deviation can be estimated by the range divided by either 4 or 6. For this distribution, the range is:

Range = Largest − smallest = 50 − 2 = 48.

Dividing the range by 4, we get an estimate of the standard deviation to be 48/4 = 12.

Dividing the range by 6, we get an estimate of the standard deviation to be 48/6 = 8.

Thus, the standard deviation should be somewhere between 8 and 12. For this problem, the standard deviation is $s = 10.64$. This value falls in the estimated range of 8 to 12.

c. First, we calculate the number of standard deviations from the mean the value of 40 years is. To do this, we first subtract the mean and then divide by the value of the standard deviation.

Number of standard deviations is $\dfrac{40 - \bar{x}}{s} = \dfrac{40 - 18.2}{10.64} = 2.05 \approx 2$

Using Chebyshev's Rule, we know that at most $1/k^2$ or $1/2^2 = 1/4$ of the data will be more than 2 standard deviations from the mean. Thus, this would indicate that at most 25% of the Generation Xers responded with 40 years or more.

Next, we calculate the number of standard deviations from the mean the value of 8 years is.

Number of standard deviations is $\dfrac{8 - \bar{x}}{s} = \dfrac{8 - 18.2}{10.64} = -.96 \approx -1$

Using Chebyshev's Rule, we get no information about the data within 1 standard deviation of the mean. However, we know the median (15) is more than 8. By definition, 50% of the data are larger than the median. Thus, at least 50% of the Generation Xers responded with 8 years or more. No additional information can be obtained with the information given.

2.67 a. More than half of the spillage amounts are less than or equal to 48 metric tons and almost all (44 out of 50) are below 104 metric tons. There appear to be three outliers, values which are much different than the others. These three values are larger than 216 metric tons.

b. From the graph in part **a**, the data are not mound shaped. Thus, we must use Chebyshev's Rule. This says that at least 8/9 of the measurements will fall within 3 standard deviations of the mean. Since most of the observations will be within 3 standard deviations of the mean, we could use this interval to predict the spillage amount of the next major oil spill. From the printout, the mean is 59.820 and the standard deviation is 53.362. The interval would be:

$\bar{x} \pm 3s \Rightarrow 59.82 \pm 3(53.362) \Rightarrow 59.82 \pm 160.086 \Rightarrow (-100.266, 219.906)$

Since an oil spillage amount cannot be negative, we would predict that the spillage amount of the next major oil spill will be between 0 and 219.906 metric tons.

2.69 a. Since the data are not mound-shaped, the Empirical Rule would not be appropriate for describing bankruptcy times.

b. Chebyshev's Rule says that at least 75% of the data will fall within 2 standard deviations of the mean. From the printout, the mean is 2.549 and the standard deviation is 1.828. The interval $\bar{x} \pm 2s$ is $2.549 \pm 2(1.828)$ or $(-1.107, 6.205)$. Thus, at least 75% of the bankruptcy times should fall within -1.107 and 6.205 months. Since the number of months cannot be negative, at least 95% of the bankruptcy times are less than 6.205 months.

c. From the data in Exercise 2.24, 47 of the 49 observations fall in this interval or $47/49 = .959$ or 95.9%. This is at least 75%. It is also very close to the 95% used with the Empirical Rule.

d. Because the data set is skewed to the right, the median is a better estimate of the center of the distribution than the mean. Thus, we would estimate that a firm would be in bankruptcy approximately 1.7 months. From the interval in part **b**, we would be very confident that the firm would be in bankruptcy no more than 6.2 months.

2.71 a. Since no information is given about the distribution of the velocities of the Winchester bullets, we can only use Chebyshev's Rule to describe the data. We know that at least 3/4 of the velocities will fall within the interval:

$$\bar{x} \pm 2s \Rightarrow 936 \pm 2(10) \Rightarrow 936 \pm 20 \Rightarrow (916, 956)$$

Also, at least 8/9 of the velocities will fall within the interval:

$$\bar{x} \pm 3s \Rightarrow 936 \pm 3(10) \Rightarrow 936 \pm 30 \Rightarrow (906, 966)$$

b. Since a velocity of 1,000 is much larger than the largest value in the second interval in part **a**, it is very unlikely that the bullet was manufactured by Winchester.

2.73 Since we do not know if the distribution of the heights of the trees is mound-shaped, we need to apply Chebyshev's Rule. We know $\mu = 30$ and $\sigma = 3$. Therefore,

$$\mu \pm 3\sigma \Rightarrow 30 \pm 3(3) \Rightarrow 30 \pm 9 \Rightarrow (21, 39)$$

According to Chebyshev's Rule, at least 8/9 or .89 of the tree heights on this piece of land fall within this interval and at most $\frac{1}{9}$ or .11 of the tree heights will fall above the interval. However, the buyer will only purchase the land if at least $\frac{1000}{5000}$ or .20 of the tree heights are at least 40 feet tall. Therefore, the buyer should not buy the piece of land.

2.75 We know $\mu = 25$ and $\sigma = .1$. Therefore,

$$\mu \pm 2\sigma \Rightarrow 25 \pm 2(.1) \Rightarrow 25 \pm .2 \Rightarrow (24.8, 25.2)$$

The machine is shut down for adjustment if the contents of two consecutive bags fall more than 2 standard deviations from the mean (i.e., outside the interval (24.8, 25.2)). Therefore, the machine was shut down yesterday at 11:30 (25.23 and 25.25 are outside the interval) and again at 4:00 (24.71 and 25.31 are outside the interval).

2.77 Using the definition of a percentile:

	Percentile	Percentage Above	Percentage Below
a.	75th	25%	75%
b.	50th	50%	50%
c.	20th	80%	20%
d.	84th	16%	84%

2.79 We first compute z-scores for each x value.

a. $z = \dfrac{x - \mu}{\sigma} = \dfrac{100 - 50}{25} = 2$

b.　$z = \dfrac{x - \mu}{\sigma} = \dfrac{1 - 4}{1} = -3$

c.　$z = \dfrac{x - \mu}{\sigma} = \dfrac{0 - 200}{100} = -2$

d.　$z = \dfrac{x - \mu}{\sigma} = \dfrac{10 - 5}{3} = 1.67$

The above z-scores indicate that the x value in part **a** lies the greatest distance above the mean and the x value of part **b** lies the greatest distance below the mean.

2.81　Since the 90th percentile of the study sample in the subdivision was .00372 mg/L, which is less than the USEPA level of .015 mg/L, the water customers in the subdivision are not at risk of drinking water with unhealthy lead levels.

2.83　a.　To calculate the U.S. merchandise trade balance for each of the ten countries, take the exports minus the imports.

Country	U.S. Merchandise Trade Balance (in billions)
Brazil	6,289.2
China	−49,695.3
Egypt	3,177.9
France	−4,671.5
Italy	−10,412.8
Japan	−56,114.7
Mexico	−14,549.1
Panama	1,168.9
Sweden	−3,984.8
Singapore	−2,378.4

b.　To find z-scores, we must first calculate the sample mean and standard deviation.

$$\bar{x} = \frac{\sum x}{n} = \frac{-131,170.6}{10} = -13,117.06$$

$$s^2 = \frac{\sum x^2 - \dfrac{(\sum x)^2}{n}}{n - 1} = \frac{6,032,962,855 - \dfrac{(131,170.6)^2}{10}}{10 - 1} = \frac{4,312,390,225}{9}$$
$$= 479,154,469.4$$

$$s = \sqrt{479,154,469.4} = 21,889.6$$

Japan:　$z = \dfrac{x - \bar{x}}{s} = \dfrac{-56,114.7 - (-13,117.06)}{21,889.6} = -1.96$

The relative position of the U.S. trade balance with Japan is 1.96 standard deviations below the mean. This indicates that this observation is small compared to the other U.S. trade balances.

Egypt: $z = \dfrac{x - \bar{x}}{s} = \dfrac{3{,}177.9 - (-13{,}117.06)}{21{,}889.6} = .74$

The relative position of the U.S. trade balance with Egypt is .74 standard deviations above the mean. This indicates that this observation is larger than the average of the U.S. trade balances.

2.85   a.   From the printout, the 10th percentile is 0. Ten percent of the observations are less than or equal to 0.

       b.   From the printout, the 95% percentile is 21. Ninety-five percent of the observations are less than or equal to 21.

       c.   The z-score for the county with 48 Superfund sites is:

$$z = \frac{x - \bar{x}}{s} = \frac{48 - 5.24}{7.224} = 5.90$$

       d.   Yes. A score of 48 is almost 6 standard deviations from the mean. We know that for any data set almost all (at least 8/9 using Chebyshev's Rule) of the observations are within 3 standard deviations of the mean. To be almost 6 standard deviations from the mean is very unusual.

2.87   To determine if the measurements are outliers, compute the z-score.

       a. $z = \dfrac{x - \bar{x}}{s} = \dfrac{65 - 57}{11} = .727$ Since this z-score is less than 3 in magnitude, 65 is not an outlier.

       b. $z = \dfrac{x - \bar{x}}{s} = \dfrac{21 - 57}{11} = -3.273$ Since this z-score is more than 3 in magnitude, 21 is an outlier.

       c. $z = \dfrac{x - \bar{x}}{s} = \dfrac{72 - 57}{11} = 1.364$ Since this z-score is less than 3 in magnitude, 72 is not an outlier.

       d. $z = \dfrac{x - \bar{x}}{s} = \dfrac{98 - 57}{11} = 3.727$ Since this z-score is more than 3 in magnitude, 98 is an outlier.

2.89   The interquartile range is IQR $= Q_U - Q_L = 85 - 60 = 25$.

The lower inner fence $= Q_L - 1.5(\text{IQR}) = 60 - 1.5(25) = 22.5$.

The upper inner fence $= Q_U + 1.5(\text{IQR}) = 85 + 1.5(25) = 122.5$.

The lower outer fence $= Q_L - 3(\text{IQR}) = 60 - 3(25) = -15$.

The upper outer fence $= Q_U + 3(\text{IQR}) = 85 + 3(25) = 160$.

With only this information, the box plot would look something like the following:

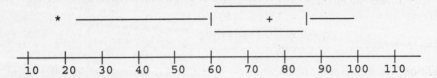

The whiskers extend to the inner fences unless no data points are that small or that large. The upper inner fence is 122.5. However, the largest data point is 100, so the whisker stops at 100. The lower inner fence is 22.5. The smallest data point is 18, so the whisker extends to 22.5. Since 18 is between the inner and outer fences, it is designated with a *. We do not know if there is any more than one data point below 22.5, so we cannot be sure that the box plot is entirely correct.

2.91   a.   Using MINITAB, the box plot for sample A is given below.

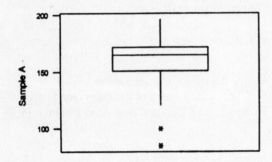

Using MINITAB, the box plot for sample B is given below.

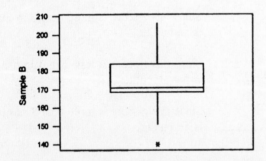

b.   The range for sample A is larger than the range for sample B. The descriptive measures for sample A (Q_L, median, and Q_U) are all smaller than those of sample B. Both samples look somewhat symmetric (excluding outliers) since the whiskers on each box plot are the same length on both sides.

In sample A, the measurement 85 is an outlier. It lies outside the outer fence.

$$\begin{aligned} \text{Lower outer fence} &= \text{Lower hinge} - 3(\text{IQR}) \\ &\approx 151 - 3(172 - 151) \\ &= 151 - 3(21) \\ &= 88 \end{aligned}$$

In addition, the observation of 100 may be an outlier. It lies outside the inner fence, but inside the outer fence.

In Sample B, the observation of 140 may be an outlier. It lies outside the inner fence, but inside the outer fence.

2.93 a. The median bankruptcy times for "Prepack" and "Joint" firms are almost the same. They are both less than the median bankruptcy time of the "None" firms.

b. The range of the "Prepack" firms is less than the other two, while the range of the "None" firms is the largest. The interquartile range of the "Prepack" firms is less than the other two, while the interquartile range of the "Joint" firms is larger than the other two.

c. No. The interquartile range for the "Prepack" firms is the smallest which corresponds to the smallest standard deviation. However, the second smallest interquartile range corresponds to the "none" firms. The second smallest standard deviation corresponds to the "Joint" firms.

d. Yes. There is evidence of two outliers in the "Prepack" firms. These are indicated by the two *'s. There is also evidence of two outliers in the "None" firms. These are indicated by the two *'s.

2.95 a. Using MINITAB, the box plot is:

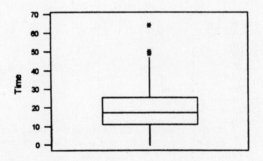

The median is about 18. The data appear to be skewed to the right since there are 3 suspect outliers to the right and none to the left. The variability of the data is fairly small because the IQR is fairly small, approximately $26 - 10 = 16$.

b. The customers associated with the suspected outliers are customers 268, 269, and 264.

c.   In order to find the z-scores, we must first find the mean and standard deviation.

$$\bar{x} = \frac{\sum x}{n} = \frac{815}{40} = 20.375$$

$$s^2 = \frac{\sum x^2 - \frac{(\sum x)^2}{n}}{n - 1} = \frac{24129 - \frac{815^2}{40}}{40 - 1} = 192.90705$$

$$s = \sqrt{192.90705} = 13.89$$

The z-scores associated with the suspected outliers are:

Customer 268 $z = \dfrac{49 - 20.375}{13.89} = 2.06$

Customer 269 $z = \dfrac{50 - 20.375}{13.89} = 2.13$

Customer 264 $z = \dfrac{64 - 20.375}{13.89} = 3.14$

All the z-scores are greater than 2. These are very unusual values.

2.97   The relative frequency histogram is:

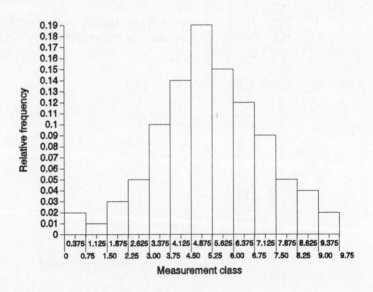

2.99   a. $z = \dfrac{x - \mu}{\sigma} = \dfrac{50 - 60}{10} = -1$

$z = \dfrac{70 - 60}{10} = 1$

$z = \dfrac{80 - 60}{10} = 2$

b. $z = \dfrac{x - \mu}{\sigma} = \dfrac{50 - 60}{5} = -2$

$z = \dfrac{70 - 60}{5} = 2$

$z = \dfrac{80 - 60}{5} = 4$

c. $z = \dfrac{x - \mu}{\sigma} = \dfrac{50 - 40}{10} = 1$

$z = \dfrac{70 - 40}{10} = 3$

$z = \dfrac{80 - 40}{10} = 4$

d. $z = \dfrac{x - \mu}{\sigma} = \dfrac{50 - 40}{100} = .1$

$z = \dfrac{70 - 40}{100} = .3$

$z = \dfrac{80 - 40}{100} = .4$

2.101   a. $\sum x = 13 + 1 + 10 + 3 + 3 = 30$

$\sum x^2 = 13^2 + 1^2 + 10^2 + 3^2 + 3^2 = 288$

$\bar{x} = \sum x = \dfrac{30}{5} = 6$

$s^2 = \dfrac{\sum x^2 - \dfrac{\left(\sum x\right)^2}{n}}{n - 1} = \dfrac{288 - \dfrac{30^2}{5}}{5 - 1} = \dfrac{108}{4} = 27 \qquad s = \sqrt{27} = 5.20$

b. $\sum x = 13 + 6 + 6 + 0 = 25$

$\sum x^2 = 13^2 + 6^2 + 6^2 + 0^2 = 241$

$\bar{x} = \dfrac{\sum x}{n} = \dfrac{25}{4} = 6.25$

$s^2 = \dfrac{\sum x^2 - \dfrac{\left(\sum x\right)^2}{n}}{n - 1} = \dfrac{241 - \dfrac{25^2}{4}}{4 - 1} = \dfrac{84.75}{3} = 28.25 \qquad s = \sqrt{28.25} = 5.32$

c. $\sum x = 1 + 0 + 1 + 10 + 11 + 11 + 15 = 49$

$\sum x^2 = 1^2 + 0^2 + 1^2 + 10^2 + 11^2 + 11^2 + 15^2 = 569$

$\bar{x} = \dfrac{\sum x}{n} = \dfrac{49}{7} = 7$

$s^2 = \dfrac{\sum x^2 - \dfrac{\left(\sum x\right)^2}{n}}{n - 1} = \dfrac{569 - \dfrac{49^2}{7}}{7 - 1} = \dfrac{226}{6} = 37.67 \qquad s = \sqrt{37.67} = 6.14$

d. $\sum x = 3 + 3 + 3 + 3 = 12$

$\sum x^2 = 3^2 + 3^2 + 3^2 + 3^2 = 36$

$\bar{x} = \dfrac{\sum x}{n} = \dfrac{12}{4} = 3$

$s^2 = \dfrac{\sum x^2 - \dfrac{\left(\sum x\right)^2}{n}}{n-1} = \dfrac{36 - \dfrac{12^2}{4}}{4-1} = \dfrac{0}{3} = 0 \qquad\qquad s = \sqrt{0} = 0$

2.103   The range is found by taking the largest measurement in the data set and subtracting the smallest measurement. Therefore, it only uses two measurements from the whole data set. The standard deviation uses every measurement in the data set. Therefore, it takes every measurement into account—not just two. The range is affected by extreme values more than the standard deviation.

2.105   a.   To display the status, we use a pie chart. From the pie chart, we see that 58% of the Beanie babies are retired and 42% are current.

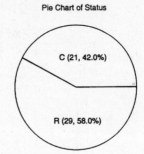

Pie Chart of Status

C (21, 42.0%)

R (29, 58.0%)

b.   Using Minitab, a histogram of the values is:

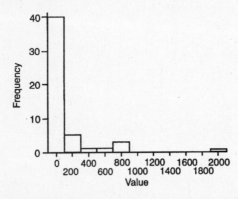

Most (40 of 50) Beanie babies have values less than $100. Of the remaining 10, 5 have values between $100 and $300, 1 has a value between $300 and $500, 1 has a value between $500 and $700, 2 have values between $700 and $900, and 1 has a value between $1900 and $2100.

c.   A plot of the value versus the age of the Beanie Baby is as follows:

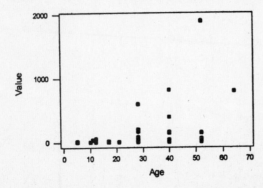

From the plot, it appears that as the age increases, the value tends to increase.

2.107 a. First, we must compute the total processing times by adding the processing times of the three departments. The total processing times are as follows:

Request	Total Processing Time	Request	Total Processing Time	Request	Total Processing Time
1	13.3	17	19.4*	33	23.4*
2	5.7	18	4.7	34	14.2
3	7.6	19	9.4	35	14.3
4	20.0*	20	30.2	36	24.0*
5	6.1	21	14.9	37	6.1
6	1.8	22	10.7	38	7.4
7	13.5	23	36.2*	39	17.7*
8	13.0	24	6.5	40	15.4
9	15.6	25	10.4	41	16.4
10	10.9	26	3.3	42	9.5
11	8.7	27	8.0	43	8.1
12	14.9	28	6.9	44	18.2*
13	3.4	29	17.2*	45	15.3
14	13.6	30	10.2	46	13.9
15	14.6	31	16.0	47	19.9*
16	14.4	32	11.5	48	15.4
				49	14.3*
				50	19.0

The stem-and-leaf displays with the appropriate leaves circled are as follows:

Stem-and-leaf of Mkt
Leaf Unit = 0.10

```
   6     0   112446
   7     1   3
  14     2   (0)024699
  16     3   2(5)
  22     4   (0)(0)(1)577
 (10)    5   0344556889
  18     6   000(2)2247(9)(9)
   8     7   003(8)
   4     8   (0)7
   2     9
   2    10   0
   1    11   0
```

Stem-and-leaf of Engr
Leaf Unit = 0.10

```
   7     0   4466699
  14     1   333378(8)
  19     2   (1)22(4)6
  23     3   1568
  (5)    4   24688
  22     5   233
  19     6   (0)12(3)9
  14     7   (2)(2)379
   9     8
   9     9   66
   7    10   0
   6    11   3
   5    12   02(3)
   2    13   (0)
   1    14   (4)
```

	Stem-and-leaf of Accnt			Stem-and-leaf of Total	
	Leaf Unit = 0.10			Leaf Unit = 1.00	

```
      19   0  11111111111(2)2333444    1    0  1
      (8)  0  55556(8)88                3    0  33
      23   1  00                        5    0  45
      21   1  7(9)                      11   0  666677
      19   2  00(2)3                    17   0  888999
      15   2                            21   1  0000
      15   3  23                        (5)   1  33333
      13   3  78                        24   1  4(4)44445555
      11   4                            14   1  66(7)(7)
      11   4                            10   1  (8)9(9)(9)
      11   5                            6    2  (0)
      11   5  8                         5    2  (3)
      10   6  2                         4    2  (4)4
       9   6                           HI   30,(36)
       9   7  (0)
       8   7
       8   8  4
      HI  (99), (105), (135), 144,
          (182), 220, (300)
```

Of the 50 requests, 10 were lost. For each of the three departments, the processing times for the lost requests are scattered throughout the distributions. The processing times for the departments do not appear to be related to whether the request was lost or not. However, the total processing times for the lost requests appear to be clustered towards the high side of the distribution. It appears that if the total processing time could be kept under 17 days, 76% of the data could be maintained, while reducing the number of lost requests to 1.

b. For the Marketing department, if the maximum processing time was set at 6.5 days, 78% of the requests would be processed, while reducing the number of lost requests by 4. For the Engineering department, if the maximum processing time was set at 7.0 days, 72% of the requests would be processed, while reducing the number of lost requests by 5. For the Accounting department, if the maximum processing time was set at 8.5 days, 86% of the requests would be processed, while reducing the number of lost requests by 5.

2.109 a. One reason the plot may be interpreted differently is that no scale is given on the vertical axis. Also, since the plot almost reaches the horizontal axis at 3 years, it is obvious that the bottom of the plot has been cut off. Another important factor omitted is who responded to the survey.

b. A scale should be added to the vertical axis. Also, that scale should start at 0.

2.111 a. Since the mean is greater than the median, the distribution of the radiation levels is skewed to the right.

b. $\bar{x} \pm s \Rightarrow 10 \pm 3 \Rightarrow (7, 13)$; $\bar{x} \pm 2s \Rightarrow 10 \pm 2(3) \Rightarrow (4, 16)$; $\bar{x} \pm 3s \Rightarrow 10 \pm 3(3) \Rightarrow (1, 19)$

Interval	Chebyshev's	Empirical
(7, 13)	At least 0	$\approx 68\%$
(4, 16)	At least 75%	$\approx 95\%$
(1, 19)	At least 88.9%	$\approx 100\%$

Since the data are skewed to the right, Chebyshev's Rule is probably more appropriate in this case.

c. The background level is 4. Using Chebyshev's Rule, at least 75% or .75(50) $\approx$ 38 homes are above the background level. Using the Empirical Rule, $\approx$ 97.5% or .975(50) $\approx$ 49 homes are above the background level.

d. $z = \dfrac{x - \bar{x}}{s} = \dfrac{20 - 10}{3} = 3.333$

It is unlikely that this new measurement came from the same distribution as the other 50. Using either Chebyshev's Rule or the Empirical Rule, it is very unlikely to see any observations more than 3 standard deviations from the mean.

2.113 a. Using MINITAB, the stem-and-leaf plot for an NFL team's current value is:

Character Stem-and-Leaf Display

```
Stem-and-leaf of Value    N = 30
Leaf Unit = 10

    2    2  99
   12    3  0000111222
   (9)   3  566779999
    9    4  0124
    5    4  68
    3    5  0
    2    5
    2    6  0
    1    6  6
```

b. Yes. Most of the values are in the neighborhood of $300 to $400 million. However, there are a few teams with very large values. The distribution is skewed to the right.

c. From the stem-and-leaf display above, the median is the average of the 15th and 16th values. The values from the plot are 360 and 370, giving a median of 365. The actual values are 369 and 371. The average of 369 and 371 is 370. Thus, the median is 370.

d. To calculate the z-scores for the Denver Broncos, we must first compute the means and standard deviations for the two variables.

Current Value:

$$\bar{x} = \frac{\sum x}{n} = \frac{11,560}{30} = 385.33$$

$$s^2 = \frac{\sum x^2 - \dfrac{\left(\sum x\right)^2}{n}}{n - 1} = \frac{4,688,054 - \dfrac{(11,560)^2}{30}}{30 - 1} = \frac{233,600.667}{29} = 8,055.1954$$

$$s = \sqrt{8,055.1954} = 89.751$$

The z-score for the Denver Broncos current value is:

$$z = \frac{x - \bar{x}}{s} = \frac{427 - 385.33}{89.751} = 0.46$$

Operating Income:

$$\bar{x} = \frac{\sum x}{n} = \frac{590.40}{30} = 19.68$$

$$s^2 = \frac{\sum x^2 - \frac{(\sum x)^2}{n}}{n - 1} = \frac{16,782.94 - \frac{(590.4)^2}{30}}{30 - 1} = \frac{5,163.868}{29} = 178.0644$$

$$s = \sqrt{178.0644} = 13.344$$

The z-score for the Denver Broncos operating income is:

$$z = \frac{x - \bar{x}}{s} = \frac{5.0 - 19.68}{13.344} = -1.10$$

e. The z-score for the current value is 0.46. The Denver Broncos' current value is .46 standard deviations above the mean current value of all NFL teams. The z-score for operating income is -1.10. The Denver Broncos' operating income is 1.10 standard deviations below the mean operating income of all NFL teams.

f. There are several teams that have a positive current value z-score (value above the mean of 385.33) and a negative operating income z-score (value below the mean of 19.68). These teams are:

Carolina Panthers
New England Patriots
Denver Broncos
Seattle Seahawks
Pittsburgh Steelers
Cincinnati Bengals

g. Using MINITAB, the box plot is:

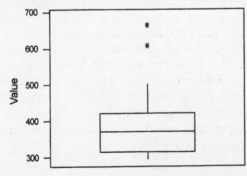

From the box plot, there are 2 potential outliers. These 2 points lie outside the inner fences but inside the outer fences. These potential outliers are associated with the Dallas Cowboys (663) and the Washington Redskins (607). The z-scores associated with these potential outliers are:

The z-score for the Dallas Cowboys' current value is:

$$z = \frac{x - \bar{x}}{s} = \frac{663 - 385.33}{89.751} = 3.09$$

The z-score for the Washington Redskins' current value is:

$$z = \frac{x - \bar{x}}{s} = \frac{607 - 385.33}{89.751} = 2.47$$

Using the z-score value, the current value associated with the Dallas Cowboys is an outlier.

h. To investigate the trend between an NFL team's current value and its operating income, we will construct a plot of the current value against the operating income.

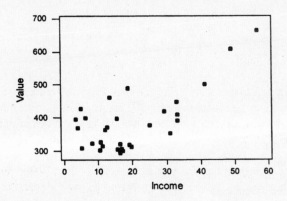

From the plot, it appears that as a team's operating income tends to increase, the current value also tends to increase.

2.115 a. Frequency bar chart.

b. It presents the number of napkins (out of 1000) that fall into each of four categories.

c. Of the 1000 napkins printed, 700 were successful. Another way of saying this is 700/1000 × 100% = 70% of the imprints were successful.

2.119 a. The histograms for both baseball teams are skewed to the right. Most players have relatively low salaries while only a few have relatively high salaries. However, the shapes of the two histograms are quite different. For the Tampa Bay Devil Rays, 22 of the 33 players (66.7%) make $250,000 or less. For the Baltimore Orioles, only 5 of the 28 players (17.9%) make $500,000 or less. For the Tampa Bay Devil Rays, only 3 of 33 players (9.1%) make more than $2,500,000. However, for the Baltimore Orioles, 13 of the 28 players (46.4%) make more than $2,500,000. These percents are quite different for the two teams.

b.   For the Baltimore Orioles, the average salary is $2,685,200 and the standard deviation is $2,222,790. Two standard deviations is 2($2,222,790) = $4,445,580. By Chebyshev's Rule, at least 75% of the salaries of the Baltimore Orioles will fall within 2 standard deviations of the mean or between $0 and $7,130,780.

For the Tampa Bay Devil Rays, the average salary is $830,700 and the standard deviation is $1,349,450. Two standard deviations is 2($1,349,450) = $2,698,900. By Chebyshev's Rule, at least 75% of the salaries of the Tampa Bay Devil Rays will fall within 2 standard deviations of the mean or between $0 and $3,529,600.

2.121   The time series plot for the data is:

Of the 25 observations, only 7 are less than the claimed number of 12 minutes. Thus, the claim that "your hood will be open less than 12 minutes when we service your car" is probably not true.

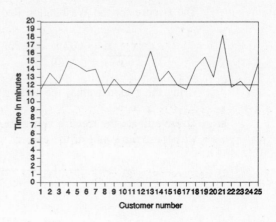

2.123   a.   A relative frequency histogram is:

From the histogram, about a third of the sample scored in the "Very relaxed/confident" category. About an equal amount scored in categories "Very anxious," "Some mild anxiety," and "Generally relaxed/comfortable." Very few scored in the "Anxious/tense" category.

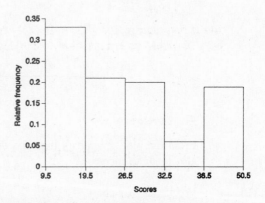

b.   From the tables, the means and standard deviations for the male and female teachers are very similar. The mean for the females is slightly lower than the mean for the males, but the standard deviation is slightly larger. Thus, the average female has a little less anxiety towards computers, but the distribution of female scores is slightly wider than that of the males. But again, these differences are so small that there probably is no difference between male and female teachers concerning their anxiety toward computers.

Probability

3.1 a. Since the probabilities must sum to 1,

$$P(E_3) = 1 - P(E_1) - P(E_2) - P(E_4) - P(E_5) = 1 - .1 - .2 - .1 - .1 = .5$$

b. $P(E_3) = 1 - P(E_3) - P(E_2) - P(E_4) - P(E_5)$
$$\Rightarrow 2P(E_3) = 1 - .1 - .2 - .1 \Rightarrow 2P(E_3) = .6 \Rightarrow P(E_3) = .3$$

c. $P(E_3) = 1 - P(E_1) - P(E_2) - P(E_4) - P(E_5) = 1 - .1 - .1 - .1 - .1 = .6$

3.3 $P(A) = P(1) + P(2) + P(3) = .05 + .20 + .30 = .55$
$P(B) = P(1) + P(3) + P(5) = .05 + .30 + .15 = .50$
$P(C) = P(1) + P(2) + P(3) + P(5) = .05 + .20 + .30 + .15 = .70$

3.5 If we denote the marbles as B_1, B_2, R_1, R_2, R_3, then the ten equally likely sample points in the sample space would be:

$$S: \begin{bmatrix} (B_1, B_2), (B_1, R_1), (B_1, R_2), (B_1, R_3), (B_2, R_1) \\ (B_2, R_2), (B_2, R_3), (R_1, R_2), (R_1, R_3), (R_2, R_3) \end{bmatrix}$$

Notice that order is ignored, as the only concern is whether or not a marble is selected. Each of these 10 would be equally likely, implying that each occurs with a probability 1/10.

$$P(A) = \frac{1}{10} \qquad P(B) = 6\left[\frac{1}{10}\right] = \frac{6}{10} = \frac{3}{5} \qquad P(C) = 3\left[\frac{1}{10}\right] = \frac{3}{10}$$

3.7 a. The experiment consists of selecting 159 employees and asking each to indicate how strongly he/she agreed or disagreed with the statement "I believe that management is committed to CQI." There are five sample points: "Strongly agree," "Agree," "Neither agree nor disagree," "Disagree," and "Strongly disagree."

b. Since we have frequencies for each of the sample points, good estimates of the probabilities are the relative frequencies. To find the relative frequencies, divide all of the frequencies by the sample size of 159. The estimates of the probabilities are:

Strongly Agree	Agree	Neither Agree Nor Disagree	Disagree	Strongly Disagree
.189	.403	.258	.113	.038

c. The probability that an employee agrees or strongly agrees with the statement is $.189 + .403 = .592$.

d. The probability that an employee does not strongly agree with the statement is equal to the sum of all the probabilities except that for "strongly agree" $= .403 + .258 + .113 + .038 = .812$.

3.9   There are $\begin{bmatrix} 6 \\ 3 \end{bmatrix} = \dfrac{6!}{3!3!} = \dfrac{6 \cdot 5 \cdot 4 \cdot 3 \cdot 2 \cdot 1}{3 \cdot 2 \cdot 1 \cdot 3 \cdot 2 \cdot 1} = 20$ possible ways to select 3 cars

from 6. Only one of these combinations includes all three lemons, so the probability that dealer A receives all three lemons is 1/20.

3.11 a. Define the following events:

H: {news story was related to Hispanics}

N: {news story was not related to Hispanics}

Of the 11,855 news stories, 118 were related to Hispanics and 11,855 - 118 = 11,737 were not related to Hispanics. Thus,

$P(N) = 11,737/11,855 = .990$

$P(H) = 118/11,855 = .010$

b. Define the following events:

C: {Hispanic news story focused on crime}

D: {Hispanic news story focused on drugs}

P: {Hispanic news story focused on politics}

Thus, $P(C) = 23/118 = .195$.

The probability that the news story focused on crime or drugs is

$P(C) + P(D) = 23/118 + 1/118 = 24/118 = .203$.

The probability that the news story did not focus on politics or crime is

10/118 + 10/118 + 1/118 + 5/118 + 1/118 + 3/118 + 3/118 + 3/118 + 11/118 + 5/118 + 5/118 + 10/118 + 1/118 = 68/118 = .576

3.13 a. The odds in favor of an Oxford Shoes win are $\dfrac{1}{3}$ to $1 - \dfrac{1}{3} = \dfrac{2}{3}$ or 1 to 2.

b. If the odds in favor of Oxford Shoes are 1 to 1, then the probability that Oxford Shoes wins is $\dfrac{1}{1 + 1} = \dfrac{1}{2}$.

c. If the odds against Oxford Shoes are 3 to 2, then the odds in favor of Oxford Shoes are 2 to 3. Therefore, the probability that Oxford Shoes wins is $\dfrac{2}{2 + 3} = \dfrac{2}{5}$.

3.15 a. The four classifications are:

(1) Raise a broad mix of crops
(2) Raise livestock
(3) Use chemicals sparingly
(4) Use techniques for regenerating the soil

Let us define the following events:

A_1: Raise a broad mix of crops
A_2: Do not raise a broad mix of crops
B_1: Raise livestock
B_2: Do not raise livestock
C_1: Use chemical sparingly
C_2: Do not use chemical sparingly
D_1: Use techniques for regenerating the soil
D_2: Do not use techniques for regenerating the soil

Each farmer is classified as using or not using each of the four techniques. Thus, the sample points are:

$A_1B_1C_1D_1, A_1B_1C_1D_2, A_1B_1C_2D_1, A_1B_2C_1D_1, A_2B_1C_1D_1, A_1B_1C_2D_2,$
$A_1B_2C_1D_2, A_2B_1C_1D_2, A_1B_2C_2D_1, A_2B_1C_2D_1, A_2B_2C_1D_1, A_1B_2C_2D_2,$
$A_2B_1C_2D_2, A_2B_2C_1D_2, A_2B_2C_2D_1, A_2B_2C_2D_2$

b. Since there are 16 classification sets or 16 sample points, the probability of any one sample point is 1/16. The probability that a farmer will be classified as unlikely on all four criteria is:

$P(A_2B_2C_2D_2) = 1/16$

c. The probability that a farmer will be classified as likely on at least three of the criteria is:

$P(A_1B_1C_1D_1) + P(A_1B_1C_1D_2) + P(A_1B_1C_2D_1) + P(A_1B_2C_1D_1) + P(A_2B_1C_1D_1)$
$= 1/16 + 1/16 + 1/16 + 1/16 + 1/16 = 5/16$

3.17 Two events are mutually exclusive if they have no sample points in common. A possible Venn diagram of two mutually exclusive events is:

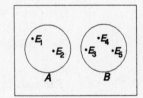

3.19 a. $P(A) = P(E_1) + P(E_2) + P(E_3) + P(E_5) + P(E_6) = \dfrac{1}{5} + \dfrac{1}{5} + \dfrac{1}{5} + \dfrac{1}{20} + \dfrac{1}{10} = \dfrac{15}{20} = \dfrac{3}{4}$

b. $P(B) = P(E_2) + P(E_3) + P(E_4) + P(E_7) = \dfrac{1}{5} + \dfrac{1}{5} + \dfrac{1}{20} + \dfrac{1}{5} = \dfrac{13}{20}$

c. $P(A \cup B) = P(E_1) + P(E_2) + P(E_3) + P(E_4) + P(E_5) + P(E_6) + P(E_7)$
$= \dfrac{1}{5} + \dfrac{1}{5} + \dfrac{1}{5} + \dfrac{1}{20} + \dfrac{1}{20} + \dfrac{1}{10} + \dfrac{1}{5} = 1$

d. $P(A \cap B) = P(E_2) + P(E_3) = \dfrac{1}{5} + \dfrac{1}{5} = \dfrac{2}{5}$

e. $P(A^c) = 1 - P(A) = 1 - \dfrac{3}{4} = \dfrac{1}{4}$

f. $P(B^c) = 1 - P(B) = 1 - \dfrac{13}{20} = \dfrac{7}{20}$

g. $P(A \cup A^c) = P(E_1) + P(E_2) + P(E_3) + P(E_4) + P(E_5) + P(E_6) + P(E_7)$
$$= \dfrac{1}{5} + \dfrac{1}{5} + \dfrac{1}{5} + \dfrac{1}{20} + \dfrac{1}{20} + \dfrac{1}{10} + \dfrac{1}{5} = 1$$

h. $P(A^c \cap B) = P(E_4) + P(E_7) = \dfrac{1}{20} + \dfrac{1}{5} = \dfrac{5}{20} = \dfrac{1}{4}$

3.21 a. $P(A) = .50 + .10 + .05 = .65$

b. $P(B) = .10 + .07 + .50 + .05 = .72$

c. $P(C) = .25$

d. $P(D) = .05 + .03 = .08$

e. $P(A^c) = .25 + .07 + .03 = .35$ (Note: $P(A^c) = 1 - P(A) = 1 - .65 = .35$)

f. $P(A \cup B) = P(B) = .10 + .07 + .50 + .05 = .72$

g. $P(A \cap C) = 0$

h. Two events are mutually exclusive if they have no sample points in common or if the probability of their intersection is 0.

$P(A \cap B) = P(A) = .50 + .10 + .05 = .65$. Since this is not 0, A and B are not mutually exclusive.

$P(A \cap C) = 0$. Since this is 0, A and C are mutually exclusive.

$P(A \cap D) = .05$. Since this is not 0, A and D are not mutually exclusive.

$P(B \cap C) = 0$. Since this is 0, B and C are mutually exclusive.

$P(B \cap D) = .05$. Since this is not 0, B and D are not mutually exclusive.

$P(C \cap D) = 0$. Since this is 0, C and D are mutually exclusive.

3.23 a. $B \cap C$

b. A^c

c. $C \cup B$

d. $A \cap C^c$

3.25   a. $P(A) = 8/28.44 = .281$

$P(B) = 7.84/28.44 = .276$

$P(C) = 1.24/28.44 = .044$

$P(D) = (1.0 + 1.24)/28.44 = 2.24/28.44 = .079$

$P(E) = 1.24/28.44 = .044$

b. $P(A \cap B) = 0/28.44 = 0$

c. $P(A \cup B) = (7.84 + 8)/28.44 = 15.84/28.44 = .557$

d. $P(B^c \cap E) = 0$

e. $P(A \cup E) = 9.24/28.44 = .325$

f.   Two events are mutually exclusive if they have no sample points in common or if the probability of their intersection is 0.

$P(A \cap B) = 0$. Since this is 0, A and B are mutually exclusive.

$P(A \cap C) = 0$. Since this is 0, A and C are mutually exclusive.

$P(A \cap D) = 0$. Since this is 0, A and D are mutually exclusive.

$P(A \cap E) = 0$. Since this is 0, A and E are mutually exclusive.

$P(B \cap C) = 1.24/28.44 = .044$. Since this is not 0, B and C are not mutually exclusive.

$P(B \cap D) = 2.24/28.44 = .079$. Since this is not 0, B and D are not mutually exclusive.

$P(B \cap E) = 1.24/28.44 = .044$. Since this is not 0, B and E are not mutually exclusive.

$P(C \cap D) = 1.24/28.44 = .044$. Since this is not 0, C and D are not mutually exclusive.

$P(C \cap E) = 1.24/28.44 = .044$. Since this is not 0, C and E are not mutually exclusive.

$P(D \cap E) = 1.24/28.44 = .044$. Since this is not 0, D and E are not mutually exclusive.

3.27   a.   A sample point is an event that cannot be decomposed into two or more other events. In this example, there are nine sample points. Let 1 be Warehouse 1, 2 be Warehouse 2, 3 be Warehouse 3, and let R be Regular, S be Stiff, and E be Extra stiff. The sample points are:

(1, R)   (1, S)   (1, E)
(2, R)   (2, S)   (2, E)
(3, R)   (3, S)   (3, E)

b.   The *sample space* of an experiment is the collection of all its sample points.

c. $P(C) = P(3, R) + P(3, S) + P(3, E)$
$ = .11 + .07 + .06$
$ = .24$

d. $P(F) = P(1, E) + P(2, E) + P(3, E)$
$ = 0 + .04 + .06$
$ = .10$

e. $P(A) = P(1, R) + P(1, S) + P(1, E)$
$ = .41 + .06 + 0$
$ = .47$

f. $P(D) = P(1, R) + P(2, R) + P(3, R)$
$ = .41 + .10 + .11$
$ = .62$

g. $P(E) = P(1, S) + P(2, S) + P(3, S)$
$ = .06 + .15 + .07$
$ = .28$

3.29 a. Define the following events:

D: {manufacturer is DaimlerChrysler}

F: {manufacturer is Ford}

G: {manufacturer is General Motors}

C: {type is car}

T: {type is truck}

There are 6 sample points: D,C D,T F,C F,T G,C G,T

b. $P(C) = 1,050,100/2,333,200 = .450$

$P(T) = 1,283,100/2,333,200 = .550$

$P(F) = 788,600/2,333,200 = .338$

c. $P(D \cup F) = P(D) + P(F) = (560,200 + 788,600)/2,333,200 = 1,348,800/2,333,200$
$ = .578$

$P(D \cap F) = 0$

d. $P(C \cap G) = 550,500/2,333,200 = .236$

$P(T \cap G) = 433,900/2,333,200 = .186$

3.31 a. Yes, the probabilities in the table sum to 1.
$.05 + .16 + .05 + .19 + .32 + .05 + .11 + .05 + .02 = 1$

b. $P(A) = .05 + .16 + .05 = .26$
$P(B) = .05 + .19 + .11 = .35$
$P(C) = .05 + .16 + .19 + .32 = .72$
$P(D) = .05 + .05 + .11 + .05 + .02 = .28$
$P(E) = .05$

c. $P(A \cup B) = .05 + .16 + .05 + .19 + .11 = .56$
   $P(A \cap B) = .05$
   $P(A \cup C) = .05 + .16 + .05 + .19 + .32 = .77$

d. $P(A^c) = 1 - P(A) = 1 - .26 = .74$

The probability that a managerial prospect is not highly motivated is .74. Only about 1/4 of the prospects are highly motivated.

e. The pairs of events that are mutually exclusive have no sample points in common.

$A \cap B$ contains the event "Prospect places in the high motivation category and in the high talent category." Therefore, A and B are not mutually exclusive.

$A \cap C$ contains the event "Prospect places in the high motivation category and in the medium or high talent category." Therefore, A and C are not mutually exclusive.

$A \cap D$ contains the event "Prospect places in the high motivation category and in the low talent category." Therefore, A and D are not mutually exclusive.

$A \cap E$ contains the event "Prospect places in the high motivation category and in the high talent category." Therefore, A and E are not mutually exclusive.

$B \cap C$ contains the event "Prospect places in the high talent category and in the medium or high motivation category." Therefore, B and C are not mutually exclusive.

$B \cap D$ contains the event "Prospect places in the high talent category and in the low motivation category." Therefore, B and D are not mutually exclusive.

$B \cap E$ contains the event "Prospect places in the high talent category and in the high motivation category." Therefore, B and E are not mutually exclusive.

$C \cap D$ contains no events. Therefore, C and D are mutually exclusive.

$C \cap E$ contains the event "Prospect places in the high talent category and in the high motivation category." Therefore, C and E are not mutually exclusive.

$D \cap E$ contains no events. Therefore, D and E are mutually exclusive.

3.33 a. $P(A) = P(E_1) + P(E_2) + P(E_3)$
   $\quad\quad = \quad .2 \quad + \quad .3 \quad + \quad .3$
   $\quad\quad = .8$

$P(B) = P(E_2) + P(E_3) + P(E_5)$
   $\quad\quad = \quad .3 \quad + \quad .3 \quad + \quad .1$
   $\quad\quad = .7$

$P(A \cap B) = P(E_2) + P(E_3)$
   $\quad\quad\quad = \quad .3 \quad + \quad .3$
   $\quad\quad\quad = .6$

b. $P(E_1 \mid A) = \dfrac{P(E_1 \cap A)}{P(A)} = \dfrac{P(E_1)}{P(A)} = \dfrac{.2}{.8} = .25$

$P(E_2 \mid A) = \dfrac{P(E_2 \cap A)}{P(A)} = \dfrac{P(E_2)}{P(A)} = \dfrac{.3}{.8} = .375$

$P(E_3 \mid A) = \dfrac{P(E_3 \cap A)}{P(A)} = \dfrac{P(E_3)}{P(A)} = \dfrac{.3}{.8} = .375$

The original sample point probabilities are in the proportion .2 to .3 to .3 or 2 to 3 to 3.

The conditional probabilities for these sample points are in the proportion .25 to .375 to .375 or 2 to 3 to 3.

    c.   (1) $P(B \mid A) = P(E_2 \mid A) + P(E_3 \mid A)$
$$= \quad .375 \quad + \quad .375 \quad \text{(from part \textbf{b})}$$
$$= .75$$

            (2) $P(B \mid A) = \dfrac{P(A \cap B)}{P(A)} = \dfrac{.6}{.8} = .75$ (from part **a**)

The two methods do yield the same result.

    d.   If A and B are independent events, $P(B \mid A) = P(B)$.

From part **c**, $P(B \mid A) = .75$. From part **a**, $P(B) = .7$.

Since $.75 \neq .7$, A and B are not independent events.

3.35   a. $P(A) = P(E_1) + P(E_3) = .22 + .15 = .37$

        b. $P(B) = P(E_2) + P(E_3) + P(E_4) = .31 + .15 + .22 = .68$

        c. $P(A \cap B) = P(E_3) = .15$

        d. $P(A \mid B) = \dfrac{P(A \cap B)}{P(B)} = \dfrac{.15}{.68} = .2206$

        e. $P(B \cap C) = 0$

        f. $P(C \mid B) = \dfrac{P(C \cap B)}{P(B)} = \dfrac{0}{.68} = 0$

        g.   For pair A and B: A and B are not independent because $P(A \mid B) \neq P(A)$ or $.2206 \neq .37$.

For pair A and C:
$$P(A \cap C) = P(E_1) = .22$$
$$P(C) = P(E_1) + P(E_5) = .22 + .1 = .32$$
$$P(A \mid C) = \dfrac{P(A \cap C)}{P(C)} = \dfrac{.22}{.32} = .6875$$

A and C are not independent because $P(A \mid C) \neq P(A)$ or $.6875 \neq .37$.

For pair B and C: B and C are not independent because $P(C \mid B) \neq P(C)$ or $0 \neq .32$.

3.37   a. $P(A \cap C) = 0 \Rightarrow A$ and C are mutually exclusive.
$P(B \cap C) = 0 \Rightarrow B$ and C are mutually exclusive.

        b. $P(A) = P(1) + P(2) + P(3) = .20 + .05 + .30 = .55$
$P(B) = P(3) + P(4) = .30 + .10 = .40$
$P(C) = P(5) + P(6) = .10 + .25 = .35$

$$P(A \cap B) = P(3) = .30$$

$$P(A \mid B) = \frac{P(A \cap B)}{P(B)} = \frac{.30}{.40} = .75$$

A and B are independent if $P(A \mid B) = P(A)$. Since $P(A \mid B) = .75$ and $P(A) = .55$, A and B are not independent.

Since A and C are mutually exclusive, they are not independent. Similarly, since B and C are mutually exclusive, they are not independent.

c. Using the probabilities of sample points,
$$P(A \cup B) = P(1) + P(2) + P(3) + P(4) = .20 + .05 + .30 + .10 = .65$$

Using the additive rule,
$$P(A \cup B) = P(A) + P(B) - P(A \cap B) = .55 + .40 - .30 = .65$$

Using the probabilities of sample points,
$$P(A \cup C) = P(1) + P(2) + P(3) + P(5) + P(6)$$
$$= .20 + .05 + .30 + .10 + .25 = .90$$

Using the additive rule,
$$P(A \cup C) = P(A) + P(C) - P(A \cap C) = .55 + .35 - 0 = .90$$

3.39 a. $P(A \cap B) = P(A) \cdot P(B) = (.4)(.2) = .08$
$P(A \mid B) = P(A) = .4$
$P(A \cup B) = P(A) + P(B) - P(A \cap B) = .4 + .2 - .08 = .52$

b. $P(A \cap B) = P(A \mid B) \cdot P(B) = (.6)(.2) = .12$
$$P(B \mid A) = \frac{P(A \cap B)}{P(A)} = \frac{.12}{.40} = .30$$

3.41 a. Define the following events:

E: {winner was from Eastern Division}

C: {winner was from Central Division}

W: {winner was from Western Division}

N: {winner was from National League}

A: {winner was from American League}

$$P(E \mid A) = \frac{P(E \cap A)}{P(A)} = \frac{5/9}{6/9} = \frac{5}{6} = .833$$

b. $$P(N \mid C) = \frac{P(N \cap C)}{P(C)} = \frac{1/9}{2/9} = \frac{1}{2} = .5$$

c. $$P(C \cup W \mid N) = \frac{P([C \cup W] \cap N)}{P(N)} = \frac{1/9}{3/9} = \frac{1}{3} = .333$$

3.43   First, define the following event:

A: {CVSA correctly determines the veracity of a suspect} $P(A) = .98$ (from claim)

a.   The event that the CVSA is correct for all four suspects is the event $A \cap A \cap A \cap A$.
$P(A \cap A \cap A \cap A) = .98(.98)(.98)(.98) = .9224$

b.   The event that the CVSA is incorrect for at least one of the four suspects is the event
$(A \cap A \cap A \cap A)^c$. $P(A \cap A \cap A \cap A)^c = 1 - P(A \cap A \cap A \cap A)$
$= 1 - .9224 = .0776$

3.45   a.   We will define the events the same as in Exercise 3.10.

There are a total of $9 \times 2 = 18$ sample points for this experiment. There are 9 sources of
CO poisoning, and each source of poisoning has 2 possible outcomes, fatal or nonfatal.
Suppose we introduce some notation to make it easier to write down the sample points. Let
FI = Fire, AU = Auto exhaust, FU = Furnace, K = Kerosene or spaceheater,
AP = Appliance, OG = Other gas-powered motors, FP = Fireplace, O = Other, and
U = Unknown. Also, let F = Fatal and N = Nonfatal. The 18 sample points are:

| FI, F | AU, F | FU, F | K, F | AP, F | OG, F | FP, F | O, F | U, F |
| FI, N | AU, N | FU, N | K, N | AP, N | OG, N | FP, N | O, N | U, N |

$P(F \mid FI) = 63/116 = .543$

b. $P(AU \mid N) = 178/807 = .221$

c. $P(U \mid F) = 9/174 = .052$

d.   The event "not fire or fireplace" would include AU, FU, K, AP, OG, O, and U.

$P(AU \cup FU \cup K \cup AP \cup OG \cup O \cup U \mid N)$
$= (178 + 345 + 18 + 63 + 73 + 19 + 42)/807 = 738/807 = .914$

3.47   Let us define the following events:

S: {School is a subscriber}
N: {School never uses the CCN broadcast}
F: {School uses the CCN broadcast more than five times per week}

From the problem, $P(S) = .40$, $P(N \mid S) = .05$, and $P(F \mid S) = .20$.

a. $P(S \cap N) = P(N \mid S) \, P(S) = .05(.40) = .02$

b. $P(S \cap F) = P(F \mid S) \, P(S) = .20(.40) = .08$

3.49   Define the following events:

A: {Seed carries single spikelets}
B: {Seed carries paired spikelets}
C: {Seed produces ears with single spikelets}
D: {Seed produces ears with paired spikelets}

From the problem, $P(A) = .4$, $P(B) = .6$, $P(C \mid A) = .29$, $P(D \mid A) = .71$, $P(C \mid B) = .26$, and
$P(D \mid B) = .74$.

a. $P(A \cap C) = P(C \mid A)P(A) = .29(.4) = .116$

b. $P(D) = P(A \cap D) + P(B \cap D) = P(D \mid A)P(A) + P(D \mid B)P(B) = .71(.4) + .74(.6)$
          $= .284 + .444 = .728$

3.51   Define the following events:

        A: {Selected firm implemented TQM}
        B: {Selected firm's sales increased}

From the information given, $P(A) = 30/100 = .3$, $P(B) = 60/100 = .6$, and $P(A \mid B) = 20/60$ $= 1/3$.

a. $P(A) = 30/100 = .3$
      $P(B) = 60/100 = .6$

b.   If A and B are independent, $P(A \mid B) = P(A)$. However, $P(A \mid B) = 1/3 \neq P(A) = .3$. Thus, A and B are not independent.

c.   Now, $P(A \mid B) = 18/60 = .3$. Since $P(A \mid B) = .3 = P(A) = .3$, A and B are independent.

3.53   a.   The number of samples of size $n = 3$ elements that can be selected from a population of $N = 600$ is:

$$\begin{pmatrix} N \\ n \end{pmatrix} = \begin{pmatrix} 600 \\ 3 \end{pmatrix} = \frac{600!}{3!597!} = \frac{600(599)(598)}{3(2)(1)} = 35,820,200$$

     b.   If random sampling is employed, then each sample is equally likely. The probability that any sample is selected is 1/35,820,200.

     c.   To draw a random sample of three elements from 600, we will number the elements from 1 to 600. Then, starting in an arbitrary position in Table I, Appendix B, we will select three numbers by going either down a column or across a row. Suppose that we start in the first three positions of column 8 and row 17. We will proceed down the column until we select three different numbers, skipping 000 and any numbers between 601 and 999. The first sample drawn will be 448, 298, and 136 (skip 987). The second sample drawn will be 47, 263, and 287. The 20 samples selected are:

Sample Number	Items Selected	Sample Number	Items Selected
1	448, 298, 136	11	345, 420, 152
2	47, 263, 287	12	144, 68, 485
3	153, 147, 222	13	490, 54, 178
4	360, 86, 357	14	428, 297, 549
5	205, 587, 254	15	186, 256, 261
6	563, 408, 258	16	90, 383, 232
7	428, 356, 543	17	438, 430, 352
8	248, 410, 197	18	129, 493, 496
9	542, 355, 208	19	440, 253, 81
10	399, 313, 563	20	521, 300, 15

None of the samples contain the same three elements. Because the probability in part **b** was so small, it would be very unlikely to have any two samples with the same elements.

3.55 a. If we randomly select one account from the 5,382 accounts, the probability of selecting account 3,241 is $1/5,382 = .000186$.

b. To draw a random sample of 10 accounts from 5,382, we will number the accounts from 1 to 5,382. Then, starting in an arbitrary position in Table I, Appendix B, we will select 10 numbers by going either down a column or across a row. Suppose that we start in the first four positions of column 10 and row 5. We will proceed down the column until we select 10 different numbers, skipping 0000 and any numbers between 5,382 and 9,999. The sample drawn will be:

$$1505, 4884, 1256, 1798, 3159, 2084, 0827, 2635, 4610, 2217$$

c. No. If the samples are randomly selected, any sample of size 10 is equally likely. The total number of ways to select 10 accounts from 5,382 is:

$$\binom{N}{n} = \binom{5,382}{10} = \frac{5,382!}{10!5,372!} = \frac{5,382(5381)(5380)\ldots(5373)}{10(9)(8)\ldots(1)}$$
$$= 5.572377607 \times 10^{30}$$

The probability that any one sample is selected is $1/5.572377607 \times 10^{30}$. Each of the two samples shown have the same probability of occurring.

3.57 a. Give each stock in the NYSE-Composite Transactions table of the Wall Street Journal a number (1 to m). Using Table I of Appendix B, pick a starting point and read down using the same number of digits as in m until you have n different numbers between 1 and m, inclusive.

3.59 (1) The probabilities of all sample points must lie between 0 and 1, inclusive.
(2) The probabilities of all the sample points in the sample space must sum to 1.

3.61 $P(A \cap B) = .4$, $P(A \mid B) = .8$

Since the $P(A \mid B) = \dfrac{P(A \cap B)}{P(B)}$, substitute the given probabilities into the formula and solve for $P(B)$.

$$.8 = \frac{.4}{P(B)} \Rightarrow P(B) = \frac{.4}{.8} = .5$$

3.63 a. $P(A \cap B) = 0$

$P(B \cap C) = P(2) = .2$

$P(A \cup C) = P(1) + P(2) + P(3) + P(5) + P(6) = .3 + .2 + .1 + .1 + .2 = .9$

$P(A \cup B \cup C) = P(1) + P(2) + P(3) + P(4) + P(5) + P(6)$
$= .3 + .2 + .1 + .1 + .1 + .2 = 1$

$P(B^c) = P(1) + P(3) + P(5) + P(6) = .3 + .1 + .1 + .2 = .7$

$P(A^c \cap B) = P(2) + P(4) = .2 + .1 = .3$

$P(B \mid C) = \dfrac{P(B \cap C)}{P(C)} = \dfrac{P(2)}{P(2) + P(5) + P(6)} = \dfrac{.2}{.2 + .1 + .2} = \dfrac{.2}{.5} = .4$

$P(B \mid A) = \dfrac{P(B \cap A)}{P(A)} = \dfrac{0}{P(A)} = 0$

b. Since $P(A \cap B) = 0$, and $P(A) \cdot P(B) > 0$, these two would not be equal, implying A and B are not independent. However, A and B are mutually exclusive, since $P(A \cap B) = 0$.

c. $P(B) = P(2) + P(4) = .2 + .1 = .3$. But $P(B \mid C)$, calculated above, is $.4$. Since these are not equal, B and C are not independent. Since $P(B \cap C) = .2$, B and C are not mutually exclusive.

3.65 a. $6! = 6 \cdot 5 \cdot 4 \cdot 3 \cdot 2 \cdot 1 = 720$

b. $\dbinom{10}{9} = \dfrac{10!}{9!(10-9)!} = \dfrac{10 \cdot 9 \cdot 8 \cdot \;\cdots\; \cdot 1}{9 \cdot 8 \cdot 7 \cdot \;\cdots\; \cdot 1 \cdot 1} = 10$

c. $\dbinom{10}{1} = \dfrac{10!}{1!(10-1)!} = \dfrac{10 \cdot 9 \cdot 8 \cdot \;\cdots\; \cdot 1}{1 \cdot 9 \cdot 8 \cdot \;\cdots\; \cdot 1} = 10$

d. $\dbinom{6}{3} = \dfrac{6!}{3!(6-3)!} = \dfrac{6 \cdot 5 \cdot 4 \cdot 3 \cdot 2 \cdot 1}{3 \cdot 2 \cdot 1 \cdot 3 \cdot 2 \cdot 1} = 20$

e. $0! = 1$

3.67 a. From the problem, it states the 25% of American adults smoke cigarettes. Thus, $P(A) = .25$.

b. Again, from the problem, it says that of the smokers, 13% attempted to quit smoking. Thus, $P(B \mid A) = .13$.

c. $P(A^c) = 1 - P(A) = 1 - .25 = .75$. The probability that an American adult does not smoke is .75.

d. $P(A \cap B) = P(B \mid A)\, P(A) = .13(.25) = .0325$.

3.69 Define the following events:

T: {Technical staff}
N: {Nontechnical staff}
U: {Under 20 years with company}
O: {Over 20 years with company}
R_1: {Retire at age 65}
R_2: {Retire at age 68}

The probabilities for each sample point are given in table form.

	U		O	
	T	N	T	N
R_1	$\dfrac{31}{200}$	$\dfrac{5}{200}$	$\dfrac{45}{200}$	$\dfrac{12}{200}$
R_2	$\dfrac{59}{200}$	$\dfrac{25}{200}$	$\dfrac{15}{200}$	$\dfrac{8}{200}$

Each sample point consists of three characteristics: type of staff (T or N), years with the company, (U or O), and age plan to retire (R_1 or R_2).

a. $P(T) = P(T \cap U \cap R_1) + P(T \cap U \cap R_2) + P(T \cap O \cap R_1) + P(T \cap O \cap R_2)$

$$= \frac{31}{200} + \frac{59}{200} + \frac{45}{200} + \frac{15}{200} = \frac{150}{200} = .75$$

b. $P(O) = P(O \cap T \cap R_1) + P(O \cap T \cap R_2) + P(O \cap N \cap R_1) + P(O \cap N \cap R_2)$

$$= \frac{45}{200} + \frac{15}{200} + \frac{12}{200} + \frac{8}{200} = \frac{80}{200} = .4$$

$$P(R_2 \cap O) = P(R_2 \cap O \cap T) + P(R_2 \cap O \cap N) = \frac{15}{200} + \frac{8}{200} = \frac{23}{200} = .115$$

Thus, $P(R_2 \mid O) = \dfrac{P(R_2 \cap O)}{P(O)} = \dfrac{.115}{.4} = .2875$

c. $P(T) = .75$ from **a**.

$$P(U \cap T) = P(U \cap T \cap R_1) + P(U \cap T \cap R_2) = \frac{31}{200} + \frac{59}{200} = \frac{90}{200} = .45$$

Thus, $P(U \mid T) = \dfrac{P(U \cap T)}{P(T)} = \dfrac{.45}{.75} = .6$

d. $P(O \cap N \cap R_1) = \dfrac{12}{200} = .06$

e. If A and B are independent, then $P(A \mid B) = P(A)$ or $P(R_2 \mid T) = P(R_2)$.

$$P(A \mid B) = \frac{P(A \cap B)}{P(B)} = \frac{\dfrac{59}{200} + \dfrac{15}{200}}{\dfrac{31}{200} + \dfrac{59}{200} + \dfrac{45}{200} + \dfrac{15}{200}} = \frac{\dfrac{74}{200}}{\dfrac{150}{200}} = \frac{74}{150} = .4933$$

$$P(A) = \frac{59}{200} + \frac{25}{200} + \frac{15}{200} + \frac{8}{200} = \frac{107}{200} = .535$$

$.4933 \neq .535$; therefore, A and B are not independent events.

f. The employee does not plan to retire at age 68 or the employee is not on the technical staff.

g. Yes, B and E are mutually exclusive events. An employee cannot be on the technical staff and on the nontechnical staff at the same time.

3.71 Suppose we define the following events:

    A: {Southwest Airline is selected}
    B: {Continental Airline is selected}
    C: {Flight arrived on time}
    D: {Flight was late}

a. Since one airline is to be selected at random, each airline is equally likely. Thus, the probability of selecting any one airline is 1/10.

    $P(A) = 1/10$
    $P(B) = 1/10$

b. $P(C \mid B) = 64.1/100 = .641$
$P(D \mid B) = (100 - 64.1)/100 = 35.9/100 = .359$

c. Since these figures are reported by the airline, these are probably upper bounds. The airlines would want to have a high "on-time" percentage. Thus, they would probably report a percentage that is higher than the actual percentage.

3.73 Define the following events:

A: {The watch is accurate}
N: {The watch is not accurate}

Assuming the manufacturer's claim is correct,

$$P(N) = .05 \text{ and } P(A) = 1 - P(N) = 1 - .05 = .95$$

The sample space for the purchase of four of the manufacturer's watches is listed below.

(A, A, A, A)	(N, A, A, A)	(A, N, N, A)	(N, A, N, N)
(A, A, A, N)	(A, A, N, N)	(N, A, N, A)	(N, N, A, N)
(A, A, N, A)	(A, N, A, N)	(N, N, A, A)	(N, N, N, A)
(A, N, A, A)	(N, A, A, N)	(A, N, N, N)	(N, N, N, N)

a. All four watches not being accurate as claimed is the sample point (N, N, N, N).

Assuming the watches purchased operate independently and the manufacturer's claim is correct,

$$P(N, N, N, N) = P(N)P(N)P(N)P(N) = .05^4 = .00000625$$

b. The sample points in the sample space that consist of exactly two watches failing to meet the claim are listed below.

(A, A, N, N)	(N, A, A, N)
(A, N, A, N)	(N, A, N, A)
(A, N, N, A)	(N, N, A, A)

The probability that exactly two of the four watches fail to meet the claim is the sum of the probabilities of these six sample points.

Assuming the watches purchased operate independently and the manufacturer's claim is correct,

$$P(A, A, N, N) = P(A)P(A)P(N)P(N) = (.95)(.95)(.05)(.05) = .00225625$$

All six of the sample points will have the same probability. Therefore, the probability that exactly two of the four watches fail to meet the claim when the manufacturer's claim is correct is

$$6(0.00225625) = .0135$$

c.   The sample points in the sample space that consist of three of the four watches failing to meet the claim are listed below.

$$(A, N, N, N) \quad (N, N, A, N)$$
$$(N, A, N, N) \quad (N, N, N, A)$$

The probability that three of the four watches fail to meet the claim is the sum of the probabilities of the four sample points.

Assuming the watches purchased operate independently and the manufacturer's claim is correct,

$$P(A, N, N, N) = P(A)P(N)P(N)P(N) = (.95)(.05)(.05)(.05) = .00011875$$

All four of the sample points will have the same probability. Therefore, the probability that three of the four watches fail to meet the claim when the manufacturer's claim is correct is

$$4(.00011875) = .000475$$

If this event occurred, we would tend to doubt the validity of the manufacturer's claim since its probability of occurring is so small.

d.   All four watches tested failing to meet the claim is the sample point (N, N, N, N).

Assuming the watches purchased operate independently and the manufacturer's claim is correct,

$$P(N, N, N, N) = P(N)P(N)P(N)P(N) = (.05)^4 = .00000625$$

Since the probability of observing this event is so small if the claim is true, we have strong evidence against the validity of the claim. However, we do not have conclusive proof that the claim is false. There is still a chance the event can occur (with probability .00000625) although it is extremely small.

3.75   Define the following events:

   A: {Acupoll predicts the success of a particular product}
   B: {Product is successful}

From the problem, we know

   $P(A \mid B) = .89$ and $P(B) = .90$

Thus, $P(A \cap B) = P(A \mid B)P(B) = .89(.90) = .801$

3.77   Define the following events:

   G: {regularly use the golf course}
   T: {regularly use the tennis courts}

Given: $P(G) = .7$ and $P(T) = .5$

The event "uses neither facility" can be written as $G^c \cap T^c$ or $(G \cup T)^c$. We are given $P(G^c \cap T^c) = P[(G \cup T)^c] = .05$. The complement of the event "uses neither facility" is the event "uses at least one of the two facilities" which can be written as $G \cup T$.

$$P(G \cup T) = 1 - P[(G \cup T)^c] = 1 - .05 = .95$$

From the additive rule, $P(G \cup T) = P(G) + P(T) - P(G \cap T)$
$$\Rightarrow .95 = .7 + .5 - P(G \cap T)$$
$$\Rightarrow P(G \cap T) = .25$$

a.   The Venn Diagram is:

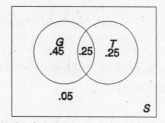

b. $P(G \cup T) = .95$ from above.

c. $P(G \cap T) = .25$ from above.

d. $P(G \mid T) = \dfrac{P(G \cap T)}{P(T)} = \dfrac{.25}{.5} = .5$

3.79   Define the following events:

   A: {Family with young children has income above the poverty line, but less than $25,000}
   B: {Family with young children has unemployed parents or no parents}
   C: {Family with young children has income below the poverty line}

a. $P(A) = (2\% + 22\%)/100\% = 24\%/100\% = .24$

b. $P(B) = (1\% + 7\% + 2\%)/100\% = 10\%/100\% = .1$

c. $P(C) = (7\% + 7\%)/100\% = 14\%/100\% = .14$

3.81   Define the following events:

   S_1: {Salesman makes sale on the first visit}
   S_2: {Salesman makes a sale on the second visit}

$P(S_1) = .4 \qquad P(S_2 \mid S_1^c) = .65$

The sample points of the experiment are:

$$S_1 \cap S_2^c$$
$$S_1^c \cap S_2$$
$$S_1^c \cap S_2^c$$

The probability the salesman will make a sale is:

$$P(S_1 \cap S_2^c) + P(S_1^c \cap S_2) = P(S_1) + P(S_2 \mid S_1^c)P(S_1^c) = .4 + .65(1 - .4) = .4 + .39 = .79$$

3.83   Define the following events:

O_1: {Component #1 operates properly}
O_2: {Component #2 operates properly}
O_3: {Component #3 operates properly}

$P(O_1) = 1 - P(O_1^c) = 1 - .12 = .88$
$P(O_2) = 1 - P(O_2^c) = 1 - .09 = .91$
$P(O_3) = 1 - P(O_3^c) = 1 - .11 = .89$

a. $P(\text{System operates properly}) = P(O_1 \cap O_2 \cap O_3)$
$= P(O_1)P(O_2)P(O_3)$
(since the three components operate independently)
$= (.88)(.91)(.89) = .7127$

b. $P(\text{System fails}) = 1 - P(\text{system operates properly})$
$= 1 - .7127$ (see part **a**)
$= .2873$

3.85   a. The possible pairs of accounts that could be obtained are:

(0001, 0002) (0001, 0003) (0001, 0004) (0001, 0005)
(0002, 0003) (0002, 0004) (0002, 0005)
(0003, 0004) (0003, 0005)
(0004, 0005)

b. There are 10 possible pairs of accounts that could be obtained. In a random sample, all 10 pairs of accounts have an equal chance of being selected. The probability of selecting any one of the 10 pairs is 1/10. Therefore, the probability of selecting accounts 0001 and 0004 is 1/10.

c. Since only two accounts have a balance of $1,000 (0001 and 0004), the probability of selecting two accounts that each have a balance of $1,000 is 1/10.

Since there are only three accounts that do not have a balance of $1,000 (0002, 0003, and 0005), there are three possible pairs of accounts in which each has a balance other than $1,000 (0002, 0003), (0002, 0005), and (0003, 0005)). Therefore, the probability of selecting a pair of accounts in which each has a balance other than $1,000 is 3/10.

3.87   Define the following events:

A: {Take tough action early}
B: {Take tough action late}
C: {Never take tough action}
D: {Wisconsin}
E: {Illinois}
F: {Arkansas}
G: {Louisiana}

a. $P(D \cup G) = P(D) + P(G)$ (since D and G are mutually exclusive)

$= \dfrac{0}{151} + \dfrac{37}{151} + \dfrac{9}{151} + \dfrac{1}{151} + \dfrac{21}{151} + \dfrac{15}{151} = \dfrac{83}{151} = .550$

b. $P((D \cup G)^c) = 1 - P(D \cup G)$

$\qquad = 1 - \dfrac{83}{151} = \dfrac{68}{151} = .450$

c. $P(C) = \dfrac{9}{151} + \dfrac{11}{151} + \dfrac{6}{151} + \dfrac{15}{151} = \dfrac{41}{151} = .272$

d. $P(F \cap C) = \dfrac{6}{151} = .040$

e. $P(C \mid F) = \dfrac{P(F \cap C)}{P(F)} = \dfrac{\frac{6}{151}}{\frac{33}{151}} = \dfrac{6}{33} = .182$

f. $P((F \cup G) \mid A) = \dfrac{P((F \cup G) \cap A)}{P(A)} = \dfrac{\frac{5}{151} + \frac{1}{151}}{\frac{7}{151}} = \dfrac{6}{7} = .857$

g. $P(C \mid F) = \dfrac{P(F \cap C)}{P(F)} = \dfrac{\frac{6}{151}}{\frac{33}{151}} = \dfrac{6}{33} = .182$

Discrete Random Variables   *Chapter 4*

4.1   A random variable is a rule that assigns one and only one value to each sample point of an experiment.

4.3   a.   The closing price of a particular stock on the New York Stock Exchange is discrete. It can take on only a countable number of values.

        b.   The number of shares of a particular stock that are traded on a particular day is discrete. It can take on only a countable number of values.

        c.   The quarterly earnings of a particular firm is discrete. It can take on only a countable number of values.

        d.   The percentage change in yearly earnings between 1996 and 1997 for a particular firm is continuous. It can take on any value in an interval.

        e.   The number of new products introduced per year by a firm is discrete. It can take on only a countable number of values.

        f.   The time until a pharmaceutical company gains approval from the U.S. Food and Drug Administration to market a new drug is continuous. It can take on any value in an interval of time.

4.5   The number of occupied units in an apartment complex at any time is a discrete random variable, as is the number of shares of stock traded on the New York Stock Exchange on a particular day. Two examples of continuous random variables are the length of time to complete a building project and the weight of a truckload of oranges.

4.7   An economist might be interested in the percentage of the work force that is unemployed, or the current inflation rate, both of which are continuous random variables.

4.9   The manager of a clothing store might be concerned with the number of employees on duty at a specific time of day, or the number of articles of a particular type of clothing that are on hand.

4.11   a.   We know $\sum p(x) = 1$. Thus, $p(2) + p(3) + p(5) + p(8) + p(10) = 1$
               $$\Rightarrow p(5) = 1 - p(2) - p(3) - p(8) - p(10) = 1 - .15 - .10 - .25 - .25 = .25$$

        b. $P(x = 2 \text{ or } x = 10) = P(x = 2) + P(x = 10) = .15 + .25 = .40$

        c. $P(x \leq 8) = P(x = 2) + P(x = 3) + P(x = 5) + P(x = 8) = .15 + .10 + .25 + .25 = .75$

4.13   a.   The sample points are (where H = head, T = tail):

                       HHH HHT HTH THH HTT THT TTH TTT
               x = # heads   3   2   2   2   1   1   1   0

b. If each event is equally likely, then $P(\text{sample point}) = \dfrac{1}{n} = \dfrac{1}{8}$

$$p(3) = \frac{1}{8},\ p(2) = \frac{1}{8} + \frac{1}{8} + \frac{1}{8} = \frac{3}{8},\ p(1) = \frac{1}{8} + \frac{1}{8} + \frac{1}{8} = \frac{3}{8},\ \text{and}\ p(0) = \frac{1}{8}$$

c.

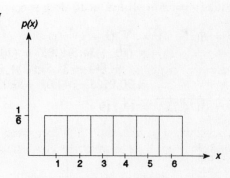

d. $P(x = 2\text{ or }x = 3) = p(2) + p(3) = \dfrac{3}{8} + \dfrac{1}{8} = \dfrac{4}{8} = \dfrac{1}{2}$

4.15   a. When a die is tossed, the number of spots observed on the upturned face can be 1, 2, 3, 4, 5, or 6. Since the six sample points are equally likely, each one has a probability of 1/6.

The probability distribution of x may be summarized in tabular form:

x	1	2	3	4	5	6
$p(x)$	$\dfrac{1}{6}$	$\dfrac{1}{6}$	$\dfrac{1}{6}$	$\dfrac{1}{6}$	$\dfrac{1}{6}$	$\dfrac{1}{6}$

b. The probability distribution of x may also be presented in graphical form:

4.17   a. $P(x = 4) = .2592$

b. $P(x < 2) = P(x = 0) + P(x = 1) = .0102 + .0768 = .0870$

c. $P(x \geq 3) = P(x = 3) + P(x = 4) + P(x = 5) = .3456 + .2592 + .0778 = .6826$

4.19   a. Since the number of observations is very large, the relative frequencies or proportions should reflect the probabilities very well.

b. Let x = household income. Then $P(x > \$200{,}000) = 1.1/100 = .011$
$P(x > \$100{,}000) = 4.1/100 + 1.1/100 = 5.2/100 = .052$
$P(x < \$100{,}000) = 18.5/100 + 19.0/100 + 15.9/100 + 12.8/100 + 9.1/100 + 13.8/100$
                 $+ 5.7/100 = 94.8/100 = .948$
$P(\$30{,}000 < x < \$49{,}999) = 12.8/100 + 9.1/100 = 21.9/100 = .219$

c.

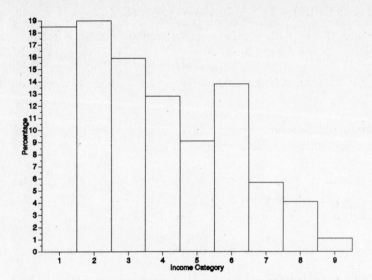

d. P(category 6) $= P(\$50,000 < x < \$74,999) = 13.8/100 = .138$
    P(category 1 or 9) $= P(x < \$10,000) + P(x \geq \$200,000)$
    $$= 18.5/100 + 1.1/100 = 19.6/100 = .196$$

4.21   The population mean, μ, is equal to the expected value of x, $E(x)$. The sample mean, $\overline{x}$, is calculated from a sample.

4.23   a. $\mu = E(x) = \sum xp(x)$
    $= 10(.05) + 20(.20) + 30(.30) + 40(.25) + 50(.10) + 60(.10)$
    $= .5 + 4 + 9 + 10 + 5 + 6 = 34.5$

    $\sigma^2 = E(x - \mu)^2 = \sum (x - \mu)^2 p(x)$
    $= (10 - 34.5)^2(.05) + (20 - 34.5)^2(.20) + (30 - 34.5)^2(.30)$
    $\quad + (40 - 34.5)^2(.25) + (50 - 34.5)^2(.10) + (60 - 34.5)^2(.10)$
    $= 30.0125 + 42.05 + 6.075 + 7.5625 + 24.025 + 65.025 = 174.75$

    $\sigma = \sqrt{174.75} = 13.219$

b.

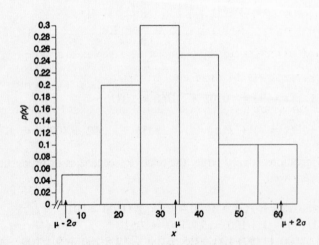

c. $\mu \pm 2\sigma \Rightarrow 34.5 \pm 2(13.219) \Rightarrow 34.5 \pm 26.438 \Rightarrow (8.062, 60.938)$

$$P(8.062 < x < 60.938) = p(10) + p(20) + p(30) + p(40) + p(50) + p(60)$$
$$= .05 + .20 + .30 + .25 + .10 + .10 = 1.00$$

4.25   a.   It would seem that the mean of both would be 1 since they both are symmetric distributions centered at 1.

      b. $P(x)$ seems more variable since there appears to be greater probability for the two extreme values of 0 and 2 than there is in the distribution of y.

      c.   For x: $\mu = E(x) = \sum xp(x) = 0(.3) + 1(.4) + 2(.3) = 0 + .4 + .6 = 1$

$$\sigma^2 = E[(x - \mu)^2] = \sum (x - \mu)^2 p(x)$$
$$= (0 - 1)^2(.3) + (1 - 1)^2(.4) + (2 - 1)^2(.3) = .3 + 0 + .3 = .6$$

For y: $\mu = E(y) = \sum yp(y) = 0(.1) + 1(.8) + 2(.1) = 0 + .8 + .2 = 1$

$$\sigma^2 = E[(y - \mu)^2] = \sum (y - \mu)^2 p(y)$$
$$= (0 - 1)^2(.1) + (1 - 1)^2(.8) + (2 - 1)^2(.1) = .1 + 0 + .1 = .2$$

The variance for x is larger than that for y.

4.27   Let x = bookie's earnings per dollar wagered. Then x can take on values \$1 (you lose) and \$-5 (you win). The only way you win is if you pick 3 winners in 3 games. If the probability of picking 1 winner in 1 game is .5, then $P(www) = p(w)p(w)p(w) = .5(.5)(.5) = .125$ (assuming games are independent).

Thus, the probability distribution for x is:

x	$p(x)$
\$1	.875
\$-5	.125

$E(x) = \sum xp(x) = 1(.875) - 5(.125) = .875 - .625 = \$.25$

4.29   a.   Let x = number of training units necessary to master the complex computer software program.

$$\mu = E(x) = \sum xp(x) = 1(.1) + 2(.25) + 3(.4) + 4(.15) + 5(.1)$$
$$= .1 + .5 + 1.2 + .6 + .5 = 2.9$$

This is the average number of units necessary to master the complex software program.

Median = 3 (first observation where the cumulative probability is $\geq$ .5)

At least half of the observations are less than or equal to 3 and at least half of the observations are greater than or equal to 3.

      b. $P(x \leq k) \geq .75 \Rightarrow k = 3$
$P(x \leq k) \geq .90 \Rightarrow k = 4$

      c. $\mu = E(x) = \sum xp(x) = 1(.25) + 2(.35) + 3(.40) = .25 + .70 + 1.2 = 2.15$

This is smaller than the answer in part a. Again, this is the average number of units necessary to master the complex software program.

Median = 2 (first observation where the cumulative probability is $\geq .5$)

$P(x \leq k) \geq .75 \Rightarrow k = 3$
$P(x \leq k) \geq .90 \Rightarrow k = 3$

4.31 **For ARC a_1:** $\mu = E(x) = \sum xp(x) = 0(.05) + 1(.10) + 2(.25) + 3(.60) = 2.4$
The mean capacity for ARC a_1 is 2.4

For ARC a_2: $\mu = E(x) = \sum xp(x) = 0(.10) + 1(.30) + 2(.60) = 1.5$
The mean capacity for ARC a_2 is 1.5

For ARC a_3: $\mu = E(x) = \sum xp(x) = 0(.10) + 1(.90) = .90$
The mean capacity for ARC a_3 is .90

For ARC a_4: $\mu = E(x) = \sum xp(x) = 0(.10) + 1(.90) = .90$
The mean capacity for ARC a_4 is .90

For ARC a_5: $\mu = E(x) = \sum xp(x) = 0(.10) + 1(.90) = .90$
The mean capacity for ARC a_5 is .90

For ARC a_6: $\mu = E(x) = \sum xp(x) = 0(.05) + 1(.25) + 2(.70) = 1.65$
The mean capacity for ARC a_6 is 1.65

4.33 a. Since there are 20 possible outcomes that are all equally likely, the probability of any of the 20 numbers is 1/20. The probability distribution of x is:

$P(x = 5) = 1/20 = .05;$ $P(x = 10) = 1/20 = .05;$ etc.

x	5	10	15	20	25	30	35	40	45	50	55	60	65	70	75	80	85	90	95	100
$p(x)$	.05	.05	.05	.05	.05	.05	.05	.05	.05	.05	.05	.05	.05	.05	.05	.05	.05	.05	.05	.05

b. $E(x) = \sum xp(x) = 5(.05) + 10(.05) + 15(.05) + 20(.05) + 25(.05) + 30(.05) + 35(.05)$
$+ 40(.05) + 45(.05) + 50(.05) + 55(.05) + 60(.05) + 65(.05) + 70(.05) + 75(.05)$
$+ 80(.05) + 85(.05) + 90(.05) + 95(.05) + 100(.05) = 52.5$

c. $\sigma^2 = E(x - \mu)^2 = \sum (x - \mu)^2 p(x) = (5 - 52.5)^2(.05) + (10 - 52.5)^2(.05)$
$+ (15 - 52.5)^2(.05) + (20 - 52.5)^2(.05) + (25 - 52.5)^2(.05) + (30 - 52.5)^2(.05)$
$+ (35 - 52.5)^2(.05) + (40 - 52.5)^2(.05) + (45 - 52.5)^2(.05) + (50 - 52.5)^2(.05)$
$+ (55 - 52.5)^2(.05) + (60 - 52.5)^2(.05) + (65 - 52.5)^2(.05) + (70 - 52.5)^2(.05)$
$+ (75 - 52.5)^2(.05) + (80 - 52.5)^2(.05) + (85 - 52.5)^2(.05) + (90 - 52.5)^2(.05)$
$+ (95 - 52.5)^2(.05) + (100 - 52.5)^2(.05)$
$= 831.25$

$\sigma = \sqrt{\sigma^2} = \sqrt{831.25} = 28.83$

Since the uniform distribution is not mound-shaped, we will use Chebyshev's theorem to describe the data. We know that at least 8/9 of the observations will fall with 3 standard deviations of the mean and at least 3/4 of the observations will fall within 2 standard deviations of the mean. For this problem,

$\mu \pm 2\sigma \Rightarrow 52.5 \pm 2(28.83) \Rightarrow 52.5 \pm 57.66 \Rightarrow (-5.16, 110.16)$. Thus, at least 3/4 of the data will fall between -5.16 and 110.16. For our problem, all of the observations will fall within 2 standard deviations of the mean. Thus, x is just as likely to fall within any interval of equal length.

d. If a player spins the wheel twice, the total number of outcomes will be 20(20) = 400. The sample space is:

5, 5	10, 5	15, 5	20, 5	25, 5...	100, 5
5,10	10,10	15,10	20,10	25,10...	100,10
5,15	10,15	15,15	20,15	25,15...	100,15
⋮	⋮	⋮	⋮	⋮	⋮
5,100	10,100	15,100	20,100	25,100...	100,100

Each of these outcomes are equally likely, so each has a probability of 1/400 = .0025.

Now, let x equal the sum of the two numbers in each sample. There is one sample with a sum of 10, two samples with a sum of 15, three samples with a sum of 20, etc. If the sum of the two numbers exceeds 100, then x is zero. The probability distribution of x is:

x	$p(x)$
0	.5250
10	.0025
15	.0050
20	.0075
25	.0100
30	.0125
35	.0150
40	.0175
45	.0200
50	.0225
55	.0250
60	.0275
65	.0300
70	.0325
75	.0350
80	.0375
85	.0400
90	.0425
95	.0450
100	.0475

e. We assumed that the wheel is fair, or that all outcomes are equally likely.

f. $\mu = E(x) = \sum x\, p(x) = 0(.5250) + 10(.0025) + 15(.0050) + 20(.0075) + ... + 100(.0475)$
$= 33.25$

$\sigma^2 = E(x - \mu)^2 = \sum (x - \mu)^2\, p(x) = (0 - 33.25)^2(.525) + (10 - 33.25)^2(.0025)$
$+ (15 - 33.25)^2(.0050) + (20 - 33.25)^2(.0075) + ... + (100 - 33.25)^2(.0475)$
$= 1471.3125$

$\sigma = \sqrt{\sigma^2} = \sqrt{1471.3125} = 38.3577$

g. $P(x = 0) = .525$

h.   Given that the player obtains a 20 on the first spin, the possible values for x (sum of the two spins) are 0 (player spins 85, 90, 95, or 100 on the second spin), 25, 30, ..., 100. In order to get an x of 25, the player would spin a 5 on the second spin. Similarly, the player would have to spin a 10 on the second spin order to get an x of 30, etc. Since all of the outcomes are equally likely on the second spin, the distribution of x is:

x	$p(x)$
0	.20
25	.05
30	.05
35	.05
40	.05
45	.05
50	.05
55	.05
60	.05
65	.05
70	.05
75	.05
80	.05
85	.05
90	.05
95	.05
100	.05

i.   The probability that the players total score will exceed one dollar is the probability that x is zero. $P(x = 0) = .20$

j.   Given that the player obtains a 65 on the first spin, the possible values for x (sum of the two spins) are 0 (player spins 40, 45, 50, up to 100 on second spin), 70, 75, 80,..., 100. In order to get an x of 70, the player would spin a 5 on the second spin. Similarly, the player would have to spin a 10 on the second spin in order to get an x of 75, etc. Since all of the outcomes are equally likely on the second spin, the distribution of x is:

x	$p(x)$
0	.65
70	.05
75	.05
80	.05
85	.05
90	.05
95	.05
100	.05

The probability that the players total score will exceed one dollar is the probability that x is zero. $P(x = 0) = .65$.

4.35 a. $\dfrac{6!}{2!(6-2)!} = \dfrac{6!}{2!4!} = \dfrac{6 \cdot 5 \cdot 4 \cdot 3 \cdot 2 \cdot 1}{(2 \cdot 1)(4 \cdot 3 \cdot 2 \cdot 1)} = 15$

     b. $\begin{bmatrix} 5 \\ 2 \end{bmatrix} = \dfrac{5!}{2!(5-2)!} = \dfrac{5!}{2!3!} = \dfrac{5 \cdot 4 \cdot 3 \cdot 2 \cdot 1}{(2 \cdot 1)(3 \cdot 2 \cdot 1)} = 10$

     c. $\begin{bmatrix} 7 \\ 0 \end{bmatrix} = \dfrac{7!}{0!(7-0)!} = \dfrac{7!}{0!7!} = \dfrac{7 \cdot 6 \cdot 5 \cdot 4 \cdot 3 \cdot 2 \cdot 1}{(1)(7 \cdot 6 \cdot 5 \cdot 4 \cdot 3 \cdot 2 \cdot 1)} = 1$
                        (Note: $0! = 1$)

     d. $\begin{bmatrix} 6 \\ 6 \end{bmatrix} = \dfrac{6!}{6!(6-6)!} = \dfrac{6!}{6!0!} = \dfrac{6 \cdot 5 \cdot 4 \cdot 3 \cdot 2 \cdot 1}{(6 \cdot 5 \cdot 4 \cdot 3 \cdot 2 \cdot 1)(1)} = 1$

     e. $\begin{bmatrix} 4 \\ 3 \end{bmatrix} = \dfrac{4!}{3!(4-3)!} = \dfrac{4!}{3!1!} = \dfrac{4 \cdot 3 \cdot 2 \cdot 1}{(3 \cdot 2 \cdot 1)(1)} = 4$

4.37 a. $P(x = 1) = \dfrac{5!}{1!4!}(.2)^1(.8)^4 = \dfrac{5 \cdot 4 \cdot 3 \cdot 2 \cdot 1}{(1)(4 \cdot 3 \cdot 2 \cdot 1)}(.2)^1(.8)^4 = 5(.2)^1(.8)^4 = .4096$

     b. $P(x = 2) = \dfrac{4!}{2!2!}(.6)^2(.4)^2 = \dfrac{4 \cdot 3 \cdot 2 \cdot 1}{(2 \cdot 1)(2 \cdot 1)}(.6)^2(.4)^2 = 6(.6)^2(.4)^2 = .3456$

     c. $P(x = 0) = \dfrac{3!}{0!3!}(.7)^0(.3)^3 = \dfrac{3 \cdot 2 \cdot 1}{(1)(3 \cdot 2 \cdot 1)}(.7)^0(.3)^3 = 1(.7)^0(.3)^3 = .027$

     d. $P(x = 3) = \dfrac{5!}{3!2!}(.1)^3(.9)^2 = \dfrac{5 \cdot 4 \cdot 3 \cdot 2 \cdot 1}{(3 \cdot 2 \cdot 1)(2 \cdot 1)}(.1)^3(.9)^2 = 10(.1)^3(.9)^2 = .0081$

     e. $P(x = 2) = \dfrac{4!}{2!2!}(.4)^2(.6)^2 = \dfrac{4 \cdot 3 \cdot 2 \cdot 1}{(2 \cdot 1)(2 \cdot 1)}(.4)^2(.6)^2 = 6(.4)^2(.6)^2 = .3456$

     f. $P(x = 1) = \dfrac{3!}{1!2!}(.9)^1(.1)^2 = \dfrac{3 \cdot 2 \cdot 1}{(1)(2 \cdot 1)}(.9)^1(.1)^2 = 3(.9)^1(.1)^2 = .027$

4.39 a. $\mu = np = 25(.5) = 12.5$

       $\sigma^2 = np(1-p) = 25(.5)(.5) = 6.25$

       $\sigma = \sqrt{\sigma^2} = \sqrt{6.25} = 2.5$

     b. $\mu = np = 80(.2) = 16$

       $\sigma^2 = np(1-p) = 80(.2)(.8) = 12.8$

       $\sigma = \sqrt{\sigma^2} = \sqrt{12.8} = 3.578$

     c. $\mu = np = 100(.6) = 60$

       $\sigma^2 = np(1-p) = 100(.6)(.4) = 24$

       $\sigma = \sqrt{\sigma^2} = \sqrt{24} = 4.899$

d. $\mu = np = 70(.9) = 63$

$\sigma^2 = np(1 - p) = 70(.9)(.1) = 6.3$

$\sigma = \sqrt{\sigma^2} = \sqrt{6.3} = 2.510$

e. $\mu = np = 60(.8) = 48$

$\sigma^2 = np(1 - p) = 60(.8)(.2) = 9.6$

$\sigma = \sqrt{\sigma^2} = \sqrt{9.6} = 3.098$

f. $\mu = np = 1,000(.04) = 40$

$\sigma^2 = np(1 - p) = 1,000(.04)(.96) = 38.4$

$\sigma = \sqrt{\sigma^2} = \sqrt{38.4} = 6.197$

4.41 x is a binomial random variable with $n = 4$.

a. If the probability distribution of x is symmetric, $p(0) = p(4)$ and $p(1) = p(3)$.

Since $p(x) = \begin{bmatrix} n \\ x \end{bmatrix} p^x q^{n-x} \quad x = 0, 1, \ldots , n,$

When $n = 4$,

$\begin{bmatrix} 4 \\ 0 \end{bmatrix} p^0 q^4 = \begin{bmatrix} 4 \\ 4 \end{bmatrix} p^4 q^0 \Rightarrow \dfrac{4!}{0!4!} p^0 q^4 = \dfrac{4!}{4!0!} p^4 q^0 \Rightarrow q^4 = p^4 \Rightarrow p = q$

Since $p + q = 1, p = .5$

Therefore, the probability distribution of x is symmetric when $p = .5$.

b. If the probability distribution of x is skewed to the right, then the mean is greater than the median. Therefore, there are more small values in the distribution (0, 1) than large values (3, 4). Therefore, p must be smaller than .5. Let $p = .2$ and the probability distribution of x will be skewed to the right.

c. If the probability distribution of x is skewed to the left, then the mean is smaller than the median. Therefore, there are more large values in the distribution (3, 4) than small values (0, 1). Therefore, p must be larger than .5. Let $p = .8$ and the probability distribution of x will be skewed to the left.

d. In part a, x is a binomial random variable with $n = 4$ and $p = .5$.

$p(x) = \begin{bmatrix} 4 \\ x \end{bmatrix} .5^x .5^{4-x} \quad x = 0, 1, 2, 3, 4$

$p(0) = \begin{bmatrix} 4 \\ 0 \end{bmatrix} .5^0 .5^4 = \dfrac{4!}{0!4!} .5^4 = 1(.5)^4 = .0625$

$p(1) = \begin{bmatrix} 4 \\ 1 \end{bmatrix} .5^1 .5^3 = \dfrac{4!}{1!3!} .5^4 = 4(.5)^4 = .25$

$p(2) = \begin{bmatrix} 4 \\ 2 \end{bmatrix} .5^2 .5^2 = \dfrac{4!}{2!2!} .5^4 = 6(.5)^4 = .375$

$p(3) = p(1) = .25$ (since the distribution is symmetric)

$p(4) = p(0) = .0625$

The probability distribution of x in tabular form is:

x	0	1	2	3	4
$p(x)$	.0625	.25	.375	.25	.0625

$\mu = np = 4(.5) = 2$

The graph of the probability distribution of x when $n = 4$ and $p = .5$ is as follows.

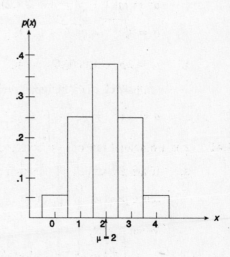

In part **b**, x is a binomial random variable with $n = 4$ and $p = .2$.

$$p(x) = \begin{bmatrix} 4 \\ x \end{bmatrix} .2^x .8^{4-x} \qquad x = 0, 1, 2, 3, 4$$

$$p(0) = \begin{bmatrix} 4 \\ 0 \end{bmatrix} .2^0 .8^4 = 1(1).8^4 = .4096$$

$$p(1) = \begin{bmatrix} 4 \\ 1 \end{bmatrix} .2^1 .8^3 = 4(.2)(.8)^3 = .4096$$

$$p(2) = \begin{bmatrix} 4 \\ 2 \end{bmatrix} .2^2 .8^2 = 6(.2)^2(.8)^2 = .1536$$

$$p(3) = \begin{bmatrix} 4 \\ 3 \end{bmatrix} .2^3 .8^1 = 4(.2)^3(.8) = .0256$$

$$p(4) = \begin{bmatrix} 4 \\ 4 \end{bmatrix} .2^4 .8^0 = 1(.2)^4(1) = .0016$$

The probability distribution of x in tabular form is:

x	0	1	2	3	4
$p(x)$	.4096	.4096	.1536	.0256	.0016

$\mu = np = 4(.2) = .8$

The graph of the probability distribution of x when $n = 4$ and $p = .2$ is as follows:

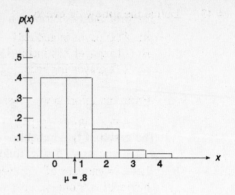

In part **c**, x is a binomial random variable with $n = 4$ and $p = .8$.

$$p(x) = \begin{bmatrix} 4 \\ x \end{bmatrix} .8^x .2^{4-x} \qquad x = 0, 1, 2, 3, 4$$

$$p(0) = \begin{bmatrix} 4 \\ 0 \end{bmatrix} .8^0 .2^4 = 1(1).2^4 = .0016$$

$$p(1) = \begin{bmatrix} 4 \\ 1 \end{bmatrix} .8^1 .2^3 = 4(.8)(.2)^3 = .0256$$

$$p(2) = \begin{bmatrix} 4 \\ 2 \end{bmatrix} .8^2 .2^2 = 6(.8)^2(.2)^2 = .1536$$

$$p(3) = \begin{bmatrix} 4 \\ 3 \end{bmatrix} .8^3 .2^1 = 4(.8)^3(.2) = .4096$$

$$p(4) = \begin{bmatrix} 4 \\ 4 \end{bmatrix} .8^4 .2^0 = 1(.8)^4(1) = .4096$$

The probability distribution of x in tabular form is:

x	0	1	2	3	4
$p(x)$	.0016	.0256	.1536	.4096	.4096

Note: The distribution of x when $n = 4$ and $p = .2$ is the reverse of the distribution of x when $n = 4$ and $p = .8$.

$$\mu = np = 4(.8) = 3.2$$

The graph of the probability distribution of x when $n = 4$ and $p = .8$ is as follows:

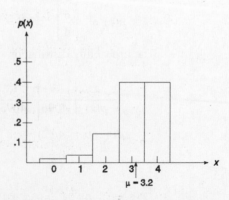

e. In general, when $p = .5$, a binomial distribution will be symmetric regardless of the value of n. When p is less than .5, the binomial distribution will be skewed to the right; and when p is greater than .5, it will be skewed to the left. (Refer to parts **a**, **b**, and **c**.)

4.43   Define the following events:

> A: {Taxpayer is audited}
> B: {Taxpayer has income less than \$100,000)
> C: {Taxpayer has income of \$100,000 or higher}

a.   From the information given in the problem,

$$P(A \mid B) = 15/1000 = .015$$
$$P(A \mid C) = 30/1000 = .030$$

b.   Let x = number of taxpayers with incomes under \$100,000 who are audited. Then x is a binomial random variable with $n = 5$ and $p = .015$.

$$P(x = 1) = \binom{5}{1} .015^1 .985^{(5-1)} \frac{5!}{1!4!} .015^1 .985^{(4)} = .0706$$

$$P(x > 1) = 1 - [P(x = 0) + P(x = 1)]$$

$$= 1 - \left[\left[\binom{5}{0} .015^0 .985^{(5-0)} + .0706 \right] \right.$$

$$= 1 - \left[\frac{5!}{0!5!} .015^0 .985^5 + .0706 \right]$$

$$= 1 - [.9272 + .0706] = 1 - .9978 = .0022$$

c.   Let x = number of taxpayers with incomes of \$100,000 or more who are audited. Then x is a binomial random variable with $n = 5$ and $p = .030$.

$$P(x = 1) = \binom{5}{1} .03^1 .97^{(5-1)} \frac{5!}{1!4!} .03^1 .97^4 = .1328$$

$$P(x > 1) = 1 - [P(x = 0) + P(x = 1)]$$

$$= 1 - \left[\left[\binom{5}{0} .03^0 .97^{(5-0)} + .1328 \right] \right.$$

$$= 1 - \left[\frac{5!}{0!5!} .03^0 .97^5 + .1328 \right]$$

$$= 1 - [.8587 + .1328] = 1 - .9915 = .0085$$

d.   Let x = number of taxpayers with incomes under \$100,000 who are audited. Then x is a binomial random variable with $n = 2$ and $p = .015$.

Let y = number of taxpayers with incomes \$100,000 or more who are audited. Then y is a binomial random variable with $n = 2$ and $p = .030$.

$$P(x = 0) = \binom{2}{0} .015^0 .985^{(2-0)} = \frac{2!}{0!2!} .015^0 .985^2 = .9702$$

$$P(y = 0) = \binom{2}{0} .03^0 .97^{(2-0)} = \frac{2!}{0!2!} .03^0 .97^2 = .9409$$

$$P(x = 0)P(y = 0) = .9702(.9409) = .9129$$

e. We must assume that the variables defined as x and y are binomial random variables. We must assume that the trials are identical, the probability of success is the same from trial to trial, and that the trials are independent.

4.45 a. In order to be a binomial random variable, the five characteristics must hold.

1. For this problem, there are 5 American adults surveyed. We will assume that these 5 trials are identical.

2. For each person surveyed, there are 2 possible outcomes: adult believes children will have a higher standard of living (S) or adult does not believe children will have a higher standard of living (F).

3. The probability that an adult believes his/her children will have a higher standard of living remains constant from trial to trial. For this problem, we will assume that this probability is $P(S) = .60$ for each trial.

4. We will assume that the opinion of one adult is independent of any other.

5. The random variable x is the number of adults who believe their children will have a higher standard of living in 5 trials.

Thus, x is a binomial random variable.

b. The value of p, the probability an adult believes his/her children will have a higher standard of living is .60.

c. Using Table II, Appendix B, with $n = 5$ and $p = .6$,

$$P(x = 3) = P(x \le 3) - P(x \le 2) = .663 - .317 = .346$$

d. Using Table II, Appendix B, with $n = 5$ and $p = .6$,

$$P(x \le 2) = .317$$

4.47 a. We must assume that the probability that a specific type of ball meets the requirements is always the same from trial to trial and the trials are independent. To use the binomial probability distribution, we need to know the probability that a specific type of golf ball meets the requirements.

b. For a binomial distribution,

$$\mu = np$$
$$\sigma = \sqrt{npq}$$

In this example, n = two dozen = $2 \cdot 12 = 24$.

$p = .10$ (Success here means the golf ball *does not* meet standards.)
$q = .90$
$\mu = np = 24(.10) = 2.4$
$\sigma = \sqrt{npq} = \sqrt{24(.10)(.90)} = 1.47$

c. In this situation,

p = Probability of success
= Probability golf ball *does* meet standards
= .90
$q = 1 - .90 = .10$
$n = 24$
$E(x) = \mu = np = 24(.90) = 21.60$
$\sigma = \sqrt{npq} = \sqrt{24(.10)(.90)} = 1.47$ (Note that this is the same as in part **b**.)

4.49 Assuming the supplier's claim is true,

$\mu = np = 500(.001) = .5$
$\sigma = \sqrt{npq} = \sqrt{500(.001)(.999)} = \sqrt{.4995} = .707$

If the supplier's claim is true, we would only expect to find .5 defective switches in a sample of size 500. Therefore, it is not likely we would find 4.

Based on the sample, the guarantee is probably inaccurate.

Note: $z = \dfrac{x - \mu}{\sigma} = \dfrac{4 - .5}{.707} = 4.95$

This is an unusually large z-score.

4.51 a. $\mu = E(x) = np = 800(.65) = 520$
$\sigma = \sqrt{npq} = \sqrt{800(.65)(.35)} = 13.491$

b. Half of the 800 food items is 400. A value of $x = 400$ would have a z-score of:

$z = \dfrac{x - \mu}{\sigma} = \dfrac{400 - 520}{13.491} = -8.895$

Since the z-score associated with 400 items is so small (-8.895), it would be virtually impossible to observe less than half without any traces of pesticides if the 65% value was correct.

4.53 a. The random variable x is discrete since it can assume a countable number of values
(0, 1, 2, ...).

b. This is a Poisson probability distribution with $\lambda = 3$.

c. In order to graph the probability distribution, we need to know the probabilities for the possible values of x. Using Table III of Appendix B with $\lambda = 3$:

$p(0) = .050$
$p(1) = P(x \le 1) - P(x = 0) = .199 - .050 = .149$
$p(2) = P(x \le 2) - P(x \le 1) = .423 - .199 = .224$
$p(3) = P(x \le 3) - P(x \le 2) = .647 - .423 = .224$
$p(4) = P(x \le 4) - P(x \le 3) = .815 - .647 = .168$
$p(5) = P(x \le 5) - P(x \le 4) = .916 - .815 = .101$
$p(6) = P(x \le 6) - P(x \le 5) = .966 - .916 = .050$
$p(7) = P(x \le 7) - P(x \le 6) = .988 - .966 = .022$
$p(8) = P(x \le 8) - P(x \le 7) = .996 - .988 = .008$
$p(9) = P(x \le 9) - P(x \le 8) = .999 - .996 = .003$
$p(10) \approx .001$

The probability distribution of x in graphical form is:

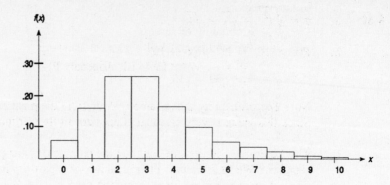

d. $\mu = \lambda = 3$
    $\sigma^2 = \lambda = 3$

    $\sigma = \sqrt{3} = 1.7321$

e. The mean of x is the same as the mean of the probability distribution, $\mu = \lambda = 3$.

    The standard deviation of x is the same as the standard deviation of the probability distribution, $\sigma = 1.7321$.

4.55 $\mu = \lambda = 1.5$

Using Table III of Appendix B:

a. $P(x \leq 3) = .934$

b. $P(x \geq 3) = 1 - P(x \leq 2) = 1 - .809 = .191$

c. $P(x = 3) = P(x \leq 3) - P(x \leq 2) = .934 - .809 = .125$

d. $P(x = 0) = .223$

e. $P(x > 0) = 1 - P(x = 0) = 1 - .223 = .777$

f. $P(x > 6) = 1 - P(x \leq 6) = 1 - .999 = .001$

4.57 a. $E(x) = \mu = \lambda = 4$

    $\sigma = \sqrt{\lambda} = \sqrt{4} = 2$

b. $z = \dfrac{x - \mu}{\sigma} = \dfrac{1 - 4}{2} = -1.5$

c. Using Table III, Appendix B, with $\lambda = 4$,

    $P(x \leq 6) = .889$

d. The experiment consists of counting the number of bank failures per year. We assume the probability a bank fails in a year is the same for each year. We must also assume that the number of bank failures in one year is independent of the number in any other year.

4.59   a. $\sigma = \sqrt{\sigma^2} = \sqrt{\lambda} = \sqrt{4} = 2$

        b. $P(x > 10) = 1 - P(x \le 10)$
                        $= 1 - .977$ (Table III, Appendix B)
                        $= .003$

              No. The probability that a sample of air from the plant exceeds the EPA limit is only .003.
              Since this value is very small, it is not very likely that this will occur.

        c.   The experiment consists of counting the number of parts per million of vinyl chloride in air
              samples. We must assume the probability of a part of vinyl chloride appearing in a million
              parts of air is the same for each million parts of air. We must also assume the number of
              parts of vinyl chloride in one million parts of air is independent of the number in any other
              one million parts of air.

4.61   a.   In the problem, it is stated that $E(x) = .03$. This is also the value of λ.

              $\sigma^2 = \lambda = .03$

        b.   The experiment consists of counting the number of deaths or missing persons in a three- year
              interval. We must assume that the probability of a death or missing person in a three-year
              period is the same for any three-year period. We must also assume that the number of deaths
              or missing persons in any three-year period is independent of the number of deaths or missing
              persons in any other three-year period.

        c. $P(x = 1) = \dfrac{\lambda^1 e^{-\lambda}}{1!} = \dfrac{.03^1 e^{-.03}}{1!} = .0291$

              $P(x = 0) = \dfrac{\lambda^0 e^{-\lambda}}{0!} = \dfrac{.03^0 e^{-.03}}{0!} = .9704$

4.63   a.   From the problem, $\lambda = .37$. Thus, $\sigma = \sqrt{\lambda} = \sqrt{.37} = .6083$

        b.   In order to plot the distribution of x, we must first calculate the probabilities.

              $P(x = 0) = \dfrac{\lambda^0 e^{-\lambda}}{0!} = \dfrac{.37^0 e^{-.37}}{0!} = .6907$

              $P(x = 1) = \dfrac{.37^1 e^{-.37}}{1!} = .2556$

              $P(x = 2) = \dfrac{.37^2 e^{-.37}}{2!} = .0473$

              $P(x = 3) = \dfrac{.37^3 e^{-.37}}{3!} = .0058$

              $P(x = 4) = \dfrac{.37^4 e^{-.37}}{4!} = .0005$

              $P(x = 5) = \dfrac{.37^5 e^{-.37}}{5!} = .00004$

The plot of the distribution is:

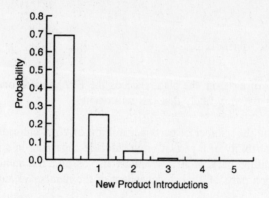

c. $P(x > 2) = 1 - P(x \le 2) = 1 - .6907 - .2556 - .0473 = .0064$

Since this probability is so small, it would be very unlikely that a mainframe manufacturer would introduce more than 2 new products per year.

$P(x < 1) = P(x = 0) = .6907$

Since this probability is not small, it would not be unusual for a mainframe manufacturer to introduce less than 1 new product per year.

4.65 $\mu = \lambda = 3$, using Table III, Appendix B:

$P(x = 3) = P(x \le 3) - P(x \le 2) = .647 - .423 = .224$
$P(x = 0) = .050$

The probability that no bulbs fail in one hour is .050. If we let y = number of one hour intervals out of 8 that have no bulbs fail, then y is a binomial random variable with $n = 8$ and $p = .05$. Then, the probability that no bulbs fail in an 8 hour shift is

$$P(y = 8) = \begin{bmatrix} 8 \\ 8 \end{bmatrix} .05^8 .95^{(8-8)} = \frac{8!}{8!(8-8)!} .05^8 .95^0$$

$$= \frac{8 \cdot 7 \cdot 6 \cdot 5 \cdot 4 \cdot 3 \cdot 2 \cdot 1}{8 \cdot 7 \cdot 6 \cdot 5 \cdot 4 \cdot 3 \cdot 2 \cdot 1 \cdot 1} .05^8 .95^0 = .05^8$$

We must assume that the 8 one-hour intervals are independent and identical, and that the probability that no bulbs fail is the same for each one-hour interval.

4.67 $p(x) = \begin{bmatrix} n \\ x \end{bmatrix} p^x q^{n-x}$ $x = 0, 1, 2, \ldots, n$

a. $P(x = 3) = p(3) = \begin{bmatrix} 7 \\ 3 \end{bmatrix} .5^3 .5^4 = \frac{7!}{3!4!} .5^3 .5^4 = 35(.125)(.0625) = .2734$

b. $P(x = 3) = p(3) = \begin{bmatrix} 4 \\ 3 \end{bmatrix} .8^3 .2^1 = \frac{4!}{3!1!} .8^3 .2^1 = 4(.512)(.2) = .4096$

c. $P(x = 1) = p(1) = \begin{bmatrix} 15 \\ 1 \end{bmatrix} .1^1 .9^{14} = \frac{15!}{1!14!} .1^1 .9^{14} = 15(.1)(.228768) = .3432$

4.69   From Table II, Appendix B:

a. $P(x = 14) = P(x \le 14) - P(x \le 13) = .584 - .392 = .192$

b. $P(x \le 12) = .228$

c. $P(x > 12) = 1 - P(x \le 12) = 1 - .228 = .772$

d. $P(9 \le x \le 18) = P(x \le 18) - P(x \le 8) = .992 - .005 = .987$

e. $P(8 < x < 18) = P(x \le 17) - P(x \le 8) = .965 - .005 = .960$

f. $\mu = np = 20(.7) = 14$

$\sigma^2 = npq = 20(.7)(.3) = 4.2, \sigma = \sqrt{4.2} = 2.049$

g. $\mu \pm 2\sigma \Rightarrow 14 \pm 2(2.049) \Rightarrow 14 \pm 4.098 \Rightarrow (9.902, 18.098)$

$$P(9.902 < x < 18.098) = P(10 \le x \le 18) = P(x \le 18) - P(x \le 9)$$
$$= .992 - .017 = .975$$

4.71   a.   Discrete — The number of damaged inventory items is countable.

b.   Continuous — The average monthly sales can take on any value within an acceptable limit.

c.   Continuous — The number of square feet can take on any positive value.

d.   Continuous — The length of time we must wait can take on any positive value.

4.73   a.   Define the following events:

N: {Household has not broken either law}
B: {Household has broken at least one of the laws}

$P(B) = .1 \qquad P(N) = 1 - P(B) = 1 - .1 = .9$

The sample space for this problem is:

$S = \{N, BN, BBN, BBBN, BBBBN, etc.\}$

Thus, x can take on the values 1, 2, 3, 4, ...

b. $P(x < 3) = P(x = 1) + P(x + 2) = P(N) + P(BN) = .9 + .1(.9) = .99$

c. $P(x > 2) = 1 - P(x \le 2) = 1 - .99 = .01$

d. $P(x = 1) = .9$
$P(x = 2) = .1(.9) = .09$
$P(x = 3) = .1^2(.9) = .009$
$P(x = 4) = .1^3(.9) = .0009$
$P(x = 5) = .1^4(.9) = .00009$
$P(x = 6) = .1^5(.9) = .000009$
$P(x = 7) = .1^6(.9) = .0000009$
$P(x = 8) = .1^7(.9) = .00000009$

$$P(x = 9) = .1^8(.9) = .000000009$$
$$P(x = 10) = .1^9(.9) = .0000000009$$

x can exceed 10, but $P(x > 10) = 1 - .9999999999 = .0000000001$

The graph of the probability distribution for x is:

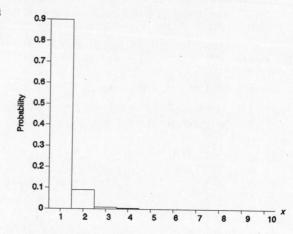

4.75   Define x as the number of invoices in the sample that contain arithmetic errors. The random variable x is a binomial random variable since it fits the characteristics (the invoices are independently chosen with only two possible outcomes). If the accountant's theory is valid, $n = 25$ and $p = .10$.

$$P(x \geq 7) = 1 - P(x \leq 6) = 1 - \sum_{x=0}^{6} p(x) = 1 - .991 \quad \text{(Table II)}$$
$$= .009$$

4.77   a.   The number of cars that have mileages within 2 miles per gallon of their EPA projections in a sample of 20 chosen from a finite population is not a binomial random variable since the sample is chosen without replacement from a finite population. However, since the sample is small compared to the population, we could treat it like a binomial random variable for convenience. Therefore, the statement is true.

b.   Let x be the number of cars that have mileages within 2 miles per gallon of their EPA projections. For convenience, assume the random variable x is binomial with $n = 20$ and $p = .70$. Using Table II, Appendix B, with $n = 20$ and $p = .70$,

$$P(x < 10) = P(x \leq 9) = .017$$

Therefore, the probability is approximately .017.

4.79   a.   In order for the number of deaths to follow a Poisson distribution, we must assume that the probability of a death is the same for any week. We must also assume that the number of deaths in any week is independent of any other week.

The first assumption may not be valid. The probability of a death may not be the same for every week. The number of passengers varies from week to week, so the probability of a death may change. Also, things such as weather, which varies from week to week may increase or decrease the chance of derailment.

b. $E(x) = \lambda = 20$

$$\sigma = \sqrt{\lambda} = \sqrt{20} = 4.4721$$

c.   The z-score corresponding to $x = 4$ is:

$$z = \frac{4 - 20}{4.4721} = -3.55$$

Since this z-score is more than 3 standard deviations from the mean, it would be very unlikely that only 4 or fewer deaths occur next week.

d.   Using Table III, Appendix B with $\lambda = 20$,

$$P(x \leq 4) = 0.000$$

This probability is consistent with the answer in part **c**. The probability of 4 or fewer deaths is essentially zero, which is very unlikely.

4.81   a. $\mu = n \cdot p = 25(.05) = 1.25$

$\sigma = \sqrt{npq} = \sqrt{25(.05)(.95)} = 1.09$

Since μ is not an integer, x could not equal its mean.

b.   The event is $(x \geq 5)$. From Table II with $n = 25$ and $p = .05$:

$$P(x \geq 5) = 1 - P(x \leq 4) = 1 - .993 = .007$$

c.   Since the probability obtained in part **b** is so small, it is unlikely that 5% applies to this agency. The percentage is probably greater than 5%.

4.83   Using Table II with $n = 25$ and $p = .8$:

a. $P(x < 15) = P(x \leq 14) = .006$

b.   Since the probability of such an event is so small when $p = .8$, if less than 15 insects die we would conclude that the insecticide is not as effective as claimed.

4.85   Let x = the number of delivery truck breakdowns today and y = the number of delivery truck breakdowns tomorrow. The random variables x and y are Poisson with $\mu = \lambda = 1.5$. Using Table III, Appendix B:

a. $P(x = 2 \cap y = 3) = P(x = 2)P(y = 3)$ (by independence)
$= [P(x \leq 2) - P(x \leq 1)][P(y \leq 3) - P(y \leq 2)]$
$= (.809 - .558)(.934 - .809) = .251(.125) = .0314$

b. $P(x < 2 \cap y > 2) = P(x < 2)P(y > 2)$ (by independence)
$= P(x \leq 1)[1 - P(y \leq 2)]$
$= .558(1 - .809) = .558(.191) = .1066$

5.1   a. $f(x) = \dfrac{1}{d - c}$ $(c \leq x \leq d)$

$$\frac{1}{d - c} = \frac{1}{45 - 20} = \frac{1}{25} = .04$$

So, $f(x) = \begin{cases} .04 & (20 \leq x \leq 45) \\ 0 & \text{otherwise} \end{cases}$

b. $\mu = \dfrac{c + d}{2} = \dfrac{20 + 45}{2} = \dfrac{65}{2} = 32.5$

$\sigma = \dfrac{d - c}{\sqrt{12}} = \dfrac{45 - 20}{\sqrt{12}} = 7.2169$

$\sigma^2 = (7.2169)^2 = 52.0833$

c.

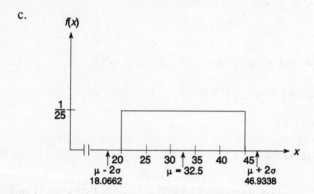

$\mu \pm 2\sigma \Rightarrow 32.5 \pm 2(7.2169) \Rightarrow (18.0662, 46.9338)$

$P(18.0662 < x < 46.9338) = P(20 < x < 45) = (45 - 20).04 = 1$

5.3   a. $f(x) = \dfrac{1}{d - c}$ $(c \leq x \leq d)$

$$\frac{1}{d - c} = \frac{1}{7 - 3} = \frac{1}{4}$$

$f(x) = \begin{cases} \dfrac{1}{4} & (3 \leq x \leq 7) \\ 0 & \text{otherwise} \end{cases}$

b. $\mu = \dfrac{c + d}{2} = \dfrac{3 + 7}{2} = \dfrac{10}{2} = 5$

$\sigma = \dfrac{d - c}{\sqrt{12}} = \dfrac{7 - 3}{\sqrt{12}} = \dfrac{4}{\sqrt{12}} = 1.155$

c. $\mu \pm \sigma \Rightarrow 5 \pm 1.155 \Rightarrow (3.845, 6.155)$

$P(\mu - \sigma \leq x \leq \mu + \sigma) = P(3.845 \leq x \leq 6.155) = \dfrac{b - a}{d - c} = \dfrac{6.155 - 3.845}{7 - 3} = \dfrac{2.31}{4}$
$= .5775$

5.5 $f(x) = \dfrac{1}{d - c} = \dfrac{1}{200 - 100} = \dfrac{1}{100} = .01$

$f(x) = \begin{cases} .01 & (100 \leq x \leq 200) \\ 0 & \text{otherwise} \end{cases}$

$\mu = \dfrac{c + d}{2} = \dfrac{100 + 200}{2} = \dfrac{300}{2} = 150$

$\sigma = \dfrac{d - c}{\sqrt{12}} = \dfrac{200 - 100}{\sqrt{12}} = \dfrac{100}{\sqrt{12}} = 28.8675$

a. $\mu \pm 2\sigma \Rightarrow 150 \pm 2(28.8675) \Rightarrow 150 \pm 57.735 \Rightarrow (92.265, 207.735)$

$P(x < 92.265) + P(x > 207.735) = P(x < 100) + P(x > 200)$
$\phantom{P(x < 92.265) + P(x > 207.735)} = 0 + 0$
$\phantom{P(x < 92.265) + P(x > 207.735)} = 0$

b. $\mu \pm 3\sigma \Rightarrow 150 \pm 3(28.8675) \Rightarrow 150 \pm 86.6025 \Rightarrow (63.3975, 236.6025)$

$P(63.3975 < x < 236.6025) = P(100 < x < 200) = (200 - 100)(.01) = 1$

c.   From a, $\mu \pm 2\sigma \Rightarrow (92.265, 207.735)$.

$P(92.265 < x < 207.735) = P(100 < x < 200) = (200 - 100)(.01) = 1$

5.7   a.   For layer 2, let x = amount loss. Since the amount of loss is random between .01 and .05 million dollars, the uniform distribution for x is:

$f(x) = \dfrac{1}{d - c} \quad (c \leq x \leq d)$

$\dfrac{1}{d - c} = \dfrac{1}{.05 - .01} = \dfrac{1}{.04} = 25$

Therefore, $f(x) = \begin{cases} 25 & (.01 \leq x \leq .05) \\ 0 & \text{otherwise} \end{cases}$

A graph of the distribution looks like the following:

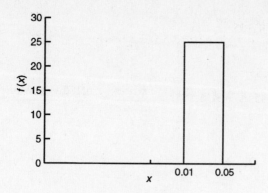

$$\mu = \frac{c + d}{2} = \frac{.01 + .05}{2} = .03$$

$$\sigma = \frac{d - c}{\sqrt{12}} = \frac{.05 - .01}{\sqrt{12}} = .0115, \ \sigma^2 = (.0115)^2 = .00013$$

The mean loss for layer 2 is .03 million dollars and the variance of the loss for layer 2 is .00013 million dollars squared.

b.   For layer 6, let x = amount loss. Since the amount of loss is random between .50 and 1.00 million dollars, the uniform distribution for x is:

$$f(x) = \frac{1}{d - c} \quad (c \leq x \leq d)$$

$$\frac{1}{d - c} = \frac{1}{1.00 - .50} = \frac{1}{.50} = 2$$

Therefore, $f(x) = \begin{cases} 2 & (.50 \leq x \leq 1.00) \\ 0 & \text{otherwise} \end{cases}$

A graph of the distribution looks like the following:

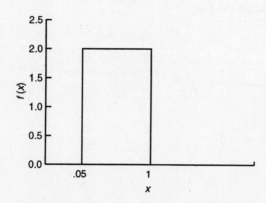

$$\mu = \frac{c + d}{2} = \frac{.50 + 1.00}{2} = .75$$

$$\sigma = \frac{d - c}{\sqrt{12}} = \frac{1.00 - .50}{\sqrt{12}} = .1443, \; \sigma^2 = (.1443)^2 = .0208$$

The mean loss for layer 6 is .75 million dollars and the variance of the loss for layer 6 is .0208 million dollars squared.

c. A loss of $10,000 corresponds to $x = .01$. $P(x > .01) = 1$

A loss of $25,000 corresponds to $x = .025$.

$$P(x < .025) = (\text{Base})(\text{Height}) = (x - c)\left[\frac{1}{d - c}\right] = (.025 - .01)\left[\frac{1}{.05 - .01}\right]$$
$$= .015(25) = .375$$

d. A loss of $750,000 corresponds to $x = .75$. A loss of $1,000,000 corresponds to $x = 1$.

$$P(.75 < x < 1) = (\text{Base})(\text{Height}) = (d - x)\left[\frac{1}{d - c}\right] = (1.00 - .75)\left[\frac{1}{1.00 - .50}\right]$$
$$= .25(2) = .5$$

A loss of $900,000 corresponds to $x = .90$.

$$P(x > .9) = (\text{Base})(\text{Height}) = (d - x)\left[\frac{1}{d - c}\right] = (1.00 - .90)\left[\frac{1}{1.00 - .50}\right]$$
$$= .10(2) = .20$$

$$P(x = .9) = 0$$

5.9 To construct a relative frequency histogram for the data, we can use 7 measurement classes.

$$\text{Interval width} = \frac{\text{Largest number} - \text{smallest number}}{\text{Number of classes}} = \frac{98.0716 - .7434}{7} = 13.9$$

We will use an interval width of 14 and a starting value of .74335.

The measurement classes, frequencies, and relative frequencies are given in the table below.

Class	Measurement Class	Class Frequency	Class Relative Frequency
1	.74335 − 14.74335	6	6/40 = .15
2	14.74335 − 28.74335	4	.10
3	28.74335 − 42.74335	6	.15
4	42.74335 − 56.74335	6	.15
5	56.74335 − 70.74335	5	.125
6	70.74335 − 84.74335	4	.10
7	84.74335 − 98.74335	9	.225
		40	1.000

The histogram looks like the data could be from a uniform distribution. The last class (84.74335 − 98.74335) has a few more observations in it than we would expect. However, we cannot expect a perfect graph from a sample of only 40 observations.

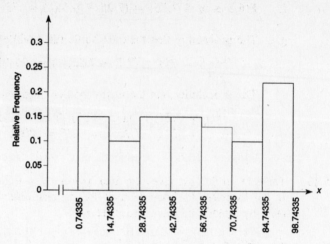

5.11   a.   The amount dispensed by the beverage machine is a continuous random variable since it can take on any value between 6.5 and 7.5 ounces.

b.   Since the amount dispensed is random between 6.5 and 7.5 ounces, x is a uniform random variable.

$$f(x) = \frac{1}{d-c} \quad (c \le x \le d)$$

$$\frac{1}{d-c} = \frac{1}{7.5 - 6.5} = \frac{1}{1} = 1$$

Therefore, $f(x) = \begin{cases} 1 & (6.5 \le x \le 7.5) \\ 0 & \text{otherwise} \end{cases}$

The graph is as follows:

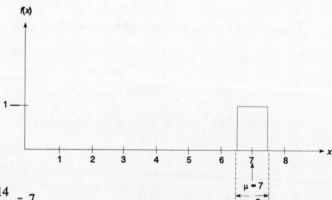

c. $\mu = \dfrac{c+d}{2} = \dfrac{6.5 + 7.5}{2} = \dfrac{14}{2} = 7$

$\sigma = \dfrac{d-c}{\sqrt{12}} = \dfrac{7.5 - 6.5}{\sqrt{12}} = .2887$

$\mu \pm 2\sigma \Rightarrow 7 \pm 2(.2887) \Rightarrow 7 \pm .5774 \Rightarrow (6.422, 7.577)$

d. $P(x \ge 7) = (7.5 - 7)(1) = .5$

e. $P(x < 6) = 0$

f. $P(6.5 \leq x \leq 7.25) = (7.25 - 6.5)(1) = .75$

g. The probability that the next bottle filled will contain more than 7.25 ounces is:

$$P(x > 7.25) = (7.5 - 7.25)(1) = .25$$

The probability that the next 6 bottles filled will contain more than 7.25 ounces is:

$$P[(x > 7.25) \cap (x > 7.25) \cap (x > 7.25) \cap (x > 7.25) \cap (x > 7.25) \cap (x > 7.25)]$$
$$= [P(x > 7.25)]^6 = .25^6 = .0002$$

5.13 Table IV in the text gives the area between $z = 0$ and $z = z_0$. In this exercise, the answers may thus be read directly from the table by looking up the appropriate z.

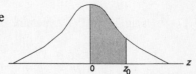

a. $P(0 < z < 2.0) = .4772$

b. $P(0 < z < 3.0) = .4987$

c. $P(0 < z < 1.5) = .4332$

d. $P(0 < z < .80) = .2881$

5.15 Using Table IV, Appendix B:

a. $P(z > 1.46) = .5 - P(0 < z \leq 1.46)$
    $= .5 - .4279 = .0721$

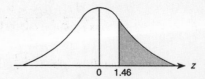

b. $P(x < -1.56) = .5 - P(-1.56 \leq z < 0)$
    $= .5 - .4406 = .0594$

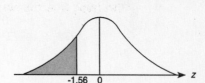

c. $P(.67 \leq z \leq 2.41)$
    $= P(0 < z \leq 2.41) - P(0 < z < .67)$
    $= .4920 - .2486 = .2434$

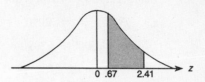

d. $P(-1.96 \leq z < -.33)$
    $= P(-1.96 \leq z < 0) - P(-.33 \leq z < 0)$
    $= .4750 - .1293 = .3457$

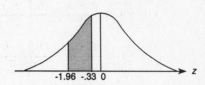

e. $P(z \geq 0) = .5$

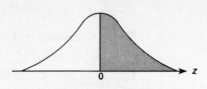

f. $P(-2.33 < z < 1.50)$
$= P(-2.33 < z < 0) + P(0 < z < 1.50)$
$= .4901 + .4332 = .9233$

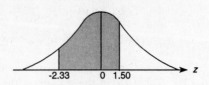

5.17 Using Table IV, Appendix B:

a. $P(-1 \leq z \leq 1)$
$= P(-1 \leq z \leq 0) + P(0 < z \leq 1)$
$= .3413 + .3413 = .6826$

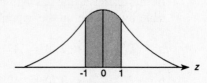

b. $P(-1.96 \leq z \leq 1.96)$
$= P(-1.96 \leq z < 0) + P(0 \leq z \leq 1.96)$
$= .4750 + .4750 = .9500$

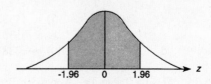

c. $P(-1.645 \leq z \leq 1.645)$
$= P(-1.645 \leq z < 0) + P(0 \leq z \leq 1.645)$
$= .4500 + .4500 = .90$
(using interpolation)

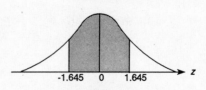

d. $P(-2 \leq z \leq 2)$
$= P(-2 \leq z < 0) + P(0 \leq z \leq 2)$
$= .4772 + .4772 = .9544$

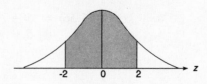

5.19 Using Table IV of Appendix B:

a. $P(z \leq z_0) = .2090$

$A = .5000 - .2090 = .2910$

Look up the area .2910 in the body of Table IV;
$z_0 = -.81$.

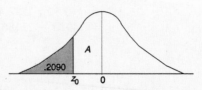

(z_0 is negative since the graph shows z_0 is on the left side of 0.)

b. $P(z \leq z_0) = .7090$

$P(z \leq z_0) = P(z \leq 0) + P(0 \leq z \leq z_0)$
$= .5 + P(0 \leq z \leq z) = .7090$

Therefore, $P(0 \leq z \leq z_0) = .7090 - .5 = .2090$

Look up the area .2090 in the body of Table IV;
$z_0 \approx .55$.

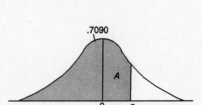

c. $P(-z_0 \leq z < z_0) = .8472$

$P(-z_0 \leq z < z_0) = 2P(0 \leq z \leq z_0)$
$2P(0 \leq z \leq z_0) = .8472$

Therefore, $P(0 \leq z \leq z_0) = .4236$.

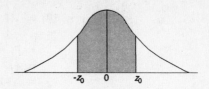

Look up the area .4236 in the body of Table IV; $z_0 = 1.43$.

d. $P(-z_0 \leq z < z_0) = .1664$

$P(-z_0 \leq z \leq z_0) = 2P(0 \leq z \leq z_0)$
$2P(0 \leq z \leq z_0) = .1664$

Therefore, $P(0 \leq z \leq z_0) = .0832$.

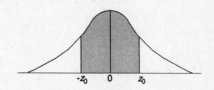

Look up the area .0832 in the body of Table IV; $z_0 = .21$.

e. $P(z_0 \leq z \leq 0) = .4798$

$P(z_0 \leq z \leq 0) = P(0 \leq z \leq -z_0)$

Look up the area .4798 in the body of Table IV;
$z_0 = -2.05$.

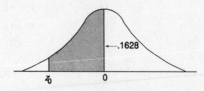

f. $P(-1 < z < z_0) = .5328$

$P(-1 < z < z_0)$
   $= P(-1 < z < 0) + P(0 < z < z_0)$
   $= .5328$

$P(0 < z < 1) + P(0 < z < z_0) = .5328$

Thus, $P(0 < z < z_0) = .5328 - .3413 = .1915$

Look up the area .1915 in the body of Table IV; $z_0 = .50$.

5.21 a. If $x = 20$, $z = \dfrac{x - \mu}{\sigma} = \dfrac{20 - 30}{4} = -2.5$

b. If $x = 30$, $z = \dfrac{x - \mu}{\sigma} = \dfrac{30 - 30}{4} = 0$

c. If $x = 27.5$, $z = \dfrac{x - \mu}{\sigma} = \dfrac{27.5 - 30}{4} = -.625$

d. If $x = 15$, $z = \dfrac{x - \mu}{\sigma} = \dfrac{15 - 30}{4} = -3.75$

e. If $x = 35$, $z = \dfrac{x - \mu}{\sigma} = \dfrac{35 - 30}{4} = 1.25$

f. If $x = 25$, $z = \dfrac{x - \mu}{\sigma} = \dfrac{25 - 30}{4} = -1.25$

5.23   a. $P(10 \leq x \leq 12) = P\left[\dfrac{10 - 11}{2} \leq z \leq \dfrac{12 - 11}{2}\right]$

$= P(-0.50 \leq z \leq 0.50)$
$= A_1 + A_2$
$= .1915 + .1915 = .3830$

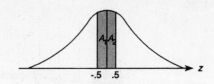

b. $P(6 \leq x \leq 10) = P\left[\dfrac{6 - 11}{2} \leq z \leq \dfrac{10 - 11}{2}\right]$

$= P(-2.50 \leq z \leq -0.50)$
$= P(-2.50 \leq z \leq 0)$
$\qquad - P(-0.50 \leq z \leq 0)$
$= .4938 - .1915 = .3023$

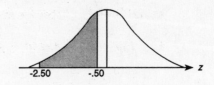

c. $P(13 \leq x \leq 16) = P\left[\dfrac{13 - 11}{2} \leq z \leq \dfrac{16 - 11}{2}\right]$

$= P(1.00 \leq z \leq 2.50)$
$= P(0 \leq z \leq 2.50)$
$\qquad - P(0 \leq z \leq 1.00)$
$= .4938 - .3413 = .1525$

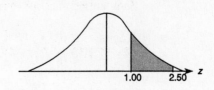

d. $P(7.8 \leq x \leq 12.6)$
$= P\left[\dfrac{7.8 - 11}{2} \leq z \leq \dfrac{12.6 - 11}{2}\right]$
$= P(-1.60 \leq z \leq 0.80)$
$= A_1 + A_2$
$= .4452 + .2881 = .7333$

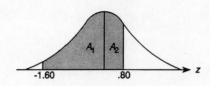

e. $P(x \geq 13.24) = P\left[z \geq \dfrac{13.24 - 11}{2}\right]$

$= P(z \geq 1.12)$
$= A_2 = .5 - A_1$
$= .5000 - .3686 = .1314$

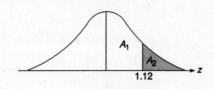

f. $P(x \geq 7.62) = P\left[z \geq \dfrac{7.62 - 11}{2}\right]$

$= P(z \geq -1.69)$
$= A_1 + A_2$
$= .4545 + .5000 = .9545$

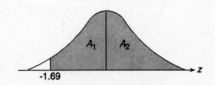

5.25

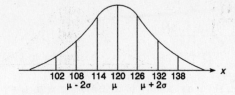

102 108 114 120 126 132 138 → x

μ - 2σ   μ   μ + 2σ

Using Table IV, Appendix B:

a. $P(\mu - 2\sigma \leq x \leq \mu + 2\sigma) = P(-2 \leq z \leq 2)$
$$= P(-2 \leq z \leq 0) + P(0 \leq z \leq 2)$$
$$= .4772 + .4772 = .9544$$

b. $P(x \geq 128) = P\left(z \geq \dfrac{128 - 120}{6}\right) = P(z \geq 1.33) = .5 - .4082 = .0918$

c. $P(x \leq 108) = P\left(z \leq \dfrac{108 - 120}{6}\right) = P(z \leq -2) = .5 - .4772 = .0228$

d. $P(112 \leq x \leq 130) = P\left(\dfrac{112 - 120}{6} \leq z \leq \dfrac{130 - 120}{6}\right) = P(-1.33 \leq z \leq 1.67)$
$$= P(-1.33 \leq z \leq 0) + P(0 \leq z \leq 1.67)$$
$$= .4082 + .4525 = .8607$$

e. $P(114 \leq x \leq 116) = P\left(\dfrac{114 - 120}{6} \leq z \leq \dfrac{116 - 120}{6}\right) = P(-1 \leq z \leq -.67)$
$$= P(-1 \leq z \leq 0) - P(-.67 \leq z \leq 0)$$
$$= .3413 - .2486 = .0927$$

f. $P(115 \leq x \leq 128) = P\left(\dfrac{115 - 120}{6} \leq z \leq \dfrac{128 - 120}{6}\right) = P(-.83 \leq z \leq 1.33)$
$$= P(-.83 \leq z \leq 0) + P(0 \leq z \leq 1.33)$$
$$= .2967 + .4082 = .7049$$

5.27 a. Let x = crop yield. The random variable x has a normal distribution with μ = 1,500 and σ = 250.

$P(x < 1,600) = P\left(z < \dfrac{1,600 - 1,500}{250}\right) = P(z < .4) = .5 + .1554 = .6554$
(Using Table IV)

b. Let x_1 = crop yield in first year and x_2 = crop yield in second year. If x_1 and x_2 are independent, then the probability that the farm will lose money for two straight years is:

$P(x_1 < 1,600)\, P(x_2 < 1,600) = P\left(z_1 < \dfrac{1,600 - 1,500}{250}\right) P\left(z_2 < \dfrac{1,600 - 1,500}{250}\right)$

$= P(z_1 < .4)\, P(z_2 < .4) = (.5 + .1554)(.5 + .1554) = .6554(.6554) = .4295$
(Using Table IV)

c. $P(1,500 - 2\sigma \leq x \leq 1,500 + 2\sigma) =$

$$P\left[\frac{[1,500 - 2\sigma] - 1,500}{\sigma} \leq z \leq \frac{[1,500 + 2\sigma] - 1,500}{\sigma}\right]$$
$$= P(-2 \leq z \leq 2) = 2P(0 \leq z \leq 2) = 2(.4772) = .9544 \qquad \text{(Using Table IV)}$$

5.29   a.   Let x = passenger demand. The random variable x has a normal distribution with $\mu = 125$ and $\sigma = 45$.

For the Boeing 727, the probability that the passenger demand will exceed the capacity is:

$$P(x > 148) = P\left[z > \frac{148 - 125}{45}\right] = P(z > .51) = .5 - .1950 = .3050$$

$$\text{(using Table IV)}$$

For the Boeing 757, the probability that the passenger demand will exceed the capacity is:

$$P(x > 182) = P\left[z > \frac{182 - 125}{45}\right] = P(z > 1.27) = .5 - .3890 = .1020$$

b.   For the Boeing 727, the probability that the flight will depart with one or more empty seats is:

$$P(x \leq 147) = P\left[z \leq \frac{147 - 125}{45}\right] = P(z \leq .49) = .5 + .1879 = .6879$$

For the Boeing 757, the probability that the flight will depart with one or more empty seats is:

$$P(x \leq 181) = P\left[z \leq \frac{181 - 125}{45}\right] = P(z \leq 1.24) = .5 + .3925 = .8925$$

c.   For the Boeing 727, the probability that the spill is more than 100 passengers is:

$$P(x > 248) = P\left[z > \frac{248 - 125}{45}\right] = P(z > 2.73) = .5 - .4968 = .0032$$

5.31   a.   Using Table IV, Appendix B, with $\mu = 20.2$ and $\sigma = .65$,

$$P(20 < x < 21) = P\left[\frac{20 - 20.2}{.65} < z < \frac{21 - 20.2}{.65}\right] = P(-.31 < z < 1.23)$$
$$= P(-.31 < z < 0) + P(0 \leq z < 1.23) = .1217 + .3907 = .5124$$

b. $P(x \leq 19.84) = P\left[z \leq \dfrac{19.84 - 20.2}{.65}\right] = P(z \leq -.55) = .5 - .2088 = .2912$

Since the probability of observing a sardine with a length of 19.84 cm or smaller is not small ($p = .2912$), this is not an unusual event if the sardine was, in fact, two years old. Thus, it is likely that the sardine is two years old.

c. $P(x \geq 22.01) = P\left[z \geq \dfrac{22.01 - 20.2}{.65}\right] = P(z \geq 2.78) = .5 - .4973 = .0027$

Since the probability of observing a sardine with a length of 22.01 cm or larger is so small ($p = .0027$), this would be a very unusual event if the sardine was, in fact, two years old. Thus, it is unlikely that the sardine is two years old.

5.33   a.   Using Table IV, Appendix B, with $\mu = 8.72$ and $\sigma = 1.10$,

$$P(x < 6) = P\left[z < \frac{6 - 8.72}{1.10}\right] = P(z < -2.47) = .5 - .4932 = .0068$$

Thus, approximately .68% of the games would result in fewer than 6 hits.

b.   The probability of observing fewer than 6 hits in a game is $p = .0068$. The probability of observing 0 hits would be even smaller. Thus, it would be extremely unusual to observe a no hitter.

5.35   Let $x =$ the amount of dye discharged. The random variable x is normally distributed with $\sigma = 4$.

We want $P(\text{shade is unacceptable}) \leq .01$

$\Rightarrow P(x > 6) \leq .01$

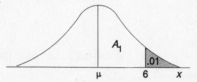

Then $A_1 = .50 - .01 = .49$. Look up the area .49 in the body of Table IV, Appendix B; (take the closest value) $z_0 = 2.33$.

To find μ, substitute into the z-score formula:

$$z = \frac{x - \mu}{\sigma}$$

$$2.33 = \frac{6 - \mu}{.4}$$

$$\mu = 6 - .4(2.33) = 5.068$$

5.37   a.   If z is a standard normal random variable,

$Q_L = z_L$ is the value of the standard normal distribution which has 25% of the data to the left and 75% to the right.

Find z_L such that $P(z < z_L) = .25$

$A_1 = .50 - .25 = .25$.

Look up the area $A_1 = .25$ in the body of Table IV of Appendix B; $z_L = -.67$ (taking the closest value). If interpolation is used, $-.675$ would be obtained.

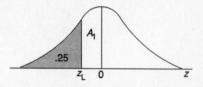

$Q_U = z_U$ is the value of the standard normal distribution which has 75% of the data to the left and 25% to the right.

Find z_U such that $P(z < z_U) = .75$

$A_1 + A_2 = P(z \leq 0) + P(0 \leq z \leq z_U)$
$\qquad\quad = .5 + P(0 \leq z \leq z_U)$
$\qquad\quad = .75$

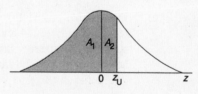

Therefore, $P(0 \leq z \leq z_U) = .25$.

Look up the area .25 in the body of Table IV of Appendix B; $z_U = .67$ (taking the closest value).

b. Recall that the inner fences of a box plot are located $1.5(Q_U - Q_L)$ outside the hinges (Q_L and Q_U).

To find the lower inner fence,

$$Q_L - 1.5(Q_U - Q_L) = -.67 - 1.5(.67 - (-.67))$$
$$= -.67 - 1.5(1.34)$$
$$= -2.68 \ (-2.70 \text{ if } z_L = -.675 \text{ and } z_U = +.675)$$

The upper inner fence is:

$$Q_U + 1.5(Q_U - Q_L) = .67 + 1.5(.67 - (-.67))$$
$$= .67 + 1.5(1.34)$$
$$= 2.68 \ (+2.70 \text{ if } z_L = -.675 \text{ and } z_U = +.675)$$

c. Recall that the outer fences of a box plot are located $3(Q_U - Q_L)$ outside the hinges (Q_L and Q_U).

To find the lower outer fence,

$$Q_L - 3(Q_U - Q_L) = -.67 - 3(.67 - (-.67))$$
$$= -.67 - 3(1.34)$$
$$= -4.69 \ (-4.725 \text{ if } z_L = -.675 \text{ and } z_U = +.675)$$

The upper outer fence is:

$$Q_U + 3(Q_U - Q_L) = .67 + 3(.67 - (-.67))$$
$$= .67 + 3(1.34)$$
$$= 4.69 \ (4.725 \text{ if } z_L = -.675 \text{ and } z_U = +.675)$$

d. $P(z < -2.68) + P(z > 2.68)$
    $= 2P(z > 2.68)$
    $= 2(.5000 - .4963)$
        (Table IV, Appendix B)
    $= 2(.0037) = .0074$

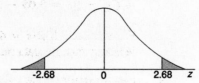

(or $2(.5000 - .4965) = .0070$ if -2.70 and 2.70 are used)

$P(z < -4.69) + P(z > 4.69)$
$= 2P(z > 4.69)$
$\approx 2(.5000 - .5000) \approx 0$

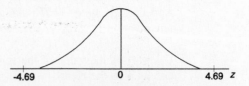

e. In a normal probability distribution, the probability of an observation being beyond the inner fences is only .0074 and the probability of an observation being beyond the outer fences is approximately zero. Since the probability is so small, there should not be any observations beyond the inner and outer fences. Therefore, they are probably outliers.

5.39 a. $IQR = Q_U - Q_L = 195 - 72 = 123$

b. $IQR/s = 123/95 = 1.295$

c. Yes. Since IQR is approximately 1.3, this implies that the data are approximately normal.

5.41   a.   Using MINITAB, the stem-and-leaf display is:

```
Stem-and-leaf of X        N = 28
Leaf Unit = 0.10


     5        11266
     6    2   1
     8    3   35
    11    4   035
    14    5   039
    14    6   3457
    10    7   346
     7    8   24469
     2        47
```

Since the data do not form a mound-shape, it indicates that the data may not be normally distributed.

b.   Using MINITAB, the descriptive statistics are:

Variable	N	Mean	Median	TrMean	StDev	SE Mean
X	28	5.511	6.100	5.519	2.765	0.5230

Variable	Minimum	Maximum	Q1	Q3
X	1.100	9.700	3.350	8.050

The standard deviation is 2.765.

c.   Using the printout from MINITAB in part **b**, $Q_L = 3.35$, and $Q_U = 8.05$. The IQR $= Q_U - Q_L = 8.05 - 3.35 = 4.7$. If the data are normally distributed, then IQR/$s \approx 1.3$.

For this data, IQR/$s = 4.7/2.765 = 1.70$. This is a fair amount larger than 1.3, which indicates that the data may not be normally distributed.

d.   Using MINITAB, the normal probability plot is:

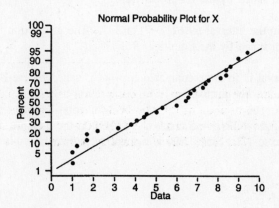

The data at the extremes are not particularly on a straight line. This indicates that the data are not normally distributed.

5.43   Using MINITAB, the stem-and-leaf display for the data is:

```
Stem-and-leaf of Score    N = 121
Leaf Unit = 1.0

   1    3   6
   1    4
   1    4
   1    5
   1    5
   1    6
   1    6
   3    7   04
   7    7   5889
   8    8   1
  38    8   66666667777778888888888999999999
 (56)   9   00000001111111111111222222222333333333333333333333444444444
  27    9   5555555555556666666667777889
```

From the plot, the data appear to be very skewed to the left. This implies that the data are not normal.

Using MINITAB, the descriptive statistics are:

Variable	N	Mean	Median	TrMean	StDev	SE Mean
Score	121	90.504	92.000	91.321	6.961	0.633

Variable	Minimum	Maximum	Q1	Q3
Score	36.000	99.000	88.500	94.000

$\bar{x} \pm s \Rightarrow 90.504 \pm 6.961 \Rightarrow (83.543, 97.465)$

$\bar{x} \pm 2s \Rightarrow 90.504 \pm 2(6.961) \Rightarrow 90.504 \pm 13.922 \Rightarrow (76.582, 104.426)$

$\bar{x} \pm 3s \Rightarrow 90.504 \pm 3(6.961) \Rightarrow 90.504 \pm 20.883 \Rightarrow (69.621, 111.387)$

Of the 121 measurements, 110 are in the interval 83.543 − 97.465. The proportion is 110/121 = .909. This is much larger than the proportion stated by the Empirical Rule.

Of the 121 measurements, 117 are in the interval 76.582 − 104.426. The proportion is 117/121 = .967. This is close to the proportion stated by the Empirical Rule.

Of the 121 measurements, 120 are in the interval 69.621 − 111.387. The proportion is 120/121 = .992. This is close to the proportion stated by the Empirical Rule.

Since the proportion in the first interval is so large compared to what is stated by the Empirical Rule, this would imply that the data are not normal.

IQR $= Q_U - Q_L = 94 - 88.5 = 5.5$. IQR/$s = 5.5/6.961 = .790$. If the data are normally distributed, this ratio should be close to 1.3. Since .790 is not fairly close to 1.3, this indicates that the data are not normal.

Using MINITAB, the normal probability plot is:

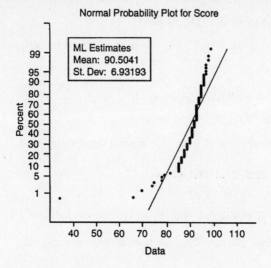

Normal Probability Plot for Score

ML Estimates
Mean: 90.5041
St. Dev: 6.93193

The data do not form a straight line. This indicates that the data are not normally distributed.

5.45   Let x = maximum number of years one expects to spend with any one employer. For this problem, $\mu = 18.2$ and $\sigma = 10.64$. The minimum value for x is 0, which has a z-score of:

$$z = \frac{x - \mu}{\sigma} = \frac{0 - 18.2}{10.64} = -1.71$$

Since the smallest possible value of x is only 1.71 standard deviations from the mean, it is very unlikely that the data are normal. A normal distribution will have about .0436 or 4.36% of the observations more than 1.71 standard deviations below the mean.

$$(P(z < -1.71) = .5 - .4564 = .0436)$$

For this data set, there are no observations more than 1.71 standard deviations below the mean.

5.47   a. $\mu = np = 100(.01) = 1.0$, $\sigma = \sqrt{npq} = \sqrt{100(.01)(.99)} = .995$

$\mu \pm 3\sigma \Rightarrow 1 \pm 3(.995) \Rightarrow 1 \pm 2.985 \Rightarrow (-1.985, 3.985)$

Since this interval does not fall in the interval $(0, n = 100)$, the normal approximation is not appropriate.

b. $\mu = np = 20(.6) = 12$, $\sigma = \sqrt{npq} = \sqrt{20(.6)(.4)} = 2.191$

$\mu \pm 3\sigma \Rightarrow 12 \pm 3(2.191) \Rightarrow 12 \pm 6.573 \Rightarrow (5.427, 18.573)$

Since this interval falls in the interval $(0, n = 20)$, the normal approximation is appropriate.

c. $\mu = np = 10(.4) = 4$, $\sigma = \sqrt{npq} = \sqrt{10(.4)(.6)} = 1.549$

$\mu \pm 3\sigma \Rightarrow 4 \pm 3(1.549) \Rightarrow 4 \pm 4.647 \Rightarrow (-.647, 8.647)$

Since this interval does not fall within the interval $(0, n = 10)$, the normal approximation is not appropriate.

d. $\mu = np = 1000(.05) = 50$, $\sigma = \sqrt{npq} = \sqrt{1000(.05)(.95)} = 6.892$

$\mu \pm 3\sigma \Rightarrow 50 \pm 3(6.892) \Rightarrow 50 \pm 20.676 \Rightarrow (29.324, 70.676)$

Since this interval falls within the interval $(0, n = 1000)$, the normal approximation is appropriate.

e. $\mu = np = 100(.8) = 80$, $\sigma = \sqrt{npq} = \sqrt{100(.8)(.2)} = 4$

$\mu \pm 3\sigma \Rightarrow 80 \pm 3(4) \Rightarrow 80 \pm 12 \Rightarrow (68, 92)$

Since this interval falls within the interval $(0, n = 100)$, the normal approximation is appropriate.

f. $\mu = np = 35(.7) = 24.5$, $\sigma = \sqrt{npq} = \sqrt{35(.7)(.3)} = 2.711$

$\mu \pm 3\sigma \Rightarrow 24.5 \pm 3(2.711) \Rightarrow 24.5 \pm 8.133 \Rightarrow (16.367, 32.633)$

Since this interval falls within the interval $(0, n = 35)$, the normal approximation is appropriate.

5.49 a. Using Table II, $P(x \leq 11) = .345$

$$\mu = np = 25(.5) = 12.5, \sigma = \sqrt{npq} = \sqrt{25(.5)(.5)} = 2.5$$

Using the normal approximation,

$$P(x \leq 11) \approx P\left[z \leq \frac{(11 + .5) - 12.5}{2.5}\right] = P(z \leq -.40) = .5 - .1554 = .3446$$

b. Using Table II, $P(x \geq 16) = 1 - P(x \leq 15) = 1 - .885 = .115$

Using the normal approximation,

$$P(x \geq 16) \approx P\left[z \geq \frac{(16 - .5) - 12.5}{2.5}\right] = P(z \geq 1.2) = .5 - .3849 = .1151$$
$$\text{(from Table IV, Appendix B)}$$

c. Using Table II, $P(8 \leq x \leq 16) = P(x \leq 16) - P(x \leq 7) = .946 - .022 = .924$

Using the normal approximation,

$$P(8 \leq x \leq 16) \approx P\left[\frac{(8 - .5) - 12.5}{2.5} \leq z \leq \frac{(16 + .5) - 12.5}{2.5}\right]$$
$$= P(-2.0 \leq z \leq 1.6) = .4772 + .4452 = .9224$$
$$\text{(from Table IV, Appendix B)}$$

5.51 $\mu = np = 1000(.5) = 500$, $\sigma = \sqrt{npq} = \sqrt{1000(.5)(.5)} = 15.811$

a. Using the normal approximation,

$$P(x > 500) \approx P\left[z > \frac{(500 + .5) - 500}{15.811}\right] = P(z > .03) = .5 - .0120 = .4880$$
$$\text{(from Table IV, Appendix B)}$$

b. $P(490 \leq x < 500) \approx P\left[\frac{(490 - .5) - 500}{15.811} \leq z \leq \frac{(500 - .5) - 500}{15.811}\right]$
$$= P(-.66 \leq z < -.03) = .2454 - .0120 = .2334$$
$$\text{(from Table IV, Appendix B)}$$

c. $P(x > 550) \approx P\left[z > \dfrac{(550 + .5) - 500}{15.811}\right] = P(z > 3.19) \approx .5 - .5 = 0$
(from Table IV, Appendix B)

5.53   Let x = number of items with incorrect prices in 10,000 trials. Thus, x is a binomial random variable with n = 10,000 and p = 1/30 = .033.

$$\mu \pm 3\sigma \Rightarrow np \pm 3\sqrt{npq} \Rightarrow 10,000(.033) \pm 3\sqrt{10,000(.033)(.967)}$$
$$\Rightarrow 330 \pm 3\sqrt{319.11} \Rightarrow 330 \pm 3(17.864) \Rightarrow 330 \pm 53.591 \Rightarrow (276.409, 383.591)$$

Since the interval lies in the range 0 to 10,000, we can use the normal approximation to approximate the probabilities.

a. $P(x \geq 100) \approx P\left[z \geq \dfrac{(100 - .5) - 330}{17.864}\right] = P(z \geq -12.90)$

$= P(-12.90 \leq z < 0) + .5 \approx .5 + .5 = 1$

b.   Let x = number of items with incorrect prices in 100 trials. Thus, x is a binomial random variable with n = 100 and p = 1/30 = .033.

$$\mu \pm 3\sigma \Rightarrow np \pm 3\sqrt{npq} \Rightarrow 100(.033) \pm 3\sqrt{100(.033)(.967)}$$
$$\Rightarrow 3.3 \pm 3\sqrt{3.191} \Rightarrow 3.3 \pm 3(1.786) \Rightarrow 3.3 \pm 5.358 \Rightarrow (-2.058, 8.658)$$

Since the interval does not lie in the range 0 to 100, the normal approximation will not be appropriate.

5.55   a.   Let x_1 = number of patients out of 500,000 who experience serious post-laser vision problems after being operated on by corneal specialists. Then x_1 is a binomial random variable with n = 500,000 and p_1 = .01

$E(x_1) = np_1 = 500,000(.01) = 5,000$

Let x_2 = number of patients out of 500,000 who experience serious post-laser vision problems after being operated on by opthalmologists. Then x_2 is a binomial random variable with n = 500,000 and p_2 = .05

$E(x_2) = np_2 = 500,000(.05) = 25,000$

b.   Let x_2 = number of patients out of 400 who experience serious post-laser vision problems after being operated on by opthalmologists. Then x_2 is a binomial random variable with n = 400 and p_2 = .05.

$$\mu \pm 3\sigma \Rightarrow np_2 \pm 3\sqrt{np_2 q_2} \Rightarrow 400(.05) \pm 3\sqrt{400(.05)(.95)} \Rightarrow 20 \pm 3(4.3589)$$
$$\Rightarrow 20 \pm 13.0767 \Rightarrow (6.9233, 33.0767)$$

Since the interval lies in the range 0 to 400, we can use the normal approximation to approximate the probability.

$$P(x \geq 20) \approx P\left[z \geq \dfrac{(20 - .5) - 20}{4.3589}\right] = P(z \geq -.11) = .5 + .0438 = .5438$$

c. Let x_1 = number of patients out of 400 who experience serious post-laser vision problems after being operated on by corneal specialists. Then x_1 is a binomial random variable with $n = 400$ and $p_1 = .01$.

$$\mu \pm 3\sigma \Rightarrow np_1 \pm 3\sqrt{np_1q_1} \Rightarrow 400(.01) \pm 3\sqrt{400(.01)(.99)} \Rightarrow 4 \pm 3(1.99)$$
$$\Rightarrow 4 \pm 5.97 \Rightarrow (-1.97, 9.97)$$

Since the interval does not lie in the range 0 to 400, we cannot use the normal approximation to approximate the probability.

5.57 Let x equal the number of catastrophes due to booster failure.

a. In order to approximate the binomial distribution with the normal distribution, the interval $\mu \pm 3\sigma$ should lie in the range 0 to n.

$$\mu \pm 3\sigma \Rightarrow np \pm 3\sqrt{npq} \Rightarrow 25\left[\frac{1}{35}\right] \pm 3\sqrt{25\left[\frac{1}{35}\right]\left[1 - \frac{1}{35}\right]}$$
$$\Rightarrow .714 \pm 3(.833) \Rightarrow (-1.785, 3.213)$$

Since the interval calculated does not lie in the range 0 to 25, we should not use the normal approximation.

b. $P(x \geq 1) \approx P\left[z \geq \dfrac{(1 - .5) - .714}{.833}\right]$

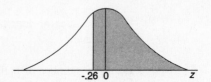

$ = P(z \geq -.26)$
$ = .5000 + .1026 = .6026$
(Using Table IV in Appendix B.)

The exact probability is .5155 and the approximate probability is .6026. The approximation is quite a bit off, but this is not surprising since in part **a** we decided that we should not use the normal approximation.

c. Referring to part **a**, recalculate the interval $\mu \pm 3\sigma$ using $n = 100$ instead of $n = 25$.

$$\mu \pm 3\sigma \Rightarrow np \pm 3\sqrt{npq} \Rightarrow 100\left[\frac{1}{35}\right] \pm 3\sqrt{100\left[\frac{1}{35}\right]\left[1 - \frac{1}{35}\right]}$$
$$\Rightarrow 2.857 \pm 3(1.666) \Rightarrow (-2.141, 7.855)$$

Since the interval calculated does not lie in the range 0 to 100 we should not use the normal approximation when $n = 100$.

Recalculate the interval $\mu \pm 3\sigma$ using $n = 500$.

$$\mu \pm 3\sigma \Rightarrow np \pm 3\sqrt{npq} \Rightarrow 500\left[\frac{1}{35}\right] \pm 3\sqrt{500\left[\frac{1}{35}\right]\left[1 - \frac{1}{35}\right]}$$
$$\Rightarrow 14.286 \pm 3(3.725) \Rightarrow (3.111, 25.461)$$

Since the interval calculated does lie in the range 0 to 500, we can use the normal approximation when $n = 500$.

Since we can use the normal approximation when $n = 500$, we can use it when $n = 1,000$.

$$\mu \pm 3\sigma \Rightarrow np \pm 3\sqrt{npq} \;\Rightarrow\; 1000\left[\frac{1}{35}\right] \pm 3\sqrt{1000\left[\frac{1}{35}\right]\left[1 - \frac{1}{35}\right]}$$

$$\Rightarrow 28.571 \pm 3(5.268) \Rightarrow (12.767, 44.375)$$

Since the interval calculated does lie in the range 0 to 1,000, we can use the normal approximation when $n = 1,000$.

d. x is a binomial random variable with $n = 1000$ and $p = \dfrac{1}{35}$.

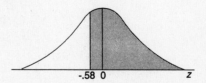

$$P(x > 25) \approx P\left[z > \frac{(25 + .5) - 28.571}{5.268}\right]$$
$$= P(z > -.58)$$
$$= .5000 + .2190 = .7190$$
(Using Table IV in Appendix B.)

5.59   a.   If 80% of the passengers pass through without their luggage being inspected, then 20% will be detained for luggage inspection. The expected number of passengers detained will be:

$$E(x) = np = 1,500(.2) = 300$$

b.   For $n = 4,000$, $E(x) = np = 4,000(.2) = 800$

c. $P(x > 600) \approx P\left[z > \dfrac{(600 + .5) - 800}{\sqrt{4000(.2)(.8)}}\right] = P(z > -7.89) = .5 + .5 = 1.0$

5.61   a.   If $\lambda = 1$, $a = 1$, then $e^{-\lambda a} = e^{-1} = .367879$

b.   If $\lambda = 1$, $a = 2.5$, then $e^{-\lambda a} = e^{-2.5} = .082085$

c.   If $\lambda = 2.5$, $a = 3$, then $e^{-\lambda a} = e^{-7.5} = .000553$

d.   If $\lambda = 5$, $a = .3$, then $e^{-\lambda a} = e^{-1.5} = .223130$

5.63   Using Table V in Appendix B:

a. $P(x \le 3) = 1 - P(x > 3) = 1 - e^{-2.5(3)} = 1 - e^{-7.5} = 1 - .000553 = .999447$

b. $P(x \le 4) = 1 - P(x > 4) = 1 - e^{-2.5(4)} = 1 - e^{-10} = 1 - .000045 = .999955$

c. $P(x \le 1.6) = 1 - P(x > 1.6) = 1 - e^{-2.5(1.6)} = 1 - e^{-4} = 1 - .018316 = .981684$

d. $P(x \le .4) = 1 - P(x > .4) = 1 - e^{-2.5(.4)} = 1 - e^{-1} = 1 - .367879 = .632121$

5.65 $f(x) = \lambda e^{-\lambda x} = e^{-x}$ $(x > 0)$

$\mu = \dfrac{1}{\lambda} = \dfrac{1}{1} = 1$, $\sigma = \dfrac{1}{\lambda} = \dfrac{1}{1} = 1$

a. $\mu \pm 3\sigma \Rightarrow 1 \pm 3(1) \Rightarrow (-2, 4)$

Since $\mu - 3\sigma$ lies below 0, find the probability that x is more than $\mu + 3\sigma = 4$.

$P(x > 4) = e^{-1(4)} = e^{-4} = .018316$ (using Table V in Appendix B)

b. $\mu \pm 2\sigma \Rightarrow 1 \pm 2(1) \Rightarrow (-1, 3)$

Since $\mu - 2\sigma$ lies below 0, find the probability that x is between 0 and 3.

$$P(x < 3) = 1 - P(x \geq 3) = 1 - e^{-1(3)} = 1 - e^{-3} = 1 - .049787 = .950213$$
(using Table V in Appendix B)

c. $\mu \pm .5\sigma \Rightarrow 1 \pm .5(1) \Rightarrow (.5, 1.5)$

$$P(.5 < x < 1.5) = P(x > .5) - P(x > 1.5)$$
$$= e^{-.5} - e^{-1.5}$$
$$= .606531 - .223130$$
$$= .383401 \quad \text{(using Table V in Appendix B)}$$

5.67 a. $\lambda = 1/\mu = 1/10.54 = .0949$

b. $\mu = 10.54; \quad \sigma = 1/\lambda = 1/.0949 = 10.54$

On average, the University of Michigan hockey team scored every 10.54 minutes.

Since we know the distribution of time-between-goals is not symmetric, we use Chebyshev's Rule to describe the data. We know at least 75% of all times-between-goals will fall within 2 standard deviations of the mean.

$$\mu \pm 2\sigma \Rightarrow 10.54 \pm 2(10.54) \Rightarrow 10.54 \pm 21.08 \Rightarrow (-10.54, 31.62)$$

Since we know that no time can be negative, we know that at least 75% of all times-between-goals are less than 31.62 minutes.

c. To graph the exponential distribution of x when $\lambda = .0949$ we need to calculate $f(x)$ for certain values of x. Using a calculator:

$$f(x) = \lambda e^{-\lambda x} = .0949 \, e^{-.0949x}$$

$$f(1) = .0949 \, e^{-.0949(1)} = .0863$$

$$f(5) = .0949 \, e^{-.0949(5)} = .0590$$

$$f(10) = .0949 \, e^{-.0949(10)} = .0367$$

$$f(15) = .0949 \, e^{-.0949(15)} = .0229$$

$$f(20) = .0949 \, e^{-.0949(20)} = .0142$$

$$f(25) = .0949 \, e^{-.0949(25)} = .0088$$

$$f(30) = .0949 \, e^{-.0949(30)} = .0055$$

The graph of the exponential distribution is:

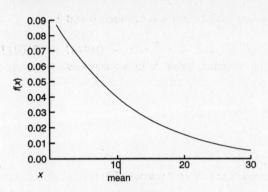

d. $P(x < 2) = 1 - e^{-.0949(2)} = 1 - e^{-.1898} = 1 - .8271 = .1729$

5.69   a. $P(x) = e^{-\lambda x} = e^{-.5x}$

b. $P(x \geq 4) = e^{-.5(4)} = e^{-2} = .135335$ (Table V, Appendix B)

c. $\mu = \dfrac{1}{\lambda} = \dfrac{1}{.5} = 2$

$P(x > \mu) = P(x > 2) = e^{-.5(2)} = e^{-1} = .367879$ (Table V, Appendix B)

d.   For all exponential distributions, $\mu = \dfrac{1}{\lambda}$

$P(x > \mu) = P\left[x > \dfrac{1}{\lambda}\right] = e^{-\lambda(1/\lambda)} = e^{-1} = .367879.$ Thus,

regardless of the value of λ, the probability that x is larger than the mean is always .367879.

e. $P(x > 5) = e^{-.5(5)} = e^{-2.5} = .082085$ (Table V, Appendix B)

If 10,000 units are sold, approximately $10,000(.082085) = 820.85$ will perform satisfactorily for more than 5 years.

$P(x \leq 1) = 1 - P(x > 1) = 1 - e^{-.5(1)} = 1 - e^{-.5} = 1 - .606531 = .39469$

If 10,000 units are sold, approximately $10,000(.393469) = 3934.69$ will fail within 1 year.

f. $P(x < a) \leq .05$
$\Rightarrow 1 - P(x \geq a) \leq .05$
$\Rightarrow P(x \geq a) \geq .95$
$\Rightarrow e^{-.5a} \geq .95$

Using Table V, Appendix B, $e^{-.05}$ is closest to .95 (yet larger).

Thus, $.05 = .5a \Rightarrow a = .1$

The warranty should be for approximately .1 year or $.1(365) = 36.5$ or 37 days.

5.71   a.   Let x = interarrival time of jobs. Then x has an exponential distribution with a mean of $\mu = 1.25$ minutes and $\lambda = 1/1.25$.

$P(x \leq 1) = 1 - P(x > 1) = 1 - e^{-1/1.25} = 1 - e^{-.8} = 1 - .449329 = .550671$

       b.   Let y = amount of time the machine operates before breaking down. Then y has an exponential distribution with a mean of $\mu = 540$ minutes and $\lambda = 1/540$.

$P(y > 720) = e^{-720/540} = e^{-1.333333} = .263597$

5.73   a. $\mu = 1/\lambda = 1/.004 = 250$

       b.   Let x = lifelength of the new halogen bulb. Then x has an exponential distribution with $\lambda = .004$.

$P(x > 500) = e^{-.004(500)} = e^{-2} = .135335$ (from Table V, Appendix B)

       c.   First, we must find the probability of each individual event. Let x = lifelength of the first bulb, and y = lifelength of the second bulb.

$P(x > 300) = e^{-.004(300)} = e^{-1.2} = .301194$ (from Table V, Appendix B)

$P(y > 200) = e^{-.004(200)} = e^{-.8} = .449329$ (from Table V, Appendix B)

Since the two events are independent, $P(x > 300 \text{ and } y > 200) = P(x > 300)P(y > 200) = .301194(.449329) = .135335$

       d.   For $a = 300$ and $b = 200$, $P(x > a + b) = P(x > 300 + 200) = P(x > 500) = .135335$

From part c, $P(x > 300)P(x > 200) = .135335$.

Thus, $P(x > 500) = P(x > 300)P(x > 200)$.

       e.   Let $a = 100$ and $b = 400$. $P(x > a + b) = P(x > 100 + 400) = P(x > 500) = .135335$

$P(x > 100) = e^{-.004(100)} = e^{-.4} = .670320$ (from Table V, Appendix B)

$P(x > 400) = e^{-.004(400)} = e^{-1.6} = .201897$ (from Table V, Appendix B)

Since the two events are independent, $P(x > 100 \text{ and } x > 400) = P(x > 100)P(x > 400) = .670320(.201897) = .135336$

       f.   In general, $P(x > a + b) = e^{-\lambda(a+b)}$

$P(x > a) = e^{-\lambda a}$ and $P(x > b) = e^{-\lambda b}$.

If the two events are independent,
$$P(x > a \text{ and } x > b) = P(x > a)P(x > b) = e^{-\lambda a}e^{-\lambda b} = e^{-\lambda(a+b)} = P(x > a + b).$$

5.75   a. $f(x) = \begin{cases} \dfrac{1}{d - c} = \dfrac{1}{90 - 10} = \dfrac{1}{80}, & 10 \leq x \leq 90 \\ 0 & \text{otherwise} \end{cases}$

b. $\mu = \dfrac{c + d}{2} = \dfrac{10 + 90}{2} = 50$

$\sigma = \dfrac{d - c}{\sqrt{12}} = \dfrac{90 - 10}{\sqrt{12}} = 23.094011$

c. The interval $\mu \pm 2\sigma \Rightarrow 50 \pm 2(23.094) \Rightarrow 50 \pm 46.188 \Rightarrow (3.812, 96.188)$ is indicated on the graph.

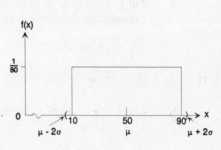

d. $P(x \le 60) = \text{Base(height)} = (60 - 10)\dfrac{1}{80} = \dfrac{5}{8} = .625$

e. $P(x \ge 90) = 0$

f. $P(x \le 80) = \text{Base(height)} = (80 - 10)\dfrac{1}{80} = \dfrac{7}{8} = .875$

g. $P(\mu - \sigma \le x \le \mu + \sigma) = P(50 - 23.094 \le x \le 50 + 23.094)$
$= P(26.906 \le x \le 73.094)$
$= \text{Base(height)}$

$= (73.094 - 26.906)\left[\dfrac{1}{80}\right] = \dfrac{46.188}{80} = .577$

h. $P(x > 75) = \text{Base(height)} = (90 - 75)\dfrac{1}{80} = \dfrac{15}{80} = .1875$

5.77 a. $P(z \le z_0) = .5080$
$\Rightarrow P(0 \le z \le z_0) = .5080 - .5 = .0080$
Looking up the area .0080 in Table IV,
$\Rightarrow \qquad z_0 = .02$

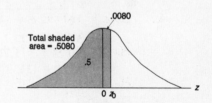

b. $P(z \ge z_0) = .5517$
$\Rightarrow P(z_0 \le z \le 0) = .5517 - .5 = .0517$

Looking up the area .0517 in Table IV, $z_0 = -.13$.

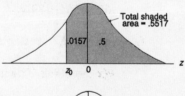

c. $P(z \ge z_0) = .1492$
$\Rightarrow P(0 \le z \le z_0) = .5 - .1492 = .3508$
Looking up the area .3508 in Table IV,
$\Rightarrow \qquad z_0 = 1.04$

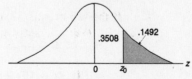

d. $P(z_0 \leq z \leq .59) = .4773$

   $\Rightarrow P(z_0 \leq z \leq 0) + P(0 \leq z \leq .59) = .4773$

   $P(0 \leq z \leq .59) = .2224$

   Thus, $P(z_0 \leq z \leq 0) = .4773 - .2224 = .2549$
   Looking up the area .2549 in Table IV, $z_0 = -.69$

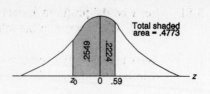

5.79 $\mu = np = 100(.5) = 50$, $\sigma = \sqrt{npq} = \sqrt{100(.5)(.5)} = 5$

a. $P(x \leq 48) = P\left[z \leq \dfrac{(48 + .5) - 50}{5}\right]$

   $= P(z \leq -.30)$
   $= .5 - .1179 = .3821$

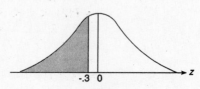

b. $P(50 \leq x \leq 65)$

   $= P\left[\dfrac{(50 - .5) - 50}{5} \leq z \leq \dfrac{(65 + .5) - 50}{5}\right]$

   $= P(-.10 \leq z \leq 3.10)$
   $= .0398 + .5000 = .5398$

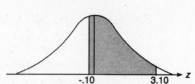

c. $P(x \geq 70) = P\left[z \geq \dfrac{(70 - .5) - 50}{5}\right]$

   $= (z \geq 3.90)$
   $= .5 - .5 = 0$

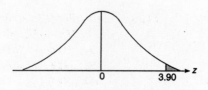

d. $P(55 \leq x \leq 58)$

   $= P\left[\dfrac{(55 - .5) - 50}{5} \leq z \leq \dfrac{(58 + .5) - 50}{5}\right]$

   $= P(.90 \leq z \leq 1.70)$
   $= P(0 \leq z \leq 1.70) - P(0 \leq z \leq .90)$
   $= .4554 - .3159 = .1395$

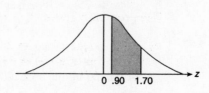

e. $P(x = 62)$

   $= P\left[\dfrac{(62 - .5) - 50}{5} \leq z \leq \dfrac{(62 + .5) - 50}{5}\right]$

   $= P(2.30 \leq z \leq 2.50)$
   $= P(0 \leq z \leq 2.50) - (0 \leq z \leq 2.30)$
   $= .4938 - .4893 = .0045$

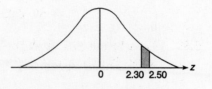

f. $P(x \leq 49$ or $x \geq 72)$

   $= P\left[z \leq \dfrac{(49 + .5) - 50}{5}\right] + P\left[z \geq \dfrac{(72 - .5) - 50}{5}\right]$

   $= P(z \leq -.10) + P(z \geq 4.30)$
   $= (.5 - .0398) + (.5 - .5) = .4602$

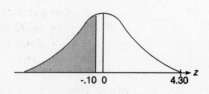

5.81 Let y be the profit on a metal part that is produced. Then y is \$10, \$$-2$, or \$$-1$, depending where it falls with respect to the tolerance limits.

Let x be the tensile strength of a particular metal part. The random variable x is normally distributed with $\mu = 25$ and $\sigma = 2$.

$$z = \frac{x - \mu}{\sigma} = \frac{21 - 25}{2} = -2$$

$$z = \frac{x - \mu}{\sigma} = \frac{30 - 25}{2} = 2.5$$

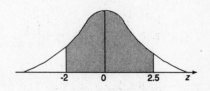

$$\begin{aligned}
P(y = 10) &= P(x \text{ falls within the tolerance limits}) \\
&= P(21 < x < 30) = P(-2 < z < 2.5) \\
&= P(-2 < z < 0) + P(0 < z < 2.5) \\
&= P(0 < z < 2) + P(0 < z < 2.5) \\
&= .4772 + .4938 \\
&= .9710
\end{aligned}$$

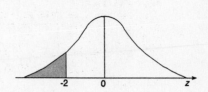

$$\begin{aligned}
P(y = -2) &= P(x \text{ falls below the lower tolerance limit}) \\
&= P(x < 21) = P(z < -2) \\
&= .5000 - P(-2 < z < 0) \\
&= .5000 - P(0 < z < 2) \\
&= .5000 - .4772 \\
&= .0228
\end{aligned}$$

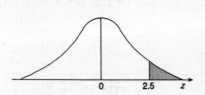

$$\begin{aligned}
P(y = -1) &= P(x \text{ falls above the upper tolerance limit}) \\
&= P(x > 30) = P(z > 2.5) \\
&= .5000 - P(0 < z < 2.5) \\
&= .5000 - .4938 \\
&= .0062
\end{aligned}$$

The probability distribution of y is given below:

y	10	-2	-1
$p(y)$	.9710	.0228	.0062

$$\begin{aligned}
E(y) = \sum yp(y) &= 10(.9710) + -2(.0228) + -1(.0062) \\
&= 9.71 - .0456 - .0062 \\
&= \$9.6582
\end{aligned}$$

5.83 Let x be the noise level per jet takeoff in a neighborhood near the airport. The random variable x is approximately normally distributed with $\mu = 100$ and $\sigma = 6$.

a. $$\begin{aligned}
P(x > 108) &= P\left[z > \frac{108 - 100}{6}\right] \\
&= P(z > 1.33) \\
&= .5000 - P(0 \le z \le 1.33) \\
&= .5000 - .4082 \\
&= .0918
\end{aligned}$$

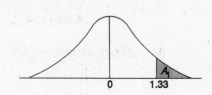

b. $P(x = 100) = 0$

c. Given $P(x < 105) = .95$ and $\sigma = 6$,

$$P(x < 105) = P(x < \mu) + P(\mu < x < 105)$$
$$= .5 + .45 = A_1 + A_2$$

Looking up the area $A_2 = .45$ in Table IV, $z_0 = 1.645$.

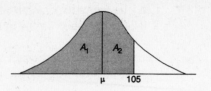

Since $z = 1.645$, $x = 105$ and $\sigma = 6$,

$$z_0 = \frac{x_0 - \mu}{\sigma} \Rightarrow 1.645 = \frac{105 - \mu}{6} \Rightarrow 9.87 = 105 - \mu$$

Hence, $\mu = 95.13$

Since $\mu = 100$, the mean level of noise must be lowered $100 - 95.13 = 4.87$ decibels.

5.85 Let x = interarrival time between patients. Then x is an exponential random variable with a mean of 4 minutes and $\lambda = 1/4$.

a. $P(x < 1) = 1 - P(x \geq 1)$
$\qquad = 1 - e^{-1/4}$
$\qquad = 1 - e^{-.25}$
$\qquad = 1 - .778801$
$\qquad = .221199$

b. Assuming that the interarrival times are independent,
$\qquad P(\text{next 4 interarrival times are all less than 1 minute})$
$\qquad\qquad = \{P(x < 1)\}^4$
$\qquad\qquad = .221199^4$
$\qquad\qquad = .002394$

c. $P(x > 10) = e^{-10(1/4)}$
$\qquad\qquad = e^{-2.5}$
$\qquad\qquad = .082085$

5.87 Let x equal the difference between the actual weight and recorded weight (the error of measurement). The random variable x is normally distributed with $\mu = 592$ and $\sigma = 628$.

a. We want to find the probability that the weigh-in-motion equipment understates the actual weight of the truck. This would be true if the error of measurement is positive.

$$P(x > 0) = P\left[z > \frac{0 - 592}{628}\right]$$
$$= P(z > -.94)$$
$$= .5000 + .3264$$
$$= .8264$$

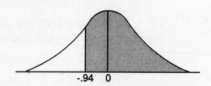

b. $P(\text{overstate the weight}) = 1 - P(\text{understate the weight})$
$\qquad\qquad\qquad\qquad\qquad\quad = 1 - .8264$
$\qquad\qquad\qquad\qquad\qquad\quad = .1736 \qquad$ (Refer to part a.)

For 100 measurements, approximately $100(.1736) = 17.36$ or 17 times the weight would be overstated.

c. $P(x > 400) = P\left(z > \dfrac{400 - 592}{628}\right)$

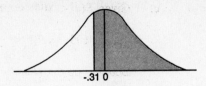

$= P(z > -.31)$
$= .5000 + .1217$
$= .6217$

d. We want $P(\text{understate the weight}) = .5$

To understate the weight, $x > 0$. Thus, we want to find μ so that $P(x > 0) = .5$

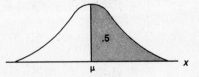

$$P(x > 0) = P\left(z > \dfrac{0 - \mu}{628}\right) = .5$$

From Table IV, Appendix B, $z_0 = 0$. To find μ, substitute into the z-score formula:

$$z_0 = \dfrac{x_0 - \mu}{\sigma} \Rightarrow 0 = \dfrac{0 - \mu}{628} \Rightarrow \mu = 0$$

Thus, the mean error should be set at 0.

We want $P(\text{understate the weight}) = .4$

To understate the weight, $x > 0$. Thus, we want to find μ so that $P(x > 0) = .4$

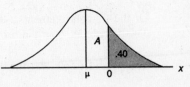

$A = .5 - .40 = .1$. Look up the area .1000 in the body of Table IV, Appendix B, $z_0 = .25$.

To find μ, substitute into the z-score formula:

$$z_0 = \dfrac{x_0 - \mu}{\sigma} \Rightarrow .25 = \dfrac{0 - \mu}{628} \Rightarrow \mu = 0 - (.25)628 = -157$$

Thus, the mean error should be set at -157.

5.89 Using MINITAB, the stem-and-leaf display is:

```
Stem-and-leaf of Time       N  = 49
Leaf Unit = 0.10


 (26)    1 00001122222344444445555679
  23     2 11446799
  15     3 002899
   9     4 11125
   4     5 24
   2     6
   2     7 8
   1     8
   1     9
   1    10 1
```

The data are skewed to the right, and do not appear to be normally distributed.

Using MINITAB, the descriptive statistics are:

```
Variable   N       Mean      Median    TrMean    StDev    SE Mean
Time       49      2.549     1.700     2.333     1.828    0.261

Variable           Minimum   Maximum   Q1        Q3
Time               1.000     10.100    1.350     3.500
```

$\bar{x} \pm s \Rightarrow 2.549 \pm 1.828 \Rightarrow (0.721, 4.377)$

$\bar{x} \pm 2s \Rightarrow 2.549 \pm 2(1.828) \Rightarrow 2.549 \pm 3.656 \Rightarrow (-1.107, 6.205)$

$\bar{x} \pm 3s \Rightarrow 2.549 \pm 3(1.828) \Rightarrow 2.549 \pm 5.484 \Rightarrow (-2.935, 8.033)$

Of the 49 measurements, 44 are in the interval (0.721, 4.377). The proportion is 44/49 = .898. This is much larger than the proportion (.68) stated by the Empirical Rule.

Of the 49 measurements, 47 are in the interval (−1.107, 6.205). The proportion is 47/49 = .959. This is close to the proportion (.95) stated by the Empirical Rule.

Of the 49 measurements, 48 are in the interval (−2.935, 8.033). The proportion is 48/49 = .980. This is smaller than the proportion (1.00) stated by the Empirical Rule.

This would imply that the data are not normal.

$IQR = Q_U - Q_L = 3.500 - 1.350 = 2.15$. $IQR/s = 2.15/1.828 = 1.176$. If the data are normally distributed, this ratio should be close to 1.3. Since 1.176 is smaller than 1.3, this indicates that the data may not be normal.

Using MINITAB, the normal probability plot is:

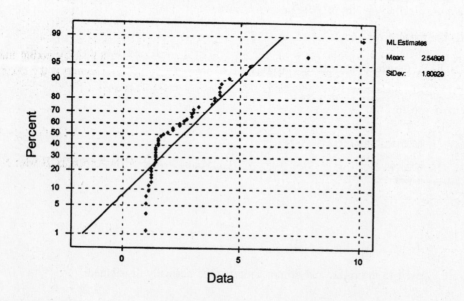

Normal Probability Plot for Time

Since this plot is not a straight line, the data are not normal.

All four checks indicate that the data are not normal.

5.91 a. (i) $P(0 < z < 1.2) \approx 1.2(4.4 - 1.2)/10 = .384$
   (ii) $P(0 < z < 2.5) = .49$
   (iii) $P(z > .8) = .5 - P(0 < z < .8) = .5 - .8(4.4 - .8)/10 = .5 - .288 = .212$
   (iv) $P(z < 1.0) = .5 + P(0 < z < 1) = .5 + 1(4.4 - 1)/10 = .5 + .34 = .84$

   b. Using Table IV, Appendix B:
   (i) $P(0 < z < 1.2) = .3849$
   (ii) $P(0 < z < 2.5) = .4938$
   (iii) $P(z > .8) = .5 - P(0 < z < .8) = .5 - .2881 = .2119$
   (iv) $P(z < 1.0) = .5 + P(0 < z < 1) = .5 + .3413 = .8413$

   c. For each part, we will take the approximate probability minus the exact probability:
   (i) $| .384 - .3849 | = .0009$
   (ii) $| .49 - .4938 | = .0038$
   (iii) $| .212 - .2119 | = .0001$
   (iv)) $| .84 - .8413 | = .0013$

   All of the absolute differences are less than .0052.

5.93 For $n = 1600$ and $p = .2$, $\mu = np = 1600(.2) = 320$ and $\sigma = \sqrt{npq} = \sqrt{1600(.2)(.8)} = 16$

   Using the normal approximation to the binomial and Table IV,

$$P(x \geq 400) \approx P\left[z \geq \frac{(400 - .5) - 320}{16}\right] = P(z \geq 4.97) = .5 - .5 = 0$$

   If $p = .2$, the probability of observing 400 or more consumers who favor the product is essentially 0. This implies that p is probably not .2 but larger than .2.

5.95 a. Define $x = $ the number of serious accidents per month. Then x has a Poisson distribution with $\lambda = 2$. If we define $y = $ the time between adjacent serious accidents, then y has an exponential distribution with $\mu = 1/\lambda = 1/2$. If an accident occurs today, the probability that the next serious accident will **not** occur during the next month is:

$$P(y > 1) = e^{-1(2)} = e^{-2} = .135335$$

   Alternatively, we could solve the problem in terms of the random variable x by noting that the probability that the next serious accident will **not** occur during the next month is the same as the probability that the number of serious accident next month is zero, i.e.,

$$P(y > 1) = P(x = 0) = \frac{e^{-2}2^0}{0!} = e^{-2} = .135335$$

   b. $P(x > 1) = 1 - P(x \leq 1) = 1 - .406 = .594$ (Using Table III in Appendix B with $\lambda = 2$)

Sampling Distributions

6.1   a–b.   The different samples of $n = 2$ with replacement and their means are:

Possible Samples	$\bar{x}$	Possible Samples	$\bar{x}$
0, 0	0	4, 0	2
0, 2	1	4, 2	3
0, 4	2	4, 4	4
0, 6	3	4, 6	5
2, 0	1	6, 0	3
2, 2	2	6, 2	4
2, 4	3	6, 4	5
2, 6	4	6, 6	6

c.   Since each sample is equally likely, the probability of any 1 being selected is $\dfrac{1}{4}\left(\dfrac{1}{4}\right) = \dfrac{1}{16}$

d.
$$P(\bar{x} = 0) = \frac{1}{16}$$

$$P(\bar{x} = 1) = \frac{1}{16} + \frac{1}{16} = \frac{2}{16}$$

$$P(\bar{x} = 2) = \frac{1}{16} + \frac{1}{16} + \frac{1}{16} = \frac{3}{16}$$

$$P(\bar{x} = 3) = \frac{1}{16} + \frac{1}{16} + \frac{1}{16} + \frac{1}{16} = \frac{4}{16}$$

$$P(\bar{x} = 4) = \frac{1}{16} + \frac{1}{16} + \frac{1}{16} = \frac{3}{16}$$

$$P(\bar{x} = 5) = \frac{1}{16} + \frac{1}{16} = \frac{2}{16}$$

$$P(\bar{x} = 6) = \frac{1}{16}$$

$\bar{x}$	$p(\bar{x})$
0	1/16
1	2/16
2	3/16
3	4/16
4	3/16
5	2/16
6	1/16

e.

6.3   If the observations are independent of each other, then

$$P(1, 1) = p(1)p(1) = .2(.2) = .04$$
$$P(1, 2) = p(1)p(2) = .2(.3) = .06$$
$$P(1, 3) = p(1)p(3) = .2(.2) = .04$$
     etc.

a.

Possible Samples	$\bar{x}$	$p(\bar{x})$	Possible Samples	$\bar{x}$	$p(\bar{x})$
1, 1	1	.04	3, 4	3.5	.04
1, 2	1.5	.06	3, 5	4	.02
1, 3	2	.04	4, 1	2.5	.04
1, 4	2.5	.04	4, 2	3	.06
1, 5	3	.02	4, 3	3.5	.04
2, 1	1.5	.06	4, 4	4	.04
2, 2	2	.09	4, 5	4.5	.02
2, 3	2.5	.06	5, 1	3	.02
2, 4	3	.06	5, 2	3.5	.03
2, 5	3.5	.03	5, 3	4	.02
3, 1	2	.04	5, 4	4.5	.02
3, 2	2.5	.06	5, 5	5	.01
3, 3	3	.04			

Summing the probabilities, the probability distribution of $\bar{x}$ is:

$\bar{x}$	$p(\bar{x})$
1	.04
1.5	.12
2	.17
2.5	.20
3	.20
3.5	.14
4	.08
4.5	.04
5	.01

b.

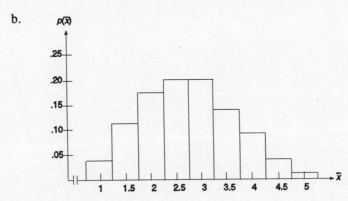

c. $P(\bar{x} \geq 4.5) = .04 + .01 = .05$

d.   No. The probability of observing $\bar{x} = 4.5$ or larger is small (.05).

6.5 a. For a sample of size $n = 2$, the sample mean and sample median are exactly the same. Thus, the sampling distribution of the sample median is the same as that for the sample mean (see Exercise 6.3a).

b. The probability histogram for the sample median is identical to that for the sample mean (see Exercise 6.3b).

6.9 a. $\mu = \sum xp(x) = 2\left[\dfrac{1}{3}\right] + 4\left[\dfrac{1}{3}\right] + 9\left[\dfrac{1}{3}\right] = \dfrac{15}{3} = 5$

b. The possible samples of size $n = 3$, the sample means, and the probabilities are:

Possible Samples	$\bar{x}$	$p(\bar{x})$	m	Possible Samples	$\bar{x}$	$p(\bar{x})$	m
2, 2, 2	2	1/27	2	4, 4, 4	4	1/27	4
2, 2, 4	8/3	1/27	2	4, 4, 9	17/3	1/27	4
2, 2, 9	13/3	1/27	2	4, 9, 2	5	1/27	4
2, 4, 2	8/3	1/27	2	4, 9, 4	17/3	1/27	4
2, 4, 4	10/3	1/27	4	4, 9, 9	22/3	1/27	9
2, 4, 9	5	1/27	4	9, 2, 2	13/3	1/27	2
2, 9, 2	13/3	1/27	2	9, 2, 4	5	1/27	4
2, 9, 4	5	1/27	4	9, 2, 9	20/3	1/27	9
2, 9, 9	20/3	1/27	9	9, 4, 2	5	1/27	4
4, 2, 2	8/3	1/27	2	9, 4, 4	17/3	1/27	4
4, 2, 4	10/3	1/27	4	9, 4, 9	22/3	1/27	9
4, 2, 9	5	1/27	4	9, 9, 2	20/3	1/27	9
4, 4, 2	10/3	1/27	4	9, 9, 4	22/3	1/27	9
				9, 9, 9	9	1/27	9

The sampling distribution of $\bar{x}$ is:

$\bar{x}$	$p(\bar{x})$
2	1/27
8/3	3/27
10/3	3/27
4	1/27
13/3	3/27
5	6/27
17/3	3/27
20/3	3/27
22/3	3/27
9	1/27
	27/27

$$E(\bar{x}) = \sum \bar{x}p(\bar{x}) = 2\left[\frac{1}{27}\right] + \frac{8}{3}\left[\frac{3}{27}\right] + \frac{10}{3}\left[\frac{3}{27}\right] + 4\left[\frac{1}{27}\right] + \frac{13}{3}\left[\frac{3}{27}\right]$$

$$+ 5\left[\frac{6}{27}\right] + \frac{17}{3}\left[\frac{3}{27}\right] + \frac{20}{3}\left[\frac{3}{27}\right] + \frac{22}{3}\left[\frac{3}{27}\right] + 9\left[\frac{1}{27}\right]$$

$$= \frac{2}{27} + \frac{8}{27} + \frac{10}{27} + \frac{4}{27} + \frac{13}{27} + \frac{30}{27} + \frac{17}{27} + \frac{20}{27} + \frac{22}{27} + \frac{9}{27}$$

$$= \frac{135}{27} = 5$$

Since $\mu = 5$ in part **a**, and $E(\bar{x}) = \mu = 5$, $\bar{x}$ is an unbiased estimator of μ.

c. The median was calculated for each sample and is shown in the table in part **b**. The sampling distribution of m is:

m	$p(m)$
2	7/27
4	13/27
9	7/27
	27/27

$$E(m) = \sum mp(m) = 2\left[\frac{7}{27}\right] + 4\left[\frac{13}{27}\right] + 9\left[\frac{7}{27}\right] = \frac{14}{27} + \frac{52}{27} + \frac{63}{27} = \frac{129}{27} = 4.778$$

$E(m) = 4.778 \neq \mu = 5$. Thus, m is a biased estimator of μ.

d. Use the sample mean, $\bar{x}$. It is an unbiased estimator.

6.13 a. Refer to the solution to Exercise 6.3. The values of s^2 and the corresponding probabilities are listed below:

$$s^2 = \frac{\sum (x^2) - \frac{(\sum x)^2}{n}}{n - 1}$$

For sample 1, 1, $s^2 = \dfrac{2 - \frac{2^2}{2}}{1} = 0$

For sample 1, 2, $s^2 = \dfrac{5 - \frac{3^2}{2}}{1} = .5$

The rest of the values are calculated and shown:

s^2	$p(s^2)$	s^2	$p(s^2)$
0.0	.04	0.5	.04
0.5	.06	2.0	.02
2.0	.04	4.5	.04
4.5	.04	2.0	.06
8.0	.02	0.5	.04
0.5	.06	0.0	.04
0.0	.09	0.5	.02
0.5	.06	8.0	.02
2.0	.06	4.5	.03
4.5	.03	2.0	.02
2.0	.04	0.5	.02
0.5	.06	0.0	.01
0.0	.04		

The sampling distribution of s^2 is:

s^2	$p(s^2)$
0.0	.22
0.5	.36
2.0	.24
4.5	.14
8.0	.04

b. $\sigma^2 = \sum (x - \mu)^2 p(x) = (1 - 2.7)^2(.2) + (2 - 2.7)^2(.3) + (3 - 2.7)^2(.2)$
$$+ (4 - 2.7)^2(.2) + (5 - 2.7)^2(.1)$$
$$= 1.61$$

c. $E(s^2) = \sum s^2 p(s^2) = 0(.22) + .5(.36) + 2(.24) + 4.5(.14) + 8(.04) = 1.61$

d. The sampling distribution of s is listed below, where $s = \sqrt{s^2}$:

s	$p(s)$
0.000	.22
0.707	.36
1.414	.24
2.121	.14
2.828	.04

e. $E(s) = \sum s p(s) = 0(.22) + .707(.36) + 1.414(.24) + 2.121(.14) + 2.828(.04)$
$$= 1.00394$$

Since $E(s) = 1.00394$ is not equal to $\sigma = \sqrt{\sigma^2} = \sqrt{1.61} = 1.269$, s is a biased estimator of σ.

6.15 a. $\mu_{\bar{x}} = \mu = 100$, $\sigma_{\bar{x}} = \dfrac{\sigma}{\sqrt{n}} = \dfrac{\sqrt{100}}{\sqrt{4}} = 5$

b. $\mu_{\bar{x}} = \mu = 100$, $\sigma_{\bar{x}} = \dfrac{\sigma}{\sqrt{n}} = \dfrac{\sqrt{100}}{\sqrt{25}} = 2$

c. $\mu_{\bar{x}} = \mu = 100$, $\sigma_{\bar{x}} = \dfrac{\sigma}{\sqrt{n}} = \dfrac{\sqrt{100}}{\sqrt{100}} = 1$

d. $\mu_{\bar{x}} = \mu = 100$, $\sigma_{\bar{x}} = \dfrac{\sigma}{\sqrt{n}} = \dfrac{\sqrt{100}}{\sqrt{50}} = 1.414$

e. $\mu_{\bar{x}} = \mu = 100$, $\sigma_{\bar{x}} = \dfrac{\sigma}{\sqrt{n}} = \dfrac{\sqrt{100}}{\sqrt{500}} = .447$

f. $\mu_{\bar{x}} = \mu = 100$, $\sigma_{\bar{x}} = \dfrac{\sigma}{\sqrt{n}} = \dfrac{\sqrt{100}}{\sqrt{1000}} = .316$

6.17 a. $\mu = \sum xp(x) = 1(.1) + 2(.4) + 3(.4) + 8(.1) = 2.9$

$\sigma^2 = \sum (x - \mu)^2 p(x) = (1 - 2.9)^2(.1) + (2 - 2.9)^2(.4) + (3 - 2.9)^2(.4) + (8 - 2.9)^2(.1)$
$= .361 + .324 + .004 + 2.601 = 3.29$

$\sigma = \sqrt{3.29} = 1.814$

b.   The possible samples, values of $\bar{x}$, and associated probabilities are listed:

Possible Samples	$\bar{x}$	$p(\bar{x})$	Possible Samples	$\bar{x}$	$p(\bar{x})$
1, 1	1	.01	3, 1	2	.04
1, 2	1.5	.04	3, 2	2.5	.16
1, 3	2	.04	3, 3	3	.16
1, 8	4.5	.01	3, 8	5.5	.04
2, 1	1.5	.04	8, 1	4.5	.01
2, 2	2	.16	8, 2	5	.04
2, 3	2.5	.16	8, 3	5.5	.04
2, 8	5	.04	8, 8	8	.01

$P(1, 1) = p(1)p(1) = .1(.1) = .01$
$P(1, 2) = p(1)p(2) = .1(.4) = .04$
$P(1, 3) = p(1)p(3) = .1(.4) = .04$
    etc.

The sampling distribution of $\bar{x}$ is:

$\bar{x}$	$p(\bar{x})$
1	.01
1.5	.08
2	.24
2.5	.32
3	.16
4.5	.02
5	.08
5.5	.08
8	.01
	1.00

c. $\mu_{\bar{x}} = E(\bar{x}) = \sum \bar{x}p(\bar{x}) = 1(.01) + 1.5(.08) + 2(.24) + 2.5(.32) + 3(.16) + 4.5(.02)$
$$+ 5(.08) + 5.5(.08) + 8(.01)$$
$$= 2.9 = \mu$$

$\sigma_{\bar{x}}^2 = \sum (\bar{x} - \mu_{\bar{x}})^2 p(\bar{x}) = (1 - 2.9)^2(.01) + (1.5 - 2.9)^2(.08) + (2 - 2.9)^2(.24)$
$$+ (2.5 - 2.9)^2(.32) + (3 - 2.9)^2(.16) + (4.5 - 2.9)^2(.02)$$
$$+ (5 - 2.9)^2(.08) + (5.5 - 2.9)^2(.08) + (8 - 2.9)^2(.01)$$
$$= .0361 + .1568 + .1944 + .0512 + .0016 + .0512 + .3528$$
$$+ .5408 + .2601$$
$$= 1.645$$

$\sigma_{\bar{x}} = \sqrt{1.645} = 1.283$

$\sigma_{\bar{x}} = \sigma/\sqrt{n} = 1.814/\sqrt{2} = 1.283$

6.19 a. $\mu_{\bar{x}} = \mu = 20$, $\sigma_{\bar{x}} = \sigma/\sqrt{n} = 16/\sqrt{64} = 2$

b. By the Central Limit Theorem, the distribution of $\bar{x}$ is approximately normal. In order for the Central Limit Theorem to apply, n must be sufficiently large. For this problem, $n = 64$ is sufficiently large.

c. $z = \dfrac{\bar{x} - \mu_{\bar{x}}}{\sigma_{\bar{x}}} = \dfrac{15.5 - 20}{2} = -2.25$

d. $z = \dfrac{\bar{x} - \mu_{\bar{x}}}{\sigma_{\bar{x}}} = \dfrac{23 - 20}{2} = 1.50$

6.21 By the Central Limit Theorem, the sampling distribution of $\bar{x}$ is approximately normal with $\mu_{\bar{x}} = \mu = 30$ and $\sigma_{\bar{x}} = \sigma/\sqrt{n} = 16/\sqrt{100} = 1.6$. Using Table IV, Appendix B:

a. $P(\bar{x} \geq 28) = P\left(z \geq \dfrac{28 - 30}{1.6}\right) = P(z \geq -1.25) = .5 + .3944 = .8944$

b. $P(22.1 \leq \bar{x} \leq 26.8) = P\left(\dfrac{22.1 - 30}{1.6} \leq z \leq \dfrac{26.8 - 30}{1.6}\right) = P(-4.94 \leq z \leq -2)$
$$= .5 - .4772 = .0228$$

c. $P(\bar{x} \le 28.2) = P\left(z \le \dfrac{28.2 - 30}{1.6}\right) = P(z \le -1.13) = .5 - .3708 = .1292$

d. $P(\bar{x} \ge 27.0) = P\left(z \ge \dfrac{27.0 - 30}{1.6}\right) = P(z \ge -1.88) = .5 + .4699 = .9699$

6.25 a. By the Central Limit Theorem, the sampling distribution of $\bar{x}$ is approximately normal with

$\mu_{\bar{x}} = \mu$ and $\sigma_{\bar{x}} = \sigma/\sqrt{n}$.

b. Let $\mu = 18.5$. Since we do not know σ we will estimate it with $s = 6$.

$P(\bar{x} \ge 19.1) \approx P\left(z \ge \dfrac{19.1 - 18.5}{6/\sqrt{344}}\right) = P(z \ge 1.85) = .5 - .4678 = .0322$

c. Let $\mu = 19.5$. Since we do not know σ we will estimate it with $s = 6$.

$P(\bar{x} \ge 19.1) \approx P\left(z \ge \dfrac{19.1 - 19.5}{6/\sqrt{344}}\right) = P(z \ge -1.24) = .5 + .3925 = .8925$

d. If $P(\bar{x} \ge 19.1) = .5$, then the population mean must be equal to 19.1. (For a normal distribution, half of the distribution is above the mean and half is below the mean.)

e. If $P(\bar{x} \ge 19.1) = .2$, then the population mean is less than 19.1. We know the probability that $\bar{x}$ is greater than the mean is .5. Since $P(x \ge 19.1) = .2$ which is less than .5, we know that 19.1 must be to the right of the mean. Thus, the population mean must be less than 19.1.

6.27 a. For $n = 36$, $\mu_{\bar{x}} = \mu = 406$ and $\sigma_{\bar{x}} = \sigma/\sqrt{n} = 10.1/\sqrt{36} = 1.6833$. By the Central Limit Theorem, the sampling distribution is approximately normal (n is large).

b. $P(\bar{x} \le 400.8) = P\left(z \le \dfrac{400.8 - 406}{1.6833}\right) = P(z \le -3.09) = .5 - .4990 = .0010$

(using Table IV, Appendix B)

c. The first. If the true value of μ is 406, it would be extremely unlikely to observe an $\bar{x}$ as small as 400.8 or smaller (probability .0010). Thus, we would infer that the true value of μ is less than 406.

6.29 a. By the Central Limit Theorem, the sampling distribution of $\bar{x}$ is approximately normal with

$\mu_{\bar{x}} = \mu$ and $\sigma_{\bar{x}} = \sigma/\sqrt{n} = \sigma/\sqrt{50}$.

b. $\mu_{\bar{x}} = \mu = 40$ and $\sigma_{\bar{x}} = \sigma/\sqrt{50} = 12/\sqrt{50} = 1.6971$.

$P(\bar{x} \ge 44) = P\left(z \ge \dfrac{44 - 40}{1.6971}\right) = P(z \ge 2.36) = .5 - .4909 = .0091$

(using Table IV, Appendix B)

c. $\mu \pm 2\sigma/\sqrt{n} \Rightarrow 40 \pm 2(1.6971) \Rightarrow 40 \pm 3.3942 \Rightarrow (36.6058, 43.3942)$

$$P(36.6058 \leq \bar{x} \leq 43.3942) = P\left[\frac{36.6058 - 40}{1.6971} \leq z \leq \frac{43.3942 - 40}{1.6971}\right]$$
$$= P(-2 \leq z \leq 2) = 2(.4772) = .9544$$

(using Table IV, Appendix B)

6.31   a.   "The sampling distribution of the sample statistic A" is the probability distribution of the variable A.

b.   "A" is an unbiased estimator of α if the mean of the sampling distribution of A is α.

c.   If both A and B are unbiased estimators of α, then the statistic whose standard deviation is smaller is a better estimator of α.

d.   No. The Central Limit Theorem applies only to the sample mean. If A is the sample mean, $\bar{x}$, and n is sufficiently large, then the Central Limit Theorem will apply. However, both A and B cannot be sample means. Thus, we cannot apply the Central Limit Theorem to both A and B.

6.33   By the Central Limit Theorem, the sampling distribution of $\bar{x}$ is approximately normal.

$$\mu_{\bar{x}} = \mu = 19.6, \; \sigma_{\bar{x}} = \frac{3.2}{\sqrt{68}} = .388$$

a. $P(\bar{x} \leq 19.6) = P\left[z \leq \dfrac{19.6 - 19.6}{.388}\right] = P(z \leq 0) = .5$ (using Table IV, Appendix B)

b. $P(\bar{x} \leq 19) = P\left[z \leq \dfrac{19 - 19.6}{.388}\right] = P(z \leq -1.55) = .5 - .4394 = .0606$

(using Table IV, Appendix B)

c. $P(\bar{x} \geq 20.1) = P\left[z \geq \dfrac{20.1 - 19.6}{.388}\right] = P(z \geq 1.29) = .5 - .4015 = .0985$

(using Table IV, Appendix B)

d. $P(19.2 \leq \bar{x} \leq 20.6) = P\left[\dfrac{19.2 - 19.6}{.388} \leq z \leq \dfrac{20.6 - 19.6}{.388}\right]$

$$= P(-1.03 \leq z \leq 2.58) = .3485 + .4951 = .8436$$

(using Table IV, Appendix B)

6.37   Given: $\mu = 100$ and $\sigma = 10$

n	1	5	10	20	30	40	50
$\dfrac{\sigma}{\sqrt{n}}$	10	4.472	3.162	2.236	1.826	1.581	1.414

The graph of $\sigma/\sqrt{n}$ against n is given here:

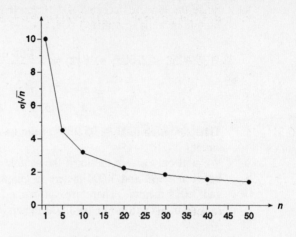

6.39   a.   The distribution of x has a mean of $\mu = 26$ and a standard deviation of σ. There is no information given to indicate the shape of the distribution.

b.   The distribution of $\bar{x}$ has a mean of $\mu_{\bar{x}} = \mu = 26$ and a standard deviation of $\sigma_{\bar{x}} = \sigma/\sqrt{n}$. Since $n = 200$ is sufficiently large, the Central Limit Theorem says that the sampling distribution of $\bar{x}$ is approximately normal.

c.   If $\sigma = 20$, then $\sigma_{\bar{x}} = \sigma/\sqrt{n} = 20/\sqrt{200} = 1.4142$.

$$P(\bar{x} > 26.8) = P\left(z > \frac{26.8 - 26}{1.4142}\right) = P(z > .57) = .5 - .2157 = .2843$$

d.   If $\sigma = 10$, then $\sigma_{\bar{x}} = \sigma/\sqrt{n} = 10/\sqrt{200} = .7071$

$$P(\bar{x} > 26.8) = P\left(z > \frac{26.8 - 26}{.7071}\right) = P(z > 1.13) = .5 - .3708 = .1292$$

6.41   By the Central Limit Theorem, the sampling distribution of $\bar{x}$ is approximately normal.

$$\mu_{\underline{\bar{x}}} = \mu = 7;\ \sigma_{\underline{\bar{x}}} = \frac{\sigma}{\sqrt{n}} = \frac{2}{\sqrt{100}} = .2$$

a. $P(\bar{x} \le 6.4) = P\left(z \le \frac{6.4 - 7}{.2}\right) = P(z \le -3.00) = .5 - .4987 = .0013$

b.   Since the probability of observing the sample mean 6.4 or less is only .0013, it would be reasonable to conclude that the program did decrease the mean number of sick days taken by the company's employees.

6.43   The mean, μ, of the length of the steel rods is 3 meters with a standard deviation, σ, of .03. By the Central Limit Theorem, the sampling distribution of $\bar{x}$ is approximately normal since $n \ge 30$, and

$$\mu_{\bar{x}} = \mu = 3 \text{ and } \sigma_{\bar{x}} = \frac{\sigma}{\sqrt{n}} = \frac{.03}{\sqrt{100}} = .003$$

a. Since the lots are accepted if the sample mean is 3.005 meters or more and returned if the sample mean is less than 3.005,

$$P(\bar{x} < 3.005) = P\left[z < \frac{3.005 - 3}{.003}\right]$$
$$= P(z < 1.67) = .5 + P(0 < z < 1.67)$$
$$= .5 + .4525 = .9525$$

Thus, $.9525 \times 100 = 95.25\%$ of the lots will be returned to the vendor.

b. We will only accept the lot if the sample mean is 3.005 meters or more. If all the rods are between 2.999 and 3.004 meters in length, then the sample mean must also be between 2.999 and 3.004 meters. Therefore, all of the lots (100%) will be returned to the vendor since the sample mean will never be 3.005 meters or more.

6.45 a. The mean, μ, diameter of the bearings is unknown with a standard deviation, σ, of .001 inch. By the Central Limit Theorem, the sampling distribution of $\bar{x}$ is approximately normal since $n \geq 30$, with

$$\mu_{\bar{x}} = \mu \qquad \sigma_{\bar{x}} = \frac{\sigma}{\sqrt{n}} = \frac{.001}{\sqrt{36}} = .000167$$

Having the sample mean fall within .0001 inch of μ implies $|\bar{x} - \mu| \leq .0001$ or $-.0001 \leq \bar{x} - \mu \leq .0001$.

$$P(-.0001 \leq \bar{x} - \mu \leq .0001)$$
$$= P\left[\frac{-.0001}{.000167} \leq z \leq \frac{.0001}{.000167}\right] = P(-.60 \leq z \leq .60)$$
$$= 2P(0 \leq z \leq .60) = 2(.2257) = .4514$$

b. It will not be affected. Since $n \geq 30$, the sampling distribution of $\bar{x}$ is approximately normal by the Central Limit Theorems regardless of the shape of the distribution of x.

6.47 The mean, μ, of the percentage of alkali in a test specimen of soap is 2% with a standard deviation, σ, of 1%. The sampling distribution of $\bar{x}$ is approximately normal since x is approximately normal and if $n = 4$,

$$\mu_{\bar{x}} = \mu = 2 \qquad \sigma_{\bar{x}} = \frac{\sigma}{\sqrt{n}} = \frac{1}{\sqrt{4}} = .5$$

a. The control limits are located $3\sigma_{\bar{x}}$ above and below μ.

$$3\sigma_{\bar{x}} = 3(.5) = 1.5$$

Therefore, the upper and lower control limits are located 1.5% above and below μ.

b. $\overline{x}$ will fall outside the control limits if it is smaller than $\mu - 3\sigma_{\overline{x}}$ or larger than $\mu + 3\sigma_{\overline{x}}$. If the process is in control,

$$P(\overline{x} < \mu - 3\sigma_{\overline{x}}) + P(\overline{x} > \mu + 3\sigma_{\overline{x}})$$

$$= P\left(z < \frac{\mu - 3\sigma_{\overline{x}} - \mu}{\sigma_{\overline{x}}}\right) + P\left(z > \frac{\mu + 3\sigma_{\overline{x}} - \mu}{\sigma_{\overline{x}}}\right)$$

$$= P(z < -3) + P(z > 3)$$
$$= 2(z > 3)$$
$$= 2(.5 - P(0 < z < 3))$$
$$= 2(.5 - .4987)$$
$$= 2(.0013)$$
$$= .0026$$

c.   The process is deemed to be out of control if $\overline{x}$ is outside the control limits. The control limits are located at $\mu \pm 3\sigma_{\overline{x}} \Rightarrow 2 \pm 1.5 \Rightarrow (.5, 3.5)$. If the mean shifts to $\mu = 3\%$,

$$P(\overline{x} < .5) + P(\overline{x} > 3.5)$$

$$= P\left(z < \frac{.5 - 3}{.5}\right) + P\left(z > \frac{3.5 - 3}{.5}\right)$$

$$= P(z < -5) + P(z > 1)$$
$$= .5 - .5 + .5 - .3413$$
$$= .1587$$

6.49   Referring to Exercises 6.47 and 6.48, the mean, μ, of the percentage of alkali in a test specimen of soap is 2% with a standard deviation, σ, of 1%. The sampling distribution of $\overline{x}$ is approximately normal since x is approximately normal and if $n = 4$,

$$\mu_{\overline{x}} = \mu = 2 \qquad \sigma_{\overline{x}} = \frac{\sigma}{\sqrt{n}} = \frac{1}{\sqrt{4}} = .5$$

a. $\overline{x}$ will fall outside the warning limits if it is smaller than $\mu - 1.96\sigma_{\overline{x}}$ or larger than $\mu + 1.96\sigma_{\overline{x}}$. If the process is in control,

$$P(\overline{x} < \mu - 1.96\sigma_{\overline{x}}) + P(\overline{x} > \mu + 1.96\sigma_{\overline{x}})$$

$$= P\left(z < \frac{\mu - 1.96\sigma_{\overline{x}} - \mu}{\sigma_{\overline{x}}}\right) + P\left(z > \frac{\mu + 1.96\sigma_{\overline{x}} - \mu}{\sigma_{\overline{x}}}\right)$$

$$= P(z < -1.96) + P(z > 1.96)$$
$$= 2P(z > 1.96)$$
$$= 2(.5 - .4750)$$
$$= 2(.025)$$
$$= .05$$

b. $P(\overline{x} > \mu + 1.96\sigma_{\overline{x}}) = P(z > 1.96) = .025$ (Refer to part a.)

Therefore, $40 \times .025 = 1$ of the next 40 values of $\overline{x}$ is expected to fall above the upper warning limit.

c. P(next two values of $\overline{x}$ fall below the lower warning limit)
$$= P(\overline{x} < \mu - 1.96\sigma_{\overline{x}})P(\overline{x} < \mu - 1.96\sigma_{\overline{x}}) \text{ (by independence)}$$
$$= P(z < -1.96)P(z < -1.96)$$
$$= .025(.025) \text{ (Refer to part a).}$$
$$= .000625$$

6.51   a.   If x is an exponential random variable, then $\mu = E(x) = 1/\lambda = 60$. The standard deviation of x is $\sigma = 1/\lambda = 60$.

Then, $E(\overline{x}) = \mu_{\overline{x}} = \mu = 60$;

$$V = \sigma_{\overline{x}}^2 = \frac{\sigma^2}{n} = \frac{60^2}{100} = 36$$

b.   Because the sample size is fairly large, the Central Limit Theorem says that the sampling distribution of $\overline{x}$ is approximately normal.

c. $P(\overline{x} \leq 30) = P\left[z \leq \dfrac{30 - 60}{\sqrt{36}} \right] = P(z \leq -5.0) \approx .5 - .5 = 0$

Inferences Based on a Single Sample: Estimation with Confidence Intervals   *Chapter 7*

7.1 a.   For $\alpha = .10$, $\alpha/2 = .10/2 = .05$. $z_{\alpha/2} = z_{.05}$ is the z-score with .05 of the area to the right of it. The area between 0 and $z_{.05}$ is $.5 - .05 = .4500$. Using Table IV, Appendix B, $z_{.05} = 1.645$.

   b.   For $\alpha = .01$, $\alpha/2 = .01/2 = .005$. $z_{\alpha/2} = z_{.005}$ is the z-score with .005 of the area to the right of it. The area between 0 and $z_{.005}$ is $.5 - .005 = .4950$. Using Table IV, Appendix B, $z_{.005} = 2.58$.

   c.   For $\alpha = .05$, $\alpha/2 = .05/2 = .025$. $z_{\alpha/2} = z_{.025}$ is the z-score with .025 of the area to the right of it. The area between 0 and $z_{.025}$ is $.5 - .025 = .4750$. Using Table IV, Appendix B, $z_{.025} = 1.96$.

   d.   For $\alpha = .20$, $\alpha/2 = .20/2 = .10$. $z_{\alpha/2} = z_{.10}$ is the z-score with .10 of the area to the right of it. The area between 0 and $z_{.10}$ is $.5 - .10 = .4000$. Using Table IV, Appendix B, $z_{.10} = 1.28$.

7.3 a.   For confidence coefficient .95, $\alpha = .05$ and $\alpha/2 = .05/2 = .025$. From Table IV, Appendix B, $z_{.025} = 1.96$. The confidence interval is:

$$\bar{x} \pm z_{.025}\frac{s}{\sqrt{n}} \Rightarrow 28 \pm 1.96\frac{\sqrt{12}}{\sqrt{75}} \Rightarrow 28 \pm .784 \Rightarrow (27.216, 28.784)$$

   b. $\bar{x} \pm z_{.025}\dfrac{s}{\sqrt{n}} \Rightarrow 102 \pm 1.96\dfrac{\sqrt{22}}{\sqrt{200}} \Rightarrow 102 \pm .65 \Rightarrow (101.35, 102.65)$

   c. $\bar{x} \pm z_{.025}\dfrac{s}{\sqrt{n}} \Rightarrow 15 \pm 1.96\dfrac{.3}{\sqrt{100}} \Rightarrow 15 \pm .0588 \Rightarrow (14.9412, 15.0588)$

   d. $\bar{x} \pm z_{.025}\dfrac{s}{\sqrt{n}} \Rightarrow 4.05 \pm 1.96\dfrac{.83}{\sqrt{100}} \Rightarrow 4.05 \pm .163 \Rightarrow (3.887, 4.213)$

   e.   No. Since the sample size in each part was large (n ranged from 75 to 200), the Central Limit Theorem indicates that the sampling distribution of $\bar{x}$ is approximately normal.

7.5 a.   For confidence coefficient .95, $\alpha = .05$ and $\alpha/2 = .05/2 = .025$. From Table IV, Appendix B, $z_{.025} = 1.96$. The confidence interval is:

$$\bar{x} \pm z_{\alpha/2}\frac{s}{\sqrt{n}} \Rightarrow 26.2 \pm 1.96\frac{4.1}{\sqrt{70}} \Rightarrow 26.2 \pm .96 \Rightarrow (25.24, 27.16)$$

   b.   The confidence coefficient of .95 means that in repeated sampling, 95% of all confidence intervals constructed will include μ.

c. For confidence coefficient .99, $\alpha = .01$ and $\alpha/2 = .01/2 = .005$. From Table IV, Appendix B, $z_{.005} = 2.58$. The confidence interval is:

$$\bar{x} \pm z_{\alpha/2}\frac{s}{\sqrt{n}} \Rightarrow 26.2 \pm 2.58\frac{4.1}{\sqrt{70}} \Rightarrow 26.2 \pm 1.26 \Rightarrow (24.94, \ 27.46)$$

d. As the confidence coefficient increases, the width of the confidence interval also increases.

e. Yes. Since the sample size is 70, the Central Limit Theorem applies. This ensures the distribution of $\bar{x}$ is normal, regardless of the original distribution.

7.7 A point estimator is a single value used to estimate the parameter, μ. An interval estimator is two values, an upper and lower bound, which define an interval with which we attempt to enclose the parameter, μ. An interval estimate also has a measure of confidence associated with it.

7.9 Yes. As long as the sample size is sufficiently large, the Central Limit Theorem says the distribution of $\bar{x}$ is approximately normal regardless of the original distribution.

7.11 a. The population from which the sample was drawn is the set of all adult smokers in the U.S.

b. The 95% confidence interval is (19.7, 20.3). We are 95% confident that the mean number of cigarettes smoked per day by all smokers is between 19.7 and 20.3.

c. Since the sample size is so large ($n = 11,000$), no assumptions are necessary. The Central Limit Theorem indicates that the sampling distribution of $\bar{x}$ is approximately normal.

d. Since the entire 95% confidence interval is above the value of 15, the claim made by the tobacco industry researcher is probably not true.

7.13 a. For confidence coefficient .90, $\alpha = .10$ and $\alpha/2 = .05$. From Table IV, Appendix B, $z_{.05} = 1.645$. The confidence interval is:

$$\bar{x} \pm z_{\alpha/2}\frac{s}{\sqrt{n}} \Rightarrow 3.39 \pm 1.645\frac{.80}{\sqrt{797}} \Rightarrow 3.39 \pm .0466 \Rightarrow (3.3434, \ 3.4366)$$

Since the sample size was so large, no assumptions are necessary.

b. We are 90% confident that the mean risk is between 3.3434 and 3.4366. Since all values included in the interval exceed 2.5, the researchers would conclude that students in these grades exhibit an awareness of risk involved in bicycling.

7.15 From the printout, the 95% confidence interval is (.3526, .4921). We are 95% confident that the true mean correlation coefficient between appraisal participation and a subordinate's satisfaction with the appraisal is between .3526 and .4921.

7.17 a. Some preliminary calculations are:

$$\bar{x} = \frac{\sum x}{n} = \frac{2406}{36} = 66.83$$

$$s^2 = \frac{\sum x^2 - \frac{(\sum x)^2}{n}}{n - 1} = \frac{168,016 - \frac{(2406)^2}{36}}{36 - 1} = 206.143$$

$$s = \sqrt{206.143} = 14.3577$$

For confidence coefficient .95, $\alpha = 1 - .95 = .05$ and $\alpha/2 = .05/2 = .025$. From Table IV, Appendix B, $z_{.025} = 1.96$. The confidence interval is:

$$\bar{x} \pm z_{.025}\frac{s}{\sqrt{n}} \Rightarrow 66.83 \pm 1.96\frac{14.3577}{\sqrt{36}} \Rightarrow 66.83 \pm 4.69 \Rightarrow (62.14, 71.52)$$

We are 95% confident that the mean raw test score for all twenty-five year olds is between 62.14 and 71.52.

b. We must assume that the sample is random and that the observations are independent.

c. From the printout, the 95% confidence interval is (41.009, 49.602). We are 95% confident that the mean raw test score for all sixty year olds is between 41.009 and 49.602.

7.19 a. For confidence coefficient .80, $\alpha = 1 - .80 = .20$ and $\alpha/2 = .20/2 = .10$. From Table IV, Appendix B, $z_{.10} = 1.28$. From Table VI, with df $= n - 1 = 5 - 1 = 4$, $t_{.10} = 1.533$.

b. For confidence coefficient .90, $\alpha = 1 - .90 = .05$ and $\alpha/2 = .10/2 = .05$. From Table IV, Appendix B, $z_{.05} = 1.645$. From Table VI, with df $= n - 1 = 5 - 1 = 4$, $t_{.05} = 2.132$.

c. For confidence coefficient .95, $\alpha = 1 - .95 = .05$ and $\alpha/2 = .05/2 = .025$. From Table IV, Appendix B, $z_{.025} = 1.96$. From Table VI, with df $= n - 1 = 5 - 1 = 4$, $t_{.025} = 2.776$.

d. For confidence coefficient .98, $\alpha = 1 - .98 = .02$ and $\alpha/2 = .02/2 = .01$. From Table IV, Appendix B, $z_{.01} = 2.33$. From Table VI, with df $= n - 1 = 5 - 1 = 4$, $t_{.01} = 3.747$.

e. For confidence coefficient .99, $\alpha = 1 - .99 = .02$ and $\alpha/2 = .02/2 = .005$. From Table IV, Appendix B, $z_{.005} = 2.575$. From Table VI, with df $= n - 1 = 5 - 1 = 4$, $t_{.005} = 4.604$.

f. Both the t- and z-distributions are symmetric around 0 and mound-shaped. The t-distribution is more spread out than the z-distribution.

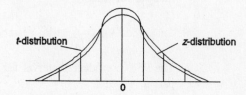

7.21 a. $P(-t_0 < t < t_0) = .95$ where df $= 10$

Because of symmetry, the statement can be written

$$P(0 < t < t_0) = .475 \text{ where df} = 10$$
$$\Rightarrow P(t \geq t_0) = .025$$
$$t_0 = 2.228$$

b. $P(t \leq -t_0 \text{ or } t \geq t_0) = .05$ where df $= 10$

$$\Rightarrow 2P(t \geq t_0) = .05$$
$$\Rightarrow P(t \geq t_0) = .025 \text{ where df} = 10$$
$$t_0 = 2.228$$

c. $P(t \leq t_0) = .05$ where df $= 10$

Because of symmetry, the statement can be written

$$\Rightarrow P(t \geq -t_0) = .05 \text{ where df} = 10$$
$$t_0 = -1.812$$

d. $P(t < -t_0 \text{ or } t > t_0) = .10$ where df = 20
$$\Rightarrow 2P(t > t_0) = .10$$
$$\Rightarrow P(t > t_0) = .05 \text{ where df} = 20$$
$$t_0 = 1.725$$

e. $P(t \leq -t_0 \text{ or } t \geq t_0) = .01$ where df = 5
$$\Rightarrow 2P(t \geq t_0) = .01$$
$$\Rightarrow P(t \geq t_0) = .005 \text{ where df} = 5$$
$$t_0 = 4.032$$

7.23   For this sample,

$$\bar{x} = \frac{\sum x}{n} = \frac{1567}{16} = 97.9375$$

$$s^2 = \frac{\sum x^2 - \frac{(\sum x)^2}{n}}{n-1} = \frac{155,867 - \frac{1567^2}{16}}{16-1} = 159.9292$$

$$s = \sqrt{s^2} = 12.6463$$

a.   For confidence coefficient, .80, $\alpha = 1 - .80 = .20$ and $\alpha/2 = .20/2 = .10$. From Table VI, Appendix B, with df $= n - 1 = 16 - 1 = 15$, $t_{.10} = 1.341$. The 80% confidence interval for μ is:

$$\bar{x} \pm t_{.10}\frac{s}{\sqrt{n}} \Rightarrow 97.94 \pm 1.341\frac{12.6463}{\sqrt{16}} \Rightarrow 97.94 \pm 4.240 \Rightarrow (93.700, 102.180)$$

b.   For confidence coefficient, .95, $\alpha = 1 - .95 = .05$ and $\alpha/2 = .05/2 = .025$. From Table VI, Appendix B, with df $= n - 1 = 24 - 1 = 23$, $t_{.025} = 2.131$. The 95% confidence interval for μ is:

$$\bar{x} \pm t_{.025}\frac{s}{\sqrt{n}} \Rightarrow 97.94 \pm 2.131\frac{12.6463}{\sqrt{16}} \Rightarrow 97.94 \pm 6.737 \Rightarrow (91.203, 104.677)$$

The 95% confidence interval for μ is wider than the 80% confidence interval for μ found in part **a**.

c.   For part **a**:

We are 80% confident that the true population mean lies in the interval 93.700 to 102.180.

For part **b**:

We are 95% confident that the true population mean lies in the interval 91.203 to 104.677.

The 95% confidence interval is wider than the 80% confidence interval because the more confident you want to be that μ lies in an interval, the wider the range of possible values.

7.25   a.   First, we must compute some preliminary satistics:

$$\bar{x} = \frac{\sum x}{n} = \frac{28.856}{10} = 2.8856$$

$$s^2 = \frac{\sum x^2 - \frac{\left(\sum x\right)^2}{n}}{n-1} = \frac{221.90161 - \frac{(28.856)^2}{10}}{10-1} = 15.4039$$

$$s = \sqrt{s^2} = \sqrt{15.4039} = 3.925$$

For confidence coefficient .99, $\alpha = .01$ and $\alpha/2 = .01/2 = .005$. From Table VI, Appendix B, with df $= n - 1 = 10 - 1 = 9$, $t_{.005} = 3.250$. The confidence interval is:

$$\bar{x} \pm t_{.005}\frac{s}{\sqrt{n}} \Rightarrow 2.8856 \pm 3.250\frac{3.925}{\sqrt{10}} \Rightarrow 2.8856 \pm 4.034 \Rightarrow (-1.148, 6.919)$$

b.   First, we must compute some preliminary statistics:

$$\bar{x} = \frac{\sum x}{n} = \frac{4.083}{10} = .4083$$

$$s^2 = \frac{\sum x^2 - \frac{\left(\sum x\right)^2}{n}}{n-1} = \frac{2.227425 - \frac{(4.083)^2}{10}}{10-1} = .06226$$

$$s = \sqrt{s^2} = \sqrt{.06226} = .2495$$

For confidence coefficient .99, $\alpha = .01$ and $\alpha/2 = .01/2 = .005$. From Table VI, Appendix B, with df $= n - 1 = 10 - 1 = 9$, $t_{.005} = 3.250$. The confidence interval is:

$$\bar{x} \pm t_{.005}\frac{s}{\sqrt{n}} \Rightarrow .4083 \pm 3.250\frac{.2495}{\sqrt{10}} \Rightarrow .4083 \pm .2564 \Rightarrow (.1519, .6647)$$

c.   We are 99% confident that the mean lead level in water specimens from Crystal Lake Manors is between -1.148 and 6.919 or 0 and 6.919 μ/L since no value can be less than 0.

We are 99% confident that the mean copper level in water specimens from Crystal Lake Manors is between .1519 and .6647 mg/L.

d.   The phrase "99% confident" means that if repeated samples of size n were selected and 99% confidence intervals constructed for the mean, 99% of all intervals constructed would contain the mean.

7.27   a.   For confidence coefficient .99, $\alpha = .01$ and $\alpha/2 = .01/2 = .005$. From Table VI, Appendix B, with df $= n - 1 = 3 - 1 = 2$, $t_{.005} = 9.925$. The confidence interval is:

$$\bar{x} \pm t_{.005}\frac{s}{\sqrt{n}} \Rightarrow 49.3 \pm 9.925\frac{1.5}{\sqrt{3}} \Rightarrow 49.3 \pm 8.60 \Rightarrow (40.70, 57.90)$$

b.   We are 99% confident that the mean percentage of B(a)p removed from all soil specimens using the poison is between 40.70% and 57.90%.

c.   We must assume that the distribution of the percentages of B(a)p removed from all soil specimens using the poison is normal.

7.29   First we make some preliminary calculations:

$$\bar{x} = \frac{\sum x}{n} = \frac{1479.9}{8} = 184.9875$$

$$s^2 = \frac{\sum x^2 - \frac{(\sum x)^2}{n}}{n-1} = \frac{453,375.17 - \frac{1479.9^2}{8}}{8-1} = 25,658.88124$$

$$s = \sqrt{25,658.88124} = 160.1839$$

For confidence coefficient .95, $\alpha = .05$ and $\alpha/2 = .025$. From Table VI, Appendix B, with df $= n - 1 = 8 - 1 = 7$, $t_{.025} = 2.365$. The 95% confidence interval is:

$$\bar{x} \pm t_{.05}\frac{s}{\sqrt{n}} \Rightarrow 184.9875 \pm 2.365\frac{160.1839}{\sqrt{8}} \Rightarrow 184.9875 \pm 133.9384 \Rightarrow (51.0491, 318.9259)$$

We must assume that the population of private colleges' and universities' endowments are normally distributed.

7.31   a.   For confidence coefficient .99, $\alpha = .01$ and $\alpha/2 = .01/2 = .005$. From Table VI, Appendix B, with df $= n - 1 = 22 - 1 = 21$, $t_{.005} = 2.831$. The confidence interval is:

$$\bar{x} \pm t_{\alpha/2}\frac{s}{\sqrt{n}} \Rightarrow 22.455 \pm 2.831\frac{18.518}{\sqrt{22}} \Rightarrow 22.455 \pm 11.177 \Rightarrow (11.278, 33.632)$$

b.   We are 99% confident that the mean number of full-time employees at office furniture dealers in Tampa is between 11.278 and 33.632.

c.   In order for the confidence interval to be valid, we must assume that the distribution of the number of full-time employees at all office furniture dealers in Tampa is normal and that the sample was a random sample.

d.   If the 22 observations in the sample were the top-ranked furniture dealers in Tampa, then the sample was not a random sample. Thus, the validity of the interval is suspect.

7.33   An unbiased estimator is one in which the mean of the sampling distribution is the parameter of interest, i.e., $E(\hat{p}) = p$.

7.35   The sample size is large enough if $\hat{p} \pm 3\sigma_{\hat{p}}$ lies within the interval (0, 1).

$$\hat{p} \pm 3\sigma_{\hat{p}} \Rightarrow \hat{p} \pm 3\sqrt{\frac{pq}{n}} \Rightarrow \hat{p} \pm 3\sqrt{\frac{\hat{p}\hat{q}}{n}}$$

a.   When $n = 400$, $\hat{p} = .10$:

$$.10 \pm 3\sqrt{\frac{.10(1 - .10)}{400}} \Rightarrow .10 \pm .045 \Rightarrow (.055, .145)$$

Since the interval lies completely in the interval (0, 1), the normal approximation will be adequate.

b. When $n = 50$, $\hat{p} = .10$:

$$.10 \pm 3 \sqrt{\frac{.10(1 - .10)}{50}} \Rightarrow .10 \pm .127 \Rightarrow (-.027, .227)$$

Since the interval does not lie completely in the interval $(0, 1)$, the normal approximation will not be adequate.

c. When $n = 20$, $\hat{p} = .5$:

$$.5 \pm 3 \sqrt{\frac{.5(1 - .5)}{20}} \Rightarrow .5 \pm .335 \Rightarrow (.165, .835)$$

Since the interval lies completely in the interval $(0, 1)$, the normal approximation will be adequate.

d. When $n = 20$, $\hat{p} = .3$:

$$.3 \pm 3 \sqrt{\frac{.3(1 - .3)}{20}} \Rightarrow .3 \pm .307 \Rightarrow (-.007, .607)$$

Since the interval does not lie completely in the interval $(0, 1)$, the normal approximation will not be adequate.

7.37 a. The sample size is large enough if the interval $\hat{p} \pm 3\sigma_{\hat{p}}$ does not include 0 or 1.

$$\hat{p} \pm 3\sigma_{\hat{p}} \Rightarrow \hat{p} \pm 3 \sqrt{\frac{pq}{n}} \Rightarrow \hat{p} \pm 3 \sqrt{\frac{\hat{p}\hat{q}}{n}} \Rightarrow .46 \pm 3 \sqrt{\frac{.46(1 - .46)}{225}} \Rightarrow .46 \pm .0997$$
$$\Rightarrow (.3603, .5597)$$

Since the interval lies within the interval $(0, 1)$, the normal approximation will be adequate.

b. For confidence coefficient .95, $\alpha = .05$ and $\alpha/2 = .025$. From Table IV, Appendix B, $z_{.025} = 1.96$. The 95% confidence interval is:

$$\hat{p} \pm z_{.025} \sqrt{\frac{pq}{n}} \Rightarrow \hat{p} \pm 1.96 \sqrt{\frac{\hat{p}\hat{q}}{n}} \Rightarrow .46 \pm 1.96 \sqrt{\frac{.46(1 - .46)}{225}} \Rightarrow .46 \pm .065$$
$$\Rightarrow (.395, .525)$$

c. We are 95% confident the true value of p will fall between .395 and .525.

d. "95% confidence interval" means that if repeated samples of size 225 were selected from the population and 95% confidence intervals formed, 95% of all confidence intervals will contain the true value of p.

7.39 a. Of the 1000 observations, 29% said they would never give personal information to a company $\Rightarrow \hat{p} = .29$

To see if the sample size is sufficiently large:

$$\hat{p} \pm 3\sigma_{\hat{p}} \approx \hat{p} \pm 3 \sqrt{\frac{\hat{p}\hat{q}}{n}} \Rightarrow .29 \pm 3 \sqrt{\frac{.29(.71)}{1000}} \Rightarrow .29 \pm .043 \Rightarrow (.247, .333)$$

Since this interval is wholly contained in the interval $(0, 1)$, we may conclude that the normal approximation is reasonable.

Inferences Based on a Single Sample: Estimation with Confidence Intervals

b. For confidence coefficient .95, $\alpha = 1 - .95 = .05$ and $\alpha/2 = .05/2 = .025$. From Table IV, Appendix B, $z_{.025} = 1.96$. The 95% confidence interval is:

$$\hat{p} \pm z_{.025}\sqrt{\frac{\hat{p}\hat{q}}{n}} \Rightarrow .29 \pm 1.96\sqrt{\frac{.29(.71)}{1000}} \Rightarrow .29 \pm .028 \Rightarrow (.262, .318)$$

We are 95% confident that the proportion of Internet users who would never give personal information to a company is between .262 and .318.

c. We must assume that the sample is a random sample from the population.

7.41 a. The point estimate for the proportion of major oil spills that are caused by hull failure is:

$$\hat{p} = \frac{x}{n} = \frac{12}{50} = .24$$

b. To see if the sample size is sufficiently large:

$$\hat{p} \pm 3\sigma_{\hat{p}} \approx \hat{p} \pm 3\sqrt{\frac{\hat{p}\hat{q}}{n}} \Rightarrow .24 \pm 3\sqrt{\frac{.24(.76)}{50}} \Rightarrow .24 \pm .181 \Rightarrow (.059, .421)$$

Since this interval is wholly contained in the interval (0, 1), we may conclude that the normal approximation is reasonable.

For confidence coefficient .95, $\alpha = .05$ and $\alpha/2 = .05/2 = .025$. From Table IV, Appendix B, $z_{.025} = 1.96$. The confidence interval is:

$$\hat{p} \pm z_{.025}\sqrt{\frac{pq}{n}} \approx \hat{p} \pm 1.96\sqrt{\frac{\hat{p}\hat{q}}{n}} \Rightarrow .24 \pm 1.96\sqrt{\frac{.24(.76)}{50}} \Rightarrow .24 \pm .118$$
$$\Rightarrow (.122, .358)$$

We are 95% confident that the true percentage of major oil spills that are caused by hull failure is between .122 and .358.

7.43 a. Of the 72 observations, 50 admitted having employees whose performance was affected by drugs or alcohol $\Rightarrow \hat{p} = 50/72 = .694$.

To see if the sample size is sufficiently large:

$$\hat{p} \pm \sigma_{\hat{p}} \Rightarrow \hat{p} \pm 3\sqrt{\frac{pq}{n}} \Rightarrow \hat{p} \pm 3\sqrt{\frac{\hat{p}\hat{q}}{n}} \Rightarrow .694 \pm 3\sqrt{\frac{.694(.306)}{72}} \Rightarrow .694 \pm .163$$
$$\Rightarrow (.531, .857)$$

Since the interval lies within the interval (0, 1), the normal approximation will be adequate.

For confidence coefficient .95, $\alpha = .05$ and $\alpha/2 = .05/2 = .025$. From Table IV, Appendix B, $z_{.025} = 1.96$. The confidence interval is:

$$\hat{p} \pm z_{.05}\sqrt{\frac{pq}{n}} \Rightarrow \hat{p} \pm 1.96\sqrt{\frac{\hat{p}\hat{q}}{n}} \Rightarrow .694 \pm 1.96\sqrt{\frac{.694(.306)}{72}} \Rightarrow .694 \pm .106$$
$$\Rightarrow (.588, .800)$$

b. We must assume that the sample size is sufficiently large and that the sample was randomly selected.

c. We are 95% confident that the proportion of all New Jersey companies with substance abuse problems is between .588 and .800.

d. In repeated sampling, 95% of all intervals constructed will contain the true proportion.

e. One must look at the interval constructed with some skepticism. The problem states that questionnaires were sent to all New Jersey businesses that were members of the Governor's Council. However, the total number mailed out is not given. There were 72 respondents. If there were only 80 questionnaires mailed out, then a return rate of 72 would be quite high. On the other hand, if 500 questionnaires were mailed out a return rate of 72 would not be very good. Also, this sample was self selected, not random. It may not be representative of the entire population. Thus, the interval constructed in part **a** should be looked at with caution.

7.45 First, we must compute $\hat{p}$: $\hat{p} = \dfrac{x}{n} = \dfrac{282{,}200}{332{,}000} = .85$

To see if the sample size is sufficiently large:

$$\hat{p} \pm 3\sigma_{\hat{p}} \approx \hat{p} \pm 3\sqrt{\frac{\hat{p}\hat{q}}{n}} \Rightarrow .85 \pm 3\sqrt{\frac{.85(.15)}{332{,}000}} \Rightarrow .85 \pm .002 \Rightarrow (.848, .852)$$

Since this interval is wholly contained in the interval $(0, 1)$, we may conclude that the normal approximation is reasonable.

For confidence coefficient .99, $\alpha = .01$ and $\alpha/2 = .01/2 = .005$. From Table IV, Appendix B, $z_{.005} = 2.58$. The confidence interval is:

$$\hat{p} \pm z_{.005}\sqrt{\frac{pq}{n}} \approx \hat{p} \pm 2.58\sqrt{\frac{\hat{p}\hat{q}}{n}} \Rightarrow .85 \pm 2.58\sqrt{\frac{.85(.15)}{332{,}000}} \Rightarrow .85 \pm .002 \Rightarrow (.848, .852)$$

We are 99% confident that the true percentage of items delivered on time by the U.S. Postal Service is between 84.8% and 85.2%.

7.47 To compute the necessary sample size, use

$$n = \frac{(z_{\alpha/2})^2 \sigma^2}{B^2} \text{ where } \alpha = 1 - .95 = .05 \text{ and } \alpha/2 = .05/2 = .025.$$

From Table IV, Appendix B, $z_{.025} = 1.96$. Thus,

$$n = \frac{(1.96)^2(7.2)}{.3^2} = 307.328 \approx 308$$

You would need to take 308 samples.

7.49   a.   An estimate of σ is obtained from:

$$\text{range} \approx 4s$$

$$s \approx \frac{\text{range}}{4} = \frac{34 - 30}{4} = 1$$

To compute the necessary sample size, use

$$n = \frac{(z_{\alpha/2})^2 \sigma^2}{B^2} \quad \text{where } \alpha = 1 - .90 = .10 \text{ and } \alpha/2 = .05.$$

From Table IV, Appendix B, $z_{.05} = 1.645$. Thus,

$$n = \frac{(1.645)^2(1)^2}{.2^2} = 67.65 \approx 68$$

b.   A less conservative estimate of σ is obtained from:

$$\text{range} \approx 6s$$

$$s \approx \frac{\text{range}}{6} = \frac{34 - 30}{6} = .6667$$

Thus, $n = \dfrac{(z_{\alpha/2})^2 \sigma^2}{B^2} = \dfrac{(1.645)^2(.6667)^2}{.2^2} = 30.07 \approx 31$

7.51   For confidence coefficient .90, $\alpha = .10$ and $\alpha/2 = .05$. From Table IV, Appendix B, $z_{.05} = 1.645$.

We know $\hat{p}$ is in the middle of the interval, so $\hat{p} = \dfrac{.54 + .26}{2} = .4$

The confidence interval is $\hat{p} \pm z_{.05} \sqrt{\dfrac{\hat{p}\hat{q}}{n}} \Rightarrow .4 \pm 1.645 \sqrt{\dfrac{.4(.6)}{n}}$

We know $.4 - 1.645 \sqrt{\dfrac{.4(.6)}{n}} = .26$

$\Rightarrow .4 - \dfrac{.8059}{\sqrt{n}} = .26$

$\Rightarrow .4 - .26 = \dfrac{.8059}{\sqrt{n}} \Rightarrow \sqrt{n} = \dfrac{.8059}{.14} = 5.756$

$\Rightarrow n = 5.756^2 = 33.1 \approx 34$

7.53   a.   The width of a confidence interval is $2B = 2z_{\alpha/2} \dfrac{\sigma}{\sqrt{n}}$

For confidence coefficient .95, $\alpha = 1 - .95 = .05$ and $\alpha/2 = .05/2 = .025$. From Table IV, Appendix B, $z_{.025} = 1.96$.

For $n = 16$,

$$W = 2z_{\alpha/2} \frac{\sigma}{\sqrt{n}} = 2(1.96)\frac{1}{\sqrt{16}} = 0.98$$

For $n = 25$,

$$W = 2z_{\alpha/2}\frac{\sigma}{\sqrt{n}} = 2(1.96)\frac{1}{\sqrt{25}} = 0.784$$

For $n = 49$,

$$W = 2z_{\alpha/2}\frac{\sigma}{\sqrt{n}} = 2(1.96)\frac{1}{\sqrt{49}} = 0.56$$

For $n = 100$,

$$W = 2z_{\alpha/2}\frac{\sigma}{\sqrt{n}} = 2(1.96)\frac{1}{\sqrt{100}} = 0.392$$

For $n = 400$,

$$W = 2z_{\alpha/2}\frac{\sigma}{\sqrt{n}} = 2(1.96)\frac{1}{\sqrt{400}} = 0.196$$

b.

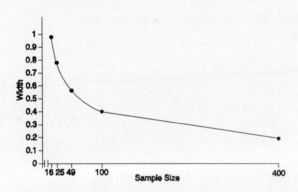

7.55   a.   Of the 13,000 observations, 2,938 indicated that they were definitely not willing to pay such fees, $\Rightarrow \hat{p} = 2,938/13,000 = .226$.

To see if the sample size is sufficiently large:

$$\hat{p} \pm 3\sigma_{\hat{p}} \Rightarrow \hat{p} \pm 3\sqrt{\frac{pq}{n}} \Rightarrow \hat{p} \pm 3\sqrt{\frac{\hat{p}\hat{q}}{n}} \Rightarrow .226 \pm 3\sqrt{\frac{.226(.774)}{13,000}} \Rightarrow .226 \pm .011$$
$$\Rightarrow (.215, .237)$$

Since the interval lies within the interval $(0, 1)$, the normal approximation will be adequate.

For confidence coefficient .95, $\alpha = .05$ and $\alpha/2 = .05/2 = .025$. From Table IV, Appendix B, $z_{.025} = 1.96$. The confidence interval is:

$$\hat{p} \pm z_{.05}\sqrt{\frac{pq}{n}} \Rightarrow \hat{p} \pm 1.96\sqrt{\frac{\hat{p}\hat{q}}{n}} \Rightarrow .226 \pm 1.96\sqrt{\frac{.226(.774)}{13,000}} \Rightarrow .226 \pm .007$$
$$\Rightarrow (.219, .233)$$

We are 95% confident that the proportion definitely unwilling to pay fees is between .219 and .233.

b.   The width of the interval is $.233 - .219 = .014$. Since the interval is unnecessarily small, this indicates that the sample size was extremely large.

c. The bound is $B = .02$. For confidence coefficient .95, $\alpha = .05$ and $\alpha/2 = .05/2 = .025$. From Table IV, Appendix B, $z_{.025} = 1.96$. Thus,

$$n = \frac{(z_{\alpha/2})^2 pq}{B^2} = \frac{1.96^2\,.226(.774)}{.02^2} = 1,679.97 \approx 1,680.$$

Thus, we would need a sample size of 1,680.

7.57 For confidence coefficient .90, $\alpha = .10$ and $\alpha/2 = .10/2 = .05$. From Table IV, Appendix B, $z_{.05} = 1.645$. Since we have no estimate given for the value of p, we will use .5. The sample size is:

$$n = \frac{z_{\alpha/2}^2 pq}{B^2} = \frac{1.645^2(.5)(.5)}{.02^2} = 1,691.3 \approx 1,692$$

7.59 To compute the needed sample size, use

$$n = \frac{(z_{\alpha/2})^2 \sigma^2}{B^2} \text{ where } \alpha = 1 - .95 = .05 \text{ and } \alpha/2 = .05/2 = .025.$$

From Table IV, Appendix B, $z_{.025} = 1.96$.

Thus, for $s = 10$, $n = \dfrac{(1.96)^2(10)^2}{3^2} = 42.68 \approx 43$

For $s = 20$, $n = \dfrac{(1.96)^2(20)^2}{3^2} = 170.74 \approx 171$

For $s = 30$, $n = \dfrac{(1.96)^2(30)^2}{3^2} = 384.16 \approx 385$

7.61 To compute the necessary sample size, use

$$n = \frac{(z_{\alpha/2})^2 \sigma^2}{B^2} \text{ where } \alpha = 1 - .90 = .10 \text{ and } \alpha/2 = .05.$$

From Table IV, Appendix B, $z_{.05} = 1.645$. Thus,

$$n = \frac{(1.645)^2(10)^2}{1^2} = 270.6 \approx 271$$

7.63 The bound is $B = .05$. For confidence coefficient .99, $\alpha = 1 - .99 = .01$ and $\alpha/2 = .01/2 = .005$. From Table IV, Appendix B, $z_{.005} = 2.575$.

We estimate p with $\hat{p} = 11/27 = .407$. Thus,

$$n = \frac{(z_{\alpha/2})^2 pq}{B^2} = \frac{2.575^2(.407)(.593)}{.05^2} \approx 640.1 \Rightarrow 641$$

The necessary sample size would be 641. The sample was not large enough.

7.65 $\sigma_{\bar{x}} = \dfrac{\sigma}{\sqrt{n}} \sqrt{\dfrac{N-n}{N}}$

    a. $\sigma_{\bar{x}} = \dfrac{200}{\sqrt{1000}} \sqrt{\dfrac{2500 - 1000}{2500}} = 4.90$

    b. $\sigma_{\bar{x}} = \dfrac{200}{\sqrt{1000}} \sqrt{\dfrac{5000 - 1000}{5000}} = 5.66$

    c. $\sigma_{\bar{x}} = \dfrac{200}{\sqrt{1000}} \sqrt{\dfrac{10,000 - 1000}{10,000}} = 6.00$

    d. $\sigma_{\bar{x}} = \dfrac{200}{\sqrt{1000}} \sqrt{\dfrac{100,000 - 1000}{100,000}} = 6.293$

7.67   a. $\hat{\sigma}_{\bar{x}} = \dfrac{s}{\sqrt{n}} \sqrt{\dfrac{N-n}{N}} = \dfrac{50}{\sqrt{2000}} \sqrt{\dfrac{10,000 - 2000}{10,000}} = 1.00$

    b. $\hat{\sigma}_{\bar{x}} = \dfrac{50}{\sqrt{4000}} \sqrt{\dfrac{10,000 - 4000}{10,000}} = .6124$

    c. $\hat{\sigma}_{\bar{x}} = \dfrac{50}{\sqrt{10,000}} \sqrt{\dfrac{10,000 - 10,000}{10,000}} = 0$

    d.   As n increases, $\sigma_{\bar{x}}$ decreases.

    e.   We are computing the standard error of $\bar{x}$. If the entire population is sampled, then $\bar{x} = \mu$. There is no sampling error, so $\sigma_{\bar{x}} = 0$.

7.69   The approximate 95% confidence interval for p is

$$\hat{p} \pm 2\hat{\sigma}_{\hat{p}} \Rightarrow \hat{p} \pm 2\sqrt{\dfrac{\hat{p}(1-\hat{p})}{n}} \sqrt{\dfrac{N-n}{N}}$$

$$\Rightarrow .42 \pm 2\sqrt{\dfrac{.42(.58)}{1600}} \sqrt{\dfrac{6000 - 1600}{6000}} \Rightarrow .42 \pm .021 \Rightarrow (.399, .441)$$

7.71   a.   The point estimate of the mean value of the parts inventory is $\bar{x} = 156.46$.

    b.   The estimated standard error is:

$$\hat{\sigma}_{\bar{x}} = \dfrac{s}{\sqrt{n}} \sqrt{\dfrac{N-n}{N}} = \dfrac{209.10}{\sqrt{100}} \sqrt{\dfrac{500 - 100}{500}} = 18.7025$$

c. The approximate 95% confidence interval is:

$$\bar{x} \pm 2\hat{\sigma}_{\bar{x}} \Rightarrow \bar{x} \pm 2\left[\frac{s}{\sqrt{n}}\right]\sqrt{\frac{N-n}{N}} \Rightarrow 156.46 \pm 2(18.7025) \Rightarrow 156.46 \pm 37.405$$

$$\Rightarrow (119.055, 193.865)$$

We are 95% confident that the mean value of the parts inventory is between $119.06 and $193.87.

d. Since the interval in part **c** does not include $300, the value of $300 is not a reasonable value for the mean value of the parts inventory.

7.73   For $N = 1,500$, $n = 35$, $\bar{x} = 1$, and $s = 124$, the 95% confidence interval is:

$$\bar{x} \pm 2\hat{\sigma}_{\bar{x}} \Rightarrow \bar{x} \pm 2\left[\frac{s}{\sqrt{n}}\right]\sqrt{\frac{N-n}{N}} \Rightarrow 1 \pm 2\left[\frac{124}{\sqrt{35}}\right]\sqrt{\frac{1,500-35}{1,500}}$$

$$\Rightarrow 1 \pm 41.43 \Rightarrow (-40.43, 42.43)$$

We are 95% confident that the mean error of the new system is between $-$40.43 and $42.43.

7.75   For $N = 251$, $n = 72$, $\hat{p} = .694$, the 95% confidence interval is:

$$\hat{p} \pm 2\hat{\sigma}_{\hat{p}} \Rightarrow \hat{p} \pm 2\sqrt{\frac{\hat{p}(1-\hat{p})}{n}}\sqrt{\frac{(N-n)}{N}}$$

$$\Rightarrow .694 \pm 2\sqrt{\frac{.694(.306)}{72}}\sqrt{\frac{(251-72)}{251}} \Rightarrow .694 \pm .092 \Rightarrow (.602, .786)$$

We are 95% confident that the proportion of all New Jersey's Council business members that have employees with substance abuse problems is between .602 and .786.

7.77   a. $P(t \leq t_0) = .05$ where df $= 20$
$$t_0 = -1.725$$

b. $P(t \geq t_0) = .005$ where df $= 9$
$$t_0 = 3.250$$

c. $P(t \leq -t_0 \text{ or } t \geq t_0) = .10$ where df $= 8$ is equivalent to
$$P(t \geq t_0) = .10/2 = .05 \text{ where df} = 8$$
$$t_0 = 1.860$$

d. $P(t \leq -t_0 \text{ or } t \geq t_0) = .01$ where df $= 17$ is equivalent to
$$P(t \geq t_0) = .01/2 = .005 \text{ where df} = 17$$
$$t_0 = 2.898$$

7.79   a. For confidence coefficient .99, $\alpha = .01$ and $\alpha/2 = .005$. From Table IV, Appendix B, $z_{.005} = 2.58$. The confidence interval is:

$$\bar{x} \pm z_{\alpha/2}\frac{s}{\sqrt{n}} \Rightarrow 32.5 \pm 2.58\frac{30}{\sqrt{225}} \Rightarrow 32.5 \pm 5.16 \Rightarrow (27.34, 37.66)$$

b. The sample size is $n = \dfrac{(z_{\alpha/2})^2\sigma^2}{B^2} = \dfrac{2.58^2(30)^2}{.5^2} = 23{,}963.04 \approx 23{,}964$

c. "99% confidence" means that if repeated samples of size 225 were selected from the population and 99% confidence intervals constructed for the population mean, then 99% of all the intervals constructed will contain the population mean.

7.81 a. The finite population correction factor is:

$$\sqrt{\dfrac{(N-n)}{N}} = \sqrt{\dfrac{(2{,}000 - 50)}{2{,}000}} = .9874$$

b. The finite population correction factor is:

$$\sqrt{\dfrac{(N-n)}{N}} = \sqrt{\dfrac{(100 - 20)}{100}} = .8944$$

c. The finite population correction factor is:

$$\sqrt{\dfrac{(N-n)}{N}} = \sqrt{\dfrac{(1{,}500 - 300)}{1{,}500}} = .8944$$

7.83 a. The 95% confidence interval is (298.6, 582.3).

b. We are 95% confident that the mean sales price is between \$298,600 and \$582,300.

c. "95% confidence" means that in repeated sampling, 95% of all confidence intervals constructed will contain the true mean salary and 5% will not.

d. Since the sample size is small ($n = 20$), we must assume that the distribution of sales prices is normal. From the stem-and-leaf display, it does not appear that the data come from a normal distribution. Thus, this confidence interval is probably not valid.

7.85 a. First we must compute $\hat{p}$: $\hat{p} = \dfrac{x}{n} = \dfrac{89{,}582}{102{,}263} = .876$

To see if the sample size is sufficiently large:

$$\hat{p} \pm 3\sigma_{\hat{p}} \approx \hat{p} \pm 3\sqrt{\dfrac{\hat{p}\hat{q}}{n}} \Rightarrow .876 \pm 3\sqrt{\dfrac{.876(.124)}{102{,}263}} \Rightarrow .876 \pm .003 \Rightarrow (.873, .879)$$

Since this interval is wholly contained in the interval (0, 1), we may conclude that the normal approximation is reasonable.

For confidence coefficient .99, $\alpha = .01$ and $\alpha/2 = .01/2 = .005$. From Table IV, Appendix B, $z_{.005} = 2.58$. The confidence interval is:

$$\hat{p} \pm z_{.005}\sqrt{\dfrac{pq}{n}} \approx \hat{p} \pm 2.58\sqrt{\dfrac{\hat{p}\hat{q}}{n}} \Rightarrow .876 \pm 2.58\sqrt{\dfrac{.876(.124)}{102{,}263}} \Rightarrow .876 \pm .003$$
$$\Rightarrow (.873, .879)$$

We are 99% confident that the true proportion of American adults who believe their health to be good to excellent is between .873 and .879.

7.87 a. For confidence coefficient .95, $\alpha = .05$ and $\alpha/2 = .025$. From Table IV, Appendix B, $z_{.025} = 1.96$. The confidence interval is:

$$\bar{x} \pm z_{\alpha/2}\frac{s}{\sqrt{n}}$$

Men: $7.4 \pm 1.96\dfrac{6.3}{\sqrt{159}} \Rightarrow 7.4 \pm .979 \Rightarrow (6.421, 8.379)$

We are 95% confident that the average distance to work for men in the central city is between 6.421 and 8.379 miles.

Women: $4.5 \pm 1.96\dfrac{4.2}{\sqrt{119}} \Rightarrow 4.5 \pm .755 \Rightarrow (3.745, 5.255)$

We are 95% confident that the average distance to work for women in the central city is between 3.745 and 5.255 miles.

b. Men: $9.3 \pm 1.96\dfrac{7.1}{\sqrt{138}} \Rightarrow 9.3 \pm 1.185 \Rightarrow (8.115, 10.485)$

We are 95% confident that the average distance to work for men in the suburbs is between 8.115 and 10.485 miles.

Women: $6.6 \pm 1.96\dfrac{5.6}{\sqrt{93}} \Rightarrow 6.6 \pm 1.138 \Rightarrow (5.462, 7.738)$

We are 95% confident that the average distance to work for women in the suburbs is between 5.462 and 7.738 miles.

7.89 a. For confidence coefficient .90, $\alpha = .10$ and $\alpha/2 = .05$. From Table IV, Appendix B, $z_{.05} = 1.645$. The 90% confidence interval is:

$$\bar{x} \pm z_{.05}\frac{\sigma}{\sqrt{n}} \Rightarrow \bar{x} \pm 1.645\frac{s}{\sqrt{n}} \Rightarrow 12.2 \pm 1.645\frac{10}{\sqrt{100}} \Rightarrow 12.2 \pm 1.645$$

$$\Rightarrow (10.555, 13.845)$$

b. For confidence coefficient .99, $\alpha = .01$ and $\alpha/2 = .005$. From Table IV, Appendix B, $z_{.005} = 2.58$.

The sample size is $n = \dfrac{(z_{\alpha/2})^2\sigma^2}{B^2} = \dfrac{(2.58)^2(10)^2}{2^2} = 166.4 \approx 167$

You would need to take $n = 167$ samples.

7.91 a. Of the 24 observations, 20 were 2 weeks of vacation $\Rightarrow \hat{p} = 20/24 = .833$.

To see if the sample size is sufficiently large:

$$\hat{p} \pm 3\sigma_{\hat{p}} \Rightarrow \hat{p} \pm 3\sqrt{\frac{pq}{n}} \Rightarrow \hat{p} \pm 3\sqrt{\frac{\hat{p}\hat{q}}{n}} \Rightarrow .833 \pm 3\sqrt{\frac{.833(.167)}{24}} \Rightarrow .833 \pm .228$$

$$\Rightarrow (.605, 1.061)$$

Since the interval does not lie within the interval $(0, 1)$, the normal approximation will not be adequate.

b.   The bound is $B = .02$. For confidence coefficient .95, $\alpha = .05$ and $\alpha/2 = .05/2 = .025$. From Table IV, Appendix B, $z_{.025} = 1.96$. Thus,

$$n = \frac{(z_{\alpha/2})^2 pq}{B^2} = \frac{1.96^2\ .833(.167)}{.02^2} = 1,336.02 \approx 1,337.$$

Thus, we would need a sample size of 1,337.

7.93 a.   First, we must estimate the standard deviation. The only information that we have is the values of the 20th, 50th, and 80th percentiles. Since the 20th percentile \$35,100 is closer to the median, \$50,000, than the 80th percentile, \$73,000, the data are skewed. From Chebyshev's Rule, we know that at least $1 - 1/k^2$ of the observations are within k standard deviations of the mean. Thus, we want to find k such that $1 - 1/k^2 = .8 - .2 = .6$.

$$1 - 1/k^2 = .6 \Rightarrow k^2 = 1/.4 = 2.5 \Rightarrow k \approx 1.6$$

Thus, there are $2(1.6) = 3.2$ standard deviations in the interval from the 20th percentile to the 80th percentile. The standard deviation can be estimated by:

$$s \approx \frac{80\text{th} - 20\text{th}}{3.2} = \frac{73,000 - 35,100}{3.2} = 11,843.75$$

For confidence coefficient .98, $\alpha = .02$ and $\alpha/2 = .02/2 = .01$. From Table IV, Appendix B, $z_{.01} = 2.33$. Thus,

$$n = \frac{(z_{\alpha/2})^2 \sigma^2}{B^2} = \frac{2.33^2 (11,843.75)^2}{2,000^2} = 190.4 \approx 191$$

Thus, we would need a sample size of 191.

b.   See part **a**.

c.   We must assume that the distribution of salaries next year has a similar shape to the distribution of salaries in the sixth annual salary survey.

7.95 a.   We would have to assume that the sample was a random sample. Since n is large, the Central Limit Theorem applies.

b. $\bar{x} = \dfrac{\sum x}{n} = \dfrac{586}{180} = 3.256$

$$s^2 = \frac{\sum x^2 - \dfrac{\left(\sum x\right)^2}{n}}{n - 1} = \frac{2,640 - \dfrac{586^2}{180}}{180 - 1} = 4.0908; \quad s = \sqrt{4.0908} = 2.0226$$

For confidence coefficient .98, $\alpha = .02$ and $\alpha/2 = .02/2 = .01$. From Table IV, Appendix B, $z_{.01} = 2.33$. The 98% confidence interval is:

$$\bar{x} \pm 2.33 \hat{\sigma}_{\bar{x}} \Rightarrow \bar{x} \pm 2.33 \left[\frac{s}{\sqrt{n}} \right] \sqrt{\frac{N - n}{N}} \Rightarrow 3.256 \pm 2.33 \left[\frac{2.0226}{\sqrt{180}} \right] \sqrt{\frac{8,521 - 180}{8,521}}$$

$$\Rightarrow 3.256 \pm .348 \Rightarrow (2.908, 3.604)$$

We are 98% confident that the mean subscription length is between 2.908 and 3.604 years.

c.   Since this is a mail-in survey, the sample is self-selected. Thus, it may not be representative of the population.

7.99   a.   For confidence coefficient .99, $\alpha = 1 - .99 = .01$ and $\alpha/2 = .01/2 = .005$. From Table VI, Appendix B, with df $= n - 1 = 9 - 1 = 8$. $t_{.005} = 3.355$. The 99% confidence interval is:

$$\bar{x} \pm t_{.005}\frac{s}{\sqrt{n}} \Rightarrow 985.6 \pm 3.355\frac{22.9}{\sqrt{9}} \Rightarrow 985.6 \pm 25.610 \Rightarrow (959.990, 1011.210)$$

        b.   Since 1000 is in the 99% confidence interval, it is not an unusual value for the mean. Thus, based on this confidence interval, the process should not be considered out of control.

        c.   (a)   For confidence coefficient .90, $\alpha = 1 - .90 = .10$ and $\alpha/2 = .10/2 = .05$. From Table VI, Appendix B, with df $= n - 1 = 9 - 1 = 8$, $t_{.05} = 1.860$. The 90% confidence interval is:

$$\bar{x} \pm t_{.05}\frac{s}{\sqrt{n}} \Rightarrow 985.6 \pm 1.860\frac{22.9}{\sqrt{9}} \Rightarrow 985.6 \pm 14.198 \Rightarrow (971.402, 999.798)$$

                (b)   Since 1000 is not in the 90% confidence interval, it is an unusual value for the mean. Thus, it appears the process is out of control based on the 90% confidence interval.

        d.   We would use the 99% confidence interval. We would have a smaller probability of concluding that the process is out of control when it is not.

        e.   We must assume that the samples are random and that the breaking strengths are normally distributed.

7.101   For confidence coefficient .95, $\alpha = .05$ and $\alpha/2 = .025$. From Table IV, Appendix B, $z_{.025} = 1.96$. From Exercise 7.100, a good approximation for p is .094. Also, $B = .02$.

The sample size is $n = \dfrac{(z_{\alpha/2})^2 pq}{B^2} = \dfrac{(1.96)^2(.094)(.906)}{.02^2} = 817.9 \approx 818$

You would need to take $n = 818$ samples.

Inferences Based on a Single Sample: Tests of Hypothesis

Chapter 8

8.1   The null hypothesis is the "status quo" hypothesis, while the alternative hypothesis is the research hypothesis.

8.3   The "level of significance" of a test is α. This is the probability that the test statistic will fall in the rejection region when the null hypothesis is true.

8.5   The four possible results are:

1.   Rejecting the null hypothesis when it is true. This would be a Type I error.
2.   Accepting the null hypothesis when it is true. This would be a correct decision.
3.   Rejecting the null hypothesis when it is false. This would be a correct decision.
4.   Accepting the null hypothesis when it is false. This would be a Type II error.

8.7   When you reject the null hypothesis in favor of the alternative hypothesis, this does not prove the alternative hypothesis is correct. We are $100(1 - \alpha)\%$ confident that there is sufficient evidence to conclude that the alternative hypothesis is correct.

If we were to repeatedly draw samples from the population and perform the test each time, approximately $100(1 - \alpha)\%$ of the tests performed would yield the correct decision.

8.9   Let p = student loan default rate in 2000. To see if the student loan default rate is less than .10, we test:

$$H_0: \ p = .10$$

$$H_a: \ p < .10$$

8.11   a.   A Type I error is rejecting the null hypothesis when it is true. In a murder trial, we would be concluding that the accused is guilty when, in fact, he/she is innocent.

A Type II error is accepting the null hypothesis when it is false. In this case, we would be concluding that the accused is innocent when, in fact, he/she is guilty.

b.   Both errors are bad. However, if an innocent person is found guilty of murder and is put to death, there is no way to correct the error. On the other hand, if a guilty person is set free, he/she could murder again.

c.   In a jury trial, α is assumed to be smaller than β. The only way to convict the accused is for a unanimous decision of guilt. Thus, the probability of convicting an innocent person is set to be small.

d.   In order to get a unanimous vote to convict, there has to be overwhelming evidence of guilt. The probability of getting a unanimous vote of guilt if the person is really innocent will be very small.

e. If a jury is predjuced against a guilty verdict, the value of α will decrease. The probability of convicting an innocent person will be even smaller if the jury if predjudiced against a guilty verdict.

f. If a jury is predjudiced against a guilty verdict, the value of β will increase. The probability of declaring a guilty person innocent will be larger if the jury is prejudiced against a guilty verdict.

8.13 a. Since the company must give proof the drug is safe, the null hypothesis would be the drug is unsafe. The alternative hypothesis would be the drug is safe.

b. A Type I error would be concluding the drug is safe when it is not safe. A Type II error would be concluding the drug is not safe when it is. α is the probability of concluding the drug is safe when it is not. β is the probability of concluding the drug is not safe when it is.

c. In this problem, it would be more important for α to be small. We would want the probability of concluding the drug is safe when it is not to be as small as possible.

8.15 a.

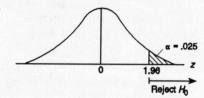

b.

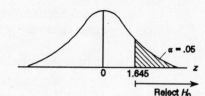

c.

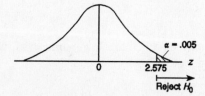

d.

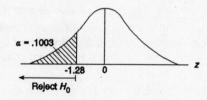

e.

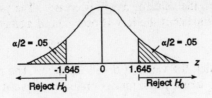

f.

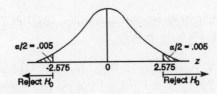

g. $P(z > 1.96) = .025$
    $P(z > 1.645) = .05$
    $P(z > 2.575) = .005$
    $P(z < -1.28) = .1003$
    $P(z < -1.645 \text{ or } z > 1.645) = .10$
    $P(z < -2.575 \text{ or } z > 2.575) = .01$

8.17 a. H_0: $\mu = 100$
          H_a: $\mu > 100$

The test statistic is $z = \dfrac{\bar{x} - \mu_0}{\sigma_{\bar{x}}} = \dfrac{\bar{x} - \mu_0}{\sigma/\sqrt{n}} = \dfrac{110 - 100}{60/\sqrt{100}} = 1.67$

The rejection region requires $\alpha = .05$ in the upper tail of the z-distribution. From Table IV, Appendix B, $z_{.05} = 1.645$. The rejection region is $z > 1.645$.

Since the observed value of the test statistic falls in the rejection region, ($z = 1.67 > 1.645$), H_0 is rejected. There is sufficient evidence to indicate the true population mean is greater than 100 at $\alpha = .05$.

b. H_0: $\mu = 100$
    H_a: $\mu \neq 100$

The test statistic is $z = \dfrac{\bar{x} - \mu_0}{\sigma_{\bar{x}}} = \dfrac{110 - 100}{60/\sqrt{100}} = 1.67$

The rejection region requires $\alpha/2 = .05/2 = .025$ in each tail of the z-distribution. From Table IV, Appendix B, $z_{.025} = 1.96$. The rejection region is $z < -1.96$ or $z > 1.96$.

Since the observed value of the test statistic does not fall in the rejection region, ($z = 1.67 \not> 1.96$), H_0 is not rejected. There is insufficient evidence to indicate μ does not equal 100 at $\alpha = .05$.

c. In part **a**, we rejected H_0 and concluded the mean was greater than 100. In part **b**, we did not reject H_0. There was insufficient evidence to conclude the mean was different from 100. Because the alternative hypothesis in part **a** is more specific than the one in **b**, it is easier to reject H_0.

8.19   To determine if the mean point-spread error is different from 0, we test:

$$H_0: \ \mu = 0$$
$$H_a: \ \mu \neq 0$$

The test statistic is $z = \dfrac{\bar{x} - \mu_0}{\sigma_{\bar{x}}} = \dfrac{-1.6 - 0}{13.3/\sqrt{240}} = -1.86$

The rejection region requires $\alpha/2 = .01/2 = .005$ in each tail of the z distribution. From Table IV, Appendix B, $z_{.005} = 2.575$. The rejection region is $z > 2.575$ or $z < -2.575$.

Since the observed value of the test statistic does not fall in the rejection region ($z = -1.86 \nless -2.575$), H_0 is not rejected. There is insufficient evidence to indicate that the true mean point-spread error is different from 0 at $\alpha = .01$.

8.21   a.   To determine whether the true mean PTSD score of all World War II aviator POWs is less than 16, we test:

$$H_0: \ \mu = 16$$
$$H_a: \ \mu < 16$$

b.   The test statistic is $z = \dfrac{\bar{x} - \mu_0}{\sigma_{\bar{x}}} = \dfrac{9 - 16}{9.32/\sqrt{33}} = -4.31$

The rejection region requires $\alpha = .10$ in the lower tail of the z-distribution. From Table IV, Appendix B, $z_{.10} = 1.28$. The rejection region is $z < -1.28$.

Since the observed value of the test statistic falls in the rejection region ($z = -4.31 < -1.28$), H_0 is rejected. There is sufficient evidence to indicate that the true mean PTSD score of all World War II aviator POWs is less than 16 at $\alpha = .10$.

The practical implications of the test are that the World War II aviator POWs have a lower level PTSD level on the average than the POWs from Vietnam.

c.   The sample used in this study was a self-selected sample—only 33 of the 239 located survivors responded. Very often, self-selected respondents are not representative of the population. Here, those former POWs who are more comfortable with their lives may be more willing to respond than those who are less comfortable. Those who are less comfortable may be suffering more from PTSD than those who are more comfortable. Also, it may not be fair to compare the survivors from World War II to the survivors of Vietnam. The World War II survivors are more removed from their imprisonment than those from the Vietnam war. Also, many of the World War II POWs probably are no longer living. Again, those still alive may be the ones who are more comfortable with their lives.

8.23   a.   To determine if the process is not operating satisfactorily, we test:

$$H_0: \ \mu = .250$$
$$H_a: \ \mu \neq .250$$

The test statistic is $z = \dfrac{\bar{x} - \mu_0}{\sigma_{\bar{x}}} = \dfrac{.252475 - .250}{.00223/\sqrt{40}} = 7.02$

The rejection region requires $\alpha/2 = .01/2 = .005$ in each tail of the z-distribution. From Table IV, Appendix B, $z_{.005} = 2.58$. The rejection region is $z < -2.58$ or $z > 2.58$.

Since the observed value of the test statistic falls in the rejection region ($z = 7.02 > 2.58$), H_0 is rejected. There is sufficient information to indicate the process is performing in an unsatisfactory manner at $\alpha = .01$.

    b. α is the probability of a Type I error. A Type I error, in this case, is to say the process is unsatisfactory when, in fact, it is satisfactory. The risk, then, is to the producer since he will be spending time and money to repair a process that is not in error.

β is the probability of a Type II error. A Type II error, in this case, is to say the process is satisfactory when it, in fact, is not. This is the consumer's risk since he could unknowingly purchase a defective product.

8.25   a.   To determine if the sample data refute the manufacturer's claim, we test:

$$H_0: \ \mu = 10$$
$$H_a: \ \mu < 10$$

    b.   A Type I error is concluding the mean number of solder joints inspected per second is less than 10 when, in fact, it is 10 or more.

A Type II error is concluding the mean number of solder joints inspected per second is at least 10 when, in fact, it is less than 10.

    c. $H_0: \ \mu = 10$
$H_a: \ \mu < 10$

The test statistic is $z = \dfrac{\bar{x} - \mu_0}{\sigma_{\bar{x}}} = \dfrac{9.29 - 10}{2.10/\sqrt{48}} = -2.34$

The rejection region requires $\alpha = .05$ in the lower tail of the z-distribution. From Table IV, Appendix B, $z_{.05} = 1.645$. The rejection region is $z < -1.645$.

Since the observed value of the test statistic falls in the rejection region ($z = -2.34 < -1.645$), H_0 is rejected. There is sufficient evidence to indicate the mean number of inspections per second is less than 10 at $\alpha = .05$.

8.27   a.   Since the standard deviation is almost the same as the mean, and we know that fat intake cannot be negative, the distribution of fat intake per day is skewed to the right.

    b.   To determine if the mean fat intake for middle-age men on weight-control programs exceeds 30 grams, we test:

$$H_0: \ \mu = 30$$
$$H_a: \ \mu > 30$$

The test statistic is $z = \dfrac{\bar{x} - \mu_0}{\sigma_{\bar{x}}} = \dfrac{37 - 30}{32/\sqrt{64}} = 1.75$

The rejection statistics requires $\alpha = .10$ in the upper tail of the z-distribution. From Table IV, Appendix B, $z_{.10} = 1.28$. The rejection region is $z > 1.28$

Since the observed value of the test statistic falls in the rejection region ($z = 1.75 > 1.28$), H_0 is rejected. There is sufficient evidence to indicate the mean fat intake for middle-age men on weight-control programs exceeds 30 grams at $\alpha = .10$.

c. For $\alpha = .05$, the rejection region requires $\alpha = .05$ in the upper tail of the z-distribution. From Table IV, Appendix B, $z_{.05} = 1.645$. The rejection region is $z > 1.645$. Since the observed value of the test statistic falls in the rejection region ($z = 1.75 > 1.645$), H_0 is rejected. The conclusion is the same.

For $\alpha = .01$, the rejection region requires $\alpha = .01$ in the upper tail of the z-distribution. From Table IV, Appendix B, $z_{.01} = 2.33$. The rejection region is $z > 2.33$. Since the observed value of the test statistic does not fall in the rejection region ($z = 1.75 \ngtr 2.33$), H_0 is not rejected. The conclusion is now different.

8.29 a. Since the p-value $= .10$ is greater than $\alpha = .05$, H_0 is not rejected.

b. Since the p-value $= .05$ is less than $\alpha = .10$, H_0 is rejected.

c. Since the p-value $= .001$ is less than $\alpha = .01$, H_0 is rejected.

d. Since the p-value $= .05$ is greater than $\alpha = .025$, H_0 is not rejected.

e. Since the p-value $= .45$ is greater than $\alpha = .10$, H_0 is not rejected.

8.31 p-value $= P(z \geq 2.17) = .5 - P(0 < z < 2.17) = .5 - .4850 = .0150$

(using Table IV, Appendix B)

8.33 $z = \dfrac{\bar{x} - \mu_0}{\sigma_{\bar{x}}} = \dfrac{49.4 - 50}{4.1/\sqrt{100}} = -1.46$

p-value $= P(z \geq -1.46) = .5 + .4279 = .9279$

There is no evidence to reject H_0 for $\alpha \leq .10$.

8.35 a. The p-value reported by SAS is for a two-tailed test. Thus, $P(z \leq -1.63) + P(z \geq 1.63)$ $= .1032$. For this one-tailed test, the p-value $= P(z \leq -1.63) = .1032/2 = .0516$.

Since the p-value $= .0516 > \alpha = .05$, H_0 is not rejected. There is insufficient evidence to indicate $\mu < 75$ at $\alpha = .05$.

b. For this one-tailed test, the p-value $= P(z \leq 1.63)$. Since $P(z \leq -1.63) = .1032/2$ $= .0516$, $P(z \leq 1.63) = 1 - .0516 = .9484$.

Since the p-value $= .9484 > \alpha = .10$, H_0 is not rejected. There is insufficient evidence to indicate $\mu < 75$ at $\alpha = .10$.

c. For this one-tailed test, the p-value $= P(z \geq 1.63) = .1032/2 = .0516$.

Since the p-value $= .0516 < \alpha = .10$, H_0 is rejected. There is sufficient evidence to indicate $\mu > 75$ at $\alpha = .10$.

d. For this two-tailed test, the p-value $= .1032$.

Since the p-value $= .1032 > \alpha = .01$, H_0 is not rejected. There is insufficient evidence to indicate $\mu \neq 75$ at $\alpha = .01$.

8.37   a. $z = \dfrac{\bar{x} - \mu_0}{\sigma_{\bar{x}}} = \dfrac{10.2 - 0}{31.3/\sqrt{50}} = 2.30$

       b.   For this two-sided test, the p-value = $P(z \geq 2.30) + P(z \leq -2.30) = (.5 - .4893) + (.5 - .4893) = .0214$. Since this value is so small, there is evidence to reject H_0. There is sufficient evidence to indicate the mean level of feminization is different from 0% for any value of $\alpha > .0214$.

       c. $z = \dfrac{\bar{x} - \mu_0}{\sigma_{\bar{x}}} = \dfrac{15.0 - 0}{25.1/\sqrt{50}} = 4.23$

            For this two-sided test, the p-value = $P(z \geq 4.23) + P(z \leq -4.23) \approx (.5 - .5) + (.5 - .5) = 0$. Since this value is so small, there is evidence to reject H_0. There is sufficient evidence to indicate the mean level of feminization is different from 0% for any value of $\alpha > 0.0$.

8.39   a.   To determine if children in this age group perceive a risk associated with failure to wear helmets, we test:

            H_0: $\mu = 2.5$
            H_a: $\mu > 2.5$

       b.   The test statistic is $z = \dfrac{\bar{x} - \mu_0}{\sigma_{\bar{x}}} = \dfrac{3.39 - 2.5}{.80/\sqrt{797}} = 31.41$

            p-value = $P(z \geq 31.41) \approx .5 - .5 = 0$

       c.   There is strong evidence to reject H_0 for any reasonable value of α. There is strong evidence to indicate the mean perceived risk associated with failure to wear helmets is greater than 2.5 for any reasonable value of α.

8.41   a.   To determine whether Chinese smokers smoke, on average, more cigarettes a day in 1997 than in 1995, we test:

            H_0: $\mu = 16.5$
            H_a: $\mu > 16.5$

       b.   The test statistic is $z = \dfrac{\bar{x} - \mu_0}{\sigma_{\bar{x}}} = \dfrac{17.05 - 16.5}{5.21/\sqrt{200}} = 1.49$

            The observed significance level is $p = P(z \geq 1.49) = .5 - .4319 = .0681$ (using Table IV, Appendix B).

            Since the observed significance level (.0681) is not less than $\alpha = .05$, H_0 is not rejected. There is insufficient evidence to indicate that Chinese smokers smoke, on average, more cigarettes a day in 1997 than in 1995 at $\alpha = .05$.

            If we used $\alpha = .10$, we would reject H_0. There is sufficient evidence to indicate that Chinese smokers smoke, on average, more cigarettes a day in 1997 than in 1995 at $\alpha = .10$.

       c.   The two-tailed test is inappropriate because we are interested in whether Chinese smokers, on average, smoke more cigarettes now than in 1995. This specifies only one-tail for the test.

8.43   We should use the t-distribution in testing a hypothesis about a population mean if the sample size is small, the population being sampled from is normal, and the variance of the population is unknown.

8.45   a. $P(t > 1.440) = .10$
            (Using Table VI, Appendix B, with df = 6)

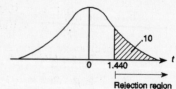

        b. $P(t < -1.782) = .05$
            (Using Table VI, Appendix B, with df = 12)

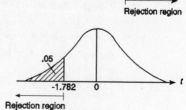

        c. $P(t < -2.060) = P(t > 2.060) = .025$
            (Using Table VI, Appendix B, with df = 25)

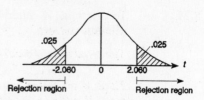

8.47   a.   The rejection region requires $\alpha/2 = .05/2 = .025$ in each tail of the t-distribution with df = $n - 1 = 14 - 1 = 13$. From Table VI, Appendix B, $t_{.025} = 2.160$. The rejection region is $t < -2.160$ or $t > 2.160$.

        b.   The rejection region requires $\alpha = .01$ in the upper tail of the t-distribution with df = $n - 1$ = $24 - 1 = 23$. From Table VI, Appendix B, $t_{.01} = 2.500$. The rejection region is $t > 2.500$.

        c.   The rejection region requires $\alpha = .10$ in the upper tail of the t-distribution with df = $n - 1$ = $9 - 1 = 8$. From Table VI, Appendix B, $t_{.10} = 1.397$. The rejection region is $t > 1.397$.

        d.   The rejection region requires $\alpha = .01$ in the lower tail of the t-distribution with df = $n - 1$ = $12 - 1 = 11$. From Table VI, Appendix B, $t_{.01} = 2.718$. The rejection region is $t < -2.718$.

        e.   The rejection region requires $\alpha/2 = .10/2 = .05$ in each tail of the t-distribution with df = $n - 1 = 20 - 1 = 19$. From Table VI, Appendix B, $t_{.05} = 1.729$. The rejection region is $t < -1.729$ or $t > 1.729$.

        f.   The rejection region requires $\alpha = .05$ in the lower tail of the t-distribution with df = $n - 1$ = $4 - 1 = 3$. From Table VI, Appendix B, $t_{.05} = 2.353$. The rejection region is $t < -2.353$.

8.49   a.   We must assume that a random sample was drawn from a normal population.

       b.   The hypotheses are:

$$H_0: \ \mu = 1000$$
$$H_a: \ \mu > 1000$$

The test statistic is $t = 1.894$.

The p-value is .0382.

There is evidence to reject H_0 for $\alpha > .0382$. There is evidence to indicate the mean is greater than 1000 for $\alpha > .0382$.

       c.   The hypotheses are:

$$H_0: \ \mu = 1000$$
$$H_a: \ \mu \neq 1000$$

The test statistic is $t = 1.894$.

The p-value is $2(.0382) = .0764$.

There is no evidence to reject H_0 for $\alpha = .05$. There is insufficient evidence to indicate the mean is different than 1000 for $\alpha = .05$.

There is evidence to reject H_0 for $\alpha > .0764$. There is evidence to indicate the mean is different than 1000 for $\alpha > .0764$.

8.51   a.   To determine if the mean repellency percentage of the new mosquito repellent is less than 95, we test:

$$H_0: \mu = 95$$
$$H_a: \mu < 95$$

The test statistic is $t = \dfrac{\bar{x} - \mu_0}{s/\sqrt{n}} = \dfrac{83 - 95}{15/\sqrt{5}} = -1.79$

The rejection region requires $\alpha = .10$ in the lower tail of the t distribution. From Table VI, Appendix B, with df $= n - 1 = 5 - 1 = 4$, $t_{.10} = 1.533$. The rejection region is $t < -1.533$.

Since the observed value of the test statistic falls in the rejection region ($t = -1.79 < -1.533$), H_0 is rejected. There is sufficient evidence to indicate that the true mean repellency percentage of the new mosquito repellent is less than 95 at $\alpha = .10$.

       b.   We must assume that the population of percent repellencies is normally distributed.

8.53   Some preliminary calculations:

$$\bar{x} = \frac{\sum x}{n} = \frac{489}{5} = 97.8 \qquad s^2 = \frac{\sum x^2 - \dfrac{(\sum x)^2}{n}}{n - 1} = \frac{47,867 - \dfrac{489^2}{5}}{5 - 1} = 10.7$$

$$s = \sqrt{10.7} = 3.271$$

Inferences Based on a Single Sample: Tests of Hypothesis

To determine if the mean recovery percentage of Aldrin exceeds 85% using the new MSPD method, we test:

H_0: $\mu = 85$
H_a: $\mu > 85$

The test statistic is $t = \dfrac{\bar{x} - \mu_0}{s/\sqrt{n}} = \dfrac{97.8 - 85}{3.271/\sqrt{5}} = 8.75$

The rejection region requires $\alpha = .05$ in the upper tail of the t-distribution with df $= n - 1$ $= 5 - 1 = 4$. From Table VI, Appendix B, $t_{.05} = 2.132$. The rejection region is $t > 2.132$.

Since the observed value of the test statistic falls in the rejection region ($t = 8.75 > 2.132$), H_0 is rejected. There is sufficient evidence to indicate that the true mean recovery percentage of Aldrin exceeds 85% using the new MSPD method at $\alpha = .05$.

8.55   a.   To determine if the plants meet the current OSHA standard, we test:

H_0: $\mu = .004$
H_a: $\mu > .004$

b.   First, compute the sample mean and standard deviation for plant 1's arsenic level:

$$\bar{x} = \frac{\sum x}{n} = \frac{.015}{2} = .0075$$

$$s^2 = \frac{\sum x^2 - \dfrac{(\sum x)^2}{n}}{n - 1} = \frac{.000125 - \dfrac{.015^2}{2}}{2 - 1} = .0000125$$

$$s = \sqrt{s^2} = .003536$$

The test statistic is $t = \dfrac{\bar{x} - \mu_0}{s/\sqrt{n}} = \dfrac{.0075 - .004}{.003536/\sqrt{2}} = 1.40$

The p-value $= P(t \geq 1.40)$. From Table VI, Appendix B, with df $= n - 1 = 2 - 1 = 1$, the p-value $> .10$.

Next, compute the sample mean and standard deviation for plant 2's arsenic level:

$$\bar{x} = \frac{\sum x}{n} = \frac{.14}{2} = .07$$

$$s^2 = \frac{\sum x^2 - \dfrac{(\sum x)^2}{n}}{n - 1} = \frac{.0106 - \dfrac{.14^2}{2}}{2 - 1} = .0008$$

$$s = \sqrt{s^2} = .0283$$

The test statistic is $t = \dfrac{\bar{x} - \mu_0}{s/\sqrt{n}} = \dfrac{.07 - .004}{.0283/\sqrt{2}} = 3.3$

The p-value $= P(t \geq 3.30)$. From Table VI, Appendix B, with df $= n - 1 = 2 - 1 = 1$, the $.05 < p$-value $< .10$.

c.   For plant 1, the test statistic is $t = 1.40$ and the p-value $= .200$. There is no evidence to reject H_0 for $\alpha \leq .10$. There is insufficient evidence to indicate the mean level is greater than .004 for $\alpha \leq .10$.

For plant 2, the test statistic is $t = 3.30$ and the p-value $= .094$. There is no evidence to reject H_0 for $\alpha = .05$. There is insufficient evidence to indicate the mean level is greater than .004 for $\alpha = .05$. There is evidence to reject H_0 for $\alpha = .10$. There is sufficient evidence to indicate the mean level is greater than .004 for $\alpha = .10$.

8.57   The sample size is large enough if the interval $p_0 \pm 3\sigma_{\hat{p}}$ is contained in the interval $(0, 1)$.

a. $p_0 \pm 3\sqrt{\dfrac{p_0 q_0}{n}} \Rightarrow .975 \pm 3\sqrt{\dfrac{(.975)(.025)}{900}} \Rightarrow .975 \pm .016 \Rightarrow (.959, .991)$

Since the interval is contained in the interval $(0, 1)$, the sample size is large enough.

b. $p_0 \pm 3\sqrt{\dfrac{p_0 q_0}{n}} \Rightarrow .01 \pm 3\sqrt{\dfrac{(.01)(.99)}{125}} \Rightarrow .01 \pm .027 \Rightarrow (-.017, .037)$

Since the interval is not contained in the interval $(0, 1)$, the sample size is not large enough.

c. $p_0 \pm 3\sqrt{\dfrac{p_0 q_0}{n}} \Rightarrow .75 \pm 3\sqrt{\dfrac{(.75)(.25)}{40}} \Rightarrow .75 \pm .205 \Rightarrow (.545, .955)$

Since the interval is contained in the interval $(0, 1)$, the sample size is large enough.

d. $p_0 \pm 3\sqrt{\dfrac{p_0 q_0}{n}} \Rightarrow .75 \pm 3\sqrt{\dfrac{(.75)(.25)}{15}} \Rightarrow .75 \pm .335 \Rightarrow (.415, 1.085)$

Since the interval is not contained in the interval $(0, 1)$, the sample size is not large enough.

e. $p_0 \pm 3\sqrt{\dfrac{p_0 q_0}{n}} \Rightarrow .62 \pm 3\sqrt{\dfrac{(.62)(.38)}{12}} \Rightarrow .62 \pm .420 \Rightarrow (.120, 1.040)$

Since the interval is not contained in the interval $(0, 1)$, the sample size is not large enough.

8.59   a. $z = \dfrac{\hat{p} - p_0}{\sqrt{\dfrac{p_0 q_0}{n}}} = \dfrac{.83 - .9}{\sqrt{\dfrac{.9(.1)}{100}}} = -2.33$

b.   The denominator in Exercise 8.54 is $\sqrt{\dfrac{.7(.3)}{100}} = .0458$ as compared to $\sqrt{\dfrac{.9(.1)}{100}} = .03$ in part **a**. Since the denominator in this problem is smaller, the absolute value of z is larger.

c.   The rejection region requires $\alpha = .05$ in the lower tail of the z-distribution. From Table IV, Appendix B, $z_{.05} = 1.645$. The rejection region is $z < -1.645$.

Inferences Based on a Single Sample: Tests of Hypothesis

Since the observed value of the test statistic falls in the rejection region ($z = -2.33 < -1.645$), H_0 is rejected. There is sufficient evidence to indicate the population proportion is less than .9 at $\alpha = .05$.

d. The p-value $= P(z \leq -2.33) = .5 - .4901 = .0099$ (from Table IV, Appendix B). Since the p-value is less than $\alpha = .05$, H_0 is rejected.

8.61 From Exercise 7.36, $n = 50$ and since p is the proportion of consumers who do not like the snack food, $\hat{p}$ will be:

$$\hat{p} = \frac{\text{Number of 0's in sample}}{n} = \frac{29}{50} = .58$$

First, check to see if the normal approximation will be adequate:

$$p_0 \pm 3\sigma_{\hat{p}} \Rightarrow p_0 \pm 3\sqrt{\frac{pq}{n}} \approx p_0 \pm 3\sqrt{\frac{p_0 q_0}{n}} \Rightarrow .5 \pm 3\sqrt{\frac{.5(1 - .5)}{50}} \Rightarrow .5 \pm .2121$$
$$\Rightarrow (.2879, .7121)$$

Since the interval lies completely in the interval $(0, 1)$, the normal approximation will be adequate.

a. H_0: $p = .5$
   H_a: $p > .5$

The test statistic is $z = \dfrac{\hat{p} - p_0}{\sigma_{\hat{p}}} = \dfrac{\hat{p} - p_0}{\sqrt{\dfrac{p_0 q_0}{n}}} = \dfrac{.58 - .5}{\sqrt{\dfrac{.5(1 - .5)}{50}}} = 1.13$

The rejection region requires $\alpha = .10$ in the upper tail of the z-distribution. From Table IV, Appendix B, $z_{.10} = 1.28$. The rejection region is $z > 1.28$.

Since the observed value of the test statistic does not fall in the rejection region ($z = 1.13 \not> 1.28$), H_0 is not rejected. There is insufficient evidence to indicate the proportion of customers who do not like the snack food is greater than .5 at $\alpha = .10$.

b. p-value $= P(z \geq 1.13) = .5 - .3708 = .1292$

8.63 a. Some preliminary calculations are:

$$\hat{p} = x/n = 23/33 = .697$$

First we check to see if the normal approximation is adequate:

$$p_0 \pm 3\sigma_{\hat{p}} \Rightarrow p_0 \pm 3\sqrt{\frac{p_0 q_0}{n}} \Rightarrow .6 \pm 3\sqrt{\frac{.6(.4)}{33}} \Rightarrow .6 \pm .256 \Rightarrow (.344, .856)$$

Since the interval falls completely in the interval $(0, 1)$, the normal distribution will be adequate.

To determine if the cream will improve the skin of more than 60% of women over age 40, we test:

H_0: $p = .60$
H_a: $p > .60$

The test statistic is $z = \dfrac{\hat{p} - p_0}{\sqrt{\dfrac{p_0 q_0}{n}}} = \dfrac{.697 - .60}{\sqrt{\dfrac{.60(.40)}{33}}} = 1.14$

The rejection region requires $\alpha = .05$ in the upper tail of the z distribution. From Table IV, Appendix B, $z_{.05} = 1.645$. The rejection region is $z > 1.645$.

Since the observed value of the test statistic does not fall in the region ($z = 1.14 \not> 1.645$), H_0 is not rejected. There is insufficient evidence to indicate that the cream will improve the skin of more than 60% of women over age 40 at $\alpha = .05$.

b.   The p-value is $p = P(z \geq 1.14) = .5 - P(0 < z < 1.14) = .5 - .3729 = .1271$. (using Table IV) The probability of observing our test statistic or anything more unusual, given H_0 is true, is .1271. Since this p-value is not very small, there is no evidence to indicate that H_0 is false.

8.65   Let p = proportion of patients taking the pill who reported an improved condition.

First we check to see if the normal approximation is adequate:

$$p_0 \pm 3\sigma_{\hat{p}} \Rightarrow p_0 \pm 3\sqrt{\frac{p_0 q_0}{n}} \Rightarrow .5 \pm 3\sqrt{\frac{.5(.5)}{7000}} \Rightarrow .5 \pm .018 \Rightarrow (.482, .518)$$

Since the interval falls completely in the interval $(0, 1)$, the normal distribution will be adequate.

To determine if there really is a placebo effect at the clinic, we test:

H_0: $p = .5$
H_a: $p > .5$

The test statistic is $z = \dfrac{\hat{p} - p_0}{\sqrt{\dfrac{p_0 q_0}{n}}} = \dfrac{.7 - .5}{\sqrt{\dfrac{.5(.5)}{7000}}} = 33.47$

The rejection region requires $\alpha = .05$ in the upper tail of the z distribution. From Table IV, Appendix B, $z_{.05} = 1.645$. The rejection region is $z > 1.645$.

Since the observed value of the test statistic falls in the rejection region ($z = 33.47 > 1.645$), H_0 is rejected. There is sufficient evidence to indicate that there really is a placebo effect at the clinic at $\alpha = .05$.

8.67   a. $\hat{p} = 15/60 = .25$

To determine if the proportion of shoppers who fail in their attempts to purchase merchandise online is less than .39, we test:

H_0: $p = .39$
H_a: $p < .39$

The test statistic is $z = \dfrac{\hat{p} - p_0}{\sqrt{\dfrac{p_0 q_0}{n}}} = \dfrac{.25 - .39}{\sqrt{\dfrac{.39(.61)}{60}}} = -2.22$

The rejection region requires $\alpha = .01$ in the lower tail of the z-distribution. From Table IV, Appendix B, $z_{.05} = 2.33$. The rejection region is $z < -2.33$.

Since the observed value of the test statistic does not fall in the rejection region ($z = -2.22 \not< -2.33$), H_0 is not rejected. There is insufficient evidence to indicate the proportion of shoppers who fail in their attempts to purchase merchandise online is less than .39 at $\alpha = .01$.

b.   The observed significance level of the test is p-value = $P(z \leq -2.22) = .5 - .4868 = .0132$. Since the p-value is greater than $\alpha = .01$, H_0 is not rejected.

8.69   First, check to see if the normal approximation is adequate:

$$p_0 \pm 3\sigma_{\hat{p}} \Rightarrow p_0 \pm 3\sqrt{\dfrac{p_0 q_0}{n}} \Rightarrow .5 \pm 3\sqrt{\dfrac{(.5)(.5)}{100}} \Rightarrow .5 \pm .15 \Rightarrow (.35, .65)$$

Since the interval falls completely in the interval $(0,1)$, the normal distribution will be adequate.

$$\hat{p} = \dfrac{x}{n} = \dfrac{56}{100} = .56$$

To determine if more than half of all Diet Coke drinkers prefer Diet Pepsi, we test:

H_0: $p = .5$
H_a: $p > .5$

The test statistic is $z = \dfrac{\hat{p} - p_0}{\sqrt{\dfrac{p_0 q_0}{n}}} = \dfrac{.56 - .5}{\sqrt{\dfrac{.5(.5)}{100}}} = 1.20$

The rejection region requires $\alpha = .05$ in the upper tail of the z-distribution. From Table IV, Appendix B, $z_{.05} = 1.645$. The rejection region is $z > 1.645$.

Since the observed value of the test statistic does not fall in the rejection region ($z = 1.20 \not> 1.645$), H_0 is not rejected. There is insufficient evidence to indicate that more than half of all Diet Coke drinkers prefer Diet Pepsi at $\alpha = .05$.

Since H_0 was not rejected, there is no evidence that Diet Coke drinkers prefer Diet Pepsi.

8.71 a. By the Central Limit Theorem, the sampling distribution of $\bar{x}$ is approximately normal with $\mu_{\bar{x}} = \mu = 500$ and

$$\sigma_{\bar{x}} = \frac{\sigma}{\sqrt{n}} = \frac{100}{\sqrt{25}} = 20.$$

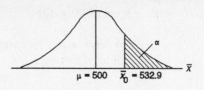

b. $\bar{x}_0 = \mu_0 + z_\alpha \sigma_{\bar{x}} = \mu_0 + z_\alpha \dfrac{\sigma}{\sqrt{n}}$ where $z_\alpha = z_{.05} = 1.645$ from Table IV, Appendix B.

Thus, $\bar{x}_0 = 500 + 1.645 \dfrac{100}{\sqrt{25}} = 532.9$

c. The sampling distribution of $\bar{x}$ is approximately normal by the Central Limit Theorem with $\mu_{\bar{x}} = \mu = 550$ and

$$\sigma_{\bar{x}} = \frac{\sigma}{\sqrt{n}} = \frac{100}{\sqrt{25}} = 20.$$

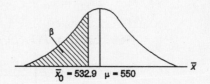

d. $\beta = P(\bar{x}_0 < 532.9 \text{ when } \mu = 550) = P\left(z < \dfrac{532.9 - 550}{100/\sqrt{25}} \right) = P(z < -.86)$

$$= .5 - .3051 = .1949$$

e. Power $= 1 - \beta = 1 - .1949 = .8051$

8.73 a. The sampling distribution of $\bar{x}$ will be approximately normal (by the Central Limit Theorem) with $\mu_{\bar{x}} = \mu = 75$ and $\sigma_{\bar{x}} = \dfrac{\sigma}{\sqrt{n}} = \dfrac{15}{\sqrt{49}} = 2.143$.

b. The sampling distribution of $\bar{x}$ will be approximately normal (by the Central Limit Theorem) with $\mu_{\bar{x}} = \mu = 70$ and $\sigma_{\bar{x}} = \dfrac{\sigma}{\sqrt{n}} = \dfrac{15}{\sqrt{49}} = 2.143$.

c. First, find $\bar{x}_0 = \mu_0 - z_\alpha \sigma_{\bar{x}} = \mu_0 - z_\alpha \dfrac{\sigma}{\sqrt{n}}$ where $z_{.10} = 1.28$ from Table IV, Appendix B.

Thus, $\bar{x}_0 = 75 - 1.28 \dfrac{15}{\sqrt{49}} = 72.257$

Now, find $\beta = P(\bar{x}_0 > 72.257 \text{ when } \mu = 70) = P\left(z > \dfrac{72.257 - 70}{15/\sqrt{49}} \right)$

$$= P(z > 1.05) = .5 - .3531 = .1469$$

d. Power $= 1 - \beta = 1 - .1469 = .8531$

8.75 a. The sampling distribution of $\bar{x}$ will be approximately normal (by the Central Limit Theorem) with $\mu_{\bar{x}} = \mu = 30$ and $\sigma_{\bar{x}} = \dfrac{\sigma}{\sqrt{n}} = \dfrac{1.2}{\sqrt{121}} = .109.$

b. The sampling distribution of $\bar{x}$ will be approximately normal (CLT) with $\mu_{\bar{x}} = \mu = 29.8$ and $\sigma_{\bar{x}} = \dfrac{\sigma}{\sqrt{n}} = \dfrac{1.2}{\sqrt{121}} = .109$.

c. First, find $\bar{x}_{\text{O,L}} = \mu_0 - z_{\alpha/2}\sigma_{\bar{x}} = \mu_0 - z_{\alpha/2}\dfrac{\sigma}{\sqrt{n}}$

where $z_{.05/2} = z_{.025} = 1.96$ from Table IV, Appendix B.

Thus, $\bar{x}_{\text{O,L}} = 30 - 1.96\dfrac{1.2}{\sqrt{121}} = 29.79$

$$\bar{x}_{\text{O,U}} = \mu_0 + z_{\alpha/2}\sigma_{\bar{x}} = \mu_0 + z_{\alpha/2}\dfrac{\sigma}{\sqrt{n}} = 30 + 1.96\dfrac{1.2}{\sqrt{121}} = 30.21$$

Now, find $\beta = P(29.79 < \bar{x} < 30.21$ when $\mu = 29.8)$

$$= P\left[\dfrac{29.79 - 29.8}{1.2/\sqrt{121}} < z < \dfrac{30.21 - 29.8}{1.2/\sqrt{121}}\right]$$
$$= P(-.09 < z < 3.76)$$
$$= .0359 + .5 = .5359$$

d. $\beta = P(29.79 < \bar{x} < 30.21$ when $\mu = 30.4) = P\left[\dfrac{29.79 - 30.4}{1.2/\sqrt{121}} < z < \dfrac{30.21 - 30.4}{1.2/\sqrt{121}}\right]$
$$= P(-5.59 < z < -1.74)$$
$$= .5 - .4591 = .0409$$

8.77 a. We have failed to reject H_0 when it is not true. This is a Type II error.

To compute β, first find:

$$\bar{x}_0 = \mu_0 - z_\alpha \sigma_{\bar{x}} = \mu_0 - z_\alpha \dfrac{\sigma}{\sqrt{n}} \text{ where } z_{.05} = 1.645 \text{ from Table IV, Appendix B.}$$

Thus, $\bar{x}_0 = 5.0 - 1.645\dfrac{.01}{\sqrt{100}} = 4.998355$

Then find:

$$\beta = P(\bar{x}_0 > 4.998355 \text{ when } \mu = 4.9975) = P\left[z > \dfrac{4.998355 - 4.9975}{.01/\sqrt{100}}\right]$$
$$= P(z > .86) = .5 - .3051 = .1949$$

b. We have rejected H_0 when it is true. This is a Type I error. The probability of a Type I error is $\alpha = .05$.

c. A departure of .0025 below 5.0 is $\mu = 4.9975$. Using **a**, β when $\mu = 4.9975$ is .1949. The power of the test is $1 - \beta = 1 - .1949 = .8051$

8.79   First, find $\bar{x}_0$ such that $P(\bar{x} < \bar{x}_0) = .05$.

$$P(\bar{x} < \bar{x}_0) = P\left(z < \frac{\bar{x}_0 - 10}{1.2/\sqrt{48}}\right) = P(z < z_0) = .05.$$

From Table IV, Appendix B, $z_0 = -1.645$.

Thus, $z_0 = \dfrac{\bar{x}_0 - 10}{1.2/\sqrt{48}} \Rightarrow \bar{x}_0 = -1.645(.173) + 10 = 9.715$

The probability of a Type II error is:

$$\beta = P(\bar{x} \geq 9.715 \mid \mu = 9.5) = P\left(z \geq \frac{9.715 - 9.5}{1.2/\sqrt{48}}\right) = P(z \geq 1.24) = .5 - .3925$$
$$= .1075$$

8.81   a.   df $= n - 1 = 16 - 1 = 15$; reject H_0 if $\chi^2 < 6.26214$ or $\chi^2 > 27.4884$

b.   df $= n - 1 = 23 - 1 = 22$; reject H_0 if $\chi^2 > 40.2894$

c.   df $= n - 1 = 15 - 1 = 14$; reject H_0 if $\chi^2 > 21.0642$

d.   df $= n - 1 = 13 - 1 = 12$; reject H_0 if $\chi^2 < 3.57056$

e.   df $= n - 1 = 7 - 1 = 6$; reject H_0 if $\chi^2 < 1.63539$ or $\chi^2 > 12.5916$

f.   df $= n - 1 = 25 - 1 = 24$; reject H_0 if $\chi^2 < 13.8484$

8.83   a. H_0: $\sigma^2 = 1$
H_a: $\sigma^2 > 1$

The test statistic is $\chi^2 = \dfrac{(n - 1)s^2}{\sigma_0^2} = \dfrac{(100 - 1)4.84}{1} = 479.16$

The rejection region requires $\alpha = .05$ in the upper tail of the χ^2 distribution with df $= n - 1$ $= 100 - 1 = 99$. From Table VII, Appendix B, $\chi_{.05}^2 \approx 124.324$. The rejection region is $\chi^2 > 124.324$.

Since the observed value of the test statistic falls in the rejection region ($\chi^2 = 479.16 > 124.324$), H_0 is rejected. There is sufficient evidence to indicate the variance is larger than 1 at $\alpha = .05$.

b.   In part **b** of Exercise 8.82, the test statistic was $\chi^2 = 29.04$. The conclusion was to reject H_0 as it was in this problem.

8.85   a.   To determine if the true standard deviation of the point-spread errors exceed 15 (variance exceeds 225), we test:

H_0: $\sigma^2 = 225$
H_a: $\sigma^2 > 225$

b. The test statistic is $\chi^2 = \dfrac{(n-1)s^2}{\sigma_0^2} = \dfrac{(240-1)13.3^2}{225} = 187.896$

c. The rejection region requires α in the upper tail of the χ^2 distribution with df $= n - 1$ $= 240 - 1 = 239$. The maximum value of df in Table VII is 100. Thus, we cannot find the rejection region using Table VII. Using a statistical package, the p-value associated with $\chi^2 = 187.896$ is .9938.

Since the p-value is so large, there is no evidence to reject H_0. There is insufficient evidence to indicate that the true standard deviation of the point-spread errors exceeds 15 for any reasonable value of α.

(Since the observed variance (or standard deviation) is less than the hypothesized value of the variance (or standard deviation) under H_0, there is no way H_0 will be rejected for any reasonable value of α.)

8.87 To determine if the diameters of the ball bearings are more variable when produced by the new process, test:

H_0: $\sigma^2 = .00156$
H_a: $\sigma^2 > .00156$

The test statistic is $\chi^2 = \dfrac{(n-1)s^2}{\sigma_0^2} = \dfrac{99(.00211)}{.00156} = 133.90$

The rejection region requires use of the upper tail of the χ^2 distribution with df $= n - 1$ $= 100 - 1 = 99$. We will use df $= 100 \approx 99$ due to the limitations of the table. From Table VII, Appendix B, $\chi^2_{.025} = 129.561 < 133.90 < 135.807 = \chi^2_{.010}$. The p-value of the test is between .010 and .025. The decision made depends on the desired α. For $\alpha < .010$, there is not enough evidence to show that the variance in the diameters is greater than .00156; the reverse decision would be made for $\alpha \geq .025$.

8.89 First, we need to estimate the value of the sample standard deviation. We know that the sample standard deviation can be estimated by dividing the range by 4 or 6. We will use the range divided by 4 as our estimate. Thus, $s \approx$ Range/4 $= (3.0 - .03)/4 = 2.97/4 = .7425$.

To determine if the SNR variance exceeds .54, we test:

H_0: $\sigma^2 = .54$
H_a: $\sigma^2 > .54$

The test statistic is $\chi^2 = \dfrac{(n-1)s^2}{\sigma_0^2} = \dfrac{(41-1).7425^2}{.54} = 40.8375$

The rejection region requires $\alpha = .10$ in the upper tail of the χ^2 distribution with df $= n - 1$ $= 41 - 1 = 40$. From Table VII, Appendix B, $\chi^2_{.10} = 51.8050$. The rejection region is $\chi^2 > 51.8050$.

Since the observed value of the test statistic does not fall in the rejection region $(\chi^2 = 40.8375 \not> 51.8050)$, H_0 is not rejected. There is insufficient evidence to indicate that the SNR variance exceeds .54 at $\alpha = .10$.

8.91   The smaller the p-value associated with a test of hypothesis, the stronger the support for the **alternative** hypothesis. The p-value is the probability of observing your test statistic or anything more unusual, given the null hypothesis is true. If this value is small, it would be very unusual to observe this test statistic if the null hypothesis were true. Thus, it would indicate the alternative hypothesis is true.

8.93   There is not a direct relationship between α and β. That is, if α is known, it does not mean β is known because β depends on the value of the parameter in the alternative hypothesis and the sample size. However, as α decreases, β increases for a fixed value of the parameter and a fixed sample size.

8.95   a. H_0: $\mu = 80$
       H_a: $\mu < 80$

The test statistic is $t = \dfrac{\bar{x} - \mu_0}{s/\sqrt{n}} = \dfrac{72.6 - 80}{\sqrt{19.4}/\sqrt{20}} = -7.51$

The rejection region requires $\alpha = .05$ in the lower tail of the t-distribution with df $= n - 1 = 20 - 1 = 19$. From Table VI, Appendix B, $t_{.05} = 1.729$. The rejection region is $t < -1.729$.

Since the observed value of the test statistic falls in the rejection region ($-7.51 < -1.729$), H_0 is rejected. There is sufficient evidence to indicate that the mean is less than 80 at $\alpha = .05$.

       b. H_0: $\mu = 80$
       H_a: $\mu \neq 80$

The test statistic is $t = \dfrac{\bar{x} - \mu_0}{s/\sqrt{n}} = \dfrac{72.6 - 80}{\sqrt{19.4}/\sqrt{20}} = -7.51$

The rejection region requires $\alpha/2 = .01/2 = .005$ in each tail of the t-distribution with df $= n - 1 = 20 - 1 = 19$. From Table VI, Appendix B, $t_{.005} = 2.861$. The rejection region is $t < -2.861$ or $t > 2.861$.

Since the observed value of the test statistic falls in the rejection region ($-7.51 < -2.861$), H_0 is rejected. There is sufficient evidence to indicate that the mean is different from 80 at $\alpha = .01$.

8.97   a. H_0: $\mu = 8.3$
       H_a: $\mu \neq 8.3$

The test statistic is $z = \dfrac{\bar{x} - \mu_0}{\sigma_{\bar{x}}} = \dfrac{8.2 - 8.3}{.79/\sqrt{175}} = -1.67$

The rejection region requires $\alpha/2 = .05/2 = .025$ in each tail of the z-distribution. From Table IV, Appendix B, $z_{.025} = 1.96$. The rejection region is $z < -1.96$ or $z > 1.96$.

Since the observed value of the test statistic does not fall in the rejection region ($-1.67 \nless -1.96$), H_0 is not rejected. There is insufficient evidence to indicate that the mean is different from 8.3 at $\alpha = .05$.

b. H_0: $\mu = 8.4$
H_a: $\mu \neq 8.4$

The test statistic is $z = \dfrac{\bar{x} - \mu_0}{\sigma_{\bar{x}}} = \dfrac{8.2 - 8.4}{.79/\sqrt{175}} = -3.35$

The rejection region is the same as part **b**, $z < -1.96$ or $z > 1.96$.

Since the observed value of the test statistic falls in the rejection region $(-3.35 < -1.96)$, H_0 is rejected. There is sufficient evidence to indicate that the mean is different from 8.4 at $\alpha = .05$.

8.99 a. H_0: $\sigma^2 = 30$
H_a: $\sigma^2 > 30$

The test statistic is $\chi^2 = \dfrac{(n-1)s^2}{\sigma_0^2} = \dfrac{(41-1)(6.9)^2}{30} = 63.48$

The rejection region requires $\alpha = .05$ in the upper tail of the χ^2 distribution with

df $= n - 1 = 40$. From Table VII, Appendix B, $\chi^2_{.05} = 55.7585$. The rejection region is $\chi^2 > 55.7585$.

Since the observed value of the test statistic falls in the rejection region $(\chi^2 = 63.48 > 55.7585)$, H_0 is rejected. There is sufficient evidence to indicate the variance is larger than 30 at $\alpha = .05$.

b. H_0: $\sigma^2 = 30$
H_a: $\sigma^2 \neq 30$

The test statistic is $\chi^2 = 63.48$ (from part **c**).

The rejection region requires $\alpha/2 = .05/2 = .025$ in each tail of the χ^2 distribution with

df $= n - 1 = 40$. From Table VII, Appendix B, $\chi^2_{.025} = 59.3417$ and $\chi^2_{.975} = 24.4331$. The rejection region is $\chi^2 < 24.4331$ or $\chi^2 > 59.3417$.

Since the observed value of the test statistic falls in the rejection region $(\chi^2 = 63.48 > 59.3417)$, H_0 is rejected. There is sufficient evidence to indicate the variance is not 30 at $\alpha = .05$.

8.101 a. To determine if the claim can be rejected, we test:

H_0: $\mu = .25$
H_a: $\mu < .25$

The test statistic is $z = \dfrac{\hat{p} - p_0}{\sqrt{\dfrac{p_0 q_0}{n}}} = \dfrac{.190 - .25}{\sqrt{\dfrac{.25(.75)}{195}}} = -1.93$

Since no α was given, we will use $\alpha = .05$. The rejection region requires $\alpha = .05$ in the lower tail of the z-distribution. From Table IV, Appendix B, $z_{.05} = 1.645$. The rejection region is $z < -1.645$.

Since the observed value of the test statistic falls in the rejection region ($z = -1.93 < -1.645$), H_0 is rejected. There is sufficient evidence to reject the claim that the "more than 25% of all U.S. businesses will have Web sites by the middle of 1995" at $\alpha = .05$.

b. This sample was self-selected and may not be representative of the population. The sample of readers who received the questionnaires was randomly selected. However, only 195 out of 1,500 returned the questionnaires. Usually those who return questionnaires have strong opinions one way or another, and thus, those responding to the questionnaire may not be representative.

8.103 a. First, check to see if the normal approximation is adequate:

$$p_0 \pm 3\sigma_{\hat{p}} \Rightarrow p_0 \pm 3\sqrt{\frac{p_0 q_0}{n}} \Rightarrow .25 \pm 3\sqrt{\frac{(.25)(.75)}{159}} \Rightarrow .25 \pm .103 \Rightarrow (.147, .353)$$

Since the interval falls completely in the interval $(0, 1)$, the normal distribution will be adequate.

$$\hat{p} = \frac{x}{n} = \frac{124}{159} = .786$$

To determine if the percentage of truckers who suffer from sleep apnea differs from 25%, we test:

H_0: $p = .25$
H_a: $p \neq .25$

The test statistic is $z = \dfrac{\hat{p} - p_0}{\sqrt{\dfrac{p_0 q_0}{n}}} = \dfrac{.786 - .25}{\sqrt{\dfrac{(.25)(.75)}{159}}} = 15.61$

The rejection region requires $\alpha/2 = .10/2 = .05$ in each tail of the z-distribution. From Table IV, Appendix B, $z_{.05} = 1.645$. The rejection region is $z < -1.645$ or $z > 1.645$.

Since the observed value of the test statistic falls in the rejection region ($z = 15.61 > 1.645$), H_0 is rejected. There is sufficient evidence to indicate that the percentage of truckers who suffer from sleep apnea differs from 25% at $\alpha = .05$.

b. The observed significance level is the p-value and is:

$$p\text{-value} = P(z \geq 15.61) + P(z \leq -15.61) \approx (.5 - .5) + (.5 - .5) = 0$$

Since the p-value is so small, we would reject H_0 for any reasonable value of α. There is sufficient evidence to indicate that the percentage of truckers who suffer from sleep apnea differs from 25%.

c. The inference from a confidence interval and a test of hypothesis must agree because the same numbers are used in both if the same level of significance is used.

8.105   a.   The test statistic is $t = \dfrac{\bar{x} - \mu_0}{s/\sqrt{n}} = \dfrac{1173.6 - 1100}{36.3/\sqrt{3}} = 3.512$

The p-value $= P(t \geq 3.512)$. From Table VI with df $= n - 1 = 3 - 1 = 2$, $.025 < p$-value $< .05$.

b.   The p-value $= .0362 = P(t \geq 3.512)$. Since this p-value is fairly small, there is evidence to reject H_0 for $\alpha > .0362$. There is evidence to indicate the mean length of life of a certain mechanical component is longer than 1100 hours.

c.   A Type I error would be of most concern for this test. A Type I error would be concluding the mean lifetime is greater than 1100 hours when in fact the mean lifetime is not greater than 1100.

d.   It is rather questionable whether a sample of 3 is representative of the population. If the sample is representative, then the conclusion is warranted.

8.107   a.   First, check to see if n is large enough:

$$p_0 \pm 3\sigma_{\hat{p}} \Rightarrow p_0 \pm 3\sqrt{\frac{p_0 q_0}{n}} \Rightarrow .5 \pm 3\sqrt{\frac{.5(.5)}{250}} \Rightarrow .5 \pm .095 \Rightarrow (.405, .595)$$

Since the interval lies within the interval $(0, 1)$, the normal approximation will be adequate.

To determine if there is evidence to reject the claim that no more than half of all manufacturers are dissatisfied with their trade promotion spending, we test:

H_0: $p = .5$
H_a: $p > .5$

The test statistic is $z = \dfrac{\hat{p} - p_0}{\sqrt{\dfrac{p_0 q_0}{n}}} = \dfrac{.91 - .5}{\sqrt{\dfrac{.5(.5)}{250}}} = 12.97$

The rejection region requires $\alpha = .02$ in the upper tail of the z-distribution. From Table IV, Appendix B, $z_{.02} = 2.05$. The rejection region is $z > 2.05$.

Since the observed value of the test statistic falls in the rejection region ($z = 12.97 > 2.05$), H_0 is rejected. There is sufficient evidence to reject the claim that no more than half of all manufacturers are dissatisfied with their trade promotion spending at $\alpha = .02$.

b.   The observed significance level is p-value $= P(z \geq 12.97) \approx .5 - .5 = 0$. Since this p-value is so small, H_0 will be rejected for any reasonable value of α.

c.   First, we must define the rejection region in terms of $\hat{p}$.

$$\hat{p} = p_0 + z_\alpha \, \sigma_{\hat{p}} = .5 + 2.05\sqrt{\frac{.5(.5)}{250}} = .565$$

$$\beta = P(\hat{p} < .565 \mid p = .55) = P\left(z < \frac{.565 - .55}{\sqrt{\frac{.55(.45)}{250}}}\right) = P(z < .48) = .5 + .1844 = .6844$$

8.109 a. To determine if the production process should be halted, we test:

H_0: $\mu = 3$
H_a: $\mu > 3$

where μ = mean amount of PCB in the effluent.

The test statistic is $z = \dfrac{\bar{x} - \mu_0}{\sigma_{\bar{x}}} = \dfrac{3.1 - 3}{.5/\sqrt{50}} = 1.41$

The rejection region requires $\alpha = .01$ in the upper tail of the z-distribution. From Table IV, Appendix B, $z_{.01} = 2.33$. The rejection region is $z > 2.33$.

Since the observed value of the test statistic does not fall in the rejection region, ($z = 1.41 \not> 2.33$), H_0 is not rejected. There is insufficient evidence to indicate the mean amount of PCB in the effluent is more than 3 parts per million at $\alpha = .01$. Do not halt the manufacturing process.

b. As plant manager, I do not want to shut down the plant unnecessarily. Therefore, I want $\alpha = P$(shut down plant when $\mu = 3$) to be small.

c. The p-value is $p = P(z \geq 1.41) = .5 - .4207 = .0793$. Since the p-value is not less than $\alpha = .01$, H_0 is not rejected.

8.111 a. No, it increases the risk of falsely rejecting H_0, i.e., closing the plant unnecessarily.

b. First, find $\bar{x}_0$ such that $P(\bar{x} > \bar{x}_0) = P(z > z_0) = .05$.

From Table IV, Appendix B, $z_0 = 1.645$

$$z = \frac{\bar{x}_0 - \mu}{\sigma/\sqrt{n}} \Rightarrow 1.645 = \frac{\bar{x}_0 - 3}{.5/\sqrt{50}} \Rightarrow \bar{x}_0 = 3.116$$

Then, compute:

$$\beta = P(\bar{x}_0 \leq 3.116 \text{ when } \mu = 3.1) = P\left(z \leq \frac{3.116 - 3.1}{.5/\sqrt{50}}\right) = P(z \leq .23) = .5 + .0910 = .5910$$

Power $= 1 - \beta = 1 - .5910 = .4090$

c. The power of the test increases as α increases.

8.113 a. Type II error is concluding the newsletter does not significantly increase the odds of winning when in fact it does.

b. First, calculate the value of $\hat{p}$ that corresponds to the border between the acceptance region and the rejection region.

$P(\hat{p} > p_0) = P(z > z_0) = .05$. From Table IV, Appendix B, $z_0 = 1.645$.

$$z = \frac{\hat{p} - p_0}{\sqrt{\dfrac{p_0 q_0}{n}}} \Rightarrow \hat{p}_0 = p_0 + 1.645\sigma_{\hat{p}} = .5 + 1.645\sqrt{\frac{.5(.5)}{50}} = .5 + .116 = .616$$

$$\beta = P(\hat{p} \le .616 \text{ when } p = .55)$$

$$= P\left[z < \frac{.616 - .55}{\sqrt{\frac{.55(.45)}{50}}}\right] = P(z \le .94) = .5 + .3264 = .8264$$

c. If n increases, the probability of a Type II error would decrease.

First, calculate the value of $\hat{p}$ that corresponds to the border between the acceptance region and the rejection region.

$$\hat{p} = p_0 + 1.645\sigma_{\hat{p}_0} = .5 + 1.645\sqrt{\frac{.5(.5)}{100}} = .5 + .082 = .582$$

$$\beta = P(\hat{p} \le .582 \text{ when } p = .55)$$

$$= P\left[z \le \frac{.582 - .55}{\sqrt{\frac{.55(.45)}{100}}}\right] = P(z \le .64) = .5 + .2389 = .7389$$

8.115   a.   The value of the test statistic is $t = 2.408$. The p-value is .0304, which corresponds to a two-tailed test.

$P(t \ge 2.408) + P(t \le -2.408) = .0304$. Since the p-value is less than $\alpha = .10$, H_0 is rejected. There is sufficient evidence to indicate the mean beta coefficient of high technology stock is different than 1.

b.   The p-value would be $.0304/2 = .0152$.

8.117   a.   To determine if the mean price of a new home in November 2000 exceeds $209,700, we test:

$$H_0: \ \mu = 209,700$$

$$H_a: \ \mu > 209,700$$

b.   The test statistic is $z = \dfrac{\bar{x} - \mu_0}{\sigma_{\bar{x}}} = \dfrac{216,981 - 209,700}{19,805/\sqrt{32}} = 2.08$

The p-value $= P(z \ge 2.08) = .5 - .4812 = .0188$.

Since the p-value is fairly small, there is evidence to reject H_0. There is sufficient evidence to indicate the mean price of a new home in November 2000 exceeds $209,700 for any value of $\alpha > .0188$.

9.1　a.　$\mu_1 \pm 2\sigma_{\bar{x}_1} \Rightarrow \mu_1 \pm 2\dfrac{\sigma_1}{\sqrt{n_1}} \Rightarrow 150 \pm 2\dfrac{\sqrt{900}}{\sqrt{100}} \Rightarrow 150 \pm 6 \Rightarrow (144, 156)$

　　　b.　$\mu_2 \pm 2\sigma_{\bar{x}_2} \Rightarrow \mu_2 \pm 2\dfrac{\sigma_2}{\sqrt{n_2}} \Rightarrow 150 \pm 2\dfrac{\sqrt{1600}}{\sqrt{100}} \Rightarrow 150 \pm 8 \Rightarrow (142, 158)$

　　　c.　$\mu_{\bar{x}_1 - \bar{x}_2} = \mu_1 - \mu_2 = 150 - 150 = 0$

$$\sigma_{\bar{x}_1 - \bar{x}_2} = \sqrt{\frac{\sigma_1^2}{n_1} + \frac{\sigma_2^2}{n_2}} = \sqrt{\frac{900}{100} + \frac{1600}{100}} = \sqrt{\frac{2500}{100}} = 5$$

　　　d.　$(\mu_1 - \mu_2) \pm 2\sqrt{\dfrac{\sigma_1^2}{n_1} + \dfrac{\sigma_2^2}{n_2}} \Rightarrow (150 - 150) \pm 2\sqrt{\dfrac{900}{100} + \dfrac{1600}{100}} \Rightarrow 0 \pm 10 \Rightarrow (-10, 10)$

　　　e.　The variability of the difference between the sample means is greater than the variability of the individual sample means.

9.3　a.　For confidence coefficient .95, $\alpha = .05$ and $\alpha/2 = .025$. From Table IV, Appendix B, $z_{.025} = 1.96$. The confidence interval is:

$$(\bar{x}_1 - \bar{x}_2) \pm z_{.025}\sqrt{\frac{\sigma_1^2}{n_1} + \frac{\sigma_2^2}{n_2}} \Rightarrow (5,275 - 5,240) \pm 1.96\sqrt{\frac{150^2}{400} + \frac{200^2}{400}}$$

$$\Rightarrow 35 \pm 24.5 \Rightarrow (10.5, 59.5)$$

We are 95% confident that the difference between the population means is between 10.5 and 59.5.

　　　b.　The test statistic is $z = \dfrac{(\bar{x}_1 - \bar{x}_2) - (\mu_1 - \mu_2)}{\sqrt{\dfrac{\sigma_1^2}{n_1} + \dfrac{\sigma_2^2}{n_2}}} = \dfrac{(5275 - 5240) - 0}{\sqrt{\dfrac{150^2}{400} + \dfrac{200^2}{400}}} = 2.8$

The p-value of the test is $P(z \le -2.8) + P(z \ge 2.8) = 2P(z \ge 2.8) = 2(.5 - .4974)$
$= 2(.0026) = .0052$

Since the p-value is so small, there is evidence to reject H_0. There is evidence to indicate the two population means are different for $\alpha > .0052$.

c. The p-value would be half of the p-value in part **b**. The p-value $= P(z \geq 2.8) = .5 - .4974$ $= .0026$. Since the p-value is so small, there is evidence to reject H_0. There is evidence to indicate the mean for population 1 is larger than the mean for population 2 for $\alpha > .0026$.

d. The test statistic is $z = \dfrac{(\bar{x}_1 - \bar{x}_2) - (\mu_1 - \mu_2)}{\sqrt{\dfrac{\sigma_1^2}{n_1} + \dfrac{\sigma_2^2}{n_2}}} = \dfrac{(5275 - 5240) - 25}{\sqrt{\dfrac{150^2}{400} + \dfrac{200^2}{400}}} = .8$

The p-value of the test is $P(z \leq -.8) + P(z \geq .8) = 2P(z \geq .8) = 2(.5 - .2881)$
$= 2(.2119) = .4238$

Since the p-value is so large, there is no evidence to reject H_0. There is no evidence to indicate that the difference in the 2 population means is different from 25 for $\alpha \leq .10$.

e. We must assume that we have two independent random samples.

9.5 a. No. Both populations must be normal.

b. No. Both populations variances must be equal.

c. No. Both populations must be normal.

d. Yes.

e. No. Both populations must be normal.

9.7 Some preliminary calculations are:

$$\bar{x}_1 = \frac{\sum x_1}{n_1} = \frac{11.8}{5} = 2.36 \qquad s_1^2 = \frac{\sum x_1^2 - \dfrac{\left(\sum x_1\right)^2}{n_1}}{n_1 - 1} = \frac{30.78 - \dfrac{(11.8)^2}{5}}{5 - 1} = .733$$

$$\bar{x}_2 = \frac{\sum x_2}{n_2} = \frac{14.4}{4} = 3.6 \qquad s_2^2 = \frac{\sum x_2^2 - \dfrac{\left(\sum x_2\right)^2}{n_2}}{n_2 - 1} = \frac{53.1 - \dfrac{(14.4)^2}{4}}{4 - 1} = .42$$

a. $s_p^2 = \dfrac{(n_1 - 1)s_1^2 + (n_2 - 1)s_2^2}{n_1 + n_2 - 2} = \dfrac{(5 - 1).773 + (4 - 1).42}{5 + 4 - 2} = \dfrac{4.192}{7} = .5989$

b. H_0: $\mu_1 - \mu_2 = 0$
H_a: $\mu_1 - \mu_2 < 0$

The test statistic is $t = \dfrac{(\bar{x}_1 - \bar{x}_2) - D_0}{\sqrt{s_p^2\left(\dfrac{1}{n_1} + \dfrac{1}{n_2}\right)}} = \dfrac{(2.36 - 3.6) - 0}{\sqrt{.5989\left(\dfrac{1}{5} + \dfrac{1}{4}\right)}} = \dfrac{-1.24}{.5191} = -2.39$

The rejection region requires $\alpha = .10$ in the lower tail of the t-distribution with df $= n_1 + n_2 - 2 = 5 + 4 - 2 = 7$. From Table VI, Appendix B, $t_{.10} = 1.415$. The rejection region is $t < -1.415$.

Since the test statistic falls in the rejection region ($t = -2.39 < -1.415$), H_0 is rejected. There is sufficient evidence to indicate that $\mu_2 > \mu_1$ at $\alpha = .10$.

c. A small sample confidence interval is needed because $n_1 = 5 < 30$ and $n_2 = 4 < 30$.

For confidence coefficient .90, $\alpha = .10$ and $\alpha/2 = .05$. From Table VI, Appendix B, with df $= n_1 + n_2 - 2 = 5 + 4 - 2 = 7$, $t_{.05} = 1.895$. The 90% confidence interval for $(\mu_1 - \mu_2)$ is:

$$\left(\bar{x}_1 - \bar{x}_2\right) \pm t_{.05}\sqrt{s_p^2\left[\frac{1}{n_1} + \frac{1}{n_2}\right]} \Rightarrow (2.36 - 3.6) \pm 1.895\sqrt{.5989\left[\frac{1}{5} + \frac{1}{4}\right]}$$
$$\Rightarrow -1.24 \pm .98 \Rightarrow (-2.22, -0.26)$$

d. The confidence interval in part c provides more information about $(\mu_1 - \mu_2)$ than the test of hypothesis in part b. The test in part b only tells us that μ_2 is greater than μ_1. However, the confidence interval estimates what the difference is between μ_1 and μ_2.

9.9 a. The test statistic is $z = -1.576$ and the p-value $= .1150$. Since the p-value is not small, there is no evidence to reject H_0 for $\alpha \le .10$. There is insufficient evidence to indicate the two population means differ for $\alpha \le .10$.

b. If the alternative hypothesis had been one-tailed, the p-value would be half of the value for the two-tailed test. Here, p-value $= .1150/2 = .0575$.

There is no evidence to reject H_0 for $\alpha = .05$. There is insufficient evidence to indicate the mean for population 1 is less than the mean for population 2 at $\alpha = .05$.

There is evidence to reject H_0 for $\alpha > .0575$. There is sufficient evidence to indicate the mean for population 1 is less than the mean for population 2 at $\alpha > .0575$.

9.11 a. $s_p^2 = \dfrac{(n_1 - 1)s_1^2 + (n_2 - 1)s_2^2}{n_1 + n_2 - 2} = \dfrac{(17 - 1)3.4^2 + (12 - 1)4.8^2}{17 + 12 - 2} = 16.237$

The test statistic is $t = \dfrac{\left(\bar{x}_1 - \bar{x}_2\right) - 0}{\sqrt{s_p^2\left[\dfrac{1}{n_1} + \dfrac{1}{n_2}\right]}} = \dfrac{(5.4 - 7.9) - 0}{\sqrt{16.237\left[\dfrac{1}{17} + \dfrac{1}{12}\right]}} = -1.646$

The p-value $= P(t \le -1.646) + P(t \ge 1.646) = 2P(t \ge 1.646)$.

Using Table VI with df $= n_1 + n_2 = 17 + 12 - 2 = 27$, $P(t \ge 1.646)$ is between .05 and .10. Thus, $2(.05) < p$-value $< 2(.10)$ or $.10 < p$-value $< .20$.

These values correspond to those found in the printout.

Since the p-value is not small, there is no evidence to reject H_0. There is no evidence to indicate the means are different for $\alpha \le .10$.

b. For confidence coefficient .95, $\alpha = .05$ and $\alpha/2 = .025$. From Table VI, Appendix B, with $df = n_1 + n_2 - 2 = 17 + 12 - 2 = 27$, $t_{.025} = 2.052$. The confidence interval is:

$$(\bar{x}_1 - \bar{x}_2) \pm t_{.025}\sqrt{s_p^2\left[\frac{1}{n_1} + \frac{1}{n_2}\right]} \quad \text{where } t \text{ has 27 df}$$

$$\Rightarrow (5.4 - 7.9) \pm 2.052\sqrt{16.237\left[\frac{1}{17} + \frac{1}{12}\right]} \Rightarrow -2.50 \pm 3.12 \Rightarrow (-5.62, 0.62)$$

9.13 a. Let $\mu_1 =$ mean ingratiatory score for managers and $\mu_2 =$ mean ingratiatory score for clerical personnel. To determine if there is a difference in ingratiatory behavior between managers and clerical personnel, we test:

H_0: $\mu_1 = \mu_2$

H_a: $\mu_1 \neq \mu_2$

b. The test statistic is $z = \dfrac{(\bar{x}_1 - \bar{x}_2) - D_o}{\sqrt{\dfrac{s_1^2}{n_1} + \dfrac{s_2^2}{n_2}}} = \dfrac{(2.41 - 1.90) - 0}{\sqrt{\dfrac{(.74)^2}{288} + \dfrac{(.59)^2}{110}}} = 7.17$

The rejection region requires $\alpha/2 = .05/2 = .025$ in each tail of the z-distribution. From Table IV, Appendix B, $z_{.025} = 1.96$. The rejection region is $z < -1.96$ or $z > 1.96$.

Since the observed value of the test statistic falls in the rejection region ($z = 7.17 > 1.96$), H_0 is rejected. There is sufficient evidence to indicate a difference in ingratiatory behavior between managers and clerical personnel at $\alpha = .05$.

c. For confidence coefficient .95, $\alpha = .05$ and $\alpha/2 = .05/2 = .025$. From Table IV, Appendix B, $z_{.025} = 1.96$. The 95% confidence interval is:

$$(\bar{x}_1 - \bar{x}_2) \pm z_{.025}\sqrt{\frac{s_1^2}{n_1} + \frac{s_2^2}{n_2}} \Rightarrow (2.41 - 1.90) \pm 1.96\sqrt{\frac{.74^2}{288} + \frac{.59^2}{110}}$$

$$\Rightarrow .51 \pm .14 \Rightarrow (.37, .65)$$

We are 95% confident that the difference in mean ingratiatory scores between managers and clerical personnel is between .37 and .65. Since this interval does not contain 0, it is consistent with the test of hypothesis which rejected the hypothesis that there was no difference in mean scores for the two groups.

9.15 a. Let $\mu_1 =$ mean age of nonpurchasers and $\mu_2 =$ mean age of purchasers.

To determine if there is a difference in the mean age of purchasers and nonpurchasers, we test:

H_0: $\mu_1 - \mu_2 = 0$
H_a: $\mu_1 - \mu_2 \neq 0$

The test statistic is $t = 1.9557$ (from printout).

The rejection region requires $\alpha/2 = .10/2 = .05$ in each tail of the t-distribution with df = $n_1 + n_2 - 2 = 20 + 20 - 2 = 38$. From Table VI, Appendix B, $t_{.05} \approx 1.684$. The rejection region is $t < -1.684$ or $t > 1.684$.

Since the observed value of the test statistic falls in the rejection region ($t = 1.9557 > 1.684$), H_0 is rejected. There is sufficient evidence to indicate the mean age of purchasers and nonpurchasers differ at $\alpha = .10$.

b. The necessary assumptions are:

1. Both sampled populations are approximately normal.
2. The population variances are equal.
3. The samples are randomly and independently sampled.

c. The observed significance level is $p = .0579$. Since the p-value is less than α ($.0579 < .10$), H_0 is rejected. This is the same result as in part **a**.

d. For confidence coefficient .90, $\alpha = 1 - .90 = .10$ and $\alpha/2 = .10/2 = .05$. From Table VI, Appendix B, with df = 38, $t_{.05} \approx 1.684$. The confidence interval is:

$$(\bar{x}_2 - \bar{x}_1) \pm t_{.05} \sqrt{s_p^2 \left[\frac{1}{n_2} + \frac{1}{n_1} \right]} \Rightarrow (39.8 - 47.2) \pm 1.684 \sqrt{143.1684 \left[\frac{1}{20} + \frac{1}{20} \right]}$$

$$\Rightarrow -7.4 \pm 6.382 \Rightarrow (-13.772, -1.028)$$

We are 90% confident that the difference in mean ages between purchasers and nonpurchasers is between -13.772 and -1.028.

9.17 a. Yes. The mean wastes for cities of industrialized countries are all greater than 2 while the mean wastes for cities of middle-income countries are all less than 1.0.

b. Let μ_1 = mean waste for cities in industrialized countries and μ_2 = mean waste for cities in middle-income countries. To determine if the mean waste generation rates of cities in industrialized and middle-income countries differ, we test:

$H_0: \mu_1 - \mu_2 = 0$
$H_a: \mu_1 - \mu_2 \neq 0$

The test statistic is $t = \dfrac{(\bar{x}_1 - \bar{x}_2) - D_0}{\sqrt{s_p^2 \left[\frac{1}{n_1} + \frac{1}{n_2} \right]}} = 19.73$ (from printout)

The rejection region is $t < -2.228$ or $t > 2.228$ (from printout).

Since the observed value of the test statistic falls in the rejection region ($t = 19.73 > 2.228$), H_0 is rejected. There is sufficient evidence to indicate that the mean waste generation rates of cities in industrialized and middle-income countries differ at $\alpha = .05$.

Inferences Based on Two Samples: Confidence Intervals and Tests of Hypotheses 161

9.19 a. Let μ_1 = mean change in bond prices handled by underwriter 1 and μ_2 = mean change in bond prices handled by underwriter 2.

$$s_p^2 = \frac{(n_1 - 1)s_1^2 + (n_2 - 1)s_2^2}{n_1 + n_2 - 2} = \frac{(27 - 1).0098 + (23 - 1).002465}{27 + 23 - 2} = \frac{.30903}{48}$$
$$= .006438$$

To determine if there is a difference in the mean change in bond prices handled by the 2 underwriters, we test:

H_0: $\mu_1 - \mu_2 = 0$
H_a: $\mu_1 - \mu_2 \neq 0$

The test statistic is $t = \dfrac{(\bar{x}_1 - \bar{x}_2) - D_0}{\sqrt{s_p^2 \left[\dfrac{1}{n_1} + \dfrac{1}{n_2} \right]}} = \dfrac{-.0491 - (-.0307) - 0}{\sqrt{.006438 \left[\dfrac{1}{27} + \dfrac{1}{23} \right]}} = -.81$

The rejection region requires $\alpha/2 = .05/2 = .025$ in each tail of the t-distribution with df = $n_1 + n_2 - 2 = 27 + 23 - 2 = 48$. From Table VI, Appendix B, $t_{.025} \approx 1.96$. The rejection region is $t < -1.96$ or $t > 1.96$.

Since the observed value of the test statistic does not fall in the rejection region ($t = -.81 \not< -1.96$), H_0 is not rejected. There is insufficient evidence to indicate there is a difference in the mean change in bond prices handled by the 2 underwriters at $\alpha = .05$.

b. For confidence coefficient .95, $\alpha = 1 - .95 = .05$ and $\alpha/2 = .05/2 = .025$. From Table VI, Appendix B, with df = 48, $t_{.025} \approx 1.96$. The confidence interval is:

$$(\bar{x}_1 - \bar{x}_2) \pm t_{.025} \sqrt{s_p^2 \left[\frac{1}{n_1} + \frac{1}{n_2} \right]}$$

$$\Rightarrow (-.0491 - (-.0307)) \pm 1.96 \sqrt{.006438 \left[\frac{1}{27} + \frac{1}{23} \right]}$$

$$\Rightarrow -.0184 \pm .0446 \Rightarrow (-.063, .0262)$$

We are 95% confident the difference in the mean bond prices handled by underwriter 1 and underwriter 2 is somewhere between $-.063$ and $.0262$.

9.21 a. Let μ_1 = mean number of cigarettes per week for the treatment group and μ_2 = mean number of cigarettes per week for the control group.

For confidence coefficient .95, $\alpha = .05$ and $\alpha/2 = .025$. From Table VI, Appendix B, with df = $n_1 + n_2 - 2 = 35 + 17 - 2 = 50$, $t_{.025} \approx 2.021$. The confidence interval is:

$$(\bar{x}_1 - \bar{x}_2) \pm t_{.025} \sqrt{s_p^2 \left[\frac{1}{n_1} + \frac{1}{n_2} \right]}$$

For Beginning time period:

$$s_p^2 = \frac{(n_1 - 1)s_1^2 + (n_2 - 1)s_2^2}{n_1 + n_2 - 2} = \frac{(35 - 1)71.20^2 + (17 - 1)67.45^2}{35 + 17 - 2} = 4903.06$$

$$\Rightarrow (165.09 - 159.00) \pm 2.021 \sqrt{4903.06\left[\frac{1}{35} + \frac{1}{17}\right]}$$

$$\Rightarrow 6.09 \pm 41.835 \Rightarrow (-35.745, 47.925)$$

We are 95% confident that the difference in the mean number of cigarettes smoked per week for the two groups is between -35.745 and 47.925.

For First follow-up period:

$$s_p^2 = \frac{(n_1 - 1)s_1^2 + (n_2 - 1)s_2^2}{n_1 + n_2 - 2} = \frac{(35 - 1)69.08^2 + (17 - 1)66.80^2}{35 + 17 - 2} = 4672.91$$

$$\Rightarrow (105.00 - 157.24) \pm 2.021 \sqrt{4672.91\left[\frac{1}{35} + \frac{1}{17}\right]}$$

$$\Rightarrow -52.24 \pm 40.842 \Rightarrow (-93.082, -11.398)$$

We are 95% confident that the difference in the mean number of cigarettes smoked per week for the two groups is between -93.082 and -11.398.

For Second follow-up period:

$$s_p^2 = \frac{(n_1 - 1)s_1^2 + (n_2 - 1)s_2^2}{n_1 + n_2 - 2} = \frac{(35 - 1)69.08^2 + (17 - 1)65.73^2}{35 + 17 - 2} = 4627.53$$

$$\Rightarrow (111.11 - 159.52) \pm 2.021 \sqrt{4627.53\left[\frac{1}{35} + \frac{1}{17}\right]}$$

$$\Rightarrow -48.41 \pm 40.643 \Rightarrow (-89.053, -7.767)$$

We are 95% confident that the difference in the mean number of cigarettes smoked per week for the two groups is between -89.053 and -7.767.

For Third follow-up period:

$$s_p^2 = \frac{(n_1 - 1)s_1^2 + (n_2 - 1)s_2^2}{n_1 + n_2 - 2} = \frac{(35 - 1)67.59^2 + (17 - 1)64.41^2}{35 + 17 - 2} = 4434.08$$

$$\Rightarrow (120.20 - 157.88) \pm 2.021 \sqrt{4434.08\left[\frac{1}{35} + \frac{1}{17}\right]}$$

$$\Rightarrow -37.68 \pm 39.784 \Rightarrow (-77.464, 2.104)$$

We are 95% confident that the difference in the mean number of cigarettes smoked per week for the two groups is between -77.464 and 2.104.

For Fourth follow-up period:

$$s_p^2 = \frac{(n_1 - 1)s_1^2 + (n_2 - 1)s_2^2}{n_1 + n_2 - 2} = \frac{(35 - 1)74.09^2 + (17 - 1)67.01^2}{35 + 17 - 2} = 5169.65$$

$$\Rightarrow (123.63 - 162.17) \pm 2.021 \sqrt{5169.65 \left(\frac{1}{35} + \frac{1}{17} \right)}$$

$$\Rightarrow -38.54 \pm 42.958 \Rightarrow (-81.498, 4.418)$$

We are 95% confident that the difference in the mean number of cigarettes smoked per week for the two groups is between -81.498 and 4.418.

b.   For each time period, we must make the following assumptions:

   1.   Both populations being sampled from are normal
   2.   The two population variances are equal.
   3.   Independent random samples are selected from each population.

9.23   a.   Let μ_1 = mean rate for cable companies with no competition and μ_2 = mean rate for cable companies with competition.

   To determine if the mean rate for cable companies with no competition is higher than that for companies with competition, we test:

   H_0: $\mu_1 - \mu_2 = 0$
   H_a: $\mu_1 - \mu_2 > 0$

b.   Some preliminary calculations are:

$$\bar{x}_1 = \frac{\sum x_1}{n_1} = \frac{144.83}{6} = 24.138$$

$$s_1^2 = \frac{\sum x_1^2 - \frac{\left(\sum x_1\right)^2}{n_1}}{n_1 - 1} = \frac{3552.3193 - \frac{144.83^2}{6}}{5} = 11.2729$$

$$\bar{x}_2 = \frac{\sum x_2}{n_2} = \frac{119.2}{6} = 19.867$$

$$s_2^2 = \frac{\sum x_2^2 - \frac{\left(\sum x_2\right)^2}{n_2}}{n_2 - 1} = \frac{2391.7322 - \frac{119.2^2}{6}}{5} = 4.7251$$

$$s_p^2 = \frac{(n_1 - 1)s_1^2 + (n_2 - 1)s_2^2}{n_1 + n_2 - 2} = \frac{5(11.2729) + 5(4.7251)}{6 + 6 - 2} = 7.999$$

The test statistic is $t = \dfrac{(\bar{x}_1 - \bar{x}_2) - D_0}{\sqrt{s_p^2 \left(\frac{1}{n_1} + \frac{1}{n_2} \right)}} = \dfrac{24.138 - 19.867 - 0}{\sqrt{7.999 \left(\frac{1}{6} + \frac{1}{6} \right)}} = 2.616$

The p-value $= P(t \geq 2.616)$. Using Table VI, Appendix B, with df $= n_1 + n_2 - 2 = 6 + 6 - 2 = 10$, $.01 < p$-value $< .025$. Since the p-value is less than $\alpha = .05$, there is evidence to reject H_0. There is sufficient evidence to indicate the mean rate for cable companies with no competition is higher than that for companies with competition for $\alpha = .05$.

c.   We must assume:

   1.   Both populations sampled from are normally distributed.
   2.   The variances for the two populations are equal.
   3.   Independent random samples were selected from each population.

9.25   a.   The rejection region requires $\alpha = .05$ in the upper tail of the t-distribution with df $= n_D - 1 = 12 - 1 = 11$. From Table VI, Appendix B, $t_{.05} = 1.796$. The rejection region is $t > 1.796$.

   b.   From Table VI, with df $= n_D - 1 = 24 - 1 = 23$, $t_{.10} = 1.319$. The rejection region is $t > 1.319$.

   c.   From Table VI, with df $= n_D - 1 = 4 - 1 = 3$, $t_{.025} = 3.182$. The rejection region is $t > 3.182$.

   d.   From Table VI, with df $= n_D - 1 = 8 - 1 = 7$, $t_{.01} = 2.998$. The rejection region is $t > 2.998$.

9.27   Let $\mu_1 =$ mean of population 1 and $\mu_2 =$ mean of population 2.

   a. H_0: $\mu_D = 0$
        H_a: $\mu_D < 0$ where $\mu_D = \mu_1 - \mu_2$

   b.   The test statistic is $t = -5.29$ and the p-value $= .0002$.

   Since the p-value is so small, there is evidence to reject H_0. There is evidence to indicate the mean for population 2 is larger than the mean for population 1 for $\alpha > .0002$.

   c.   The confidence interval is $(-5.284, -2.116)$. We are 95% confident the difference in the 2 population means is between -5.284 and -2.116.

   d.   We must assume that the population of differences is normal, and the sample of differences is randomly selected.

9.29   Some preliminary calculations:

Pair	Difference $x - y$
1	$55 - 44 = 11$
2	$68 - 55 = 13$
3	$40 - 25 = 15$
4	$55 - 56 = -1$
5	$75 - 62 = 13$
6	$52 - 38 = 14$
7	$49 - 31 = 18$

Inferences Based on Two Samples: Confidence Intervals and Tests of Hypotheses

$$\bar{x}_D = \frac{\sum x_D}{n_D} = \frac{83}{7} = 11.86$$

$$s_D^2 = \frac{\sum x_D^2 - \frac{\left(\sum x_D\right)^2}{n_D}}{n_D - 1} = \frac{1205 - \frac{83^2}{7}}{7 - 1} = 36.8095$$

$$s_D = \sqrt{s_D^2} = \sqrt{36.8095} = 6.0671$$

a. H_0: $\mu_D = 10$
       H_a: $\mu_D \neq 10$ where $\mu_D = (\mu_1 - \mu_2)$

The test statistic is $t = \dfrac{\bar{x}_D - D_0}{s_D/\sqrt{n_D}} = \dfrac{11.86 - 10}{6.0671/\sqrt{7}} = \dfrac{1.86}{2.2931} = .81$

The rejection region requires $\alpha/2 = .05/2 = .025$ in each tail of the t-distribution with df $= n_D - 1 = 7 - 1 = 6$. From Table VI, Appendix B, $t_{.025} = 2.447$. The rejection region is $t < -2.447$ or $t > 2.447$.

Since the observed value of the test statistic does not fall in the rejection region ($t = .81 \not> 2.447$), H_0 is not rejected. There is insufficient evidence to conclude $\mu_D \neq 10$ at $\alpha = .05$.

b. p-value $= P(t \leq -.81) + P(t \geq .81) = 2P(t \geq .81)$

Using Table VI, Appendix B, with df $= 6$, $P(t \geq .81)$ is greater than $.10$.

Thus, $2P(t \geq .81)$ is greater than $.20$.

The probability of observing a value of t as large as $.81$ or as small as $-.81$ if, in fact, $\mu_D = 10$ is greater than $.20$. We would conclude that there is insufficient evidence to suggest $\mu_D \neq 10$.

9.31   Some preliminary calculations are:

Operator	Difference (Before - After)
1	5
2	3
3	9
4	7
5	2
6	−2
7	−1
8	11
9	0
10	5

$$\bar{x}_D = \frac{\sum x_D}{n_D} = \frac{39}{10} = 3.9$$

$$s_{D^2} = \frac{\sum x_{D^2} - \frac{(\sum x_D)^2}{n_D}}{n_D - 1} = \frac{319 - \frac{39^2}{10}}{10 - 1} = 18.5444$$

$$s_D = \sqrt{18.5444} = 4.3063$$

a. To determine if the new napping policy reduced the mean number of customer complaints, we test:

H_0: $\mu_D = 0$
H_a: $\mu_D > 0$

The test statistic is $t = \dfrac{\bar{x}_D - 0}{\dfrac{s_D}{\sqrt{n_D}}} = \dfrac{3.9 - 0}{\dfrac{4.3063}{\sqrt{10}}} = 2.864$

The rejection region requires $\alpha = .05$ in the upper tail of the t-distribution with df $= n_D - 1$ $= 10 - 1 = 9$. From Table VI, Appendix B, $t_{.05} = 1.833$. The rejection region is $t > 1.833$.

Since the observed value of the test statistic falls in the rejection region ($t = 2.864 > 1.833$), H_0 is rejected. There is sufficient evidence to indicate the new napping policy reduced the mean number of customer complaints at $\alpha = .05$.

b. In order for the above test to be valid, we must assume that

1. The population of differences is normal
2. The differences are randomly selected

9.33 a. To determine if on average, the economists were more optimistic about the prospects for low inflation in late 1999 than they were for Spring 2000, we test:

H_0: $\mu_D = 0$
H_a: $\mu_D < 0$

b. Some preliminary calculations are:

Economist	Difference (1999 - 2000)
1	−.4
2	0
3	0
4	−.5
5	−.1
6	−.5
7	0
8	−.3
9	−.1

$$\bar{x}_D = \frac{\sum x_D}{n_D} = \frac{-1.9}{9} = -.211$$

$$s_{D^2} = \frac{\sum x_{D^2} - \frac{\left(\sum x_D\right)^2}{n_D}}{n_D - 1} = \frac{.77 - \frac{(-1.9)^2}{9}}{9 - 1} = .0461$$

$$s_D = \sqrt{.0461} = .2147$$

The test statistic is $t = \dfrac{\bar{x}_D - 0}{\dfrac{s_D}{\sqrt{n_D}}} = \dfrac{-.211 - 0}{\dfrac{.2147}{\sqrt{9}}} = -2.948$

The rejection region requires $\alpha = .05$ in the lower tail of the t-distribution with df $= n_D - 1$ $= 9 - 1 = 8$. From Table VI, Appendix B, $t_{.05} = 1.860$. The rejection region is $t < -1.860$.

Since the observed value of the test statistic falls in the rejection region ($t = -2.948 <$ -1.860), H_0 is rejected. There is sufficient evidence to indicate on average, the economists were more optimistic about the prospects for low inflation in late 1999 than they were for Spring 2000 at $\alpha = .05$.

9.35   a.   Let μ_D = mean difference in pupil dilation between pattern 1 and pattern 2.

To determine if the pupil dilation differs for the two patterns, we test:

H_0: $\mu_D = 0$
H_a: $\mu_D \neq 0$

b.   The test statistic is $t = 5.76$ and the p-value $= .000$. Since the p-value is so small, there is strong evidence to reject H_0. There is evidence to indicate that the pupil dilation differs for the two patterns for $\alpha > .0000$.

The p-value is not exactly 0. The p-value $= P(t \leq -5.76) + P(t \geq 5.76)$. Rounded off to 4 decimal places, the p-value is .0000.

The 95% confidence interval is (.150, .328). We are 95% confident that the mean difference in pupil dilation is between .150 and .328. Since both values are greater than zero, there is evidence to indicate the mean pupil dilation for pattern 1 is greater than the mean dilation for pattern 2.

c.   The paired difference design is better. There is much variation in pupil dilation from person to person. By using the paired difference design, we can eliminate the person to person differences.

9.37   Let μ_1 = mean number of swims by male rat pups and μ_2 = mean number of swims by female rat pups. Then $\mu_D = \mu_1 - \mu_2$. To determine if there is a difference in the mean number of swims required by male and female rat pups, we test:

$$H_0: \ \mu_D = 0$$
$$H_a: \ \mu_D \neq 0$$

The test statistic is $t = 0.46$ (from printout)

The p-value is $p = 0.65$.

Since the p-value is greater than α $(p = .65 > .10)$, H_0 is not rejected. There is insufficient evidence to indicate there is a difference in the mean number of swims required by male and female rat pups at $\alpha = .10$.

9.39   Remember that $\hat{p}_1$ and $\hat{p}_2$ can be viewed as means of the number of successes per n trials in the respective samples. Therefore, when n_1 and n_2 are large, $\hat{p}_1 - \hat{p}_2$ is approximately normal by the Central Limit Theorem.

9.41   a.   The rejection region requires $\alpha = .01$ in the lower tail of the z-distribution. From Table IV, Appendix B, $z_{.01} = 2.33$. The rejection region is $z < -2.33$.

       b.   The rejection region requires $\alpha = .025$ in the lower tail of the z-distribution. From Table IV, Appendix B, $z_{.025} = 1.96$. The rejection region is $z < -1.96$.

       c.   The rejection region requires $\alpha = .05$ in the lower tail of the z-distribution. From Table IV, Appendix B, $z_{.05} = 1.645$. The rejection region is $z < -1.645$.

       d.   The rejection region requires $\alpha = .10$ in the lower tail of the z-distribution. From Table IV, Appendix B, $z_{.10} = 1.28$. The rejection region is $z < -1.28$.

9.43   For confidence coefficient .95, $\alpha = 1 - .95 = .05$ and $\alpha/2 = .05/2 = .025$. From Table IV, Appendix B, $z_{.025} = 1.96$. The 95% confidence interval for $p_1 - p_2$ is approximately:

   a. $(\hat{p}_1 - \hat{p}_2) \pm z_{\alpha/2} \sqrt{\dfrac{\hat{p}_1 \hat{q}_1}{n_1} + \dfrac{\hat{p}_2 \hat{q}_2}{n_2}} \Rightarrow (.65 - .58) \pm 1.96 \sqrt{\dfrac{.65(1 - .65)}{400} + \dfrac{.58(1 - .58)}{400}}$

$$\Rightarrow .07 \pm .067 \Rightarrow (.003, .137)$$

   b. $(\hat{p}_1 - \hat{p}_2) \pm z_{\alpha/2} \sqrt{\dfrac{\hat{p}_1 \hat{q}_1}{n_1} + \dfrac{\hat{p}_2 \hat{q}_2}{n_2}} \Rightarrow (.31 - .25) \pm 1.96 \sqrt{\dfrac{.31(1 - .31)}{180} + \dfrac{.25(1 - .25)}{250}}$

$$\Rightarrow .06 \pm .086 \Rightarrow (-.026, .146)$$

   c. $(\hat{p}_1 - \hat{p}_2) \pm z_{\alpha/2} \sqrt{\dfrac{\hat{p}_1 \hat{q}_1}{n_1} + \dfrac{\hat{p}_2 \hat{q}_2}{n_2}} \Rightarrow (.46 - .61) \pm 1.96 \sqrt{\dfrac{.46(1 - .46)}{100} + \dfrac{.61(1 - .61)}{120}}$

$$\Rightarrow -.15 \pm .131 \Rightarrow (-.281, -.019)$$

9.45 $\hat{p} = \dfrac{n_1 \hat{p}_1 + n_2 \hat{p}_2}{n_1 + n_2} = \dfrac{55(.7) + 65(.6)}{55 + 65} = \dfrac{78}{120} = .65$ $\hat{q} = 1 - \hat{p} = 1 - .65 = .35$

$$H_0: \ p_1 - p_2 = 0$$
$$H_a: \ p_1 - p_2 > 0$$

Inferences Based on Two Samples: Confidence Intervals and Tests of Hypotheses   169

The test statistic is $z = \dfrac{(\hat{p}_1 - \hat{p}_2) - 0}{\sqrt{\hat{p}\hat{q}\left[\dfrac{1}{n_1} + \dfrac{1}{n_2}\right]}} = \dfrac{(.7 - .6) - 0}{\sqrt{.65(.35)\left[\dfrac{1}{55} + \dfrac{1}{65}\right]}} = \dfrac{.1}{.08739} = 1.14$

The rejection region requires $\alpha = .05$ in the upper tail of the z-distribution. From Table IV, Appendix B, $z_{.05} = 1.645$. The rejection region is $z > 1.645$.

Since the observed value of the test statistic does not fall in the rejection region ($z = 1.14 \not> 1.645$), H_0 is not rejected. There is insufficient evidence to indicate the proportion from population 1 is greater than that for population 2 at $\alpha = .05$.

9.47 a. Let p_1 = death rate of Operation Crossroads sailors and p_2 = death rate of a comparable group of sailors. The parameter of interest for this problem is $p_1 - p_2$, or the difference in the death rates for the two groups.

b. "The increase was not statistically significant" means that even though the sample death rate of Operation Crossroads sailors is 4.6% higher than the sample death rate of a comparable group of sailors, we could not reject the null hypothesis that there is no difference in the death rates of the two groups of soldiers. For the given samples sizes, the test statistic did not fall in the rejection region.

9.49 a. Let p_{1999} = proportion of adult Americans who would vote for a woman president in 1999 and p_{1975} = proportion of adult Americans who would vote for a woman president in 1975.

b. To see if the samples are sufficiently large:

$\hat{p}_{1999} \pm 3\sigma_{\hat{p}_{1999}} \Rightarrow \hat{p}_{1999} \pm 3\sqrt{\dfrac{p_{1999}q_{1999}}{n_{1999}}} \Rightarrow \hat{p}_{1999} \pm 3\sqrt{\dfrac{\hat{p}_{1999}\hat{q}_{1999}}{n_{1999}}} \Rightarrow .92 \pm 3\sqrt{\dfrac{.92(.08)}{2000}}$
$\Rightarrow .92 \pm .02 \Rightarrow (.90, .94)$

$\hat{p}_{1975} \pm 3\sigma_{\hat{p}_{1975}} \Rightarrow \hat{p}_{1975} \pm 3\sqrt{\dfrac{p_{1975}q_{1975}}{n_{1975}}} \Rightarrow \hat{p}_{1975} \pm 3\sqrt{\dfrac{\hat{p}_{1975}\hat{q}_{1975}}{n_{1975}}} \Rightarrow .73 \pm 3\sqrt{\dfrac{.73(.27)}{1500}}$
$\Rightarrow .73 \pm .03 \Rightarrow (.70, .76)$

Since both intervals are contained within the interval (0, 1), the normal approximation will be adequate.

c. For confidence coefficient .90, $\alpha = .10$ and $\alpha/2 = .10/2 = .05$. From Table IV, Appendix B, $z_{.05} = 1.645$. The 90% confidence interval is:

$(\hat{p}_1 - \hat{p}_2) \pm z_{.05}\sqrt{\dfrac{\hat{p}_1\hat{q}_1}{n_1} + \dfrac{\hat{p}_2\hat{q}_2}{n_2}} \Rightarrow (.92 - .73) \pm 1.645\sqrt{\dfrac{.92(.08)}{2000} + \dfrac{.73(.27)}{1500}}$
$\Rightarrow .19 \pm .02 \Rightarrow (.17, .21)$

We are 90% confident that the difference in the proportions of adult Americans who would vote for a woman president between 1999 and 1975 is between .17 and .21.

d. To see if the samples are sufficiently large:

$$\hat{p}_{1999} \pm 3\sigma_{\hat{p}_{1999}} \Rightarrow \hat{p}_{1999} \pm 3\sqrt{\frac{p_{1999}q_{1999}}{n_{1999}}} \Rightarrow \hat{p}_{1999} \pm 3\sqrt{\frac{\hat{p}_{1999}\hat{q}_{1999}}{n_{1999}}} \Rightarrow .92 \pm 3\sqrt{\frac{.92(.08)}{20}}$$

$$\Rightarrow .92 \pm .18 \Rightarrow (.74, 1.10)$$

$$\hat{p}_{1975} \pm 3\sigma_{\hat{p}_{1975}} \Rightarrow \hat{p}_{1975} \pm 3\sqrt{\frac{p_{1975}q_{1975}}{n_{1975}}} \Rightarrow \hat{p}_{1975} \pm 3\sqrt{\frac{\hat{p}_{1975}\hat{q}_{1975}}{n_{1975}}} \Rightarrow .73 \pm 3\sqrt{\frac{.73(.27)}{50}}$$

$$\Rightarrow .73 \pm .19 \Rightarrow (.54, .92)$$

Since the first interval is not contained within the interval $(0, 1)$, the normal approximation will not be adequate.

9.51 a. Let p_1 = error rate for supermarkets and p_2 = error rate for department stores. To see if the samples are sufficiently large:

$$\hat{p}_1 \pm 3\sigma_{\hat{p}_1} \Rightarrow \hat{p}_1 \pm 3\sqrt{\frac{p_1q_1}{n_1}} \Rightarrow \hat{p}_1 \pm 3\sqrt{\frac{\hat{p}_1\hat{q}_1}{n_1}} \Rightarrow .0347 \pm 3\sqrt{\frac{.0347(.9653)}{800}}$$

$$\Rightarrow .0347 \pm .0194 \Rightarrow (.0153, .0541)$$

$$\hat{p}_2 \pm 3\sigma_{\hat{p}_2} \Rightarrow \hat{p}_2 \pm 3\sqrt{\frac{p_2q_2}{n_2}} \Rightarrow \hat{p}_2 \pm 3\sqrt{\frac{\hat{p}_2\hat{q}_2}{n_2}} \Rightarrow .0915 \pm 3\sqrt{\frac{.0915(.9085)}{900}}$$

$$\Rightarrow .0915 \pm .0288 \Rightarrow (.0627, .1203)$$

Since both intervals lie within the interval $(0, 1)$, the normal approximation will be adequate.

b. For confidence coefficient .98, $\alpha = .02$ and $\alpha/2 = .02/2 = .01$. From Table IV, Appendix B, $z_{.01} = 2.33$. The 95% confidence interval is:

$$(\hat{p}_1 - \hat{p}_2) \pm z_{.01}\sqrt{\frac{\hat{p}_1\hat{q}_1}{n_1} + \frac{\hat{p}_2\hat{q}_2}{n_2}}$$

$$\Rightarrow (.0347 - .0915) \pm 2.33\sqrt{\frac{.0347(.9653)}{800} + \frac{.0915(.9085)}{900}} \Rightarrow -.0568 \pm .0270$$

$$\Rightarrow (-.0838, -.0298)$$

We are 98% confident that the difference in the error rates between supermarkets and department stores is between $-.0838$ and $-.0298$.

c. We must assume that the sample sizes are sufficiently large and that the two samples were independently and randomly selected.

9.53 To determine if there is a difference in the proportions of consumer/commercial and industrial product managers who are at least 40 years old, we could use either a test of hypothesis or a confidence interval. Since we are asked only to determine if there is a difference in the proportions, we will use a test of hypothesis.

Let p_1 = proportion of consumer/commercial product managers at least 40 years old and p_2 = proportion of industrial product managers at least 40 years old.

$$\hat{p}_1 = .40 \qquad \hat{q}_1 = 1 - \hat{p}_1 = 1 - .40 = .60$$

$$\hat{p}_2 = .54 \qquad \hat{q}_2 = 1 - \hat{p}_2 = 1 - .54 = .46$$

$$\hat{p} = \frac{n_1\hat{p}_1 + n_2\hat{p}_2}{n_1 + n_2} = \frac{93(.40) + 212(.54)}{93 + 212} = .497 \qquad \hat{q} = 1 - \hat{p} = 1 - .497 = .503$$

To see if the samples are sufficiently large:

$$\hat{p}_1 \pm 3\sigma_{\hat{p}_1} \Rightarrow \hat{p}_1 \pm 3\sqrt{\frac{p_1 q_1}{n_1}} \Rightarrow \hat{p}_1 \pm 3\sqrt{\frac{\hat{p}_1 \hat{q}_1}{n_1}} \Rightarrow .40 \pm 3\sqrt{\frac{.40(.60)}{93}}$$

$$\Rightarrow .40 \pm .152 \Rightarrow (.248, .552)$$

$$\hat{p}_2 \pm 3\sigma_{\hat{p}_2} \Rightarrow \hat{p}_2 \pm 3\sqrt{\frac{p_2 q_2}{n_2}} \Rightarrow \hat{p}_2 \pm 3\sqrt{\frac{\hat{p}_2 \hat{q}_2}{n_2}} \Rightarrow .54 \pm 3\sqrt{\frac{.54(.46)}{212}}$$

$$\Rightarrow .54 \pm .103 \Rightarrow (.437, .643)$$

Since both intervals lie within the interval (0, 1), the normal approximation will be adequate.

To determine if there is a difference in the proportions of consumer/commercial and industrial product managers who are at least 40 years old, we test:

$$H_0: \ p_1 - p_2 = 0$$
$$H_a: \ p_1 - p_2 \neq 0$$

The test statistic is $z = \dfrac{(\hat{p}_1 - \hat{p}_2) - 0}{\sqrt{\hat{p}\hat{q}\left[\dfrac{1}{n_1} + \dfrac{1}{n_2}\right]}} = \dfrac{(.40 - .54) - 0}{\sqrt{.497(.503)\left[\dfrac{1}{93} + \dfrac{1}{212}\right]}} = -2.25$

We will use $\alpha = .05$. The rejection region requires $\alpha/2 = .05/2 = .025$ in each tail of the z-distribution. From Table IV, Appendix B, $z_{.025} = 1.96$. The rejection region is $z < -1.96$ or $z > 1.96$.

Since the observed value of the test statistic falls in the rejection region ($z = -2.25 < -1.96$), H_0 is rejected. There is sufficient evidence to indicate that there is a difference in the proportions of consumer/commercial and industrial product managers who are at least 40 years old at $\alpha = .05$.

Since the test statistic is negative, there is evidence to indicate that the industrial product managers tend to be older than the consumer/commercial product managers.

9.55 $\quad n_1 = n_2 = \dfrac{(z_{\alpha/2})^2(\sigma_1^2 + \sigma_2^2)}{B^2}$

For confidence coefficient .95, $\alpha = 1 - .95 = .05$ and $\alpha/2 = .05/2 = .025$. From Table IV, Appendix B, $z_{.025} = 1.96$.

$$n_1 = n_2 = \frac{1.96^2(14 + 14)}{1.8^2} = 33.2 \approx 34$$

9.57 a. For confidence coefficient .99, $\alpha = 1 - .99 = .01$ and $\alpha/2 = .01/2 = .005$. From Table IV, Appendix B, $z_{.005} = 2.58$.

$$n_1 = n_2 = \frac{(z_{\alpha/2})^2(p_1q_1 + p_2q_2)}{B^2} = \frac{2.58^2(.4(1 - .4) + .7(1 - .7))}{.01^2} = \frac{2.99538}{.0001}$$
$$= 29,953.8 \approx 29,954$$

b. For confidence coefficient .90, $\alpha = 1 - .90 = .10$ and $\alpha/2 = .10/2 = .05$. From Table IV, Appendix B, $z_{.05} = 1.645$. Since we have no prior information about the proportions, we use $p_1 = p_2 = .5$ to get a conservative estimate. For a width of .05, the bound is .025.

$$n_1 = n_2 = \frac{(z_{\alpha/2})^2(p_1q_1 + p_2q_2)}{B^2} = \frac{(1.645)^2(.5(1 - .5) + .5(1 - .5))}{.025^2} = 2164.82 \approx 2165$$

c. From part **b**, $z_{.05} = 1.645$.

$$n_1 = n_2 = \frac{(z_{\alpha/2})^2(p_1q_1 + p_2q_2)}{B^2} = \frac{(1.645)^2(.2(1 - .2) + .3(1 - .3))}{.03^2} = \frac{1.00123}{.0009}$$
$$= 1112.48 \approx 1113$$

9.59 For confidence coefficient .95, $\alpha = .05$ and $\alpha/2 = .05/2 = .025$. From Table IV, Appendix B, $z_{.025} = 1.96$.

$$n_1 = n_2 = \frac{(z_{\alpha/2})^2(\sigma_1^2 + \sigma_2^2)}{B^2} = \frac{1.96^2(3.189^2 + 2.355^2)}{1.5^2} = 26.8 \approx 27$$

We would need to sample 27 specimens from each location.

9.61 For confidence coefficient .90, $\alpha = 1 - .90 = .10$ and $\alpha/2 = .10/2 = .05$. From Table IV, Appendix B, $z_{.05} = 1.645$. Since no information is given about the values of p_1 and p_2, we will be conservative and use .5 for both. A width of .04 means the bound is $.04/2 = .02$.

$$n_1 = n_2 = \frac{(z_{\alpha/2})^2(p_1q_1 + p_2q_2)}{B^2} = \frac{(1.645)^2(.5(.5) + .5(.5))}{.02^2} = 3,382.5 \approx 3,383$$

9.63 For confidence coefficient .90, $\alpha = 1 - .90 = .10$ and $\alpha = .10/2 = .05$. From Table IV, Appendix B, $z_{.05} = 1.645$. Since prior information is given about the values of p_1 and p_2, we will use these values as estimators. Thus, $p_1 = p_2 = .5$. A width of .10 means the bound is $.10/2 = .05$.

$$n_1 = n_2 = \frac{(z_{\alpha/2})^2(p_1q_1 + p_2q_2)}{B^2} = \frac{(1.645)^2(.5(.5) + .5(.5))}{.05^2} = 541.2 \approx 542$$

9.65 For confidence coefficient .95, $\alpha = 1 - .95 = .05$ and $\alpha/2 = .025$. From Table IV, Appendix B, $z_{.025} = 1.96$.

$$n_1 = n_2 = \frac{(z_{\alpha/2})^2(\sigma_1^2 + \sigma_2^2)}{B^2} = \frac{(1.96)^2(35^2 + 80^2)}{10^2} = 292.9 \approx 293$$

9.67   a.   With $v_1 = 2$ and $v_2 = 30$,
             $P(F \geq 5.39) = .01$ (Table XI, Appendix B)

       b.   With $v_1 = 24$ and $v_2 = 10$,
             $P(F \geq 2.74) = .05$ (Table IX, Appendix B)

             Thus, $P(F < 2.74) = 1 - P(F \geq 2.74) = 1 - .05 = .95$.

       c.   With $v_1 = 7$ and $v_2 = 1$,
             $P(F \geq 236.8) = .05$ (Table VIII, Appendix B)

             Thus, $P(F < 236.8) = 1 - P(F \geq 236.8) = 1 - .05 = .95$.

       d.   With $v_1 = 40$ and $v_2 = 40$,
             $P(F > 2.11) = .01$ (Table XI, Appendix B)

9.69   To test H_0: $\sigma_1^2 = \sigma_2^2$ against H_a: $\sigma_1^2 \neq \sigma_2^2$, the rejection region is $F > F_{\alpha/2}$ with $v_1 = 10$ and $v_2 = 12$.

       a. $\alpha = .20$, $\alpha/2 = .10$
             Reject H_0 if $F > F_{.10} = 2.19$ (Table VIII, Appendix B)

       b. $\alpha = .10$, $\alpha/2 = .05$
             Reject H_0 if $F > F_{.05} = 2.75$ (Table IX, Appendix B)

       c. $\alpha = .05$, $\alpha/2 = .025$
             Reject H_0 if $F > F_{.025} = 3.37$ (Table X, Appendix B)

       d. $\alpha = .02$, $\alpha/2 = .01$
             Reject H_0 if $F > F_{.01} = 4.30$ (Table XI, Appendix B)

9.71   a.   To determine if a difference exists between the population variances, we test:

             H_0: $\sigma_1^2 = \sigma_2^2$
             H_a: $\sigma_1^2 \neq \sigma_2^2$

             The test statistic is $F = \dfrac{s_2^2}{s_1^2} = \dfrac{8.75}{3.87} = 2.26$

             The rejection region requires $\alpha/2 = .10/2 = .05$ in the upper tail of the F-distribution with $v_1 = n_2 - 1 = 27 - 1 = 26$ and $v_2 = n_1 - 1 = 12 - 1 = 11$. From Table IX, Appendix B, $F_{.05} \approx 2.60$. The rejection region is $F > 2.60$.

             Since the observed value of the test statistic does not fall in the rejection region ($F = 2.26 \not> 2.60$), H_0 is not rejected. There is insufficient evidence to indicate a difference between the population variances.

       b.   The p-value is $2P(F \geq 2.26)$. From Tables VIII and IX, with $v_1 = 26$ and $v_2 = 11$,

             $$2(.05) < 2P(F \geq 2.26) < 2(.10) \Rightarrow .10 < 2P(F \geq 2.26) < .20$$

             There is no evidence to reject H_0 for $\alpha \leq .10$.

9.73 a. Using MINITAB, the descriptive statistics are:

Descriptive Statistics

Variable	N	Mean	Median	TrMean	StDev	SE Mean
Banking	8	20.77	16.95	20.77	15.70	5.55
Energy	9	26.1	3.2	26.1	83.4	27.8

Variable	Minimum	Maximum	Q1	Q3
Banking	-2.40	46.50	10.57	33.87
Energy	-56.6	231.7	-20.4	40.5

The standard deviation tells how different the growth rates of net incomes are within each industry. If the standard deviation is small, this indicates that the growth rates are similar within an industry. If the standard deviation is large, this indicates that the growth rates are very different within an industry.

b. To determine if the variability of net income growth rates differ for the two industries, we test:

$$H_0: \ \sigma_1^2 = \sigma_2^2$$
$$H_a: \ \sigma_1^2 \neq \sigma_2^2$$

c. The test statistic is $F = \dfrac{s_2^2}{s_1^2} = \dfrac{83.4^2}{15.7^2} = 28.22$

The rejection region requires $\alpha/2 = .05/2 = .025$ in the upper tail of the F-distribution with $v_1 = n_2 - 1 = 9 - 1 = 8$ and $v_2 = n_1 - 1 = 8 - 1 = 7$. From Table X, Appendix B, $F_{.025} = 4.90$. The rejection region is $F > 4.90$.

Since the observed value of the test statistic falls in the rejection region ($F = 28.22 > 4.90$), H_0 is rejected. There is sufficient evidence to indicate the variability of net income growth rates differ for the two industries at $\alpha = .05$.

d. We must assume that:

1. Both samples populations are normally distributed
2 The samples are random and independent

9.75 a. Let σ_1^2 = variance in inspection errors for novice inspectors and σ_2^2 = variance in inspection errors for experienced inspectors. Since we wish to determine if the data support the belief that the variance is lower for experienced inspectors than for novice inspectors, we test:

$$H_0: \ \sigma_1^2 = \sigma_2^2$$
$$H_a: \ \sigma_1^2 > \sigma_2^2$$

The test statistic is $F = \dfrac{\text{Larger sample variance}}{\text{Smaller sample variance}} = \dfrac{s_1^2}{s_2^2} = \dfrac{8.643^2}{5.744^2} = 2.26$

The rejection region requires $\alpha = .05$ in the upper tail of the F-distribution with $v_1 = n_1 - 1 = 12 - 1 = 11$ and $v_2 = n_2 - 1 = 12 - 1 = 11$. From Table IX, Appendix B, $F_{.05} \approx 2.82$ (using interpolation). The rejection region is $F > 2.82$.

Since the observed value of the test statistic does not fall in the rejection region ($F = 2.26 \not> 2.82$), H_0 is not rejected. The sample data do not support her belief at $\alpha = .05$.

b. The p-value $= P(F \geq 2.26)$ with $v_1 = 11$ and $v_2 = 11$. Checking Tables VIII, IX, X, and XI in Appendix B, we find $F_{.10} = 2.23$ and $F_{.05} = 2.82$. Since the observed value of F exceeds $F_{.10}$ but is less than $F_{.05}$, the observed significance level for the test is less than .10. So $.05 < p$-value $< .10$.

9.77 a. Let $\sigma_1^2 =$ variance of the order-to-delivery times for the Persian Gulf War and $\sigma_2^2 =$ variance of the order-to-delivery times for Bosnia.

To determine if the variances of the order-to-delivery times for the Persian Gulf and Bosnia shipments are equal, we test:

$$H_0: \quad \frac{\sigma_1^2}{\sigma_2^2} = 1$$

$$H_a: \quad \frac{\sigma_1^2}{\sigma_2^2} \neq 1$$

The test statistic is $F = 8.29$ (from printout).

The p-value is $p = 0.007$ (from printout). Since the p-value is less than α ($p = .007 < .05$), H_0 is rejected. There is sufficient evidence to indicate the variances of the order-to-delivery times for the Persian Gulf and Bosnia shipments differ at $\alpha = .05$.

b. No. One assumption necessary for the small sample confidence interval for $(\mu_1 - \mu_2)$ is that $\sigma_1^2 = \sigma_2^2$. For this problem, there is evidence to indicate that $\sigma_1^2 \neq \sigma_2^2$.

9.79 a. $s_p^2 = \dfrac{(n_1 - 1)s_1^2 + (n_1 - 1)s_2^2}{n_1 + n_2 - 2} = \dfrac{11(74.2) + 13(60.5)}{12 + 14 - 2} = 66.7792$

$H_0: \mu_1 - \mu_2 = 0$
$H_a: \mu_1 - \mu_2 > 0$

The test statistic is $t = \dfrac{(\bar{x}_1 - \bar{x}_2) - 0}{\sqrt{s_p^2 \left[\dfrac{1}{n_1} + \dfrac{1}{n_2} \right]}} = \dfrac{(17.8 - 15.3) - 0}{\sqrt{66.7792 \left[\dfrac{1}{12} + \dfrac{1}{14} \right]}} = .78$

The rejection region requires $\alpha = .05$ in the upper tail of the t-distribution with df $= n_1 + n_2 - 2 = 12 + 14 - 2 = 24$. From Table VI, Appendix B, for df $= 24$, $t_{.05} = 1.711$. The rejection region is $t > 1.711$.

Since the observed value of the test statistic does not fall in the rejection region ($0.78 \not> 1.711$), H_0 is not rejected. There is insufficient evidence to indicate that $\mu_1 > \mu_2$ at $\alpha = .05$.

b. For confidence coefficient .99, $\alpha = .01$ and $\alpha/2 = .01/2 = .005$. From Table VI, Appendix B, with df $= n_1 + n_2 - 2 = 12 + 14 - 2 = 24$, $t_{.005} = 2.797$. The confidence interval is:

$$(\bar{x}_1 - \bar{x}_2) \pm t_{.005}\sqrt{s_p^2\left[\frac{1}{n_1} + \frac{1}{n_2}\right]} \Rightarrow (17.8 - 15.3) \pm 2.797\sqrt{66.7792\left[\frac{1}{12} + \frac{1}{14}\right]}$$

$$\Rightarrow 2.50 \pm 8.99 \Rightarrow (-6.49, 11.49)$$

c. For confidence coefficient .99, $\alpha = .01$ and $\alpha/2 = .01/2 = .005$. From Table IV, Appendix B, $z_{.005} = 2.58$.

$$n_1 = n_2 = \frac{(z_{\alpha/2})^2(\sigma_1^2 + \sigma_2^2)}{B^2} = \frac{(2.58)^2(74.2 + 60.5)}{2^2} = 224.15 \approx 225$$

9.81 a. For confidence coefficient .90, $\alpha = .10$ and $\alpha/2 = .05$. From Table IV, Appendix B, $z_{.05} = 1.645$. The confidence interval is:

$$(\bar{x}_1 - \bar{x}_2) \pm z_{.05}\sqrt{\frac{s_1^2}{n_1} + \frac{s_2^2}{n_2}} \Rightarrow (12.2 - 8.3) \pm 1.645\sqrt{\frac{2.1}{135} + \frac{3.0}{148}}$$

$$\Rightarrow 3.90 \pm .31 \Rightarrow (3.59, 4.21)$$

b. H_0: $\mu_1 - \mu_2 = 0$
H_a: $\mu_1 - \mu_2 \neq 0$

The test statistic is $z = \dfrac{(\bar{x}_1 - \bar{x}_2 0) - 0}{\sqrt{\dfrac{s_1^2}{n_1} + \dfrac{s_2^2}{n_2}}} = \dfrac{(12.2 - 8.3) - 0}{\sqrt{\dfrac{2.1}{135} + \dfrac{3.0}{148}}} = 20.60$

The rejection region requires $\alpha/2 = .01/2 = .005$ in each tail of the z-distribution. From Table IV, Appendix B, $z_{.005} = 2.58$. The rejection region is $z < -2.58$ or $z > 2.58$.

Since the observed value of the test statistic falls in the rejection region ($20.60 > 2.58$), H_0 is rejected. There is sufficient evidence to indicate that $\mu_1 \neq \mu_2$ at $\alpha = .01$.

c. For confidence coefficient .90, $\alpha = .10$ and $\alpha/2 = .05$. From Table IV, Appendix B, $z_{.05} = 1.645$.

$$n_1 = n_2 = \frac{(z_{\alpha/2})^2(\sigma_1^2 + \sigma_2^2)}{B^2} = \frac{(1.645)^2(2.1 + 3.0)}{.2^2} = 345.02 \approx 346$$

9.83 a. This is a paired difference experiment.

Pair	Difference (Pop. 1 − Pop. 2)
1	6
2	4
3	4
4	3
5	2

$$\bar{x}_D = \frac{\sum x_D}{n_D} = \frac{19}{5} = 3.8 \qquad s_D^2 = \frac{\sum x_D^2 - \frac{\left(\sum x_D\right)^2}{n_D}}{n_D - 1} = \frac{81 - \frac{19^2}{5}}{5 - 1} = 2.2$$

$$s_D = \sqrt{2.2} = 1.4832$$

$H_0: \mu_D = 0$
$H_a: \mu_D \neq 0$

The test statistic is $t = \dfrac{\bar{x}_D - 0}{s_D/\sqrt{n_D}} = \dfrac{3.8 - 0}{1.4832/\sqrt{5}} = 5.73$

The rejection region requires $\alpha/2 = .05/2 = .025$ in each tail of the t-distribution with df $= n - 1 = 5 - 1 = 4$. From Table VI, Appendix B, $t_{.025} = 2.776$. The rejection region is $t < -2.776$ or $t > 2.776$.

Since the observed value of the test statistic falls in the rejection region ($5.73 > 2.776$), H_0 is rejected. There is sufficient evidence to indicate that the population means are different at $\alpha = .05$.

b. For confidence coefficient .95, $\alpha = .05$ and $\alpha/2 = .025$. Therefore, we would use the same t value as above, $t_{.025} = 2.776$. The confidence interval is:

$$\bar{x}_D \pm t_{\alpha/2}\frac{s_D}{\sqrt{n_D}} \Rightarrow 3.8 \pm 3.8 \pm 2.776\frac{1.4832}{\sqrt{5}} \Rightarrow 3.8 \pm 1.84 \Rightarrow (1.96, 5.64)$$

c. The sample of differences must be randomly selected from a population of differences which has a normal distribution.

9.85 If the p-value is less than α, reject H_0. Otherwise, do not reject H_0.

a. p-value $= .0429 < .05 \Rightarrow$ Reject H_0

b. p-value $= .1984 \nless .05 \Rightarrow$ Do not reject H_0

c. p-value $= .0001 < .05 \Rightarrow$ Reject H_0

d. p-value $= .0344 < .05 \Rightarrow$ Reject H_0

e. p-value $= .0545 \nless .05 \Rightarrow$ Do not reject H_0

f. p-value $= .9633 \nless .05 \Rightarrow$ Do not reject H_0

g. We must assume:
   1. Both sampled populations are normal.
   2. Both population variances are equal.
   3. Samples are random and independent.

9.87 a. To determine if there is a difference in the mean strength of the two types of shocks, we test:

$H_0: \mu_D = 0$
$H_a\ \mu_D \neq 0$

The test statistic is $t = 7.679$ (from the printout)

The p-value for the test is $p = .000597$. Since the p-value is less than $\alpha = .05$, H_0 is rejected. There is sufficient evidence to indicate a difference in the mean strength of the two types of shocks at $\alpha = .05$.

b. The p-value for the test is $p = .000597$. Since the p-value is less than $\alpha = .05$, H_0 is rejected. There is sufficient evidence to indicate a difference in the mean strength of the two types of shocks at $\alpha = .05$.

c. The necessary assumptions are:

   1. The population of difference is normal.
   2. The differences are randomly and independently selected.

d. For confidence coefficient .95, $\alpha = 1 - .95 = .05$ and $\alpha/2 = .05/2 = .025$. From Table VI, Appendix B, with df $= 5$, $t_{.025} = 2.571$. The confidence interval is:

$$\bar{x}_D \pm t_{.025} \frac{s_D}{\sqrt{n_D}} \Rightarrow .4167 \pm 2.571 \left[\frac{.1329}{\sqrt{6}} \right] \Rightarrow .4167 \pm .1395 \Rightarrow (.2772, .5562)$$

We are 95% confident the difference in mean strength between the manufacturer's shock and that of the competitor's shock is between .2772 and .5562.

9.89 a. Let $\mu_1 =$ mean GPA for traditional students and $\mu_2 =$ mean GPA for nontraditional students. To determine whether the mean GPAs of traditional and nontraditional students differ, we test:

$H_0: \mu_1 - \mu_2 = 0$
$H_a: \mu_1 - \mu_2 \neq 0$

b. The test statistic is $z = \dfrac{(\bar{x}_1 - \bar{x}_2) - D_0}{\sqrt{\dfrac{s_1^2}{n_1} + \dfrac{s_2^2}{n_2}}} = \dfrac{(2.9 - 3.5) - 0}{\sqrt{\dfrac{.5^2}{94} + \dfrac{.5^2}{73}}} = -7.69$

The rejection region requires $\alpha/2 = .01/2 = .005$ in each tail of the z-distribution. From Table IV, Appendix B, $z_{.005} = 2.58$. The rejection region is $z < -2.58$ or $z > 2.58$.

Since the observed value of the test statistic falls in the rejection region ($z = -7.69 < -2.58$), H_0 is rejected. There is sufficient evidence to indicate that the mean GPAs of traditional and nontraditional students differ for $\alpha = .01$.

c. We must assume that the two samples are randomly and independently selected from the populations of GPAs.

9.91 a. Since there are large differences among the canisters, a paired difference experiment was conducted to eliminate the differences from canister to canister.

b. To determine if there is a difference in the mean exhalation rates between PCHD and EERF, we test

$H_0: \mu_1 - \mu_2 = 0$
$H_a: \mu_1 - \mu_2 \neq 0$

The test statistic is $t = \dfrac{\bar{x}_D - 0}{s_D/\sqrt{n_D}} = \dfrac{84.17 - 0}{408.92/\sqrt{15}} = .80$

The rejection region requires $\alpha/2 = .05/2 = .025$ in each tail of the t-distribution with df $= n_D - 1 = 15 - 1 = 14$. From Table VI, Appendix B, $t_{.025} = 2.145$. The rejection region is $t < -2.145$ or $t > 2.145$.

Since the observed value of the test statistic does not fall in the rejection region ($.80 \not> 2.145$), H_0 is not rejected. There is insufficient evidence to indicate that there is a difference in the mean exhalation rates between PCHD and EERF at $\alpha = .05$.

c. For confidence coefficient .95, $\alpha = .05$ and $\alpha/2 = .025$. From Table VI, Appendix B, with df $= n_D - 1 = 15 - 1 = 14$, $t_{.025} = 2.145$. The confidence interval is:

$$\bar{x}_D \pm t_{\alpha/2} s_D/\sqrt{n_D} \Rightarrow 84.17 \pm (2.145)\dfrac{408.92}{\sqrt{15}} \Rightarrow 84.17 \pm 226.47 \Rightarrow (-142.30, 310.64)$$

We are 95% confident the difference in mean measurements between PCHD and EERF is between -142.30 and 310.64. Since 0 is in the interval, it implies there is no significant difference between the mean measurements. This supports the test in part **b**.

9.93 Let μ_1 = mean initial performance of stayers and μ_2 = mean initial performance of leavers.

To determine if the mean initial performance differs for stayers and leavers, we test:

H_0: $\mu_1 - \mu_2 = 0$
H_a: $\mu_1 - \mu_2 \neq 0$

The test statistic is $z = \dfrac{(\bar{x}_1 - \bar{x}_2) - 0}{\sqrt{\dfrac{s_1^2}{n_1} + \dfrac{s_2^2}{n_2}}} = \dfrac{(3.51 - 3.24) - 0}{\sqrt{\dfrac{.51^2}{174} + \dfrac{.52^2}{355}}} = 5.68$

Since no α is given, we will use $\alpha = .05$. The rejection region requires $\alpha/2 = .05/2 = .025$ in each tail of the z-distribution. For Table IV, Appendix B, $z_{.025} = 1.96$. The rejection region is $z < -1.96$ or $z > 1.96$.

Since the observed value of the test statistic falls in the rejection region ($z = 5.68 > 1.96$), H_0 is rejected. There is sufficient evidence to indicate the mean initial performance differs for stayers and leavers at $\alpha = .05$.

Let μ_1 = mean rate of career advancement of stayers and μ_2 = mean rate of career advancement of leavers.

To determine if the mean rate of career advancement differs for stayers and leavers, we test:

H_0: $\mu_1 - \mu_2 = 0$
H_a: $\mu_1 - \mu_2 \neq 0$

The test statistic is $z = \dfrac{(\bar{x}_1 - \bar{x}_2) - 0}{\sqrt{\dfrac{s_1^2}{n_1} + \dfrac{s_2^2}{n_2}}} = \dfrac{(0.43 - 0.31) - 0}{\sqrt{\dfrac{.20^2}{174} + \dfrac{.31^2}{355}}} = 5.36$

Since no α is given, we will use $\alpha = .05$. The rejection region is $z < -1.96$ or $z > 1.96$ (from above).

Since the observed value of the test statistic falls in the rejection region ($z = 5.36 > 1.96$), H_0 is rejected. There is sufficient evidence to indicate the mean rate of career advancement differs for stayers and leavers at $\alpha = .05$.

Let μ_1 = mean final performance appraisal of stayers and μ_2 = mean final performance appraisal of leavers.

To determine if the mean final performance appraisal differs for stayers and leavers, we test:

H_0: $\mu_1 - \mu_2 = 0$
H_a: $\mu_1 - \mu_2 \neq 0$

The test statistic is $z = \dfrac{(\bar{x}_1 - \bar{x}_2) - 0}{\sqrt{\dfrac{s_1^2}{n_1} + \dfrac{s_2^2}{n_2}}} = \dfrac{(3.78 - 3.15) - 0}{\sqrt{\dfrac{.62^2}{174} + \dfrac{.68^2}{355}}} = 10.63$

Since no α is given, we will use $\alpha = .05$. The rejection region is $z < -1.96$ or $z > 1.96$ (from above).

Since the observed value of the test statistic falls in the rejection region ($z = 10.63 > 1.96$), H_0 is rejected. There is sufficient evidence to indicate the mean final performance appraisal differs for stayers and leavers at $\alpha = .05$.

9.95   Some preliminary calculations are:

Supervisor	Difference (Pre-test − Post-test)
1	−15
2	1
3	−7
4	−8
5	−4
6	−13
7	−8
8	2
9	−10
10	−7

$$\bar{x}_D = \frac{\sum x_D}{n_D} = \frac{-69}{10} = -6.9$$

$$s_D^2 = \frac{\sum x_D^2 - \frac{\left(\sum x_D\right)^2}{n_D}}{n_D - 1} = \frac{741 - \frac{(-69)^2}{10}}{10 - 1} = \frac{264.9}{9} = 29.4333$$

$$s_D = \sqrt{29.4333} = 5.4252$$

a. To determine if the training program is effective in increasing supervisory skills, we test:

H_0: $\mu_D = 0$
H_a: $\mu_D < 0$

The test statistic is $t = \dfrac{\bar{x}_D - 0}{\dfrac{s_D}{\sqrt{n_D}}} = \dfrac{-6.9 - 0}{\dfrac{5.4252}{\sqrt{10}}} = -4.02$

The rejection region requires $\alpha = .10$ in the lower tail of the t-distribution with df = $n_D - 1$ = $10 - 1 = 9$. From Table VI, Appendix B, $t_{.10} = 1.383$. The rejection region is $t < -1.383$.

Since the observed value of the test statistic falls in the rejection region ($t = -4.02 < -1.383$), H_0 is rejected. There is sufficient evidence to indicate the training program is effective in increasing supervisory skills at $\alpha = .10$.

b. From the printout, the p-value is $p = .0030$. The probability of observing a test statistic of -4.02 or anything lower is .0030 when H_0 is true. This is very unusual if H_0 is true. There is evidence to reject H_0 for $\alpha > .003$.

9.97 For probability .95, $\alpha = 1 - .95 = .05$ and $\alpha/2 = .05/2 = .025$. From Table IV, Appendix B, $z_{.025} = 1.96$. Since we have no prior information about the proportions, we use $p_1 = p_2 = .5$ to get a conservative estimate.

$$n_1 = n_2 = \frac{(z_{\alpha/2})^2(p_1 q_1 + p_2 q_2)}{B^2} = \frac{(1.96)^2(.5(1 - .5) + .5(1 - .5))}{.02^2} = \frac{1.9208}{.0004} = 4,802$$

9.99 Let p_1 = unemployment rate for the urban industrial community and p_2 = unemployment rate for the university community.

Some preliminary calculations are:

$$\hat{p}_1 = \frac{x_1}{n_1} = \frac{47}{525} = .0895 \qquad \hat{p}_2 = \frac{x_2}{n_2} = \frac{22}{375} = .0587$$

For confidence coefficient .95, $\alpha = 1 - .95 = .05$ and $\alpha/2 = .05/2 = .025$. From Table IV, Appendix B, $z_{.025} = 1.96$. The confidence interval is:

$$(\hat{p}_1 - \hat{p}_2) \pm z_{.025}\sqrt{\frac{\hat{p}_1 \hat{q}_1}{n_1} + \frac{\hat{p}_2 \hat{q}_2}{n_2}}$$

$$\Rightarrow (.0895 - .0587) \pm 1.96\sqrt{\frac{.0895(.9105)}{525} + \frac{.0587(.9413)}{375}}$$

$$\Rightarrow .0308 \pm .0341 \Rightarrow (-.0033, .0649)$$

We are 95% confident the difference in unemployment rates in the two communities is between $-.0033$ and $.0649$.

9.101 a. Define the following parameters:

p_1 = proportion of earthquake-insured residents in Contra Costa County
p_2 = proportion of earthquake-insured residents in Santa Clara County
p_3 = proportion of earthquake-insured residents in Los Angeles County
p_4 = proportion of earthquake-insured residents in San Bernardino County

$$\hat{p}_1 = \frac{x_1}{n_1} = \frac{117}{521} = .225 \qquad \hat{p}_2 = \frac{x_2}{n_2} = \frac{222}{556} = .399$$

$$\hat{p}_3 = \frac{x_3}{n_3} = \frac{133}{337} = .395 \qquad \hat{p}_4 = \frac{x_4}{n_4} = \frac{109}{372} = .293$$

For confidence coefficient $.95$, $\alpha = .05$ and $\alpha/2 = .025$. From Table IV, Appendix B, $z_{.025} = 1.96$. The form of the confidence interval is:

Comparing Los Angeles County with Contra Costa County:

$$(\hat{p}_3 - \hat{p}_1) \pm z_{.025} \sqrt{\frac{\hat{p}_3 \hat{q}_3}{n_3} + \frac{\hat{p}_1 \hat{q}_1}{n_1}}$$

$$\Rightarrow (.395 - .225) \pm 1.96 \sqrt{\frac{.395(.605)}{337} + \frac{.225(.775)}{521}}$$

$$\Rightarrow .17 \pm .063 \Rightarrow (.107, .233)$$

We are 95% confident that the difference in the proportions of earthquake-insured residents between Los Angeles County and Contra Costa County is between $.107$ and $.233$.

Comparing Los Angeles County with Santa Clara County:

$$(\hat{p}_3 - \hat{p}_2) \pm z_{.025} \sqrt{\frac{\hat{p}_3 \hat{q}_3}{n_3} + \frac{\hat{p}_2 \hat{q}_2}{n_2}}$$

$$\Rightarrow (.395 - .399) \pm 1.96 \sqrt{\frac{.395(.605)}{337} + \frac{.399(.601)}{556}}$$

$$\Rightarrow -.004 \pm .066 \Rightarrow (-.070, .062)$$

We are 95% confident that the difference in the proportions of earthquake-insured residents between Los Angeles County and Santa Clara County is between $-.070$ and $.062$.

Comparing Los Angeles County with San Bernardino County:

$$(\hat{p}_3 - \hat{p}_4) \pm z_{.025} \sqrt{\frac{\hat{p}_3 \hat{q}_3}{n_3} + \frac{\hat{p}_4 \hat{q}_4}{n_4}}$$

$$\Rightarrow (.395 - .293) \pm 1.96 \sqrt{\frac{.395(.605)}{337} + \frac{.293(.707)}{372}}$$

$$\Rightarrow .102 \pm .070 \Rightarrow (.032, .172)$$

We are 95% confident that the difference in the proportions of earthquake-insured residents between Los Angeles County and San Bernardino County is between $.032$ and $.172$.

b. Two of the three confidence intervals do not contain 0. These two intervals compare Los Angeles County with Contra Costa County and San Bernardino County. Since 0 is not in the 95% confidence interval, there is evidence to indicate that the proportion of earthquake-insured residents in Los Angeles County is greater than the proportion in either Contra Costa County or San Bernardino County. Since 0 is in the interval comparing Los Angeles County with Santa Clara County, there is no evidence to indicate that the proportion of earthquake-insured residents in Los Angeles County is greater than the proportion in Santa Clara County.

9.103 a. For each of the three measures, let μ_1 = mean score for males seeing the first advertisement and μ_2 = mean score for males seeing the second advertisement. Also, let $\mu_D = \mu_1 - \mu_2$. To determine whether the first ad will be more effective when shown to males, we test:

H_0: $\mu_D = 0$
H_a: $\mu_D > 0$

b. This experiment was a paired difference experiment. Each male was shown both advertisements.

c. Attitude towards the Advertisement:

The p-value = .091. There is no evidence to reject H_0 for α = .05. There is no evidence to indicate the first ad will be more effective when shown to males for α = .05. There is evidence to reject H_0 for α = .10. There is evidence to indicate the first ad will be more effective when shown to males for α = .10.

Attitude toward Brand of Soft Drink:

The p-value = .032. There is evidence to reject H_0 for $\alpha > .032$. There is evidence to indicate the first ad will be more effective when shown to males for $\alpha > .032$.

Intention to Purchase the Soft Drink:

The p-value = .050. There is no evidence to reject H_0 for α = .05. There is no evidence to indicate the first ad will be more effective when shown to males for α = .05. There is evidence to reject H_0 for $\alpha > .050$. There is evidence to indicate the first ad will be more effective when shown to males for $\alpha > .050$.

d. We must assume that the sample of differences is randomly selected.

10.1   a.

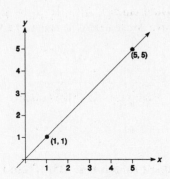

      b.

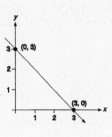

   c.

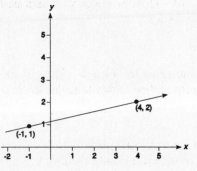

      d.

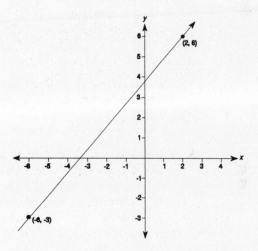

10.3   The two equations are:

$$4 = \beta_0 + \beta_1(-2) \text{ and } 6 = \beta_0 + \beta_1(4)$$

Subtracting the first equation from the second, we get

$$
\begin{array}{r}
6 = \beta_0 + 4\beta_1 \\
-(4 = \beta_0 - 2\beta_1) \\
\hline
2 = 6\beta_1
\end{array}
\Rightarrow \beta_1 = \frac{2}{6} = \frac{1}{3}
$$

Substituting $\beta_1 = \frac{1}{3}$ into the first equation, we get:

$$4 = \beta_0 + \frac{1}{3}(-2) \Rightarrow \beta_0 = 4 + \frac{2}{3} = \frac{14}{3}$$

The equation for the line is $y = \frac{14}{3} + \frac{1}{3}x$.

10.5   To graph a line, we need two points. Pick two values for x, and find the corresponding y values by substituting the values of x into the equation.

a.   Let $x = 0 \Rightarrow y = 4 + (0) = 4$
     and $x = 2 \Rightarrow y = 4 + (2) = 6$

b.   Let $x = 0 \Rightarrow y = 5 - 2(0) = 5$
     and $x = 2 \Rightarrow y = 5 - 2(2) = 1$

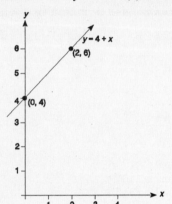

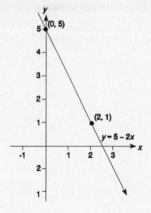

c.   Let $x = 0 \Rightarrow y = -4 + 3(0) = -4$
     and $x = 2 \Rightarrow y = -4 + 3(2) = 2$

d.   Let $x = 0 \Rightarrow y = -2(0) = 0$
     and $x = 2 \Rightarrow y = -2(2) = -4$

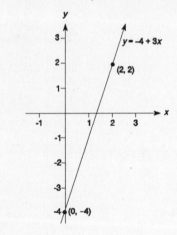

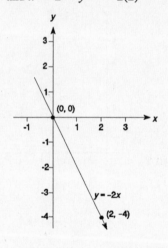

e.   Let $x = 0 \Rightarrow y = 0$
     and $x = 2 \Rightarrow y = 2$

f.   Let $x = 0 \Rightarrow y = .5 + 1.5(0) = .5$
     and $x = 2 \Rightarrow y = .5 + 1.5(2) = 3.5$

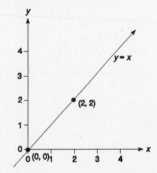

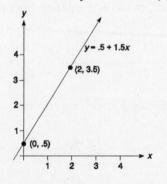

10.7   A deterministic model does not allow for random error or variation, whereas a probabilistic model does. An example where a deterministic model would be appropriate is:

Let y = cost of a 2×4 piece of lumber and
x = length (in feet)

The model would be $y = \beta_1 x$. There should be no variation in price for the same length of wood.

An example where a probabilistic model would be appropriate is:

Let y = sales per month of a commodity and
x = amount of money spent advertising

The model would be $y = \beta_0 + \beta_1 x + \epsilon$. The sales per month will probably vary even if the amount of money spent on advertising remains the same.

10.9   No. The random error component, ϵ, allows the values of the variable to fall above or below the line.

10.11   From Exercise 10.10, $\hat{\beta}_0 = 7.10$ and $\hat{\beta}_1 = -.78$.

The fitted line is $\hat{y} = 7.10 - .78x$. To obtain values for $\hat{y}$, we substitute values of x into the equation and solve for $\hat{y}$.

a.

x	y	$\hat{y} = 7.10 - .78x$	$(y - \hat{y})$	$(y - \hat{y})^2$
7	2	1.64	.36	.1296
4	4	3.98	.02	.0004
6	2	2.42	−.42	.1764
2	5	5.54	−.54	.2916
1	7	6.32	.68	.4624
1	6	6.32	−.32	.1024
3	5	4.76	.24	.0576

$$\sum(y - \hat{y}) = 0.02 \qquad \text{SSE} = \sum(y - \hat{y})^2 = 1.2204$$

b.

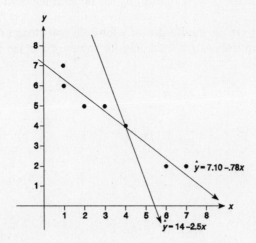

c.

x	y	$\hat{y} = 14 - 2.5x$	$(y - \hat{y})$	$(y - \hat{y})^2$
7	2	−3.5	5.5	30.25
4	4	4	0	0
6	2	−1	3	9
2	5	9	−4	16
1	7	11.5	−4.5	20.25
1	6	11.5	−5.5	30.25
3	5	6.5	−1.5	2.25
			$\sum(y - \hat{y}) = -7$	SSE = 108.00

10.13 a.

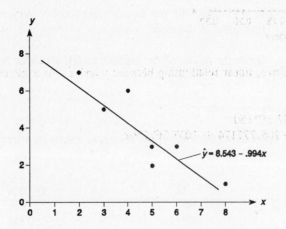

b. Looking at the scattergram, x and y appear to have a negative linear relationship.

c. From the printout, $\hat{\beta}_1 = -.9939$ and $\hat{\beta}_0 = 8.543$

d. The least squares line is $\hat{y} = 8.543 - .994x$. The line is plotted in part **a**. It appears to fit the data well.

e. $\hat{\beta}_0 = 8.543$ Since $x = 0$ is not in the observed range, $\hat{\beta}_0$ has no meaning other than the y-intercept.

   $\hat{\beta}_1 = -.994$ The estimated change in the mean value of y for each unit change in x is −.994. These interpretations are valid only for values of x in the range from 2 to 8.

10.15   a.   The slope should be positive. As batting averages increase, one would expect the number of games won to increase.

   b.

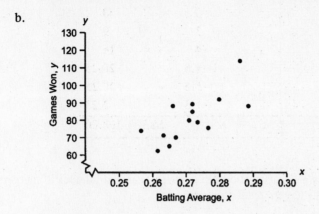

Yes; There appears to be a positive, linear relationship between y and x. As x increases, y tends to increase.

   c. $\hat{\beta}_0 = -205.777174$, $\hat{\beta}_1 = 1057.367150$
The least squares line is $\hat{y} = -205.777174 + 1057.367150x$

   d.

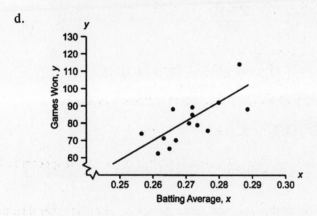

Yes; The least squares line seems to fit the points on the scattergram.

   e.   Yes; The points on the scattergram are clustered fairly closely around the least squares line.

   f. $\hat{\beta}_0 = -205.777174$. Since $x = 0$ is not in the observed range, $\hat{\beta}_0$ has no interpretation other than being the y-intercept.

$\hat{\beta}_1 = 1057.367150$. For each additional increase of 1 in batting average, the mean number of games won increases by an estimated 1057.367150 games. Since no one has a batting average of 1, a better interpretation would be as follows: For each additional increase of .01 in batting average, the mean number of games won is estimated to increase by 10.57367150 (or approximately 10 games).

10.17 a. Using MINITAB, the scattergram is:

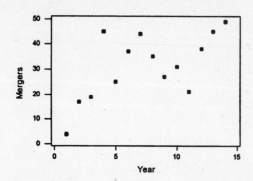

From the plot, it appears that there is a linear relationship between year and number of mergers. As the year increases, the number of mergers tends to increase.

b. $\sum x = 105$ $\qquad$ $\sum y = 437$ $\qquad$ $\sum xy = 3,721$ $\qquad$ $\sum x^2 = 1,015$

$$\bar{x} = \frac{\sum x}{n} = \frac{105}{14} = 7.5 \qquad \bar{y} = \frac{\sum y}{n} = \frac{437}{14} = 31.21428571$$

$$SS_{xy} = \sum xy - \frac{(\sum x)(\sum y)}{n} = 3,721 - \frac{105(437)}{14} = 3,721 - 3,277.5 = 443.5$$

$$SS_{xx} = \sum x^2 - \frac{(\sum x)^2}{n} = 1,015 - \frac{105^2}{14} = 1,015 - 787.5 = 227.5$$

$$\hat{\beta}_1 = \frac{SS_{xy}}{SS_{xx}} = \frac{443.5}{227.5} = 1.949450549 \approx 1.949$$

$$\hat{\beta}_0 = \bar{y} - \hat{\beta}_1 \bar{x} = 31.21428571 - 1.949450549(7.5) = 31.21428571 - 14.62087912$$
$$= 16.59340659 \approx 16.593$$

The fitted regression line is $\hat{y} = 16.593 + 1.949x$

c. Using MINITAB, the least squares line is:

Regression Plot

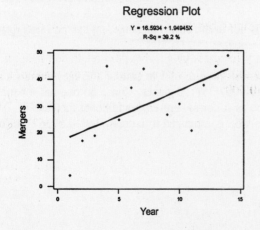

Y = 16.5934 + 1.94945X
R-Sq = 39.2 %

d.   For $x = 15$, $\hat{y} = 16.593 + 1.949(15) = 45.828$. This compares very favorably to the actual number of mergers in 1994 of 42.

10.19   a.   It appears as salary increases, the retaliation index decreases.

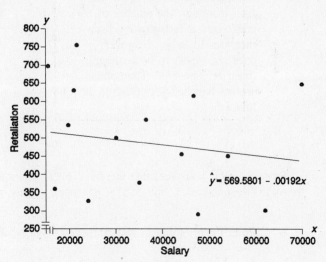

b. $\sum x = 544,100$ $\sum y = 7,497$ $\sum xy = 263,977,000$

$\sum x^2 = 23,876,290,000$

$$\bar{x} = \frac{\sum x}{n} = \frac{544,100}{15} = 36,273.333 \qquad \bar{y} = \frac{\sum y}{n} = \frac{7,497}{15} = 499.8$$

$$SS_{xy} = \sum xy - \frac{(\sum x)(\sum y)}{n} = 263,977,000 - \frac{(544,100)(7,497)}{15}$$
$$= 263,977,000 - 271,941,180 = -7,964,180$$

$$SS_{xx} = \sum x^2 - \frac{(\sum x)^2}{n} = 23,876,290,000 - \frac{(544,100)^2}{15}$$
$$= 23,876,290,000 - 19,736,320,670 = 4,139,969,330$$

$$\hat{\beta}_1 = \frac{SS_{xy}}{SS_{xx}} = \frac{-7,964,180}{4,139,969,330} = -.001923729 \approx -.00192$$

$$\hat{\beta}_0 = \bar{y} - \hat{\beta}_1\bar{x} = 499.8 - (-.001923729)(36,273.333)$$
$$= 499.8 + 69.78007144 = 569.5800714 \approx 569.5801$$

$$\hat{y} = 569.5801 - .00192x$$

c.   The least squares line supports the answer because the line has a negative slope.

d. $\hat{\beta}_0 = 569.5801$ This has no meaning because $x = 0$ is not in the observed range.

e. $\hat{\beta}_1 = -.00192$ When the salary increases by \$1, the mean retaliation index is estimated to decrease by .00192. This is meaningful for the range of x from \$16,900 to \$70,000.

10.21 a. The plot of the data is:

It appears that as the age of the firm increases, the number of employees at fast-growing firms increases linearly. However, it does not appear to be a strong linear relationship. The points are not bunched very close to the line.

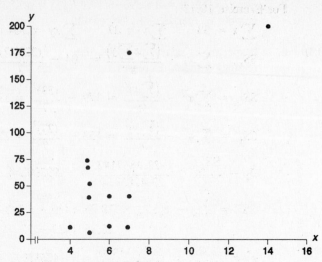

b. From the printout, $\hat{\beta}_0 = -51.361607$ and $\hat{\beta}_1 = 17.754464$.

$\hat{\beta}_0 = -51.361607$. Since $x = 0$ is not in the observed range, $\hat{\beta}_0$ is just an estimate of the y-intercept.

$\hat{\beta}_1 = 17.754464$. For each additional year of age, the mean number of employees is estimated to increase by 17.754464.

10.23 a. $s^2 = \dfrac{SSE}{n - 2} = \dfrac{8.34}{26 - 2} = .3475$

b. We would expect most of the observations to be within $2s$ of the least squares line. This is:

$2s = 2\sqrt{.3475} \approx 1.179$

10.25 $SSE = SS_{yy} - \hat{\beta}_1 SS_{xy}$

where $SS_{yy} = \sum y_i^2 - \dfrac{\left(\sum y_i\right)^2}{n}$

For Exercise 10.10,

$\sum y_i^2 = 159 \qquad \sum y_i = 31$

$SS_{yy} = 159 - \dfrac{31^2}{7} = 159 - 137.2857143 = 21.7142857$

$SS_{xy} = -26.2857143 \qquad \hat{\beta}_1 = -.779661017$

Therefore, $SSE = 21.7142857 - (-.779661017)(-26.2857143) = 1.22033896 \approx 1.2203$

$s^2 = \dfrac{SSE}{n - 2} = \dfrac{1.22033896}{7 - 2} = .244067792, \quad s = \sqrt{.244067792} = .4960$

We would expect most of the observations to fall within $2s$ or $2(.4940)$ or $.988$ units of the least squares prediction line.

For Exercise 10.13,

$$\sum x = 33 \qquad \sum y = 27 \qquad \sum xy = 104 \qquad \sum x^2 = 179 \qquad \sum y^2 = 133$$

$$SS_{xy} = \sum xy - \frac{\left(\sum x \sum y\right)}{n} = 104 - \frac{(23)(27)}{7} = 104 - 127.2857143 = -23.2857143$$

$$SS_{xx} = \sum x^2 - \frac{\left(\sum x\right)^2}{n} = 179 - \frac{(33)^2}{7} = 179 - 155.5714286 = 23.4285714$$

$$SS_{yy} = \sum y^2 - \frac{\left(\sum y\right)^2}{n} = 133 - \frac{(27)^2}{7} = 133 - 104.1428571 = 28.8571429$$

$$\hat{\beta}_1 = \frac{SS_{xy}}{S_{xx}} = \frac{-23.2857143}{23.4285714} = -.99390244$$

$$SSE = SS_{yy} - \hat{\beta}_1 SS_{xy} = 28.8571429 - (.99390244)(-23.2857143)$$
$$= 28.8571429 - 23.14372824 = 5.71341466$$

$$s^2 = \frac{SSE}{n-2} = \frac{5.71341466}{7-2} = 1.142682932 \qquad s = \sqrt{1.142682932} = 1.0690$$

We would expect most of the observations to fall within $2s$ or $2(1.0690)$ or 2.1380 units of the least squares prediction line.

10.27 a. $\hat{\beta}_1 = \dfrac{SS_{xy}}{SS_{xx}} = \dfrac{1,419,492.796}{3,809,368.452} = .372632055 \approx .373$

$\hat{\beta}_0 = \bar{y} - \hat{\beta}_1 \bar{x} = 302.52 - .372632055(792.04) = 7.3805068 \approx 7.381$

The least squares line is $\hat{y} = 7.381 + .373x$

The graph of the data is:

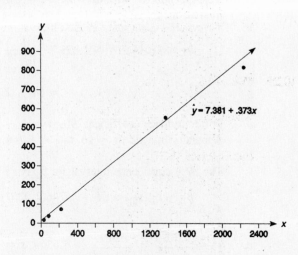

b. For $x = \$1,600$ billion, $\hat{y} = 7.381 + .373(1,600) = \$604.181$ billion.

c. $SSE = SS_{yy} - \hat{\beta}_1 SS_{xy} = 531,174.148 - .372632055(1,419,492.796) = 2225.6298$

$s^2 = \dfrac{SSE}{n-2} = \dfrac{2225.6298}{5-2} = 741.8766 \qquad s = \sqrt{741.8766} = 27.237$

d. We would expect almost all of the observed values of y to fall within $2s$ or $2(27.237)$ or 54.474 dollars of their least squares predicted values.

10.29 a. From the printout, SSE = 20,554.41518, s^2 = MSE = 2,055.44152, and s = ROOT MSE = 45.33698.

b. We would expect that most of the observations will fall within $2s$ or $2(45.33698) = 90.67396$ employees of their predicted values.

10.31 a. For confidence coefficient .95, $\alpha = 1 - .95 = .05$ and $\alpha/2 = .05/2 = .025$. From Table VI, Appendix B, with df = $n - 2 = 12 - 2 = 10$, $t_{.025} = 2.228$.

The 95% confidence interval for β_1 is:

$$\hat{\beta}_1 \pm t_{.025}s_{\hat{\beta}_1} \text{ where } s_{\hat{\beta}_1} = \frac{s}{\sqrt{SS_{xx}}} = \frac{3}{\sqrt{35}} = .5071$$

$$\Rightarrow 31 \pm 2.228(.5071) \Rightarrow 31 \pm 1.13 \Rightarrow (29.87, 32.13)$$

For confidence coefficient .90, $\alpha = 1 - .90 = .10$ and $\alpha/2 = .10/2 = .05$. From Table VI, Appendix B, with df = 10, $t_{.05} = 1.812$.

The 90% confidence interval for β_1 is:

$$\hat{\beta}_1 \pm t_{.05}s_{\hat{\beta}_1} \Rightarrow 31 \pm 1.812(.5071) \Rightarrow 31 \pm .92 \Rightarrow (30.08, 31.92)$$

b. $s^2 = \dfrac{SSE}{n-2} = \dfrac{1960}{18-2} = 122.5$, $s = \sqrt{s^2} = 11.0680$

For confidence coefficient, .95, $\alpha = 1 - .95 = .05$ and $\alpha/2 = .05/2 = .025$. From Table VI, Appendix B, with df = $n - 2 = 18 - 2 = 16$, $t_{.025} = 2.120$. The 95% confidence interval for β_1 is:

$$\hat{\beta}_1 \pm t_{.025}s_{\hat{\beta}_1} \text{ where } s_{\hat{\beta}_1} = \frac{s}{\sqrt{SS_{xx}}} = \frac{11.0680}{\sqrt{30}} = 2.0207$$

$$\Rightarrow 64 \pm 2.120(2.0207) \Rightarrow 64 \pm 4.28 \Rightarrow (59.72, 68.28)$$

For confidence coefficient .90, $\alpha = 1 - .90 = .10$ and $\alpha/2 = .10/2 = .05$. From Table VI, Appendix B, with df = 16, $t_{.05} = 1.746$.

The 90% confidence interval for β_1 is:

$$\hat{\beta}_1 \pm t_{.05}s_{\hat{\beta}_1} \Rightarrow 64 \pm 1.746(2.0207) \Rightarrow 64 \pm 3.53 \Rightarrow (60.47, 67.53)$$

c. $s^2 = \dfrac{SSE}{n-2} = \dfrac{146}{24-2} = 6.6364$, $s = \sqrt{s^2} = 2.5761$

For confidence coefficient .95, $\alpha = 1 - .95 = .05$ and $\alpha/2 = .05/2 = .025$. From Table VI, Appendix B, with df = $n - 2 = 24 - 2 = 22$, $t_{.025} = 2.074$. The 95% confidence interval for β_1 is:

$$\hat{\beta}_1 \pm t_{.025}s_{\hat{\beta}_1} \text{ where } s_{\hat{\beta}_1} = \frac{s}{\sqrt{SS_{xx}}} = \frac{2.5761}{\sqrt{64}} = .3220$$

$$\Rightarrow -8.4 \pm 2.074(.322) \Rightarrow -8.4 \pm .67 \Rightarrow (-9.07, -7.73)$$

For confidence coefficient .90, $\alpha = 1 - .90 = .10$ and $\alpha/2 = .10/2 = .05$. From Table VI, Appendix B, with df = 22, $t_{.05} = 1.717$.

The 90% confidence interval for β_1 is:

$$\hat{\beta}_1 \pm t_{.05}s_{\hat{\beta}_1} \Rightarrow -8.4 \pm 1.717(.322) \Rightarrow -8.4 \pm .55 \Rightarrow (-8.95, -7.85)$$

10.33   From Exercise 10.32 $\hat{\beta}_1 = .8214$, $s = 1.1922$, $SS_{xx} = 28$, and $n = 7$.

For confidence coefficient .80, $\alpha = 1 - .80 = .20$ and $\alpha/2 = .20/2 = .10$. From Table VI, Appendix B, with df = $n - 2 = 7 - 2 = 5$, $t_{.10} = 1.476$. The 80% confidence interval for β_1 is:

$$\hat{\beta}_1 \pm t_{.025}s_{\hat{\beta}_1} \text{ where } s_{\hat{\beta}_1} = \frac{s}{\sqrt{SS_{xx}}} = \frac{1.1922}{\sqrt{28}} = .2253$$

$$\Rightarrow .8214 \pm 1.476(.2253) \Rightarrow .8214 \pm .3325 \Rightarrow (.4889, 1.1539)$$

For confidence coefficient .98, $\alpha = 1 - .98 = .02$ and $\alpha/2 = .02/2 = .01$. From Table VI, Appendix B, with df = 5, $t_{.01} = 3.365$.

The 98% confidence interval for β_1 is:

$$\hat{\beta}_1 \pm t_{.01}s_{\hat{\beta}_1} \Rightarrow .8214 \pm 3.365(.2253) \Rightarrow .8214 \pm .7581 \Rightarrow (.0633, 1.5795)$$

10.35   a.   Using MINITAB, the scattergram is:

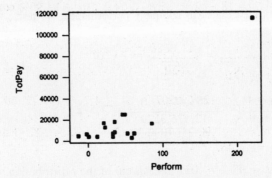

It appears that as performance increases, CEO pay tends to increase.

b. $\sum x = 755.9 \qquad \sum y = 285,412 \qquad \sum xy = 32,460,260 \qquad \sum x^2 = 77,402.39$

$\sum y^2 = 16,051,516,284$

$$\bar{x} = \frac{\sum x}{n} = \frac{755.9}{17} = 44.46470588 \qquad \bar{y} = \frac{\sum y}{n} = \frac{285,412}{17} = 16,788.94118$$

$$SS_{xy} = \sum xy - \frac{(\sum x)(\sum y)}{n} = 32,460,260 - \frac{755.9(285,412)}{17}$$

$$= 32,460,260 - 12,690,760.64 = 19,769,499.3$$

$$SS_{xx} = \sum x^2 - \frac{(\sum x)^2}{n} = 77,402.39 - \frac{755.9^2}{17}$$
$$= 77,402.39 - 33,619.87118 = 43,791.51882$$

$$\hat{\beta}_1 = \frac{SS_{xy}}{SS_{xx}} = \frac{19,769,499.3}{43,791.51882} = 451.4458483 \approx 451.446$$

$$\hat{\beta}_0 = \bar{y} - \hat{\beta}_1\bar{x} = 16,788.94118 - 451.4458483(44.46470588)$$
$$= 16,788.94118 - 20,073.40687 = -3,284.46569 \approx -3,284.466$$

The fitted regression line is $\hat{y} = -3,284.466 + 451.446x$

c. $$SS_{yy} = \sum y^2 - \frac{(\sum y)^2}{n} = 16,051,516,284 - \frac{285,412^2}{17}$$
$$= 16,051,516,284 - 4,791,765,279 = 11,259,751,005$$

$$SSE = SS_{yy} - \hat{\beta}_1 SS_{xy} = 11,259,751,005 - 451.4458483(19,769,499.3)$$
$$= 11,259,751,005 - 8,924,858,409 = 2,334,892,596$$

$$s^2 = \frac{SSE}{n-2} = \frac{2,334,892,596}{17-2} = 155,659,506.4$$

$$s = \sqrt{s^2} = \sqrt{155,659,506.4} = 12,476.3579$$

To determine if CEO compensation is related to company performance, we test:

H_0: $\beta_1 = 0$
H_a: $\beta_1 \neq 0$

The test statistic is $t = \dfrac{\hat{\beta}_1 - 0}{s_{\hat{\beta}_1}} = \dfrac{451.446 - 0}{\dfrac{12,476.3579}{\sqrt{43,791.51882}}} = 7.572$

The rejection region requires $\alpha/2 = .05/2 = .025$ in each tail of the t-distribution with df $= n - 2 = 17 - 2 = 15$. From Table VI, Appendix B, $t_{.025} = 2.131$. The rejection region is $t < -2.131$ or $t > 2.131$.

Since the observed value of the test statistic falls in the rejection region ($t = 7.572 > 2.131$), H_0 is rejected. There is sufficient evidence to indicate that CEO compensation is related to company performance at $\alpha = .05$.

d. $\hat{\beta}_1 = 451.446$. For each percent increase in performance, the mean total pay is estimated to increase by 451.446 thousand dollars.

e.   For confidence coefficient .90, $\alpha = .10$ and $\alpha/2 = .10/2 = .05$. From Table VI, Appendix B, with df $= n - 2 = 17 - 2 = 15$, $t_{.05} = 1.753$. The 90% confidence interval is:

$$\hat{\beta}_1 \pm t_{.05}s_{\hat{\beta}_1} \Rightarrow 451.446 \pm 1.753\frac{12,476.3579}{\sqrt{43,791.51882}}$$
$$\Rightarrow 451.446 \pm 104.514 \Rightarrow (346.932, 555.960)$$

We are 90% confident that the change in the mean CEO compensation for each percent increase in performance is between 346.932 and 555.960 thousand dollars.

f.   We would expect the variability among the CEO compensations in the same industry to be smaller than that from many industries. Thus, we would expect the width of the confidence interval in part **e** to be smaller.

10.37   a.   Using MINITAB, the scattergram of the data is:

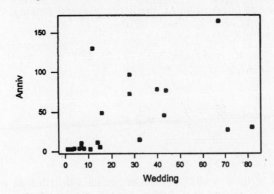

If the players' rankings remained the same, then the scattergram would be a straight line with a slope of 1. If the claim is true, then the scattergram would reveal points that would lie above this imaginary line. From the plot, there appears to be more points above this line than below it, which would support the claim.

b. $\sum x = 541$ $\sum y = 851$ $\sum xy = 32,145$ $\sum x^2 = 25,401$

$$\bar{x} = \frac{\sum x}{n} = \frac{541}{22} = 24.59090909 \qquad \bar{y} = \frac{\sum y}{n} = \frac{851}{22} = 38.68181818$$

$$SS_{xy} = \sum xy - \frac{(\sum x)(\sum y)}{n} = 32,145 - \frac{541(851)}{22}$$
$$= 32,145 - 20,926.86364 = 11,218.13636$$

$$SS_{xx} = \sum x^2 - \frac{(\sum x)^2}{n} = 25,401 - \frac{541^2}{22}$$
$$= 25,401 - 13,303.68182 = 12,097.31818$$

$$SS_{yy} = \sum y^2 - \frac{(\sum y)^2}{n} = 77,931 - \frac{851^2}{22}$$
$$= 77,931 - 32,918.22727 = 45,012.77273$$

$$\hat{\beta}_1 = \frac{SS_{xy}}{SS_{xx}} = \frac{11,218.13636}{12,097.31818} = .927324237 \approx .927$$

$$\hat{\beta}_0 = \bar{y} - \hat{\beta}_1\bar{x} = 38.68181818 - .927324237(24.59090909) = 15.87807217 \approx 15.878$$

The fitted model is: $\hat{y} = 15.878 + .927x$

c. $SSE = SS_{yy} - \hat{\beta}_1 SS_{xy} = 45,012.77273 - .927324237(11,218.13636)$

$$= 45,012.77273 - 10,402.84974 = 34,609.92299$$

$$s^2 = \frac{SSE}{n-2} = \frac{34,609.92299}{22-2} = 1730.49615 \qquad s = \sqrt{s^2} = \sqrt{1,730.49615} = 41.5992$$

To determine if the model contributes information for predicting players' rankings on their first anniversary, we test:

$H_0: \beta_1 = 0$
$H_a: \beta_1 \neq 0$

The test statistic is $t = \dfrac{\hat{\beta}_1 - 0}{s_{\hat{\beta}_1}} = \dfrac{.927 - 0}{\dfrac{41.5992}{\sqrt{12,097.31818}}} = 2.451$

The rejection region requires $\alpha/2 = .05/2 = .025$ in each tail of the t-distribution with df $= n - 2 = 22 - 2 = 20$. From Table VI, Appendix B, $t_{.025} = 2.086$. The rejection region is $t < -2.086$ or $t > 2.086$.

Since the observed value of the test statistic falls in the rejection region ($t = 2.451 > 2.086$), H_0 is rejected. There is sufficient evidence to indicate the model contributes information for predicting players' rankings on their first anniversary at $\alpha = .05$.

d. If there were no changes whatsoever in the rankings of the sample players after getting married, the true value of β_0 would be 0 and the true value of β_1 would be 1.

10.39 a. To determine if x and y are linearly related, we test:

$H_0: \beta_1 = 0$
$H_a: \beta_1 \neq 0$

The test statistic is $t = 4.98$.

The p-value is .001. Since the p-value is less than $\alpha = .01$, H_0 is rejected at $\alpha = .01$. There is sufficient evidence to indicate that x and y are linearly related.

b. Since the model is adequate, it is reasonable to use it to predict values of y.

For $x = 3$, $\hat{y} = .202 + .135x = .202 + .135(3) = .607$. This value is meaningful only if $x = 3$ is within the observed range.

10.41   a.   To determine whether the number of employees is positively linearly related to age of a fast-growing firm, we test:

$$H_0: \beta_1 = 0$$
$$H_a: \beta_1 > 0$$

The test statistic is $t = \dfrac{\hat{\beta}_1 - 0}{s_{\hat{\beta}_1}} = 3.384$ (from printout).

The p-value is $.0070/2 = .0035$. Since the p-value is less than $\alpha = .01$, H_0 is rejected. There is sufficient evidence to indicate that the number of employees is positively linearly related to age of a fast-growing firm at $\alpha > .0035$.

  b.   For confidence coefficient .99, $\alpha = 1 - .99 = .01$ and $\alpha/2 = .005$. From Table VI, Appendix B, with df $= n - 2 = 12 - 2 = 10$, $t_{.005} = 3.169$. The confidence interval is:

$$\beta_1 \pm t_{.005}\, s_{\hat{\beta}_1} \Rightarrow 17.754 \pm 3.169\,(5.2467) \Rightarrow 17.754 \pm 16.627 \Rightarrow (1.127, 34.381)$$

We are 99% confident that for each additional year of age, the mean number of employees will increase by anywhere from 1.127 to 34.381.

10.43   From Exercise 10.19,

$$SS_{xx} = 4,362,209,330 \qquad \hat{\beta}_1 = -.002186456$$
$$SS_{xy} = -9,537,780$$

$$\sum y_i = 7497 \qquad \sum y_i^2 = 4,061,063$$

$$SS_{yy} = \sum y_i^2 - \frac{\left(\sum y_i\right)^2}{n} = 4,061,063 - \frac{7497^2}{15} = 314062.4$$

$$SSE = SS_{yy} - \hat{\beta}_1 SS_{xy} = 314062.4 - (-.002186456)(-9,537,780) = 293208.4637$$

$$s^2 = \frac{SSE}{n-2} = \frac{293208.4637}{15-2} = 22554.49721 \quad s = \sqrt{22554.49721} = 150.1815$$

To determine if extent of retaliation is related to whistle blower's power, we test:

$$H_0: \beta_1 = 0$$
$$H_a: \beta_1 \neq 0$$

The test statistic is $t = \dfrac{\hat{\beta}_1 - 0}{s_{\hat{\beta}_1}} = \dfrac{-.0022}{\dfrac{150.1815}{\sqrt{4362209330}}} = -.96$

The rejection region requires $\alpha/2 = .05/2 = .025$ in each tail of the t-distribution with df $= n - 2 = 15 - 2 = 13$. From Table VI, Appendix B, $t_{.025} = 2.160$. The rejection region is $t > 2.160$ or $t < -2.160$.

Since the observed value of the test statistic does not fall in the rejection region ($t = -.96 \not< -2.160$), H_0 is not rejected. There is insufficient evidence to indicate the extent of retaliation is related to the whistle blower's power at $\alpha = .05$. This agrees with Near and Miceli.

10.45 a. If $r = .7$, there is a positive relationship between x and y. As x increases, y tends to increase. The slope is positive.

b. If $r = -.7$, there is a negative relationship between x and y. As x increases, y tends to decrease. The slope is negative.

c. If $r = 0$, there is a 0 slope. There is no relationship between x and y.

d. If $r^2 = .64$, then r is either $.8$ or $-.8$. The relationship between x and y could be either positive or negative.

10.47 a. From Exercises 10.10 and 10.25,

$$r^2 = 1 - \frac{SSE}{SS_{yy}} = 1 - \frac{1.22033896}{21.7142857} = 1 - .0562 = .9438$$

94.38% of the total sample variability around $\overline{y}$ is explained by the linear relationship between y and x.

b. From Exercises 10.13 and 10.25,

$$r^2 = 1 - \frac{SSE}{SS_{yy}} = 1 - \frac{5.71341466}{28.8571429} = .8020$$

80.20% of the total sample variability around $\overline{y}$ is explained by the linear relationship between y and x.

10.49 a. $r = .14$. Because this value is close to 0, there is a very weak positive linear relationship between math confidence and computer interest for boys.

b. $r = .33$. Because this value is fairly close to 0, there is a weak positive linear relationship between math confidence and computer interest for girls.

10.51 a. Using MINITAB, the scattergram is:

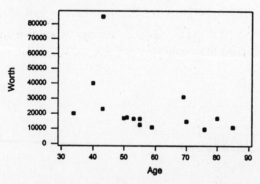

It appears from this scattergram that the relationship between net worth and age is a negative relationship. This relationship could be either linear or possibly quadratic. If any relationship exists, it is very weak.

b. $\sum x = 863$ $\sum y = 343,300$ $\sum xy = 18,039,900$ $\sum x^2 = 52,957$

$\sum y^2 = 12,876,790,000$

$$SS_{xy} = \sum xy - \frac{(\sum x)(\sum y)}{n} = 18{,}039{,}900 - \frac{863(343{,}300)}{15}$$
$$= 18{,}039{,}900 - 19{,}751{,}193.33 = -1{,}711{,}293.33$$

$$SS_{xx} = \sum x^2 - \frac{(\sum x)^2}{n} = 52{,}957 - \frac{863^2}{15}$$
$$= 52{,}957 - 49{,}651.26667 = 3{,}305.73333$$

$$SS_{yy} = \sum y^2 - \frac{(\sum y)^2}{n} = 12{,}876{,}790{,}000 - \frac{343{,}300^2}{15}$$
$$= 12{,}876{,}790{,}000 - 7{,}856{,}992{,}667 = 5{,}019{,}797{,}333$$

$$r = \frac{SS_{xy}}{\sqrt{SS_{xx}SS_{yy}}} = \frac{-1{,}711{,}293.33}{\sqrt{3{,}305.73333(5{,}019{,}797{,}333)}} = -.420$$

This correlation coefficient indicates that there is a moderately weak negative linear relationship between age and net worth.

c.   The only change would be that the relationship would be a moderately weak positive linear relationship.

d.   The coefficient of determination is: $r^2 = (-.420)^2 = .1764$. About 17.6% of the sample variation in net worth can be explained by the linear relationship between age and net worth.

10.53   From the printout, $r^2 = $ R-SQUARED $ = 0.2935$.

29.4% of the sample variability around the sample mean S&P 500 stock composite average is explained by the linear relationship between the interest rate and the S&P 500 stock composite average.

From the printout, $r = -.5418$

The relationship between interest rate and S&P stock composite average is negative since $r < 0$. The relationship is not particularly strong because $-.5418$ is not that close to -1.

10.55   a.   Using MINITAB, the scattergram is:

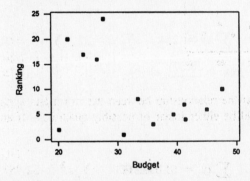

From the scattergram, there appears to be a relatively weak negative linear relationship between rankings and athletic department budget.

b. $\sum x = 435$ $\sum y = 123$ $\sum xy = 3{,}773.2$ $\sum x^2 = 15{,}547.3$

$\sum y^2 = 1{,}825$

$$SS_{xy} = \sum xy - \frac{(\sum x)(\sum y)}{n} = 3{,}773.2 - \frac{435(123)}{13}$$
$$= 3{,}773.2 - 4{,}115.769231 = -342.569231$$

$$SS_{xx} = \sum x^2 - \frac{(\sum x)^2}{n} = 15{,}547.3 - \frac{435^2}{13}$$
$$= 15{,}547.3 - 14{,}555.76923 = 991.53077$$

$$SS_{yy} = \sum y^2 - \frac{(\sum y)^2}{n} = 1{,}825 - \frac{123^2}{13}$$
$$= 1{,}825 - 1{,}163.769231 = 661.230769$$

$$r = \frac{SS_{xy}}{\sqrt{SS_{xx}SS_{yy}}} = \frac{-342.569231}{\sqrt{991.53077(661.230769)}} = -.423$$

This correlation coefficient indicates that there is a moderately weak negative linear relationship between AP rankings and athletic department budget.

10.57   a.

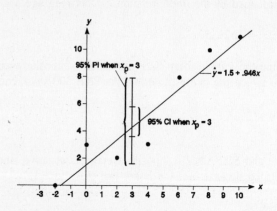

b.   Some preliminary calculations are:

$$\sum x = 28 \quad\quad \sum x^2 = 224 \quad \sum xy = 254 \quad \sum y = 37 \quad \sum y^2 = 307$$

$$SS_{xy} = \sum xy - \frac{\sum x \sum y}{n} = 254 - \frac{28(37)}{7} = 106$$

$$SS_{xx} = \sum x^2 - \frac{(\sum x)^2}{n} = 224 - \frac{28^2}{7} = 112$$

$$SS_{yy} = \sum y^2 - \frac{(\sum y)^2}{n} = 307 - \frac{37^2}{7} = 111.4285714$$

$$\hat{\beta}_1 = \frac{SS_{xy}}{SS_{xx}} = \frac{106}{112} = .946428571$$

$$\hat{\beta}_0 = \bar{y} - \hat{\beta}_1 \bar{x} = \frac{37}{7} - .946428571\left[\frac{28}{7}\right] = 1.5$$

The least squares line is $\hat{y} = 1.5 + .946x$.

c. $SSE = SS_{yy} - \hat{\beta}_1 SS_{xy} = 111.4285714 - (.946428571)(106) = 11.1071429$

$$s^2 = \frac{SSE}{n-2} = \frac{11.1071429}{7-2} = 2.22143$$

d.   The form of the confidence interval is:

$$\hat{y} \pm t_{\alpha/2}s\sqrt{\frac{1}{n} + \frac{(x_p - \bar{x})^2}{SS_{xx}}} \text{ where } s = \sqrt{s^2} = \sqrt{2.22143} = 1.4904$$

For $x_p = 3$, $\hat{y} = 1.5 + .946(3) = 4.338$ and $\bar{x} = \frac{28}{7} = 4$

For confidence coefficient .90, $\alpha = 1 - .90 = .10$ and $\alpha/2 = .10/2 = .05$. From Table VI, Appendix B, $t_{.05} = 2.015$ with df $= n - 2 = 7 - 2 = 5$.

The 90% confidence interval is:

$$4.338 \pm 2.015(1.4904)\sqrt{\frac{1}{7} + \frac{(3-4)^2}{112}} \Rightarrow 4.338 \pm 1.170 \Rightarrow (3.168, 5.508)$$

e.   The form of the prediction interval is:

$$\hat{y} \pm t_{\alpha/2}s\sqrt{1 + \frac{1}{n} + \frac{(x_p - \bar{x})^2}{SS_{xx}}}$$

The 90% prediction interval is:

$$4.338 \pm 2.015(1.4904)\sqrt{1 + \frac{1}{7} + \frac{(3-4)^2}{112}} \Rightarrow 4.338 \pm 3.223 \Rightarrow (1.115, 7.561)$$

f.   The 95% prediction interval for y is wider than the 95% confidence interval for the mean value of y when $x_p = 3$.

The error of predicting a particular value of y will be larger than the error of estimating the mean value of y for a particular x value. This is true since the error in estimating the mean value of y for a given x value is the distance between the least squares line and the true line of means, while the error in predicting some future value of y is the sum of two errors—the error of estimating the mean of y plus the random error that is a component of the value of y to be predicted.

10.59 a.   The form of the confidence interval is:

$$\bar{y} \pm t_{\alpha/2}\frac{s}{\sqrt{n}} \quad \text{where } \bar{y} = \frac{\sum y}{n} = \frac{22}{10} = 2.2$$

$$s^2 = \frac{\sum y^2 - \frac{(\sum y)^2}{n}}{n-1} = \frac{82 - \frac{(22)^2}{10}}{10-1} = 3.7333 \text{ and } s = 1.9322$$

For confidence coefficient .95, $\alpha = 1 - .95 = .05$ and $\alpha/2 = .05/2 = .025$. From Table VI, Appendix B, $t_{.025} = 2.262$ with df $= n - 1 = 10 - 1 = 9$. The 95% confidence interval is:

$$2.2 \pm 2.262\frac{1.9322}{\sqrt{10}} \Rightarrow 2.2 \pm 1.382 \Rightarrow (.818, 3.582)$$

b.

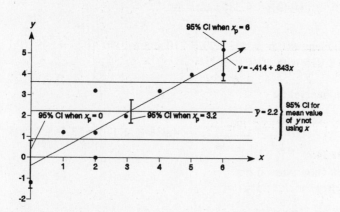

c.   The confidence intervals computed in Exercise 10.58 are much narrower than that found in part **a**. Thus, x appears to contribute information about the mean value of y.

d.   From Exercise 10.58, $\hat{\beta}_1 = .843$, $s = .8619$, SS$_{xx} = 38.9$, and $n = 10$.

H_0: $\beta_1 = 0$
H_a: $\beta_1 \neq 0$

The test statistic is $t = \dfrac{\hat{\beta}_1 - 0}{s_{\hat{\beta}_1}} = \dfrac{\hat{\beta}_1 - 0}{\dfrac{s}{\sqrt{\text{SS}_{xx}}}} = \dfrac{.843 - 0}{\dfrac{.8619}{\sqrt{38.9}}} = 6.10$

The rejection region requires $\alpha/2 = .05/2 = .025$ in each tail of the t-distribution with df $= n - 2 = 10 - 2 = 8$. From Table VI, Appendix B, $t_{.025} = 2.306$. The rejection region is $t > 2.306$ or $t < -2.306$.

Since the observed value of the test statistic falls in the rejection region ($t = 6.10 > 2.306$), H_0 is rejected. There is sufficient evidence to indicate the straight-line model contributes information for the prediction of y at $\alpha = .05$.

10.61 a. Using MINITAB, the scattergram is:

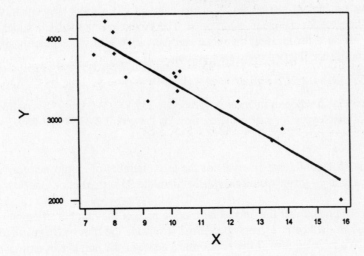

Regression Plot

Y = 5566.13 - 210.346X
R-Sq = 84.4 %

b. From the printout, the least squares line is:

$$\hat{y} = 5566.13 - 210.346x$$

See the plot in part a.

c. To determine if mortgage interest rates contribute information for the prediction of annual sales of existing single-family homes, we test:

H_0: $\beta_1 = 0$

H_a: $\beta_1 \neq 0$

The test statistic is $t = -8.69$ (from printout)

The p-value is $p = 0.0000$. Since the p-value is less than α ($p = 0.0000 < .05$), H_0 is rejected. There is sufficient evidence to indicate the mortgage interest rates contribute information for the prediction of annual sales of existing single-family homes at $\alpha = .05$.

d. From the printout, $r^2 = .8437$.

84.37% of the sample variability of the annual sales of existing single-family homes about their means is explained by the linear relationship between interest rates and annual sales of existing single-family homes.

e. From the printout, the confidence interval is: (3714.7, 4052.0)

We are 95% confident that the mean number of existing single-family homes sold when the average annual mortgage rate is 8% is between 3714.7 and 4052.0.

f. From the printout, the prediction interval is: (3364.1, 4402.7)

    We are 95% confident that the actual number of existing single-family homes sold when the average annual mortgage rate is 8% is between 3364.1 and 4402.7.

g. The width of the prediction interval for an actual value of y is always larger than the width of the confidence interval for the mean value of y. The prediction interval takes into account two variances - the variance for locating the mean and the variance of y once the mean has been located. The confidence interval takes into account only one variance – the variance in locating the mean.

10.63 a. For $x = 10$, the 95% prediction interval is (12.6384, 239.7). We are 95% confident that the actual number of employees for fast-growing firms is between 12.6384 and 239.7 when the age is 10 years.

b. The width of the 95% confidence interval for the mean number of employees for fast-growing firms when the age is 10 years would be smaller than the 95% prediction interval.

c. We would not recommend that this model be used to predict the number of employees for fast-growing firms when the age is 2 years, because 2 is outside the observed ages (ages ranged from 4 to 14). We have no idea if the relationship between the number of employees and age is the same outside the observed range.

10.65 a. To determine if the average hourly wage rate contributes information to predict quit rates, we test:

$$H_0: \beta_1 = 0$$
$$H_a: \beta_1 \neq 0$$

The test statistic is $t = \dfrac{\hat{\beta}_1 - 0}{s_{\hat{\beta}_1}} = -5.91$ (from printout).

The rejection region requires $\alpha/2 = .05/2 = .025$ in each tail of the t-distribution with df $= n - 2 = 15 - 2 = 13$. From Table VI, Appendix B, $t_{.025} = 2.160$. The rejection region is $t < -2.160$ or $t > 2.160$.

Since the observed value of the test statistic falls in the rejection region ($t = -5.91 < -2.160$), H_0 is rejected. There is sufficient evidence to indicate that the average hourly wage rate contributes information to predict quit ratio at $\alpha = .05$.

Since the slope is negative ($\hat{\beta}_1 = -.3466$), the model suggests that x and y have a negative relationship. As the average hourly wage rate increases, the quit rate tends to decrease.

b. From the printout, the 95% prediction interval is (.656, 2.829). We are 95% confident that the quit rate in an industry with an average hourly wage of $9.00 is between .656 and 2.829.

c. From the printout, the 95% confidence interval is (1.467, 2.018). We are 95% confident that the mean quit rate of all industries with an average hourly wage of $9.00 is between 1.467 and 2.018.

10.67 a. $\hat{\beta}_1 = \dfrac{SS_{xy}}{SS_{xx}} = \dfrac{-88}{55} = -1.6$, $\hat{\beta}_0 = \bar{y} - \hat{\beta}_1 \bar{x} = 35 - (-1.6)(1.3) = 37.08$

The least squares line is $\hat{y} = 37.08 - 1.6x$.

b.

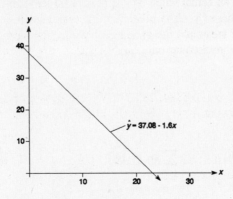

c. $SSE = SS_{yy} - \hat{\beta}_1 SS_{xy} = 198 - (-1.6)(-88) = 57.2$

d. $s^2 = \dfrac{SSE}{n-2} = \dfrac{57.2}{15-2} = 4.4$

e. For confidence coefficient .90, $\alpha = 1 - .90 = .10$ and $\alpha/2 = .10/2 = .05$. From Table VI, Appendix B, with df $= n - 2 = 15 - 2 = 13$, $t_{.05} = 1.771$. The 90% confidence interval for β_1 is:

$$\hat{\beta}_1 \pm t_{\alpha/2} \dfrac{s}{\sqrt{SS_{xx}}} \Rightarrow -1.6 \pm 1.771 \dfrac{\sqrt{4.4}}{\sqrt{55}} \Rightarrow -1.6 \pm .501 \Rightarrow (-2.101, -1.099)$$

We are 90% confident the change in the mean value of y for each unit change in x is between -2.101 and -1.099.

f. For $x_p = 15$, $\hat{y} = 37.08 - 1.6(15) = 13.08$

The 90% confidence interval is:

$$\hat{y} \pm t_{\alpha/2} s \sqrt{\dfrac{1}{n} + \dfrac{(x_p - \bar{x})^2}{SS_{xx}}} \Rightarrow 13.08 \pm 1.771(\sqrt{4.4}) \sqrt{\dfrac{1}{15} + \dfrac{(15 - 1.3)^2}{55}}$$

$$\Rightarrow 13.08 \pm 6.929 \Rightarrow (6.151, 20.009)$$

g. The 90% prediction interval is:

$$\hat{y} \pm t_{\alpha/2} s \sqrt{1 + \dfrac{1}{n} + \dfrac{(x_p - \bar{x})^2}{SS_{xx}}} \Rightarrow 13.08 \pm 1.771(\sqrt{4.4}) \sqrt{1 + \dfrac{1}{15} + \dfrac{(15 - 1.3)^2}{55}}$$

$$\Rightarrow 13.08 \pm 7.862 \Rightarrow (5.218, 20.942)$$

10.69   a.

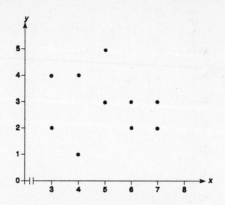

b.   Some preliminary calculations are:

$$\sum x = 50 \qquad \sum x^2 = 270 \qquad \sum xy = 143$$
$$\sum y = 29 \qquad \sum y^2 = 97$$

$$SS_{xy} = \sum xy - \frac{\sum x \sum y}{n} = 143 - \frac{50(29)}{10} = -2$$

$$SS_{xx} = \sum x^2 - \frac{(\sum x)^2}{n} = 270 - \frac{50^2}{10} = 20$$

$$SS_{yy} = \sum y^2 - \frac{(\sum y)^2}{n} = 97 - \frac{29^2}{10} = 12.9$$

$$r = \frac{SS_{xy}}{\sqrt{SS_{xx}SS_{yy}}} = \frac{-2}{\sqrt{20(12.9)}} - .1245$$

$$r^2 = 2(-.1245)^2 = .0155$$

c.   Some preliminary calculations are:

$$\hat{\beta}_1 = \frac{SS_{xy}}{SS_{xx}} = \frac{-2}{20} = -.1$$

$$SSE = SS_{yy} = \hat{\beta}_1 SS_{xy} = 12.9 - (-.1)(-2) = 12.7$$

$$s^2 = \frac{SSE}{n - 2} = \frac{12.7}{10 - 2} = 1.5875 \quad s = \sqrt{1.5875} = 1.25996$$

To determine if x and y are linearly correlated, we test:

H_0: $\beta_1 = 0$
H_a: $\beta_1 \neq 0$

The test statistic is $t = \dfrac{\hat{\beta}_1 - 0}{\dfrac{s}{\sqrt{SS_{xx}}}} = \dfrac{-.1 - 0}{\dfrac{1.25996}{\sqrt{20}}} = -.35$

The rejection requires $\alpha/2 = .10/2 = .05$ in the each tail of the t-distribution with df $= n - 2 = 10 - 2 = 8$. From Table VI, Appendix B, $t_{.05} = 1.86$. The rejection region is $t > 1.86$ or $t < -1.86$.

Since the observed value of the test statistic does not fall in the rejection region ($t = -.35 \not< -1.86$), H_0 is not rejected. There is insufficient evidence to indicate that x and y are linearly correlated at $\alpha = .10$.

10.71   a.   The plot of the data is:

It appears that there is a linear
relationship between order size and time.
As order size increases, the time tends to
increase.

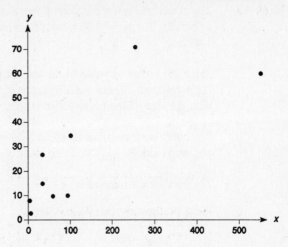

b.   Some preliminary calculations are:

$$\sum x_i = 1149 \qquad \sum x_i^2 = 398,979 \qquad \sum x_i y_i = 58,102$$

$$\sum y_i = 239 \qquad \sum y_i^2 = 11,093$$

$$SS_{xy} = \sum x_i y_i - \frac{\sum x_i \sum y_i}{n} = 58,102 - \frac{1149(239)}{9} = 27,589.66667$$

$$SS_{xx} = \sum x_i^2 - \frac{\left(\sum x_i\right)^2}{n} = 398,979 - \frac{1149^2}{9} = 252,290$$

$$SS_{yy} = \sum y_i^2 - \frac{\left(\sum y_i\right)^2}{n} = 11,093 - \frac{239^2}{9} = 4746.222222$$

$$\hat{\beta}_1 = \frac{SS_{xy}}{SS_{xx}} = \frac{27,589.66667}{252,290} = .109356957 \approx .10936$$

$$\hat{\beta}_0 = \bar{y} - \hat{\beta}_1 \bar{x} = \frac{239}{9} - (.109356957)\frac{1149}{9} = 12.59431738 \approx 12.594$$

$$SSE = SS_{yy} - \hat{\beta}_1 SS_{xy} = 4746.222222 - (.109356957)(27,589.66667)$$
$$= 1729.10023$$

$$s^2 = \frac{SSE}{n-2} = \frac{1729.10023}{9-2} = 247.0143186 \qquad s = \sqrt{s^2} = 15.7167$$

The least squares line is $\hat{y} = 12.594 + .10936x$.

c.   To determine if the mean time to fill an order increases with the size of the order, we test:

H_0: $\beta_1 = 0$
H_a: $\beta_1 > 0$

The test statistic is $t = \dfrac{\hat{\beta}_1 - 0}{s_{\hat{\beta}_1}} = \dfrac{.1094 - 0}{\dfrac{15.7167}{\sqrt{252,290}}} = 3.50$

The rejection region requires $\alpha = .05$ in the upper tail of the t-distribution. From Table VI, Appendix B, $t_{.05} = 1.895$, with df $= n - 2 = 9 - 2 = 7$. The rejection region is $t > 1.895$.

Since the observed value of the test statistic falls in the rejection region ($t = 3.50 > 1.895$), H_0 is rejected. There is sufficient evidence to indicate the mean time to fill an order increases with the size of the order for $\alpha = .05$.

d.   For confidence coefficient .95, $\alpha = 1 - .95 = .05$ and $\alpha/2 = .05/2 = .025$. From Table VI, Appendix B, $t_{.025} = 2.365$ with df $= n - 2 = 9 - 2 = 7$.

The confidence interval is:

$$\hat{y} \pm t_{\alpha/2}s\sqrt{\frac{1}{n} + \frac{(x_p - \bar{x})^2}{SS_{xx}}}$$

For $x_p = 150$, $\hat{y} = 12.594 + .10936(150) = 28.998$, and $\bar{x} = \dfrac{1149}{9} = 127.6667$

$$28.988 \pm 2.365(15.7167)\sqrt{\frac{1}{9} + \frac{(150 - 127.6667)^2}{252,290}} \Rightarrow 28.988 \pm 12.500$$
$$\Rightarrow (16.498, 41.498)$$

10.73   Answers may vary. One possible answer may include:

The least squares line is $\hat{y} = -92.457684 + 8.346821x$. To determine if age can be used to predict market value, we test:

H_0: $\beta_1 = 0$
H_a: $\beta_1 \neq 0$

The test statistic is $t = 3.248$ with p-value $= .0021$. Reject the null hypothesis for levels of significance $\alpha > .0021$. There is sufficient evidence to indicate that age contributes information for the prediction of market value (y) at $\alpha > .0021$.

$r = .42$; Since this value is near .5, there is a moderate positive linear relationship between the value and age of the Beanie Baby.

10.75   a. $\sum x = 55$ $\qquad$ $\sum x^2 = 899$ $\qquad$ $\sum xy = 154.89$
$\sum y = 14.49$ $\qquad$ $\sum y^2 = 42.0817$

$SS_{xy} = \sum xy - \dfrac{\sum x \sum y}{n} = 154.89 - \dfrac{55(14.49)}{5} = -4.55$

$SS_{xx} = \sum x^2 - \dfrac{(\sum x)^2}{n} = 899 - \dfrac{55^2}{5} = 294$

$SS_{yy} = \sum y^2 - \dfrac{(\sum y)^2}{n} = 42.0817 - \dfrac{14.49^2}{5} = .08968$

$\hat{\beta}_1 = \dfrac{SS_{xy}}{SS_{xx}} = \dfrac{-4.55}{294} = -.01547619 \approx -.015$

$\hat{\beta}_0 = \bar{y} - \hat{\beta}_1\bar{x} = 2.898 - (-.01547619)(11) = 3.068238095 \approx 3.068$

The least squares line is $\hat{y} = 3.068 - .015x$.

b. The graph of the data is:

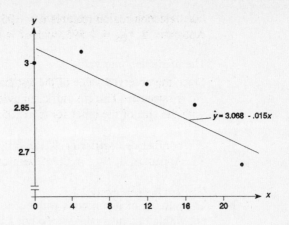

c. $SSE = SS_{yy} - \hat{\beta}_1 SS_{xy} = .08968 - (-.01547619)(-4.55) = .019263335$

$$s^2 = \frac{SSE}{n-2} = \frac{.019263335}{5-2} = .0064211 \qquad s = \sqrt{.0064211} = .0801$$

To determine whether the model is useful for predicting grade point average, we test:

$H_0: \ \beta_1 = 0$
$H_a: \ \beta_1 \neq 0$

The test statistic is $t = \dfrac{\hat{\beta}_1 - 0}{s_{\hat{\beta}_1}} = \dfrac{-.0155 - 0}{\dfrac{.0801}{\sqrt{294}}} = -3.32$

The rejection region requires $\alpha/2 = .10/2 = .05$ in each tail of the t-distribution. From Table VI, Appendix B, with df $= n - 2 = 5 - 2 = 3$, $t_{.05} = 2.353$. The rejection region is $t < -2.353$ or $t > 2.353$.

Since the observed value of the test statistic falls in the rejection region ($t = -3.32 < -2.353$), H_0 is rejected. There is sufficient evidence to indicate the model is useful for predicting grade point average at $\alpha = .10$.

d. For $x = 10$, $\hat{y} = 3.068 - .0155(10) = 2.913$.

For confidence coefficient .90, $\alpha = .10$ and $\alpha/2 = .10/2 = .05$. From Table VI, Appendix B, with df $= n - 2 = 5 - 2 = 3$, $t_{.05} = 2.353$. The 90% prediction interval is:

$$\hat{y} \pm t_{\alpha/2} s \sqrt{1 + \frac{1}{n} + \frac{(x_p - \bar{x})^2}{SS_{xx}}} \Rightarrow 2.913 \pm 2.353(.0801)\sqrt{1 + \frac{1}{5} + \frac{(10-11)^2}{294}}$$

$$\Rightarrow 2.913 \pm .207 \Rightarrow (2.706, 3.120)$$

We are 90% confident that the actual grade point average of a high school student who works 10 hours per week is between 2.706 and 3.120.

10.77 a. For confidence coefficient .90, $\alpha = 1 - .90 = .10$ and $\alpha/2 = .10/2 = .05$. From Table VI, Appendix B, $t_{.05} = 1.740$ with df $= n - 2 = 19 - 2 = 17$.

The prediction interval is:

$$\hat{y} \pm t_{\alpha/2}s\sqrt{1 + \frac{1}{n} + \frac{(x_p - \bar{x})^2}{SS_{xx}}} \quad \text{where } \hat{y} = 44.13 + .2366(55) = 57.143$$

$$\Rightarrow 57.143 \pm 1.74(19.40)\sqrt{1 + \frac{1}{19} + \frac{(55 - 44.1579)^2}{10,824.5263}} \Rightarrow 57.143 \pm 34.818$$

$$\Rightarrow (22.325, 91.961)$$

b. The number of interactions with outsiders in the study went from 10 to 82. The value 110 is not within this interval. We do not know if the relationship between x and y is the same outside the observed range. Also, the farther x_p lies from $\bar{x}$ the larger will be the error of prediction. The prediction interval for a particular value of y will be very wide when $x_p = 110$.

c. The prediction interval for a manager's success index will be narrowest when the number of contacts with people outside her work unit is $\bar{x} = 44.1579$ (44).

10.79 Some preliminary calculations are:

$$\sum x = 4305 \qquad \sum x^2 = 1,652,025 \qquad \sum xy = 76,652,695$$
$$\sum y = 201,558 \qquad \sum y^2 = 3,571,211,200$$

a. $$\hat{\beta}_1 = \frac{\sum xy}{\sum x^2} = \frac{76,652,695}{1,652,025} = 46.39923427 \approx 46.3992$$

The least squares line is $\hat{y} = 46.3992x$.

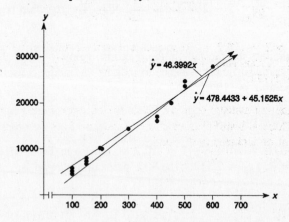

b. $SS_{xy} = \sum xy - \dfrac{\sum x \sum y}{n} = 76,652,695 - \dfrac{4305(201,558)}{15} = 18,805,549$

$SS_{xx} = \sum x^2 - \dfrac{(\sum x)^2}{n} = 1,652,025 - \dfrac{4305^2}{15} = 416,490$

$\hat{\beta}_1 = \dfrac{SS_{xy}}{SS_{xx}} = \dfrac{18,805,549}{416,490} = 45.15246224 \approx 45.1525$

$\hat{\beta}_0 = \bar{y} - \hat{\beta}_1 \bar{x} = \dfrac{201,558}{15} - 45.15246224 \left(\dfrac{4305}{15} \right) = 478.4433$

The least squares line is $\hat{y} = 478.4433 + 45.1525x$.

c. Because $x = 0$ is not in the observed range, we are trying to represent the data on the observed interval with the best fitting line. We are not concerned with whether the line goes through $(0, 0)$ or not.

d. Some preliminary calculations are:

$$SS_{yy} = \sum y^2 - \dfrac{(\sum y)^2}{n} = 3,571,211,200 - \dfrac{201,558^2}{15} = 862,836,042$$

$$SSE = SS_{yy} - \hat{\beta}_1 SS_{xy} = 862,836,042 - 45.15246224(18,805,549) = 13,719,200.88$$

$$s^2 = \dfrac{SSE}{n-2} = \dfrac{13,719,200.88}{15-2} = 1,055,323.145 \qquad s = 1027.2892$$

H_0: $\beta_0 = 0$
H_a: $\beta_0 \neq 0$

The test statistic is $t = \dfrac{\hat{\beta}_0 - 0}{s\sqrt{\dfrac{1}{n} + \dfrac{\bar{x}^2}{SS_{xx}}}} = \dfrac{478.443}{1027.2892\sqrt{\dfrac{1}{15} + \dfrac{287^2}{416,490}}} = .906$

The rejection region requires $\alpha/2 = .10/2 = .05$ in each tail of the t-distribution with df $= n - 2 = 15 - 2 = 13$. From Table VI, Appendix B, $t_{.05} = 1.771$. The rejection region is $t < -1.771$ or $t > 1.771$.

Since the observed value of the test statistic does not fall in the rejection region ($t = .906 \not> 1.771$), H_0 is not rejected. There is insufficient evidence to indicate β_0 is different from 0 at $\alpha = .10$. Thus, β_0 should not be included in the model.

10.81   Using MINITAB, the two regression analyses are:

Regression Analysis

The regression equation is
Ind.Costs = 301 + 10.3 Mach-Hours

Predictor	Coef	StDev	T	P
Constant	301.0	229.8	1.31	0.219
Mach-Hou	10.312	3.124	3.30	0.008

S = 170.5   R-Sq = 52.1%   R-Sq(adj) = 47.4%

Analysis of Variance

Source	DF	SS	MS	F	P
Regression	1	316874	316874	10.90	0.008
Residual Error	10	290824	29082		
Total	11	607698			

Regression Analysis
The regression equation is
Ind.Costs = 745 + 7.72 Direct-Hours

Predictor	Coef	StDev	T	P
Constant	744.7	217.6	3.42	0.007
Direct-H	7.716	5.396	1.43	0.183

S = 224.6   R-Sq = 17.0%   R-Sq(adj) = 8.7%

Analysis of Variance

Source	DF	SS	MS	F	P
Regression	1	103187	103187	2.05	0.183
Residual Error	10	504511	50451		
Total	11	607698			

Unusual Observations

Obs	Direct-H	Ind.Cost	Fit	StDev Fit	Residual	St Resid
9	70.0	1316.0	1284.8	181.9	31.2	0.24 X

X denotes an observation whose X value gives it large influence.

From these two cost functions, the model containing Machine-Hours should be used to predict Indirect Manufacturing Labor Costs. There is a significant linear relationship between Indirect Manufacturing Labor Costs and Machine-Hours $(t = 3.30, p = 0.008)$. There is not a significant linear relationship between Indirect Manufacturing Labor Costs and Direct Manufacturing Labor-Hours $(t = 1.43, p = 0.183)$. The r^2 for the first model is .521 while the r^2 for the second model is .170. In addition, the standard deviation for the first model is 170.5 while the standard deviation for the second model is 224.6. All of these lead to the better model as the model containing Machine-Hours as the independent variable.

Multiple Regression and Model Building

Chapter 11

11.1   a. $E(y) = \beta_0 + \beta_1 x_1 + \beta_2 x_2$

      b. $E(y) = \beta_0 + \beta_1 x_1 + \beta_2 x_2 + \beta_3 x_3 + \beta_4 x_4$

      c. $E(y) = \beta_0 + \beta_1 x_1 + \beta_2 x_2 + \beta_3 x_3 + \beta_4 x_4 + \beta_5 x_5$

11.3   a.   We are given $\hat{\beta}_2 = 2.7$, $s_{\hat{\beta}_2} = 1.86$, and $n = 30$.

$$H_0: \beta_2 = 0$$
$$H_a: \beta_2 \neq 0$$

The test statistic is $t = \dfrac{\hat{\beta}_2 - 0}{s_{\hat{\beta}_2}} = \dfrac{2.7}{1.86} = 1.45$

The rejection region requires $\alpha/2 = .05/2 = .025$ in each tail of the t distribution with df $= n - (k + 1) = 30 - (3 + 1) = 26$. From Table VI, Appendix B, $t_{.025} = 2.056$. The rejection region is $t < -2.056$ or $t > 2.056$.

Since the observed value of the test statistic does not fall in the rejection region ($t = 1.45 \not> 2.056$), H_0 is not rejected. There is insufficient evidence to indicate $\beta_2 \neq 0$ at $\alpha = .05$.

      b.   We are given $\beta_3 = .93$, $s_{\beta_3} = .29$, and $n = 30$.

Test $H_0: \beta_3 = 0$
              $H_a: \beta_3 \neq 0$

The test statistic is $t = \dfrac{\hat{\beta}_3 - 0}{s_{\beta_3}} = \dfrac{.93}{.29} = 3.21$

The rejection region is the same as part **a**, $t < -2.056$ or $t > 2.056$.

Since the observed value of the test statistic falls in the rejection region ($t = 3.21 > 2.056$), H_0 is rejected. There is sufficient evidence to indicate $\beta_3 \neq 0$ at $\alpha = .05$.

      c. $\hat{\beta}_3$ has a smaller estimated standard error than $\hat{\beta}_2$. Therefore, the test statistic is larger for $\hat{\beta}_3$ even though $\hat{\beta}_3$ is smaller than $\hat{\beta}_2$.

11.5   The number of degrees of freedom available for estimating σ^2 is $n - (k + 1)$ where k is the number of independent variables in the regression model. Each additional independent variable placed in the model causes a corresponding decrease in the degrees of freedom.

11.7 a. The first-order model is: $E(y) = \beta_0 + \beta_1 x_1 + \beta_2 x_2$

From the printout, the least squares prediction equation is:

$$\hat{y} = -20.352 + 13.3504\, x_1 + 243.714\, x_2$$

$\hat{\beta}_0 = -20.352$. This has no meaning since $x_1 = 0$ and $x_2 = 0$ are not in the observed range.

$\hat{\beta}_1 = 13.3504$. For each additional year of age, the mean annual earnings is predicted to increase by \$13.3504, holding hours worked per day constant.

$\hat{\beta}_2 = 243.714$. For each additional hour worked per day, the mean annual earnings is predicted to increase by \$243.714, holding age constant.

To determine if age is a useful predictor of annual earnings, we test:

$$H_0: \beta_1 = 0$$
$$H_a: \beta_1 \neq 0$$

The test statistic is $t = 1.74$.

The p-value is $p = .1074$. Since the p-value is greater than $\alpha = .01$ $(p = .1074 > \alpha = .01)$, H_0 is not rejected. There is insufficient evidence to indicate that age is a useful predictor of annual earnings, adjusted for hours worked per day, at $\alpha = .01$.

e. For confidence coefficient .99, $\alpha = .01$ and $\alpha/2 = .01/2 = .005$. From Table VI, Appendix B, with df $= n - 3 = 15 - 3 = 12$, $t = 3.055$. The 99% confidence interval is:

$$\hat{\beta}_2 \pm t_{.005} s_{\hat{\beta}_2} \Rightarrow 243.714 \pm 3.055(63.5117) \Rightarrow 243.714 \pm 194.028 \Rightarrow (49.686, 437.742)$$

We are 99% confident that the change in the mean annual earnings for each additional hour worked per day will be somewhere between \$49.686 and \$437.742, holding age constant.

11.9 a. Using MINITAB, the output is:

Regression Analysis

```
The regression equation is
y = 20.9 + 0.261 x1 - 7.8 x2 + 0.0042 x3

Predictor       Coef        StDev           T          P
Constant       20.88        24.16        0.86      0.395
x1            0.2614       0.2394        1.09      0.284
x2             -7.85        13.28       -0.59      0.560
x3           0.00415      0.01042        0.40      0.693

S = 14.01       R-Sq = 9.7%      R-Sq(adj) = 0.0%

Analysis of Variance

Source            DF           SS          MS         F        P
Regression         3        566.5       188.8      0.96    0.425
Residual Error    27       5302.3       196.4
Total             30       5868.8

Source         DF     Seq SS
x1              1      372.3
x2              1      162.9
x3              1       31.2
```

The least squares prediction equation is:

$$\hat{y} = 20.9 + 0.261x_1 - 7.8x_2 + .0042x_3.$$

b. From the printout, the standard deviation is $s = 14.01$. Most of the observed values of the price of Ford stock will fall within $\pm 2s$ or $\pm 2(14.01)$ or ± 28.02 units of their predicted values.

c. To determine if the price of Ford stock decreases as the yen rate increases, we test:

H_0: $\beta_1 = 0$
H_a: $\beta_1 < 0$

The test statistic is $t = 1.09$.

The p-value for the test is $p = 1 - .284/2 = 1 - .142 = .858$. Since the p-value is greater than $\alpha = .05$ ($p = .858 > \alpha = .05$), H_0 is not rejected. There is insufficient evidence to indicate that the price of Ford stock decreases as the yen rate increases holding the Deutsche Mark exchange rate and the S & P 500 Index constant at $\alpha = .05$.

d. $\hat{\beta}_2 = -7.8$. The mean price of Ford stock is estimated to decrease by 7.8 for each unit increase in Deutsche mark exchange rate, holding the yen exchange rate and the S & P 500 Index constant.

11.11 a. $\hat{y} = 12.2 - .0265x_1 - .458x_2$

b. $\hat{\beta}_0 = 12.2 =$ the estimate of the y-intercept

$\hat{\beta}_1 = -.0265$. We estimate that the mean weight change will decrease by .0265% for each additional increase of 1% in digestion efficiency, with acid-detergent fibre held constant.

$\hat{\beta}_2 = -.458$. We estimate that the mean weight change will decrease by .458% for each additional increase of 1% in acid-detergent fibre, with digestion efficiency held constant.

c. To determine if digestion efficiency is a useful predictor of weight change, we test:

H_0: $\beta_1 = 0$
H_a: $\beta_1 \neq 0$

The test statistic is $t = -.50$. The p-value is $p = .623$. Since the p-value is greater than α ($p = .623 > .01$), H_0 is not rejected. There is insufficient evidence to indicate that digestion efficiency is a useful linear predictor of weight change at $\alpha = .01$.

d. For confidence coefficient .99, $\alpha = 1 - .99 = .01$ and $\alpha/2 = .01/2 = .005$. From Table VI, Appendix B, with df $= n - (k + 1) = 42 - (2 + 1) = 39$, $t_{.005} \approx 2.704$. The 99% confidence interval is:

$$\hat{\beta}_2 \pm t_{.005}\, s_{\hat{\beta}_2} \Rightarrow -.4578 \pm 2.704\,(.1283) \Rightarrow -.4578 \pm .3469 \Rightarrow (-.8047, -.1109)$$

We are 99% confident that the change in mean weight change for each unit change in acid-detergent fiber, holding digestion efficiency constant is between $-.8047\%$ and $-.1109\%$.

11.13 $\hat{\beta}_0 = 39.05 =$ the estimate of the y-intercept

$\hat{\beta}_1 = -5.41$. We estimate that the mean operating margin will decrease by 5.41% for each additional increase of 1 unit of x_1, the state population divided by the total number of inns in the state (with all other variables held constant).

$\hat{\beta}_2 = 5.86$. We estimate that the mean operating margin will increase by 5.86% for each additional increase of 1 unit of x_2, the room rate (with all other variables held constant).

$\hat{\beta}_3 = -3.09$. We estimate that the mean operating margin will decrease by 3.09% for each additional increase of 1 unit of x_3, the square root of the median income of the area (with all other variables held constant).

$\hat{\beta}_4 = 1.75$. We estimate that the mean operating margin will increase by 1.75% for each additional increase of 1 unit of x_4, the number of college students within four miles of the inn (with all other variables held constant).

11.15 a. The SAS printout for the model is:

DEPENDENT VARIABLE: Y

SOURCE	DF	SUM OF SQUARES	MEAN SQUARE	F VALUE
MODEL	5	1052894700508.240	210578940101.648	190.75
ERROR	19	20975246806.001	1103960358.211	PR > F
CORRECTED TOTAL	24	1073869947314.240		0.0001

R-SQUARE	C.V.	ROOT MSE	Y MEAN
0.980468	11.4346	33225.899	290573.52000000

PARAMETER	ESTIMATE	T FOR HO: PARAMETER=0	PR > |T|	STD ERROR OF ESTIMATE
INTERCEPT	93073.85223495	3.24	0.0043	28720.89686205
X1	4152.20700875	2.78	0.0118	1491.62587008
X2	-854.94161450	-2.86	0.0099	298.44765134
X3	0.92424393	0.32	0.7515	2.87673442
X4	2692.46175182	1.71	0.1041	1577.28622584
X5	15.54276851	10.62	0.0001	1.46287006

The least squares prediction equation is:

$$\hat{y} = 93{,}074 + 4152x_1 - 855x_2 + .924x_3 + 2692x_4 + 15.5x_5$$

b. $s =$ ROOT MSE $= 33{,}225.9$. We would expect about 95% of the observations to fall within $\pm 2s$ or $\pm 2(33{,}225.9)$ or $\pm 66{,}452$ units of the regression line.

c. To determine if the value increases with the number of units, we test:

$H_0:\ \beta_1 = 0$
$H_a:\ \beta_1 > 0$

The test statistic is $t = \dfrac{\hat{\beta}_1 - 0}{s_{\hat{\beta}_1}} = \dfrac{4152 - 0}{1491.626} = 2.78$

The observed significance level or p-value is $.0118/2 = .0059$. Since this value is less than $\alpha = .05$, H_0 is rejected. There is sufficient evidence to indicate that the value increases as the number of units increases at $\alpha = .05$.

d. $\hat{\beta}_1$:   We estimate the mean value will increase by \$4,152 for each additional apartment unit, all other variables held constant.

e.   Using SAS, the plot is:

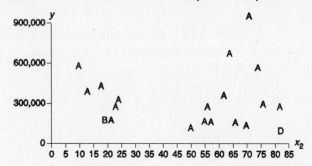

PLOT IF Y*X2   LEGEND: A = 1 OBS, B = 2 OBS, ETC.

It appears from the graph that there is not much of a linear relationship between value (y) and age (x_2).

f. H_0: $\beta_2 = 0$
      H_a: $\beta_2 < 0$

The test statistic is $t = \dfrac{\hat{\beta}_2 - 0}{s_{\hat{\beta}_2}} = \dfrac{-855 - 0}{298.447} = -2.86$

The observed significance level or p-value is $.0099/2 = .00495$. Since this value is less than $\alpha = .01$, H_0 is rejected. There is sufficient evidence to indicate that the value and age are negatively related, all other variables in the model held constant, at $\alpha = .01$.

A one-tailed test is reasonable because the older the building, the lower the sales price (market value), at least for certain values of age.

g.   The p-value is $.0099/2 = .00495$ (because we had a one-tailed test).

11.17 a. $R^2 = .8911$

89.11% of the total sample variability of y is explained by the linear relationship between y and the two independent variables x_1 and x_2.

b. $R_a^2 = .8775$

87.75% of the total sample variability of y is explained by the linear relationship between y and the two independent variables x_1 and x_2, adjusting for the sample size and the number of independent variables.

c. H_0: $\beta_1 = \beta_2 = 0$
      H_a: At least one $\beta_i \neq 0$, for $i = 1, 2$

The test statistic is $F = \dfrac{R^2/k}{(1 - R^2)/[n - (k + 1)]} = \dfrac{.8911/2}{(1 - .8911)/[19 - (2 + 1)]} = 65.462$

The rejection region requires $\alpha = .05$ in the upper tail of the F distribution with df $= \nu_1 = k = 2$ and $\nu_2 = n - (k + 1) = 19 - (2 + 1) = 16$. From Table IX, Appendix B, $F_{.05} = 3.63$. The rejection region is $F > 3.63$.

Since the observed value of the test statistic falls in the rejection region ($F = 65.462 > 3.63$), H_0 is rejected. There is sufficient evidence to indicate the model is useful in predicting y at $\alpha = .05$.

The test statistic can also be calculated by $\dfrac{MS(Model)}{MS(Error)} = \dfrac{12.11167}{0.18497} = 65.479$

From the printout, $F = 65.478$.

d. Prob $> F = p$-value $\leq .0001$

The probability of observing a test statistic of 65.478 or anything higher is less than .0001. This is very unusual if H_0 is true. This is very significant. There is strong evidence to reject H_0 for $\alpha > .0001$.

11.19 a. Some preliminary calculations are:

$SSE = \sum (y_i - \hat{y}_i)^2 = 12.35$, df $= n - (k + 1) = 20 - (2 + 1) = 17$

$SS(Total) = \sum (y - \bar{y})^2 = 24.44$, df $= n - 1 = 20 - 1 = 19$

$SS(Model) = SS(Total) - SSE = 24.44 - 12.35 = 12.09$, df $= k = 2$

$MS(Model) = \dfrac{SS(Model)}{k} = \dfrac{12.09}{2} = 6.045$

$MS(Error) = \dfrac{SSE}{n - (k + 1)} = \dfrac{12.35}{17} = .72647$

$F = \dfrac{MS(Model)}{MS(Error)} = \dfrac{6.045}{.72647} = 8.321$

$R^2 = 1 - \dfrac{SSE}{SS(Total)} = 1 - \dfrac{12.35}{24.44} = .4947$

$R_a^2 = 1 - \left[\dfrac{n - 1}{n - (k + 1)} \right] (1 - R^2)$

$\quad = 1 - \left[\dfrac{20 - 1}{20 - (2 + 1)} \right] (1 - .4947)$

$\quad = .4352$

The test statistic could also be calculated by:

$F = \dfrac{R^2/k}{(1 - R^2)/[n - (k + 1)]} = \dfrac{.4947/2}{(1 - .4947)/17} = 8.32$

The analysis of variance table is:

Source	df	SS	MS	F
Model	2	12.09	6.045	8.321
Error	17	12.35	.72647	
Total	19	24.44		

b. H_0: $\beta_1 = \beta_2 = 0$
H_a: At least one $\beta_i \neq 0$, $i = 1, 2$

The test statistic is $F = \dfrac{MS(Model)}{MS(Error)} = \dfrac{6.045}{.72647} = 8.321$

The rejection region requires $\alpha = .05$ in the upper tail of the F distribution with df = $\nu_1 = k$ = 2 and $\nu_2 = n - (k + 1) = 17$. From Table IX, Appendix B, $F_{.05} = 3.59$. The rejection region is $F > 3.59$.

Since the observed value of the test statistic falls in the rejection region ($F = 8.321 > 3.59$), H_0 is rejected. There is sufficient evidence to indicate the model is useful in predicting y at $\alpha = .05$.

11.21   a.   From the printout, R^2 = R Square = .8168492. This means that 81.68% of the sample variation of the total pay is explained by the linear relationship between total pay and the independent variables company performance and company sales.

b.   To determine if at least one of the variables in the model is useful in predicting total pay, we test:

H_0: $\beta_1 = \beta_2 = 0$
H_a: At least one of the coefficients is nonzero

c.   The test statistic is $F = \dfrac{MS(Model)}{MSE} = 31.22$

The p-value is $p = 6.91292E\text{-}06 = .0000069$.

d.   Since the p-value is less than $\alpha = .05$ ($p = .0000069 < .05$), H_0 is rejected. There is sufficient evidence to indicate the model is useful in predicting total pay at $\alpha = .05$.

11.23   a.   The least squares prediction equation is:

$$\hat{y} = -4.30 - .002x_1 + .336x_2 + .384x_3 + .067x_4 - .143x_5 + .081x_6 + .134x_7$$

b.   To determine if the model is adequate, we test:

H_0: $\beta_1 = \beta_2 = \beta_3 = \beta_4 = \beta_5 = \beta_6 = \beta_7 = 0$
H_a: At least one $\beta_i \neq 0$, $i = 1, 2, 3, ..., 7$

The test statistic is $F = 111.1$ (from table).

Since no α was given, we will use $\alpha = .05$. The rejection region requires $\alpha = .05$ in the upper tail of the F-distribution with $\nu_1 = k = 7$ and $\nu_2 = n - (k + 1) = 268 - (7 + 1) = 260$. From Table IX, Appendix B, $F_{.05} \approx 2.01$. The rejection region is $F > 2.01$.

Since the observed value of the test statistic falls in the rejection region ($F = 111.1 > 2.01$), H_0 is rejected. There is sufficient evidence to indicate that the model is adequate for predicting the logarithm of the audit fees at $\alpha = .05$.

c.　$\hat{\beta}_3 = .384.$　　For each additional subsidiary of the auditee, the mean of the logarithm of audit fee is estimated to increase by .384 units.

d.　To determine if the $\beta_4 > 0$, we test:

$$H_0: \beta_4 = 0$$
$$H_a: \beta_4 > 0$$

The test statistic is $t = 1.76$ (from table).

The p-value for the test is .079. Since the p-value is not less than α ($p = .079 \not< \alpha = .05$), H_0 is not rejected. There is insufficient evidence to indicate that $\beta_4 > 0$, holding all the other variables constant, at $\alpha = .05$.

e.　To determine if the $\beta_1 < 0$, we test:

$$H_0: \beta_1 = 0$$
$$H_a: \beta_1 < 0$$

The test statistic is $t = -0.049$ (from table).

The p-value for the test is .961. Since the p-value is not less than α ($p = .961 \not< \alpha = .05$), H_0 is not rejected. There is insufficient evidence to indicate that $\beta_1 < 0$, holding all the other variables constant, at $\alpha = .05$. There is insufficient evidence to indicate that the new auditors charge less than incumbent auditors.

11.25　a.　$R^2 = .51$. 51% of the variability in the operating margins can be explained by the model containing these four independent variables.

b.　To determine if the model is adequate, we test:

$$H_0: \beta_1 = \beta_2 = \beta_3 = \beta_4 = 0$$
$$H_a: \text{At least one } \beta_i \neq 0, i = 1, 2, 3, 4$$

The test statistic is

$$F = \frac{R^2/k}{(1 - R^2)/[n - (k + 1)]} = \frac{.51/4}{(1 - .51)/[57 - (4 + 1)]} = 13.53$$

The rejection region requires $\alpha = .05$ in the upper tail of the F distribution with $v_1 = k = 4$ and $v_2 = n - (k + 1) = 57 - (4 + 1) = 52$. From Table IX, Appendix B, $F_{.05} \approx 2.61$. The rejection region is $F > 2.61$.

Since the observed value of the test statistic falls in the rejection region ($F = 13.53 > 2.61$), H_0 is rejected. There is sufficient evidence that the model is useful in predicting operating margins at $\alpha = .05$.

11.27 To determine if the model is useful, we test:

$$H_0: \beta_1 = \beta_2 = \cdots = \beta_{18} = 0$$
$$H_a: \text{At least one } \beta_i \neq 0, \, i = 1, 2, \ldots, 18$$

The test statistic is $F = \dfrac{R^2/k}{(1 - R^2)/[n - (k + 1)]} = \dfrac{.95/18}{(1 - .95)/[20 - (18 + 1)]} = 1.06$

The rejection region requires $\alpha = .05$ in the upper tail of the F distribution with $\nu_1 = k = 18$ and $\nu_2 = n - (k + 1) = 20 - (18 + 1) = 1$. From Table IX, Appendix B, $F_{.05} \approx 245.9$. The rejection region is $F > 245.9$.

Since the observed value of the test statistic does not fall in the rejection region ($F = 1.06 \not> 247$), H_0 is not rejected. There is insufficient evidence to indicate the model is adequate at $\alpha = .05$.

Note: Although R^2 is large, there are so many variables in the model that ν_2 is small.

11.29 a. $R^2 = .529$. 52.9% of the total variability of weight change is explained by the model containing the two independent variables.

$R_a^2 = .505$. This statistic has a similar interpretation to that of R^2, but is adjusted for both the sample size n and the number of β parameters in the model.

The R_a^2 statistic is the preferred measure of model fit because it takes into account the sample size and the number of β parameters.

b. $H_0: \beta_1 = \beta_2 = 0$
$H_a: \text{At least one } \beta_i \neq 0, \, i = 1, 2$

The test statistic is $F = 21.88$ with p-value $= .000$. Since the p-value is so small, H_0 is rejected for any $\alpha > .000$. There is sufficient evidence to indicate that the model is adequate.

11.31 a. The 95% prediction interval is $(1{,}759.7, 4{,}275.4)$. We are 95% confident that the true actual annual earnings for a vendor who is 45 years old and who works 10 hours per day is between $1,759.7 and $4,275.4.

b. The 95% confidence interval is $(2{,}620.3, 3{,}414.9)$. We are 95% confident that the true mean annual earnings for vendors who are 45 years old and who work 10 hours per day is between $2,620.3 and $3,414.9.

c. Yes. The prediction interval for the ACTUAL value of y is always wider than the confidence interval for the MEAN value of y.

11.33 The first order model is:

$$E(y) = \beta_0 + \beta_1 x_1 + \beta_2 x_2 + \beta_3 x_5$$

We want to find a 95% prediction interval for the actual voltage when the volume fraction of the disperse phase is at the high level ($x_1 = 80$), the salinity is at the low level ($x_2 = 1$), and the amount of surfactant is at the low level ($x_5 = 2$).

Using MINITAB, the output is:

```
The regression equation is
y = 0.993 - 0.0243 x1 + 0.142 x2 + 0.385 x5

Predictor         Coef        StDev          T          P
Constant        0.9326       0.2482       3.76      0.002
x1             -0.024272     0.004900     -4.95      0.000
x2              0.14206      0.07573      1.88      0.080
x5              0.38457      0.09801      3.92      0.001

S = 0.4796      R-Sq = 66.6%      R-Sq(adj) = 59.9%

Analysis of Variance

Source           DF          SS          MS         F          P
Regression        3        6.8701      2.2900     9.95      0.001
Residual Error   15        3.4509      0.2301
Total            18       10.3210

Source        DF      Seq SS
x1             1      1.4016
x2             1      1.9263
x5             1      3.5422

Unusual Observations
Obs         x1          y        Fit    StDev Fit    Residual    St Resid
  3        40.0      3.200      2.068      0.239       1.132       2.72R

R denotes an observation with a large standardized residual

Predicted Values

   Fit    StDev Fit      95.0% CI           95.0% PI
 -0.098      0.232    ( -0.592,  0.396)  ( -1.233,  1.038)
```

The 95% prediction interval is $(-1.233, 1.038)$. We are 95% confident that the actual voltage is between -1.233 and 1.038 kw/cm when the volume fraction of the disperse phase is at the high level $(x_1 = 80)$, the salinity is at the low level $(x_2 = 1)$, and the amount of surfactant is at the low level $(x_5 = 2)$.

11.35   a.   To determine if the model is useful for predicting the number of man-hours needed, we test:

H_0: $\beta_1 = \beta_2 = \beta_3 = \beta_4 = 0$
H_a: At least one $\beta_i \neq 0$, $i = 1, 2, 3, 4$

The test statistic is $F = 72.11$ with p-value $= .000$. Since the p-value is less than $\alpha = .01$, we can reject H_0. There is sufficient evidence that the model is useful for predicting man-hours at $\alpha = .01$.

b.   The confidence interval is (1449, 2424).

With 95% confidence, we can conclude that the mean number of man-hours for all boilers with characteristics $x_1 = 150,000$, $x_2 = 500$, $x_3 = 1$, $x_4 = 0$ will fall between 1449 hours and 2424 hours.

The prediction interval is (47, 3825).

With 95% confidence, we can conclude that the number of man-hours for an individual boiler with characteristics $x_1 = 150,000$, $x_2 = 500$, $x_3 = 1$, $x_4 = 0$ will fall between 47 hours and 3825 hours.

11.37 a. $E(y) = \beta_0 + \beta_1 x_1 + \beta_2 x_2 + \beta_3 x_1 x_2$

       b. $E(y) = \beta_0 + \beta_1 x_1 + \beta_2 x_2 + \beta_3 x_3 + \beta_4 x_1 x_2 + \beta_5 x_1 x_3 + \beta_6 x_2 x_3$

11.39 a.   The response surface is a twisted surface in three-dimensional space.

       b.   For $x_1 = 0$, $E(y) = 3 + 0 + 2x_2 - 0x_2 = 3 + 2x_2$
            For $x_1 = 1$, $E(y) = 3 + 1 + 2x_2 - 1x_2 = 4 + x_2$
            For $x_1 = 2$, $E(y) = 3 + 2 + 2x_2 - 2x_2 = 5$

            The plot of the lines is:

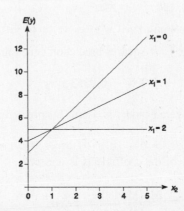

       c.   The lines are not parallel because interaction between x_1 and x_2 is present. Interaction between x_1 and x_2 means that the effect of x_2 on y depends on what level x_1 takes on.

       d.   For $x_1 = 0$, as x_2 increases from 0 to 5, $E(y)$ increases from 3 to 13.
            For $x_1 = 1$, as x_2 increases from 0 to 5, $E(y)$ increases from 4 to 9.
            For $x_1 = 2$, as x_2 increases from 0 to 5, $E(y) = 5$.

       e.   For $x_1 = 2$ and $x_2 = 4$, $E(y) = 5$
            For $x_1 = 0$ and $x_2 = 5$, $E(y) = 13$

            Thus, $E(y)$ changes from 5 to 13.

11.41 a.   CEO income (x_1) and stock percentage (x_2) are said to interact if the effect of one variable, say CEO income, on the dependent variable profit (y) depends on the level of the second variable, stock percentage.

       b.   Using MINITAB, the output is:

```
Regression Analysis

The regression equation is
y = 1161 + 0.122 x1 + 6.0 x2 - 0.0353 x1x2

Predictor      Coef      StDev        T        P
Constant      1160.5     983.1      1.18    0.272
x1           0.12176    0.04234     2.88    0.021
x2              6.03     61.19      0.10    0.924
x1x2        -0.03528    0.01168    -3.02    0.017

S = 2311     R-Sq = 57.0%     R-Sq(adj) = 40.9%
```

```
Analysis of Variance

Source          DF        SS          MS         F        P
Regression       3    56744919    18914973     3.54    0.068
Residual Error   8    42734541     5341818
Total           11    99479461

Source     DF     Seq SS
x1          1    2051170
x2          1    5955824
x1x2        1   48737925

Unusual Observations
Obs    x1     y       Fit   StDev Fit   Residual   St Resid
3     855    346      204       2303        142       0.74 X
```

denotes an observation whose X value gives it large influence.

From the printout, the least squares prediction equation is:

$$\hat{y} = 1161 + 0.122\, x_1 + 6.0\, x_2 - 0.0353\, x_1 x_2$$

To determine if the overall model is useful for predicting company profit, we test:

$H_0: \beta_1 = \beta_2 = \beta_3 = 0$
$H_a:$ At least one of the coefficients is nonzero

The test statistic is $F = \dfrac{\text{MS(Model)}}{\text{MSE}} = 3.54$

The p-value is $p = .068$. Since the p-value is less than $\alpha = .10$ ($p = .068 < .10$), H_0 is rejected. There is sufficient evidence to indicate the model is useful in predicting company profit at $\alpha = .10$.

c. To determine if CEO income and stock percentage interact, we test:

$H_0: \beta_1 = 0$
$H_a: \beta_1 \neq 0$

The test statistic is $t = -3.02$

The p-value is $p = 0.017$. Since the p-value is less than $\alpha = .10$ ($p = .017 < \alpha = .10$), H_0 is rejected. There is sufficient evidence to indicate that CEO income and stock percentage interact, at $\alpha = .10$.

d. When $x_2 = 2\%$, the least squares prediction equation becomes:

$$\hat{y} = 1161 + 0.122\, x_1 + 6.0\,(2) - 0.0353\, x_1(2)$$
$$= 1161 + 0.122\, x_1 + 12 - 0.0706\, x_1 = 1173 + 0.0514\, x_1$$

When the CEO owns 2% of the company's stock ($x_2 = 2\%$), then the change in profit for every one thousand dollar increase in a CEO's income is estimated to be 0.0514 million dollars or \$51,400.

11.43 a. A model including the interaction term is:

$$E(y) = \beta_0 + \beta_1 x_1 + \beta_2 x_2 + \beta_3 x_1 x_2$$

b. To determine if the effect of treatment on spelling score depends on disease intensity, we test:

$$H_0: \ \beta_3 = 0$$
$$H_a: \ \beta_3 \neq 0$$

The test statistic is $t = 1.6$.

The p-value is $p = .02$. Since the p-value is less than α ($p = .02 < .05$), H_0 is rejected. There is sufficient evidence to indicate that the effect of treatment on spelling score depends on disease intensity at $\alpha = .05$.

c. Since the two variables interact, the main effects may be covered up by the interaction effect. Thus, tests on main effects should not be made. Also, the coefficients of the main effects should be interpreted with caution. Since the independent variables interact, the effect of one independent variable on the dependent variable depends on the level of the second independent variable.

11.45 a. By including the interaction terms, it implies that the relationship between voltage and volume fraction of the disperse phase depends on the levels of salinity and surfactant concentration.

A possible sketch of the relationship is:

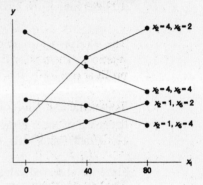

b. Using SAS, the printout is:

Model: MODEL1
Dependent Variable: Y

Analysis of Variance

Source	DF	Sum of Squares	Mean Square	F Value	Prob>F
Model	5	7.01028	1.40206	5.505	0.0061
Error	13	3.31073	0.25467		
C Total	18	10.32101			

Root MSE	0.50465	R-square	0.6792
Dep Mean	0.97684	Adj R-sq	0.5558
C.V.	51.66138		

Parameter Estimates

Variable	DF	Parameter Estimate	Standard Error	T for H0: Parameter=0	Prob > |T|
INTERCEP	1	0.905732	0.28546326	3.173	0.0073
X1	1	-0.022753	0.00831751	-2.736	0.0170
X2	1	0.304719	0.23660006	1.288	0.2202
X5	1	0.274741	0.22704807	1.210	0.2478
X1X2	1	-0.002804	0.00378998	-0.740	0.4725
X1X5	1	0.001579	0.00394692	0.400	0.6956

Multiple Regression and Model Building

Obs	X1	X2	X5	Dep Var Y	Predict Value	Std Err Predict	Lower95% Predict	Upper95% Predict	Residual
1	40	1	2	0.6400	0.8640	0.185	-0.2969	2.0248	-0.2240
2	80	1	4	0.8000	0.7701	0.309	-0.5082	2.0484	0.0299
3	40	4	4	3.2000	2.1174	0.264	0.8869	3.3480	1.0826
4	80	4	2	0.4800	0.2092	0.305	-1.0645	1.4828	0.2708
5	40	1	4	1.7200	1.5398	0.309	0.2617	2.8178	0.1802
6	80	1	2	0.3200	-0.0320	0.283	-1.2820	1.2181	0.3520
7	40	4	2	0.6400	1.4416	0.292	0.1824	2.7009	-0.8016
8	80	4	4	0.6800	1.0113	0.298	-0.2553	2.2779	-0.3313
9	40	1	2	0.1200	0.8640	0.185	-0.2969	2.0248	-0.7440
10	80	1	4	0.8800	0.7701	0.309	-0.5082	2.0484	0.1099
11	40	4	4	2.3200	2.1174	0.264	0.8869	3.3480	0.2026
12	80	4	2	0.4000	0.2092	0.305	-1.0645	1.4828	0.1908
13	40	1	4	1.0400	1.5398	0.309	0.2617	2.8178	-0.4998
14	80	1	2	0.1200	-0.0320	0.283	-1.2820	1.2181	0.1520
15	40	4	2	1.2800	1.4416	0.292	0.1824	2.7009	-0.1616
16	80	4	4	0.7200	1.0113	0.298	-0.2553	2.2779	-0.2913
17	0	0	0	1.0800	0.9057	0.285	-0.3468	2.1583	0.1743
18	0	0	0	1.0800	0.9057	0.285	-0.3468	2.1583	0.1743
19	0	0	0	1.0400	0.9057	0.285	-0.3468	2.1583	0.1343

Sum of Residuals	0
Sum of Squared Residuals	3.3107
Predicted Resid SS (Press)	6.5833

The fitted regression line is:

$$\hat{y} = .906 - .023x_1 + .305x_2 + .275x_5 - .003x_1x_2 + .002x_1x_5$$

To determine if the model is useful, we test:

H_0: $\beta_1 = \beta_2 = \beta_3 = \beta_4 = \beta_5 = 0$
H_a: At least one $\beta_i \neq 0$, for $i = 1, 2, ..., 5$

The test statistic is $F = 5.505$.

Since no α was given, $\alpha = .05$ will be used. The rejection region requires $\alpha = .05$ in the upper tail of the F-distribution with $\nu_1 = k = 5$ and $\nu_2 = n - (k + 1) = 19 - (5 + 1) = 13$. From Table VIII, Appendix B, $F_{.05} = 3.03$. The rejection region is $F > 3.03$.

Since the observed value of the test statistic falls in the rejection region ($F = 5.505 > 3.03$), H_0 is rejected. There is sufficient evidence to indicate the model is useful for predicting voltage at $\alpha = .05$.

$R^2 = .6792$. Thus, 67.92% of the sample variation of voltage is explained by the model containing the three independent variables and two interaction terms.

The estimate of the standard deviation is $s = .505$.

Comparing this model to that fit in Exercise 11.14, the model in Exercise 11.14 appears to fit the data better. The model in Exercise 11.14 has a higher R^2 (.7710 vs .6792) and a smaller estimate of the standard deviation (.464 vs .505).

c. $\hat{\beta}_0 = .906$.   This is simply the estimate of the y-intercept.

$\hat{\beta}_1 = -.023$.   For each unit increase in disperse phase volume, we estimate that the mean voltage will decrease by .023 units, holding salinity and surfactant concentration at 0.

$\hat{\beta}_2 = .305$.   For each unit increase in salinity, we estimate that the mean voltage will increase by .305 units, holding disperse phase volume and surfactant concentration at 0.

$\hat{\beta}_3 = .275.$ For each unit increase in surfactant concentration, we estimate that the mean voltage will increase by .275 units, holding disperse phase volume and salinity at 0.

$\hat{\beta}_4 = -.003.$ This estimates the difference in the slope of the relationship between voltage and disperse phase volume for each unit increase in salinity, holding surfactant concentration constant.

$\hat{\beta}_5 = .002.$ This estimates the difference in the slope of the relationship between voltage and disperse phase volume for each unit increase in surfactant concentration, holding salinity constant.

11.47   a. H_0: $\beta_2 = 0$
H_a: $\beta_2 \neq 0$

The test statistic is $t = \dfrac{\hat{\beta}_2 - 0}{s_{\hat{\beta}_2}} = \dfrac{.47 - 0}{.15} = 3.133$

The rejection region requires $\alpha/2 = .05/2 = .025$ in each tail of the t distribution with df = $n - (k + 1) = 25 - (2 + 1) = 22$. From Table VI, Appendix B, $t_{.025} = 2.074$. The rejection region is $t < -2.074$ or $t > 2.074$.

Since the observed value of the test statistic falls in the rejection region ($t = 3.133 > 2.074$), H_0 is rejected. There is sufficient evidence to indicate the quadratic term should be included in the model at $\alpha = .05$.

b. H_0: $\beta_2 = 0$
H_a: $\beta_2 > 0$

The test statistic is the same as in part a, $t = 3.133$.

The rejection region requires $\alpha = .05$ in the upper tail of the t distribution with df = 22. From Table VI, Appendix B, $t_{.05} = 1.717$. The rejection region is $t > 1.717$.

Since the observed value of the test statistic falls in the rejection region ($t = 3.133 > 1.717$), H_0 is rejected. There is sufficient evidence to indicate the quadratic curve opens upward at $\alpha = .05$.

11.49   a.

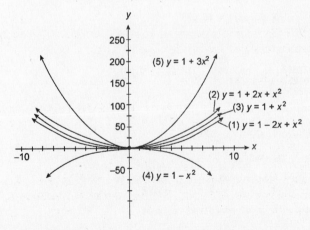

b.   It moves the graph to the right ($-2x$) or to the left ($+2x$) compared to the graph of $y = 1 + x^2$.

c.   It controls whether the graph opens up ($+x^2$) or down ($-x^2$). It also controls how steep the curvature is, i.e., the larger the absolute value of the coefficient of x^2, the narrower the curve is.

11.51. a.   A first order model is:

$$E(y) = \beta_0 + \beta_1 x$$

b.   A second order model is:

$$E(y) = \beta_0 + \beta_1 x + \beta_2 x^2$$

c.   Using MINITAB, a scattergram of these data is:

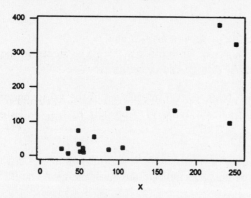

From the plot, it appears that the first order model might fit the data better. There does not appear to be much of a curve to the relationship.

d.   Using MINITAB, the output is:

```
Regression Analysis

The regression equation is
y = 1.5 + 0.38 x + 0.00293 x-sq

Predictor        Coef       StDev          T        P
Constant         1.51       67.97       0.02    0.983
x               0.375       1.360       0.28    0.787
x-sq         0.002925    0.004771       0.61    0.551

S = 71.44      R-Sq = 67.5%     R-Sq(adj) = 62.0%

Analysis of Variance

Source            DF          SS          MS        F        P
Regression         2      127012       63506    12.44    0.001
Residual Error    12       61252        5104
Total             14      188264

Source            DF      Seq SS
x                  1      125093
x-sq               1        1919

Unusual Observations
Obs     x      y     Fit   StDev Fit    Residual    St Resid
  2   243   98.2   264.9        41.4      -166.7       -2.86R
  3   229  382.5   241.0        35.3       141.5        2.28R

R denotes an observation with a large standardized residual
```

To investigate the usefulness of the model, we test:

H_0: $\beta_1 = \beta_2 = 0$
H_a: At least one $\beta_i \neq 0$, $i = 1, 2$

The test statistic is $F = 12.44$.

The p-value is $p = .001$. Since the p-value is so small, we reject H_0. There is sufficient evidence to indicate the model is useful for predicting foreign gross revenue.

To determine if a curvilinear relationship exists between foreign and domestic gross revenues, we test:

H_0: $\beta_2 = 0$
H_a: $\beta_2 \neq 0$

The test statistic is $t = 0.61$

The p-value is $p = 0.551$. Since the p-value is greater than $\alpha = .05$
($p = .551 > \alpha = .05$), H_0 is not rejected. There is insufficient evidence to indicate that a curvilinear relationship exists between foreign and domestic gross revenues at $\alpha = .05$.

e. From the analysis in part **d**, the first-order model better explains the variation in foreign gross revenues. In part **d**, we concluded that the second-order term did not improve the model.

11.53 a. $E(y) = \beta_0 + \beta_1 x_1 + \beta_2 x_2 + \beta_3 x_1 x_2 + \beta_4 x_1^2 + \beta_5 x_2^2$

b. $\beta_4 x_1^2$ and $\beta_5 x_2^2$

11.55 a.

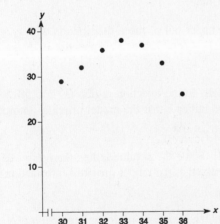

b. If information were available only for $x = 30, 31, 32,$ and 33, we would suggest a first-order model where $\beta_1 > 0$. If information was available only for $x = 33, 34, 35,$ and 36, we would again suggest a first-order model where $\beta_1 < 0$. If all the information was available, we would suggest a second-order model.

11.57 The model would be $E(y) = \beta_0 + \beta_1 x + \beta_2 x^2$. Since the value of y is expected to increase and then decrease as x gets larger, β_2 will be negative. A sketch of the model would be:

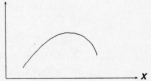

11.59 a.   A scatterplot of the data is:

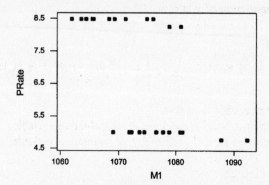

b.   From the plot, it appears that there is a somewhat linear relationship between prime rate and M1. Thus, a proposed model is:

$$E(y) = \beta_0 + \beta_1 M_1$$

c.   The model fit was a quadratic model $E(y) = \beta_0 + \beta_1 M_1 + \beta_2 M_1^2$. To determine if the model provides information for the prediction of y, we test:

H_0: $\beta_1 = \beta_2 = 0$
H_a: At least one $\beta_i \neq 0$, for $i = 1, 2$

The test statistic is $F = 5.58$.

The rejection region requires $\alpha = .05$ in the upper tail of the F-distribution with $\nu_1 = k = 2$ and $\nu_2 = n - (k + 1) = 24 - (2 + 1) = 21$. From Table IX, Appendix B, $F_{.05} = 3.47$. The rejection region is $F > 3.47$.

Since the observed value of the test statistic falls in the rejection region ($F = 5.58 > 3.47$), H_0 is rejected. There is sufficient evidence to indicate that the model provides information for the prediction of y at $\alpha = .05$.

d.   The observed significance level is $p = .0114$. Since the p-value is less than $\alpha = .05$, H_0 is rejected. There is sufficient evidence to indicate that the model provides information for the prediction of y at $\alpha = .05$.

e.   To determine if the second-order term contributes information for the prediction of y, we test:

H_0: $\beta_2 = 0$
H_a: $\beta_2 \neq 0$

The test statistic is $t = .76$.

The rejection region requires $\alpha/2 = .05/2 = .025$ in each tail of the t-distribution with df $= n - (k + 1) = 24 - (2 + 1) = 21$ From Table VI, Appendix B, $t_{.025} = 2.080$. The rejection region is $t < -2.080$ or $t > 2.080$.

Since the observed value of the test statistic does not fall in the rejection region ($t = .76 \not> 2.080$), H_0 is not rejected. There is insufficient evidence to indicate that the second-order term contributes information for the prediction of y at $\alpha = .05$.

f. The observed significance level is $p = .4562$. Since the p-value is not less than $\alpha = .05$, H_0 is not rejected. There is insufficient evidence to indicate that the second-order term contributes information for the prediction of y at $\alpha = .05$.

11.61 The model is $E(y) = \beta_0 + \beta_1 x_1 + \beta_2 x_2$

where $x_1 = \begin{cases} 1 & \text{if the variable is at level 2} \\ 0 & \text{otherwise} \end{cases}$ $x_2 = \begin{cases} 1 & \text{if the variable is at level 3} \\ 0 & \text{otherwise} \end{cases}$

β_0 = mean value of y when qualitative variable is at level 1.
β_1 = difference in mean value of y between level 2 and level 1 of qualitative variable.
β_2 = difference in mean value of y between level 3 and level 1 of qualitative variable.

11.63 a. The least squares prediction equation is:

$$\hat{y} = 80 + 16.8x_1 + 40.4x_2$$

b. $\hat{\beta}_1$ estimates the difference in the mean value of the dependent variable between level 2 and level 1 of the independent variable.

$\hat{\beta}_2$ estimates the difference in the mean value of the dependent variable between level 3 and level 1 of the independent variable.

c. The hypothesis H_0: $\beta_1 = \beta_2 = 0$ is the same as H_0: $\mu_1 = \mu_2 = \mu_3$.

The hypothesis H_a: At least one of the parameters β_1 and β_2 differs from 0 is the same as H_a: At least one mean (μ_1, μ_2, or μ_3) is different.

d. The test statistic is $F = \dfrac{\text{MSR}}{\text{MSE}} = \dfrac{2059.5}{83.3} = 24.72$

Since no α was given, we will use $\alpha = .05$. The rejection region requires $\alpha = .05$ in the upper tail of the test statistic with numerator df $= k = 2$ and denominator df $= n - (k + 1)$ $= 15 - (2 + 1) = 12$. From Table IX, Appendix B, $F_{.05} = 3.89$. The rejection region is $F > 3.89$.

Since the observed value of the test statistic falls in the rejection region ($F = 24.72 > 3.89$), H_0 is rejected. There is sufficient evidence to indicate at least one of the means is different at $\alpha = .05$.

11.65 a. Let $x_1 = \begin{cases} 1 & \text{if no} \\ 0 & \text{if yes} \end{cases}$

The model would be $E(y) = \beta_0 + \beta_1 x_1$

In this model, β_0 is the mean job preference for those who responded 'yes' to the question "Flextime of the position applied for" and β_1 is the difference in the mean job preference between those who responded 'no' to the question and those who answered 'yes' to the question.

b. Let $x_1 = \begin{cases} 1 & \text{if referral} \\ 0 & \text{if not} \end{cases}$ $x_2 = \begin{cases} 1 & \text{if on-premise} \\ 0 & \text{if not} \end{cases}$

The model would be $E(y) = \beta_0 + \beta_1 x_1 + \beta_2 x_2$

In this model, β_0 is the mean job preference for those who responded 'none' to level of day care support required, β_1 is the difference in the mean job preference between those who responded 'referral' and those who responded 'none', and β_2 is the difference in the mean job preference between those who responded 'on-premise' and those who responded 'none'.

c.   Let $x_1 = \begin{cases} 1 \text{ if counseling} \\ 0 \text{ if not} \end{cases}$ $x_2 = \begin{cases} 1 \text{ if active search} \\ 0 \text{ if not} \end{cases}$

The model would be $E(y) = \beta_0 + \beta_1 x_1 + \beta_2 x_2$

In this model, β_0 is the mean job preference for those who responded 'none' to spousal transfer support required, β_1 is the difference in the mean job preference between those who responded 'counseling' and those who responded 'none', and β_2 is the difference in the mean job preference between those who responded 'active search' and those who responded 'none'.

d.   Let $x_1 = \begin{cases} 1 \text{ if not married} \\ 0 \text{ if married} \end{cases}$

The model would be $E(y) = \beta_0 + \beta_1 x_1$

In this model, β_0 is the mean job preference for those who responded 'married' to marital status and β_1 is the difference in the mean job preference between those who responded 'not married' and those who answered 'married'.

e.   Let $x_1 = \begin{cases} 1 \text{ if female} \\ 0 \text{ if male} \end{cases}$

The model would be $E(y) = \beta_0 + \beta_1 x_1$

In this model, β_0 is the mean job preference for males and β_1 is the difference in the mean job preference between females and males.

11.67   a.   Let $x_1 = \begin{cases} 1 \text{ if automotive} \\ 0 \text{ if not} \end{cases}$ $x_2 = \begin{cases} 1 \text{ if pharmaceuticals} \\ 0 \text{ if not} \end{cases}$

$x_3 = \begin{cases} 1 \text{ if telecommunications} \\ 0 \text{ if not} \end{cases}$

The model would be $E(y) = \beta_0 + \beta_1 x_1 + \beta_2 x_2 + \beta_3 x_3$

b.   In this model, β_0 is the mean total pay for the CEOs in the utilities industry, β_1 is the difference in the mean total pay between CEOs in the automotive industry and the utilities industry, β_2 is the difference in the mean total pay between CEOs in the pharmaceutical industry and the utilities industry, and β_3 is the difference in the mean total pay between CEOs in the telecommunications industry and the utilities industry.

c. Using MINITAB, the printout is:

Regression Analysis

```
The regression equation is
y = 1780 + 2759 x1 + 9589 x2 + 10909 x3

Predictor       Coef      StDev          T       P
Constant        1780       2313       0.77   0.453
x1              2759       3272       0.84   0.412
x2              9589       3272       2.93   0.010
x3             10909       3272       3.33   0.004

S = 5173      R-Sq = 49.3%     R-Sq(adj) = 39.8%

Analysis of Variance

Source           DF          SS          MS       F       P
Regression        3   416735105   138911702    5.19   0.011
Residual Error   16   428122266    26757642
Total            19   844857371

Source     DF     Seq SS
x1          1   62236461
x2          1   56972032
x3          1  297526612

Unusual Observations
Obs     x1      y      Fit   StDev Fit    Residual   St Resid
 10   0.00  21116    11369        2313        9747      2.11R
 14   0.00  22441    12689        2313        9752      2.11R

R denotes an observation with a large standardized residual
```

The least squares prediction equation is:

$$\hat{y} = 1780 + 2759 x_1 + 9589 x_2 + 10909 x_3$$

d. To determine if the model is useful in predicting total pay, we test:

$H_0: \beta_1 = \beta_2 = \beta_3 = 0$
$H_a:$ At least one of the coefficients is nonzero

The test statistic is $F = \dfrac{\text{MS(Model)}}{\text{MSE}} = 5.19$

No α is given in the problem. We will use $\alpha = .05$. The p-value is $p = .011$. Since the p-value is less than $\alpha = .05$ ($p = .011 < .05$), H_0 is rejected. There is sufficient evidence to indicate the model is useful in predicting total pay at $\alpha = .05$.

e. For the telecommunications industry, $x_1 = 0$, $x_2 = 0$, and $x_3 = 1$. Using the least squares prediction equation, we get:

$$\hat{y} = 1780 + 2759(0) + 9589(0) + 10909(1)$$
$$= 12{,}689$$

f. The difference in the mean pay of CEOs in the pharmaceutical industry and the utilities industry is β_2. For confidence coefficient .95, $\alpha = .05$ and $\alpha/2 = .05/2 = .025$. From Table VI, Appendix B, with df $= n - 4 = 20 - 4 = 16$, $t_{.025} = 2.120$. The 95% confidence interval is:

$$\hat{\beta}_2 \pm t_{.025} s_{\hat{\beta}_2} \Rightarrow 9{,}589 \pm 2.120(3272) \Rightarrow 9{,}589 \pm 6{,}936.64 \Rightarrow (2{,}652.36,\ 16{,}525.64)$$

We are 95% confident that the difference in mean pay of CEOs in the pharmaceutical and utilities industries is between 2,652.36 and 16,525.64 thousand dollars.

11.69 a. Let $x_1 = \begin{cases} 1 & \text{if pond is enriched} \\ 0 & \text{if otherwise} \end{cases}$

The model is $E(y) = \beta_0 + \beta_1 x_1$

b. β_0 = mean mosquito larvae in the natural pond
β_1 = difference in the mean mosquito larvae between the enriched pond and the natural pond

c. To determine if the mean larval density for the enriched pond exceeds the mean for the natural pond, we test:

H_0: $\beta_1 = 0$
H_a: $\beta_1 > 0$

d. The p-value for the global F test is $p = .004$. Thus, the p-value for this test is $p = .004/2 = .002$. Since the p-value is so small, there is evidence to reject H_0. There is sufficient evidence to indicate that the mean larval densities are larger for the enriched pond than the natural pond at $\alpha > .002$.

11.71 a. To determine if there is a difference in mean monthly sales among the three incentive plans, we test:

H_0: $\beta_1 = \beta_2 = 0$
H_a: At least one $\beta_i \neq 0$, $i = 1, 2$

The test statistic is $F = \dfrac{\text{MSR}}{\text{MSE}} = \dfrac{201.8}{42} = 4.80$

The rejection region requires $\alpha = .05$ in the upper tail of the F distribution with numerator df $= k = 2$ and denominator df $= n - (k + 1) = 15 - (2 + 1) = 12$. From Table IX, Appendix B, $F_{.05} = 3.89$. The rejection region is $F > 3.89$.

Since the observed value of the test statistic falls in the rejection region ($F = 4.80 > 3.89$), H_0 is rejected. There is sufficient evidence to conclude that there is a difference in mean monthly sales among the three incentive plants at $\alpha = .05$.

b. The least squares prediction equation is:

$\hat{y} = 20.0 - 8.60x_1 + 3.80x_2$

$x_1 = 1$ if salesperson is paid a straight salary and $x_2 = 0$.

Thus, an estimate of the mean sales for those on a straight salary is:

$\hat{y} = 20.0 - 8.60(1) + 3.80(0) = 11.4$

Thus, the mean sales is estimated to be $11,400.

c. For those on commission only, $x_1 = 0$ and $x_2 = 0$. The estimate of the mean sales for those on commission only is:

$\hat{y} = 20.0 - 8.60(0) + 3.80(0) = 20.0$

Thus, the mean sales is estimated to be $20,000.

11.73   a.   The first-order model is $E(y) = \beta_0 + \beta_1 x_1$

b.   The new model is $E(y) = \beta_0 + \beta_1 x_1 + \beta_2 x_2 + \beta_3 x_3$

where $x_2 = \begin{cases} 1 & \text{if level 2} \\ 0 & \text{otherwise} \end{cases}$ $x_3 = \begin{cases} 1 & \text{if level 3} \\ 0 & \text{otherwise} \end{cases}$

c.   To allow for interactions, the model is:

$$E(y) = \beta_0 + \beta_1 x_1 + \beta_2 x_2 + \beta_3 x_3 + \beta_4 x_1 x_2 + \beta_5 x_1 x_3$$

d.   The response lines will be parallel if $\beta_4 = \beta_5 = 0$

e.   There will be one response line if $\beta_2 = \beta_3 = \beta_4 = \beta_5 = 0$

11.75   a.   When $x_2 = x_3 = 0$, $E(y) = \beta_0 + \beta_1 x_1$
When $x_2 = 1$ and $x_3 = 0$, $E(y) = \beta_0 + \beta_1 x_1 + \beta_2$
When $x_2 = 0$ and $x_3 = 1$, $E(y) = \beta_0 + \beta_1 x_1 + \beta_3$

b.   The least squares prediction equation is:

$$\hat{y} = 44.803 + 2.173 x_1 + 9.413 x_2 + 15.632 x_3$$

c.   For level 1, $\hat{y} = 44.803 + 2.173 x_1$
For level 2, $\hat{y} = 44.803 + 2.173 x_1 + 9.413$
$\qquad = 54.216 + 2.173 x_1$
For level 3, $\hat{y} = 44.803 + 2.173 x_1 + 15.632$
$\qquad = 60.435 + 2.173 x_1$

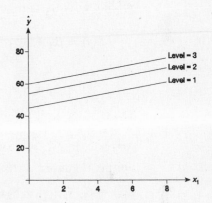

11.77   The model is $E(y) = \beta_0 + \beta_1 x_1 + \beta_2 x_1^2 + \beta_3 x_2 + \beta_4 x_3 + \beta_5 x_4$
where x_1 is the quantitative variable and

$x_2 = \begin{cases} 1 \text{ if level 2 of qualitative variable} \\ 0 \text{ otherwise} \end{cases}$

$x_3 = \begin{cases} 1 \text{ if level 3 of qualitative variable} \\ 0 \text{ otherwise} \end{cases}$

$x_4 = \begin{cases} 1 \text{ if level 4 of qualitative variable} \\ 0 \text{ otherwise} \end{cases}$

11.79   a.   For obese smokers, $x_2 = 0$. The equation of the hypothesized line relating mean REE to time after smoking for obese smokers is:

$$E(y) = \beta_0 + \beta_1 x_1 + \beta_2(0) + \beta_3 x_1(0) = \beta_0 + \beta_1 x_1$$

The slope of the line is β_1.

b. For normal weight smokers, $x_2 = 1$. The equation of the hypothesized line relating mean REE to time after smoking for normal smokers is:

$$E(y) = \beta_0 + \beta_1 x_1 + \beta_2(1) + \beta_3 x_1(1) = (\beta_0 + \beta_2) + (\beta_1 + \beta_3)x_1$$

The slope of the line is $\beta_1 + \beta_3$.

c. The reported p-value is .044. Since the p-value is small, there is evidence to indicate that interaction between time and weight is present for $\alpha > .044$.

11.81   a.   Let x_1 = sales volume

$$x_2 = \begin{cases} 1 \text{ if NW} \\ 0 \text{ if not} \end{cases} \qquad x_3 = \begin{cases} 1 \text{ if S} \\ 0 \text{ if not} \end{cases}$$

$$x_4 = \begin{cases} 1 \text{ if W} \\ 0 \text{ if not} \end{cases}$$

The complete second order model for the sales price of a single-family home is:

$$E(y) = \beta_0 + \beta_1 x_1 + \beta_2 x_1^2 + \beta_3 x_2 + \beta_4 x_3 + \beta_5 x_4 + \beta_6 x_1 x_2 + \beta_7 x_1 x_3 + \beta_8 x_1 x_4$$
$$+ \beta_9 x_1^2 x_2 + \beta_{10} x_1^2 x_3 + \beta_{11} x_1^2 x_4$$

For the West, $x_2 = 0$, $x_3 = 0$, and $x_4 = 1$. The equation would be:

$$E(y) = \beta_0 + \beta_1 x_1 + \beta_2 x_1^2 + \beta_3(0) + \beta_4(0) + \beta_5(0) + \beta_6 x_1(0) + \beta_7 x_1(0)$$
$$+ \beta_8 x_1(0) + \beta_9 x_1^2(0) + \beta_{10} x_1^2(0) + \beta_{11} x_1^2(0)$$

$$= \beta_0 + \beta_1 x_1 + \beta_2 x_1^2 + \beta_5 + \beta_8 x_1 + \beta_{11} x_1^2$$

$$= \beta_0 + \beta_5 + \beta_1 x_1 + \beta_8 x_1 + \beta_2 x_1^2 + \beta_{11} x_1^2$$
$$= (\beta_0 + \beta_5) + (\beta_1 + \beta_8)x_1 + (\beta_2 + \beta_{11})x_1^2$$

For the Northwest, $x_2 = 1$, $x_3 = 0$, and $x_4 = 0$. The equation would be:

$$E(y) = \beta_0 + \beta_1 x_1 + \beta_2 x_1^2 + \beta_3(1) + \beta_4(0) + \beta_5(0) + \beta_6 x_1(1) + \beta_7 x_1(0)$$
$$+ \beta_8 x_1(0) + \beta_9 x_1^2(1) + \beta_{10} x_1^2(0) + \beta_{11} x_1^2(0)$$

$$= \beta_0 + \beta_1 x_1 + \beta_2 x_1^2 + \beta_3 + \beta_6 x_1 + \beta_9 x_1^2$$

$$= \beta_0 + \beta_3 + \beta_1 x_1 + \beta_6 x_1 + \beta_2 x_1^2 + \beta_9 x_1^2$$
$$= (\beta_0 + \beta_3) + (\beta_1 + \beta_6)x_1 + (\beta_2 + \beta_9)x_1^2$$

The parameters β_3, β_4, and β_5 allow for the y-intercepts of the 4 regions to be different. The parameters β_6, β_7, and β_8 allow for the peaks of the curves to be a different values of sales volume (x_1) for the four regions. The parameters β_9, β_{10}, and β_{11} allow for the shapes of the curves to be different for the four regions. Thus, all the parameters from β_3 through β_{11} allow for differences in mean sales prices among the four regions.

e.   Using MINITAB, the printout is:

Regression Analysis

```
The regression equation is
y = 1854740 - 70.4 x1 +0.000721 x1sq + 159661 x2 + 5291908 x3
    + 3663319 x4 + 22.2 x1x2 - 23.9 x1x3 - 37 x1x4
    -0.000421 x1sqx2 -0.000404 x1sqx3 -0.000181 x1sqx4


Predictor         Coef         StDev           T        P
Constant       1854740       1984278        0.93    0.364
x1              -70.44         72.09       -0.98    0.343
x1sq         0.0007211     0.0006515        1.11    0.285
x2              159661       2069265        0.08    0.939
x3             5291908       4812586        1.10    0.288
x4             3663319       4478880        0.82    0.425
x1x2             22.25         73.74        0.30    0.767
x1x3            -23.86         92.09       -0.26    0.799
x1x4             -37.2         103.0       -0.36    0.723
x1sqx2      -0.0004210     0.0006589       -0.64    0.532
x1sqx3      -0.0004044     0.0006777       -0.60    0.559
x1sqx4      -0.0001810     0.0007333       -0.25    0.808

S = 24366      R-Sq = 85.0%     R-Sq(adj) = 74.6%

Analysis of Variance

Source            DF           SS            MS         F        P
Regression        11  53633628997    4875784454      8.21    0.000
Residual Error    16   9499097458     593693591
Total             27  63132726455

Source      DF      Seq SS
x1           1     3591326
x1sq         1       64275360
x2           1  11338642654
x3           1  10081000583
x4           1     241539024
x1x2         1  18258475317
x1x3         1   5579187440
x1x4         1   7566169810
x1sqx2       1     138146367
x1sqx3       1     326425228
x1sqx4       1        36175888

Unusual Observations
Obs    x1       y        Fit    StDev Fit    Residual    St Resid
 2   1025   185900    241659       18746      -55759       -3.58R
 5  60324   295300    229697       15712       65603        3.52R
 7  61025   190855    191084       24360        -229       -0.42 X

R denotes an observation with a large standardized residual
X denotes an observation whose X value gives it large influence.
```

To determine if the model is useful for predicting sales price, we test:

H_0: $\beta_1 = \beta_2 = ... = \beta_{11} = 0$
H_a: At least one of the coefficients is nonzero

The test statistic is $F = \dfrac{\text{MS(Model)}}{\text{MSE}} = 8.21$

The p-value is $p = .000$. Since the p-value is less than $\alpha = .01$ ($p = .000 < .01$), H_0 is rejected. There is sufficient evidence to indicate the model is useful in predicting sales price at $\alpha = .01$.

11.83 a. Let $x_2 = \begin{cases} 1 & \text{if Developing} \\ 0 & \text{otherwise} \end{cases}$

The model would be:

$$E(y) = \beta_0 + \beta_1 x_1 + \beta_2 x_2 + \beta_3 x_1 x_2$$

b. Using SAS, the plot of the data is:

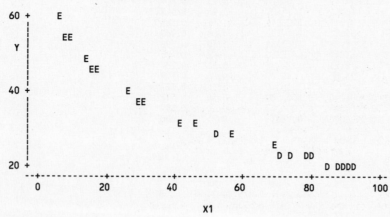

Plot of Y*X1. Symbol is value of X2.

NOTE: 7 obs hidden.

From the plot, it appears that the model is appropriate. The two lines appear to have different slopes.

c. Using SAS, the output from fitting the model is:

Model: MODEL1
Dependent Variable: Y

Analysis of Variance

Source	DF	Sum of Squares	Mean Square	F Value	Prob>F
Model	3	4596.51074	1532.17025	216.342	0.0001
Error	26	184.13626	7.08216		
C Total	29	4780.64700			

Root MSE	2.66123	R-square	0.9615
Dep Mean	32.91000	Adj R-sq	0.9570
C.V.	8.08640		

Parameter Estimates

Variable	DF	Parameter Estimate	Standard Error	T for H0: Parameter=0	Prob > |T|
INTERCEP	1	56.917056	1.18055383	48.212	0.0001
X1	1	-0.557425	0.03668862	-15.193	0.0001
X2	1	-18.293440	5.48687666	-3.334	0.0026
X1X2	1	0.353682	0.07614777	4.645	0.0001

The fitted regression model is:

$$\hat{y} = 56.917 - .557x_1 - 18.293x_2 + .354x_1x_2$$

For the emerging countries, $x_2 = 0$. The fitted model is:

$$\hat{y} = 56.917 - .557x_1 - 18.293(0) + .354x_1(0) = 56.917 - .557x_1$$

For the developed countries, $x_2 = 1$. The fitted model is:

$$\hat{y} = 56.917 - .557x_1 - 18.293(1) + .354x_1(1) = 38.624 - .203x_1$$

d. The plot of the fitted lines is:

```
Plot of Y*X1.    Symbol is value of X2.
Plot of YHAT*X1. Symbol used is '*'.
```

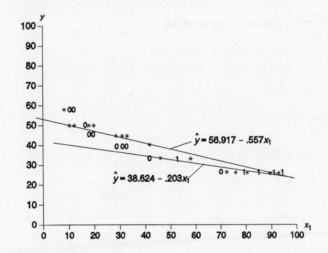

```
NOTE: 14 obs hidden.
```

e. To determine if the slope of the linear relationship between volatility and credit rating depends on market type, we test:

H_0: $\beta_3 = 0$
H_a: $\beta_3 \neq 0$

The test statistic is $t = 4.645$.

The p-value is 0.0001. Since the p-value is less than $\alpha = .01$, H_0 is rejected. There is sufficient evidence to indicate that the slope of the linear relationship between volatility and credit rating depends on market type at $\alpha = .01$.

11.85 The models in parts **a** and **b** are nested:

The complete model is $E(y) = \beta_0 + \beta_1x_1 + \beta_2x_2$
The reduced model is $E(y) = \beta_0 + \beta_1x_1$

The models in parts **a** and **d** are nested.

The complete model is $E(y) = \beta_0 + \beta_1x_1 + \beta_2x_2 + \beta_3x_1x_2$
The reduced model is $E(y) = \beta_0 + \beta_1x_1 + \beta_2x_2$

The models in parts **a** and **e** are nested.

The complete model is $E(y) = \beta_0 + \beta_1x_1 + \beta_2x_2 + \beta_3x_1x_2 + \beta_4x_1^2 + \beta_5x_2^2$
The reduced model is $E(y) = \beta_0 + \beta_1x_1 + \beta_2x_2$

The models in parts **b** and **c** are nested.

The complete model is $E(y) = \beta_0 + \beta_1 x_1 + \beta_2 x_1^2$

The reduced model is $E(y) = \beta_0 + \beta_1 x_1$

The models in parts **b** and **d** are nested.

The complete model is $E(y) = \beta_0 + \beta_1 x_1 + \beta_2 x_2 + \beta_3 x_1 x_2$

The reduced model is $E(y) = \beta_0 + \beta_1 x_1$

The models in parts **b** and **e** are nested.

The complete model is $E(y) = \beta_0 + \beta_1 x_1 + \beta_2 x_2 + \beta_3 x_1 x_2 + \beta_4 x_1^2 + \beta_5 x_2^2$

The reduced model is $E(y) = \beta_0 + \beta_1 x_1$

The models in parts **c** and **e** are nested.

The complete model is $E(y) = \beta_0 + \beta_1 x_1 + \beta_2 x_2 + \beta_3 x_1 x_2 + \beta_4 x_1^2 + \beta_5 x_2^2$

The reduced model is $E(y) = \beta_0 + \beta_1 x_1 + \beta_2 x_1^2$

The models in parts **d** and **e** are nested.

The complete model is $E(y) = \beta_0 + \beta_1 x_1 + \beta_2 x_2 + \beta_3 x_1 x_2 + \beta_4 x_1^2 + \beta_5 x_2^2$

The reduced model is $E(y) = \beta_0 + \beta_1 x_1 + \beta_2 x_2 + \beta_3 x_1 x_2$

11.87   a.   The least squares prediction equation for the complete model is:

$$\hat{y} = 14.6 - .611 x_1 + .439 x_2 - .080 x_3 - .064 x_4$$

The least squares prediction equation for the reduced model is:

$$\hat{y} = 14.0 - .642 x_1 + .396 x_2$$

b. $SSE_R = 160.44$ and $SSE_C = 152.66$

The sum of the squared deviations from the mean for the complete model is 152.66 while the sum of the squared deviations from the mean for the reduced model is 160.44.

c.   Including β_0, there are five β parameters in the complete model and three in the reduced model.

d.   The hypotheses are:

H_0: $\beta_3 = \beta_4 = 0$
H_a: At least one $\beta_i \neq 0$, $i = 3, 4$

e.   The test statistic is $F = \dfrac{(SSE_R - SSE_C)/(k - g)}{SSE_C / [n - (k + 1)]}$

$$= \frac{(160.44 - 152.66)/(4 - 2)}{152.66/[20 - (4 + 1)]} = \frac{3.89}{10.1773} = .38$$

The rejection region requires $\alpha = .05$ in the upper tail of the F distribution with numerator df $= k - g = 4 - 2 = 2$ and denominator df $= n - (k + 1) = 20 - (4 + 1) = 15$. From Table IX, Appendix B, $F_{.05} = 3.68$. The rejection region is $F > 3.68$.

Since the observed value of the test statistic does not fall in the rejection region ($F = .38 \not> 3.68$), H_0 is not rejected. There is insufficient evidence to indicate the complete model is better than the reduced model at $\alpha = .05$.

f. The p-value $= P(F \geq .38)$. With numerator df $= 2$ and denominator df $= 15$, $P(F \geq .38) > .10$ from Table VIII, Appendix B.

11.89 a. Using MINITAB, the output from fitting a complete second-order model is:

```
* NOTE *     X1 is highly correlated with other  predictor variables
* NOTE *     X2 is highly correlated with other  predictor variables
* NOTE *     X1X2 is highly correlated with other  predictor variables

The regression equation is
Y = 172788 - 10739 X1 - 499 X2 - 20.2 X1X2 + 198 X1SQ + 14.7 X2SQ

Predictor       Coef       Stdev     t-ratio       p
Constant      172788       97785        1.77   0.084
X1            -10739        2789       -3.85   0.000
X2              -499        1444       -0.35   0.731
X1X2          -20.20       21.36       -0.95   0.350
X1SQ          197.57       22.60        8.74   0.000
X2SQ          14.678       8.819        1.66   0.103

s = 13132      R-sq = 95.9%     R-sq(adj) = 95.5%

Analysis of Variance

SOURCE        DF          SS            MS          F        p
Regression     5  1.70956E+11   34191134720     198.27    0.000
Error         42  7242915328     172450368
Total         47  1.78199E+11

SOURCE        DF       SEQ SS
X1             1  1.56067E+11
X2             1     13214024
X1X2           1   1686339840
X1SQ           1  12711371776
X2SQ           1    477704384

Unusual Observations
Obs.    X1         Y         Fit Stdev.Fit  Residual    St.Resid
 14    62.9    203288     235455     6002    -32167       -2.75R
 22    45.4     27105      58567     3603    -31462       -2.49R
 34    28.2     28722      15156    11311     13566        2.03RX
 43    64.3    230329     248054     8790    -17725       -1.82 X
 47    63.9    212309     240469     4904    -28160       -2.31R

R denotes an obs. with a large st. resid.
X denotes an obs. whose X value gives it large influence.
```

b.   To test the hypothesis H_0: $\beta_4 = \beta_5 = 0$, we must fit the reduced model

$$E(y) = \beta_0 + \beta_1 x_1 + \beta_2 x_2 + \beta_3 x_1 x_2$$

Using MINITAB, the output from fitting the reduced model is:

```
* NOTE *     X1X2 is highly correlated with other  predictor variables

The regression equation is
Y = - 476768 + 11458 X1 + 3404 X2 - 64.4 X1X2

Predictor       Coef       Stdev    t-ratio       p
Constant     -476768      100852      -4.73   0.000
X1             11458        1874       6.11   0.000
X2              3404        1814       1.88   0.067
X1X2           -64.35       33.77     -1.91   0.063

s = 21549      R-sq = 88.5%    R-sq(adj) = 87.8%

Analysis of Variance

SOURCE       DF          SS           MS         F       p
Regression    3  1.57767E+11  52588867584    113.25   0.000
Error        44  20431990784    464363424
Total        47  1.78199E+11

SOURCE       DF      SEQ SS
X1            1  1.56067E+11
X2            1    13214024
X1X2          1  1686339840

Unusual Observations
Obs.      X1          Y       Fit Stdev.Fit  Residual  St.Resid
 34      28.2     28722    -59713    11922     88435     4.93RX
 38      66.5    290411    250350     9553     40061     2.07R
 43      64.3    230329    202899    11574     27430     1.51 X

R denotes an obs. with a large st. resid.
X denotes an obs. whose X value gives it large influence.
```

The test is:

H_0: $\beta_4 = \beta_5 = 0$
H_a: At least one $\beta_i \neq 0$, for $i = 4, 5$

The test statistic is $F = \dfrac{(\text{SSE}_R - \text{SSE}_C)/(k - g)}{\text{SSE}_C /[n - (k + 1)]}$

$$= \frac{(20,431,990,784 - 7,242,915,328)/(5 - 3)}{7,242,915,328/[48 - (5 + 1)]} = 38.24$$

The rejection region requires $\alpha = .05$ in the upper tail of the F-distribution with $v_1 = k - g$ $= 5 - 3 = 2$ and $v_2 = n - (k + 1) = 48 - (5 + 1) = 42$. From Table IX, Appendix B, $F_{.05} \approx 3.23$. The rejection region is $F > 3.23$.

Since the observed value of the test statistic falls in the rejection region ($F = 38.24 > 3.23$), H_0 is rejected. There is sufficient evidence to indicate that at least one of the quadratic terms contributes to the prediction of monthly collision claims at $\alpha = .05$.

c.   From part **b**, we know at least one of the quadratic terms is significant. From part **a**, it appears that none of the terms involving x_2 may be significant.

Thus, we will fit the model with just x_1 and x_1^2. The MINITAB output is:

```
The regression equation is
Y = 185160 - 11580 X1 + 196 X1SQ

Predictor      Coef       Stdev     t-ratio       p
Constant     185160       54791        3.38    0.002
X1           -11580        2182       -5.31    0.000
X1SQ         195.54       21.64        9.04    0.000

s = 13219       R-sq = 95.6%      R-sq(adj) = 95.4%

Analysis of Variance

SOURCE        DF          SS          MS         F        p
Regression     2  1.70335E+11  85167357952    487.36    0.000
Error         45  7863868416     174752624
Total         47  1.78199E+11

SOURCE        DF      SEQ SS
X1             1  1.56067E+11
X1SQ           1  14267676672

Unusual Observations
Obs.     X1        Y       Fit  Stdev.Fit  Residual   St.Resid
 10    35.8    28957     21200      5825      7757       0.65 X
 14    62.9   203288    230397      4044    -27109      -2.15R
 22    45.4    27105     62456      2856    -35351      -2.74R
 34    28.2    28722     14099     11344     14623       2.15RX
 38    66.5   290411    279798      6189     10613       0.91 X
 47    63.9   212309    243611      4570    -31302      -2.52R

R denotes an obs. with a large st. resid.
X denotes an obs. whose X value gives it large influence.
```

To see if any of the terms involving x_2 are significant, we test:

H_0: $\beta_2 = \beta_3 = \beta_5 = 0$
H_a: At least one $\beta_i \neq 0$, for $i = 2, 3, 5$

The test statistic is
$$F = \frac{(\text{SSE}_R - \text{SSE}_C)/(k - g)}{\text{SSE}_C / [n - (k + 1)]}$$
$$= \frac{(7{,}863{,}868{,}416 - 7{,}242{,}915{,}328)/(5 - 2)}{7{,}242{,}915{,}328/[48 - (5 + 1)]} = 1.20$$

The rejection region requires $\alpha = .05$ in the upper tail of the F-distribution with $v_1 = k - g = 5 - 2 = 3$ and $v_2 = n - (k + 1) = 48 - (5 + 1) = 42$. From Table IX, Appendix B, $F_{.05} \approx 2.84$. The rejection region is $F > 2.84$

Since the observed value of the test statistic does not fall in the rejection region ($F = 1.20 \not> 2.84$), H_0 is not rejected. There is insufficient evidence to indicate that any of the terms involving x_2 contribute to the model at $\alpha = .05$.

Thus, it appears that the best model is $E(y) = \beta_0 + \beta_1 x_1 + \beta_2 x_1^2$. The model does not support the analyst's claim. In the model above, the estimate for β_2 is positive. This would indicate that the higher claims are for both the young and the old. Also, there is no evidence to support the claim that there are more claims when the temperature goes down.

11.91   a.   To determine whether the complete model contributes information for the prediction of y, we test:

H_0: $\beta_1 = \beta_2 = \beta_3 = \beta_4 = \beta_5 = 0$
H_a: At least one of the β's is not 0, $i = 1, 2, 3, 4, 5$

   b.   The test statistic is $F = \dfrac{\text{MSR}}{\text{MSE}} = \dfrac{982.31}{53.84} = 18.24$

The rejection region requires $\alpha = .05$ in the upper tail of the F distribution with numerator df $= k = 5$ and denominator df $= n - (k + 1) = 40 - (5 + 1) = 34$. From Table IX, Appendix B, $F_{.05} \approx 2.53$. The rejection region is $F > 2.53$.

Since the observed value of the test statistic falls in the rejection region ($F = 18.24 > 2.53$), H_0 is rejected. There is sufficient evidence to indicate that the complete model contributes information for the prediction of y at $\alpha = .05$.

   c.   To determine whether a second-order model contributes more information than a first-order model for the prediction of y, we test:

H_0: $\beta_3 = \beta_4 = \beta_5 = 0$
H_a: At least one of the parameters, β_3, β_4, or β_5, is not 0

   d.   The test statistic is $F = \dfrac{(\text{SSE}_R - \text{SSE}_C)/(k - g)}{\text{SSE}_C /[n - (k + 1)]} = \dfrac{(3197.16 - 1830.44)/(5 - 2)}{1830.44/(40 - (5 + 1))}$

$$= \frac{455.5733}{53.8365} = 8.46$$

The rejection region requires $\alpha = .05$ in the upper tail of the F distribution with numerator df $= k - g = 3$ and denominator df $= n - (k + 1) = 40 - (5 + 1) = 34$. From Table IX, Appendix B, $F_{.05} \approx 2.92$. The rejection region is $F > 2.92$.

Since the observed value of the test statistic falls in the rejection region ($F = 8.46 > 2.92$), H_0 is rejected. There is sufficient evidence to indicate the second-order model contributes more information than a first-order model for the prediction of y at $\alpha = .05$.

   e.   The second-order model, based on the test result in part **d**.

11.93   a.   To determine whether there is a nonconstant rate of increase of mean salary with experience, we test:

H_0: $\beta_2 = \beta_5 = 0$
H_a: At least one of the parameters β_2 and β_5 is not 0

   b.   To determine whether there are differences in mean salaries that are attributable to gender, we test:

H_0: $\beta_3 = \beta_4 = \beta_5 = 0$
H_a: At least one of the parameters β_3, β_4, and β_5 is not 0

   c.   To determine if there is a nonconstant rate of change of mean salary with experience, we test:

H_0: $\beta_2 = \beta_5 = 0$
H_a: At least one $\beta_i \neq 0$, $i = 2, 5$

The test statistic is $F = \dfrac{(\text{SSE}_R - \text{SSE}_C)/(k - g)}{\text{SSE}_C/[n - (k + 1)]} = \dfrac{(448.0 - 358.4)/(5 - 3)}{358.4/[100 - (5 + 1)]} = 11.75$

The rejection region requires $\alpha = .05$ in the upper tail of the F distribution with numerator df $= k - g = 5 - 3 = 2$ and denominator df $= n - (k + 1) = 100 - (5 + 1) = 94$. From Table IX, Appendix B, $F_{.05} \approx 3.15$. The rejection region is $F > 3.15$.

Since the observed value of the test statistic falls in the rejection region ($F = 11.75 > 3.15$), H_0 is rejected. There is insufficient evidence to support the claim that the rate of change of mean salary with experience is not constant at $\alpha = .05$.

11.95   a.   To determine whether the rate of increase of emotional distress with experience is different for the two groups, we test:

H_0: $\beta_4 = \beta_5 = 0$
H_a: At least one $\beta_i \neq 0$, $i = 4, 5$

b.   To determine whether there are differences in mean emotional distress levels that are attributable to exposure group, we test:

H_0: $\beta_3 = \beta_4 = \beta_5 = 0$
H_a: At least one $\beta_i \neq 0$, $i = 3, 4, 5$

c.   To determine whether there are differences in mean emotional distress levels that are attributable to exposure group, we test:

H_0: $\beta_3 = \beta_4 = \beta_5 = 0$
H_a: At least one $\beta_i \neq 0$, $i = 3, 4, 5$

The test statistic is $F = \dfrac{(\text{SSE}_R - \text{SSE}_C)/(k - g)}{\text{SSE}_C/[n - (k + 1)]} = \dfrac{(795.23 - 783.9)/(5 - 2)}{783.9/[200 - (5 + 1)]} = .93$

The rejection region requires $\alpha = .05$ in the upper tail of the F distribution with $\nu_1 = k - g = 5 - 2 = 3$ and $\nu_2 = n - (k + 1) = 200 - (5 + 1) = 194$. From Table IX, Appendix B, $F_{.05} \approx 2.60$. The rejection region is $F > 2.60$.

Since the observed value of the test statistic does not fall in the rejection region ($F = .93 \not> 2.60$), H_0 is not rejected. There is insufficient evidence to indicate that there are differences in mean emotional distress levels that are attributable to exposure group at $\alpha = .05$.

11.97   a.   In Step 1, all one-variable models are fit to the data. These models are of the form:

$E(y) = \beta_0 + \beta_1 x_i$

Since there are 7 independent variables, 7 models are fit. (Note: There are actually only 6 independent variables. One of the qualitative variables has three levels and thus two dummy variables. Some statistical packages will allow one to bunch these two variables together so that they are either both in or both out. In this answer, we are assuming that each x_i stands by itself.

b. In Step 2, all two-varirable models are fit to the data, where the variable selected in Step 1, say x_1, is one of the variables. These models are of the form:

$$E(y) = \beta_0 + \beta_1 x_1 + \beta_2 x_i$$

Since there are 6 independent variables remaining, 6 models are fit.

c. In Step 3, all three-variable models are fit to the data, where the variables selected in Step 2, say x_1 and x_2, are two of the variables. These models are of the form:

$$E(y) = \beta_0 + \beta_1 x_1 + \beta_2 x_2 + \beta_3 x_i$$

Since there are 5 independent variables remaining, 5 models are fit.

d. The procedure stops adding independent variables when none of the remaining variables, when added to the model, have a p-value less than some predetermined value. This predetermined value is usually $\alpha = .05$.

e. Two major drawbacks to using the final stepwise model as the "best" model are:

(1) An extremely large number of single β parameter t-tests have been conducted. Thus, the probability is very high that one or more errors have been made in including or excluding variables.

(2) Often the variables selected to be included in a stepwise regression do not include the high-order terms. Consequently, we may have initially omitted several important terms from the model.

11.99 a. First, we must note that 3 of the variables are qualitative – Status (fixed or competitive), District (1, 2, 3, 4, or 5), and Subcontractor utilization (yes or no). Since Status and Sub contractor have only two levels each and are coded as 0 or 1, they can be used in the regression model as is. However, since District has 5 levels, 4 dummy variables must be created and used in the regression model. Let

$$D_1 = \begin{cases} 1 \text{ if District 1} \\ 0 \text{ if not} \end{cases} \quad D_2 = \begin{cases} 1 \text{ if District 2} \\ 0 \text{ if not} \end{cases} \quad D_3 = \begin{cases} 1 \text{ if District 3} \\ 0 \text{ if not} \end{cases} \quad D_4 = \begin{cases} 1 \text{ if District 4} \\ 0 \text{ if not} \end{cases}$$

Using SAS and grouping D_1, D_2, D_3, and D_4 so they must enter or leave the regression model together, the output from the Stepwise regression is (using the significance level of .15 for entry):

```
              Stepwise Procedure for Dependent Variable LOWBID

Step 1   Group GROUP3   Entered    R-square = 0.29873974   C(p) = 55.30668707

                        DF      Sum of Squares    Mean Square      F     Prob>F

          Regression    1          1.80641503     1.80641503    91.59   0.0001
          Error       215          4.24037022     0.01972265
          Total       216          6.04678525

                        Parameter      Standard       Type II
          Variable      Estimate         Error     Sum of Squares    F     Prob>F

          INTERCEP     0.90960784      0.01135369   126.59012353   6418.51  0.0001
          --- Group GROUP3  ---                       1.80641503     91.59  0.0001
          STATUS       0.20007966      0.02090628     1.80641503     91.59  0.0001

Bounds on condition number:           1,         1
```

Step 2   Group GROUP11   Entered   R-square = 0.33104874   C(p) = 44.94505445

	DF	Sum of Squares	Mean Square	F	Prob>F
Regression	2	2.00178064	1.00089032	52.95	0.0001
Error	214	4.04500461	0.01890189		
Total	216	6.04678525			

Variable	Parameter Estimate	Standard Error	Type II Sum of Squares	F	Prob>F
INTERCEP	0.88344751	0.01377515	77.74525439	4113.09	0.0001
--- Group GROUP3 ---			1.23250211	65.21	0.0001
STATUS	0.17599296	0.02179486	1.23250211	65.21	0.0001
--- Group GROUP11 ---			0.19536561	10.34	0.0015
MOBIL	0.00984633	0.00306269	0.19536561	10.34	0.0015

Bounds on condition number: 1.134004,   4.536016

Step 3   Group GROUP5   Entered   R-square = 0.34140466   C(p) = 42.98281325

	DF	Sum of Squares	Mean Square	F	Prob>F
Regression	3	2.06440066	0.68813355	36.81	0.0001
Error	213	3.98238460	0.01869664		
Total	216	6.04678525			

Variable	Parameter Estimate	Standard Error	Type II Sum of Squares	F	Prob>F
INTERCEP	0.92954541	0.02867345	19.64920261	1050.95	0.0001
--- Group GROUP3 ---			0.85401517	45.68	0.0001
STATUS	0.15915272	0.02354849	0.85401517	45.68	0.0001
--- Group GROUP5 ---			0.06262002	3.35	0.0686
NO_BID	-0.00745399	0.00407300	0.06262002	3.35	0.0686
--- Group GROUP11 ---			0.13934600	7.45	0.0069
MOBIL	0.00854071	0.00312844	0.13934600	7.45	0.0069

Bounds on condition number: 1.344083,   11.63597

All groups of variables left in the model are significant at the 0.1500 level.
No other group of variables met the 0.1500 significance level for entry into the model.

Summary of Stepwise Procedure for Dependent Variable LOWBID

Step	Group Entered	Removed	Number In	Partial R**2	Model R**2	C(p)	F	Prob>F
1	GROUP3		1	0.2987	0.2987	55.3067	91.5909	0.0000
2	GROUP11		2	0.0323	0.3310	44.9451	10.3358	0.0015
3	GROUP5		3	0.0104	0.3414	42.9828	3.3493	0.0686

In this analysis, GROUP3 corresponds to the variable STATUS, GROUP11 corresponds to the variable MOBIL, and GROUP5 corresponds to the variable NO_BID.

b. $\hat{\beta}_0 = .9295$. This is simply the estimate of the y-intercept.

$\hat{\beta}_1 = .1592$. The mean low bid for a competitive contract is estimated to be .1592 thousand dollars (or $159.20) greater than that for a fixed contract, all other variables held constant.

$\hat{\beta}_2 = -.0075$. For each additional bidder, the mean low bid is estimated to decrease by .0075 thousand dollars (or $7.50), all other variables held constant.

$\hat{\beta}_3 = .0085$. As the percentage of costs allocated to mobilization increases by one percent, the mean low bid for a competitive contract is estimated to be increase by .0085 thousand dollars (or $8.50), all other variables held constant.

c. First, an extremely large number of *t*-tests have been conducted, leading to a high probability of making one or more Type I or Type II errors. Second, the stepwise model does not include any higher order or interaction terms. Stepwise regression should be used only when necessary, that is, when you want to determine which of a large number of potentially important independent variables should be used in the model-building process.

11.101 Yes. x_2 and x_4 are highly correlated (.93), as well as x_4 and x_5 (.86). When highly correlated independent variables are present in a regression model, the results can be confusing. The researcher may want to include only one of the variables.

11.103 When independent variables that are highly correlated with each other are included in a regression model, the results may be confusing. Highly correlated independent variables contribute overlapping information in the prediction of the dependent variable. The overall global test can indicate that the model is useful in predicting the dependent variable, while the individual *t*-tests on the independent variables can indicate that none of the independent variables are significant. This happens because the individual *t*-tests tests for the significance of an independent variable after the other independent variables are taken into account. Usually, only one of the independent variables that are highly correlated with each other is included in the regression model.

11.105 a. Using MINITAB, the correlations among the three independent variables STATUS, NO_BID, and MOBIL are:

Correlations (Pearson)

```
          Status   No_Bid
No_Bid    -0.487
           0.000

Mobil      0.343   -0.320
           0.000    0.000
```

Cell Contents: Correlation
                       P-Value

Since all of the pairwise correlations are relatively small (all less than .5 in magnitude), there does not appear to be a problem with multicollinearity. (We note that since the variable STATUS has only two levels, the correlation coefficients computed between status and another variable are not really correlation coefficients. However, they still do give some indication as to whether both variables should be included in the model.)

b. Using MINITAB, the output from fitting a full interaction model is:

Regression Analysis

```
The regression equation is
LowBid = 0.915 + 0.180 Status - 0.00715 No_Bid + 0.0133 Mobil
 + 0.0112 Stat_NoBid - 0.0120 Stat_Mob - 0.00011 NoBid_Mob
```

Predictor	Coef	StDev	T	P
Constant	0.91529	0.02946	31.07	0.000
Status	0.18049	0.05981	3.02	0.003
No_Bid	-0.007148	0.004723	-1.51	0.131
Mobil	0.013316	0.006878	1.94	0.054
Stat_NoB	0.01120	0.01754	0.64	0.524
Stat_Mob	-0.012012	0.006053	-1.98	0.048
NoBid_Mo	-0.000107	0.001563	-0.07	0.946

```
S = 0.1362    R-Sq = 36.5%    R-Sq(adj) = 35.1%
```

```
Analysis of Variance

Source          DF        SS          MS         F        P
Regression       6     2.90113     0.48352     26.07    0.000
Residual Error  272    5.04496     0.01855
Total           278    7.94610

Source         DF     Seq SS
Status          1     2.48090
No_Bid          1     0.15568
Mobil           1     0.18189
Stat_NoB        1     0.00616
Stat_Mob        1     0.07642
NoBid_Mo        1     0.00009
```

The fitted regression model is:

$\overset{\wedge}{\text{LowBid}}$ = 0.915 + 0.180 Status - 0.00715 No_Bid + 0.0133 Mobil + 0.0112 Stat_NoBid - 0.0120 Stat_Mob - 0.00011 NoBid_Mob

We note that several terms in this model are not significant, so more analysis is needed to obtain the "best" model.

c.   Using MINITAB, the stem-and-lead display of the residuals is:

Character Stem-and-Leaf Display

```
Stem-and-leaf of RESI1    N = 279
Leaf Unit = 0.010

    4    -3 3200
   10    -2 998655
   18    -2 44222100
   32    -1 99888866555555
   62    -1 4444444333332222222211111000000
   99    -0 99999888887777777777666666666555555
  (47)   -0 44444444433333333333333222222222222111111000000000
  133     0 0000001111111222222222233333334444444
   95     0 5555666667777777888888888888999999999
   60     1 0000111111222223333333344
   37     1 55555555566777888889
   18     2 001111234
    9     2 569
    6     3 03
    4     3 55
    2     4 0
    1     4 5
```

Since the display looks fairly mound-shaped, the assumption of normality appears to be valid.

A plot of the residuals versus NO_BID is:

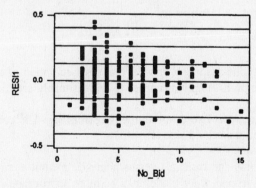

From this plot, there is no apparent curve to the residuals, so it appears that adding the Number of Bidders squared would not improve the model. There is one observation more than 3 standard deviations from the mean and a total of 14 more than 2 standard deviations from the mean. However, using the Empirical Rule, we would expect about 5% or .05(279) = 13.95 ≈ 14 observations to be more than 2 standard deviations from the mean and about .3% or .003(279) = .837 ≈ 1 to be more than 3 standard deviations from the mean. Thus, our data are what we would expect. There do not appear to be any outliers.

A plot of the residuals versus MOBIL is:

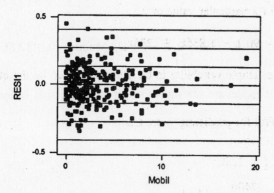

From this plot, there is no apparent curve to the residuals, so it appears that adding Percentage of costs for mobilization squared would not improve the model.

Since Status has only 2 levels, the plot of the residuals versus STATUS will not provide any useful information.

A plot of the residuals versus predicted values is:

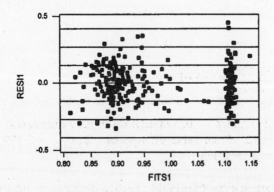

From this plot, there is no obvious cone-shape. It appears that the assumption of constant variance is valid. Thus, the standard regression assumptions appear to be reasonably satisfied.

11.107   a.   No; Income and household size do not seem to be highly correlated. The correlation coefficient between income and household size is −.137.

         b.   Yes; The residuals versus income and residuals versus homesize exhibit a curved shape. Such a pattern could indicate that a second-order model may be more appropriate.

c. No; The residuals versus the predicted values reveals varying spreads for different values of $\hat{y}$. This implies that the variance of $\in$ is not constant for all settings of the x's.

d. Yes; The outlier shows up in several plots and is the 26th household (Food consumption = \$7500, income = \$7300 and household size = 5).

e. No; The frequency distribution of the residuals shows that the outlier skews the frequency distribution to the right.

11.109 In multiple regression, as in simple regression, the confidence interval for the mean value of y is narrower than the prediction interval of a particular value of y.

11.111 a. The least squares equation is $\hat{y} = 90.1 - 1.836x_1 + .285x_2$

b. $R^2 = .916$. About 91.6% of the sample variability in the y's is explained by the model $E(y) = \beta_0 + \beta_1 x_1 + \beta_2 x_2$

c. To determine if the model is useful for predicting y, we test:

H_0: $\beta_1 = \beta_2 = 0$
H_a: At least one $\beta_i \neq 0$, $i = 1, 2$

The test statistic is $F = \dfrac{\text{MSR}}{\text{MSE}} = \dfrac{7400}{114} = 64.91$

The rejection region requires $\alpha = .05$ in the upper tail of the F distribution with $\nu_1 = k = 2$ and $\nu_2 = n - (k + 1) = 15 - (2 + 1) = 12$. From Table IX, Appendix B, $F_{.05} = 3.89$. The rejection region is $F > 3.89$.

Since the observed value of the test statistic falls in the rejection region ($F = 64.91 > 3.89$), H_0 is rejected. There is sufficient evidence to indicate the model is useful for predicting y at $\alpha = .05$.

d. H_0: $\beta_1 = 0$
H_a: $\beta_1 \neq 0$

The test statistic is $t = \dfrac{\hat{\beta}_1}{s_{\hat{\beta}_1}} = \dfrac{-1.836}{.367} = -5.01$

The rejection region requires $\alpha/2 = .05/2 = .025$ in each tail of the t distribution with df $= n - (k + 1) = 15 - (2 + 1) = 12$. From Table VI, Appendix B, $t_{.025} = 2.179$. The rejection region is $t < -2.179$ or $t > 2.179$.

Since the observed value of the test statistic falls in the rejection region ($t = -5.01 < -2.179$), H_0 is rejected. There is sufficient evidence to indicate β_1 is not 0 at $\alpha = .05$.

e. The standard deviation is $\sqrt{\text{MSE}} = \sqrt{114} = 10.677$. We would expect about 95% of the observations to fall within $2(10.677) = 21.354$ units of the fitted regression line.

11.113 The model-building step is the key to the success or failure of a regression analysis. If the model is a good model, we will have a good predictive model for the dependent variable y. If the model is not a good model, the predictive ability will not be of much use.

11.115 $E(y) = \beta_0 + \beta_1 x_1 + \beta_2 x_2 + \beta_3 x_3$

where $x_1 = \begin{cases} 1, \text{ if level 2} \\ 0, \text{ otherwise} \end{cases}$ $x_2 = \begin{cases} 1, \text{ if level 3} \\ 0, \text{ otherwise} \end{cases}$ $x_3 = \begin{cases} 1, \text{ if level 4} \\ 0, \text{ otherwise} \end{cases}$

11.117 The stepwise regression method is used to try to find the best model to describe a process. It is a screening procedure that tries to select a small subset of independent variables from a large set of independent variables that will adequately predict the dependent variable. This method is useful in that it can eliminate some unimportant independent variables from consideration.

11.119 Even though SSE $= 0$, we cannot estimate σ^2 because there are no degrees of freedom corresponding to error. With three data points, there are only two degrees of freedom available. The degrees of freedom corresponding to the model is $k = 2$ and the degrees of freedom corresponding to error is $n - (k + 1) = 3 - (2 + 1) = 0$. Without an estimate for σ^2, no inferences can be made.

11.121 a. The type of juice extractor is qualitative.
The size of the orange is quantitative.

   b. The model is $E(y) = \beta_0 + \beta_1 x_1 + \beta_2 x_2$

   where x_1 = diameter of orange

   $x_2 = \begin{cases} 1 \text{ if Brand B} \\ 0 \text{ if not} \end{cases}$

   c. To allow the lines to differ, the interaction term is added:

   $E(y) = \beta_0 + \beta_1 x_1 + \beta_2 x_2 + \beta_3 x_1 x_2$

   d. For part **b**:

   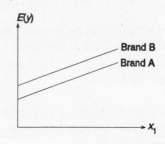

   For part **c**:

   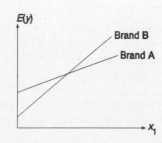

   e. To determine whether the model in part **c** provides more information for predicting yield than does the model in part **b**, we test:

   $H_0: \beta_3 = 0$
   $H_a: \beta_3 \neq 0$

f. The test statistic would be $F = \dfrac{(SSE_R - SSE_C)/(k - g)}{SSE_C/[n - (k + 1)]}$

To compute SSE_R: The model in part **b** is fit and SSE_R is the sum of squares for error.

To compute SSE_C: The model in part **c** is fit and SSE_C is the sum of squares for error.

$k - g$ = number of parameters in H_0 which is 1
$n - (k + 1)$ = degrees of freedom for error in the complete model

11.123 a. The first order model for $E(y)$ as a function of the first five independent variables is:

$$E(y) = \beta_0 + \beta_1 x_1 + \beta_2 x_2 + \beta_3 x_3 + \beta_4 x_4 + \beta_5 x_5$$

b. To test the utility of the model, we test:

H_0: $\beta_1 = \beta_2 = \beta_3 = \beta_4 = \beta_5 = 0$
H_a: At least one $\beta_i \neq 0$, $i = 1, 2, 3, 4, 5$

The test statistic is $F = 34.47$.

The p-value is $p < .001$. Since the p-value is so small, there is sufficient evidence to indicate the model is useful for predicting GSI at $\alpha > .001$.

$R^2 = .469$. 46.9% of the variability in the GSI scores is explained by the model including the first five independent variables.

c. The first order model for $E(y)$ as a function of all seven independent variables is:

$$E(y) = \beta_0 + \beta_1 x_1 + \beta_2 x_2 + \beta_3 x_3 + \beta_4 x_4 + \beta_5 x_5 + \beta_6 x_6 + \beta_7 x_7$$

d. $R^2 = .603$ 60.3% of the variability in the GSI scores is explained by the model including the first seven independent variables.

e. Since the p-values associated with the variables DES and PDEQ-SR are both less than .001, there is evidence that both variables contribute to the prediction of GSI, adjusted for all the other variables already in the model for $\alpha > .001$.

11.125 The correlation coefficient between Importance and Replace is .2682. This correlation coefficient is fairly small and would not indicate a problem with multicollinearity between Importance and Replace. The correlation coefficient between Importance and Support is .6991. This correlation coefficient is fairly large and would indicate a potential problem with multicollinearity between Importance and Support. Probably only one of these variables should be included in the regression model. The correlation coefficient between Replace and Support is $-.0531$. This correlation coefficient is very small and would not indicate a problem with multicollinearity between Replace and Support. Thus, the model could probably include Replace and one of the variables Support or Importance.

11.127 a.   Using MINITAB, the scattergram is:

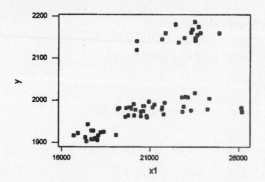

b.   Let $x_2 = \begin{cases} 1 \text{ if } 1\text{--}35W \\ 0 \text{ if not} \end{cases}$

The complete second-order model would be

$$E(y) = \beta_0 + \beta_1 x_1 + \beta_2 x_1^2 + \beta_3 x_2 + \beta_4 x_1 x_2 + \beta_5 x_1^2 x_2$$

c.   Using MINITAB, the printout is:

Regression Analysis

```
The regression equation is
  y = 776 + 0.104 x1 -0.000002 x1sq + 232 x2 - 0.0091 x1x2
        +0.000000 x1sqx2

Predictor         Coef        StDev          T        P
Constant         776.4        144.5       5.37    0.000
x1             0.10418      0.01388       7.50    0.000
x1sq        -0.00000223   0.00000033     -6.73    0.000
x2               232         1094         0.21    0.833
x1x2         -0.00914      0.09829       -0.09    0.926
x1sqx2      0.00000027   0.00000220       0.12    0.903

S = 15.58      R-Sq = 97.2%    R-Sq(adj) = 97.0%

Analysis of Variance

Source            DF          SS          MS         F        P
Regression         5      555741      111148    457.73    0.000
Residual Error    66       16027         243
Total             71      571767


Source            DF      Seq SS
x1                 1      254676
x1sq               1       21495
x2                 1      279383
x1x2               1         183
x1sqx2             1           4

Unusual Observations
Obs    x1       y       Fit StDev Fit  Residual  St Resid
 27  19062  1917.64  1953.27    2.51    -35.63     -2.32R
 48  26148  1982.02  1978.23    9.10      3.79      0.30 X
 53  26166  1972.92  1978.01    9.15     -5.09     -0.40 X
 55  20250  2120.00  2130.56   10.57    -10.56     -0.92 X
 56  20251  2140.00  2130.57   10.57      9.43      0.82 X
 63  24885  2160.02  2161.81   12.67     -1.79     -0.20 X

R denotes an observation with a large standardized residual
X denotes an observation whose X value gives it large influence.
```

The fitted model is

$$\hat{y} = 776 + .104 x_1 - .000002 x_1^2 + 232 x_2 - .0091 x_1 x_2 + .00000027 x_1^2 x_2.$$

To determine if the curvilinear relationship is different at the two locations, we test:

H_0: $\beta_3 = \beta_4 = \beta_5 = 0$
H_0: At least one of the coefficients is nonzero

In order to test this hypothesis, we must fit the reduced model

$$E(y) = \beta_0 + \beta_1 x_1 + \beta_2 x_1^2$$

Using MINITAB, the printout from fitting the reduced model is:

Regression Analysis

```
The regression equation is
y = 197 + 0.149 x1 -0.000003 x1sq

Predictor          Coef        StDev          T        P
Constant          197.5        578.9       0.34    0.734
x1              0.14921      0.05551       2.69    0.009
x1sq         -0.00000295   0.00000132      -2.24    0.028

S = 65.45      R-Sq = 48.3%    R-Sq(adj) = 46.8%

Analysis of Variance

Source             DF           SS          MS        F        P
Regression          2       276171      138085    32.23    0.000
Residual Error     69       295597        4284
Total              71       571767

Source             DF      Seq SS
x1                  1      254676
x1sq                1       21495

Unusual Observations
Obs      x1        y        Fit  StDev Fit    Residual  St Resid
 30   16691  1916.13    1865.11      23.39       51.02      0.83 X
 48   26148  1982.02    2079.68      33.08      -97.66     -1.73 X
 53   26166  1972.92    2079.59      33.31     -106.67     -1.89 X
 56   20251  2140.00    2007.88      10.43      132.12      2.04R

R denotes an observation with a large standardized residual
X denotes an observation whose X value gives it large influence.
```

The fitted regression line is $\hat{y} = 197 + .149x_1 - .000003x_1^2$

To determine if the curvilinear relationship is different at the two locations, we test:

H_0: $\beta_3 = \beta_4 = \beta_5 = 0$
H_a: At least one of the coefficients is nonzero

The test statistic is $F = \dfrac{(\text{SSE}_R - \text{SSE}_C)/(k - g)}{\text{SSE}_C/[n - (k + 1)]} = \dfrac{(295,597 - 16,027)/(5 - 2)}{16,027/[72 - (5 + 1)]}$
$= 383.76$

Since no α was given we will use $\alpha = .05$. The rejection region requires $\alpha = .05$ in the upper tail of the F-distribution with $v_1 = (k - g) = (5 - 2) = 3$ and $v_2 = n - (k + 1) = 72 - (5 + 1) = 66$. From Table IX, Appendix B, $F_{.05} \approx 2.76$. The rejection region is $F > 2.76$.

Since the observed value of the test statistic falls in the rejection region
($F = 383.76 > 2.76$), H_0 is rejected. There is sufficient evidence to indicate the curvilinear relationship is different at the two locations at $\alpha = .05$.

d. Using MINITAB, the plot of the residual versus x_1 is:

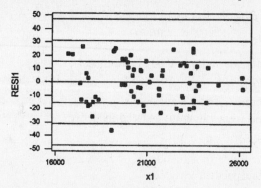

From this plot, we notice that there is only one point more than 2 standard deviations from the mean and no points that are more than 3 standard deviations from the mean. Thus, there do not appear to be any outliers. There is no curve to the residuals, so we have the appropriate model.

A stem-and-leaf display of the residuals is:

```
Character Stem-and-Leaf Display


Stem-and-leaf of RESI1     N = 72
Leaf Unit = 1.0

    1    -3 5
    1    -3
    2    -2 5
    5    -2 210
   13    -1 99877755
   23    -1 4443221100
   29    -0 996655
  (10)   -0 4432111000
   33     0 03344
   28     0 5678899
   21     1 11222244
   13     1 577
   10     2 0012334
    3     2 556
```

The stem-and-leaf display looks fairly mound-shaped, so it appears that the assumption of normality is valid.

A plot of the residuals versus the fitted values is:

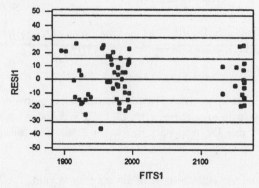

From this plot, there is no cone-shape. Thus, it appears that the assumption of constant variance is valid.

11.129 a.   The model is:

$$E(y) = \beta_0 + \beta_1 x_1 + \beta_2 x_2 + \beta_3 x_3$$

where y = market share

$$x_1 = \begin{cases} 1 \text{ if VH} \\ 0 \text{ otherwise} \end{cases} \quad x_2 = \begin{cases} 1 \text{ if H} \\ 0 \text{ otherwise} \end{cases} \quad x_3 = \begin{cases} 1 \text{ if M} \\ 0 \text{ otherwise} \end{cases}$$

We assume that the error terms (ϵ_i) or y's are normally distributed at each exposure level, with a common variance. Also, we assume the ϵ_i's have a mean of 0 and are independent.

b.   No interaction terms were included because we have only one independent variable, exposure level. Even though we have 3 x_i's in the model, they are dummy variables and correspond to different levels of the one independent variable.

c.   Using SAS to fit the model $E(y) = \beta_0 + \beta_1 x_1 + \beta_2 x_2 + \beta_3 x_3$, we get:

DEPENDENT VARIABLE: Y

SOURCE	DF	SUM OF SQUARES	MEAN SQUARE	F VALUE
MODEL	3	13.34333333	4.44777778	63.09
ERROR	20	1.41000000	0.07050000	PR > F
CORRECTED TOTAL	23	14.75333333		0.0001

R-SQUARE	C.V.	ROOT MSE	Y MEAN
0.904428	2.4065	0.26551836	11.03333333

PARAMETER		ESTIMATE	T FOR H0: PARAMETER = 0	PR > |IT|	STD ERROR OF ESTIMATE
INTERCEPT		10.23333333	94.41	0.0001	0.10839742
X	VH	0.50000000	3.26	0.0039	0.15329710
	H	2.01666667	13.16	0.0001	0.15329710
	M	0.68333333	4.46	0.0002	0.15329710

The fitted model is $\hat{y} = 10.2 + .5x_1 + 2.02x_2 + .683x_3$

$$x_1 = \begin{cases} 1 \text{ if VH} \\ 0 \text{ otherwise} \end{cases}$$

$$x_2 = \begin{cases} 1 \text{ if H} \\ 0 \text{ otherwise} \end{cases}$$

$$x_3 = \begin{cases} 1 \text{ if M} \\ 0 \text{ otherwise} \end{cases}$$

d.   To determine if the firm's expected market share differs for different levels of advertising exposure, we test:

H_0: $\beta_1 = \beta_2 = \beta_3 = 0$
H_a: At least one $\beta_i \neq 0$, $i = 1, 2, 3$

The test statistic is $F = 63.09$.

The rejection region requires $\alpha = .05$ in the upper tail of the F-distribution with $\nu_1 = k = 3$ and $\nu_2 = n - (k + 1) = 24 - (3 + 1) = 20$. From Table IX, Appendix B, $F_{.05} = 3.10$. The rejection region is $F > 3.10$.

Since the observed value of the test statistic falls in the rejection region ($F = 63.09 > 3.10$), H_0 is rejected. There is sufficient evidence to indicate the firm's expected market share differs for different levels of advertising exposure at $\alpha = .05$.

11.131 a. $\hat{\beta}_0 = -105$ has no meaning because $x_3 = 0$ is not in the observable range. $\hat{\beta}_0$ is simply the y-intercept.

$\hat{\beta}_1 = 25$. The estimated difference in mean attendance between weekends and weekdays is 25, temperature and weather constant.

$\hat{\beta}_2 = 100$. The estimated difference in mean attendance between sunny and overcast days is 100, type of day (weekend or weekday) and temperature constant.

$\hat{\beta}_3 = 10$. The estimated change in mean attendance for each additional degree of temperature is 10, type of day (weekend or weekday) and weather (sunny or overcast) held constant.

b. To determine if the model is useful for predicting daily attendance, we test:

H_0: $\beta_1 = \beta_2 = \beta_3 = 0$
H_a: At least one $\beta_i \neq 0$, $i = 1, 2, 3$

The test statistic is $F = \dfrac{R^2/k}{(1 - R^2)/[n - (k + 1)]} = \dfrac{.65/3}{(1 - .65)/[30 - (3 + 1)]} = 16.10$

The rejection region requires $\alpha = .05$ in the upper tail of the F distribution with numerator df $= k = 3$ and denominator df $= n - (k + 1) = 30 - (3 + 1) = 26$. From Table IX, Appendix B, $F_{.05} \approx 2.98$. The rejection region is $F > 2.98$.

Since the observed value of the test statistic falls in the rejection region ($F = 16.10 > 2.98$), H_0 is rejected. There is sufficient evidence to indicate the model is useful for predicting daily attendance at $\alpha = .05$.

c. To determine if mean attendance increases on weekends, we test:

H_0: $\beta_1 = 0$
H_a: $\beta_1 > 0$

The test statistic is $t = \dfrac{\hat{\beta}_1 - 0}{s_{\hat{\beta}_1}} = \dfrac{25 - 0}{10} = 2.5$

The rejection region requires $\alpha = .10$ in the upper tail of the t distribution with df $= n - (k + 1) = 30 - (3 + 1) = 26$. From Table VI, Appendix B, $t_{.10} = 1.315$. The rejection region is $t > 1.315$.

Since the observed value of the test statistic falls in the rejection region ($t = 2.5 > 1.315$), H_0 is rejected. There is sufficient evidence to indicate the mean attendance increases on weekends at $\alpha = .10$.

d. Sunny $\Rightarrow x_2 = 1$, Weekday $\Rightarrow x_1 = 0$, Temperature $95° \Rightarrow x_3 = 95$
$\hat{y} = -105 + 25(0) + 100(1) + 10(95) = 945$

e. We are 90% confident that the actual attendance for sunny weekdays with a temperature of $95°$ is between 645 and 1245.

11.133 a. $\hat{\beta}_1 = .02573$. The mean GPA is estimated to increase by .02573 for each 1 percentile point increase in verbal score, mathematics score held constant.

$\hat{\beta}_2 = .03361$. The mean GPA is estimated to increase by .03361 for each 1 percentile point increase in mathematics score, verbal score held constant.

b. The standard deviation is $\sqrt{MSE} = \sqrt{.16183} = .40228$. We would expect about 95% of the observations to fall within $2(.40228) = .80456$ units of their predicted values.

$R_a^2 = .66382$. About 66% of the sample variability in GPA's is explained by the model containing verbal and mathematics scores, adjusting for sample size and the number of parameters in the model.

c. To determine if the model is useful for predicting GPA, we test:

H_0: $\beta_1 = \beta_2 = 0$
H_a: At least one $\beta_i \neq 0$, $i = 1, 2$

The test statistic is $F = \dfrac{MSR}{MSE} = \dfrac{6.39297}{.16183} = 39.505$

The p-value is .0000. Since the p-value is so small, H_0 is rejected. There is sufficient evidence to indicate the model is useful for predicting GPA.

d. For $x_2 = 60$, $\hat{y} = -1.57 + .026x_1 + .034(60) = .47 + .026x_1$
For $x_2 = 75$, $\hat{y} = -1.57 + .026x_1 + .034(75) = .98 + .026x_1$
For $x_2 = 90$, $\hat{y} = -1.57 + .026x_1 + .034(90) = 1.49 + .026x_1$

The plot is:

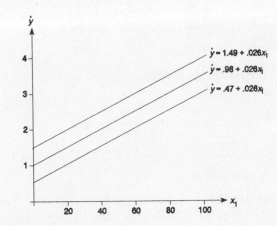

e. From the plot of the residuals against x_1, there is a general mound shape to the residuals. This indicates that adding x_1^2 to the model might provide significant information to the model. From the plot of the residuals against x_2, there is a general mound or bowl shape. This indicates that adding x_2^2 to the model might add significantly to the model.

11.135 a. $E(y) = \beta_0 + \beta_1 x_1 + \beta_2 x_6 + \beta_3 x_7$

where $x_6 = \begin{cases} 1 & \text{if condition is good} \\ 0 & \text{otherwise} \end{cases}$

$x_7 = \begin{cases} 1 & \text{if condition is fair} \\ 0 & \text{otherwise} \end{cases}$

b.   The model specified in part **a** seems appropriate. The points for E, F, and G cluster around three parallel lines.

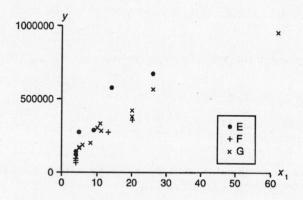

c.   Using MINITAB, the output is

```
The regression equation is
y = 188875 + 15617 x1 - 103046 x6 - 152487 x7

Predictor       Coef        StDev           T          P
Constant      188875        28588        6.61      0.000
x1             15617         1066       14.66      0.000
x6           -103046        31784       -3.24      0.004
x7           -152487        39157       -3.89      0.001

S = 64624      R-Sq = 91.8%    R-Sq(adj) = 90.7%

Analysis of Variance

Source          DF            SS           MS          F        P
Regression       3    9.86170E+11  3.28723E+11      78.71    0.000
Residual Error  21    87700442851   4176211564
Total           24    1.07387E+12

Source     DF         SeqSS
x1          1    9.15776E+11
x6          1     7061463149
x7          1    63332198206

Unusual Observations
Obs    x1        y         Fit     StDev Fit     Residual     St Resid
 10   62.0   950000    1054078        53911      -104078      -2.92RX
 23   14.0   573200     407512        26670       165688       2.81R

R denotes an observation with a large standardized residual
X denotes an observation whose X value gives it large influence.
```

The fitted model is $\hat{y} = 188,875 + 15,617 x_1 - 103,046 x_6 - 152,487 x_7$

For excellent condition, $\hat{y} = 188,875 + 15,617 x_1$
For good condition, $\hat{y} = 85,829 + 15,617 x_1$
For fair condition, $\hat{y} = 36,388 + 15,617 x_1$

d.

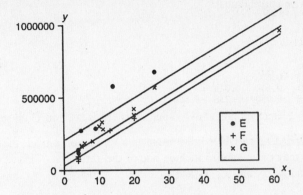

e. We must first fit a reduced model with just x_1, number of apartments. Using MINITAB, the output is:

```
The regression equation is
y = 101786 + 15525 x1

Predictor      Coef      StDev         T        P
Constant      101786     23291      4.37    0.000
x1             15525      1345     11.54    0.000

S = 82908      R-Sq = 85.3%    R-Sq(adj) = 84.6%

Analysis of Variance

Source          DF          SS           MS        F        P
Regression       1  9.15776E+11  9.15776E+11   133.23    0.000
Residual Error  23  1.58094E+11   6873656705
Total           24  1.07387E+12

Unusual Observations
Obs    x1      y       Fit    StDev Fit    Residual    St Resid
  4   26.0  676200    505433     24930      170757       2.16R
 10   62.0  950000   1064353     69058     -114353      -2.49RX
 23   14.0  573200    319140     16765      254060       3.13R

R denotes an observation with a large standardized residual
X denotes an observation whose X value gives it large influence.
```

The fitted model is $\hat{y} = 101{,}786 + 15{,}525x_1$.

To determine if the relationship between sale price and number of units differs depending on the physical condition of the apartments, we test:

H_0: $\beta_2 = \beta_3 = 0$
H_a: At least one $\beta_i \neq 0$, $i = 2, 3$

The test statistic is:

$$F = \frac{(SSE_R - SSE_C)/(k - g)}{SSE_C/[n - (k + 1)]} = \frac{(1.58094 \times 10^{11} - 87{,}700{,}442{,}851)/2}{4{,}176{,}211{,}564} = 8.43$$

The rejection region requires $\alpha = .05$ in the upper tail of the F distribution with $\nu_1 = k - g = 3 - 1 = 2$ and $\nu_2 = n - (k + 1) = 25 - (3 + 1) = 21$. From Table IX, Appendix B, $F_{.05} = 3.47$. The rejection region is $F > 3.47$.

Since the observed value of the test statistic falls in the rejection region ($F = 8.43 > 3.47$), H_0 is rejected. There is evidence to indicate that the relationship between sale price and number of units differs depending on the physical condition of the apartments at $\alpha = .05$.

f. We will look for high pairwise correlations.

	x1	x2	x3	x4	x5	x6
x2	-0.014					
x3	0.800	-0.188				
x4	0.224	-0.363	0.166			
x5	0.878	0.027	0.673	0.089		
x6	0.175	-0.447	0.271	0.112	0.020	
x7	-0.128	0.392	-0.118	0.050	-0.238	-0.564

When highly correlated independent variables are present in a regression model, the results are confusing. The researchers may only want to include one of the variables. This may be the case for the variables: x_1 and x_3, x_1 and x_5, x_3 and x_5

g. Use the following plots to check the assumptions on $\in$.

residuals vs x_1
residuals vs x_2
residuals vs x_3
residuals vs x_4
residuals vs x_5
resisduals vs predicted values
frequency distribution of the standardized residuals.

From the plots of the residuals, there do not appear to be any outliers — no standardized residuals are larger than 2.38 in magnitude. In all the plots of the residuals vs x_i, there is no trend that would indicate non-constant variance (no funnel shape). In addition, there is no U or upside-down U shape that would indicate that any of the variables should be squared. In the histogram of the residuals, the plot is fairly mound-shaped, which would indicate the residuals are approximately normally distributed. All of the assumptions appear to be met.

Residuals Versus x_1
(response is y)

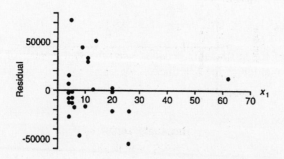

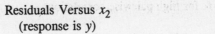

Residuals Versus x_2
(response is y)

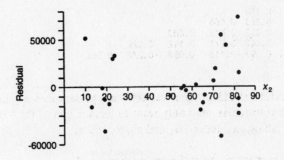

Residuals Versus x_3
(response is y)

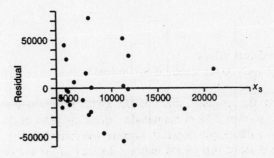

Residuals Versus x_4
(response is y)

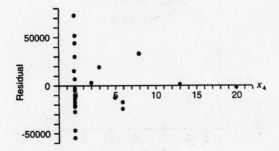

Residuals Versus x_5
(response is y)

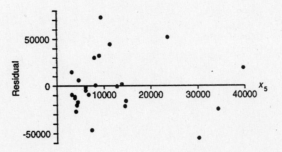

Residuals Versus the Predicted Values
(response is *y*)

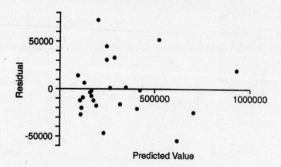

Histogram of the Residuals
(response is *y*)

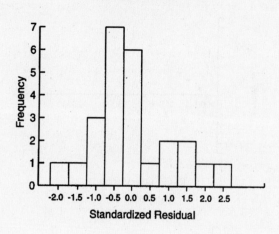

Methods for Quality Improvement

Chapter 12

12.1   A control chart is a time series plot of individual measurements or means of a quality variable to which a centerline and two other horizontal lines called control limits have been added. The center line represents the mean of the process when the process is in a state of statistical control. The upper control limit and the lower control limit are positioned so that when the process is in control the probability of an individual measurement or mean falling outside the limits is very small. A control chart is used to determine if a process is in control (only common causes of variation present) or not (both common and special causes of variation present). This information helps us to determine when to take action to find and remove special causes of variation and when to leave the process alone.

12.3   When a control chart is first constructed, it is not known whether the process is in control or not. If the process is found not to be in control, then the centerline and control limits should not be used to monitor the process in the future.

12.5   Even if all the points of an $\bar{x}$-chart fall within the control limits, the process may be out of control. Nonrandom patterns may exist among the plotted points that are within the control limits, but are very unlikely if the process is in control. Examples include six points in a row steadily increasing or decreasing and 14 points in a row alternating up and down.

12.7   Rule 1:   One point beyond Zone A: No points are beyond Zone A.

Rule 2:   Nine points in a row in Zone C or beyond: No sequence of nine points are in Zone C (on one side of the centerline) or beyond.

Rule 3:   Six points in a row steadily increasing or decreasing: No sequence of six points steadily increase or decrease.

Rule 4:   Fourteen points in a row alternating up and down: This pattern does not exist.

Rule 5:   Two out of three points in Zone A or beyond: There are no groups of three consecutive points that have two or more in Zone A or beyond.

Rule 6:   Four out of five points in a row in Zone B or beyond: Points 18 through 21 are all in Zone B or beyond. This indicates the process is out of control.

Thus, rule 6 indicates this process is out of control.

12.9   Using Table XII, Appendix B:

a.   With $n = 3$, $A_2 = 1.023$

b.   With $n = 10$, $A_2 = 0.308$

c.   With $n = 22$, $A_2 = 0.167$

12.11 a.   For each sample, we compute $\bar{x} = \dfrac{\sum x}{n}$ and R = range = largest measurement − smallest measurement. The results are listed in the table:

Sample No.	$\bar{x}$	R	Sample No.	$\bar{x}$	R
1	20.225	1.8	11	21.225	3.2
2	19.750	2.8	12	20.475	0.9
3	20.425	3.8	13	19.650	2.6
4	19.725	2.5	14	19.075	4.0
5	20.550	3.7	15	19.400	2.2
6	19.900	5.0	16	20.700	4.3
7	21.325	5.5	17	19.850	3.6
8	19.625	3.5	18	20.200	2.5
9	19.350	2.5	19	20.425	2.2
10	20.550	4.1	20	19.900	5.5

b. $\bar{\bar{x}} = \dfrac{\bar{x}_1 + \bar{x}_2 + \cdots + \bar{x}_{20}}{k} = \dfrac{402.325}{20} = 20.11625$

$\bar{R} = \dfrac{R_1 + R_2 + \cdots + R_{20}}{k} = \dfrac{66.2}{20} = 3.31$

c.   *Centerline* $= \bar{\bar{x}} = 20.116$

From Table XII, Appendix B, with $n = 4$, $A_2 = .729$.

Upper control limit $= \bar{\bar{x}} + A_2\bar{R} = 20.116 + .729(3.31) = 22.529$
Lower control limit $= \bar{\bar{x}} - A_2\bar{R} = 20.116 - .729(3.31) = 17.703$

d.   *Upper* A−B *boundary* $= \bar{\bar{x}} + \dfrac{2}{3}(A_2\bar{R}) = 20.116 + \dfrac{2}{3}(.729)(3.31) = 21.725$

Lower A−B *boundary* $= \bar{\bar{x}} - \dfrac{2}{3}(A_2\bar{R}) = 20.116 - \dfrac{2}{3}(.729)(3.31) = 18.507$

Upper B−C *boundary* $= \bar{\bar{x}} + \dfrac{1}{3}(A_2\bar{R}) = 20.116 + \dfrac{1}{3}(.729)(3.31) = 20.920$

Lower B−C *boundary* $= \bar{\bar{x}} - \dfrac{1}{3}(A_2\bar{R}) = 20.116 - \dfrac{1}{3}(.729)(3.31) = 19.312$

e. The $\bar{x}$-chart is:

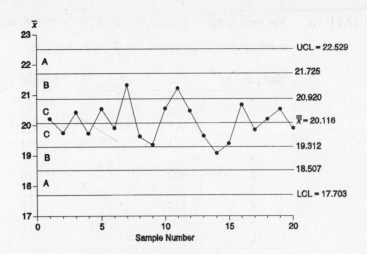

Rule 1: One point beyond Zone A: No points are beyond Zone A.
Rule 2: Nine points in a row in Zone C or beyond: No sequence of nine points are in Zone C (on one side of the centerline) or beyond.
Rule 3: Six points in a row steadily increasing or decreasing: No sequence of six points steadily increase or decrease.
Rule 4: Fourteen points in a row alternating up and down: This pattern does not exist.
Rule 5: Two out of three points in Zone A or beyond: There are no groups of three consecutive points that have two or more in Zone A or beyond.
Rule 6: Four out of five points in a row in Zone B or beyond: No sequence of five points has four or more in Zone B or beyond.

The process appears to be in control.

12.13 a. $\bar{\bar{x}} = \dfrac{\bar{x}_1 + \bar{x}_2 + \cdots + \bar{x}_{20}}{k} = \dfrac{479.942}{20} = 23.9971$

$\bar{R} = \dfrac{R_1 + R_2 + \cdots + R_{20}}{k} = \dfrac{3.63}{20} = .1815$

Centerline $= \bar{\bar{x}} = 23.9971$

From Table XII, Appendix B, with $n = 5$, $A_2 = .577$.

Upper control limit $= \bar{\bar{x}} + A_2\bar{R} = 23.9971 + .577(.1815) = 24.102$
Lower control limit $= \bar{\bar{x}} - A_2\bar{R} = 23.9971 - .577(.1815) = 23.892$

Upper A$-$B boundary $= \bar{\bar{x}} + \dfrac{2}{3}(A_2\bar{R}) = 23.9971 + \dfrac{2}{3}(.577)(.1815) = 24.067$

Lower A$-$B boundary $= \bar{\bar{x}} - \dfrac{2}{3}(A_2\bar{R}) = 23.9971 - \dfrac{2}{3}(.577)(.1815) = 23.927$

Upper B$-$C boundary $= \bar{\bar{x}} + \dfrac{1}{3}(A_2\bar{R}) = 23.9971 + \dfrac{1}{3}(.577)(.1815) = 24.032$

Lower B$-$C boundary $= \bar{\bar{x}} - \dfrac{1}{3}(A_2\bar{R}) = 23.9971 - \dfrac{1}{3}(.577)(.1815) = 23.962$

The $\bar{x}$-chart is:

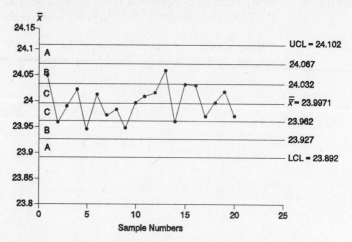

b. To determine if the process is in or out of control, we check the six rules:

Rule 1: One point beyond Zone A: No points are beyond Zone A.

Rule 2: Nine points in a row in Zone C or beyond: No sequence of nine points are in Zone C (on one side of the centerline) or beyond.

Rule 3: Six points in a row steadily increasing or decreasing: No sequence of six points steadily increase or decrease.

Rule 4: Fourteen points in a row alternating up and down: This pattern does not exist.

Rule 5: Two out of three points in Zone A or beyond: There are no groups of three consecutive points that have two or more in Zone A or beyond.

Rule 6: Four out of five points in a row in Zone B or beyond: No sequence of five points has four or more in Zone B or beyond.

The process appears to be in control.

c. Since the process is in control, these limits should be used to monitor future process output.

d. The rational subgrouping strategy used by K-Company will facilitate the identification of process variation caused by differences in the two shifts. All observations within one sample are from the same shift. The shift change is at 3:00 P.M. The samples are selected at 8:00 A.M., 11:00 A.M., 2:00 P.M., 5:00 P.M., and 8:00 P.M. No samples will contain observations from both shifts.

12.15 a.   First, we must compute the range for each sample. The range $= R =$ largest measurement $-$ smallest measurement. The results are listed in the table:

Sample No.	R	Sample No.	R	Sample No.	R
1	2.0	25	4.6	49	4.0
2	2.1	26	3.0	50	4.9
3	1.8	27	3.4	51	3.8
4	1.6	28	2.3	52	4.6
5	3.1	29	2.2	53	7.1
6	3.1	30	3.3	54	4.6
7	4.2	31	3.6	55	2.2
8	3.6	32	4.2	56	3.6
9	4.6	33	2.4	57	2.6
10	2.6	34	4.5	58	2.0
11	3.5	35	5.6	59	1.5
12	5.3	36	4.9	60	6.0
13	5.5	37	10.2	61	5.7
14	5.6	38	5.5	62	5.6
15	4.6	39	4.7	63	2.3
16	3.0	40	4.7	64	2.3
17	4.6	41	3.6	65	2.6
18	4.5	42	3.0	66	3.8
19	4.8	43	2.2	67	2.8
20	5.4	44	3.3	68	2.2
21	5.5	45	3.2	69	4.2
22	3.8	46	0.8	70	2.6
23	3.6	47	4.2	71	1.0
24	2.5	48	5.6	72	1.9

$$\bar{\bar{x}} = \frac{\bar{x}_1 + \bar{x}_2 + \cdots + \bar{x}_{72}}{k} = \frac{3537.3}{72} = 49.129$$

$$\bar{R} = \frac{R_1 + R_2 + \cdots + R_{72}}{k} = \frac{268.8}{72} = 3.733$$

Centerline $= \bar{\bar{x}} = 49.13$

From Table XII, Appendix B, with $n = 6$, $A_2 = .483$.

Upper control limit $= \bar{\bar{x}} + A_2\bar{R} = 49.129 + .483(3.733) = 50.932$
Lower control limit $= \bar{\bar{x}} - A_2\bar{R} = 49.129 - .483(3.733) = 47.326$

Upper A$-$B boundary $= \bar{\bar{x}} + \frac{2}{3}(A_2\bar{R}) = 49.129 + \frac{2}{3}(.483)(3.733) = 50.331$

Lower A$-$B boundary $= \bar{\bar{x}} - \frac{2}{3}(A_2\bar{R}) = 49.129 - \frac{2}{3}(.483)(3.733) = 47.927$

Upper B$-$C boundary $= \bar{\bar{x}} + \frac{1}{3}(A_2\bar{R}) = 49.129 + \frac{1}{3}(.483)(3.733) = 49.730$

Lower B$-$C boundary $= \bar{\bar{x}} - \frac{1}{3}(A_2\bar{R}) = 49.129 - \frac{1}{3}(.483)(3.733) = 48.528$

The $\bar{x}$-chart is:

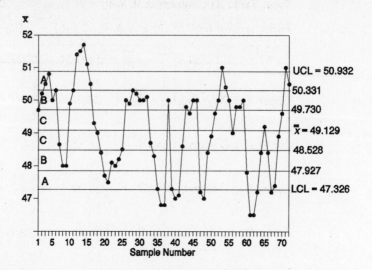

b. To determine if the process is in or out of control, we check the six rules:

Rule 1: One point beyond Zone A: There are a total of 17 points beyond Zone A.

Rule 2: Nine points in a row in Zone C or beyond: No sequence of nine points are in Zone C (on one side of the centerline) or beyond.

Rule 3: Six points in a row steadily increasing or decreasing: There is one sequence of seven points that are steadily increasing—Points 15 through 21.

Rule 4: Fourteen points in a row alternating up and down: This pattern does not exist.

Rule 5: Two out of three points in Zone A or beyond: There are four groups of at least three points in Zone A or beyond—Points 12–16, Points 35–37, Points 39–41, and Points 60–63.

Rule 6: Four out of five points in a row in Zone B or beyond: There are four groups of points that satisfy this rule—Points 10–16, Points 19–24, Points 26–32, and Points 60–64.

The process appears to be out of control. Rules 1, 3, 5, and 6 indicate that the process is out of control.

c. No. The problem does not give the times of the shifts. However, suppose we let the first shift be from 6:00 A.M. to 2:00 P.M., the second shift be from 2:00 P.M. to 10:00 P.M., and the third shift be from 10:00 P.M. to 6:00 A.M. If this is the case, the major problems are during the second shift.

12.17 a. $$\bar{\bar{x}} = \frac{\bar{x}_1 + \bar{x}_2 + \cdots + \bar{x}_{20}}{k} = \frac{1,052.933333}{20} = 52.6467$$

$$\bar{R} = \frac{R_1 + R_2 + \cdots + R_{20}}{k} = \frac{15.1}{20} = .755$$

Centerline $= \bar{\bar{x}} = 52.6467$

From Table XII, Appendix B, with $n = 3$, $A_2 = 1.023$

Upper control limit $= \bar{\bar{x}} + A_2\bar{R} = 52.6467 + 1.023(.755) = 53.419$

Lower control limit $= \bar{\bar{x}} - A_2\bar{R} = 52.6467 - 1.023(.755) = 51.874$

Upper A – B *boundary* $= \bar{\bar{x}} + \frac{2}{3}(A_2\bar{R}) = 52.6467 + \frac{2}{3}(1.023)(.755) = 53.162$

Lower A – B *boundary* $= \bar{\bar{x}} - \frac{2}{3}(A_2\bar{R}) = 52.6467 - \frac{2}{3}(1.023)(.755) = 52.132$

Upper B – C *boundary* $= \bar{\bar{x}} + \frac{1}{3}(A_2\bar{R}) = 52.6467 + \frac{1}{3}(1.023)(.755) = 52.904$

Lower B – C *boundary* $= \bar{\bar{x}} - \frac{1}{3}(A_2\bar{R}) = 52.6467 - \frac{1}{3}(1.023)(.755) = 52.389$

The $\bar{x}$-chart is:

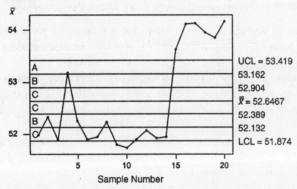

b.   To determine if the process is in or out of control, we check the six rules:

Rule 1: One point beyond Zone A: Eight points are beyond Zone A.
Rule 2: Nine points in a row in Zone C or beyond: Data points 5 through 14
        (10 points) are in Zone C (on one side of the centerline) or beyond.
Rule 3: Six points in a row steadily increasing or decreasing: No sequence of six
        points steadily increase or decrease.
Rule 4: Fourteen points in a row alternating up and down: This pattern does not
        exist.
Rule 5: Two out of three points in Zone A or beyond: There are several sets of
        three consecutive points that have two points in Zone A or beyond.
Rule 6: Four out of five points in a row in Zone B or beyond: There are several
        sets of five points where four or more are in Zone B or beyond.

Special causes of variation appear to be present. The process appears to be out of control.
Rules 1, 2, 5, and 6 indicate the process is out of control.

c.   Processes that are out of control exhibit variation that is the result of both common causes and
     special causes of variation. Common causes affect all output of the process. Special causes
     typically affect only local areas or operations within a process.

d.   Since the process is out of control, the control limits and centerline should not be used to
     monitor future output.

12.19 The control limits of the $\bar{x}$-chart are a function of and reflect the variation in the process. If the variation were unstable (i.e., out of control), the control limits would not be constant. Under these circumstances, the fixed control limits of the $\bar{x}$-chart would have little meaning. We use the R-chart to determine whether the variation of the process is stable. If it is, the $\bar{x}$-chart is meaningful. Thus, we interpret the R-chart prior to the $\bar{x}$-chart.

12.21 a. From Exercise 12.10, $\bar{R} = \dfrac{R_1 + R_2 + \cdots + R_{25}}{k} = \dfrac{198.7}{25} = 7.948$

Centerline $= \bar{R} = 7.948$

From Table XII, Appendix B, with $n = 5$, $D_4 = 2.114$ and $D_3 = 0$.

Upper control limit $= \bar{R}D_4 = 7.948(2.114) = 16.802$

Since $D_3 = 0$, the lower control limit is negative and is not included on the chart.

b. From Table XII, Appendix B, with $n = 5$, $d_2 = 2.326$, and $d_3 = .864$.

Upper A$-$B boundary $= \bar{R} + 2d_3\dfrac{\bar{R}}{d_2} = 7.948 + 2(.864)\dfrac{7.948}{2.326} = 13.853$

Lower A$-$B boundary $= \bar{R} - 2d_3\dfrac{\bar{R}}{d_2} = 7.948 - 2(.864)\dfrac{7.948}{2.326} = 2.043$

Upper B$-$C boundary $= \bar{R} + d_3\dfrac{\bar{R}}{d_2} = 7.948 + (.864)\dfrac{7.948}{2.326} = 10.900$

Lower B$-$C boundary $= \bar{R} - d_3\dfrac{\bar{R}}{d_2} = 7.948 - (.864)\dfrac{7.948}{2.326} = 4.996$

c. The R-chart is:

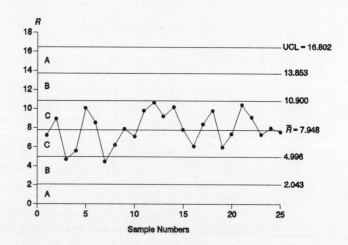

To determine if the process is in or out of control, we check the four rules:

Rule 1: One point beyond Zone A: No points are beyond Zone A.

Rule 2: Nine points in a row in Zone C or beyond: No sequence of nine points are in Zone C (on one side of the centerline) or beyond.

Rule 3: Six points in a row steadily increasing or decreasing: No sequence of six points steadily increase or decrease.

Rule 4: Fourteen points in a row alternating up and down: This pattern does not exist.

The process appears to be in control.

12.23 First, we construct an R-chart.

$$\bar{R} = \frac{R_1 + R_2 + \cdots + R_{20}}{k} = \frac{80.6}{20} = 4.03$$

Centerline $= \bar{R} = 4.03$

From Table XII, Appendix B, with $n = 7$, $D_4 = 1.924$ and $D_3 = .076$.

Upper control limit $= \bar{R}D_4 = 4.03(1.924) = 7.754$
Lower control limit $= \bar{R}D_3 = 4.03(0.076) = 0.306$

From Table XII, Appendix B, with $n = 7$, $d_2 = 2.704$ and $d_3 = .833$.

Upper A$-$B *boundary* $= \bar{R} + 2d_3\frac{\bar{R}}{d_2} = 4.03 + 2(.833)\frac{4.03}{2.704} = 6.513$

Lower A$-$B *boundary* $= \bar{R} - 2d_3\frac{\bar{R}}{d_2} = 4.03 - 2(.833)\frac{4.03}{2.704} = 1.547$

Upper B$-$C *boundary* $= \bar{R} + d_3\frac{\bar{R}}{d_2} = 4.03 + (.833)\frac{4.03}{2.704} = 5.271$

Lower B$-$C *boundary* $= \bar{R} - d_3\frac{\bar{R}}{d_2} = 4.03 - (.833)\frac{4.03}{2.704} = 2.789$

The R-chart is:

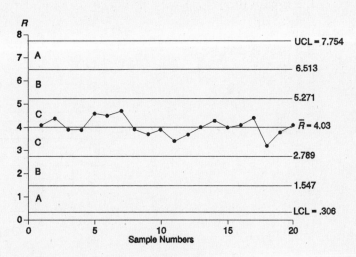

To determine if the process is in or out of control, we check the four rules:

Rule 1: One point beyond Zone A: No points are beyond Zone A.
Rule 2: Nine points in a row in Zone C or beyond: No sequence of nine points are in Zone C (on one side of the centerline) or beyond.
Rule 3: Six points in a row steadily increasing or decreasing: No sequence of six points steadily increase or decrease.
Rule 4: Fourteen points in a row alternating up and down: This pattern does not exist.

The process appears to be in control. Since the process variation is in control, it is appropriate to construct the $\bar{x}$-chart.

To construct an $\bar{x}$-chart, we first calculate the following:

$$\bar{\bar{x}} = \frac{\bar{x}_1 + \bar{x}_2 + \cdots + \bar{x}_{20}}{k} = \frac{434.56}{20} = 21.728$$

$$\bar{R} = \frac{R_1 + R_2 + \cdots + R_{20}}{k} = \frac{80.6}{20} = 4.03$$

Centerline $= \bar{\bar{x}} = 21.728$

From Table XII, Appendix B, with $n = 7$, $A_2 = .419$.

Upper control limit $= \bar{\bar{x}} + A_2\bar{R} = 21.728 + .419(4.03) = 23.417$
Lower control limit $= \bar{\bar{x}} - A_2\bar{R} = 21.728 - .419(4.03) = 20.039$

Upper A$-$B *boundary* $= \bar{\bar{x}} + \frac{2}{3}(A_2\bar{R}) = 21.728 + \frac{2}{3}(.419)(4.03) = 22.854$

Lower A$-$B *boundary* $= \bar{\bar{x}} - \frac{2}{3}(A_2\bar{R}) = 21.728 - \frac{2}{3}(.419)(4.03) = 20.602$

Upper B$-$C *boundary* $= \bar{\bar{x}} + \frac{1}{3}(A_2\bar{R}) = 21.728 + \frac{1}{3}(.419)(4.03) = 22.291$

Lower B$-$C *boundary* $= \bar{\bar{x}} - \frac{1}{3}(A_2\bar{R}) = 21.728 - \frac{1}{3}(.419)(4.03) = 21.165$

The $\bar{x}$-chart is:

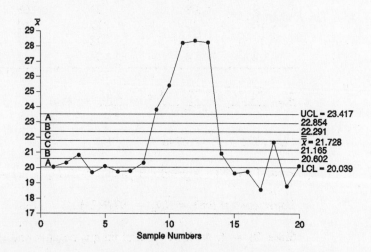

To determine if the process is in or out of control, we check the six rules:

Rule 1: One point beyond Zone A: There are 12 points beyond Zone A. This indicates the process is out of control.

Rule 2: Nine points in a row in Zone C or beyond: No sequence of nine points are in Zone C (on one side of the centerline) or beyond.

Rule 3: Six points in a row steadily increasing or decreasing: Points 6 through 12 steadily increase. This indicates the process is out of control.

Rule 4: Fourteen points in a row alternating up and down: This pattern does not exist.

Rule 5: Two out of three points in Zone A or beyond: There are several groups of three consecutive points that have two or more in Zone A or beyond. This indicates the process is out of control.

Rule 6: Four out of five points in a row in Zone B or beyond: Several sequences of five points have four or more in Zone B or beyond. This indicates the process is out of control.

Rules 1, 3, 5, and 6 indicate that the process is out of control.

12.25 a. Yes. Because all five observations in each sample were selected from the same dispenser, the rational subgrouping will enable the company to detect variation in fill caused by differences in the carbon dioxide dispensers.

b. For each sample, we compute the range = R = largest measurement − smallest measurement. The results are listed in the table:

Sample No.	R	Sample No.	R
1	.05	13	.05
2	.06	14	.04
3	.06	15	.05
4	.05	16	.05
5	.07	17	.06
6	.07	18	.06
7	.09	19	.05
8	.08	20	.08
9	.08	21	.08
10	.11	22	.12
11	.14	23	.12
12	.14	24	.15

$$\bar{R} = \frac{R_1 + R_2 + \cdots + R_{24}}{k} = \frac{1.91}{24} = .0796$$

Centerline = $\bar{R}$ = .0796

From Table XII, Appendix B, with $n = 5$, $D_4 = 2.114$, and $D_3 = 0$.

Upper control limit = $\bar{R}D_4$ = .0796(2.114) = .168

Since $D_3 = 0$, the lower control limit is negative and is not included on the chart.

From Table XII, Appendix B, with $n = 5$, $d_2 = 2.326$, and $d_3 = .864$.

$$Upper\ A-B\ boundary = \bar{R} + 2d_3 \frac{\bar{R}}{d_2} = .0796 + 2(.864)\frac{.0796}{2.326} = .139$$

$$Lower\ A-B\ boundary = \bar{R} - 2d_3 \frac{\bar{R}}{d_2} = .0796 - 2(.864)\frac{.0796}{2.326} = .020$$

$$Upper\ B-C\ boundary = \bar{R} + d_3 \frac{\bar{R}}{d_2} = .0796 + (.864)\frac{.0796}{2.326} = .109$$

$$Lower\ B-C\ boundary = \bar{R} - d_3 \frac{\bar{R}}{d_2} = .0796 - (.864)\frac{.0796}{2.326} = .050$$

The *R*-chart is:

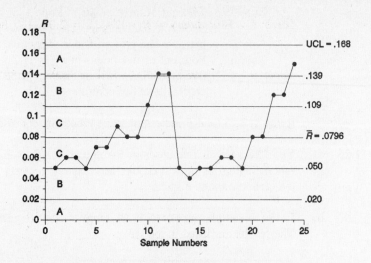

c. To determine if the process is in or out of control, we check the four rules:

Rule 1: One point beyond Zone A: No points are beyond Zone A.

Rule 2: Nine points in a row in Zone C or beyond: No sequence of nine points are in Zone C (on one side of the centerline) or beyond.

Rule 3: Six points in a row steadily increasing or decreasing: No sequence of six points steadily increase or decrease.

Rule 4: Fourteen points in a row alternating up and down: This pattern does not exist.

The process appears to be in control.

d. Since the process variation is in control, the *R*-chart should be used to monitor future process output.

e. The $\bar{x}$-chart should be constructed. The control limits of the $\bar{x}$-chart depend on the variation of the process. (In particular, they are constructed using $\bar{R}$.) If the variation of the process is in control, the control limits of the $\bar{x}$-chart are meaningful.

12.27 a. $\bar{R} = \dfrac{R_1 + R_2 + \cdots + R_{25}}{k} = \dfrac{2.5 + 1.5 + \cdots + 2.0}{25} = \dfrac{52}{25} = 2.08$

Centerline $= \bar{R} = 2.08$

From Table XII, Appendix B, with $n = 5$, $D_4 = 2.114$ and $D_3 = 0$.

Upper control limit $= \bar{R}D_4 = 2.08(2.114) = 4.397$

Since $D_3 = 0$, the lower control limit is negative and is not included on the chart.

From Table XII, Appendix B, with $n = 5$, $d_2 = 2.326$ and $d_3 = 0.864$.

Upper A – B *boundary* $= \bar{R} + 2d_3\dfrac{\bar{R}}{d_2} = 2.08 + 2(.864)\dfrac{2.08}{2.326} = 3.625$

$$\text{Lower A} - \text{B } boundary = \bar{R} - 2d_3\frac{\bar{R}}{d_2} = 2.08 - 2(.864)\frac{2.08}{2.326} = .535$$

$$\text{Upper B} - \text{C } boundary = \bar{R} + d_3\frac{\bar{R}}{d_2} = 2.08 + (.864)\frac{2.08}{2.326} = 2.853$$

$$\text{Lower B} - \text{C } boundary = \bar{R} - d_3\frac{\bar{R}}{d_2} = 2.08 - (.864)\frac{2.08}{2.326} = 1.307$$

The R-chart is:

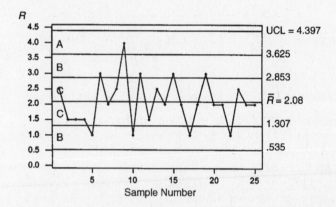

To determine if the process is in or out of control, we check the four rules:

Rule 1: One point beyond Zone A: No points are beyond Zone A.
Rule 2: Nine points in a row in Zone C or beyond: No sequence of nine points are in Zone C (on one side of the centerline) or beyond.
Rule 3: Six points in a row steadily increasing or decreasing: No sequence of six points steadily increase or decrease.
Rule 4: Fourteen points in a row alternating up and down: This pattern does not exist.

The process appears to be in control since none of the out-of-control signals are observed. No special causes of variation appear to be present.

Since the process appears to be under control, it is appropriate to construct an $\bar{x}$-chart for the data.

c. $$\bar{R} = \frac{R_1 + R_2 + \cdots + R_{25}}{k} = \frac{2.5 + 0.0 + \cdots + 2.5}{25} = \frac{42.5}{25} = 1.7$$

$Centerline = \bar{R} = 1.7$

From Table XII, Appendix B, with $n = 5$, $D_4 = 2.114$ and $D_3 = 0$.

$Upper\ control\ limit = \bar{R}D_4 = 1.7(2.114) = 3.594$

Since $D_3 = 0$, the lower control limit is negative and is not included on the chart.

From Table XII, Appendix B, with $n = 5$, $d_2 = 2.326$ and $d_3 = 0.864$.

$$Upper\ A - B\ boundary = \bar{R} + 2d_3\frac{\bar{R}}{d_2} = 1.7 + 2(.864)\frac{1.7}{2.326} = 2.963$$

$$Lower\ A - B\ boundary = \bar{R} - 2d_3\frac{\bar{R}}{d_2} = 1.7 - 2(.864)\frac{1.7}{2.326} = .437$$

$$Upper\ B - C\ boundary = \bar{R} + d_3\frac{\bar{R}}{d_2} = 1.7 + (.864)\frac{1.7}{2.326} = 2.331$$

$$Lower\ B - C\ boundary = \bar{R} - d_3\frac{\bar{R}}{d_2} = 1.7 - (.864)\frac{1.7}{2.326} = 1.069$$

The R chart is:

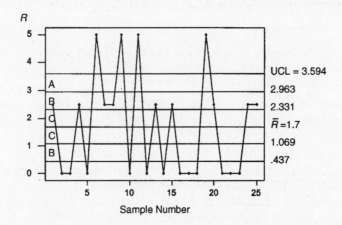

To determine if the process is in or out of control, we check the four rules:

Rule 1: One point beyond Zone A: Four points are beyond Zone A.
Rule 2: Nine points in a row in Zone C or beyond: No sequence of nine points are in Zone C (on one side of the centerline) or beyond.
Rule 3: Six points in a row steadily increasing or decreasing: No sequence of six points steadily increase or decrease.
Rule 4: Fourteen points in a row alternating up and down: This pattern does not exist.

The process appears to be out of control. Rule 1 indicates the process is out of control. Since this process is out of control, it is not appropriate to construct an x-chart for the data.

d.   We get two different answers as to whether this process is in control, depending on the accuracy of the data. When the data were measured to an accuracy of .5 gram, the process appears to be in control. However, when the data were measured to an accuracy of only 2.5 grams, the process appears to be out of control. The same data were used for each chart – just measured to different accuracies.

12.29 a. $\bar{R} = \dfrac{R_1 + R_2 + \cdots + R_{16}}{k} = \dfrac{.4 + 1.4 + \cdots + 2.6}{16} = \dfrac{44.1}{16} = 2.756$

Centerline $= \bar{R} = 2.756$

From Table XII, Appendix B, with $n = 5$, $D_4 = 2.114$ and $D_3 = 0$.

Upper control limit $= \bar{R}D_4 = 2.756(2.114) = 5.826$

Since $D_3 = 0$, the lower control limit is negative and is not included on the chart.

From Table XII, Appendix B, with $n = 5$, $d_2 = 2.326$ and $d_3 = 0.864$.

Upper A – B *boundary* $= \bar{R} + 2d_3\dfrac{\bar{R}}{d_2} = 2.756 + 2(.864)\dfrac{2.756}{2.326} = 4.803$

Lower A – B *boundary* $= \bar{R} - 2d_3\dfrac{\bar{R}}{d_2} = 2.756 - 2(.864)\dfrac{2.756}{2.326} = .709$

Upper B – C *boundary* $= \bar{R} + d_3\dfrac{\bar{R}}{d_2} = 2.756 + (.864)\dfrac{2.756}{2.326} = 3.780$

Lower B – C *boundary* $= \bar{R} - d_3\dfrac{\bar{R}}{d_2} = 2.756 - (.864)\dfrac{2.756}{2.326} = 1.732$

The *R*-chart is:

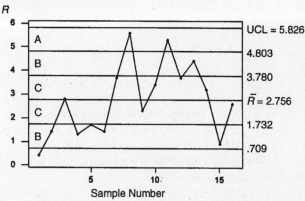

b. The *R*-chart is designed to monitor the process variation.

c. To determine if the process is in or out of control, we check the four rules:

Rule 1: One point beyond Zone A: No points are beyond Zone A.
Rule 2: Nine points in a row in Zone C or beyond: No sequence of nine points are in Zone C (on one side of the centerline) or beyond.
Rule 3: Six points in a row steadily increasing or decreasing: No sequence of six points steadily increases or decreases.
Rule 4: Fourteen points in a row alternating up and down: This pattern does not exist.

The process appears to be in control. None of the out-of-control signals are present. There is no indication that special causes of variation present.

12.31 The sample size is determined as follows:

$$n > \frac{9(1 - p_0)}{p_0} = \frac{9(1 - .08)}{.08} = 103.5 \approx 104$$

12.33 a. We must first calculate $\bar{p}$. To do this, it is necessary to find the total number of defectives in all the samples. To find the number of defectives per sample, we multiple the proportion by the sample size, 150. The number of defectives per sample are shown in the table:

Sample No.	p	No. Defectives	Sample No.	p	No. Defectives
1	.03	4.5	11	.07	10.5
2	.05	7.5	12	.04	6.0
3	.10	15.0	13	.06	9.0
4	.02	3.0	14	.05	7.5
5	.08	12.0	15	.07	10.5
6	.09	13.5	16	.06	9.0
7	.08	12.0	17	.07	10.5
8	.05	7.5	18	.02	3.0
9	.07	10.5	19	.05	7.5
10	.06	9.0	20	.03	4.5

Note: There cannot be a fraction of a defective. The proportions presented in the exercise have been rounded off. I have used the fractions to minimize the roundoff error.

To get the total number of defectives, sum the number of defectives for all 20 samples. The sum is 172.5. To get the total number of units sampled, multiply the sample size by the number of samples: 150(20) = 3000.

$$\bar{p} = \frac{\text{Total defective in all samples}}{\text{Total units sampled}} = \frac{172.5}{3000} = .0575$$

Centerline $= \bar{p} = .0575$

Upper control limit $= \bar{p} + 3\sqrt{\dfrac{\bar{p}(1 - \bar{p})}{n}} = .0575 + 3\sqrt{\dfrac{.0575(.9425)}{150}} = .1145$

Lower control limit $= \bar{p} - 3\sqrt{\dfrac{\bar{p}(1 - \bar{p})}{n}} = .0575 - 3\sqrt{\dfrac{.0575(.9425)}{150}} = .0005$

b. *Upper* A−B *boundary* $= \bar{p} + 2\sqrt{\dfrac{\bar{p}(1 - \bar{p})}{n}} = .0575 + 2\sqrt{\dfrac{.0575(.9425)}{150}} = .0955$

Lower A−B *boundary* $= \bar{p} - 2\sqrt{\dfrac{\bar{p}(1 - \bar{p})}{n}} = .0575 - 2\sqrt{\dfrac{.0575(.9425)}{150}} = .0195$

Upper B−C *boundary* $= \bar{p} + \sqrt{\dfrac{\bar{p}(1 - \bar{p})}{n}} = .0575 + \sqrt{\dfrac{.0575(.9425)}{150}} = .0765$

Lower B−C *boundary* $= \bar{p} - \sqrt{\dfrac{\bar{p}(1 - \bar{p})}{n}} = .0575 - \sqrt{\dfrac{.0575(.9425)}{150}} = .0385$

c.   The *p*-chart is:

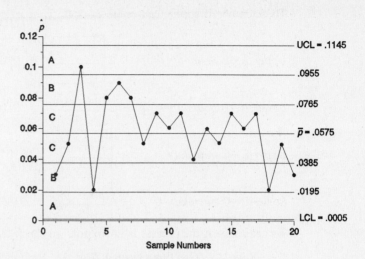

Sample Numbers

d.   To determine if the process is in or out of control, we check the four rules:

Rule 1:   One point beyond Zone A: No points are beyond Zone A.

Rule 2:   Nine points in a row in Zone C or beyond: No sequence of nine points are in Zone C (on one side of the centerline) or beyond.

Rule 3:   Six points in a row steadily increasing or decreasing: No sequence of six points steadily increase or decrease.

Rule 4:   Fourteen points in a row alternating up and down: Points 7 through 20 alternate up and down. This indicates the process is out of control.

Rule 4 indicates that the process is out of control.

e.   Since the process is out of control, the centerline and control limits should not be used to monitor future process output. The centerline and control limits are intended to represent the behavior of the process when it is under control.

12.35   a.   Yes. The minimum sample size necessary so the lower control limit is not negative is:

$$n > \frac{9(1 - p_0)}{p_0}$$

From the data, $p_0 \approx .01$

Thus, $n > \dfrac{9(1 - .01)}{.01} = 891$. Our sample size was 1000.

b. $Upper\ control\ limit = \bar{p} + 3\sqrt{\dfrac{\bar{p}(1 - \bar{p})}{n}} = .01047 + 3\sqrt{\dfrac{.01047(.98953)}{1000}} = .02013$

$Lower\ control\ limit = \bar{p} - 3\sqrt{\dfrac{\bar{p}(1 - \bar{p})}{n}} = .01047 - 3\sqrt{\dfrac{.01047(.98953)}{1000}} = .00081$

c. To determine if special causes are present, we must complete the *p*-chart.

$$\text{Upper } A-B \text{ } boundary = \overline{p} + 2\sqrt{\frac{\overline{p}(1 - \overline{p})}{n}} = .01047 + 2\sqrt{\frac{.01047(.98953)}{1000}} = .01691$$

$$\text{Lower } A-B \text{ } boundary = \overline{p} - 2\sqrt{\frac{\overline{p}(1 - \overline{p})}{n}} = .01047 - 2\sqrt{\frac{.01047(.98953)}{1000}} = .00403$$

$$\text{Upper } B-C \text{ } boundary = \overline{p} + \sqrt{\frac{\overline{p}(1 - \overline{p})}{n}} = .01047 + \sqrt{\frac{.01047(.98953)}{1000}} = .01369$$

$$\text{Lower } B-C \text{ } boundary = \overline{p} - \sqrt{\frac{\overline{p}(1 - \overline{p})}{n}} = .01047 - \sqrt{\frac{.01047(.98953)}{1000}} = .00725$$

To determine if the process is in control, we check the four rules.

Rule 1:   One point beyond Zone A: No points are beyond Zone A.

Rule 2:   Nine points in a row in Zone C or beyond: There are not nine points in a row in Zone C (on one side of the centerline) or beyond.

Rule 3:   Six points in a row steadily increasing or decreasing: No sequence of six points steadily increase or decrease.

Rule 4:   Fourteen points in a row alternating up and down: This pattern does not exist.

It appears that the process is in control.

d. The rational subgrouping strategy says that samples should be chosen so that it gives the maximum chance for the measurements in each sample to be similar and so that it gives the maximum chance for the samples to differ. By selecting 1000 consecutive chips each time, this gives the maximum chance for the measurements in the sample to be similar. By selecting the samples every other day, there is a relatively large chance that the samples differ.

12.37   a. To compute the proportion of defectives in each sample, divide the number of defectives by the number in the sample, 100:

$$\hat{p} = \frac{\text{No. of defectives}}{\text{No. in sample}}$$

The sample proportions are listed in the table:

Sample No.	$\hat{p}$	Sample No.	$\hat{p}$
1	.02	16	.02
2	.04	17	.03
3	.10	18	.07
4	.04	19	.03
5	.01	20	.02
6	.01	21	.03
7	.13	22	.07
8	.09	23	.04
9	.11	24	.03
10	.00	25	.02
11	.03	26	.02
12	.04	27	.00
13	.02	28	.01
14	.02	29	.03
15	.08	30	.04

To get the total number of defectives, sum the number of defectives for all 30 samples. The sum is 120. To get the total number of units sampled, multiply the sample size by the number of samples: $100(30) = 3000$.

$$\bar{p} = \frac{\text{Total defective in all samples}}{\text{Total units sampled}} = \frac{120}{3000} = .04$$

The centerline is $\bar{p} = .04$

$$\textit{Upper control limit} = \bar{p} + 3\sqrt{\frac{\bar{p}(1 - \bar{p})}{n}} = .04 + 3\sqrt{\frac{.04(1 - .04)}{100}} = .099$$

$$\textit{Lower control limit} = \bar{p} - 3\sqrt{\frac{\bar{p}(1 - \bar{p})}{n}} = .04 - 3\sqrt{\frac{.04(1 - .04)}{100}} = -.019$$

$$\textit{Upper A}-\textit{B boundary} = \bar{p} + 2\sqrt{\frac{\bar{p}(1 - \bar{p})}{n}} = .04 + 2\sqrt{\frac{.04(1 - .04)}{100}} = .079$$

$$\textit{Lower A}-\textit{B boundary} = \bar{p} - 2\sqrt{\frac{\bar{p}(1 - \bar{p})}{n}} = .04 - 2\sqrt{\frac{.04(1 - .04)}{100}} = .001$$

$$\textit{Upper B}-\textit{C boundary} = \bar{p} + \sqrt{\frac{\bar{p}(1 - \bar{p})}{n}} = .04 + \sqrt{\frac{.04(1 - .04)}{100}} = .060$$

$$\textit{Lower B}-\textit{C boundary} = \bar{p} - \sqrt{\frac{\bar{p}(1 - \bar{p})}{n}} = .04 - \sqrt{\frac{.04(1 - .04)}{100}} = .020$$

The *p*-chart is:

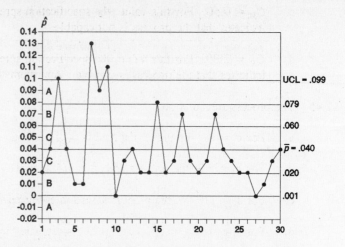

b. To determine if the process is in or out of control, we check the four rules for the *R*-chart.

Rule 1: One point beyond Zone A: There are 3 points beyond Zone A—points 2, 7, and 9.

Rule 2: Nine points in a row in Zone C or beyond: No sequence of nine points are in Zone C (on one side of the centerline) or beyond.

Rule 3: Six points in a row steadily increasing or decreasing: This pattern is not present.

Rule 4: Fourteen points in a row alternating up and down: This pattern does not exist.

The process does not appear to be in control. Rule 1 indicates that the process is out of control.

c. No. Since the process is not in control, then these control limits are meaningless.

12.39 A capability analysis is a methodology used to help determine when common cause variation is unacceptably high. If a process is not in statistical control, then both common causes and special causes of variation exist. It would not be possible to determine if the common cause variation is too high because it could not be separated from special cause variation.

12.41 One way to assess the capability of a process is to construct a frequency distribution or stem-and-leaf display for a large sample of individual measurements from the process. Then, the specification limits and the target value for the output variable are added to the graph. This is called a capability analysis diagram. A second way to assess the capability of a process is to quantify capability. The most direct way to quantify capability is to count the number of items that fall outside the specification limits in the capability analysis diagram and report the percentage of such items in the sample. Also, one can construct a capability index. This is the ratio of the difference in the specification spread and the difference in the process spread. This measure is called C_P. If C_P is less than 1, then the process is not capable.

12.43 a. $C_P = 1.00$. For this value, the specification spread is equal to the process spread. This indicates that the process is capable. Approximately 2.7 units per 1,000 will be unacceptable.

b. $C_P = 1.33$. For this value, the specification spread is greater than the process spread. This indicates that the process is capable. Approximately 63 units per 1,000,000 will be unacceptable.

c. $C_P = 0.50$. For this value, the specification spread is less than the process spread. This indicates that the process is not capable.

d. $C_P = 2.00$. For this value, the specification spread is greater than the process spread. This indicates that the process is capable. Approximately 2 units per billion will be unacceptable.

12.45 The process spread is 6σ.

a.   For $\sigma = 21$, the process spread is $6(21) = 126$

b.   For $\sigma = 5.2$, the process spread is $6(5.2) = 31.2$

c.   For $s = 110.06$, the process spread is estimated by $6(110.06) = 660.36$

d.   For $s = .0024$, the process spread is estimated by $6(.0024) = .0144$

12.47 We know that $C_P = \dfrac{USL - LSL}{6\sigma}$

Thus, if $C_P = 2$, then $2 = \dfrac{USL - LSL}{6\sigma} \Rightarrow 12\sigma = USL - LSL$. The process mean is halfway between the USL and the LSL. Since the specification spread covers 12σ, then the USL must be $12\sigma/2 = 6\sigma$ from the process mean.

12.49 a.   A capability analysis diagram is:

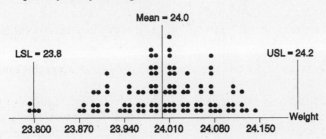

b.   From the sample, $\bar{x} = 23.997$ and $s = .077$.

$$C_P = \frac{USL - LSL}{6\sigma} \approx \frac{24.2 - 23.8}{6(.077)} = \frac{.4}{.462} = .866$$

Since the C_P value is less than 1, the process is not capable.

12.51 The quality of a good or service is indicated by the extent to which it satisfies the needs and preferences of its users. Its eight dimensions are: performance, features, reliability, conformance, durability, serviceability, aesthetics, and other perceptions that influence judgments of quality.

12.53 A process is a series of actions or operations that transform inputs to outputs. A process produces output over time. Organizational process: Manufacturing a product. Personnel Process: Balancing a checkbook.

12.55 The six major sources of process variation are: people, machines, materials, methods, measurements, and environment.

12.61   Common causes of variation are the methods, materials, equipment, personnel, and environment that make up a process and the inputs required by the process. That is, common causes are attributable to the design of the process. Special causes of variation are events or actions that are not part of the process design. Typically, they are transient, fleeting events that affect only local areas or operations within the process for a brief period of time. Occasionally, however, such events may have a persistent or recurrent effect on the process.

12.63   Control limits are a function of the natural variability of the process. The position of the limits is a function of the size of the process standard deviation. Specification limits are boundary points that define the acceptable values for an output variable of a particular product or service. They are determined by customers, management, and/or product designers. Specification limits may be either two-sided, with upper and lower limits, or one-sided with either an upper or lower limit. Specification limits are not dependent on the process in any way. The process may not be able to meet the specification limits even when it is under statistical control.

12.65   The C_p statistic is used to assess capability if the process is stable (in control) and if the process is centered on the target value.

12.67   a.   The centerline is:

$$\bar{x} = \frac{\sum x}{n} = \frac{96}{15} = 6.4$$

The time series plot is:

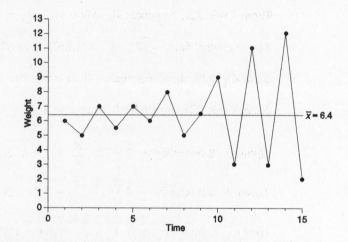

b.   The type of variation best described by the pattern in this plot is increasing variance. The spread of the measurements increases with the passing of time.

12.69   To determine if the process is in or out of control, we check the six rules:

Rule 1:   One point beyond Zone A: No points are beyond Zone A.
Rule 2:   Nine points in a row in Zone C or beyond: Points 8 through 16 are in Zone C (on one side of the centerline) or beyond. This indicates the process is out of control.
Rule 3:   Six points in a row steadily increasing or decreasing: No sequence of six points steadily increase or decrease.
Rule 4:   Fourteen points in a row alternating up and down: This pattern does not exist.
Rule 5:   Two out of three points in Zone A or beyond: No group of three consecutive points have two or more in Zone A or beyond.
Rule 6:   Four out of five points in a row in Zone B or beyond: No sequence of five points has four or more in Zone B or beyond.

Rule 2 indicates that the process is out of control. A special cause of variation appears to be present.

12.71 a. To compute the range, subtract the larger score minus the smaller score. The ranges for the samples are listed in the table:

Sample No.	R	$\bar{x}$	Sample No.	R	$\bar{x}$
1	4	343.0	11	5	357.5
2	3	329.5	12	10	330.0
3	12	349.0	13	2	349.0
4	1	351.5	14	1	336.5
5	12	354.0	15	16	337.0
6	6	339.0	16	7	354.5
7	3	329.5	17	1	352.5
8	0	344.0	18	6	337.0
9	25	346.5	19	6	338.0
10	15	353.5	20	13	351.5

The centerline is $\bar{R} = \dfrac{\sum R}{k} = \dfrac{148}{20} = 7.4$

From Table XII, Appendix B, with $n = 2$, $D_3 = 0$, and $D_4 = 3.267$.

Upper control limit $= \bar{R}D_4 = 7.4(3.267) = 24.1758$

Since $D_3 = 0$, the lower control limit is negative and is not included on the chart.

From Table XII, Appendix B, with $n = 2$, $d_2 = 1.128$, and $d_3 = .853$.

Upper A–B *boundary* $= \bar{R} + 2d_3\dfrac{\bar{R}}{d_2} = 7.4 + 2(.853)\dfrac{(7.4)}{1.128} = 18.5918$

Lower A–B *boundary* $= \bar{R} - 2d_3\dfrac{\bar{R}}{d_2} = 7.4 - 2(.853)\dfrac{(7.4)}{1.128} = -3.7918$

Upper B–C *boundary* $= \bar{R} + d_3\dfrac{\bar{R}}{d_2} = 7.4 + (.853)\dfrac{(7.4)}{1.128} = 12.9959$

Lower B–C *boundary* $= \bar{R} - d_3\dfrac{\bar{R}}{d_2} = 7.4 - (.853)\dfrac{(7.4)}{1.128} = 1.8041$

The R-chart is:

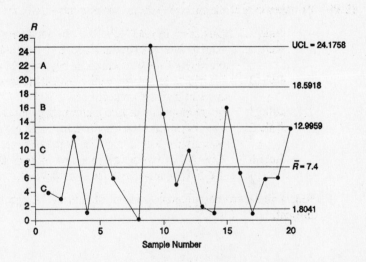

To determine if the process is in control, we check the four rules.

Rule 1: One point beyond Zone A: Point 9 is beyond Zone A. This indicates the process is out of control.

Rule 2: Nine points in a row in Zone C or beyond: There are not nine points in a row in Zone C (on one side of the centerline) or beyond.

Rule 3: Six points in a row steadily increasing or decreasing: No sequence of six points steadily increase or decrease.

Rule 4: Fourteen points in a row alternating up and down: This pattern does not exist.

Rule 1 indicates that the process is out of control. We should not use this to construct the $\bar{x}$-chart.

b. We will construct the $\bar{x}$-chart even though the R-chart indicates the variation is out of control. First, compute the mean for each sample by adding the 2 observations and dividing by 2. These values are in the table in part **a.**

The centerline is $\bar{\bar{x}} = \dfrac{\sum \bar{x}}{k} = \dfrac{6883}{20} = 344.15$

From Table XII, Appendix B, with $n = 2$, $A_2 = 1.880$.

$\bar{\bar{x}} = 344.15$ and $\bar{R} = 7.4$

Upper control limit $= \bar{\bar{x}} + A_2\bar{R} = 344.15 + 1.88(7.4) = 358.062$
Lower control limit $= \bar{\bar{x}} - A_2\bar{R} = 344.15 - 1.88(7.4) = 330.238$

Upper A–B boundary $= \bar{\bar{x}} + \dfrac{2}{3}\left(A_2\bar{R}\right) = 344.15 + \dfrac{2}{3}(1.88)(7.4) = 353.425$

Lower A–B boundary $= \bar{\bar{x}} - \dfrac{2}{3}\left(A_2\bar{R}\right) = 344.15 - \dfrac{2}{3}(1.88)(7.4) = 334.875$

Upper B–C boundary $= \bar{\bar{x}} + \dfrac{1}{3}\left(A_2\bar{R}\right) = 344.15 + \dfrac{1}{3}(1.88)(7.4) = 348.787$

Lower B–C boundary $= \bar{\bar{x}} - \dfrac{1}{3}\left(A_2\bar{R}\right) = 344.15 - \dfrac{1}{3}(1.88)(7.4) = 339.513$

The $\bar{x}$-chart is:

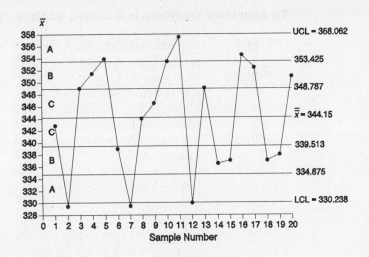

To determine if the process is in control, we check the six rules.

Rule 1: One point beyond Zone A: Points 2 and 7 are beyond Zone A. This indicates the process is out of control.

Rule 2: Nine points in a row in Zone C or beyond: There are nine points (Points 9 through 17) in a row in Zone C (on one side of the centerline) or beyond. This indicates that the process is out of control.

Rule 3: Six points in a row steadily increasing or decreasing: No sequence of six points steadily increase or decrease.

Rule 4: Fourteen points in a row alternating up and down: This pattern does not exist.

Rule 5: Two out of three points in Zone A or beyond: Points 10 and 11 are in Zone 3 or beyond. This indicates that the process is out of control.

Rule 6: Four out of five points in a row in Zone B or beyond: No sequence of five points has four or more in Zone B or beyond.

Rules 1 and 5 indicate the process is out of control. The $\bar{x}$-chart should not be used to monitor the process.

c. These control limits should not be used to monitor future output because both processes are out of control. One or more special causes of variation are affecting the process variation and process mean. These should be identified and eliminated in order to bring the processes into control.

d. Of the 40 patients sampled, 10 received care that did not conform to the hospital's requirement. The proportion is 10/40 = .25.

12.73   a.   For each sample, we compute $\bar{x} = \dfrac{\sum x}{n}$ and R = range = largest measurement − smallest measurement. The results are listed in the table:

Sample No.	$\bar{x}$	R	Sample No.	$\bar{x}$	R
1	4.36	7.1	11	3.32	4.8
2	5.10	7.7	12	4.02	4.8
3	4.52	5.0	13	5.24	7.8
4	3.42	5.8	14	3.58	3.9
5	2.62	6.2	15	3.48	5.5
6	3.94	3.9	16	5.00	3.0
7	2.34	5.3	17	3.68	6.2
8	3.26	3.2	18	2.68	3.9
9	4.06	8.0	19	3.66	4.4
10	4.96	7.1	20	4.10	5.5

$$\bar{\bar{x}} = \frac{\bar{x}_1 + \bar{x}_2 + \cdots + \bar{x}_{20}}{k} = \frac{77.34}{20} = 3.867$$

$$\bar{R} = \frac{R_1 + R_2 + \cdots + R_{20}}{k} = \frac{109.1}{20} = 5.455$$

First, we construct an R-chart.

Centerline $= \bar{R} = 5.455$

From Table XII, Appendix B, with $n = 5$, $D_4 = 2.114$, and $D_3 = 0$.

Upper control limit $= \bar{R}D_4 = 5.455(2.114) = 11.532$

Since $D_3 = 0$, the lower control limit is negative and is not included on the chart.

Upper A–B boundary $= \bar{R} + 2d_3\dfrac{\bar{R}}{d_2} = 5.455 + 2(.864)\dfrac{(5.455)}{2.326} = 9.508$

Lower A–B boundary $= \bar{R} - 2d_3\dfrac{\bar{R}}{d_2} = 5.455 - 2(.864)\dfrac{(5.455)}{2.326} = 1.402$

Upper B–C boundary $= \bar{R} + d_3\dfrac{\bar{R}}{d_2} = 5.455 + (.864)\dfrac{(5.455)}{2.326} = 7.481$

Lower B–C boundary $= \bar{R} - d_3\dfrac{\bar{R}}{d_2} = 5.455 - (.864)\dfrac{(5.455)}{2.326} = 3.429$

The *R*-chart is:

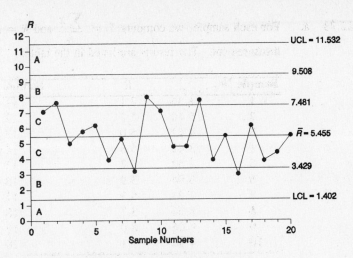

b.   To determine if the process is in or out of control, we check the four rules:

Rule 1:   One point beyond Zone A: No points are beyond Zone A.

Rule 2:   Nine points in a row in Zone C or beyond: No sequence of nine points are in Zone C (on one side of the centerline) or beyond.

Rule 3:   Six points in a row steadily increasing or decreasing: No sequence of six points steadily increase or decrease.

Rule 4:   Fourteen points in a row alternating up and down: This pattern does not exist.

The process appears to be in control. Since the process variation is in control, it is appropriate to construct the $\bar{x}$-chart.

c.   In order for the $\bar{x}$-chart to be valid, the process variation must be in control. The *R*-chart checks to see if the process variation is in control. For more details, see the answer to Exercise 12.19.

d.   To construct an $\bar{x}$-chart, we first calculate the following:

$$\bar{\bar{x}} = \frac{\bar{x}_1 + \bar{x}_2 + \cdots + \bar{x}_{20}}{k} = \frac{77.34}{20} = 3.867$$

$$\bar{R} = \frac{R_1 + R_2 + \cdots + R_{20}}{k} = \frac{109.1}{20} = 5.455$$

Centerline = $\bar{\bar{x}}$ = 3.867

From Table XII, Appendix B, with $n = 5$, $A_2 = .577$.

Upper control limit = $\bar{\bar{x}} + A_2\bar{R}$ = 3.867 + .577(5.455) = 7.015
Lower control limit = $\bar{\bar{x}} - A_2\bar{R}$ = 3.867 − .577(5.455) = .719

Upper A–B boundary = $\bar{\bar{x}} + \frac{2}{3}\left(A_2\bar{R}\right)$ = 3.867 + $\frac{2}{3}$(.577)(5.455) = 5.965

Lower A–B boundary = $\bar{\bar{x}} - \frac{2}{3}\left(A_2\bar{R}\right)$ = 3.867 − $\frac{2}{3}$(.577)(5.455) = 1.769

$$Upper \text{ B–C } boundary = \overline{\overline{x}} + \frac{1}{3}\left(A_2\overline{R}\right) = 3.867 + \frac{1}{3}(.577)(5.455) = 4.916$$

$$Lower \text{ B–C } boundary = \overline{\overline{x}} - \frac{1}{3}\left(A_2\overline{R}\right) = 3.867 - \frac{1}{3}(.577)(5.455) = 2.818$$

The $\overline{x}$-chart is:

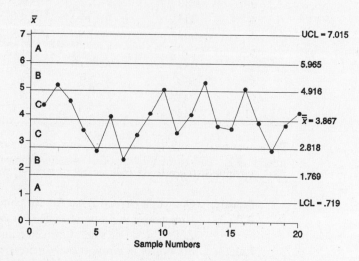

e. To determine if the process is in or out of control, we check the six rules:

Rule 1:   One point beyond Zone A: No points are beyond Zone A.

Rule 2:   Nine points in a row in Zone C or beyond: No sequence of nine points are in Zone C (on one side of the centerline) or beyond.

Rule 3:   Six points in a row steadily increasing or decreasing: No sequence of six points steadily increases or decreases.

Rule 4:   Fourteen points in a row alternating up and down: This pattern does not exist.

Rule 5:   Two out of three points in Zone A or beyond: There are no groups of three consecutive points that have two or more in Zone A or beyond.

Rule 6:   Four out of five points in a row in Zone B or beyond: No sequence of five points has four or more in Zone B or beyond.

The process appears to be in control.

f. Since both the R-chart and the $\overline{x}$-chart are in control, these control limits should be used to monitor future process output.

12.75 a. The sample size is determined by the following:

$$n > \frac{9(1 - p_0)}{p_0} = \frac{9(1 - .06)}{.06} = 141$$

The minimum sample size is 141. Since the sample size of 150 was used, it is large enough.

b. To compute the proportion of defectives in each sample, divide the number of defectives by the number in the sample, 150:

$$\hat{p} = \frac{\text{No. of defectives}}{\text{No. in sample}}$$

The sample proportions are listed in the table:

Sample No.	$\hat{p}$	Sample No.	$\hat{p}$
1	.060	11	.047
2	.073	12	.040
3	.080	13	.080
4	.053	14	.067
5	.067	15	.073
6	.040	16	.047
7	.087	17	.040
8	.060	18	.080
9	.073	19	.093
10	.033	20	.067

To get the total number of defectives, sum the number of defectives for all 20 samples. The sum is 189. To get the total number of units sampled, multiply the sample size by the number of samples: 150(20) = 3000.

$$\bar{p} = \frac{\text{Total defectives in all samples}}{\text{Total units sampled}} = \frac{189}{3000} = .063$$

$Centerline = \bar{p} = .063$

$$Upper\ control\ limit = \bar{p} + 3\sqrt{\frac{\bar{p}(1-\bar{p})}{n}} = .063 + 3\sqrt{\frac{.063(.937)}{150}} = .123$$

$$Lower\ control\ limit = \bar{p} - 3\sqrt{\frac{\bar{p}(1-\bar{p})}{n}} = .063 - 3\sqrt{\frac{.063(.937)}{150}} = .003$$

$$Upper\ A-B\ boundary = \bar{p} + 2\sqrt{\frac{\bar{p}(1-\bar{p})}{n}} = .063 + 2\sqrt{\frac{.063(.937)}{150}} = .103$$

$$Lower\ A-B\ boundary = \bar{p} - 2\sqrt{\frac{\bar{p}(1-\bar{p})}{n}} = .063 - 2\sqrt{\frac{.063(.937)}{150}} = .023$$

$$Upper\ B-C\ boundary = \bar{p} + \sqrt{\frac{\bar{p}(1-\bar{p})}{n}} = .063 + \sqrt{\frac{.063(.937)}{150}} = .083$$

$$Lower\ B-C\ boundary = \bar{p} - \sqrt{\frac{\bar{p}(1-\bar{p})}{n}} = .063 - \sqrt{\frac{.063(.937)}{150}} = .043$$

The *p*-chart is:

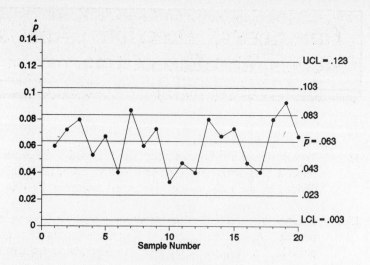

c.   To determine if the process is in or out of control, we check the four rules.

Rule 1:   One point beyond Zone A: No points are beyond Zone A.
Rule 2:   Nine points in a row in Zone C or beyond: No sequence of nine points are in Zone C (on one side of the centerline) or beyond.
Rule 3:   Six points in a row steadily increasing or decreasing: No sequence of six points steadily increase or decrease.
Rule 4:   Fourteen points in a row alternating up and down: Points 2 through 16 alternate up and down. This indicates the process is out of control.

Rule 4 indicates the process is out of control. Special causes of variation appear to be present.

e.   Since the process is out of control, the control limits should not be used to monitor future process output. It would not be appropriate to evaluate whether the process is in control using control limits determined during a period when the process was out of control.

Time Series: Descriptive Analyses, Models, and Forecasting Chapter 13

13.1   To calculate a simple index number, first obtain the prices or quantities over a time period and select a base year. For each time period, the index number is the number at that time period divided by the value at the base period multiplied by 100.

13.3   A Laspeyres index uses the purchase quantity at the base period as the weights for all other time periods. A Paasche index uses the purchase quantity at each time period as the weight for that time period. The weights at the specified time period are also used with the base period to find the index.

13.5   a.   To compute the simple index, divide each U.S. Beer Production value by the 1977 value, 171, and then multiply by 100.

Year	Simple Index	Year	Simple Index
1970	$(133/171) \times 100 = 77.78$	1983	$(195/171) \times 100 = 114.04$
1971	$(137/171) \times 100 = 80.12$	1984	$(192/171) \times 100 = 112.28$
1972	$(141/171) \times 100 = 82.46$	1985	$(194/171) \times 100 = 113.45$
1973	$(149/171) \times 100 = 87.13$	1986	$(194/171) \times 100 = 113.45$
1974	$(156/171) \times 100 = 91.23$	1987	$(196/171) \times 100 = 114.62$
1975	$(161/171) \times 100 = 94.15$	1988	$(197/171) \times 100 = 115.20$
1976	$(164/171) \times 100 = 95.91$	1989	$(198/171) \times 100 = 115.79$
1977	$(171/171) \times 100 = 100.00$	1990	$(202/171) \times 100 = 118.13$
1978	$(179/171) \times 100 = 104.68$	1991	$(204/171) \times 100 = 119.30$
1979	$(184/171) \times 100 = 107.60$	1992	$(202/171) \times 100 = 118.13$
1980	$(193/171) \times 100 = 112.87$	1993	$(202/171) \times 100 = 118.13$
1981	$(194/171) \times 100 = 113.45$	1994	$(203/171) \times 100 = 118.71$
1982	$(196/171) \times 100 = 114.62$	1995	$(200/171) \times 100 = 116.96$
		1996	$(199/171) \times 100 = 116.37$

b.   This is a quantity index because the numbers collected were the number of barrels produced rather than the price.

c.   To compute the simple index, divide each U.S. Beer Production value by the 1980 value, 193, and then multiply by 100.

Year	Simple Index	Year	Simple Index
1970	(133/193) × 100 = 68.91	1983	(195/193) × 100 = 101.04
1971	(137/193) × 100 = 70.98	1984	(192/193) × 100 = 99.48
1972	(141/193) × 100 = 73.06	1985	(194/193) × 100 = 100.52
1973	(149/193) × 100 = 77.20	1986	(194/193) × 100 = 100.52
1974	(156/193) × 100 = 80.83	1987	(196/193) × 100 = 101.55
1975	(161/193) × 100 = 83.42	1988	(197/193) × 100 = 102.07
1976	(164/193) × 100 = 84.97	1989	(198/193) × 100 = 102.59
1977	(171/193) × 100 = 88.60	1990	(202/193) × 100 = 104.66
1978	(179/193) × 100 = 92.75	1991	(204/193) × 100 = 105.70
1979	(184/193) × 100 = 95.34	1992	(202/193) × 100 = 104.66
1980	(193/193) × 100 = 100.00	1993	(202/193) × 100 = 104.66
1981	(194/193) × 100 = 100.52	1994	(203/193) × 100 = 105.18
1982	(196/193) × 100 = 101.55	1995	(200/193) × 100 = 103.63
		1996	(199/193) × 100 = 103.11

The plots of the two simple indices are:

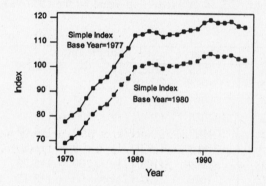

13.7 a. To compute the simple index, divide each closing price by the 1985 value, 17.84, and then multiply by 100.

Year	Simple Index	Year	Simple Index
1985	(17.84/17.84) × 100 = 100.00	1993	(25.94/17.84) × 100 = 145.40
1986	(18.46/17.84) × 100 = 103.48	1994	(27.94/17.84) × 100 = 156.61
1987	(24.09/17.84) × 100 = 135.03	1995	(27.00/17.84) × 100 = 151.35
1988	(19.03/17.84) × 100 = 106.67	1996	(34.19/17.84) × 100 = 191.65
1989	(25.32/17.84) × 100 = 141.93	1997	(39.50/17.84) × 100 = 221.41
1990	(29.95/17.84) × 100 = 167.88	1998	(57.06/17.84) × 100 = 319.83
1991	(34.13/17.84) × 100 = 191.31	1999	(54.56/17.84) × 100 = 305.83
1992	(33.56/17.84) × 100 = 188.12	2000	(46.31/17.84) × 100 = 259.59

b. The value of the index in 1985 is 100 and the value in 1989 was 141.93. Thus, the stock price increased by $141.93 - 100 = 41.93\%$.

The value of the index in 1991 is 191.31 and the value in 2000 was 259.59. Thus, the stock price increased by $259.59 - 191.31 = 68.28\%$.

13.9 a. To compute the simple index for the agricultural data, divide each farm value by the 1980 value, 3,364, and then multiply by 100. To compute the simple index for the nonagricultural data, divide each nonfarm value by the 1980 value, 95,938, and then multiply by 100. The two indices are:

Year	Farm Index	Nonfarm Index
1980	100.00	100.00
1981	100.12	101.14
1982	101.10	100.19
1983	100.56	101.58
1984	98.72	105.99
1985	94.50	108.37
1986	94.02	110.94
1987	95.36	113.86
1988	94.20	116.53
1989	95.10	118.97
1990	94.71	119.59
1991	96.11	118.46
1992	95.33	119.23
1993	91.38	121.15
1994	101.34	124.72
1995	102.26	126.60
1996	102.35	128.48
1997	101.04	131.50

b. The nonfarm segment has shown the greater percentage change in employment over the time period. The nonfarm employment in 1997 was 31.5% greater than in 1980. The farm employment in 1997 was only 1.04% greater than in 1980.

c. To compute the simple composite index, first sum the two values (farm and nonfarm) for every time period. Then, divide each sum by the sum in 1980, 99,302, and then multiply by 100. The simple composite index is:

Year	Sum	Simple Composite Index
1980	99,302	100.00
1981	100,398	101.10
1982	99,526	100.23
1983	100,833	101.54
1984	105,006	105.74
1985	107,150	107.90
1986	109,597	110.37
1987	112,440	113.23
1988	114,969	115.78
1989	117,341	118.17
1990	117,914	118.74
1991	116,877	117.70
1992	117,598	118.42
1993	119,306	120.14
1994	123,060	123.92
1995	124,900	125.78
1996	126,707	127.60
1997	129,558	130.47

Time Series: Descriptive Analyses, Models, and Forecasting

d. The simple composite index value for 1997 was 130.47. The composite employment is 30.47% higher in 1997 than in 1980.

13.11 a. The find Laspeyres index, we multiply the durable goods by 10.9, the nondurable goods by 14.02, and the services by 42.6. The three products are then summed. The index is found by dividing the weighted sum at each time period by the weighted sum of 1970, 17,108.86, and then multiplying by 100. The Laspeyres index and the simple composite index for 1970 (computed in Exercise 13.10) are:

Year	Simple Composite Index-1970	Weighted Sum	Laspeyres Index
1960	51.43	8,409.95	49.16
1965	68.77	11,442.51	66.88
1970	100.00	17,108.86	100.00
1975	158.52	27,509.89	160.79
1980	270.39	48,215.53	281.82
1985	412.59	76,167.86	445.20
1990	581.78	110,254.64	644.43
1991	603.63	115,824.36	676.98
1992	639.89	123,587.96	722.36
1993	677.22	131,182.38	766.75
1994	715.93	138,574.46	809.96
1995	957.53	186,502.36	1,090.09
1996	982.58	190,610.72	1,114.11
1997	1,021.48	196,740.79	1,149.94

b. The plot of the two indices is:

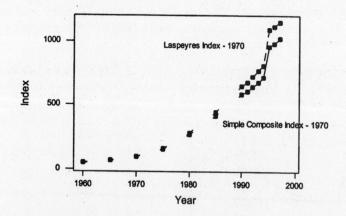

The two indices are very similar from 1960 to approximately 1980. After 1980, the difference between the two indices becomes larger, with the Laspeyres index increasing faster than the simple composite index.

13.13 a. To compute the simple index for the average hourly earnings for manufacturing workers, divide the hourly earnings for each year by the hourly earnings for the base year, 4.83, and multiply by 100. To compute the simple index for the average hourly earnings for transportation and public utilities workers, divide the hourly earnings for each year by the hourly earnings for the base year, 5.88, and multiply by 100. To compute the simple index for the average hourly earnings for wholesale trade workers, divide the hourly earnings for each year by the hourly earnings for the base year, 4.72, and multiply by 100. The three indices are:

Year	Manufacturing Index	Transportation/ Utilities Index
1975	100.00	100.0
1976	108.07	109.69
1977	117.60	118.88
1978	127.74	128.74
1979	138.72	138.78
1980	150.52	150.85
1981	165.42	164.97
1982	175.78	175.51
1983	182.82	183.50
1984	190.27	189.12
1985	197.52	193.88
1986	201.45	198.98
1987	205.18	204.59
1988	210.97	208.50
1989	216.98	214.29
1990	224.22	220.58
1991	231.47	224.83
1992	237.27	228.74
1993	243.06	231.63
1994	249.90	235.71
1995	256.11	242.01
1996	264.39	245.75
1997	272.67	253.74
1998	279.30	260.37

b. The two plots are:

The two simple earnings indices are very similar. From 1975 to 1998, the hourly earnings have increased from 160.37% for the transportation and public utilities workers to 179.30% for the manufacturing workers.

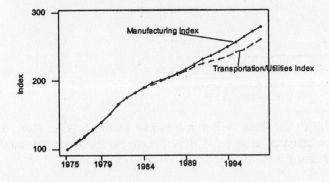

c. To compute the simple composite index for the hourly earnings, sum the earnings for the three industries for each time period. Then divide the sum at each year by the sum at the base year, 15.43, and multiply by 100. To compute the simple composite index for weekly hours, sum the weekly hours for the three industries for each time period. Then divide the sum at each year by the sum at the base year, 117.8, and multiply by 100. The two composite indices are:

Year	Earnings Sum	Hours Sum	Earnings Index	Hours Index
1975	15.43	117.80	100.00	100.00
1976	16.69	118.60	108.17	100.68
1977	18.06	119.00	117.04	101.02
1978	19.62	119.20	127.15	101.19
1979	21.25	118.90	137.72	100.93
1980	23.09	117.70	149.64	99.92
1981	25.24	117.70	163.58	99.92
1982	26.89	116.20	174.27	98.64
1983	28.16	117.60	182.50	99.83
1984	29.19	118.60	189.18	100.68
1985	30.09	118.40	195.01	100.51
1986	30.77	118.20	199.42	100.34
1987	31.53	118.30	204.34	100.42
1988	32.43	118.00	210.17	100.17
1989	33.47	117.90	216.92	100.08
1990	34.59	117.80	224.17	100.00
1991	35.55	117.50	230.40	99.75
1992	36.30	118.10	235.26	100.25
1993	37.10	119.20	240.44	101.19
1994	37.99	120.30	246.21	102.12
1995	39.03	119.40	252.95	101.36
1996	40.09	119.50	259.82	101.44
1997	41.54	120.10	269.22	101.95
1998	42.86	119.60	277.77	101.53

d. The plots of the two composite indices are:

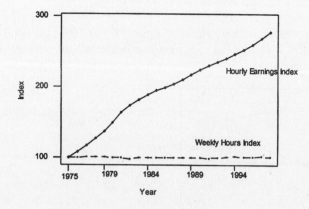

The composite earnings index has increased 177.77% from 1975 to 1998. However, the composite weekly hours has increased only 1.53% from 1975 to 1998.

13.15   a.   The exponentially smoothed employment for the first period is equal to the employment for that period. For the rest of the time periods, the exponentially smoothed employment values are found by multiplying .5 times the employment value of that time period and adding to that $(1 - .5)$ times the value of the exponentially smoothed employment figure of the previous time period.

The exponentially smoothed employment value for the time period 1987 is $.5(281.3) + (1 - .5)(280.5) = 280.9$. The rest of the values are shown in the table.

Year	Employment	Exponentially Smoothed Series $w = .5$
1986	280.5	280.5
1987	281.3	280.9
1988	250.3	265.6
1989	246.6	256.1
1990	239.8	248.0
1991	218.1	233.0
1992	218.7	225.9
1993	210.0	217.9
1994	205.0	211.5
1995	206.6	209.0
1996	200.4	204.7

b.   The graph of the time series and the exponentially smoothed series is:

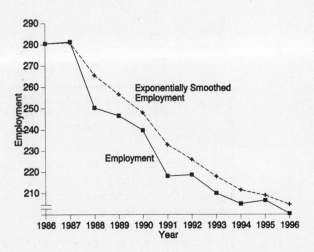

13.17   a.   The exponentially smoothed fish catch for Chile for the first period is equal to the fish catch for that period. For the rest of the time periods, the exponentially smoothed fish catch values are found by multiplying .5 times the fish catch of that time period and adding to that $(1 - .5)$ times the value of the exponentially smoothed fish catch figure of the previous time period. The exponentially smoothed fish catch for Chile for the time period 1987 is $.5(4,814.6) + (1 - .5)(5,571.6) = 5,193.10$. The rest of the values are shown in the table.

Similarly, the exponentially smoothed fish catch for Brazil for the first period is equal to the fish catch for that period. For the rest of the time periods, the exponentially smoothed fish catch values are found by multiplying .5 times the fish catch of that time period and adding to that $(1 - .5)$ times the value of the exponentially smoothed fish catch figure of the previous

time period. The exponentially smoothed fish catch for Brazil for time period 1987 is
.5(948.0) + (1 − .5)(957.6) = 952.80. The rest of the values are shown in the table.

Year	Chile Catch	Brazil Catch	Chile $w = .5$ Exponentially Smoothed Catch	Brazil $w = .5$ Exponentially Smoothed Catch
1986	5,571.6	957.6	5,571.60	957.60
1987	4,814.6	948.0	5,193.10	952.80
1988	5,209.9	830.1	5,201.50	891.45
1989	6,454.2	850.0	5,827.85	870.73
1990	5,195.4	802.9	5,511.63	836.81
1991	6,002.8	800.0	5,757.21	818.41
1992	6,501.8	790.0	6,129.51	804.20
1993	6,034.9	780.0	6,082.20	792.10
1994	7,838.5	820.0	6,960.35	806.05
1995	7,590.5	800.0	7,275.43	803.03

b. The plot of the two time series and the two exponentially smoothed series is:

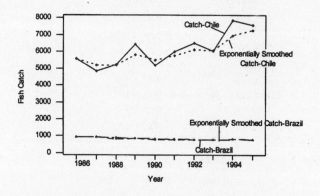

Both the time series and the exponentially smoothed series for fish catch in Brazil are fairly
stable over time. There is a fairly steady decrease over time. Both the time series and the
exponentially smoothed series for fish catch in Chile show an increase over time. The
exponentially smoothed series is more stable than is the actual time series.

13.19   a.   The exponentially smoothed expenditure for the first time period is equal to the expenditure for
that period. For the rest of the time periods, the exponentially smoothed expenditures are
found by multiplying the expenditures for the time period by $w = .2$ and adding to that
$(1 − .2)$ times the exponentially smoothed value above it. The exponentially smoothed values
for the year 1971 is .2(92.3) + (1 − .2)(80.6) = 82.94. The rest of the values appear in the
table. The process is repeated with $w = .8$.

Year	Expenditures	$w = .2$ Exponentially Smoothed Value	$w = .8$ Exponentially Smoothed Value
1970	80.6	80.60	80.60
1971	92.3	82.94	89.96
1972	105.4	87.43	102.31
1973	114.6	92.87	112.14
1974	117.9	97.87	116.75
1975	129.4	104.18	126.87
1976	155.2	114.38	149.53
1977	179.3	127.37	173.35
1978	198.1	141.51	193.15
1979	219.4	157.09	214.15
1980	236.6	172.99	232.11
1981	261.5	190.69	255.62
1982	267.3	206.01	264.96
1983	291.9	223.19	286.51
1984	319.5	242.45	312.90
1985	359.5	265.86	350.18
1986	366.3	285.95	363.08
1987	377.1	304.18	374.30
1988	406.4	324.62	399.98
1989	425.7	344.84	420.56
1990	463.3	368.53	454.75
1991	438.2	382.47	441.51
1992	466.3	399.23	461.34
1993	504.2	420.23	495.63
1994	542.2	444.62	532.89
1995	572.3	470.16	564.42
1996	602.2	496.57	594.64

b.   The plot of the two series is:

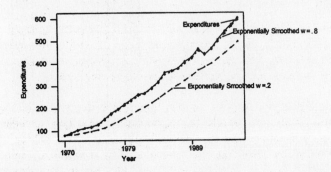

There is a steeper increase in expenditures in the 1980s and early 1990s compared with the 1970s.

13.21   If w is small (near 0), one will obtain a smooth, slowly changing series of forecasts. If w is large (near 1), one will obtain more rapidly changing forecasts that depend mostly on the current values of the series.

13.23 a.   We first compute the exponentially smoothed values $E_1, E_2, \ldots, E_t$ for years 1970–1993.

$$E_1 = Y_1 = 133.1$$

For $w = .3$, $E_2 = wY_2 + (1 - w)E_1 = .3(137) + (1 - .3)(133) = 134.20$
$$E_3 = wY_3 + (1 - w)E_2 = .3(141) + (1 - .3)(134.20) = 136.24$$

The rest of the values appear in the table.

For $w = .7$, $E_2 = wY_2 + (1 - w)E_1 = .7(137) + (1 - .7)(133) = 135.80$
$$E_3 = wY_3 + (1 - w)E_2 = .7(141) + (1 - .7)(135.80) = 139.44$$

The rest of the values appear in the table.

Year	Beer Production	Exponentially Smoothed Value $w = .3$	Exponentially Smoothed Value $w = .7$
1970	133	133.00	133.00
1971	137	134.20	135.80
1972	141	136.24	139.44
1973	149	140.07	146.13
1974	156	144.85	153.04
1975	161	149.69	158.61
1976	164	153.99	162.38
1977	171	159.09	168.42
1978	179	165.06	175.82
1979	184	170.74	181.55
1980	193	177.42	189.56
1981	194	182.39	192.67
1982	196	186.48	195.00
1983	195	189.03	195.00
1984	192	189.92	192.90
1985	194	191.15	193.67
1986	194	192.00	193.90
1987	196	193.20	195.37
1988	197	194.34	196.51
1989	198	195.44	197.55
1990	202	197.41	200.67
1991	204	199.39	203.00
1992	202	200.17	202.30
1993	202	200.72	202.09
1994	203		
1995	200		
1996	199		

To forecast using exponentially smoothed values, we use the following:

For $w = .3$:

$$F_{1994} = F_{t+1} = E_t = 200.72$$
$$F_{1995} = F_{t+2} = F_{t+1} = 200.72$$
$$F_{1996} = F_{t+3} = F_{t+1} = 200.72$$

For $w = .7$:

$$F_{1994} = F_{t+1} = E_t = 202.09$$
$$F_{1995} = F_{t+2} = F_{t+1} = 202.09$$
$$F_{1996} = F_{t+3} = F_{t+1} = 202.09$$

b. We first compute the Holt-Winters values for years 1970−1993.

With $w = .7$ and $v = .3$,

$$E_2 = Y_2 = 137$$
$$E_3 = wY_3 + (1 - w)(E_2 + T_2) = .7(141) + (1 - .7)(137 + 4) = 141$$

$$T_2 = Y_2 - Y_1 = 137 - 133 = 4$$
$$T_3 = v(E_3 - E_2) + (1 - v)T_2 = .3(141 - 137) + (1 - .3)(4) = 4.0$$

The rest of the E_t's and T_t's appear in the table that follows.

With $w = .3$ and $v = .7$,

$$E_2 = Y_2 = 137$$
$$E_3 = .3(141) + (1 - .3)(137 + 4) = 141.0$$

$$T_2 = Y_2 - Y_1 = 141 - 137 = 4$$
$$T_3 = .7(141 - 137) + (1 - .7)(4) = 4.0$$

The rest of the E_t's and T_t's appear in the table below.

Year	Beer Production	E_t $w = .7$ $v = .3$	T_t $w = .7$ $v = .3$	E_t $w = .3$ $v = .7$	T_t $w = .3$ $v = .7$
1970	133				
1971	137	137.00	4.00	137.00	4.00
1972	141	141.00	4.00	141.00	4.00
1973	149	147.80	4.84	146.20	4.84
1974	156	154.99	5.55	152.53	5.88
1975	161	160.86	5.64	159.19	6.43
1976	164	164.75	5.12	165.13	6.09
1977	171	170.66	5.35	171.15	6.04
1978	179	178.10	5.98	177.73	6.42
1979	184	184.03	5.96	184.11	6.39
1980	193	192.10	6.60	191.25	6.91
1981	194	195.41	5.61	196.91	6.04
1982	196	197.51	4.56	200.87	4.58
1983	195	197.12	3.07	202.31	2.39
1984	192	194.46	1.35	200.89	-0.28
1985	194	194.54	0.97	198.63	-1.67
1986	194	194.45	0.65	196.07	-2.29
1987	196	195.73	0.84	194.45	-1.82
1988	197	196.87	0.93	193.94	-0.90
1989	198	197.94	0.97	194.52	0.14
1990	202	201.07	1.62	196.86	1.68
1991	204	203.61	1.89	200.18	2.83
1992	202	203.05	1.16	202.70	2.61
1993	202	202.66	0.69	204.32	1.92
1994	203				
1995	200				
1996	199				

To forecast using the Holt-Winters Model:

For $w = .7$ and $v = .3$,

$$F_{1994} = F_{t+1} = E_t + T_t = 202.66 + .69 = 203.35$$
$$F_{1995} = F_{t+2} = E_t + 2T_t = 202.66 + 2(.69) = 204.04$$
$$F_{1996} = F_{t+3} = E_t + 3T_t = 202.66 + 3(.69) = 204.73$$

For $w = .3$ and $v = .7$,

$$F_{1994} = F_{t+1} = E_t + T_t = 204.32 + 1.92 = 206.24$$
$$F_{1995} = F_{t+2} = E_t + 2T_t = 204.32 + 2(1.92) = 208.16$$
$$F_{1996} = F_{t+3} = E_t + 3T_t = 204.32 + 3(1.92) = 210.08$$

13.25 a. We first compute the exponentially smoothed values $E_1, E_2, \ldots, E_t$ for 1980 through 1998.

$$E_1 = Y_1 = 104.7$$

For $w = .7$,

$$E_2 = wY_2 + (1 - w)E_1 = .7(114.6) + (1 - .7)104.70 = 111.63$$
$$E_3 = wY_3 + (1 - w)E_2 = .7(126.5) + (1 - .7)111.63 = 122.04$$

The rest of the values appear in the table:

Year	Quarter	S & P 500	Exponentially Smoothed Value $w = .7$	Exponentially Smoothed Value $w = .3$
1980	I	104.7	104.70	104.70
	II	114.6	111.63	107.67
	III	126.5	122.04	113.32
	IV	133.5	130.06	119.37
1981	I	133.2	132.26	123.52
	II	132.3	132.29	126.15
	III	118.3	122.50	123.80
	IV	123.8	123.41	123.80
1982	I	110.8	114.58	119.90
	II	109.7	111.16	116.84
	III	122.4	119.03	118.51
	IV	139.4	133.29	124.78
1983	I	151.9	146.32	132.91
	II	166.4	160.37	142.96
	III	167.2	165.15	150.23
	IV	164.4	164.63	154.48
1984	I	157.4	159.57	155.36
	II	153.1	155.04	154.68
	III	166.1	162.78	158.11
	IV	164.5	163.98	160.02
1985	I	179.4	174.78	165.84
	II	188.9	184.66	172.76
	III	184.1	184.27	176.16
	IV	207.3	200.39	185.50
1986	I	232.3	222.73	199.54
	II	245.3	238.53	213.27
	III	238.3	238.37	220.78
	IV	248.6	245.53	229.12

1987	I	292.5	278.41	248.14
	II	301.4	294.50	264.12
	III	318.7	311.44	280.49
	IV	241.0	262.13	268.64
1988	I	265.7	264.63	267.76
	II	270.7	268.88	268.64
	III	268.0	268.26	268.45
	IV	276.5	274.03	270.86
1989	I	292.7	287.10	277.42
	II	323.7	312.72	291.30
	III	347.3	336.93	308.10
	IV	348.6	345.10	320.25
1990	I	338.5	340.48	325.73
	II	360.4	354.42	336.13
	III	315.4	327.11	329.91
	IV	328.8	328.29	329.58
1991	I	372.3	359.10	342.39
	II	378.3	372.54	353.17
	III	387.2	382.80	363.38
	IV	388.5	386.79	370.91
1992	I	407.3	401.15	381.83
	II	408.27	406.13	389.76
	III	418.48	414.78	398.38
	IV	435.64	429.38	409.56
1993	I	450.2	443.95	421.75
	II	448.1	446.86	429.65
	III	459.2	455.50	438.52
	IV	466.0	462.85	446.76
1994	I	463.8	463.51	451.87
	II	454.8	457.41	452.75
	III	467.0	464.12	457.03
	IV	455.2	457.88	456.48
1995	I	493.2	482.60	467.49
	II	539.4	522.36	489.07
	III	578.8	561.87	515.99
	IV	614.6	598.78	545.57
1996	I	645.5	631.48	575.55
	II	670.63	658.89	604.07
	III	687.31	678.78	629.04
	IV	740.74	722.15	662.55
1997	I	757.12	746.63	690.92
	II	885.14	843.59	749.19
	III	947.28	916.17	808.62
	IV	970.43	954.15	857.16
1998	I	1,101.75	1,057.47	930.53
	II	1,133.84	1,110.93	991.53
	III	1,017.01	1,045.19	999.17
	IV	1,229.23	1,174.02	1,068.19
1999	I	1,286.37		
	II	1,372.71		
	III	1,282.71		
	IV	1,269.25		

The forecasts for the four quarters in 1999 based on 1980–1998 data are:

$$F_{1999,I} = F_{t+1} = E_t = 1,174.02$$
$$F_{1999,II} = F_{t+2} = E_t = 1,174.02$$
$$F_{1999,III} = F_{t+3} = E_t = 1,174.02$$
$$F_{1999,IV} = F_{t+4} = E_t = 1,174.02$$

b. We first compute the exponentially smoothed values $E_1, E_2, \ldots, E_t$ for 1980 through 1998.

$$E_1 = Y_1 = 104.7$$

For $w = .3$,

$$E_2 = wY_2 + (1 - w)E_1 = .3(114.6) + (1 - .3)104.70 = 107.67$$
$$E_3 = wY_3 + (1 - w)E_2 = .3(126.5) + (1 - .3)107.67 = 113.32$$

The rest of the values appear in the table in part a.

The forecasts for the four quarters in 1999 based on 1980–1998 data are:

$$F_{1999,I} = F_{t+1} = E_t = 1,068.19$$
$$F_{1999,II} = F_{t+2} = E_t = 1,068.19$$
$$F_{1999,III} = F_{t+3} = E_t = 1,068.19$$
$$F_{1999,IV} = F_{t+4} = E_t = 1,068.19$$

13.27 a. We first compute the exponentially smoothed values $E_1, E_2, \ldots, E_t$ for 1990 through 1999.

$$E_1 = Y_1 = 411.5$$

For $w = .5$,

$$E_2 = wY_2 + (1 - w)E_1 = .5(418.5) + (1 - .5)411.50 = 415.00$$
$$E_3 = wY_3 + (1 - w)E_2 = .5(394.4) + (1 - .5)415.00 = 404.70$$

The rest of the values appear in the table.

Year	Month	Gold Price	Exponentially Smoothed $w = .5$	Holt-Winters E_t $w = .5$	T_t $v = .5$
1990	Jan	411.5	411.50		
	Feb	418.5	415.00	418.50	7.00
	Mar	394.4	404.70	409.95	−0.78
	Apr	375.5	390.10	392.34	−9.19
	May	370.4	380.25	376.77	−12.38
	Jun	353.6	366.93	359.00	−15.08
	Jul	382.0	374.46	362.96	−5.56
	Aug	396.5	385.48	376.95	4.22
	Sep	390.8	388.14	385.98	6.63
	Oct	382.0	385.07	387.30	3.97
	Nov	383.0	384.04	387.14	1.90
	Dec	379.3	381.67	384.17	−0.53
1991	Jan	384.9	383.28	384.27	−0.22
	Feb	365.1	374.19	374.58	−4.96
	Mar	347.2	360.70	358.41	−10.56
	Apr	359.6	360.15	353.73	−7.62

	May	358.1	359.12	352.10	−4.62
	Jun	368.0	363.56	357.74	0.51
	Jul	369.7	366.63	363.97	3.37
	Aug	341.9	354.27	354.62	−2.99
	Sep	368.4	361.33	360.02	1.20
	Oct	360.1	360.72	360.66	0.92
	Nov	344.2	352.46	352.89	−3.42
	Dec	380.3	366.38	364.88	4.29
1992	Jan	355.7	361.04	362.43	0.92
	Feb	355.2	358.12	359.28	−1.12
	Mar	346.0	352.06	352.08	−4.16
	Apr	339.8	345.93	343.86	−6.19
	May	338.5	342.21	338.09	−5.98
	Jun	342.0	342.11	337.05	−3.51
	Jul	338.9	340.50	336.22	−2.17
	Aug	344.2	342.35	339.13	0.37
	Sep	346.7	344.53	343.10	2.17
	Oct	345.6	345.06	345.43	2.25
	Nov	336.3	340.68	341.99	−0.59
	Dec	335.5	338.09	338.45	−2.07
1993	Jan	330.2	334.15	333.29	−3.61
	Feb	330.9	332.52	330.29	−3.31
	Mar	331.3	331.91	329.14	−2.23
	Apr	343.2	337.56	335.06	1.84
	May	368.0	352.78	352.45	9.62
	Jun	373.2	362.99	367.63	12.40
	Jul	391.6	377.29	385.82	15.29
	Aug	379.7	378.50	390.41	9.94
	Sep	356.1	367.30	378.22	−1.12
	Oct	365.4	366.35	371.25	−4.05
	Nov	374.9	370.62	371.05	−2.12
	Dec	385.3	377.96	377.11	1.97
1994	Jan	408.3	393.13	393.69	9.27
	Feb	383.3	388.22	393.13	4.36
	Mar	385.4	386.81	391.45	1.33
	Apr	378.4	382.60	385.59	−2.26
	May	382.5	382.55	382.91	−2.47
	Jun	387.0	384.78	383.72	−0.83
	Jul	386.7	385.74	384.80	0.12
	Aug	381.7	383.72	383.31	−0.68
	Sep	393.1	388.41	387.86	1.94
	Oct	391.1	389.75	390.45	2.26
	Nov	385.7	387.73	389.21	0.51
	Dec	386.7	387.21	388.21	−0.25
1995	Jan	379.8	383.51	383.88	−2.29
	Feb	377.8	380.65	379.70	−3.23
	Mar	383.4	382.03	379.93	−1.50
	Apr	391.3	386.66	384.87	1.72
	May	386.6	386.63	386.59	1.72
	Jun	388.9	387.77	388.61	1.87
	Jul	387.7	387.73	389.09	1.17
	Aug	384.9	386.32	387.58	−0.17
	Sep	384.5	385.41	385.96	−0.89

	Oct	384.4	384.90	384.73	−1.06
	Nov	381.0	382.95	382.34	−1.73
	Dec	388.7	385.83	384.65	0.30
1996	Jan	400.9	393.36	392.92	4.28
	Feb	406.1	399.73	401.65	6.51
	Mar	397.5	398.62	402.83	3.84
	Apr	394.3	396.46	400.49	0.75
	May	393.3	394.88	397.27	−1.24
	Jun	386.6	390.74	391.32	−3.59
	Jul	384.9	387.82	386.31	−4.30
	Aug	388.7	388.26	385.36	−2.63
	Sep	384.3	386.28	383.51	−2.23
	Oct	382.4	384.34	381.84	−1.95
	Nov	379.5	381.92	379.69	−2.05
	Dec	369.3	375.61	373.47	−4.14
1997	Jan	345.5	360.55	357.42	−10.10
	Feb	358.6	359.58	352.96	−7.28
	Mar	348.2	353.89	346.94	−6.65
	Apr	340.2	347.04	340.25	−6.67
	May	345.6	346.32	339.59	−3.67
	Jun	334.6	340.46	335.26	−4.00
	Jul	326.4	333.43	328.83	−5.21
	Aug	325.4	329.42	324.51	−4.77
	Sep	332.1	330.76	325.92	−1.68
	Oct	311.4	321.08	317.82	−4.89
	Nov	296.8	308.94	304.87	−8.92
	Dec	290.2	299.57	293.07	−10.36
1998	Jan	304.9	302.23	293.81	−4.81
	Feb	297.4	299.82	293.20	−2.71
	Mar	301.0	300.41	295.74	−0.08
	Apr	310.7	305.55	303.18	3.68
	May	293.6	299.58	300.23	0.36
	Jun	296.3	297.94	298.45	−0.71
	Jul	288.9	293.42	293.32	−2.92
	Aug	273.4	283.41	281.90	−7.17
	Sep	293.9	288.65	284.32	−2.38
	Oct	294.0	291.33	287.97	0.64
	Nov	294.7	293.01	291.65	2.16
	Dec	287.8	290.41	290.81	0.66
1999	Jan	285.4	287.90	288.43	−0.86
	Feb	287.1	287.50	287.34	−0.98
	Mar	279.5	283.50	282.93	−2.69
	Apr	286.6	285.50	283.42	−1.10
	May	269.0	277.03	275.66	−4.43
	Jun	262.6	269.81	266.91	−6.59
	Jul	255.6	262.71	257.96	−7.77
	Aug	254.8	258.75	252.50	−6.62
	Sep	307.5	283.13	276.69	8.79
	Oct	299.1	291.11	292.29	12.19
	Nov	291.4	291.26	297.94	8.92
	Dec	290.3	290.78	298.58	4.78

To forecast the monthly prices for 1999 using the data through December 1998:

$$F_{t+1} = E_t, F_{t+i} = E_t, \text{ for } i = 2, 3, \dots$$
$$F_{t+1} = E_{\text{Dec},1998} = 290.41$$

Year	Month	Forecast
1999	Jan	290.41
	Feb	290.41
	Mar	290.41
	Apr	290.41
	May	290.41
	Jun	290.41
	Jul	290.41
	Aug	290.41
	Sep	290.41
	Oct	290.41
	Nov	290.41
	Dec	290.41

b. To compute the one-step-ahead forecasts for 1999, we use $F_{t+1} = E_t$, where E_t is recomputed each time period. The forecasts are obtained from the table in part **a**.

Year	Month	Forecast
1999	Jan	290.41
	Feb	287.90
	Mar	287.50
	Apr	283.50
	May	285.05
	Jun	277.03
	Jul	269.81
	Aug	262.71
	Sep	258.75
	Oct	283.13
	Nov	291.11
	Dec	291.26

c. First, we compute the Holt-Winters values for the years 1990–1999.

With $w = .5$ and $v = .5$,

$$E_2 = Y_2 = 418.5$$
$$E_3 = wY_3 + (1 - w)(E_2 + T_2) = .5(394.4) + (1 - .5)(418.5 + 7.0) = 409.95$$

$$T_2 = Y_2 - Y_1 = 418.5 - 411.5 = 7$$
$$T_3 = v(E_3 - E_2) + (1 - v)T_2 = .5(409.95 - 418.5) + (1 - .5)7 = -.775$$

The rest of the E_t's and T_t's appear in the table in part **a**.

To forecast the monthly prices for 1999 using the data through December 1998:

$$F_{t+1} = E_t + T_t = 290.81 + (.66) = 291.47$$
$$F_{t+2} = E_t + 2T_t = 290.81 + 2(.66) = 292.13$$

The rest of the values appear in the table.

Year	Month	Forecast
1999	Jan	291.47
	Feb	292.13
	Mar	292.79
	Apr	293.45
	May	294.11
	Jun	294.77
	Jul	295.43
	Aug	296.09
	Sep	296.75
	Oct	297.41
	Nov	298.07
	Dec	298.73

To compute the one-step-ahead forecasts for 1999, we use $F_{t+1} = E_t + T_t$ where E_t and T_t are recomputed each time period. The forecasts are obtained from the table in part **a**.

Year	Month	Forecast
1999	Jan	291.47
	Feb	287.57
	Mar	286.36
	Apr	280.24
	May	282.32
	Jun	271.23
	Jul	260.33
	Aug	250.19
	Sep	245.88
	Oct	285.48
	Nov	304.48
	Dec	306.86

13.29 From Exercise 13.22, the forecast for 1998 is:

$$F_{1998} = E_{1997} = 1,449.15$$

The error is the difference between the actual value and the forecasted value.

Thus, the error is $Y_{1998} - F_{1998} = 1,390 - 1,449.15 = -59.15$

13.31 a. From Exercise 13.23b, the forecasts for 1994–1996 using $w = .3$ and $v = .7$ are:

$$F_{1994} = 206.24$$
$$F_{1995} = 208.16$$
$$F_{1996} = 210.08$$

The errors are the difference between the actual values and the forecasted values. Thus, the errors are:

$$Y_{1994} - F_{1994} = 203 - 206.24 = -3.24$$
$$Y_{1995} - F_{1995} = 200 - 208.16 = -8.16$$
$$Y_{1996} - F_{1996} = 199 - 210.08 = -11.08$$

b. From Exercise 13.23b, the forecasts for 1994–1996 using $w = .7$ and $v = .3$ are:

$$F_{1994} = 203.35$$
$$F_{1995} = 204.04$$
$$F_{1996} = 204.73$$

The errors are the difference between the actual values and the forecasted values. Thus, the errors are:

$$Y_{1994} - F_{1994} = 203 - 203.35 = -.35$$
$$Y_{1995} - F_{1995} = 200 - 204.04 = -4.04$$
$$Y_{1996} - F_{1996} = 199 - 204.73 = -5.73$$

c. For the Holt-Winters forecasts using $w = .3$ and $v = .7$,

$$\text{MAD} = \frac{\sum |F_t - Y_t|}{N} = \frac{|206.24 - 203| + |208.16 - 200| + |210.08 - 199|}{3}$$
$$= \frac{22.48}{3} = 7.493$$

d. For the Holt-Winters forecasts using $w = .7$ and $v = .3$,

$$\text{MAD} = \frac{\sum |F_t - Y_t|}{N} = \frac{|203.35 - 203| + |204.04 - 200| + |204.73 - 199|}{3}$$
$$= \frac{10.12}{3} = 3.373$$

e. For the Holt-Winters forecasts using $w = .3$ and $v = .7$,

$$\text{RMSE} = \sqrt{\frac{\sum (F_t - Y_t)^2}{N}} = \sqrt{\frac{(3.24)^2 + (8.16)^2 + (11.08)^2}{3}} = 8.162$$

f. For the Holt-Winters forecasts using $w = .7$ and $v = .3$,

$$\text{RMSE} = \sqrt{\frac{\sum (F_t - Y_t)^2}{N}} = \sqrt{\frac{(.35)^2 + (4.04)^2 + (5.73)^2}{3}} = 4.053$$

13.33 a. For the forecasts using $w = .7$,

$$\text{MAD} = \frac{\sum |F_t - Y_t|}{N}$$
$$= \frac{|1,174.02 - 1,286.37| + |1,174.02 - 1,372.71| + |1,174.02 - 1,282.71| + |1,174.02 - 1,269.25|}{4}$$
$$= \frac{514.96}{4} = 128.74$$

$$\text{RMSE} = \sqrt{\frac{\sum (F_t - Y_t)^2}{N}} = \sqrt{\frac{(-112.35)^2 + (-198.69)^2 + (-108.69)^2 + (-95.23)^2}{4}} = 135.076$$

b. For the forecasts using $w = .3$,

$$\text{MAD} = \frac{\sum |F_t - Y_t|}{N}$$

$$= \frac{|1,068.19 - 1,286.37| + |1,068.19 - 1,372.71| + |1,068.19 - 1,282.71| + |1,068.19 - 1,269.25|}{4}$$

$$= \frac{938.28}{4} = 234.57$$

$$\text{RMSE} = \sqrt{\frac{\sum (F_t - Y_t)^2}{N}} = \sqrt{\frac{(-218.18)^2 + (-304.52)^2 + (-214.52)^2 + (-201.06)^2}{4}} = 238.107$$

c. Based on the MAD and RMSE values, the exponentially smoothed forecasts using $w = .7$ are better than the forecasts using $w = .3$. Both the MAD and RMSE values for the exponentially smoothed forecasts using $w = .7$ are less than the MAD and RMSE values for the forecasts using $w = .3$.

13.35   a.   First, we will look at the difference between the forecasts and the actual values for both the exponentially smoothed forecasts and the Holt-Winters forecasts:

Exponentially Smoothed forecasts:

Year	Month	Forecast	Y_t	Difference
1999	Jan	290.41	285.4	5.01
	Feb	290.41	287.1	3.31
	Mar	290.41	279.5	10.91
	Apr	290.41	286.6	3.81
	May	290.41	269.0	21.41
	Jun	290.41	262.6	27.81
	Jul	290.41	255.6	34.81
	Aug	290.41	254.8	35.61
	Sep	290.41	307.5	−17.09
	Oct	290.41	299.1	−8.69
	Nov	290.41	291.4	−0.99
	Dec	290.41	290.3	0.11

$$\text{MAD} = \frac{\sum |F_t - Y_t|}{N} = \frac{|5.01| + |3.31| + \cdots + |.11|}{12} = \frac{169.56}{12} = 14.130$$

$$\text{RMSE} = \sqrt{\frac{\sum (F_t - Y_t)^2}{N}} = \sqrt{\frac{(5.01)^2 + (3.31)^2 + \cdots + (.11)^2}{12}} = 18.81$$

Holt-Winters forecasts:

Year	Month	Forecast	Y_t	Difference
1999	Jan	291.47	285.4	6.07
	Feb	292.13	287.1	5.03
	Mar	292.79	279.5	13.29
	Apr	293.45	286.6	6.85
	May	294.11	269.0	25.11
	Jun	294.77	262.6	32.17
	Jul	295.43	255.6	39.83
	Aug	296.09	254.8	41.29
	Sep	296.75	307.5	−10.75
	Oct	297.41	299.1	−1.69
	Nov	298.07	291.4	6.67
	Dec	298.73	290.3	8.43

$$\text{MAD} = \frac{\sum |F_t - Y_t|}{N} = \frac{|6.07| + |5.03| + \cdots + |8.43|}{12} = \frac{197.18}{12} = 16.432$$

$$\text{RMSE} = \sqrt{\frac{\sum (F_t - Y_t)^2}{N}} = \sqrt{\frac{(6.07)^2 + (5.03)^2 + \cdots + (8.43)^2}{12}} = 21.36$$

The MAD value for the Holt-Winters forecasts using $w = .5$ and $v = .5$ is greater than the MAD value for the exponentially smoothed forecasts using $w = .5$. Also, the RMSE value for the Holt-Winters forecasts is greater than that for the exponentially smoothed forecasts.

b. First, we will look at the difference between the forecasts and the actual values for both the exponentially smoothed one-step-ahead forecasts and the Holt-Winters one-step-ahead forecasts:

Exponentially Smoothed forecasts:

Year	Month	Forecast	Y_t	Difference
1999	Jan	290.41	285.4	5.01
	Feb	287.90	287.1	0.80
	Mar	287.50	279.5	8.00
	Apr	283.50	286.6	−3.10
	May	285.05	269.0	16.05
	Jun	277.03	262.6	14.43
	Jul	269.81	255.6	14.21
	Aug	262.71	254.8	7.91
	Sep	258.75	307.5	−48.75
	Oct	283.13	299.1	−15.97
	Nov	291.11	291.4	−0.29
	Dec	291.26	290.3	0.96

$$\text{MAD} = \frac{\sum |F_t - Y_t|}{N} = \frac{|5.01| + |0.80| + \cdots + |0.96|}{12} = \frac{135.47}{12} = 11.289$$

$$\text{RMSE} = \sqrt{\frac{\sum (F_t - Y_t)^2}{N}} = \sqrt{\frac{(5.01)^2 + (0.80)^2 + \cdots + (0.96)^2}{12}} = 16.985$$

Holt-Winters forecasts:

Year	Month	Forecast	Y_t	Difference
1999	Jan	291.47	285.4	6.07
	Feb	287.57	287.1	0.47
	Mar	286.36	279.5	6.86
	Apr	280.24	286.6	−6.36
	May	282.32	269.0	13.32
	Jun	271.23	262.6	8.63
	Jul	260.33	255.6	4.73
	Aug	250.19	254.8	−4.61
	Sep	245.88	307.5	−61.62
	Oct	285.48	299.1	−13.62
	Nov	304.48	291.4	13.08
	Dec	306.86	290.3	16.56

$$\text{MAD} = \frac{\sum |F_t - Y_t|}{N} = \frac{|6.07| + |0.47| + \cdots + |16.56|}{12} = \frac{155.93}{12} = 12.994$$

$$\text{RMSE} = \sqrt{\frac{\sum (F_t - Y_t)^2}{N}} = \sqrt{\frac{(6.07)^2 + (0.47)^2 + \cdots + (16.56)^2}{12}} = 20.100$$

Based on the MAD and RMSE values, the exponentially smoothed one-step-ahead forecasts using $w = .5$ are better than the Holt-Winters one-step-ahead forecasts using $w = .5$ and $v = .5$. Both the MAD and RMSE values for the exponentially smoothed one-step-ahead forecasts using $w = .5$ are less than the MAD and RMSE values for the Holt-Winters one-step-ahead forecasts using $w = .5$ and $v = .5$.

13.37   The major advantage of regression forecasts over the exponentially smoothed forecasts is that prediction intervals can be formed using the regression forecasts and not using the exponentially smoothed forecasts.

13.39   a.   Let $x_1 = \begin{cases} 1 \text{ if quarter 1} \\ 0 \text{ otherwise} \end{cases}$ $x_2 = \begin{cases} 1 \text{ if quarter 2} \\ 0 \text{ otherwise} \end{cases}$ $x_3 = \begin{cases} 1 \text{ if quarter 3} \\ 0 \text{ otherwise} \end{cases}$

$t = \text{time} = 1, 2, \ldots, 40$

The model is $Y_t = \beta_0 + \beta_1 t + \beta_2 x_1 + \beta_3 x_2 + \beta_4 x_3 + \epsilon$.

b.   Using SAS, the printout is:

```
DEP VARIABLE: Y
ANALYSIS OF VARIANCE

                         SUM OF          MEAN
    SOURCE      DF       SQUARES         SQUARE       F VALUE      PROB>F

    MODEL       4      1558.78512      389.69628     1275.437     0.0001
    ERROR      35        10.69387879     0.30553939
    C TOTAL    39      1569.47900

            ROOT MSE        0.5527562      R-SQUARE        0.9932
            DEP MEAN         19.305        ADJ R-SQ        0.9924
            C.V.             2.86328

PARAMETER ESTIMATES
                         PARAMETER       STANDARD      T FOR H0:
    VARIABLE    DF       ESTIMATE         ERROR       PARAMETER=0     PROB > |T|

    INTERCEP    1       11.49333333     0.24199528       47.494        0.0001
    T           1        0.50984848     0.007607057      67.023        0.0001
    X1          1       -3.95045455     0.24825125      -15.913        0.0001
    X2          1       -2.09030303     0.24766782       -8.440        0.0001
    X3          1       -4.52015152     0.24731710      -18.277        0.0001

                              PREDICT      STD ERR    LOWER95%    UPPER95%
        OBS        ACTUAL      VALUE       PREDICT     PREDICT     PREDICT      RESIDUAL

          1        8.3000      8.0527      0.2220      6.8434      9.2620        0.2473
          2       10.3000     10.4227      0.2220      9.2134     11.6320       -0.1227
          3        8.7000      8.5027      0.2220      7.2934      9.7120        0.1973
          4       13.5000     13.5327      0.2220     12.3234     14.7420       -0.0327
          5        9.8000     10.0921      0.2047      8.8955     11.2887       -0.2921
          6       12.1000     12.4621      0.2047     11.2655     13.6587       -0.3621
          7       10.1000     10.5421      0.2047      9.3455     11.7387       -0.4421
          8       15.4000     15.5721      0.2047     14.3755     16.7687       -0.1721
          9       12.1000     12.1315      0.1906     10.9445     13.3185       -0.0315
         10       14.5000     14.5015      0.1906     13.3145     15.6885      -.001515
         11       12.7000     12.5815      0.1906     11.3945     13.7685        0.1185
         12       17.1000     17.6115      0.1906     16.4245     18.7985       -0.5115
         13       13.7000     14.1709      0.1807     12.9903     15.3515       -0.4709
```

14	16.0000	16.5409	0.1807	15.3603	17.7215	-0.5409
15	14.2000	14.6209	0.1807	13.4403	15.8015	-0.4209
16	19.2000	19.6509	0.1807	18.4703	20.8315	-0.4509
17	17.4000	16.2103	0.1755	15.0330	17.3876	1.1897
18	19.7000	18.5803	0.1755	17.4030	19.7576	1.1197
19	18.0000	16.6603	0.1755	15.4830	17.8376	1.3397
20	23.1000	21.6903	0.1755	20.5130	22.8676	1.4097
21	18.2000	18.2497	0.1755	17.0724	19.4270	-0.0497
22	20.5000	20.6197	0.1755	19.4424	21.7970	-0.1197
23	18.6000	18.6997	0.1755	17.5224	19.8770	-0.0997
24	24.0000	23.7297	0.1755	22.5524	24.9070	0.2703
25	20.0000	20.2891	0.1807	19.1085	21.4697	-0.2891
26	22.2000	22.6591	0.1807	21.4785	23.8397	-0.4591
27	20.5000	20.7391	0.1807	19.5585	21.9197	-0.2391
28	25.1000	25.7691	0.1807	24.5885	26.9497	-0.6691
29	22.3000	22.3285	0.1906	21.1415	23.5155	-0.0285
30	25.1000	24.6985	0.1906	23.5115	25.8855	0.4015
31	22.9000	22.7785	0.1906	21.5915	23.9655	0.1215
32	27.7000	27.8085	0.1906	26.6215	28.9955	-0.1085
33	24.7000	24.3679	0.2047	23.1713	25.5645	0.3321
34	26.9000	26.7379	0.2047	25.5413	27.9345	0.1621
35	25.1000	24.8179	0.2047	23.6213	26.0145	0.2821
36	29.8000	29.8479	0.2047	28.6513	31.0445	-0.0479
37	25.8000	26.4073	0.2220	25.1980	27.6166	-0.6073
38	28.7000	28.7773	0.2220	27.5680	29.9866	-0.0773
39	26.0000	26.8573	0.2220	25.6480	28.0666	-0.8573
40	32.2000	31.8873	0.2220	30.6780	33.0966	0.3127
41	.	28.4467	0.2420	27.2217	29.6716	.
42	.	30.8167	0.2420	29.5917	32.0416	.
43	.	28.8967	0.2420	27.6717	30.1216	.
44	.	33.9267	0.2420	32.7017	35.1516	.

```
SUM OF RESIDUALS              5.83311E-13
SUM OF SQUARED RESIDUALS      10.69388
PREDICTED RESID SS (PRESS)    13.59247
```

The fitted model is $\hat{Y}_t = 11.4933 + .5098t - 3.9505x_1 - 2.0903x_2 - 4.5202x_3$.

To determine if the model is adequate, we test:

H_0: $\beta_1 = \beta_2 = \beta_3 = \beta_4 = 0$
H_a: At least one $\beta_i \neq 0$, $i = 1, 2, 3, 4$

The test statistic is $F = 1275.44$.

The rejection region requires $\alpha = .05$ in the upper tail of the F-distribution with numerator df $= k = 4$ and denominator df $= n - (k + 1) = 40 - (4 + 1) = 35$. From Table VIII, Appendix B, $F_{.05} \approx 2.69$. The rejection region is $F > 2.69$.

Since the observed value of the test statistic falls in the rejection region ($F = 1275.44 > 2.69$), H_0 is rejected. There is sufficient evidence to indicate the model is useful at $\alpha = .05$.

c. The estimates and the 95% prediction intervals for the four 11th year predictions are shown in the output in part **b** (last four predictions).

13.41 a. Using SAS, the output is:

Model: MODEL1
Dependent Variable: Y

Analysis of Variance

Source	DF	Sum of Squares	Mean Square	F Value	Prob>F
Model	1	651345.68513	651345.68513	2251.496	0.0001
Error	25	7232.36672	289.29467		
C Total	26	658578.05185			

Root MSE	17.00866	R-square	0.9890
Dep Mean	306.57407	Adj R-sq	0.9886
C.V.	5.54798		

Parameter Estimates

Variable	DF	Parameter Estimate	Standard Error	T for HO: Parameter=0	Prob > ¦T¦
INTERCEP	1	47.339947	6.36886803	7.433	0.0001
T	1	19.941087	0.42025537	47.450	0.0001

Obs	YEAR	Dep Var Y	Predict Value	Std Err Predict	Lower95% Predict	Upper95% Predict	Residual
1	1970	80.6000	47.3399	6.369	9.9347	84.7452	33.2601
2	1971	92.3000	67.2810	6.012	30.1269	104.4	25.0190
3	1972	105.4	87.2221	5.664	50.3006	124.1	18.1779
4	1973	114.6	107.2	5.327	70.4554	143.9	7.4368
5	1974	117.9	127.1	5.002	90.5909	163.6	-9.2043
6	1975	129.4	147.0	4.692	110.7	183.4	-17.6454
7	1976	155.2	167.0	4.401	130.8	203.2	-11.7865
8	1977	179.3	186.9	4.132	150.9	223.0	-7.6276
9	1978	198.1	206.9	3.890	170.9	242.8	-8.7686
10	1979	219.4	226.8	3.680	191.0	262.7	-7.4097
11	1980	236.6	246.8	3.508	211.0	282.5	-10.1508
12	1981	261.5	266.7	3.380	231.0	302.4	-5.1919
13	1982	267.3	286.6	3.300	250.9	322.3	-19.3330
14	1983	291.9	306.6	3.273	270.9	342.2	-14.6741
15	1984	319.5	326.5	3.300	290.8	362.2	-7.0152
16	1985	359.5	346.5	3.380	310.7	382.2	13.0438
17	1986	366.3	366.4	3.508	330.6	402.2	-0.0973
18	1987	377.1	386.3	3.680	350.5	422.2	-9.2384
19	1988	406.4	406.3	3.890	370.3	442.2	0.1205
20	1989	425.7	426.2	4.132	390.2	462.3	-0.5206
21	1990	453.7	446.2	4.401	410.0	482.3	7.5383
22	1991	438.2	466.1	4.692	429.8	502.4	-27.9028
23	1992	466.3	486.0	5.002	449.5	522.6	-19.7439
24	1993	504.2	506.0	5.327	469.3	542.7	-1.7849
25	1994	536.6	525.9	5.664	489.0	562.8	10.6740
26	1995	572.3	545.9	6.012	508.7	583.0	26.4329
27	1996	602.2	565.8	6.369	528.4	603.2	36.3918
28	1997	.	585.7	6.733	548.1	623.4	.
29	1998	.	605.7	7.103	567.7	643.7	.
30	1999	.	625.6	7.478	587.4	663.9	.
31	2000	.	645.6	7.859	607.0	684.2	.

Sum of Residuals	0
Sum of Squared Residuals	7232.3667
Predicted Resid SS (Press)	9043.3393

The fitted model is $\hat{Y}_t = 47.3399 + 19.9411t$

b. From the printout, the predictions and confidence intervals are:

1997:	585.7	(548.1, 623.4)
1998:	605.7	(567.7, 643.7)
1999:	625.6	(587.4, 663.9)
2000:	645.6	(607.0, 684.2)

13.43   a.   Using MINITAB, the output is:

```
              Regression Analysis

        The regression equation is
        Policies = 376 + 0.603 Time

        Predictor       Coef      StDev        T        P
        Constant      376.037      5.952    63.17    0.000
        Time           0.6032     0.3715     1.62    0.117

        S = 15.04      R-Sq = 9.5%      R-Sq(adj) = 5.9%

        Analysis of Variance

        Source          DF        SS         MS        F        P
        Regression       1       595.9      595.9     2.64    0.117
        Residual Error  25      5652.8      226.1
        Total           26      6248.7


        Predicted Values

            Fit  StDev Fit        95.0% CI            95.0% PI
         392.93       5.95    ( 380.67,  405.19)  ( 359.62,  426.23)
         393.53       6.28    ( 380.60,  406.46)  ( 359.97,  427.09)
```

The fitted model is $\hat{Y} = 376.037 + .6032t$

b.   The forecasted values for 1997 and 1998 are at the bottom of the printout above:

      1997:   392.93
      1998:   393.53

c.   From the printout, the 95% prediction intervals are:

      1997:   (359.62, 426.23)
      1998:   (359.97, 427.09)

13.45   a. $d = 3.9$ indicates the residuals are very strongly negatively autocorrelated.

b. $d = .2$ indicates the residuals are very strongly positively autocorrelated.

c. $d = 1.99$ indicates the residuals are probably uncorrelated.

13.47   a.   There is a tendency for the residuals to have long positive runs and negative runs. Residuals 3 through 14 are positive, while residuals 15 through 30 are negative. Residuals 31 through 38 are positive. This indicates the error terms are correlated.

b.   From the printout, the Durbin-Watson d is $d = .0692$.

To determine if the time series residuals are autocorrelated, we test:

H_0: No first-order autocorrelation of residuals
H_a: Positive or negative first-order autocorrelation of residuals

The test statistic is $d = .0692$.

For $\alpha = .10$, the rejection region is $d < d_{L,\alpha/2} = d_{L,.05} = 1.43$ or $(4 - d) < d_{L,.05} = 1.43$. The value $d_{L,.05}$ is found in Table XIII, Appendix B, with $k = 1$, $n = 38$, and $\alpha = .10$.

Since the observed value of the test statistic falls in the rejection region ($d = .0692 < 1.43$), H_0 is rejected. There is sufficient evidence to indicate the time series residuals are autocorrelated at $\alpha = .10$.

c.   We must assume the residuals are normally distributed.

13.49 a.   The least squares line is $\hat{Y}_t = 48.3714 + .1672t$

$\hat{\beta}_0 = 48.3714$ The estimated mean sales in December 1995 is 48.3714 billion dollars.
$\hat{\beta}_1 = .1672$ The estimated increase in mean sales for each month is .1672 billion dollars.

b.   Root MSE $= .83080$. We would expect to predict annual sales to within $\pm 2s$ or $\pm 2(.83080)$ or ± 1.6616 units of its actual value.

c.   To determine if the residuals are autocorrelated, we test:

H_0: No first-order autocorrelation
H_a: Positive or negative first-order autocorrelation

The test statistic is $d = 1.334$.

For $\alpha = .10$, the rejection region is $d < d_{L,\alpha/2} = d_{L,.05} = 1.27$ or $4 - d < d_{L,.05} = 1.27$, where $d_{L,.05}$ is from Table XIII, Appendix B, for $k = 1$, $n = 24$ and $\alpha/2 = .05$.

Since the test statistic does not fall in the rejection region ($d = 1.334 \not< 1.27$), H_0 is not rejected. There is insufficient evidence to indicate the residuals are autocorrelated at $\alpha = .10$.

13.51 a.   The simple composite index is found by summing the three steel prices, dividing by 64.25, the sum for the base period, 1980, and multiplying by 100. The values appear in the table.

Year	Cold Rolled Price	Hot Rolled Price	Galvanized Price	Price Total	Index
1980	21.91	18.46	23.88	64.25	100.00
1981	23.90	20.15	26.88	70.93	110.40
1982	24.65	20.80	26.75	72.20	112.37
1983	26.36	22.23	28.43	77.02	119.88
1984	28.15	23.75	30.30	82.20	127.94
1985	28.15	23.75	30.30	82.20	127.94
1986	25.65	21.15	30.30	77.10	120.00
1987	27.38	21.64	30.49	79.51	123.75
1988	28.15	21.50	31.05	80.70	125.60
1989	28.15	21.50	32.48	82.13	127.83
1990	25.37	22.25	33.55	81.17	126.33
1991	25.75	22.88	35.35	83.98	130.71
1992	24.03	19.13	30.88	74.04	115.24
1993	23.83	17.25	30.90	71.98	112.03
1994	25.70	17.25	32.24	75.19	117.03
1995	25.70	25.32	34.47	85.49	133.06
1996	25.81	23.94	35.90	85.65	133.31

b.	This is a price index because it is based on the price of steel rather than quantity.

c.	In order to compute the Laspeyres index, we need quantities of steel for the base year 1980. To compute the Paasche index, we need quantities of steel for each of the years.

13.53	To compute the Holt-Winters series, we use:

$E_2 = Y_2 = 92.3$

$E_3 = wY_3 + (1 - w)(E_2 + T_2)$
$= .3(105.4) + .7(92.3 + 11.7)$
$= 104.42$

$T_2 = Y_2 - Y_1 = 92.3 - 80.6 = 11.7$

$T_3 = v(E_3 - E_2) + (1 - v)T_2$
$= .7(104.42 - 92.3) + .3(11.7)$
$= 11.99$

The rest of the values appear in the table:

| | | Holt-Winters | |
| | | $w = .3$ | $v = .7$ |
Year	Expenditure	E_t	T_t
1970	80.6		
1971	92.3	92.30	11.70
1972	105.4	104.42	11.99
1973	114.6	115.87	11.61
1974	117.9	124.61	9.60
1975	129.4	132.77	8.59
1976	155.2	145.51	11.50
1977	179.3	163.70	16.18
1978	198.1	185.34	20.01
1979	219.4	209.56	22.96
1980	236.6	233.75	23.81
1981	261.5	258.74	24.64
1982	267.3	278.56	21.26
1983	291.9	297.45	19.60
1984	319.5	317.78	20.12
1985	359.5	344.38	24.65
1986	366.3	368.21	24.08
1987	377.1	387.73	20.89
1988	406.4	407.96	20.42
1989	425.7	427.57	19.86
1990	453.7	449.31	21.18
1991	438.2	460.80	14.39
1992	466.3	472.53	12.53
1993	504.2	490.80	16.55
1994	536.6	516.12	22.69
1995	572.3	548.86	29.72
1996	602.2	585.67	34.68

$F_{1997} = E_{1996} + T_{1996} = 585.67 + 34.68 = 620.35$
$F_{1998} = E_{1996} + 2T_{1996} = 585.67 + 2(34.68) = 655.03$
$F_{1999} = E_{1996} + 3T_{1996} = 585.67 + 3(34.68) = 689.71$
$F_{2000} = E_{1996} + 4T_{1996} = 585.67 + 4(34.68) = 724.39$

The regression forecasts from Exercise 13.41 are:

$$\hat{Y}_{1997} = 585.7$$
$$\hat{Y}_{1998} = 605.7$$
$$\hat{Y}_{1999} = 625.6$$
$$\hat{Y}_{2000} = 645.6$$

The forecasts using the Holt-Winters estimates are larger than those using regression.

13.55   a.   Using MINITAB, the printout from fitting the model $E(Y_t) = \beta_0 + \beta_1 t$ is:

```
The regression equation is
Y = 46.8 - 0.027 t

Predictor       Coef       StDev         T        P
Constant      46.792       6.122      7.64    0.000
t            -0.0272      0.5110     -0.05    0.958

S = 13.18      R-Sq = 0.0%      R-Sq(adj) = 0.0%

Analysis of Variance

Source            DF          SS         MS        F        P
Regression         1         0.5        0.5     0.00    0.958
Residual Error    18      3125.8      173.7
Total             19      3126.3

Durbin-Watson statistic = 1.83

Predicted Values

   Fit  StDev Fit        95.0% CI              95.0% PI
 46.22       6.12    ( 33.36,   59.08)  (  15.69,   76.75)
 46.19       6.57    ( 32.38,   60.00)  (  15.25,   77.13)
```

The fitted model is $\hat{Y}_t = 46.792 - .0272t$.

b.   The plot of the data is:

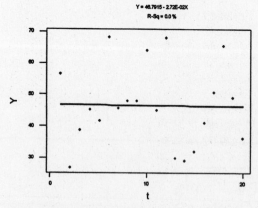

Regression Plot

c.   From the printout in part a,

$$F_{2000} = 46.22$$
$$F_{2001} = 46.19$$

d. Also from the printout in part **a**, the 95% prediction intervals are:

2000: (15.69, 76.75) We are 95% confident that the actual closing price for 2000 will be between 15.69 and 76.75.

2001: (15.25, 77.13) We are 95% confident that the actual closing price for 2001 will be between 15.25 and 77.13.

e. To determine if autocorrelation is present, we test:

H_0: Autocorrelation is not present
H_a: Autocorrelation is present

The test statistic is $d = 1.83$.

Since α is not given, we will use $\alpha = .10$. The rejection region is $d < d_{L,\alpha/2} = d_{L,.05} = 1.20$ or $4 - d < d_{L,.05} = 1.20$, where $d_{L,.05}$ is from Table XII, Appendix B, for $k = 1$, $n = 20$, and $\alpha = .10$.

Since the observed value of the test statistic does not fall in the rejection region ($d = 1.83 \nless 1.20$), H_0 is not rejected. There is insufficient evidence to indicate that autocorrelation is present at $\alpha = .10$.

13.57 To compute the Holt-Winters series using only data from 1995 through 1997, we use:

$E_2 = Y_2 = Y_{1995,II} = 7,196.50$ $\qquad$ $T_2 = Y_{1995,II} - Y_{1995,I} = 7,196.5 - 7,147.8 = 48.70$
$E_3 = wY_3 + (1 - w)(E_2 + T_2)$ $\qquad$ $T_3 = v(E_3 - E_2) + (1 - v)T_2$
$\quad = .5(7,298.5) + .5(7,196.5 + 48.7)$ $\qquad$ $\quad = .5(7,271.85 - 7,196.50) + .5(48.70)$
$\quad = 7,271.85$ $\qquad$ $\quad = 62.03$

The rest of the values are found in the following table:

| | | | Holt-Winters | |
| | | | $w = .5$ | $v = .5$ |
Year	Quarter	GPD	E_t	T_t
1995	I	7,147.8		
1995	II	7,196.5	7,196.50	48.70
1995	III	7,298.5	7,271.85	62.03
1995	IV	7,348.1	7,340.99	65.58
1996	I	7,495.3	7,450.93	87.76
1996	II	7,629.2	7,583.95	110.39
1996	III	7,703.4	7,698.87	112.65
1996	IV	7,818.4	7,814.96	114.37
1997	I	7,955.0	7,942.17	120.79
1997	II	8,063.4	8,063.18	120.90
1997	III	8,170.8	8,177.44	117.58
1997	IV	8,154.5	8,224.76	82.45

To forecast using the Holt-Winters forecasts, we use the following:

$F_{1998,I} = E_{1997,IV} + T_{1997,IV} = 8,224.76 + 82.45 = 8,307.21$
$F_{1998,II} = E_{1997,IV} + 2(T_{1997,IV}) = 8,224.76 + 2(82.45) = 8,389.66$
$F_{1998,III} = E_{1997,IV} + 3(T_{1997,IV}) = 8,224.76 + 3(82.45) = 8,472.11$
$F_{1998,IV} = E_{1997,IV} + 4(T_{1997,IV}) = 8,224.76 + 4(82.45) = 8,554.56$

13.61 a. Real income 1970 = $\dfrac{\$20,000}{38.8} \times 100 = \$51,546.39$

Real income 1997 = $\dfrac{\$60,000}{160.5} \times 100 = \$37,383.18$

The real income for 1997 was less than that for 1970. Since the real income in 1997 is less than that in 1970, you would be able to buy more in 1970 than in 1997.

b. Let x = monetary income in 1985.

Then $\dfrac{x}{160.5} = \dfrac{\$20,000}{38.8}$

Solving for x, we get $x = \$82,731.96$.

Design of Experiments and Analysis of Variance

Chapter 14

14.1 Since only one factor is utilized, the treatments are the four levels (A, B, C, D) of the qualitative factor.

14.3 a. College GPA's are measured on college students. The experimental units are college students.

b. Household income is measured on households. The experimental units are households.

c. Gasoline mileage is measured on automobiles. The experimental units are the automobiles of a particular model.

d. The experimental units are the sectors on a computer diskette.

e. The experimental units are the states.

14.5 a. The response is the opinion of the undergraduate student of the value of the discount offer.

b. There are two factors—situation at two levels (advertisements read at home vs. in-store ad) and type of comparison at two levels (comparison to previous price at same store vs. to competitor's price). Both factors are qualitative.

c. The treatments are the $2 \times 2 = 4$ combinations of situation and type of comparison.

d. The experimental units are the college students.

14.7 a. This is an observational experiment. The economist has no control over the factor levels or unemployment rates.

b. This is a designed experiment. The manager chooses only three different incentive programs to compare, and randomly assigns an incentive program to each of nine plants.

c. This is an observational experiment. Even though the marketer chooses the publication, he has no control over who responds to the ads.

d. This is an observational experiment. The load on the facility's generators is only observed, not controlled.

e. This is an observational experiment. One has no control over the distance of the haul, the goods hauled, or the price of diesel fuel.

14.9 a. From Table IX with $\nu_1 = 4$ and $\nu_2 = 4$, $F_{.05} = 6.39$.

b. From Table XI with $\nu_1 = 4$ and $\nu_2 = 4$, $F_{.01} = 15.98$.

c. From Table VIII with $\nu_1 = 30$ and $\nu_2 = 40$, $F_{.10} = 1.54$.

d.   From Table X with $\nu_1 = 15$, and $\nu_2 = 12$, $F_{.025} = 3.18$.

14.11   In the second dot diagram **b**, the difference between the sample means is small relative to the variability within the sample observations. In the first dot diagram **a**, the values in each of the samples are grouped together with a range of 4, while in the second diagram **b**, the range of values is 8.

14.13   For each dot diagram, we want to test:

$$H_0: \ \mu_1 = \mu_2$$
$$H_a: \ \mu_1 \neq \mu_2$$

From Exercise 14.12,

Diagram a	**Diagram b**
$\bar{x}_1 = 9$	$\bar{x}_1 = 9$
$\bar{x}_2 = 14$	$\bar{x}_2 = 14$
$s_1^2 = 2$	$s_1^2 = 14.4$
$s_2^2 = 2$	$s_2^2 = 14.4$

a.

Diagram a	**Diagram b**
$s_p^2 = \dfrac{s_1^2 + s_2^2}{2}$	$s_p^2 = \dfrac{s_1^2 + s_2^2}{2}$
$= \dfrac{2 + 2}{2} = 2 \quad (n_1 = n_2)$	$= \dfrac{14.4 + 14.4}{2} = 14.4 \quad (n_1 = n_2)$
In Exercise 14.12, MSE $= 2$	In Exercise 14.12, MSE $= 14.4$

The pooled variance for the two-sample t-test is the same as the MSE for the F-test.

b.

Diagram a	**Diagram b**
$t = \dfrac{\bar{x}_1 - \bar{x}_2}{\sqrt{s_p^2 \left[\frac{1}{n_1} + \frac{1}{n_2} \right]}} = \dfrac{9 - 14}{\sqrt{2 \left[\frac{1}{6} + \frac{1}{6} \right]}}$	$t = \dfrac{\bar{x}_1 - \bar{x}_2}{\sqrt{s_p^2 \left[\frac{1}{n_1} + \frac{1}{n_2} \right]}} = \dfrac{9 - 14}{\sqrt{14.4 \left[\frac{1}{6} + \frac{1}{6} \right]}}$
$= -6.12$	$= -2.28$
In Exercise 14.12, $F = 37.5$	In Exercise 14.12, $F = 5.21$

The test statistic for the F-test is the square of the test statistic for the t-test.

c.

Diagram a	**Diagram b**
For the t-test, the rejection region requires $\alpha/2 = .05/2 = .025$ in each tail of the t-distribution with df $= n_1 + n_2 - 2 = 6 + 6 - 2 = 10$. From Table VI, Appendix B, $t_{.025} = 2.228$.	For the t-test, the rejection region is the same as Diagram **a** since we are using the same α, n_1, and n_2 for both tests.

The rejection region is $t < -2.228$ or $t > 2.228$.

In Exercise 14.12, the rejection region for both diagrams using the F-test is $F > 4.96$.

The tabled F value equals the square of the tabled t value.

d.

Diagram a	Diagram b
For the *t*-test, since the test statistic falls in the rejection region ($t = -6.12 < -2.228$), we would reject H_0. In Exercise 14.12, using the *F*-test, we rejected H_0.	For the *t*-test, since the test statistic falls in the rejection region ($t = -2.28 < -2.228$), we would reject H_0. In Exercise 14.12, using the *F*-test, we rejected H_0.

e. Assumptions for the *t*-test:

1. Both populations have relative frequency distributions that are approximately normal.
2. The two population variances are equal.
3. Samples are selected randomly and independently from the populations.

Assumptions for the *F*-test:

1. Both population probability distributions are normal.
2. The two population variances are equal.
3. Samples are selected randomly and independently from the respective populations.

The assumptions are the same for both tests.

14.15 For all parts, the hypotheses are:

H_0: $\mu_1 = \mu_2 = \mu_3 = \mu_4 = \mu_5 = \mu_6$
H_a: At least two treatment means differ

The rejection region for all parts is the same.

The rejection region requires $\alpha = .10$ in the upper tail of the *F*-distribution with $v_1 = p - 1 = 6 - 1 = 5$ and $v_2 = n - p = 36 - 6 = 30$. From Table VIII, Appendix B, $F_{.10} = 2.05$. The rejection region is $F > 2.05$.

a. SST = .2(500) = 100   SSE = SS(Total) − SST = 500 − 100 = 400

$$MST = \frac{SST}{p - 1} = \frac{100}{6 - 1} = 20 \qquad MSE = \frac{SSE}{n - p} = \frac{400}{36 - 6} = 13.333$$

$$F = \frac{MST}{MSE} = \frac{20}{13.333} = 1.5$$

Since the observed value of the test statistic does not fall in the rejection region ($F = 1.5 \not> 2.05$), H_0 is not rejected. There is insufficient evidence to indicate differences among the treatment means at $\alpha = .10$.

b. SST = .5(500) = 250   SSE = SS(Total) − SST = 500 − 250 = 250

$$MST = \frac{SST}{p - 1} = \frac{250}{6 - 1} = 50 \qquad MSE = \frac{SSE}{n - p} = \frac{250}{36 - 6} = 8.333$$

$$F = \frac{MST}{MSE} = \frac{50}{8.333} = 6$$

Since the observed value of the test statistic falls in the rejection region ($F = 6 > 2.05$), H_0 is rejected. There is sufficient evidence to indicate differences among the treatment means at $\alpha = .10$.

c. $SST = .8(500) = 400$ $SSE = SS(Total) - SST = 500 - 400 = 100$

$MST = \dfrac{SST}{p-1} = \dfrac{400}{6-1} = 80$ $MSE = \dfrac{SSE}{n-p} = \dfrac{100}{36-6} = 3.333$

$F = \dfrac{MST}{MSE} = \dfrac{80}{3.333} = 24$

Since the observed value of the test statistic falls in the rejection region ($F = 24 > 2.05$), H_0 is rejected. There is sufficient evidence to indicate differences among the treatment means at $\alpha = .10$.

d.   The F-ratio increases as the treatment sum of squares increases.

14.17 a.   The number of treatments is $3 + 1 = 4$. The total sample size is $37 + 1 = 38$.

b.   To determine if the treatment means differ, we test:

H_0: $\mu_1 = \mu_2 = \mu_3 = \mu_4$
H_a: At least two treatment means differ

The test statistic is $F = 14.80$.

The rejection region requires $\alpha = .10$ in the upper tail of the F-distribution with $\nu_1 = p - 1 = 4 - 1 = 3$ and $\nu_2 = n - p = 38 - 4 = 34$. From Table VIII, Appendix B, $F_{.10} \approx 4.51$. The rejection region is $F > 4.51$.

Since the observed value of the test statistic falls in the rejection region ($F = 14.80 > 4.51$), H_0 is rejected. There is sufficient evidence to indicate differences among the treatment means at $\alpha = .10$.

c.   We need the sample means to compare specific pairs of treatment means.

14.19 a.   To determine if the mean vacancy rates of the eight office-property submarkets in Atlanta differ, we test:

H_0: $\mu_1 = \mu_2 = \mu_3 = \mu_4 = \mu_5 = \mu_6 = \mu_7 = \mu_8$
H_a: At least two means differ

b.   If quarterly data were used for nine years, there are $4 \times 9 = 36$ observations per submarket. Since there are 8 submarkets, the total sample size is $8 \times 36 = 288$. Since no value of α is given, we will use $\alpha = .05$.

The rejection region requires $\alpha = .05$ in the upper tail of the F-distribution with $\nu_1 = p - 1 = 8 - 1 = 7$ and $\nu_2 = n - p = 288 - 8 = 280$. From Table X, Appendix B, $F_{.05} \approx 2.01$. The rejection region is $F > 2.01$.

Since the observed value of the test statistic falls in the rejection region ($F = 17.54 > 2.01$), H_0 is rejected. There is sufficient evidence to indicate the mean vacancy rates of the eight office-property submarkets in Atlanta differ at $\alpha = .05$.

c.   With $\nu_1 = p - 1 = 8 - 1 = 7$ and $\nu_2 = n - p = 288 - 8 = 280$, $P(F > 17.54) < .01$, using Table XI, Appendix B. Thus, the p-value is less than .01.

d. We must assume that all eight samples are randomly drawn from normal populations, the eight populations variances are the same, and the samples are independent.

14.21 To determine if the mean ages of the powerful women differ among the three groups, we test:

H_0: $\mu_1 = \mu_2 = \mu_3$
H_a: At least two means differ

The test statistic is $F = 1.62$ (from the printout)

The p-value is $p = .209$. Since the p-value is not less than any reasonable value of α, H_0 is not .rejected. There is insufficient evidence to indicate there is a difference in the mean ages of powerful women among the three groups.

The assumptions necessary include:

1. The samples are selected randomly and independently.

    The first assumption may not be met. The 50 most powerful women in America were selected. These 50 were not randomly selected.

2. The probability distributions of ages for each group are normal.

    Looking at the stem-and-leaf displays that accompany the ANOVA table, each of the three groups of ages look fairly mound shaped. Thus, the assumption of normality is probably valid.

3. The variances of the age probability distributions for each group are equal.

    Looking at the dot plots that accompany the ANOVA table, it appears that the spread of ages for group 3 is much smaller than the spread of ages for the other 2 groups. This indicates that the variances of the three populations may not be the same.

14.23 a. To determine whether the mean scores of the four groups differ, we test:

H_0: $\mu_1 = \mu_2 = \mu_3 = \mu_4$
H_a: At least two treatment means differ

where μ_i represents the mean of the ith group.

For the variable "Infrequency":

The test statistic is $F = 155.8$.

The rejection region requires $\alpha = .05$ in the upper tail of the F-distribution with $\nu_1 = p - 1 = 4 - 1 = 3$ and $\nu_2 = n - p = 278 - 4 = 274$. Using Table IX, Appendix B, $F_{.05} \approx 2.60$. The rejection region is $F > 2.60$.

Since the observed value of the test statistic falls in the rejection region ($F = 155.5 > 2.60$), H_0 is rejected. There is sufficient evidence to indicate the mean scores on the "Infrequency" variable differ among the four groups at $\alpha = .05$.

For the variable "Obvious":

The test statistic is $F = 49.7$.

The rejection region is $F > 2.60$. (See above.)

Since the observed value of the test statistic falls in the rejection region ($F = 49.7 > 2.60$), H_0 is rejected. There is sufficient evidence to indicate the mean scores on the "Obvious" variable differ among the four groups at $\alpha = .05$.

For the variable "Subtle":

The test statistic is $F = 10.3$.

The rejection region is $F > 2.60$. (See above.)

Since the observed value of the test statistic falls in the rejection region ($F = 10.3 > 2.60$), H_0 is rejected. There is sufficient evidence to indicate the mean scores on the "Subtle" variable differ among the four groups at $\alpha = .05$.

For the variable "Obvious-Subtle":

The test statistic is $F = 45.4$.

The rejection region is $F > 2.60$. (See above.)

Since the observed value of the test statistic falls in the rejection region ($F = 45.4 > 2.60$), H_0 is rejected. There is sufficient evidence to indicate the mean scores on the "Obvious-Subtle" variable differ among the four groups at $\alpha = .05$.

For the variable "Dissimulation":

The test statistic is $F = 39.1$.

The rejection region is $F > 2.60$. (See above.)

Since the observed value of the test statistic falls in the rejection region ($F = 39.1 > 2.60$), H_0 is rejected. There is sufficient evidence to indicate the mean scores on the "Dissimulation" variable differ among the four groups at $\alpha = .05$.

b. No. No information is provided on the sample means. The test of hypotheses performed in part **a** just indicate differences exist, but do not indicate where. Further analysis would be required.

14.25   a.   To determine if the mean level of trust differs among the six treatments, we test:

H_0: $\mu_1 = \mu_2 = \mu_3 = \mu_4 = \mu_5 = \mu_6$
H_a: At least one μ_i differs

b.   The test statistic is $F = 2.21$.

The rejection region requires α in the upper tail of the F-distribution with $\nu_1 = p - 1 = 6 - 1 = 5$ and $\nu_2 = n - p = 237 - 6 = 231$. From Table IX, Appendix B, $F_{.05} \approx 2.21$. The rejection region is $F > 2.21$.

Since the observed value of the test statistic does not fall in the rejection region ($F = 2.21 \ngtr 2.21$), H_0 is not rejected. There is insufficient evidence to indicate that at least two mean trusts differ at $\alpha = .05$.

c. We must assume that all six samples are drawn from normal populations, the six population variances are the same, and that the samples are independent.

d. I would classify this experiment as designed. Each subject was randomly assigned to receive one of the six scenarios.

14.27 The number of pairwise comparisons is equal to $p(p - 1)/2$.

a. For $p = 3$, the number of comparisons is $3(3 - 1)/2 = 3$.

b. For $p = 5$, the number of comparisons is $5(5 - 1)/2 = 10$.

c. For $p = 4$, the number of comparisons is $4(4 - 1)/2 = 6$.

d. For $p = 10$, the number of comparisons is $10(10 - 1)/2 = 45$.

14.29 A comparisonwise error rate is the error rate (or the probability of declaring the means different when, in fact, they are not different) for each individual comparison. That is, if each comparison is run using $\alpha = .05$, then the comparisonwise error rate is .05.

14.31 The mean vacancy rate for the South submarket is significantly larger than the mean vacancy rates for all other submarkets. The mean vacancy rate of the Downtown submarket is significantly larger than the mean vacancy rates for all other submarkets except the South. The mean vacancy rate of the North Lake submarket is significantly larger than the mean vacancy rates for all other submarkets except the South and Downtown. The mean vacancy rate of the Midtown submarket is significantly larger than the mean vacancy rates for all other submarkets except the South, Downtown, and North Lake. There are no other significant differences.

14.33 a. There will be $c = \dfrac{3(3 - 1)}{2} = 3$ pairwise comparisons.

b. The experimentwise error rate is $\alpha = .05$. This means that the probability that at least one pair is declared significantly different when it is not is .05.

c. Yes. All sample sizes are the same. Thus, Tukey's multiple comparison is appropriate.

d. All treatments connected with a line are not significantly different. Thus, the mean cost for client A is significantly higher than the mean cost for clients B and C. No other differences are present.

14.35 a. The experimentwise error rate is given as $\alpha = .05$. This means that the probability of declaring at least two means different that are not different is .05.

b. The confidence interval for the difference between the mean sorption rates of aromatics and esters is 0.3340 and 0.8904. We are 95% confident that the difference in the mean sorption rates of aromatics and esters is between 0.3340 and 0.8904. Since 0 is not in this interval, there is evidence that the mean sorption rate for aromatics is greater than the mean sorption rate of esters.

c. The confidence intervals that do not contain 0 indicate that the pair of means are significantly different. Thus, the mean sorption rates of chloralkanes and esters are significantly different and the mean sorption rates of aromatics and esters are significantly different.

14.37 The mean number of activities for the "successful" firms is significantly greater than that for the "gave up" group and the "still trying" group. No other significant differences exist.

14.39 a.   The ANOVA table is:

Source	df	SS	MS	F
A	2	.8	.4000	3.69
B	3	5.3	1.7667	16.31
AB	6	9.6	1.6000	14.77
Error	12	1.3	.1083	
Total	23	17.0		

df for A is $a - 1 = 3 - 1 = 2$

df for $B = b - 1 = 4 - 1 = 3$

df for AB is $(a - 1)(b - 1) = 2(3) = 6$

df for Error is $n - ab = 24 - 3(4) = 12$

df for Total is $n - 1 = 24 - 1 = 23$

$SSE = SS(Total) - SSA - SSB - SSAB = 17.0 - .8 - 5.3 - 9.6 = 1.3$

$MSA = \dfrac{SSA}{a - 1} = \dfrac{.8}{3 - 1} = .40 \qquad MSB = \dfrac{SSB}{b - 1} = \dfrac{5.3}{4 - 1} = 1.7667$

$MSAB = \dfrac{SSAB}{(a - 1)(b - 1)} = \dfrac{9.6}{(3 - 1)(4 - 1)} = 1.60$

$MSE = \dfrac{SSE}{n - ab} = \dfrac{1.3}{24 - 3(4)} = .1083$

$F_A = \dfrac{MSA}{MSE} = \dfrac{.4000}{.1083} = 3.69 \qquad F_B = \dfrac{MSB}{MSE} = \dfrac{1.7667}{.1083} = 16.31$

$F_{AB} = \dfrac{MSAB}{MSE} = \dfrac{1.6000}{.1083} = 14.77$

b.   Sum of Squares for Treatment $= SSA + SSB + SSAB = .8 = 5.3 + 2.6 = 15.7$

$MST = \dfrac{SST}{ab - 1} = \dfrac{15.7}{3(4) - 1} = 1.4273 \qquad F_T = \dfrac{MST}{MSE} = \dfrac{1.4273}{.1083} = 13.18$

To determine if the treatment means differ, we test:

H_0: $\mu_1 = \mu_2 = \cdots = \mu_{12}$
H_a: At least two treatments means differ

The test statistic is $F = 13.18$.

The rejection region requires $\alpha = .05$ in the upper tail of the F-distribution with $\nu_1 = ab - 1 = 3(4) - 1 = 11$ and $\nu_2 = n - ab = 24 - 3(4) = 12$. From Table IX, Appendix B, $F_{.05} \approx 2.75$. The rejection region is $F > 2.75$.

Since the observed value of the test statistic falls in the rejection region ($F = 13.18 > 2.75$), H_0 is rejected. There is sufficient evidence to indicate the treatment means differ at $\alpha = .05$.

c. Yes. We need to partition the Treatment Sum of Squares into the Main Effects and Interaction Sum of Squares. Then we test whether factors A and B interact. Depending on the conclusion of the test for interaction, we either test for main effects or compare the treatment means.

d. Two factors are said to interact if the effect of one factor on the dependent variable is not the same at different levels of the second factor. If the factors interact, then tests for main effects are not necessary. We need to compare the treatment means for one factor at each level of the second.

e. To determine if the factors interact, we test:

H_0: Factors A and B do not interact to affect the response mean
H_a: Factors A and B do interact to affect the response mean

The test statistic is $F = \dfrac{\text{MS}AB}{\text{MSE}} = 14.77$

The rejection region requires $\alpha = .05$ in the upper tail of the F-distribution with $\nu_1 = (a-1)(b-1) = (3-1)(4-1) = 6$ and $\nu_2 = n - ab = 24 - 3(4) = 12$. From Table IX, Appendix B, $F_{.05} = 3.00$. The rejection region is $F > 3.00$.

Since the observed value of the test statistic falls in the rejection region ($F = 14.77 > 3.00$), H_0 is rejected. There is sufficient evidence to indicate the two factors interact to affect the response mean at $\alpha = .05$.

f. No. Testing for main effects is not warranted because interaction is present. Instead, we compare the treatment means of one factor at each level of the second factor.

14.41 a. The treatments for this experiment consist of a level for factor A and a level for factor B. There are six treatments—(1, 1), (1, 2), (1, 3), (2, 1), (2, 2), and (2, 3) where the first number represents the level of factor A and the second number represents the level of factor B.

The treatment means appear to be different because the sample means are quite different. The factors appear to interact because the lines are not parallel.

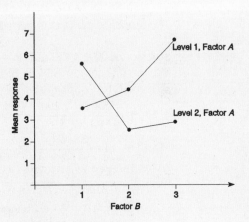

b. $\text{SST} = \text{SS}A + \text{SS}B + \text{SS}AB = 4.441 + 4.127 + 18.007 = 26.575$

$\text{MST} = \dfrac{\text{SST}}{ab-1} = \dfrac{26.575}{2(3)-1} = 5.315 \qquad F_T = \dfrac{\text{MST}}{\text{MSE}} = \dfrac{5.315}{.246} = 21.62$

To determine whether the treatment means differ, we test:

H_0: $\mu_1 = \mu_2 = \mu_3 = \mu_4 = \mu_5 = \mu_6$
H_a: At least two treatment means differ

The test statistic is $F = \dfrac{\text{MST}}{\text{MSE}} = 21.62$

The rejection region requires $\alpha = .05$ in the upper tail of the F-distribution with $v_1 = ab - 1$ $= 2(3) - 1 = 5$ and $v_2 = n - ab = 12 - 2(3) = 6$. From Table IX, Appendix B, $F_{.05} = 4.39$. The rejection region is $F > 4.39$.

Since the observed value of the test statistic falls in the rejection region ($F = 21.62 > 4.39$), H_0 is rejected. There is sufficient evidence to indicate that the treatment means differ at $\alpha = .05$. This supports the plot in **a**.

c. Yes. Since there are differences among the treatment means, we test for interaction. To determine whether the factors A and B interact, we test:

H_0: Factors A and B do not interact to affect the mean response
H_a: Factors A and B do interact to affect the mean response

The test statistic is $F = \dfrac{\text{MS}AB}{\text{MSE}} = \dfrac{9.003}{.246} = 36.60$

The rejection region requires $\alpha = .05$ in the upper tail of the F-distribution with $v_1 = (a - 1)(b - 1) = (2 - 1)(3 - 1) = 2$ and $v_2 = n - ab = 12 - 2(3) = 6$. From Table IX, Appendix B, $F_{.05} = 5.14$. The rejection region is $F > 5.14$.

Since the observed value of the test statistic falls in the rejection region ($F = 36.60 > 5.14$), H_0 is rejected. There is sufficient evidence to indicate that factors A and B interact to affect the response mean at $\alpha = .05$.

d. No. Because interaction is present, the tests for main effects are not warranted.

e. The results of the tests in parts **b** and **c** support the visual interpretation in part **a**.

14.43 a. $SSA = .2(1000) = 200$, $SSB = .1(1000) = 100$, $SSAB = .1(1000) = 100$
$SSE = SS(\text{Total}) - SSA - SSB - SSAB = 1000 - 200 - 100 - 100 = 600$
$SST = SSA + SSB + SSAB = 200 + 100 + 100 = 400$

$MSA = \dfrac{SSA}{a - 1} = \dfrac{200}{3 - 1} = 100$ $\qquad$ $MSB = \dfrac{SSB}{b - 1} = \dfrac{100}{3 - 1} = 50$

$MSAB = \dfrac{SSAB}{(a - 1)(b - 1)} = \dfrac{100}{(3 - 1)(3 - 1)} = 25$

$MSE = \dfrac{SSE}{n - ab} = \dfrac{600}{27 - 3(3)} = 33.333$ $\qquad$ $MST = \dfrac{SST}{ab - 1} = \dfrac{400}{3(3) - 1} = 50$

$F_A = \dfrac{MSA}{\text{MSE}} = \dfrac{100}{33.333} = 3.00$ $\qquad$ $F_B = \dfrac{MSB}{\text{MSE}} = \dfrac{50}{33.333} = 1.50$

$F_{AB} = \dfrac{MSAB}{\text{MSE}} = \dfrac{25}{33.333} = .75$ $\qquad$ $F_T = \dfrac{MST}{\text{MSE}} = \dfrac{50}{33.333} = 1.50$

Source	df	SS	MS	F
A	2	200	100	3.00
B	2	100	50	1.50
AB	4	100	25	.75
Error	18	600	33.333	
Total	26	1000		

To determine whether the treatment means differ, we test:

H_0: $\mu_1 = \mu_2 = \cdots = \mu_9$
H_a: At least two treatment means differ

The test statistic is $F = \dfrac{\text{MST}}{\text{MSE}} = 1.50$

Suppose $\alpha = .05$. The rejection region requires $\alpha = .05$ in the upper tail of the F-distribution with $\nu_1 = ab - 1 = 3(3) - 1 = 8$ and $\nu_2 = n - ab = 27 - 3(3) = 18$. From Table IX, Appendix B, $F_{.05} = 2.51$. The rejection region is $F > 2.51$.

Since the observed value of the test statistic does not fall in the rejection region ($F = 1.50 \not> 2.51$), H_0 is not rejected. There is insufficient evidence to indicate the treatment means differ at $\alpha = .05$. Since there are no treatment mean differences, we have nothing more to do.

b. $\text{SS}A = .1(1000) = 100$, $\text{SS}B = .1(1000) = 100$, $\text{SS}AB = .5(1000) = 500$

$\text{SSE} = \text{SS(Total)} - \text{SS}A - \text{SS}B - \text{SS}AB = 1000 - 100 - 100 - 500 = 300$

$\text{SST} = \text{SS}A + \text{SS}B + \text{SS}AB = 100 + 100 + 500 = 700$

$$\text{MS}A = \frac{\text{SS}A}{a - 1} = \frac{100}{3 - 1} = 50 \qquad\qquad \text{MS}B = \frac{\text{SS}B}{b - 1} = \frac{100}{3 - 1} = 50$$

$$\text{MS}AB = \frac{\text{SS}AB}{(a - 1)(b - 1)} = \frac{500}{(3 - 1)(3 - 1)} = 125$$

$$\text{MSE} = \frac{\text{SSE}}{n - ab} = \frac{300}{27 - 3(3)} = 16.667 \qquad \text{MST} = \frac{\text{SST}}{ab - 1} = \frac{700}{9 - 1} = 87.5$$

$$F_A = \frac{\text{MS}A}{\text{MSE}} = \frac{50}{16.667} = 3.00 \qquad\qquad F_B = \frac{\text{MS}B}{\text{MSE}} = \frac{50}{16.667} = 3.00$$

$$F_{AB} = \frac{\text{MS}AB}{\text{MSE}} = \frac{125}{16.667} = 7.50 \qquad\qquad F_T = \frac{\text{MST}}{\text{MSE}} = \frac{87.5}{16.667} = 5.25$$

Source	df	SS	MS	F
A	2	100	50	3.00
B	2	100	50	3.00
AB	4	500	125	7.50
Error	18	300	16.667	
Total	26	1000		

To determine if the treatment means differ, we test:

H_0: $\mu_1 = \mu_2 = \cdots = \mu_9$
H_a: At least two treatment means differ

The test statistic is $F = \dfrac{\text{MST}}{\text{MSE}} = 5.25$

The rejection region requires $\alpha = .05$ in the upper tail of the F-distribution with $\nu_1 = ab - 1 = 3(3) - 1 = 8$ and $\nu_2 = n - ab = 27 - 3(3) = 18$. From Table IX, Appendix B, $F_{.05} = 2.51$. The rejection region is $F > 2.51$.

Since the observed value of the test statistic falls in the rejection region ($F = 5.25 > 2.51$), H_0 is rejected. There is sufficient evidence to indicate the treatment means differ at $\alpha = .05$.

Since the treatment means differ, we next test for interaction between factors A and B. To determine if factors A and B interact, we test:

H_0: Factors A and B do not interact to affect the mean response
H_a: Factors A and B do interact to affect the mean response

The test statistic is $F = \dfrac{\text{MS}AB}{\text{MSE}} = 7.50$

The rejection region requires $\alpha = .05$ in the upper tail of the F-distribution with $\nu_1 = (a - 1)(b - 1) = (3 - 1)(3 - 1) = 4$ and $\nu_2 = n - ab = 27 - 3(3) = 18$. From Table IX, Appendix B, $F_{.05} = 2.93$. The rejection region is $F > 2.93$.

Since the observed value of the test statistic falls in the rejection region ($F = 7.50 > 2.93$), H_0 is rejected. There is sufficient evidence to indicate the factors A and B interact at $\alpha = .05$. Since interaction is present, no tests for main effects are necessary.

c. $\text{SS}A = .4(1000) = 400$, $\text{SS}B = .1(1000) = 100$, $\text{SS}AB = .2(1000) = 200$
$\text{SSE} = \text{SS(Total)} - \text{SS}A - \text{SS}B - \text{SS}AB = 1000 - 400 - 100 - 200 = 300$
$\text{SST} = \text{SS}A + \text{SS}B + \text{SS}AB = 400 + 100 + 200 = 700$

$$\text{MS}A = \frac{\text{SS}A}{a - 1} = \frac{400}{3 - 1} = 50 \qquad\qquad \text{MS}B = \frac{\text{SS}B}{b - 1} = \frac{100}{3 - 1} = 50$$

$$\text{MS}AB = \frac{\text{SS}AB}{(a - 1)(b - 1)} = \frac{200}{(3 - 1)(3 - 1)} = 50$$

$$\text{MSE} = \frac{\text{SSE}}{n - ab} = \frac{300}{27 - 3(3)} = 16.667 \qquad \text{MST} = \frac{\text{SST}}{ab - 1} = \frac{700}{3(3) - 1} = 87.5$$

$$F_A = \frac{\text{MS}A}{\text{MSE}} = \frac{200}{16.667} = 12.00 \qquad\qquad F_B = \frac{\text{MS}B}{\text{MSE}} = \frac{50}{16.667} = 3.00$$

$$F_{AB} = \frac{\text{MS}AB}{\text{MSE}} = \frac{50}{16.667} = 3.00 \qquad\qquad F_T = \frac{\text{MST}}{\text{MSE}} = \frac{87.5}{16.667} = 5.25$$

Source	df	SS	MS	F
A	2	400	200	12.00
B	2	100	50	3.00
AB	4	200	50	3.00
Error	18	300	16.667	
Total	26	1000		

To determine if the treatment means differ, we test:

H_0: $\mu_1 = \mu_2 = \cdots = \mu_9$
H_a: At least two treatment means differ

The test statistic is $F = \dfrac{\text{MST}}{\text{MSE}} = 5.25$

The rejection region requires $\alpha = .05$ in the upper tail of the F-distribution with $\nu_1 = ab - 1 = 3(3) - 1 = 8$ and $\nu_2 = n - ab = 27 - 3(3) = 18$. From Table IX, Appendix B, $F_{.05} = 2.51$. The rejection region is $F > 2.51$.

Since the observed value of the test statistic falls in the rejection region ($F = 5.25 > 2.51$), H_0 is rejected. There is sufficient evidence to indicate the treatment means differ at $\alpha = .05$.

Since the treatment means differ, we next test for interaction between factors A and B. To determine if factors A and B interact, we test:

H_0: Factors A and B do not interact to affect the mean response
H_a: Factors A and B do interact to affect the mean response

The test statistic is $F = \dfrac{\text{MS}AB}{\text{MSE}} = 3.00$

The rejection region requires $\alpha = .05$ in the upper tail of the F-distribution with $\nu_1 = (a - 1)(b - 1) = (3 - 1)(3 - 1) = 4$ and $\nu_2 = n - ab = 27 - 3(3) = 18$. From Table IX, Appendix B, $F_{.05} = 2.93$. The rejection region is $F > 2.93$.

Since the observed value of the test statistic falls in the rejection region ($F = 3.00 > 2.93$), H_0 is rejected. There is sufficient evidence to indicate the factors A and B interact at $\alpha = .05$. Since interaction is present, no tests for main effects are necessary.

d. $\text{SS}A = .4(1000) = 400$, $\text{SS}B = .4(1000) = 400$, $\text{SS}AB = .1(1000) = 100$

$\text{SSE} = \text{SS(Total)} - \text{SS}A - \text{SS}B - \text{SS}AB = 1000 - 400 - 400 - 100 = 100$

$\text{SST} = \text{SS}A + \text{SS}B + \text{SS}AB = 400 + 400 + 100 = 900$

$$\text{MS}A = \frac{\text{SS}A}{a - 1} = \frac{400}{3 - 1} = 200 \qquad \text{MS}B = \frac{\text{SS}B}{b - 1} = \frac{400}{3 - 1} = 200$$

$$\text{MS}AB = \frac{\text{SS}AB}{(a - 1)(b - 1)} = \frac{100}{(3 - 1)(3 - 1)} = 25$$

$$\text{MSE} = \frac{\text{SSE}}{n - ab} = \frac{100}{27 - 3(3)} = 5.556 \qquad \text{MST} = \frac{\text{SST}}{ab - 1} = \frac{900}{3(3) - 1} = 112.5$$

$$F_A = \frac{\text{MS}A}{\text{MSE}} = \frac{200}{5.556} = 36.00 \qquad F_B = \frac{\text{MS}B}{\text{MSE}} = \frac{200}{5.556} = 36.00$$

$$F_{AB} = \frac{\text{MS}AB}{\text{MSE}} = \frac{25}{5.556} = 4.50 \qquad F_T = \frac{\text{MST}}{\text{MSE}} = \frac{112.5}{5.556} = 20.25$$

Source	df	SS	MS	F
A	2	400	200	36.00
B	2	400	200	36.00
AB	4	100	25	4.50
Error	18	100	5.556	
Total	26	1000		

To determine if the treatment means differ, we test:

H_0: $\mu_1 = \mu_2 = \cdots = \mu_9$
H_a: At least two treatment means differ

The test statistic is $F = \dfrac{\text{MST}}{\text{MSE}} = 20.25$

The rejection region requires $\alpha = .05$ in the upper tail of the F-distribution with $\nu_1 = ab - 1 = 3(3) - 1 = 8$ and $\nu_2 = n - ab = 27 - 3(3) = 18$. From Table IX, Appendix B, $F_{.05} = 2.51$. The rejection region is $F > 2.51$.

Since the observed value of the test statistic falls in the rejection region ($F = 20.25 > 2.51$), H_0 is rejected. There is sufficient evidence to indicate the treatment means differ at $\alpha = .05$.

Since the treatment means differ, we next test for interaction between factors A and B. To determine if factors A and B interact, we test:

H_0: Factors A and B do not interact to affect the mean response
H_a: Factors A and B do interact to affect the mean response

The test statistic is $F = \dfrac{\text{MS}AB}{\text{MSE}} = 4.50$

The rejection region requires $\alpha = .05$ in the upper tail of the F-distribution with $\nu_1 = (a - 1)(b - 1) = (3 - 1)(3 - 1) = 4$ and $\nu_2 = n - ab = 27 - 3(3) = 18$. From Table IX, Appendix B, $F_{.05} = 2.93$. The rejection region is $F > 2.93$.

Since the observed value of the test statistic falls in the rejection region ($F = 4.50 > 2.93$), H_0 is rejected. There is sufficient evidence to indicate the factors A and B interact at $\alpha = .05$. Since interaction is present, no tests for main effects are necessary.

14.45 a. To determine if Herd and Season interact, we test:

H_0: Herd and Season do not interact
H_a: Herd and Season interact

The test statistic is $F = 1.2$.

The p-value is $p > .05$. Since the p-value is greater than $\alpha = .05$, H_0 is not rejected. There is insufficient evidence to indicate that herd and season interact at $\alpha = .05$.

Since the two factors do not interact, the main effect tests are run.

To determine if the mean home range differs among the four herds, we test:

H_0: $\mu_1 = \mu_2 = \mu_3 = \mu_4$
H_a: At least two treatments means differ

where μ_i is the mean home range for herd i.

The test statistic is $F = 17.2$.

The p-value is $p < .001$. Since the p-value is less than $\alpha = .05$, H_0 is rejected. There is sufficient evidence to indicate that the mean home range differs among the four herds at $\alpha = .05$.

To determine if the mean home range differs among the four seasons, we test:

H_0: $\mu_1 = \mu_2 = \mu_3 = \mu_4$
H_a: At least two treatments means differ

where μ_i is the mean home range for season i.

The test statistic is $F = 3.0$.

The p-value is $p > .05$. Since the p-value is greater than $\alpha = .05$, H_0 is not rejected. There is insufficient evidence to indicate that the mean home range differs among the four seasons at $\alpha = .05$.

b. Yes. Since herd and season do not interact, each main effect factor can be treated separately as if the second factor did not exist.

c. The mean home range for herd MTZ is significantly greater than the mean home range for the herds PLC and LGN. The mean home range for herd QMD is significantly greater than the mean home range for the herds PLC and LGN. No other differences exist.

14.47   a. The degrees of freedom for "Type of message retrieval system" is $a - 1 = 2 - 1 = 1$. The degrees of freedom for "Pricing option" is $b - 1 = 2 - 1 = 1$. The degrees of freedom for the interaction of Type of message retrieval system and Pricing option is $(a - 1)(b - 1) = (2 - 1)(2 - 1) = 1$. The degrees of freedom for error is $n - ab = 120 - 2(2) = 116$.

Source	df	SS	MS	F
Type of message retrieval system	1	-	-	2.001
Pricing Option	1	-	-	5.019
Type of system × pricing option	1	-	-	4.986
Error	116	-	-	
Total	119			

To determine if "Type of system" and "Pricing option" interact to affect the mean willingness to buy, we test:

H_0: "Type of system" and "Pricing option" do not interact

H_a: "Type of system" and "Pricing option" interact

c. The test statistic is $F = \dfrac{\text{MSAB}}{\text{MSE}} = 4.986$

The rejection region requires $\alpha = .05$ in the upper tail of the F distribution with $\nu_1 = (a - 1)(b - 1) = (2 - 1)(2 - 1) = 1$ and $\nu_2 = n - ab = 120 - 2(2) = 116$. From Table IX, Appendix B, $F_{.05} \approx 3.92$. The rejection region is $F > 3.92$.

Since the observed value of the test statistic falls in the rejection region ($F = 4.986 > 3.92$), H_0 is rejected. There is sufficient evidence to indicate "Type of system" and "Pricing option" interact to affect the mean willingness to buy at $\alpha = .05$.

d. No. Since the test in part c indicated that interaction between "Type of system" and "Pricing option" is present, we should not test for the main effects. Instead, we should proceed directly to a multiple comparison procedure to compare selected treatment means. If interaction is present, it can cover up the main effects.

14.49   a. This is a 2×2 factorial experiment.

b.   The two factors are the tent type (treated or untreated) and location (inside or outside). There are $2 \times 2 = 4$ treatments. The four treatments are (treated, inside), (treated, outside), (untreated, inside), and (untreated, outside).

c.   The response variable is the number of mosquito bites received in a 20 minute interval.

d.   There is sufficient evidence to indicate interaction is present. This indicates that the effect of the tent type on the number of mosquito bites depends on whether the person is inside or outside.

14.51   a.   Let $x_1 = \begin{cases} 1 & \text{if level 1} \\ 0 & \text{otherwise} \end{cases}$ $x_2 = \begin{cases} 1 & \text{if level 2} \\ 0 & \text{otherwise} \end{cases}$

$x_3 = \begin{cases} 1 & \text{if level 3} \\ 0 & \text{otherwise} \end{cases}$ $x_4 = \begin{cases} 1 & \text{if level 4} \\ 0 & \text{otherwise} \end{cases}$

The model is $E(y) = \beta_0 + \beta_1 x_1 + \beta_2 x_2 + \beta_3 x_3 + \beta_4 x_4$ where

β_0 = mean response for level 5 of factor
β_1 = difference in mean response between levels 1 and 5
β_2 = difference in mean response between levels 2 and 5
β_3 = difference in mean response between levels 3 and 5
β_4 = difference in mean response between levels 4 and 5

b.   Error df $= n - (k + 1) = 15 - (4 + 1) = 10$

c. H_0: $\beta_1 = \beta_2 = \beta_3 = \beta_4 = 0$

d.   The rejection region requires $\alpha = .10$ in the upper tail of the F-distribution with $\nu_1 = k = 4$ and $\nu_2 = n - (k + 1) = 15 - (4 + 1) = 10$. From Table VIII, Appendix B, $F_{.10} = 2.61$. The rejection region is $F > 2.61$.

14.53   a.   To determine if the mean costs differ among the three groups, we test:

H_0: $\beta_1 = \beta_2 = 0$
H_a: At least one $\beta_i \neq 0$, $i = 1, 2$

The test statistic is $F = 8.438$.

The rejection region requires $\alpha = .05$ in the upper tail of the F-distribution with $\nu_1 = 2$ and $\nu_2 = 27$. From Table IX, Appendix B, $F_{.05} = 3.35$. The rejection region is $F > 3.35$.

Since the observed value of the test statistic falls in the rejection region ($F = 8.438 > 3.35$), H_0 is rejected. There is sufficient evidence to indicate a difference in the treatment means among the 3 groups at $\alpha = .05$. This is the same result as found in Exercise 14.22.

b.   The observed significance level for this problem is .0014, while the observed significance level for Exercise 14.22 is .0014.

c.   SST $= 318,861.66667$ for this problem and SST $= 318,861.667$ for Exercise 14.22.
SSE $= 510,163$ for this problem and SSE $= 510,163$ for Exercise 14.22.

d. $R^2 = .3846$. 38.46% of the sample variation in costs incurred in audits is explained by the three groups.

β_0 = mean costs incurred in audits for group C

β_1 = difference in mean costs incurred in audits between groups A and C

β_2 = difference in mean costs incurred in audits between groups B and C

14.55 a.

Treatment Price, Display	Estimate of Mean Response
Regular, Normal	$\hat{\beta}_0 + \hat{\beta}_1 + \hat{\beta}_3 + \hat{\beta}_5 = 1828.67 - 626 - 250.67 + 62.67$ $= 1014.67$
Regular, Normal Plus	$\hat{\beta}_0 + \hat{\beta}_1 + \hat{\beta}_4 + \hat{\beta}_6 = 1828.67 - 626 + 681.33 - 669$ $= 1215$
Regular, Twice Normal	$\hat{\beta}_0 + \hat{\beta}_1 = 1828.67 - 626 = 1202.67$
Reduced, Normal	$\hat{\beta}_0 + \hat{\beta}_2 + \hat{\beta}_3 + \hat{\beta}_7 = 1828.67 - 323.67 - 250.67$ $+ 51.67 = 1202.66$
Reduced, Normal Plus	$\hat{\beta}_0 + \hat{\beta}_2 + \hat{\beta}_4 + \hat{\beta}_8 = 1828.67 - 323.67 + 681.33$ $- 287.67 = 1898.66$
Reduced, Twice Normal	$\hat{\beta}_0 + \hat{\beta}_2 = 1828.67 - 323.67 = 1505$
Cost, Normal	$\hat{\beta}_0 + \hat{\beta}_3 = 1828.67 - 250.67 = 1578$
Cost, Normal Plus	$\hat{\beta}_0 + \hat{\beta}_4 = 1828.67 + 681.33 = 2510$
Cost, Twice Normal	$\hat{\beta}_0 = 1828.67$

b.   The estimate of the standard deviation is $\sqrt{MSE} = \sqrt{495} = 22.2486$.

We expect most of the observed values to fall within $\pm 2s$ or $\pm 2(22.2486)$ or ± 44.4972 of their predicted values.

$R^2 = .999$. 99.9% of the sample variation in unit sales is explained by the nine different display and price combinations.

c.   To determine if the mean unit sales differ for the nine treatments, we test:

H_0: $\beta_1 = \beta_2 = \beta_3 = \cdots = \beta_8 = 0$

H_a: At least one $\beta_i \neq 0$, $i = 1, 2, \dots, 8$

The test statistic is $F = \dfrac{MSR}{MSE} = 1336.85$

The rejection region requires $\alpha = .10$ in the upper tail of the F-distribution with $\nu_1 = 8$ and $\nu_2 = 18$. From Table VIII, Appendix B, $F_{.10} = 2.04$. The rejection region is $F > 2.04$.

Since the observed value of the test statistic falls in the rejection region ($F = 1336.85 > 2.04$), H_0 is rejected. There is sufficient evidence to indicate there are differences in mean unit sales among the 9 treatments at $\alpha = .10$. This is the same result as in Exercise 15.36.

d.   The null hypothesis used to test for interaction is:

H_0: $\beta_5 = \beta_6 = \beta_7 = \beta_8 = 0$

The test statistic is $F = \dfrac{(SSE_r - SSE_c)/(k - g)}{SSE_c /[n - (k + 1)]}$

The rejection region requires $\alpha = .10$ in the upper tail of the F-distribution with $\nu_1 = 4$ and $\nu_2 = 18$. From Table VIII, Appendix B, $F_{.10} = 2.29$. The rejection region is $F > 2.29$.

e. $$F = \frac{(519{,}610.1481 - 8{,}905.3333)/(8 - 4)}{8{,}905.3333/[27 - (8 + 1)]} = \frac{127{,}676.2037}{494.7407} = 258.07$$

Since the observed value of the test statistic falls in the rejection region ($F = 258.07 > 2.29$), H_0 is rejected. There is sufficient evidence to indicate interaction is present at $\alpha = .10$. This is the same result as in Exercise 14.46.

f. No further testing is necessary. Our next step would be to compare the treatment means using Bonferroni's multiple comparisons procedure.

14.57 There are $3 \times 2 = 6$ treatments. They are A_1B_1, A_1B_2, A_2B_1, A_2B_2, A_3B_1, and A_3B_2.

14.59 a. SSE = SSTot − SST = 62.55 − 36.95 = 25.60

df Treatment = $p - 1 = 4 - 1 = 3$
df Error = $n - p = 20 - 4 = 16$
df Total = $n - 1 = 20 - 1 = 19$
MST = SST/df = $\dfrac{36.95}{3} = 12.32$

MSE = SSE/df = $\dfrac{25.60}{16} = 1.60$

$F = \dfrac{\text{MST}}{\text{MSE}} = \dfrac{12.32}{1.60} = 7.70$

The ANOVA table:

Source	df	SS	MS	F
Treatment	3	36.95	12.32	7.70
Error	16	25.60	1.60	
Total	19	62.55		

b. To determine if there is a difference in the treatment means, we test:

H_0: $\mu_1 = \mu_2 = \mu_3 = \mu_4$
H_a: At least two of the means differ

where the μ_i represents the mean for the ith treatment.

The test statistic is $F = \dfrac{\text{MST}}{\text{MSE}} = 7.70$

The rejection region requires $\alpha = .10$ in the upper tail of the F-distribution with $\nu_1 = (p - 1)$ $= (4 - 1) = 3$ and $\nu_2 = (n - p) = (20 - 4) = 16$. From Table VIII, Appendix B, $F_{.10} = 2.46$. The rejection region is $F > 2.46$.

Since the observed value of the test statistic falls in the rejection region ($F = 7.70 > 2.46$), H_0 is rejected. There is sufficient evidence to conclude that at least two of the means differ at $\alpha = .10$.

c. $\overline{x}_4 = \dfrac{\sum x_4}{n_4} = \dfrac{57}{5} = 11.4$

For confidence level .90, $\alpha = .10$ and $\alpha/2 = .10/2 = .05$. From Table VI, Appendix B, with df $= 16$, $t_{.05} = 1.746$. The confidence interval is:

$$\overline{x}_4 \pm t_{.05} \cdot \sqrt{MSE/n_4} \Rightarrow 11.4 \pm 1.746 \cdot \sqrt{1.6/5} \Rightarrow 11.4 \pm .99 \Rightarrow (10.41, 12.39)$$

14.61 a. The data are collected as a completely randomized design because five boxes of each size were randomly selected and tested.

b. Yes. The confidence intervals surrounding each of the means do not overlap. This would indicate that there is a difference in the means for the two sizes.

c. No. Several of the confidence intervals overlap. This would indicate that the mean compression strengths of the sizes that have intervals that overlap are not significantly different.

14.63 a. To determine if leadership style affects behavior of subordinates, we test:

H_0: All four treatment means are the same
H_a: At least two treatment means differ

The test statistic is $F = 30.4$.

The rejection region requires $\alpha = .05$ in the upper tail of the F-distribution with $v_1 = ab - 1 = 2(2) - 1 = 3$ and $v_2 = n - ab = 257 - 2(2) = 253$. From Table IX, Appendix B, $F_{.05} \approx 2.60$. The rejection region is $F > 2.60$.

Since the observed value of the test statistic falls in the rejection region ($F = 30.4 > 2.60$), H_0 is rejected. There is sufficient evidence to indicate that leadership style affects behavior of subordinates at $\alpha = .05$.

b. From the table, the mean response for High control, low consideration is significantly higher than for any other treatment. The mean response for Low control, low consideration is significantly higher than that for High control, high consideration and for Low control, high consideration. No other significant differences exist.

c. The assumptions for Bonferroni's method are the same as those for the ANOVA. Thus, we must assume that:

i. The populations sampled from are normal.
ii. The population variances are the same.
iii. The samples are independent.

14.65 a. This is a completely randomized design.

b. The means presented are the sample means, not the population means. The hypotheses being tested involve the population means. The sample means will almost always be different. What we must do is determine if the sample means are enough different to warrant rejection of the null hypothesis. In this case, although the sample means are different, they are not different enough to reject the null hypothesis.

14.67 a. This is a completely randomized design with a complete four-factor factorial design.

b. There are a total of $2 \times 2 \times 2 \times 2 = 16$ treatments.

c. Using SAS, the output is:

Analysis of Variance Procedure

Dependent Variable: Y

Source	DF	Sum of Squares	Mean Square	F Value	Pr > F
Model	15	546745.50	36449.70	5.11	0.0012
Error	16	114062.00	7128.88		
Corrected Total	31	660807.50			

R-Square	C.V.	Root MSE	Y Mean
0.827390	41.46478	84.433	203.63

Source	DF	Anova SS	Mean Square	F Value	Pr > F
SPEED	1	56784.50	56784.50	7.97	0.0123
FEED	1	21218.00	21218.00	2.98	0.1037
SPEED*FEED	1	55444.50	55444.50	7.78	0.0131
COLLET	1	165025.13	165025.13	23.15	0.0002
SPEED*COLLET	1	44253.13	44253.13	6.21	0.0241
FEED*COLLET	1	142311.13	142311.13	19.96	0.0004
SPEED*FEED*COLLET	1	54946.13	54946.13	7.71	0.0135
WEAR	1	378.13	378.13	0.05	0.8208
SPEED*WEAR	1	1540.13	1540.13	0.22	0.6483
FEED*WEAR	1	946.13	946.13	0.13	0.7204
SPEED*FEED*WEAR	1	528.13	528.13	0.07	0.7890
COLLET*WEAR	1	1682.00	1682.00	0.24	0.6337
SPEED*COLLET*WEAR	1	512.00	512.00	0.07	0.7921
FEED*COLLET*WEAR	1	72.00	72.00	0.01	0.9212
SPEE*FEED*COLLE*WEAR	1	1104.50	1104.50	0.15	0.6991

d. To determine if the interaction terms are significant, we must add together the sum of squares for all interaction terms as well as the degrees of freedom.

$$\text{SS(Interaction)} = 55{,}444.50 + 44{,}253.13 + 142{,}311.13 + 54{,}946.13 + 1{,}540.13 + 946.13$$
$$+ 528.13 + 1{,}682.00 + 512.00 + 72.00 + 1{,}104.50$$
$$= 303{,}339.78$$

$$\text{df(Interacton)} = 11$$

$$\text{MS(Interaction)} = \frac{\text{SS(Interacton)}}{\text{df(Interaction)}} = \frac{303{,}339.78}{11} = 27{,}576.34364$$

$$\text{F(Interacton)} = \frac{\text{MS(Interaction)}}{\text{MSE}} = \frac{27{,}576.34364}{7128.88} = 3.87$$

To determine if interaction effects are present, we test:

H_0: No interaction effects exist
H_a: Interaction effects exist

The test statistic is $F = 3.87$.

The rejection region requires $\alpha = .05$ in the upper tail of the F-distribution with $\nu_1 = 11$ and $\nu_2 = 16$. From Table IX, Appendix B, $F_{.05} \approx 2.49$. The rejection region is $F > 2.49$.

Since the observed value of the test statistic falls in the rejection region ($F = 3.87 > 2.49$), H_0 is rejected. There is sufficient evidence to indicate that interaction effects exist at $\alpha = .05$.

Since the sums of squares for a balanced factorial design are independent of each other, we can look at the SAS output to determine which of the interaction effects are significant. The three-way interaction between speed, feed, and collet is significant ($p = .0135$). There are three two-way interactions with p-values less than .05. However, all of these two-way interaction terms are imbedded in the significant three-way interaction term.

e. Yes. Since the significant interaction terms do not include wear, it would be necessary to perform the main effect test for wear. All other main effects are contained in a significant interaction term.

To determine if the mean finish measurements differ for the different levels of wear, we test:

H_0: The mean finish measurements for the two levels of wear are the same
H_a: The mean finish measurements for the two levels of wear are different

The test statistic is $t = 0.05$.

The rejection region requires $\alpha = .05$ in the upper tail of the F-distribution with $\nu_1 = 1$ and $\nu_2 = 16$. From Table IX, Appendix B, $F_{.05} = 4.49$. The rejection region is $F > 4.49$.

Since the observed value of the test statistic does not fall in the rejection region ($F = .05 \not> 4.49$), H_0 is not rejected. There is insufficient evidence to indicate that the mean finish measurements differ for the different levels of wear at $\alpha = .05$.

f. We must assume that:

i. The populations sampled from are normal.
ii. The population variances are the same.
iii. The samples are random and independent.

14.69 a. A completely randomized design was used. There are five treatments. They are the five different educational levels.

b. To determine if the mean concern ratings differ for at least two education levels, we test:

H_0: $\mu_1 = \mu_2 = \mu_3 = \mu_4 = \mu_5$
H_a: At least two treatment means differ

where μ_i represents the mean concern rating of the ith education level.

The test statistic is $F = 3.298$.

The rejection region requires $\alpha = .05$ in the upper tail of the F-distribution with $\nu_1 = p - 1 = 5 - 1 = 4$ and $\nu_2 = n - p = 315 - 5 = 310$. From Table IX, Appendix B, $F_{.05} \approx 2.37$. The rejection region is $F > 2.37$.

Since the observed value of the test statistic falls in the rejection region ($F = 3.298 > 2.37$), H_0 is rejected. There is sufficient evidence to indicate a difference in the mean concern ratings among the 5 education levels at $\alpha = .05$.

c. The mean concern rating for those with post-graduate education is significantly greater than the mean concern rating for the four other education level groups. There are no other significant differences.

14.71 a. The experiment is completely randomized. The response is the attitude test score after 1 month. The two factors are scheduling (2 levels) and payment (2 levels). Both factors are qualitative. There are $2 \times 2 = 4$ different treatments, where each treatment consists of a level of each factor, A_1B_1, A_1B_2, A_2B_1, and A_2B_2. The experimental units are the workers.

b. To determine if the treatment means differ, we test:

H_0: $\mu_1 = \mu_2 = \mu_3 = \mu_4$
H_a: At least one treatment mean differs

The test statistic is $F = \dfrac{\text{MST}}{\text{MSE}} = 12.29$

The rejection region requires $\alpha = .05$ in the upper tail of the F-distribution with $\nu_1 = ab - 1 = 2(2) - 1 = 3$ and $\nu_2 = n - ab = 16 - 2(2) = 12$. From Table IX, Appendix B, $F_{.05} = 3.49$. The rejection region is $F > 3.49$.

Since the observed value of the test statistic falls in the rejection region ($F = 12.29 > 3.49$), H_0 is rejected. There is sufficient evidence to indicate the treatment means differ at $\alpha = .05$.

c. To determine if the factors interact, we test:

H_0: Factor A and factor B do not interact to affect the response mean
H_a: Factors A and B do interact to affect the response mean

The test statistic is $F = \dfrac{\text{MS}AB}{\text{MSE}} = .02$

The rejection region requires $\alpha = .05$ in the upper tail of the F-distribution with $\nu_1 = (a - 1)(b - 1) = (2 - 1)(2 - 1) = 1$ and $\nu_2 = n - ab = 16 - 2(2) = 12$. From Table IX, Appendix B, $F_{.05} = 4.75$. The rejection region is $F > 4.75$.

Since the observed value of the test statistic does not fall in the rejection region ($F = .02 \ngtr 4.75$), H_0 is not rejected. There is insufficient evidence to indicate the factors interact at $\alpha = 05$.

To determine if the mean attitude test scores differ for the two types of scheduling, we test:

H_0: $\mu_1 = \mu_2$
H_a: $\mu_1 \neq \mu_2$

The test statistic is $F = \dfrac{\text{MS(Schedule)}}{\text{MSE}} = 7.37$

The rejection region requires $\alpha = .05$ in the upper tail of the F-distribution with $\nu_1 = (a - 1) = 2 - 1 = 1$ and $\nu_2 = n - ab = 16 - 2(2) = 12$. From Table IX, Appendix B, $F_{.05} = 4.75$. The rejection region is $F > 4.75$.

Since the observed value of the test statistic falls in the rejection region ($F = 7.37 > 4.75$), H_0 is rejected. There is sufficient evidence to indicate the mean attitude test scores differ for the two types of scheduling at $\alpha = .05$.

To determine if the mean attitude test scores differ for the two types of payments, we test:

H_0: $\mu_1 = \mu_2$
H_a: $\mu_1 \neq \mu_2$

The test statistic is $F = \dfrac{MS(\text{Payment})}{MSE} = 29.47$

The rejection region requires $\alpha = .05$ in the upper tail of the F-distribution with $\nu_1 = b - 1 = 2 - 1 = 1$ and $\nu_2 = n - ab = 16 - 2(2) = 12$. From Table IX, Appendix B, $F_{.05} = 4.75$. The rejection region is $F > 4.75$.

Since the observed value of the test statistic falls in the rejection region ($F = 29.47 > 4.75$), H_0 is rejected. There is sufficient evidence to indicate the mean attitude test scores differ for the two types of payment at $\alpha = .05$.

Since the mean attitude test scores for 8–5 is $558/8 = 69.75$ and the mean for worker-modified schedules is $634/8 = 79.25$, the mean attitude test scores for those on worker-modified schedules is significantly higher than for those on 8–5 schedules.

Since the mean attitude test scores for those on hourly rate is $520/8 = 65$ and the mean for those on hourly and piece rate is $672/8 = 84$, the mean attitude test scores for those on hourly and piece rate is significantly higher than for those on hourly rate.

d.   The necessary assumptions are:

1.   The probability distributions for each schedule-payment combination is normal.
2.   The variances for each distribution are equal.
3.   The samples are random and independent.

14.73   a.   This is an observational experiment and is completely randomized.

b.   To determine if the mean closing price differed among the three markets, we test:

H_0: $\mu_1 = \mu_2 = \mu_3$
H_a: At least two treatment means differ

The test statistic is $F = \dfrac{MST}{MSE} = 3.34$

The rejection region requires $\alpha = .10$ in the upper tail of the F-distribution with $\nu_1 = p - 1 = 3 - 1 = 2$ and $\nu_2 = n - p = 108 - 3 = 105$. From Table VIII, Appendix B, $F_{.10} \approx 2.39$. The rejection region is $F > 2.39$.

Since the observed value of the test statistic falls in the rejection region ($F = 3.34 > 2.39$), H_0 is rejected. There is sufficient evidence to indicate the mean closing price differed among the three markets at $\alpha = .10$.

c.   From the printout, the mean closing price for the NYSE is significantly higher than the mean closing price for the ASE. No other significant differences exist.

The experimentwise error rate is $\alpha = .05$.

14.75   a.   This is a completely randomized design.

b. Using the formulas in Appendix B:

$$CM = \frac{\left(\sum y_i\right)^2}{n} = \frac{497^2}{17} = 14,529.9412$$

$$SS(\text{Total}) = \sum y_i^2 - CM = 14,713 - 14,529.9412 = 183.059$$

$$SST = SS(\text{Plan}) = \frac{T_1^2}{n_1} + \frac{T_2^2}{n_2} + \frac{T_3^2}{n_3} + \frac{T_4^2}{n_4} - CM$$

$$= \frac{107^2}{4} + \frac{134^2}{5} + \frac{162^2}{5} + \frac{94^2}{3} - 14,529.9412 = 117.642$$

$$SSE = SS(\text{Total}) - SS(\text{Plan}) = 183.059 - 117.642 = 65.417$$

$$MST = MS(\text{Plan}) = \frac{SS(\text{Plan})}{p - 1} = \frac{117.642}{4 - 1} = 39.214, \ df = p - 1 = 3$$

$$MSE = \frac{SSE}{n - p} = \frac{65.417}{17 - 4} = 5.032, \ df = n - p = 13$$

$$F = \frac{MS(\text{Plan})}{MSE} = \frac{39.214}{5.032} = 7.79$$

Source	df	SS	MS	F
Treatment	3	117.642	39.214	7.79
Error	13	65.417	5.032	
Total	16	183.059		

c. To determine if the mean travel times for the four plans differ, we test:

$H_0: \ \mu_1 = \mu_2 = \mu_3 = \mu_4$
$H_a:$ At least two of the mean travel times differ

The test statistic is $F = \dfrac{MS(\text{Plan})}{MSE} = 7.79$

The rejection region requires $\alpha = .01$ in the upper tail of the F-distribution with $\nu_1 = p - 1 = 4 - 1 = 3$ and $\nu_2 = n - p = 17 - 4 = 13$. From Table XI, Appendix B, $F_{.01} = 5.74$. The rejection region is $F > 5.74$.

Since the observed value of the test statistic falls in the rejection region ($F = 7.79 > 5.74$), H_0 is rejected. There is sufficient evidence of a difference in mean travel times for the plans at $\alpha = .01$.

d.   Using SAS and $\alpha = .05$, the Tukey's multiple comparison is:

Analysis of Variance Procedure

Tukey's Studentized Range (HSD) Test for variable: Y

NOTE: This test controls the type I experimentwise error rate.

Alpha= 0.05 Confidence= 0.95 df= 13 MSE= 5.032051
Critical Value of Studentized Range= 4.151

Comparisons significant at the 0.05 level are indicated by '***'.

PLAN Comparison	Simultaneous Lower Confidence Limit	Difference Between Means	Simultaneous Upper Confidence Limit	
3 - 4	-3.742	1.067	5.875	
3 - 2	1.436	5.600	9.764	***
3 - 1	1.233	5.650	10.067	***
4 - 3	-5.875	-1.067	3.742	
4 - 2	-0.275	4.533	9.342	
4 - 1	-0.445	4.583	9.612	
2 - 3	-9.764	-5.600	-1.436	***
2 - 4	-9.342	-4.533	0.275	
2 - 1	-4.367	0.050	4.467	
1 - 3	-10.067	-5.650	-1.233	***
1 - 4	-9.612	-4.583	0.445	
1 - 2	-4.467	-0.050	4.367	

From the output, the confidence intervals that do not contain 0 indicate that the means are significantly different. The mean travel time for Plan 3 is significantly longer than the mean travel times for Plans 1 and 2. No other significant differences exist.

Nonparametric Statistics

15.1   The sign test is preferred to the *t*-test when the population from which the sample is selected is not normal.

15.3   a. $P(x \geq 7) = 1 - P(x \leq 6) = 1 - .965 = .035$

b. $P(x \geq 5) = 1 - P(x \leq 4) = 1 - .637 = .363$

c. $P(x \geq 8) = 1 - P(x \leq 7) = 1 - .996 = .004$

d. $P(x \geq 10) = 1 - P(x \leq 9) = 1 - .849 = .151$

$\mu = np = 15(.5) = 7.5$ and $\sigma = \sqrt{npq} = \sqrt{15(.5)(.5)} = 1.9365$

$P(x \geq 10) \approx P\left[z \geq \dfrac{(10 - .5) - 7.5}{1.9365}\right] = P(z \geq 1.03) = .5 - .3485 = .1515$

e. $P(x \geq 15) = 1 - P(x \leq 14) = 1 - .788 = .212$

$\mu = np = 25(.5) = 12.5$ and $\sigma = \sqrt{npq} = \sqrt{25(.5)(.5)} = 2.5$

$P(x \geq 15) \approx P\left[z \geq \dfrac{(15 - .5) - 12.5}{2.5}\right] = P(z \geq .80) = .5 - .2881 = .2119$

15.5   To determine if the median is greater than 75, we test:

$H_0: \eta = 75$
$H_a: \eta > 75$

The test statistic is $S =$ number of measurements greater than $75 = 17$.

The *p*-value $= P(x \geq 17)$ where x is a binomial random variable with $n = 25$ and $p = .5$. From Table II,

$p\text{-value} = P(x \geq 17) = 1 - P(x \leq 16) = 1 - .946 = .054$

Since the *p*-value $= .054 < \alpha = .10$, H_0 is rejected. There is sufficient evidence to indicate the median is greater than 75 at $\alpha = .10$.

We must assume the sample was randomly selected from a continuous probability distribution.

Note: Since $n \geq 10$, we could use the large-sample approximation.

15.7   a.   To determine whether the median biting rate is higher in bright, sunny weather, we test:

$H_0: \eta = 5$
$H_a: \eta > 5$

b.   The test statistic is $z = \dfrac{(S - .5) - .5n}{.5\sqrt{n}} = \dfrac{(95 - .5) - .5(122)}{.5\sqrt{122}} = 6.07$

(where S = number of observations greater than 5)

The p-value is $p = P(z \geq 6.07)$. From Table IV, Appendix B, $p = P(z \geq 6.07) \approx 0.0000$.

c.   Since the observed p-value is less than α ($p = 0.0000 < .01$), H_0 is rejected. There is sufficient evidence to indicate that the median biting rate in bright, sunny weather is greater than 5 at $\alpha = .01$.

15.9   a.   I would recommend the sign test because five of the sample measurements are of similar magnitude, but the 6th is about three times as large as the others. It would be very unlikely to observe this sample if the population were normal.

b.   To determine if the airline is meeting the requirement, we test:

H_0: $\eta = 30$
H_a: $\eta < 30$

c.   The test statistic is S = number of measurements less than $30 = 5$.

H_0 will be rejected if the p-value $< \alpha = .01$.

d.   The test statistic is $S = 5$.

The p-value $= P(x \geq 5)$ where x is a binomial random variable with $n = 6$ and $p = .5$. From Table II,

p-value $= P(x \geq 5) = 1 - P(x \leq 4) = 1 - .891 = .109$

Since the p-value $= .109$ is not less than $\alpha = .01$, H_0 is not rejected. There is insufficient evidence to indicate the airline is meeting the maintenance requirement at $\alpha = .01$.

15.11   a.   The test statistic is T_2, the rank sum of population 2 (because $n_2 < n_1$).

The rejection region is $T_2 \leq 35$ or $T_2 \geq 67$, from Table XV, Appendix B, with $n_1 = 10$, $n_2 = 6$, and $\alpha = .10$.

b.   The test statistic is T_1, the rank sum of population 1 (because $n_1 < n_2$).

The rejection region is $T_1 \geq 43$, from Table XV, Appendix B, with $n_1 = 5$, $n_2 = 7$, and $\alpha = .05$.

c.   The test statistic is T_2, the rank sum of population 2 (because $n_2 < n_1$).

The rejection region is $T_2 \geq 93$, from Table XV, Appendix B, with $n_1 = 9$, $n_2 = 8$, and $\alpha = .025$.

d. Since $n_1 = n_2 = 15$, the test statistic is:

$$z = \frac{T_1 - \dfrac{n_1(n_1 + n_2 + 1)}{2}}{\sqrt{\dfrac{n_1 n_2 (n_1 + n_2 + 1)}{12}}}$$

The rejection region is $z < -z_{\alpha/2}$ or $z > z_{\alpha/2}$. For $\alpha = .05$ and $\alpha/2 = .05/2 = .025$, $z_{.025} = 1.96$ from Table IV, Appendix B. The rejection region is $z < -1.96$ or $z > 1.96$.

15.13 The Wilcoxon rank sum test is a test of the location (center) of a distribution. The one-tailed test deals specifically with the center of one distribution being shifted in one direction (right or left) from the other distribution. The two-tailed test does not specify a particular direction of shift; we consider the possibility of a shift in either direction.

15.15 a. Some preliminary calculations:

Private Sector	Rank	Public Sector	Rank
2.58	10	5.40	15
5.05	13	2.55	9
0.05	1	9.00	16
2.10	5	10.55	17
4.30	12	1.02	2
2.25	6	5.11	14
2.50	8	12.42	18
1.94	4	1.67	3
2.33	7	3.33	11
	$T_1 = 66$		$T_2 = 105$

To determine if the distribution for public sector organizations is located to the right of the distribution for private sector firms, we test:

H_0: The two sampled populations have identical probability distributions
H_a: The probability distribution of the public sector is located to the right of that for the private sector

The test statistic is $T_2 = 105$.

The null hypothesis will be rejected if $T_2 \geq T_U$ where T_U corresponds to $\alpha = .025$ (one-tailed), and $n_1 = n_2 = 9$. From Table XV, Appendix B, $T_U = 108$. (There is no table for $\alpha = .01$. However, if we do not reject H_0 for $\alpha = .025$, we will not reject H_0 for $\alpha = .01$.)

Reject H_0 if $T_2 \geq 108$.

Since $T_2 = 105 \not\geq 108$, H_0 is not rejected. There is insufficient evidence to indicate that the distribution for public sector organizations is located to the right of the distribution for private sector firms at $\alpha = .01$.

b. The null hypothesis will be rejected if $T_2 \geq T_U$ where T_U corresponds to $\alpha = .05$ (one-tailed), and $n_1 = n_2 = 9$. From Table XV, Appendix B, $T_U = 105$. Since $T_1 = 105$, we would reject H_0. Thus, the p-value is less than or equal to $\alpha = .05$.

c. The assumptions necessary for the test are:

1. The two samples are random and independent.
2. The two probability distributions from which the samples were drawn are continuous.

15.17 a.

American Purchasing Managers		Mexican Purchasing Managers	
Sample 1	Rank	Sample 2	Rank
50	20.5	10	4.5
10	4.5	90	29
35	15.5	65	24
30	13.5	50	20.5
20	10.5	20	10.5
15	7.5	15	7.5
8	3	60	23
40	17.5	80	26.5
80	26.5	85	28
75	25	35	15.5
19	9	5	1.5
11	6	55	22
5	1.5	40	17.5
25	12	45	19
30	13.5	95	30
	$T_1 = 186$		$T_2 = 279$

These rank sums are the same as those found on the printout.

b. To determine whether American and Mexican purchasing managers perceive the given ethical situation differently, we test:

H_0: The two sampled populations have identical probability distributions

H_a: The probability distribution of the American managers is shifted to the right or left of the probability distribution of the Mexican managers.

The test statistic is $z = 1.908$ (from the printout)

The p-value is $p = .0564$. Since the p-value is greater than $\alpha = .05$, H_0 is not rejected. There is insufficient evidence to indicate American and Mexican purchasing managers perceive the given ethical situation differently at $\alpha = .05$.

c. In order to use the t-test, we need to assume that the two populations being sampled from are normal and that the variances of the two populations are equal. To check these assumptions, we will use stem-and-leaf plots and dot plots.

The stem-and-leaf plots are:

```
Stem-and-leaf of Ethics    Managers = 1    N = 15
Leaf Unit = 1.0

    2     0 58
    6     1 0159
   (2)    2 05
    7     3 005
    4     4 0
    3     5 0
    2     6
    2     7 5
    1     8 0


Stem-and-leaf of Ethics    Managers = 2    N = 15
Leaf Unit = 1.0

    1     0 5
    3     1 05
    4     2 0
    5     3 5
    7     4 05
   (2)    5 05
    6     6 05
    4     7
    4     8 05
    2     9 05
```

Neither of these two stem-and-leaf plots look mound-shaped. The assumption that the populations are normal may not be valid.

The dot plots are:

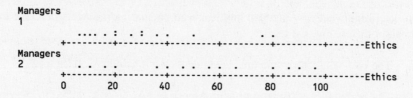

The spread of the two data sets look approximately equal. The assumption that the variances of the two populations are the same appears to be valid.

15.19

U.S. Plants		Japanese Plants	
Observation	Rank	Observation	Rank
7.11	9	3.52	4
6.06	7	2.02	2
8.00	10	4.91	6
6.87	8	3.22	3
4.77	5	1.92	1
$T_1 = 39$		$T_2 = 16$	

To determine if the distribution of American plants is shifted to the right of that for Japanese plants, we test:

H_0: The two sampled population have identical probability distributions
H_a: The probability distribution for American plants is shifted to the right of that for Japanese plants

The test statistic is $T_1 = 39$.

The rejection region is $T_1 \geq 36$ from Table XV, Appendix B, with $n_1 = n_2 = 5$, and $\alpha = .05$.

Since the observed value of the test statistic falls in the rejection region ($T_1 = 39 \geq 36$), H_0 is rejected. There is sufficient evidence to indicate the probability distribution for U.S. plants is shifted to the right of that for Japanese plants at $\alpha = .05$.

This result agrees with that from Exercise 9.20.

15.21   a.   We first rank all the data:

Firms with Successful MIS (1)				Firms with Unsuccessful MIS (2)			
Score	Rank	Score	Rank	Score	Rank	Score	Rank
52	5	90	25.5	60	10.5	65	12.5
70	15	75	17	50	4	55	7
40	1.5	80	19	55	7	70	15
80	19	95	29.5	70	15	90	25.5
82	21	90	25.5	41	3	85	22
65	12.5	86	23	40	1.5	80	19
59	9	95	29.5	55	7	90	25.5
60	10.5	93	28				
		$T_1 = 290.5$				$T_2 = 174.5$	

To determine whether the distribution of quality scores for successfully implemented systems lies above that for unsuccessfully implemented systems, we test:

H_0:   The two sampled populations have identical probability distributions
H_a: The probability distribution for successful MIS is shifted to the right of that for the unsuccessful MIS

The test statistic is $z = -1.75103$ (from printout).

The rejection region requires $\alpha = .05$ in the upper tail of the z-distribution. From Table IV, Appendix B, $z_{.05} = 1.645$. The rejection region is $z > -1.645$.

Since the observed value of the test statistic falls in the rejection region ($z = -1.75103 < -1.645$), H_0 is rejected. There is sufficient evidence to indicate the distribution of quality scores for successfully or good implemented systems lies above that for the unsuccessfully or poor implemented systems at $\alpha = .05$.

b.   We could use the two-sample t-test if:

1.   Both populations are normal.
2.   The variances of the two populations are the same.

15.23   a.   The hypotheses are:

H_0:   The two sampled populations have identical probability distributions
H_a: The probability distributions for population A is shifted to the right of that for population B

b.   Some preliminary calculations are:

Treatment A	B	Difference A − B	Rank of Absolute Difference
54	45	9	5
60	45	15	10
98	87	11	7
43	31	12	9
82	71	11	7
77	75	2	2.5
74	63	11	7
29	30	−1	1
63	59	4	4
80	82	−2	2.5
			$T_- = 3.5$

The test statistic is $T_- = 3.5$

The rejection region is $T_- \leq 8$, from Table XVI, Appendix B, with $n = 10$ and $\alpha = .025$.

Since the observed value of the test statistic falls in the rejection region ($T_- = 3.5 \leq 8$), H_0 is rejected. There is sufficient evidence to indicate the responses for A tend to be larger than those for B at $\alpha = .025$.

15.25   We assume that the probability distribution of differences is continuous so that the absolute differences will have unique ranks. Although tied (absolute) differences can be assigned average ranks, the number of ties should be small relative to the number of observations to assure validity.

15.27   a. H_0:   The two sampled populations have identical probability distributions
H_a: The probability distribution for population 1 is located to the right of that for population 2

b.   The test statistic is:

$$z = \frac{T_+ - \dfrac{n(n+1)}{4}}{\sqrt{\dfrac{n(n+1)(2n+1)}{24}}} = \frac{354 - \dfrac{30(30+1)}{4}}{\sqrt{\dfrac{30(30+1)(60+1)}{24}}} = \frac{121.5}{48.6184} = 2.499$$

The rejection region requires $\alpha = .05$ in the upper tail of the z-distribution. From Table IV, Appendix B, $z = 1.645$. The rejection region is $z > 1.645$.

Since the observed value of the test statistic falls in the rejection region ($z = 2.499 > 1.645$), H_0 is rejected. There is sufficient evidence to indicate population 1 is located to the right of that for population 2 at $\alpha = .05$.

c.   The p-value = $P(z \geq 2.499) = .5 - .4938 = .0062$ (using Table IV, Appendix B).

d.   The necessary assumptions are:

1.   The sample of differences is randomly selected from the population of differences.
2.   The probability distribution from which the sample of paired differences is drawn is continuous.

15.29

Operator	1999 Complaints	2000 Complaints	Difference	Rank of Absolute Difference
1	10	5	5	5.5
2	3	0	3	4
3	16	7	9	8
4	11	4	7	7
5	8	6	2	2.5
6	2	4	-2	2.5
7	1	2	-1	1
8	14	3	11	9
9	5	5	0	(eliminated)
10	6	1	5	5.5

Negative rank sum $T_- = 3.5$
Positive rank sum $T_+ = 41.5$

To determine if the distributions of the number of complaints differs for the two time periods, we test:

H_0: The distributions of the number of complaints for the two years are the same
H_a: The distribution of the number of complaints for 2000 is shifted to the right or left of the distribution for 1999

The test statistic is $T_- = 3.5$.

Since no α is given we will use $\alpha = .05$. The null hypothesis will be rejected if $T_- \leq T_0$ where T_0 corresponds to $\alpha = .05$ (two-tailed) and $n = 9$. From Table XVI, Appendix B, $T_0 = 6$.

Reject H_0 if $T_- \leq 6$.

Since the observed value of the test statistic falls in the rejection region ($T_- = 3.5 \leq 6$), H_0 is rejected. There is sufficient evidence to indicate the distributions of the complaints are different for the two years at $\alpha = .05$.

15.31 Some preliminary calculations are:

Employee	Before Flextime	After Flextime	Difference (B − A)	Difference
1	54	68	-14	7
2	25	42	-17	9
3	80	80	0	(Eliminated)
4	76	91	-15	8
5	63	70	-7	5
6	82	88	-6	3.5
7	94	90	4	2
8	72	81	-9	6
9	33	39	-6	3.5
10	90	93	-3	1
				$T_+ = 2$

To determine if the pilot flextime program is a success, we test:

H_0: The two probability distributions are identical
H_a: The probability distribution before is shifted to the left of that after

The test statistic is $T_+ = 2$.

The rejection region is $T_+ \leq 8$, from Table XVI, Appendix B, with $n = 9$ and $\alpha = .05$.

Since the observed value of the test statistic falls in the rejection region ($T_+ = 2 \leq 8$), H_0 is rejected. There is sufficient evidence to indicate the pilot flextime program has been a success at $\alpha = .05$.

15.33 To determine if one of the measuring facilities tends to read higher or lower than the other, we test:

H_0: The exhalation rate measurements for the two facilities are the same
H_a: The exhalation rate measurements by PCHD are shifted to the right or left of those by EERF

The test statistic is $z = -1.3631$ (from printout).

The p-value is $p = .1728$. Since the p-value is not less than α, ($p = .1728 \not< \alpha = .05$), H_0 is not rejected.

There is insufficient evidence to indicate a difference in the exhalation rate measurements for the two facilities at $\alpha = .05$.

15.35 a. A completely randomized design was used.

b. The hypotheses are:

H_0: The three probability distributions are identical
H_a: At least two of the three probability distributions differ in location

c. The rejection region requires $\alpha = .01$ in the upper tail of the χ^2 distribution with df $= p - 1$ $= 3 - 1 = 2$. From Table VII, Appendix B, $\chi^2_{.01} = 9.21034$. The rejection region is $H > 9.21034$.

d. Some preliminary calculations are:

I		II		III	
Observation	Rank	Observation	Rank	Observation	Rank
66	13	19	2	75	14.5
23	3	31	6	96	19
55	10	16	1	102	21
88	18	29	4	75	14.5
58	11	30	5	98	20
62	12	33	7	78	16
79	17	40	8		
49	9				
$R_A = 93$		$R_B = 33$		$R_C = 105$	

The test statistic is:

$$H = \frac{12}{n(n+1)} \sum \frac{R_j^2}{n_j} - 3(n+1)$$

$$= \frac{12}{21(21+1)} \left[\frac{93^2}{8} + \frac{33^2}{7} + \frac{105^2}{6} \right] - 3(21+1) = 79.85 - 66 = 13.85$$

Since the observed value of the test statistic falls in the rejection region ($H = 13.85 > 9.21034$), H_0 is rejected. There is sufficient evidence to indicate at least two of the three probability distributions differ in location at $\alpha = .01$.

15.37 a. $H = \frac{12}{n(n+1)} \sum \frac{R_j^2}{n_j} - 3(n+1)$

$$= \frac{12}{217(217+1)} \left[\frac{1804^2}{11} + \frac{6398^2}{49} + \frac{7328^2}{62} + \frac{4075^2}{39} + \frac{2660^2}{35} + \frac{1388^2}{21} \right] - 3(217+1)$$
$$= 35.23$$

b. The rejection region requires $\alpha = .01$ in the upper tail of the χ^2 distribution with df $= p - 1$ $= 6 - 1 = 5$. From Table VII, Appendix B, $\chi^2_{.01} = 15.0863$. The rejection region is $H > 15.0863$.

c. To determine if the biting rates for the six wind speed conditions differ, we test:

    H_0: The probability distributions of the number of bites are the same for the six wind
           speed conditions
    H_a: At least two of the six probability distributions differ in location

Since the observed value of the test statistic falls in the rejection region ($H = 35.23 > 15.0863$), H_0 is rejected. There is sufficient evidence to indicate that the biting rates for the six wind speed conditions differ at $\alpha = .01$.

d. The p-value is $p < .01$. Since the p-value is less than $\alpha = .01$, H_0 is rejected. This supports the inference in part c.

15.39 a. Some preliminary calculations are:

Growth		Blend		Value	
Rate	Rank	Rate	Rank	Rate	Rank
21.2	12	5.9	6	−9.2	2
37.9	17	23.5	15	−5.5	5
39.2	18	21.3	13	8.5	8
22.7	14	47.9	20	−8.5	3
44.8	19	8.2	7	9.2	9
31.8	16	17.8	11	−6.8	4
118.5	21	12.4	10	−9.6	1
$R_1 = 117$		$R_2 = 82$		$R_3 = 32$	

To determine if the rate-of-return distributions differ among the three types of mutual funds, we test:

H_0: The three probability distributions are identical
H_a: At least two of the three rate-of-return distributions differ

The test statistic is:

$$H = \frac{12}{n(n+1)}\sum \frac{R_j^2}{n_j} - 3(n+1)$$

$$= \frac{12}{21(21+1)}\left[\frac{117^2}{7} + \frac{82^2}{7} + \frac{32^2}{7}\right] - 3(21+1) = 13.544$$

The rejection region requires $\alpha = .05$ in the upper tail of the χ^2 distribution with degrees of freedom $= p - 1 = 3 - 1 = 2$. From Table VII, Appendix B, $\chi_{.05}^2 = 5.99147$. The rejection region is $H > 5.99147$.

Since the observed value of the test statistic falls in the rejection region ($H = 13.544 > 5.99147$), H_0 is rejected. There is sufficient evidence to indicate the rate-of-return distributions differ among the three types of mutual funds at $\alpha = .05$.

b. The necessary assumptions are:

1. The three samples are random and independent.
2. There are five or more measurements in each sample.
3. The three probability distributions from which the samples are drawn are continuous.

c. A Type I error would be concluding at least two of the rate-of-return distributions differ when they do not.

A Type II error would be concluding the three rate-of-return distributions are identical when they are not.

d. The F-test could be used if the three distributions were normal with equal variances.

15.41 a.

Aerospace/Defense		Electrice Utilities		Retailing		Chemical	
Ratio	Rank	Ratio	Rank	Ratio	Rank	Ratio	Rank
45.3	9	56.4	15	62.2	18	22.6	1
37.0	4	59.9	17	31.2	2	47.2	11
64.6	21	58.6	16	75.6	23	44.2	8
40.6	5	46.9	10	48.8	13	67.0	22
63.9	20	49.8	14	42.1	7	47.6	12
63.3	19	41.7	6				
		36.5	3				
$R_1 = 78$		$R_2 = 81$		$R_3 = 63$		$R_4 = 54$	

To determine if the debt/capital ratio distributions differ among the four industries, we test:

H_0: The four probability distributions are identical
H_a: At least two of the four debt/capital ratio distributions differ

The test statistic is:

$$H = \frac{12}{n(n+1)} \sum \frac{R_j^2}{n_j} - 3(n+1)$$

$$= \frac{12}{23(23+1)} \left[\frac{78^2}{6} + \frac{81^2}{7} + \frac{63^2}{5} + \frac{54^2}{5} \right] - 3(23+1) = 0.354$$

The rejection region requires $\alpha = .05$ in the upper tail of the χ^2 distribution with degrees of freedom $= p - 1 = 4 - 1 = 3$. From Table VII, Appendix B, $\chi^2_{.05} = 7.81473$. The rejection region is $H > 7.81473$.

Since the observed value of the test statistic does not fall in the rejection region ($H = 0.354 \not> 7.81473$), H_0 is not rejected. There is insufficient evidence to indicate the debt/capital ratio distributions differ among the four types of industries at $\alpha = .05$

b.   Since we concluded there was insufficient evidence of differences among the four industry populations, we do not need to make pairwise comparisons. However, if differences were found, then we should compare all pairs of distributions using the Wilcoxon rank sum test. If c comparisons are made, then each comparison would use $\alpha^* = \alpha/c$ as the level of significance.

15.43   a.   For $n = 22$, $P(r_s > .508) = .01$

b.   For $n = 28$, $P(r_s > .448) = .01$

c.   For $n = 10$, $P(r_s \le .648) = 1 - .025 = .975$

d.   For $n = 8$, $P(r_s < -.738 \text{ or } r_s > .738) = 2(.025) = .05$

15.45   Since there are no ties, we will use the shortcut formula.

a.   Some preliminary calculations are:

x Rank (u_i)	y Rank (v_i)	$d_i = u_i - v_i$	d_i^2
3	2	1	1
5	4	1	1
2	5	−3	9
1	1	0	0
4	3	1	1
			Total = 12

$$r_s = 1 - \frac{6 \sum d_i^2}{n(n^2 - 1)} = 1 - \frac{6(12)}{5(5^2 - 1)} = 1 - .6 = .4$$

b.

x Rank (u_i)	y Rank (v_i)	$d_i = u_i - v_i$	d_i^2
2	3	−1	1
3	4	−1	1
4	2	2	4
5	1	4	16
1	5	−4	16
			Total = 38

$$r_s = 1 - \frac{6 \sum d_i^2}{n(n^2 - 1)} = 1 - \frac{6(38)}{5(5^2 - 1)} = 1 - 1.9 = -.9$$

c.

x Rank (u_i)	y Rank (v_i)	$d_i = u_i - v_i$	d_i^2
1	2	−1	1
4	1	3	9
2	3	−1	1
3	4	−1	1
		Total = 12	

$$r_s = 1 - \frac{6\sum d_i^2}{n(n^2 - 1)} = 1 - \frac{6(12)}{4(4^2 - 1)} = 1 - 1.2 = -.2$$

d.

x Rank (u_i)	y Rank (v_i)	$d_i = u_i - v_i$	d_i^2
2	1	1	1
5	3	2	4
4	5	−1	1
3	2	1	1
1	4	−3	9
		Total = 16	

$$r_s = 1 - \frac{6\sum d_i^2}{n(n^2 - 1)} = 1 - \frac{6(16)}{5(5^2 - 1)} = 1 - .8 = .2$$

15.47 a. Some preliminary calculations are:

x	u	y	v	u-sq	v-sq	uv
5.2	1	220	4.5	1	20.25	4.5
5.5	7	227	7.5	49	56.25	52.5
6.0	23.5	259	15.5	552.25	240.25	364.25
5.9	20.5	210	1	420.25	1	20.5
5.8	16	224	6	256	36	96
6.0	23.5	215	3	552.25	9	70.5
5.8	16	231	9	256	81	144
5.6	10	268	19	100	361	190
5.6	10	239	11	100	121	110
5.9	20.5	212	2	420.25	4	41
5.4	5	410	24	25	576	120
5.6	10	256	14	100	196	140
5.8	16	306	22	256	484	352
5.5	7	259	15.5	49	240.25	108.5
5.3	3	284	21	9	441	63
5.3	3	383	23	9	529	69
5.7	12.5	271	20	156.25	400	250
5.5	7	264	18	49	324	126
5.7	12.5	227	7.5	156.25	56.25	93.75
5.3	3	263	17	9	289	51
5.9	20.5	232	10	420.25	100	205
5.8	16	220	4.5	256	20.25	72
5.8	16	246	13	256	169	208
5.9	20.5	241	12	420.25	144	246
$\sum u = 300$		$\sum v = 300$		$\sum u^2 = 4878$	$\sum v^2 = 4898.5$	$\sum uv = 3197.5$

$$SS_{uv} = \sum uv - \frac{(\sum u)(\sum v)}{n} = 3197.5 - \frac{300(300)}{24} = -552.5$$

$$SS_{uu} = \sum u^2 - \frac{(\sum u)^2}{n} = 4878 - \frac{300^2}{24} = 1128$$

$$SS_{vv} = \sum v^2 - \frac{(\sum v)^2}{n} = 4898.5 - \frac{300^2}{24} = 1148.5$$

$$r_s = \frac{SS_{uv}}{\sqrt{SS_{uu}SS_{vv}}} = \frac{-552.5}{\sqrt{1128(1148.5)}} = -.4854$$

Since the magnitude of the correlation coefficient is not particularly large, there is a fairly weak negative relationship between sweetness index and pectin.

b. To determine if there is a negative association between the sweetness index and the amount of pectin, we test:

H_0: $\rho_s = 0$
H_a: $\rho_s < 0$

The test statistic is $r_s = -.4854$

Reject H_0 if $r_s < -r_{s,\alpha}$ where $\alpha = .01$ and $n = 24$.

Reject H_0 if $r_s < -.485$ (from Table XVII, Appendix B)

Since the observed value of the test statistic falls in the rejection region ($r_s = -.4854 < -.485$), H_0 is rejected. There is sufficient evidence to indicate there is a negative association between the sweetness index and the amount of pectin at $\alpha = .01$.

15.49 Some preliminary calculations:

Year	u_i	v_i	$d_i = u_i - v_i$	d_i^2
1980	1	4	−3	9
1985	2	7	−5	25
1990	3	6	−3	9
1994	4	3	1	1
1995	7	1	6	36
1996	5	2	3	9
1997	6	5	1	1
				$\sum d_i^2 = 90$

$$r_s = 1 - \frac{6\sum d_i^2}{n(n^2 - 1)} = 1 - \frac{6(90)}{7(7^2 - 1)} = 1 - 1.607 = -.607$$

b. To determine if there is an association between amount spent and number employed, we test:

H_0: $\rho_s = 0$
H_a: $\rho_s \neq 0$

The test statistic is $r_s = -.607$

Reject H_0 if $r_s < -r_{s,\alpha/2}$ or $r_s > r_{s,\alpha/2}$ where $\alpha/2 = .10/2 = .05$ and $n = 7$.

Reject H_0 if $r_s < -.714$ or $r_s > .714$ (from Table XVII, Appendix B)

Since the observed value of the test statistic does not fall in the rejection region ($r_s = -.607 \not< -.714$), H_0 is not rejected. There is insufficient evidence to indicate there is an association between amount spent and number of employees at $\alpha = .10$.

15.51 b.   Some preliminary calculations:

Involvement	u_i	v_i	Differences $d_i = u_i - v_i$	d_i^2
1	8	9	-1	1
2	6	7	-1	1
3	10	10	0	0
4	2	1	1	1
5	5	5	0	0
6	9	8	1	1
7	1	2	-1	1
8	4	4	0	0
9	7	6	1	1
10	11	11	0	0
11	3	3	0	1
				$\sum d_i^2 = 6$

$$r_s = 1 - \frac{6\sum d_i^2}{n(n^2 - 1)} = 1 - \frac{6(6)}{11(11^2 - 1)} = .972$$

To determine if a positive relationship exists between participation rates and cost savings rates, we test:

H_0: $\rho_s = 0$
H_a: $\rho_s > 0$

The test statistic is $r_s = .972$.

From Table XVII, Appendix B, $r_{s,.01} = .736$, with $n = 11$. The rejection region is $r_s > .736$.

Since the observed value of the test statistic does falls in the rejection region ($r_s = .972 > .736$), H_0 is rejected. There is sufficient evidence to indicate that a positive relationship exists between participation rates and cost savings rates at $\alpha = .01$.

c.   In order for the above test to be valid, we must assume:

1.   The sample is randomly selected.
2.   The probability distributions of both of the variables are continuous.

In order to use the Pearson correlation coefficient, we must assume that both populations are normally distributed. It is very unlikely that the data are normally distributed.

15.53 Some preliminary calculations are:

Category	Crisis Intervention Rating	Rank, u_i	Clarity Rating	Rank, v_i	d_i	d_i^2
Psychosis	1.31	3	1.33	3	0	0
Drug/alcohol abuse	1.33	4	1.29	1	3	9
Depression/anxiety	1.48	5	1.59	4	1	1
Emphasis on acuteness	1.76	6	2.50	8	−2	4
Insistence on "short-term" response	2.48	7	3.22	9	−2	4
Suicide	1.13	2	1.32	2	0	0
Family problems	2.59	8	2.30	6	2	4
Violence/harm	1.06	1	1.86	5	−4	16
Miscellaneous	2.60	9	2.33	7	2	4
Nondefinition	3.57	10	3.57	10	0	0
					$\sum d_i^2 = 42$	

To determine if there is a positive relationship between the mean crisis intervention and mean clarity ratings, we test:

H_0: $\rho_s = 0$
H_a: $\rho_s > 0$

The test statistic is $r_s = 1 - \dfrac{6\sum d_i^2}{n(n^2 - 1)} = 1 - \dfrac{6(42)}{10(10^2 - 1)} = .255$

Reject H_0 if $r_s > r_{s,\alpha}$ where $\alpha = .05$ and $n = 10$:

Reject H_0 if $r_s > .564$ (using Table XVII, Appendix B).

Since the observed value of the test statistic does not fall in the rejection region ($r_s = .255 \not> .564$), H_0 is not rejected. There is insufficient evidence to indicate that there is a positive relationship between the mean crisis intervention and mean clarity ratings at $\alpha = .05$.

15.55 a. Some preliminary calculations are:

Pair	X	Rank u_i	Y	Rank v_i	u_i^2	v_i^2	$u_i v_i$
1	19	5	12	5	25	25	25
2	27	7	19	8	49	64	56
3	15	2	7	1	4	1	2
4	35	9	25	9	81	81	81
5	13	1	11	4	1	16	4
6	29	8	10	2.5	64	6.25	20
7	16	3.5	16	6	12.25	36	21
8	22	6	10	2.5	36	6.25	15
9	16	3.5	18	7	12.25	49	24.5
	$\sum u_i = 45$		$\sum v_i = 45$		$\sum u_i^2 = 284.5$	$\sum v_i^2 = 284.5$	$\sum u_i v_i = 248.5$

$$SS_{uv} = \sum u_i v_i - \frac{\sum u_i v_i}{n} = 248.5 - \frac{45(45)}{9} = 23.5$$

$$SS_{uu} = \sum u_i^2 - \frac{\left(\sum u_i\right)^2}{n} = 284.5 - \frac{45^2}{9} = 59.5$$

$$SS_{vv} = \sum v_i^2 - \frac{\left(\sum v_i\right)^2}{n} = 284.5 - \frac{45^2}{9} = 59.5$$

To determine if the Spearman rank correlation differs from 0, we test:

H_0: $\rho_s = 0$
H_a: $\rho_s \neq 0$

The test statistic is $r_s = \dfrac{SS_{uv}}{\sqrt{SS_{uu}SS_{vv}}} = \dfrac{23.5}{\sqrt{59.5(59.5)}} = .40$

Reject H_0 if $r_s < -r_{s,\alpha/2}$ or if $r_s > r_{s,\alpha/2}$ where $\alpha/2 = .025$ and $n = 9$:

Reject H_0 if $r_s < -.683$ or if $r_s > .683$ (from Table XVII, Appendix B)

Since the observed value of the test statistic does not fall in the rejection region ($r_s = .40 \ngtr$ .683), H_0 is not rejected. There is insufficient evidence to indicate that Spearman's rank correlation between x and y is significantly different from 0 at $\alpha = .05$.

b. Use the Wilcoxon signed rank test. Some preliminary calculations are:

Pair	X	Y	Difference	Rank of Absolute Difference
1	19	12	7	3
2	27	19	8	4.5
3	15	7	8	4.5
4	35	25	10	6
5	13	11	2	1.5
6	29	10	19	8
7	16	16	0	(eliminated)
8	22	10	12	7
9	16	18	−2	1.5
				$T_- = 1.5$

To determine if the probability distribution of x is shifted to the right of that for y, we test:

H_0: The probability distributions are identical for the two variables
H_a: The probability distribution of x is shifted to the right of the probability distribution of y

The test statistic is $T = T_- = 1.5$.

Reject H_0 if $T \leq T_0$ where T_0 is based on $\alpha = .05$ and $n = 8$ (one-tailed):

Reject H_0 if $T \leq 6$ (from Table XVI, Appendix B).

Since the observed value of the test statistic falls in the rejection region ($T = 1.5 \leq 6$), reject H_0 at $\alpha = .05$. There is sufficient evidence to conclude that the probability distribution of x is shifted to the right of that for y.

15.57 a. This is a paired difference problem.

  b. To determine if the problem-solving performance of video teleconferencing groups is superior to face-to-face groups, we test:

  H_0: The two sampled populations have identical probability distributions
  H_a: The probability distribution for population A (face-to-face) is shifted to the left of that for population B (video teleconferencing)

  c. Some preliminary calculations:

Group	Face-To-Face	Video Teleconferencing	Difference	Rank of Absolute Difference
1	65	75	−10	7.5
2	82	80	2	1
3	54	60	−6	6
4	69	65	4	2.5
5	40	55	−15	9
6	85	90	−5	4.5
7	98	98	0	(eliminated)
8	35	40	−5	4.5
9	85	89	−4	2.5
10	70	80	−10	7.5

Negative rank sum $T_- = 41.5$
Positive rank sum $T_+ = 3.5$

The test statistic is $T_+ = 3.5$.

The null hypothesis will be rejected if $T_+ \leq T_0$ where T_0 corresponds to $\alpha = .05$ (one-tailed) and $n = 9$. From Table XVI, Appendix B, $T_0 = 8$.

  Reject H_0 if $T_+ \leq 8$.

Since the observed value of the test statistic falls in the rejection region ($T_+ = 3.5 \leq 8$), H_0 is rejected. There is sufficient evidence to indicate that problem-solving performance of video teleconferencing groups is superior to that of groups that interact face-to-face at $\alpha = .05$.

  d. p-value $= P(T_+ \leq 3.5)$ where $n = 9$ and the test is one-tailed. Using Table XVI, locate the appropriate column for n, then find the values in that column that include the test statistic (in this case, 6 and 3). Then read the α level corresponding to these values. Thus,

  $.01 < p$-value $< .025$

15.59 Some preliminary calculations:

Urban	Rank	Suburban	Rank	Rural	Rank
4.3	4.5	5.9	14	5.1	9
5.2	10.5	6.7	17	4.8	7
6.2	15.5	7.6	19	3.9	2
5.6	12	4.9	8	6.2	15.5
3.8	1	5.2	10.5	4.2	3
5.8	13	6.8	18	4.3	4.5
4.7	6				
	$R_1 = 62.5$		$R_2 = 86.5$		$R_3 = 41$

To determine if there is a difference in the level of property taxes among the three types of school districts, we test:

H_0: The three probability distributions are identical

H_a: At least two of the three probability distributions differ in location

The test statistic is $H = \dfrac{12}{n(n+1)}\sum \dfrac{R_j^2}{n_j} - 3(n+1)$

$$= \dfrac{12}{19(19+1)}\left[\dfrac{62.5^2}{7} + \dfrac{86.5^2}{6} + \dfrac{41^2}{6}\right] - 3(20) = 65.8498 - 60$$

$$= 5.8498$$

The rejection region requires $\alpha = .05$ in the upper tail of the χ^2 distribution with df $= p - 1 = 3 - 1 = 2$. From Table VII, Appendix B, $\chi^2_{.05} = 5.99147$. The rejection region is $H > 5.99147$.

Since the observed value of the test statistic does not fall in the rejection region ($H = 5.8498 \ngtr 5.99147$), H_0 is not rejected. There is insufficient evidence to indicate that there is a difference in the level of property taxes among the three types of school districts at $\alpha = .05$.

15.61 The appropriate test for paired samples is the Wilcoxon signed rank test. Some preliminary calculations are:

Subject	Aspirin	Drug	Difference	Rank of Absolute Difference
1	15	7	8	6
2	20	14	6	3.5
3	12	13	−1	1
4	20	11	9	7
5	17	10	7	5
6	14	16	−2	2
7	17	11	6	3.5
				$T_- = 3.0$
				$T_+ = 25.0$

To determine if the probability distribution of the times required to obtain relief with aspirin is shifted to the right of the probability distribution of the times required to obtain relief with the drug, we test:

H_0: The probability distributions of length of time required for pain relief are identical for aspirin and the new drug

H_a: The probability distribution of the length of time required for pain relief with aspirin is shifted to the right of that for the new drug

The test statistic is $T_- = 3$.

Reject H_0 if $T_- \leq T_0$ where $\alpha = .05$ (one-tailed) and $n = 7$:

Reject H_0 if $T_- \leq 4$ (from Table XVI, Appendix B).

Since $T_- = 3 \leq 4$, reject H_0. There is sufficient evidence to indicate the probability distribution of time required to obtain relief with aspirin is shifted to the right of that for the new drug at $\alpha = .05$.

15.63 Some preliminary calculations are:

Type A	Rank	Type B	Rank
95	1	110	6
122	10	102	4
102	3	115	8
99	2	112	7
108	5	120	9
$T_A = 21$		$T_B = 34$	

To determine if print type A is easier to read, we test:

H_0: The two sampled populations have identical probability distributions
H_a: The probability distribution for print type A is shifted to the left of that for print type B

The test statistic is $T_A = 21$.

The rejection region is $T_A \leq 19$ form Table XV, Appendix B, with $n_A = 5$ and $n_B = 5$, and $\alpha = .05$.

Since the observed value of the test statistic does not fall in the rejection region ($T_A = 21 \nleq 19$), H_0 is not rejected. There is insufficient evidence to indicate print type A is easier to read at $\alpha = .05$.

15.65 Some preliminary calculations are:

				Supervisor			
1	Rank	2	Rank	3	Rank	4	Rank
20	21.5	17	16.5	16	14.5	8	1
19	20	11	5.5	15	12.5	12	7
20	21.5	13	8.5	13	8.5	10	3.5
18	18.5	15	12.5	18	18.5	14	10.5
17	16.5	14	10.5	11	5.5	9	2
		16	14.5			10	3.5
$R_1 = 98$		$R_2 = 68$		$R_3 = 59.5$		$R_4 = 27.5$	

a. The type of experimental design is completely randomized. The response is the rating of the leader. The factor is personality type, which has four levels and is qualitative. The treatments correspond to the four factor levels. The experimental units are the employees selected to do the ratings.

b. To determine whether the probability distributions of ratings differ for at least two of the four supervisors, we test:

H_0: The four probability distributions are identical
H_a: At least two of the four probability distributions differ in location

The test statistic is $H = \dfrac{12}{n(n+1)} \sum \dfrac{R_j^2}{n_j} - 3(n+1)$

$= \dfrac{12}{22(23)} \left[\dfrac{98^2}{5} + \dfrac{68^2}{6} + \dfrac{59.5^2}{5} + \dfrac{27.5^2}{6} \right] - 3(22+1)$

$= 83.6101 - 69 = 14.6101$

Nonparametric Statistics

The rejection region requires $\alpha = .05$ in the upper tail of the χ^2 distribution with df $= p - 1 = 4 - 1 = 3$. From Table VII, Appendix B, $\chi^2_{.05} = 7.81473$. The rejection region is $H > 7.81473$.

Since the observed value of the test statistic falls in the rejection region ($H = 14.6101 > 7.81473$), H_0 is rejected. There is sufficient evidence to indicate the probability distributions of ratings differ for at least two of the four supervisors at $\alpha = .05$.

c. The necessary assumptions are:

1. The four samples are random and independent.
2. There are five or more measurements in each sample.
3. The four probability distributions from which the samples are drawn are continuous.

d. Since we rejected H_0 in part **b**, we need to compare all pairs.

Some preliminary calculations are:

Supervisor				Supervisor				Supervisor			
1	Rank	2	Rank	1	Rank	3	Rank	1	Rank	4	Rank
20	10.5	17	6.5	20	9.5	16	4	20	10.5	8	1
19	9	11	1	19	8	15	3	19	9	12	5
20	10.5	13	2	20	9.5	13	2	20	10.5	10	3.5
18	8	15	4	18	6.5	18	6.5	18	8	14	6
17	6.5	14	3	17	5	11	1	17	7	9	2
		16	5							10	3.5
$T_1 = 44.5$		$T_2 = 21.5$		$T_1 = 38.5$		$T_3 = 16.5$		$T_1 = 45$		$T_4 = 21$	

Supervisor				Supervisor				Supervisor			
2	Rank	3	Rank	2	Rank	4	Rank	3	Rank	4	Rank
17	10	16	8.5	17	12	8	1	16	10	8	1
11	1.5	15	6.5	11	5	12	6	15	9	12	6
13	3.5	13	3.5	13	7	10	3.5	13	7	10	3.5
15	6.5	18	11	15	10	14	8.5	18	11	14	8
14	5	11	1.5	14	8.5	9	2	11	5	9	2
16	8.5			16	11	10	3.5			10	3.5
$T_2 = 35$		$T_3 = 31$		$T_2 = 53.5$		$T_4 = 24.5$		$T_3 = 42$		$T_4 = 24$	

For each pair, we test:

H_0: The two sampled populations have identical probability distributions
H_a: The probability distribution for one sampled population is shifted to the right or the left of that of the other

For supervisors 1 and 2:

The test statistic is $T_1 = 44.5$.

The rejection region is $T_1 \le 19$ or $T_1 \ge 41$ from Table XV, Appendix B, with $n_1 = 5$, $n_2 = 6$, and $\alpha = .05$.

Since the observed value of the test statistic falls in the rejection region ($T_1 = 44.5 \geq 41$), H_0 is rejected. There is sufficient evidence to indicate the probability distribution of supervisor 1 is shifted to the right of that for supervisor 2 at $\alpha = .05$.

For supervisors 1 and 3:

The test statistic is $T_1 = 38.5$.

The rejection region is $T_1 \leq 18$ or $T_1 \geq 37$ from Table XV, Appendix B, with $n_1 = n_3 = 5$ and $\alpha = .05$.

Since the observed value of the test statistic falls in the rejection region ($T_A = 38.5 \geq 37$), H_0 is rejected. There is sufficient evidence to indicate the probability distribution of supervisor 1 is shifted to the right of that for supervisor 3.

For supervisors 1 and 4:

The test statistic is $T_1 = 45$.

The rejection region is $T_1 \leq 19$ or $T_1 \geq 41$ from Table XV, Appendix B, with $n_1 = 5$, $n_4 = 6$, and $\alpha = .05$.

Since the observed value of the test statistic falls in the rejection region ($T_1 = 45 \geq 41$), H_0 is rejected. There is sufficient evidence to indicate the probability distribution of supervisor 1 is shifted to the right of that for supervisor 4 at $\alpha = .05$.

For supervisors 2 and 3:

The test statistic is $T_3 = 31$.

The rejection region is $T_3 \leq 19$ or $T_3 \geq 41$ from Table XV, Appendix B, with $n = 6$, $n = 5$, and $\alpha = .05$.

Since the observed value of the test statistic does not fall in the rejection region ($T_3 = 31 \not\leq 19$ and $\not\geq 41$), H_0 is not rejected. There is insufficient evidence to indicate the probability distribution of supervisor 2 is shifted to the right or left of that for supervisor 3 at $\alpha = .05$.

For supervisors 2 and 4:

The test statistic is $T_4 = 24.5$.

The rejection region is $T_4 \leq 26$ or $T_4 \geq 52$ from Table XV, Appendix B, with $n_2 = n_4 = 6$ and $\alpha = .05$.

Since the observed value of the test statistic falls in the rejection region ($T_4 = 24.5 \leq 26$), H_0 is rejected. There is sufficient evidence to indicate the probability distribution for supervisor 2 is shifted to the right of that for supervisor 4.

For supervisors 3 and 4:

The test statistic is $T_3 = 42$.

The rejection region is $T_3 \leq 19$ or $T_3 \geq 41$ from Table XV, Appendix B, with $n_3 = 5$, $n_4 = 6$, and $\alpha = .05$.

Since the observed value of the test statistic falls in the rejection region ($T_3 = 42 \geq 41$), H_0 is rejected. There is sufficient evidence to indicate the probability distribution for supervisor 3 is shifted to the right of that for supervisor 4.

Supervisor 1 is rated significantly higher than any of the others.

15.67   Some preliminary calculations are:

A	Rank	B	Rank
10.8	2	22.3	17
15.6	3	19.5	11
19.2	9	18.6	7
17.9	5	24.3	20
18.3	6	19.9	13
9.8	1	20.4	15
16.7	4	23.6	19
19.0	8	21.2	16
20.3	14	19.8	12
19.4	10	22.6	18
$T_1 = 62$		$T_2 = 148$	

To determine if there is a difference in location between the distributions of damage rates corresponding to the two chemicals, we test:

H_0: The two sampled populations have identical probability distributions

H_a: The probability distribution for chemical A is shifted to the right or left of that for chemical B

The test statistic is $T_1 = 62$.   (since both sample sizes are the same, either T_1 or T_2 could be used)

The null hypothesis will be rejected if $T_1 \leq T_L$ or $T_1 \geq T_U$ where T_L and T_U correspond to $\alpha = .05$ (two-tailed), $n_1 = n_2 = 10$. From Table XV, Appendix B, $T_L = 79$ and $T_U = 131$.

Reject H_0 if $T_1 \leq 79$ or $T_1 \geq 131$.

Since $T_1 = 62 \leq 79$, H_0 is rejected. There is sufficient evidence to indicate a difference in location between the distributions of damage rates corresponding to the two chemicals at $\alpha = .05$.

15.69 Some preliminary calculations are:

Before		After	
Observation	Rank	Observation	Rank
10	19	4	5.5
5	8.5	3	3.5
3	3.5	8	16.5
6	12	5	8.5
7	14.5	6	12
11	20	4	5.5
8	16.5	2	2
9	18	5	8.5
6	12	7	14.5
5	8.5	1	1
$T_{Before} = 132.5$		$T_{After} = 77.5$	

To determine if the situation has improved under the new policy, we test:

H_0: The two sampled population probability distributions are identical

H_a: The probability distribution associated with after the policy was instituted is shifted to the left of that before

The test statistic is $T_{Before} = 132.5$.

The rejection region is $T_{Before} \geq 127$ from Table XV, Appendix B, with $n_A = n_B = 10$ and $\alpha = .05$.

Since the observed value of the test statistic falls in the rejection region ($T_{Before} = 132.5 \geq 127$), H_0 is rejected. There is sufficient evidence to indicate the situation has improved under the new policy at $\alpha = .05$.

15.71 Some preliminary calculations are:

Candidate	u_i	v_i	Difference $d_i = u_i - v_i$	d_i^2
1	6	4	2	4
2	4	5	−1	1
3	5	6	−1	1
4	1	2	−1	1
5	2	1	1	1
6	3	3	0	0
			$\sum d_i^2 = 8$	

$$r_s = 1 - \frac{6 \sum d_i^2}{n(n^2 - 1)}$$

$$= 1 - \frac{6(8)}{6(36 - 1)} = .7714$$

To determine if the candidates' qualification scores are related to their interview performance, we test:

H_0: $\rho_s = 0$

H_a: $\rho_s \neq 0$

The test statistic is $r_s = .7714$

From Table XVII, Appendix B, for $\alpha/2 = .10/2 = .05$, $r_{s,.05} = .829$ for $n = 6$. The rejection region is $r_s < -.829$ or $r_s > .829$. Since the observed value of the test statistic does not fall in the rejection region ($r_s = .7714 \not> .829$), H_0 is not rejected. There is insufficient evidence to indicate the qualification scores are related to the interview performance at $\alpha = .10$.

15.73 $SS_{uv} = \sum u_i v_i - \dfrac{\sum u_i v_i}{n} = 2774.75 - \dfrac{210(210)}{20} = 569.75$

$SS_{uu} = \sum u_i^2 - \dfrac{\left(\sum u_i\right)^2}{n} = 2869.5 - \dfrac{210^2}{20} = 664.5$

$SS_{vv} = \sum v_i^2 - \dfrac{\left(\sum v_i\right)^2}{n} = 2869.5 - \dfrac{210^2}{20} = 664.5$

$r_s = \dfrac{SS_{uv}}{\sqrt{SS_{uu}SS_{vv}}} = \dfrac{569.75}{\sqrt{664.5(664.5)}} = .8574$

Since $r_s = .8574$ is greater than 0, the relationship between current importance and ideal importance is positive. The relationship is fairly strong since r_s is close to 1. This implies the views on current importance and ideal importance are very similar.

16.1   a.   The rejection region requires $\alpha = .05$ in the upper tail of the χ^2 distribution with df $= k - 1$ $= 3 - 1 = 2$. From Table VII, Appendix B, $\chi^2_{.05} = 5.99147$. The rejection region is $\chi^2 > 5.99147$.

    b.   The rejection region requires $\alpha = .10$ in the upper tail of the χ^2 distribution with df $= k - 1$ $= 5 - 1 = 4$. From Table VII, Appendix B, $\chi^2_{.10} = 7.77944$. The rejection region is $\chi^2 > 7.77944$.

    c.   The rejection region requires $\alpha = .01$ in the upper tail of the χ^2 distribution with df $= k - 1$ $= 4 - 1 = 3$. From Table VII, Appendix B, $\chi^2_{.01} = 11.3449$. The rejection region is $\chi^2 > 11.3449$.

16.3   The sample size n will be large enough so that, for every cell, the expected cell count, $E(n_i)$, will be equal to 5 or more.

16.5   Some preliminary calculations are:

    If the probabilities are the same, $p_{1,0} = p_{2,0} = p_{3,0} = p_{4,0} = .25$

$$E(n_1) = np_{1,0} = 205(.25) = 51.25$$
$$E(n_2) = E(n_3) = E(n_4) = 205(.25) = 51.25$$

    a.   To determine if the multinomial probabilities differ, we test:

H_0: $p_1 = p_2 = p_3 = p_4 = .25$
H_a: At least one of the probabilities differs from .25

The test statistic is $\chi^2 = \sum \dfrac{\left[n_i - E(n_i)\right]^2}{E(n_i)}$

$$= \frac{(43 - 51.25)^2}{51.25} + \frac{(56 - 51.25)^2}{51.25} + \frac{(59 - 51.25)^2}{51.25} + \frac{(47 - 51.25)^2}{51.25} = 3.293$$

The rejection region requires $\alpha = .05$ in the upper tail of the χ^2 distribution with df $= k - 1$ $= 4 - 1 = 3$. From Table VII, Appendix B, $\chi^2_{.05} = 7.81473$. The rejection region is $\chi^2 > 7.81473$.

Since the observed value of the test statistic does not fall in the rejection region ($\chi^2 = 3.293 \not> 7.81473$), H_0 is not rejected. There is insufficient evidence to indicate the multinomial probabilities differ at $\alpha = .05$.

    b.   The Type I error is concluding the multinomial probabilities differ when, in fact, they do not.

The Type II error is concluding the multinomial probabilities are equal, when, in fact, they are not.

16.7 a. $E(n_1) = np_{1,0} = 370(.30) = 111$

$E(n_2) = np_{2,0} = 370(.20) = 74$

$E(n_3) = np_{3,0} = 370(.20) = 74$

$E(n_4) = np_{4,0} = 370(.10) = 37$

$E(n_5) = np_{5,0} = 370(.10) = 37$

$E(n_6) = np_{6,0} = 370(.10) = 37$

b. The test statistic is $\chi^2 = \sum \dfrac{[n_i - E(n_i)]^2}{E(n_i)}$

$$= \frac{(84 - 111)^2}{111} + \frac{(79 - 74)^2}{74} + \frac{(75 - 74)^2}{74} + \frac{(49 - 37)^2}{37}$$
$$+ \frac{(36 - 37)^2}{37} + \frac{(47 - 37)^2}{37} = 13.541$$

c. To determine if the true percentages of the colors produced differ from the manufacturer's stated percentages, we test:

H_0: $p_1 = .30, p_2 = .20, p_3 = .20, p_4 = .10, p_5 = .10, p_6 = .10$
H_a: At least one p_i does not equal its hypothesized value.

The test statistic is $\chi^2 = 13.541$.

The rejection region requires $\alpha = .05$ in the upper tail of the χ^2 distribution with df $= k - 1$ $= 6 - 1 = 5$. From Table VII, Appendix B, $\chi^2_{.05} = 11.0705$. The rejection region is $\chi^2 > 11.0705$.

Since the observed value of the test statistic falls in the rejection region ($\chi^2 = 13.541 > 11.0705$), H_0 is rejected. There is sufficient evidence to indicate the true percentages of the colors produced differ from the manufacturer's stated percentages at $\alpha = .05$.

16.9 a. To determine if the opinions are not evenly divided on the issue of national health insurance, we test:

H_0: $p_1 = p_2 = p_3 = 1/3$
H_a: At least one p_i differs from its hypothesized value.

The test statistic is $\chi^2 = 87.74$ (from the printout)

The observed p-value is $p = .0000$. Since the observed p-value is less than α ($p = .0000 < \alpha = .01$), H_0 is rejected. There is sufficient evidence to indicate the opinions are not evenly divided on the issue of national health insurance at $\alpha = .01$.

b.	Let p_1 = proportion of heads of household in the U.S. population that favor national health insurance. Some preliminary calculations are:

$$\hat{p}_1 = \frac{n_1}{n} = \frac{234}{434} = .539$$

For confidence coefficient .95, $\alpha = .05$ and $\alpha/2 = .05/2 = .025$. From Table IV, Appendix B, $z_{.025} = 1.96$. The 95% confidence interval is:

$$\hat{p}_1 \pm z_{.025}\sqrt{\frac{\hat{p}_1(1 - \hat{p}_1)}{n}} \Rightarrow .539 \pm 1.96\sqrt{\frac{.539(1 - .539)}{434}}$$
$$\Rightarrow .539 \pm .047 \Rightarrow (.492, .586)$$

We are 95% confident that the true proportion of heads of household in the U.S. population that favor national health insurance is between .492 and .586.

16.11	a.	To determine if the opinions of Internet users are evenly divided among the four categories, we test:

H_0: $p_1 = p_2 = p_3 = p_4 = .25$
H_a: At least one $p_i \neq .25$, for $i = 1, 2, 3, 4$

b.	Some preliminary calculations are:

$E(n_1) = np_{1,0} = 328(.25) = 82$
$E(n_2) = E(n_3) = E(n_4) = 328(.25) = 82$

The test statistic is $\chi^2 = \sum \dfrac{[n_i - E(n_i)]^2}{E(n_i)}$

$$= \frac{(59 - 82)^2}{82} + \frac{(108 - 82)^2}{82} + \frac{(82 - 82)^2}{82} + \frac{(79 - 82)^2}{82} = 14.805$$

The rejection region requires $\alpha = .05$ in the upper tail of the χ^2 distribution with df $= k - 1$ $= 4 - 1 = 3$. From Table VII, Appendix B, $\chi^2_{.05} = 7.81473$. The rejection region is $\chi^2 > 7.81473$.

Since the observed value of the test statistic falls in the rejection region ($\chi^2 = 14.805 > 7.81473$), H_0 is rejected. There is sufficient evidence to indicate that the opinions of Internet users are not evenly divided among the four categories at $\alpha = .05$.

c.	A Type I error would be to conclude that the opinions of Internet users are not evenly divided among the four categories when, in fact, they are evenly divided.

A Type II error would be to conclude that the opinions of Internet users are evenly divided among the four categories when, in fact, they are not evenly divided.

d.	We must assume that:

1.	A multinomial experiment was conducted. This is generally satisfied by taking a random sample from the population of interest.
2.	The sample size n will be large enough so that, for every cell, the expected cell count, $E(n_i)$, will be equal to 5 or more.

16.13   To determine if the true percentages of ADEs in the five "cause" categories are different, we test:

H_0: $p_1 = p_2 = p_3 = p_4 = p_5 = .2$
H_a: At least one p_i differs from .2, $i = 1, 2, 3, 4, 5$

The test statistic is $\chi^2 = 16$ (from printout).

The p-value of the test is $p = .003019$.

Since the p-value is less than α ($p = .003019 < .10$), H_0 is rejected. There is sufficient evidence to indicate that at least one percentage of ADEs in the five "cause" categories is different at $\alpha = .10$.

16.15   a.   To determine if the number of overweight trucks per week is distributed over the 7 days of the week in direct proportion to the volume of truck traffic, we test:

H_0: $p_1 = .191, p_2 = .198, p_3 = .187, p_4 = .180, p_5 = .155, p_6 = .043, p_7 = .046$
H_a: At least one of the probabilities differs from the hypothesized value

$E(n_1) = np_{1,0} = 414(.191) = 79.074$
$E(n_2) = np_{2,0} = 414(.198) = 81.972$
$E(n_3) = np_{3,0} = 414(.187) = 77.418$
$E(n_4) = np_{4,0} = 414(.180) = 74.520$
$E(n_5) = np_{5,0} = 414(.155) = 64.170$
$E(n_6) = np_{6,0} = 414(.043) = 17.802$
$E(n_7) = np_{7,0} = 414(.046) = 19.044$

The test statistic is $\chi^2 = \sum \dfrac{[n_i - E(n_i)]^2}{E(n_i)} = \dfrac{(90 - 79.074)^2}{79.074} + \dfrac{(82 - 81.972)^2}{81.972}$

$+ \dfrac{(72 - 77.418)^2}{77.418} + \dfrac{(70 - 74.520)^2}{74.520} + \dfrac{(51 - 64.170)^2}{64.170} + \dfrac{(18 - 17.802)^2}{17.802}$

$+ \dfrac{(31 - 19.044)^2}{19.044} = 12.374$

The rejection region requires $\alpha = .05$ in the upper tail of the χ^2 distribution with df $= k - 1 = 7 - 1 = 6$. From Table VII, Appendix B, $\chi^2_{.05} = 12.5916$. The rejection region is $\chi^2 > 12.5916$.

Since the observed value of the test statistic does not fall in the rejection region ($\chi^2 = 12.374$ $\ngtr 12.5916$), H_0 is not rejected. There is insufficient evidence to indicate the number of overweight trucks per week is distributed over the 7 days of the week is not in direct proportion to the volume of truck traffic at $\alpha = .05$.

b.   The p-value is $P(\chi^2 \geq 12.374)$. From Table VII, Appendix B, with df $= k - 1 = 7 - 1 = 6$, $.05 < P(\chi^2 \geq 12.374) < .10$.

16.17   a. H_0: The row and column classifications are independent
H_a: The row and column classifications are dependent

b. The test statistic is $\chi^2 = \sum\sum \dfrac{\left[n_{ij} - \hat{E}(n_{ij})\right]^2}{\hat{E}(n_{ij})}$

The rejection region requires $\alpha = .01$ in the upper tail of the χ^2 distribution with df = $(r - 1)(c - 1) = (2 - 1)(3 - 1) = 2$. From Table VII, Appendix B, $\chi^2_{.01} = 9.21034$. The rejection region is $\chi^2 > 9.21034$.

c. The expected cell counts are:

$$\hat{E}(n_{11}) = \frac{r_1 c_1}{n} = \frac{96(25)}{167} = 14.37 \qquad E(n_{21}) = \frac{r_2 c_1}{n} = \frac{71(25)}{167} = 10.63$$

$$\hat{E}(n_{12}) = \frac{r_1 c_2}{n} = \frac{96(64)}{167} = 36.79 \qquad \hat{E}(n_{22}) = \frac{r_2 c_2}{n} = \frac{71(64)}{167} = 27.21$$

$$\hat{E}(n_{13}) = \frac{r_1 c_3}{n} = \frac{96(78)}{167} = 44.84 \qquad \hat{E}(n_{23}) = \frac{r_2 c_3}{n} = \frac{71(78)}{167} = 33.16$$

d. The test statistic is $\chi^2 = \sum\sum \dfrac{\left[n_{ij} - \hat{E}(n_{ij})\right]^2}{\hat{E}(n_{ij})}$

$$= \frac{(9 - 14.37)^2}{14.37} + \frac{(34 - 36.79)^2}{36.79} + \frac{(53 - 44.84)^2}{44.84} + \frac{(16 - 10.63)^2}{10.63}$$

$$+ \frac{(30 - 27.21)^2}{27.21} + \frac{(25 - 33.16)^2}{33.16} = 8.71$$

Since the observed value of the test statistic does not fall in the rejection region ($\chi^2 = 8.71 \not> 9.21034$), H_0 is not rejected. There is insufficient evidence to indicate the row and column classifications are dependent at $\alpha = .01$.

16.19   Some preliminary calculations are:

$$\hat{E}(n_{11}) = \frac{r_1 c_1}{n} = \frac{154(134)}{439} = 47.007 \qquad \hat{E}(n_{21}) = \frac{186(134)}{439} = 56.774$$

$$\hat{E}(n_{12}) = \frac{154(163)}{439} = 57.180 \qquad \hat{E}(n_{22}) = \frac{186(163)}{439} = 69.062$$

$$\hat{E}(n_{13}) = \frac{154(142)}{439} = 49.813 \qquad \hat{E}(n_{23}) = \frac{186(142)}{439} = 60.164$$

$$\hat{E}(n_{31}) = \frac{99(134)}{439} = 30.219 \qquad \hat{E}(n_{33}) = \frac{99(142)}{439} = 32.023$$

$$\hat{E}(n_{32}) = \frac{99(163)}{439} = 36.759$$

To determine if the row and column classifications are dependent, we test:

H_0: The row and column classifications are independent
H_a: The row and column classifications are dependent

The test statistic is $\chi^2 = \sum\sum \dfrac{\left[n_{ij} - \hat{E}(n_{ij})\right]^2}{\hat{E}(n_{ij})}$

$$= \frac{(40 - 47.007)^2}{47.007} + \frac{(72 - 57.180)^2}{57.180} + \frac{(42 - 49.813)^2}{49.813} + \frac{(63 - 56.774)^2}{56.774}$$

$$+ \frac{(53 - 69.062)^2}{69.062} + \frac{(70 - 60.164)^2}{60.164} + \frac{(31 - 30.219)^2}{30.219}$$

$$+ \frac{(38 - 36.759)^2}{36.759} + \frac{(30 - 32.023)^2}{32.023} = 12.36$$

The rejection region requires $\alpha = .05$ in the upper tail of the χ^2 distribution with df $= (r - 1)(c - 1) = (3 - 1)(3 - 1) = 4$. From Table VII, Appendix B, $\chi^2_{.05} = 9.48773$. The rejection region is $\chi^2 > 9.48773$.

Since the observed value of the test statistic falls in the rejection region ($\chi^2 = 12.36 > 9.48773$), H_0 is rejected. There is sufficient evidence to indicate the row and column classification are dependent at $\alpha = .05$.

16.21 Some preliminary calculations:

$\hat{E}(n_{11}) = \dfrac{r_1 c_1}{n} = \dfrac{2,359(1,712)}{5,026} = 803.543$ $\qquad \hat{E}(n_{12}) = \dfrac{r_1 c_2}{n} = \dfrac{2,359(3,314)}{5,026} = 1,555.457$

$\hat{E}(n_{21}) = \dfrac{r_2 c_1}{n} = \dfrac{2,667(1,712)}{5,026} = 908.457$ $\qquad \hat{E}(n_{22}) = \dfrac{r_2 c_2}{n} = \dfrac{2,667(3,314)}{5,026} = 1,758.543$

To determine if travelers who use the Internet to search for travel information are likely to be people who are college educated, we test:

H_0: Education and use of Internet for travel information are independent
H_a: Education and use of Internet for travel information are dependent

The test statistic is $\chi^2 = \sum \dfrac{\left[n_i - \hat{E}(n_i)\right]^2}{\hat{E}(n_i)}$

$$= \frac{(1,072 - 803.543)^2}{803.543} + \frac{(1,287 - 1,555.457)^2}{1,555.457} + \frac{(640 - 908.547)^2}{908.457} + \frac{(2,027 - 1,758.543)^2}{1,758.543}$$
$$= 256.336$$

The rejection region requires $\alpha = .05$ in the upper tail of the χ^2 distribution with df $= (r - 1)(c - 1) = (2 - 1)(2 - 1) = 1$. From Table VII, Appendix B, $\chi^2_{.05} = 3.84146$. The rejection region is $\chi^2 > 3.84146$.

Since the observed value of the test statistic falls in the rejection region ($\chi^2 = 256.336 > 3.814146$), H_0 is rejected. There is sufficient evidence to indicate that travelers who use the Internet to search for travel information and level of education are dependent at $\alpha = .05$. Since the proportion of college educated who use the Internet to search for travel information ($1072/2359 = .45$) is greater than the proportion of less than college educated ($640/2667 = .24$), the conclusion supports the researchers claim that travelers who use the Internet to search for travel information are likely to be people who are college educated.

The necessary assumptions are
1. The k observed counts are a random sample from the populations of interest.
2. The sample size, n, will be large enough so that, for every cell, the expected count, $E(n_{ij})$, will be equal to 5 or more.

16.23 a. The sample proportion of injured Hispanic children who were not wearing seatbelts during the accident is:

$$\hat{p} = 283/314 = .901$$

b. The sample proportion of injured non-Hispanic white children who were not wearing seatbelts during the accident is:

$$\hat{p} = 330/478 = .690$$

c. Since the proportion of injured Hispanic children who were not wearing seatbelts during the accident (.901) is .211 higher than the proportion of injured non-Hispanic white children who were not wearing seatbelts during the accident (.690), the proportions probably differ.

d. Some preliminary calculations are:

$$\hat{E}(n_{11}) = \frac{r_1 c_1}{n} = \frac{179(314)}{792} = 70.97 \qquad \hat{E}(n_{12}) = \frac{r_1 c_2}{n} = \frac{179(478)}{792} = 108.03$$

$$\hat{E}(n_{21}) = \frac{r_2 c_1}{n} = \frac{613(314)}{792} = 243.03 \qquad \hat{E}(n_{22}) = \frac{r_2 c_2}{n} = \frac{613(478)}{792} = 369.97$$

To determine whether seatbelt usage in motor vehicle accidents depends on ethnic status in the San Diego County Regionalized Trauma System, we test:

H_0: Seatbelt usage in motor vehicle accidents and ethnic status in the San Diego County Regionalized Trauma System are independent

H_a: Seatbelt usage in motor vehicle accidents and ethnic status in the San Diego County Regionalized Trauma System are dependent

The test statistic is $\chi^2 = \sum \sum \dfrac{\left[n_{ij} - \hat{E}(n_{ij})\right]^2}{\hat{E}(n_{ij})^2}$

$$= \frac{(31 - 70.97)^2}{70.97} + \frac{(148 - 108.03)^2}{108.03} + \frac{(283 - 243.03)^2}{243.03} + \frac{(330 - 369.97)^2}{369.97} = 48.191$$

The rejection region requires $\alpha = .01$ in the upper tail of the χ^2 distribution with df = $(r - 1)(c - 1) = (2 - 1)(2 - 1) = 1$. From Table VII, Appendix B, $\chi^2_{.01} = 6.63490$. The rejection region is $\chi^2 > 6.63490$.

Since the observed value of the test statistic falls in the rejection region ($\chi^2 = 48.191 > 6.63490$), H_0 is rejected. There is sufficient evidence to indicate seatbelt usage in motor vehicle accidents depends on ethnic status in the San Diego County Regionalized Trauma System at $\alpha = .01$.

e. For confidence coefficient .99, $\alpha = .01$ and $\alpha/2 = .01/2 = .005$. From Table IV, Appendix B, $z_{.005} = 2.58$. The confidence interval is:

$$(\hat{p}_1 - \hat{p}_2) \pm z_{.005} \sqrt{\frac{\hat{p}_1 \hat{q}_1}{n_1} + \frac{\hat{p}_2 \hat{q}_2}{n_2}} \Rightarrow (.901 - .690) \pm 2.58 \sqrt{\frac{.901(.099)}{314} + \frac{.690(.310)}{478}}$$

$$\Rightarrow .211 \pm .070 \Rightarrow (.141, .281)$$

We are 99% confident that the difference in the proportion of injured Hispanic children who were not wearing seatbelts and the proportion of injured non-Hispanic white children who were not wearing seatbelts is between .141 and .281.

16.25 a. Some preliminary calculations:

$$\hat{E}(n_{11}) = \frac{r_1 c_1}{n} = \frac{45(42)}{160} = 11.8 \qquad \hat{E}(n_{12}) = \frac{r_1 c_2}{n} = \frac{45(30)}{160} = 8.4$$

$$\hat{E}(n_{13}) = \frac{r_1 c_3}{n} = \frac{45(88)}{160} = 24.8 \qquad \hat{E}(n_{21}) = \frac{r_2 c_1}{n} = \frac{32(42)}{160} = 8.4$$

$$\hat{E}(n_{22}) = \frac{r_2 c_2}{n} = \frac{32(30)}{160} = 6.0 \qquad \hat{E}(n_{23}) = \frac{r_2 c_3}{n} = \frac{32(88)}{160} = 17.6$$

$$\hat{E}(n_{31}) = \frac{r_3 c_1}{n} = \frac{83(42)}{160} = 21.8 \qquad \hat{E}(n_{32}) = \frac{r_3 c_2}{n} = \frac{83(30)}{160} = 15.6$$

$$\hat{E}(n_{33}) = \frac{r_3 c_3}{n} = \frac{83(88)}{160} = 45.7$$

b. To determine whether the movie reviews of the two critics are independent, we test:

H_0: The reviews of the two critics are independent
H_a: The reviews of the two critics are dependent

The test statistic is $\chi^2 = 45.357$ (from the printout)

The p-value is $p = .000$. Since the p-value is less than $\alpha = .01$, H_0 is rejected. There is sufficient evidence to indicate the movie reviews of the two critics are dependent at $\alpha = .01$.

16.27 a. Some preliminary calculations are:

$$\hat{E}(n_{11}) = \frac{r_1 c_1}{n} = \frac{136(150)}{300} = 68 \qquad \hat{E}(n_{21}) = \frac{r_2 c_1}{n} = \frac{164(150)}{300} = 82$$

$$\hat{E}(n_{12}) = \frac{r_1 c_2}{n} = \frac{136(150)}{300} = 68 \qquad \hat{E}(n_{22}) = \frac{r_2 c_2}{n} = \frac{164(150)}{300} = 82$$

To determine whether audience gender and product identification are dependent factors for male spokespersons, we test:

H_0: Audience gender and product identification are independent factors
H_a: Audience gender and product identification are dependent factors

The test statistic is $\chi^2 = \sum\sum \dfrac{\left[n_{ij} - \hat{E}(n_{ij})\right]^2}{\hat{E}(n_{ij})^2}$

$$= \frac{(95 - 68)^3}{68} + \frac{(41 - 68)^2}{68} + \frac{(55 - 82)^2}{82} + \frac{(109 - 82)^2}{82} = 39.22$$

The rejection region requires $\alpha = .05$ in the upper tail of the χ^2 distribution with df = $(r - 1)(c - 1) = (2 - 1)(2 - 1) = 1$. From Table VII, Appendix B, $\chi^2_{.05} = 3.84146$. The rejection region is $\chi^2 > 3.84146$.

Since the observed value of the test statistic falls in the rejection region ($\chi^2 = 39.22$ > 3.84146), H_0 is rejected. There is sufficient evidence to indicate audience gender and product identification are dependent factors for $\alpha = .05$.

b. Some preliminary calculations are:

$$\hat{E}(n_{11}) = \frac{r_1 c_1}{n} = \frac{108(150)}{300} = 54 \qquad \hat{E}(n_{21}) = \frac{r_2 c_1}{n} = \frac{192(150)}{300} = 96$$

$$\hat{E}(n_{12}) = \frac{r_1 c_2}{n} = \frac{108(150)}{300} = 54 \qquad \hat{E}(n_{22}) = \frac{r_2 c_2}{n} = \frac{192(150)}{300} = 96$$

To determine whether audience gender and product identification are dependent factors for female spokespersons, we test:

H_0: Audience gender and product identification are independent factors
H_a: Audience gender and product identification are dependent factors

The test statistic is $\chi^2 = \displaystyle\sum\sum \frac{\left[n_{ij} - \hat{E}(n_{ij})\right]^2}{\hat{E}(n_{ij})}$

$$= \frac{(47 - 54)^2}{54} + \frac{(61 - 54)^2}{54} + \frac{(103 - 96)^2}{96} + \frac{(89 - 96)^2}{96} = 2.84$$

The rejection region requires $\alpha = .05$ in the upper tail of the χ^2 distribution with df = $(r - 1)(c - 1) = (2 - 1)(2 - 1) = 1$. From Table VII, Appendix B, $\chi^2_{.05} = 3.84146$. The rejection region is $\chi^2 > 3.84146$.

Since the observed value of the test statistic does not fall in the rejection region ($\chi^2 = 2.84 \not> 3.84146$), H_0 is not rejected. There is insufficient evidence to indicate audience gender and product identification are dependent factors for $\alpha = .05$.

c. When a male spokesperson is used in an advertisement, audience gender and product identification are dependent. Males tended to identify the product more frequently than females.

When a female spokesperson is used in an advertisement, there is no evidence that audience gender and product identification are dependent. Males and females tend to identify the product at the same rate.

16.29 First, we must set up the contingency table. The proportions given are the proportions of the whole group who show signs of stress and fall into a particular fitness level. Thus, the number of people showing signs of stress and falling in the poor fitness level is $np_1 = 549(.155) = 85$. The number of people showing signs of stress and falling in the average fitness level is $np_2 = 549(.133) = 73$. The number of people showing signs of stress and falling in the good fitness level is $np_3 = 549(.108) = 59$.

The contingency table is:

Fitness level	Stress		Total
	No stress	Signs of stress	
Poor	157	85	242
Average	139	73	212
Good	36	59	95
Total	332	217	549

Some preliminary calculations are:

$$\hat{E}(n_{11}) = \frac{r_1c_1}{n} = \frac{242(332)}{549} = 146.346 \qquad \hat{E}(n_{12}) = \frac{r_1c_2}{n} = \frac{242(217)}{549} = 95.654$$

$$\hat{E}(n_{21}) = \frac{r_2c_1}{n} = \frac{212(332)}{549} = 128.204 \qquad \hat{E}(n_{22}) = \frac{r_2c_2}{n} = \frac{212(217)}{549} = 83.796$$

$$\hat{E}(n_{31}) = \frac{r_3c_1}{n} = \frac{95(332)}{549} = 57.45 \qquad \hat{E}(n_{32}) = \frac{r_3c_2}{n} = \frac{95(217)}{549} = 37.55$$

To determine whether the likelihood for stress is dependent on an employee's fitness level, we test:

H_0: Likelihood for stress is independent of an employee's fitness level
H_a: Likelihood for stress is dependent on an employee's fitness level

The test statistic is $\chi^2 = \sum\sum \dfrac{\left[n_{ij} - \hat{E}(n_{ij})\right]^2}{\hat{E}(n_{ij})}$

$$= \frac{(157 - 146.346)^2}{146.346} + \frac{(85 - 95.654)^2}{95.654} + \frac{(139 - 128.204)^2}{128.204}$$

$$+ \frac{(73 - 83.796)^2}{83.796} + \frac{(36 - 57.45)^2}{57.45} + \frac{(59 - 37.55)^2}{37.55} = 24.524$$

The rejection region requires $\alpha = .05$ in the upper tail of the χ^2 distribution with df =
$(r - 1)(c - 1) = (3 - 1)(2 - 1) = 2$. From Table VII, Appendix B, $\chi^2_{.05} = 5.99147$.
The rejection region is $\chi^2 > 5.99147$.

Since the observed value of the test statistic falls in the rejection region ($\chi^2 = 24.524 > 5.99147$),
H_0 is rejected. There is sufficient evidence to indicate the likelihood for stress is dependent on an
employee's fitness level for $\alpha = .05$.

16.31   a.   Some preliminary calculations are:

If all the categories are equally likely,

$$p_{1,0} = p_{2,0} = p_{3,0} = p_{4,0} = p_{5,0} = .2$$

$$E(n_1) = E(n_2) = E(n_3) = E(n_4) = E(n_5) = np_{1,0} = 150(.2) = 30$$

To determine if the categories are not equally likely, we test:

H_0: $p_1 = p_2 = p_3 = p_4 = p_5 = .2$
H_a: At least one probability is different from .2

The test statistic is $\chi^2 = \sum \dfrac{[n_i - E(n_i)]^2}{E(n_i)}$

$$= \frac{(28 - 30)^2}{30} + \frac{(35 - 30)^2}{30} + \frac{(33 - 30)^2}{30} + \frac{(25 - 30)^2}{30} + \frac{(29 - 30)^2}{30} = 2.133$$

The rejection region requires $\alpha = .10$ in the upper tail of the χ^2 distribution with df = $k - 1 = 5 - 1 = 4$. From Table VII, Appendix B, $\chi^2_{.10} = 7.77944$. The rejection region is $\chi^2 > 7.77944$.

Since the observed value of the test statistic does not fall in the rejection region ($\chi^2 = 2.133 \not> 7.77944$), H_0 is not rejected. There is insufficient evidence to indicate the categories are not equally likely at $\alpha = .10$.

b. $\hat{p}_2 = \dfrac{35}{150} = .233$

For confidence coefficient .90, $\alpha = .10$ and $\alpha/2 = .05$. From Table IV, Appendix B, $z_{.05} = 1.645$. The confidence interval is:

$$\hat{p}_2 \pm z_{.05} \sqrt{\frac{\hat{p}_2 \hat{q}_2}{n_2}} \Rightarrow .233 \pm 1.645 \sqrt{\frac{.233(.767)}{150}} \Rightarrow .233 \pm .057 \Rightarrow (.176, .290)$$

16.33   Some preliminary calculations are:

$\hat{E}(n_{11}) = \dfrac{r_1 c_1}{n} = \dfrac{419(380)}{703} = 226.49$ $\hat{E}(n_{21}) = \dfrac{r_2 c_1}{n} = \dfrac{149(380)}{703} = 80.54$

$\hat{E}(n_{12}) = \dfrac{r_1 c_2}{n} = \dfrac{419(323)}{703} = 192.51$ $\hat{E}(n_{22}) = \dfrac{r_2 c_2}{n} = \dfrac{149(323)}{703} = 68.46$

$\hat{E}(n_{31}) = \dfrac{r_3 c_1}{n} = \dfrac{87(380)}{703} = 47.03$ $\hat{E}(n_{41}) = \dfrac{r_4 c_1}{n} = \dfrac{48(380)}{703} = 25.95$

$\hat{E}(n_{32}) = \dfrac{r_3 c_2}{n} = \dfrac{87(323)}{703} = 39.97$ $\hat{E}(n_{42}) = \dfrac{r_4 c_2}{n} = \dfrac{48(323)}{703} = 22.05$

To determine whether retirement status of a traveler and the duration of a typical trip are dependent, we test:

H_0: Retirement status of a traveler and the duration of a typical trip are independent
H_a: Retirement status of a traveler and the duration of a typical trip are dependent

The test statistic is $\chi^2 = \sum \sum \dfrac{[n_{ij} - \hat{E}(n_{ij})]^2}{\hat{E}(n_{ij})}$

$$= \frac{(247 - 226.49)^2}{226.49} + \frac{(172 - 192.51)^2}{192.51} + \frac{(82 - 80.54)^2}{80.54} + \frac{(67 - 68.46)^2}{68.46}$$

$$+ \frac{(35 - 47.03)^2}{47.03} + \frac{(52 - 39.97)^2}{39.97} + \frac{(16 - 25.95)^2}{25.95} + \frac{(32 - 22.05)^2}{22.05} = 19.10$$

The rejection region requires $\alpha = .05$ in the upper tail of the χ^2 distribution with df = $(r - 1)(c - 1) = (4 - 1)(2 - 1) = 3$. From Table VII, Appendix B, $\chi^2_{.05} = 7.81473$. The rejection region is $\chi^2 > 7.81473$.

Since the observed value of the test statistic falls in the rejection region ($\chi^2 = 19.10 > 7.81473$), H_0 is rejected. There is sufficient evidence to indicate retirement status of a traveler and the duration of a typical trip are dependent for $\alpha = .05$.

16.35 For union members:

H_0: Level of confidence and job satisfaction are independent
H_a: Level of confidence and job satisfaction are dependent

The test statistic is $\chi^2 = 13.36744$ (from printout).

The rejection region requires $\alpha = .05$ in the upper tail of the χ^2 distribution with df = $(r - 1)(c - 1) = (3 - 1)(4 - 1) = 6$. From Table VII, Appendix B, $\chi^2_{.05} = 12.5916$. The rejection region is $\chi^2 > 12.5916$.

Since the observed value of the test statistic falls in the rejection region ($\chi^2 = 13.36 > 12.5916$), H_0 is rejected. There is sufficient evidence to indicate the level of confidence and job satisfaction are related at $\alpha = .05$ for union members.

Note: This test should be viewed cautiously since three cells have expected values less than 5.

For nonunion members:

H_0: Level of confidence and job satisfaction are independent
H_a: Level of confidence and job satisfaction are dependent

The test statistic is $\chi^2 = 9.63514$ (from printout).

The rejection region is $\chi^2 > 12.5916$. Since the observed value of the test statistic does not fall in the rejection region ($\chi^2 = 9.64 \not> 12.5916$), H_0 is not rejected. There is insufficient evidence to indicate the level of confidence and job satisfaction are related for nonunion workers at $\alpha = .05$.

16.37 a. No. If January change is down, half the next 11-month changes are up and half are down.

b. The percentages of years for which the 11-month movement is up based on January change are found by dividing the numbers in the first column by the corresponding row total and multiplying by 100. We also divide the first column total by the overall total and multiply by 100.

January Change:

Up $\qquad \dfrac{25}{35} \cdot 100 = 71.4\%$

Down $\qquad \dfrac{9}{18} \cdot 100 = 50\%$

Total $\qquad \dfrac{34}{53} \cdot 100 = 64.2\%$

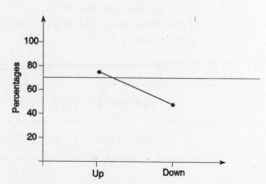

c. H_0: The January change and the next 11-month change are independent
H_a: The January change and the next 11-month change are dependent

d. Some preliminary calculations are:

$$\hat{E}(n_{11}) = \frac{r_1 c_1}{n} = \frac{35(34)}{53} = 22.453 \qquad \hat{E}(n_{12}) = \frac{35(19)}{53} = 12.547$$

$$\hat{E}(n_{21}) = \frac{18(34)}{53} = 11.547 \qquad \hat{E}(n_{22}) = \frac{18(19)}{53} = 6.453$$

The test statistic is $\chi^2 = \sum\sum \frac{[n_{ij} - \hat{E}(n_{ij})]^2}{\hat{E}(n_{ij})} = \frac{(25 - 22.453)^2}{22.453} + \frac{(9 - 11.547)^2}{11.547}$

$$+ \frac{(10 - 12.547)^2}{12.547} + \frac{(9 - 6.453)^2}{6.453} = 2.373$$

The rejection region requires $\alpha = .05$ in the upper tail of the χ^2 distribution with df = $(r - 1)(c - 1) = (2 - 1)(2 - 1) = 1$. From Table VII, Appendix B, $\chi^2_{.05} = 3.84146$. The rejection region is $\chi^2 > 3.84146$.

Since the observed value of the test statistic does not fall in the rejection region ($\chi^2 = 2.373 \ngtr 3.84146$), H_0 is not rejected. There is insufficient evidence to indicate the January change and the next 11-month change are dependent at $\alpha = .05$.

e. Yes. For $\alpha = .10$, the rejection region is $\chi^2 > \chi^2_{.10} = 2.70554$, from Table XIII, Appendix B, with df = 1. Since the observed value of the test statistic does not fall in the rejection region ($\chi^2 = 2.373 \ngtr 2.70554$), H_0 is not rejected. The conclusion is the same.

16.39 a. The contingency table is:

		Committee		
		Acceptable	Rejected	Totals
Inspector	Acceptable	101	23	124
	Rejected	10	19	29
	Totals	111	42	153

b. Yes. To plot the percentages, first convert frequencies to percentages by dividing the numbers in each column by the column total and multiplying by 100. Also, divide the row totals by the overall total and multiply by 100.

		Acceptable	Rejected	Totals
Inspector	Acceptable	$\frac{101}{111} \cdot 100 = 90.99\%$	$\frac{23}{42} \cdot 100 = 54.76\%$	$\frac{124}{153} \cdot 100 = 81.05\%$
	Rejected	$\frac{10}{111} \cdot 100 = 9.01\%$	$\frac{19}{42} \cdot 100 = 45.23\%$	$\frac{29}{153} \cdot 100 = 18.95\%$

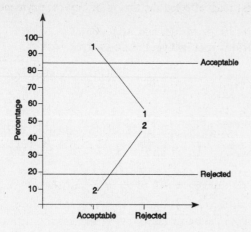

From the plot, it appears there is a relationship.

c.   Some preliminary calculations are:

$$\hat{E}(n_{11}) = \frac{r_1 c_1}{n} = \frac{124(111)}{153} = 89.691 \qquad \hat{E}(n_{12}) = \frac{r_1 c_2}{n} = \frac{124(42)}{153} = 34.039$$

$$\hat{E}(n_{21}) = \frac{r_2 c_1}{n} = \frac{29(111)}{153} = 21.039 \qquad \hat{E}(n_{22}) = \frac{r_2 c_2}{n} = \frac{29(42)}{153} = 7.961$$

To determine if the inspector's classifications and the committee's classifications are related, we test:

H_0: The inspector's and committee's classification are independent
H_a: The inspector's and committee's classifications are dependent

The test statistic is $\chi^2 = \displaystyle\sum\sum \frac{[n_{ij} - \hat{E}(n_{ij})]^2}{\hat{E}(n_{ij})}$

$$= \frac{(101 - 89.961)^2}{89.961} + \frac{(23 - 34.039)^2}{34.039} + \frac{(10 - 21.039)^2}{21.039} + \frac{(19 - 7.961)^2}{7.961}$$
$$= 26.034$$

The rejection region requires $\alpha = .05$ in the upper tail of the χ^2 distribution with df = $(r - 1)(c - 1) = (2 - 1)(2 - 1) = 1$. From Table VII, Appendix B, $\chi^2_{.05} = 3.84146$. The rejection region is $\chi^2 > 3.84146$.

Since the observed value of the test statistic falls in the rejection region ($\chi^2 = 26.034 > 3.84146$), H_0 is rejected. There is sufficient evidence to indicate the inspector's and committee's classifications are related at $\alpha = .05$. This indicates that the inspector and committee tend to make the same decisions.

16.41 a.   Some preliminary calculations are:

$E(n_1) = np_{1,0} = 200(.65) = 130 \qquad\qquad n_1 = np_1 = 200(.78) = 156$
$E(n_2) = np_{2,0} = 200(.15) = 30 \qquad\qquad n_2 = np_2 = 200(.12) = 24$
$E(n_3) = np_{3,0} = 200(.10) = 20 \qquad\qquad n_3 = np_3 = 200(.05) = 10$
$E(n_4) = np_{4,0} = 200(.07) = 14 \qquad\qquad n_4 = np_4 = 200(.02) = 4$
$E(n_5) = np_{5,0} = 200(.03) = 6 \qquad\qquad n_5 = np_5 = 200(.03) = 6$

To determine if the increase in interest rates affected the timing of buyers' payments, we test:

H_0: $p_1 = .65$, $p_2 = .15$, $p_3 = .10$, $p_4 = .07$, and $p_5 = .03$
H_a: At least one proportion differs from its hypothesized value

The test statistic is $\chi^2 = \sum \dfrac{(n_i - E(n_i))^2}{E(n_i)}$

$$= \dfrac{(156 - 130)^2}{130} + \dfrac{(24 - 30)^2}{30} + \dfrac{(10 - 20)^2}{20} + \dfrac{(4 - 14)^2}{14} + \dfrac{(6 - 6)^2}{6} = 18.54$$

The rejection region requires $\alpha = .10$ in the upper tail of the χ^2 distribution with df $=$ $k - 1 = 5 - 1 = 4$. From Table VII, Appendix B, $\chi^2_{.10} = 7.77944$. The rejection region is $\chi^2 > 7.77944$.

Since the observed value of the test statistic falls in the rejection region ($\chi^2 = 18.54 >$ 7.77944), H_0 is rejected. There is sufficient evidence to indicate the increase in interest rates affected the timing of buyers' payments at $\alpha = .10$.

b.   The observed significance level is $P(\chi^2 \geq 18.54)$. From Table VII, Appendix B, with df $=$ 4, $P(\chi^2 \geq 18.54) = p$-value $< .005$.

16.43   a.   Some preliminary calculations are:

The contingency table is:

		Defectives	Non-Defectives	
	1	25	175	200
Shift	2	35	165	200
	3	80	120	200
		140	460	600

$$\hat{E}(n_{11}) = \dfrac{r_1 c_1}{n} = \dfrac{200(140)}{600} = 46.667$$

$$\hat{E}(n_{21}) = \hat{E}(n_{31}) = \dfrac{200(140)}{600} = 46.667$$

$$\hat{E}(n_{12}) = \hat{E}(n_{22}) = \hat{E}(n_{32}) = \dfrac{200(460)}{600} = 153.333$$

To determine if quality of the filters are related to shift, we test:

H_0: Quality of filters and shift are independent
H_a: Quality of filters and shift are dependent

The test statistic is $\chi^2 = \sum\sum \dfrac{\left[n_{ij} - \hat{E}(n_{ij})\right]^2}{\hat{E}(n_{ij})} = \dfrac{(25 - 46.667)^2}{46.667} + \dfrac{(35 - 46.667)^2}{46.667}$

$$+ \dfrac{(80 - 46.667)^2}{46.667} + \dfrac{(175 - 153.333)^2}{153.333} + \dfrac{(165 - 153.333)^2}{153.333} + \dfrac{(120 - 153.333)^2}{153.333}$$

$$= 47.98$$

The rejection region requires $\alpha = .05$ in the upper tail of the χ^2 distribution with df = $(r - 1)(c - 1) = (3 - 1)(2 - 1) = 2$. From Table VII, Appendix B, $\chi^2_{.05} = 5.99147$. The rejection region is $\chi^2 > 5.99147$.

Since the observed value of the test statistic falls in the rejection region ($\chi^2 = 47.98 > 5.99147$), H_0 is rejected. There is sufficient evidence to indicate quality of filters and shift are related at $\alpha = .05$.

b. The form of the confidence interval for p is:

$$\hat{p}_1 \pm z_{\alpha/2} \sqrt{\frac{\hat{p}_1 \hat{q}_1}{n}} \text{ where } \hat{p}_1 = \frac{25}{200} = .125$$

For confidence coefficient .95, $\alpha = 1 - .95 = .05$ and $\alpha/2 = .05/2 = .025$. From Table IV, Appendix B, $z_{.025} = 1.96$. The 95% confidence interval is:

$$.125 \pm 1.96 \sqrt{\frac{.125(.875)}{200}} \Rightarrow .125 \pm .046 \Rightarrow (.079, .171)$$